Public Papers of
the Secretaries-General of
the United Nations

VOLUME VIII

U THANT

1968–1971

Public Papers of
the Secretaries-General of
the United Nations

VOLUME VIII

U THANT
1968–1971

Selected and Edited with Commentary by

ANDREW W. CORDIER
AND
MAX HARRELSON

COLUMBIA UNIVERSITY PRESS
1977
NEW YORK

The late ANDREW W. CORDIER served as Dean of the School of International Affairs at Columbia University from 1962 to 1972 and as president of the university from 1968 to 1970. From the beginning of the United Nations until 1962 Dr. Cordier was executive assistant to the Secretary-General with the rank of under-secretary. During the entire period he also had the top Secretariat responsibility for General Assembly affairs.

MAX HARRELSON served as a United Nations correspondent from 1946 until 1972, the last twenty-two years as chief correspondent of the Associated Press. Later he became a research associate in the School of International Affairs, Columbia University.

Library of Congress Cataloging in Publication Data (Revised)
Cordier, Andrew Wellington, 1901–1975 comp.
  Public papers of the Secretaries-General of the
United Nations.
    Vols.   by A. W. Cordier and M. Harrelson.
    Includes bibliographical references.
    CONTENTS: v. 1. Trygve Lie: 1946–53.—v. 2. Dag
Hammarskjöld: 1953–1956.—v. 3. Dag Hammarskjöld:
1956–1957. [etc.]
    1. United Nations—Collected works.   I. Foote,
Wilder, joint comp.   II. Harrelson, Max.   III. Lie,
Trygve, 1896–1968.   IV. Hammarskjöld, Dag, 1905–1961.
V. Thant, U., 1909–1974.   VI. Title.
JX1977.C62   341.23'08   68-8873
ISBN 0-231-04232-9

Columbia University Press
New York   Guildford, Surrey
Copyright © 1977 Columbia University Press
All rights reserved
Printed in the United States of America

Editors' Note on the Series

THE ROLE of the Secretary-General in the political life and constitutional development of the United Nations since 1945 has far exceeded the expectations of those who wrote the Charter. This has enhanced the historical significance of their public papers. These include many texts that are valuable and often indispensable as source materials in study of the Organization as a whole, of the office of Secretary-General in particular, and of the place of both in world affairs.

It is important that such papers be readily available to scholars and specialists in international affairs. In practice their accessibility has been severely limited. Some of the public papers of the Secretaries-General are included in the official documentation and some are not. In the former category are periodic and special reports to United Nations organs, proposals, and statements at meetings of the General Assembly, the Security Council, the other councils, committees, and commissions, and certain communications to governments. Not included in the official records are various other communications to governments, the Secretary-General's addresses outside the United Nations, statements to the press, press conference transcripts, radio and television broadcasts, and contributions to magazines and books. Most of the texts in this second category were issued as press releases, none as official documents.

More or less comprehensive collections of the official documents are maintained by depository libraries designated by the United Nations and located in most of the countries of the world. After more than twenty-five years it is not surprising that the volume of this documentation is immense. The record of what successive Secretaries-General have spoken or written in the official proceedings is widely dispersed throughout a great mass of records. Furthermore, it is necessary to go to the press releases for the public papers in the second category described above. The Dag Hammarskjöld Library at United Nations Headquarters maintains a comprehensive collection of press releases but it has not been the practice to include them in the deposit of official documentation in the depository libraries. Yet the press releases are usually the only source of a very important part of the public record—the Secretary-General's speeches to other groups and organizations and his press statements and press conferences. Successive Secretaries-General have frequently used these for historically significant and revealing statements.

Thus the present series of volumes of the public papers of the Secretaries-General has been undertaken to meet a real need. The project has been made possible by a grant from the Ford Foundation to the School of International Affairs of Columbia University. The series includes all texts believed by the editors to be essential or most likely to be useful in study and research about the United Nations. These have been assembled from official, semiofficial, and nonofficial sources. The texts selected for the printed series are reproduced in full except where otherwise indicated. The styles of spelling and capitalization, which were variable in the official documents and press releases, have generally been reproduced as they were in the originals. Dates have been conformed throughout to the month-day-year style. The texts are arranged for the most part in chronological order corresponding to the sequence of events to which they are related. Commentary recalling the contemporary context and giving other background for the texts is provided whenever this seems useful.

It should also be explained that the official records of the United Nations include many reports issued in the name of the Secretary-General that may more correctly be classified with the records of the organs requesting them. Such reports are factual accounts of developments or programs without personal commitments of policy or principle by the Secretary-General. There are a few borderline cases, but in general reports of this nature have not been considered as belonging with the public papers of the Secretaries-General.

Acknowledgments

PUBLICATION of the *Public Papers of the Secretaries-General of the United Nations* was made possible by a grant from the Ford Foundation to the School of International Affairs of Columbia University. The editors are deeply grateful for this financial assistance.

Our editorial and research assistant, Charlotte Carpenter, and her predecessor, Alice Smith, rendered indispensable and devoted service in assembling texts, researching the background of events for use in the commentary, finding and checking sources and references, reading proof, and supervising the reproduction of both texts and commentary.

The task of collecting the papers of U Thant included in this volume was greatly facilitated by the cooperation of the United Nations Secretariat, especially officers of the Dag Hammarskjöld Library and the Public Inquiries Unit at United Nations Headquarters.

The editors are especially grateful for the personal assistance of the late U Thant and other officials close to him in providing background material essential for the commentary. They also wish to acknowledge with appreciation the help given by the late Wilder Foote, former Research Associate in the School of International Affairs and coeditor of the preceding volumes in this series. His comments and suggestions were invaluable.

Contents

Editors' Note on the Series   v

Acknowledgments   vii

Introduction to This Volume of the Public Papers of U Thant   1

1968

The Situation in the Middle East, January   17

    Report on the Efforts of the Special Representative, January 17   18

Disarmament   20

    1. Message to the Eighteen-Nation Committee on Disarmament, Geneva, January 17   21

    2. Statement in the First Committee, April 26   22

The Situation in Vietnam, January to May   25

    1. From Transcript of Press Conference, January 18   26

    2. Statement to the Press, February 24   35

    3. Statement Recorded for Television and Radio, April 3   39

    4. Statement to the Press, April 13   39

    5. Statement to the Press, April 24   40

    6. Statement to the Press, May 3   41

    7. Excerpts from Speech at the University of Alberta, Edmonton, Alberta, May 13   41

United Nations Conference on Trade and Development   46

    1. From Statement at the Second Session of UNCTAD, New Delhi, February 9   47

    2. From Statement at the Conference of Non-Governmental Organizations, May 22   53

    3. From Statement in the Economic and Social Council, Geneva, July 8   54

Address at the International Conference on Human Rights,
Teheran, April 22   61

Statement on the Observance of Africa Day, May 27   71

From Report to the Security Council on the Situation in Cyprus,
June 11   76

The Situation in Vietnam, June and July   79

    1. From Transcript of Press Conference at Luncheon of United
       Nations Correspondents Association, June 18   80

    2. From Transcript of Press Conference, Geneva, July 10   87

From Address to the International Bar Association, Dublin, July
11   94

Nigeria–Biafra   100

    1. Message to General Yakubu Gowon, Head of the Military
       Government of Nigeria, July 13   102

    2. From Statement to Heads of State and Government of the
       Organization of African Unity, Algiers, September 13   103

Statement by a Spokesman for the Secretary-General on Soviet
Military Intervention in Czechoslovakia, August 21   106

Message to Pope Paul VI on the Occasion of the International
Eucharistic Congress, Bogotá, August 21   109

Staff Day Address, September 20   111

The Situation in Vietnam, September to November   117

    1. From Transcript of Press Conference, September 23   119

    2. Statement to the Press, November 1   128

From Introduction to the Twenty-Third Annual Report, September
24   130

Text of Identical Letters to the Foreign Ministers of France, the
United Kingdom, the United States, and the USSR Proposing a
Big Four Meeting, October 7   160

United Nations Day Message, October 24   164

The Situation in the Middle East, November   166

    Statement in the Special Political Committee, November 11   167

From Report to the Security Council on the Situation in Cyprus,
December 4   172

Contents

1969

Trygve Lie   175

  1. Message of Condolence to Per Borten, Prime Minister of
     Norway, December 30, 1968   176
  2. Address at St. Bernard's School, January 24   177

The Situation in the Middle East   179

  1. From Transcript of Press Conference, January 28   180
  2. Letter to the Foreign Minister of Israel, February 26   189
  3. Letter to the Foreign Minister of Israel, March 10   191

Letter to the Emperor of Ethiopia Regarding the Situation in
Equatorial Guinea, March 10   194

Disarmament   196

  1. From Message to the Eighteen-Nation Committee on Dis-
     armament, March 18   197
  2. From Transcript of Remarks to Non-Government Organiza-
     tions, May 27   198

From Transcript of Press Conference at Luncheon of the United
Nations Correspondents Association, April 17   201

From Speech to the United Nations Association of Great Britain,
London, April 25   214

Address at Unveiling of League of Nations Fiftieth Anniversary
Plaque, Geneva, April 30   221

Statement to the Press on the Situation in Vietnam, May 17   224

The Situation in Cyprus   226

  1. From Report to the Security Council, June 3   226
  2. From Report to the Security Council, December 3   229

Address at the Fiftieth Anniversary Conference of the International Labour Organisation, Geneva, June 18   232

Statement to the Press on Southern Rhodesia, June 21   239

Nigeria-Biafra   241

  1. Statement on Relief to Civilian Victims, July 30   242
  2. Address to the Organization of African Unity, Addis Ababa,
     September 7   243

Aerial Hijacking and Terrorism   249

1. Statement after Meeting with Representatives of the International Federation of Air Line Pilots Associations, Geneva, September 6   251
2. Statement in the Security Council, September 15   253

The Secretariat   254

1. From Staff Day Address, September 12   254
2. From Statement in the Fifth Committee, October 2   257

Views on the Situation in Vietnam, the Middle East, and Other Problems during the Autumn of 1969   261

1. Statement at Luncheon for the Hammarskjöld Memorial Scholarship Fund, September 12   264
2. From Transcript of Press Conference, September 15   267
3. From Introduction to the Twenty-Fourth Annual Report, September 15   274

Address to the Navy League, October 28   314

1970

Nigeria–Biafra   321

1. From Transcript of Press Conference, Dakar, Senegal, January 4   323
2. From Transcript of Press Conference, Accra, Ghana, January 9   325
3. Statement to the Press, Lomé, Togo, January 12   326
4. Statement to the Press, Lagos, Nigeria, January 19   327
5. Statement to the Press, Paris, January 19   328
6. Transcript of Press Conference, New York, February 17   329

Disarmament   341

1. Statement on the Occasion of the Entry into Force of the Treaty on the Non-Proliferation of Nuclear Weapons, March 5   341
2. From Statement to the Conference on Politics of Disarmament, Sponsored by the Institute on Man and Science, May 22   343

The Human Environment   345

1. Statement at Opening of the Preparatory Committee for the

United Nations Conference on the Human Environment,
March 9   346

2. From Address at the University of Texas, Austin, Texas,
May 14   350

The Situation in Vietnam   353

1. Statement to the Press, May 5   354
2. Statement to the Press, June 8   356
3. From Transcript of Remarks at Luncheon of United Nations
Correspondents Association, June 11   356
4. From Transcript of Press Conference, Geneva, July 7   369
5. Statement to the Press, November 23   379

Speech to the Royal Commonwealth Society on the Role of the
Secretary-General, London, June 15   380

The Twenty-Fifth Anniversary of the United Nations   393

1. Address at Commemorative Meeting, San Francisco, June
26   394
2. Statement at Commemorative Dinner, San Francisco, June
26   395
3. Statement in the Economic and Social Council, Geneva,
July 6   404
4. "The United Nations: Crisis of Authority," from Address to
World Association of World Federalists, Ottawa, August
23   416
5. From Statement at Commemorative Session of the General
Assembly, October 24   420
6. Statement at Special Staff Day Meeting, November 2   422
7. Transcript of Interview by Inter-Nation Television Trust of
London, November 5   427

World Youth Assembly   438

1. Statement at the Opening Meeting, July 9   439
2. Statement at the Closing Meeting, July 17   446

The Situation in the Middle East   449

1. Statement on Meeting with Secretary of State William S.
Rogers, August 4   451
2. Note on the Jarring Mission, August 7   452

From Statement on the United States Decision to Dump Nerve
Gas into the Atlantic Ocean, August 7   454

Transcript of Press Conference Dealing with the Question of a Third Term as Secretary-General and Other Subjects, September 10   456

Aerial Hijacking and Terrorism, from Statement at Dinner Inaugurating the Twenty-Fifth Anniversary of the Observance of United Nations Day, September 14   470

From Introduction to the Twenty-Fifth Annual Report, September 14   473

From Report to the Security Council on Cyprus, December 2   507

Statement to the General Assembly on the Financial Situation of the United Nations, December 17   510

1971

The Situation in the Middle East   513

    1. Report to the Security Council on Activities of the Special Representative, January 5   514
    2. Transcript of Press Conference, Geneva, April 29   525
    3. From Transcript of Press Conference, Boston, May 27   529

From Transcript of Press Conference Dealing with the Situation in Vietnam and Other Subjects, January 18   535

Statement at Ceremony Proclaiming Earth Day, March 21   544

Address to the Council for Foreign Relations Containing a Proposal for a Big Five Summit Meeting, Chicago, May 5   546

East Pakistan–Bangladesh   555

    1. Appeal for Emergency Assistance to Refugees from East Pakistan in India, May 19   557
    2. Further Appeal for Assistance, including Aid for the Population of East Pakistan, June 16   559
    3. Texts of *Aide-Mémoire* to India and Pakistan and of Memorandum to the President of the Security Council, August 2   561
    4. Statement by a United Nations Spokesman on the Impending Trial of Sheik Mujibur Rahman, August 10   566
    5. *Aide-Mémoire* on Humanitarian Aid to East Pakistan Refugees, August 13   567
    6. Text of Identical Messages to the Prime Minister of India and the President of Pakistan, October 20   569

Contents

The Second United Nations Development Decade   571

   1. From Statement to the International Symposium on the Decade, Boston, May 27   572

   2. From Statement to the St. Louis Symposium on the Decade, St. Louis, Missouri, December 16   574

From Transcript of His Final Press Conference, September 14   579

The Role of the Secretary-General   587

   1. From Speech at Luncheon for the Dag Hammarskjöld Memorial Scholarship Fund, September 16   588

   2. From Statement on the Tenth Anniversary of the Death of Dag Hammarskjöld, September 17   601

Retrospect—   604

From Introduction to the Twenty-Sixth Annual Report, September 17   605

Statement to the Press on the Question of a Third Term, October 18   672

Address at United Nations Day Concert, October 24   676

Statement to the Press on the Seating of the Representatives of the People's Republic of China, October 26   679

From Final Report to the Security Council on the Situation in Cyprus, November 30   682

Statement on the Proposed United Nations University, December 10   684

Farewell to the United Nations   689

   1. From Statement to the Staff, December 17   689

   2. From Statement at the Closing of the General Assembly, December 22   691

Index   695

Public Papers of
the Secretaries-General of
the United Nations

VOLUME VIII

U THANT

1968–1971

Introduction to This Volume
of the Public Papers of U Thant

I

U Thant had found his middle years as Secretary-General frustrating and disappointing. He was to find his final years perhaps even more so. In addition to the unsolved problems of the Middle East, Vietnam, Cyprus, finances, peace-keeping and disarmament, there were fresh problems, including eruptions of violence in Nigeria, Czechoslovakia, and East Pakistan, which brought new international tensions and added to the growing doubts as to the effectiveness of the United Nations. It is true there were a few bright spots, such as the beginning of the Vietnam talks in Paris, but the picture as a whole was far from rosy during this period as the Organization observed its twenty-fifth anniversary. Its prestige continued to erode, criticism was widespread, and at one point there was a threat that the United States would slash its financial support. Although Thant acknowledged the difficulties of the United Nations, its limitations and its shortcomings, he never lost faith in it. His dedication to the Organization is reflected repeatedly in his public papers, including his final statement to the General Assembly on December 22, 1971, when he promised to pursue during the leisure time of his retirement his efforts to strengthen it.

This volume reproduces Thant's views on the major international developments of the 1968–1971 period. The editors believe students of the United Nations will be especially interested in Thant's concept of the office of Secretary-General and his retrospective appraisals of the Organization as presented in some of his final papers, notably in a speech to the Dag Hammarskjöld Memorial Scholarship Fund of the United Nations Correspondents Association on September 16, 1971, and in the Introduction to his 1971 annual report, issued on September 17, 1971.

II

From the end of 1967 until he left office, Thant was involved almost continuously in the search for peace in the Middle East. He was assigned explicit responsibilities by the Security Council in its resolution of November 22, 1967, which requested him to designate a special representative to assist the parties in achieving a peaceful settlement and asked him to report to the Council on the progress of the special representative's efforts. The Secretary-General had named Gunnar Jarring, a highly regarded Swedish diplomat, to undertake the Middle East peace mission and Jarring had already established his headquarters in Nicosia, Cyprus, and begun his consultations by January 1968. Thant worked closely with his special representative, who pursued his efforts year after year—with a few interludes—although the initial optimism had quickly vanished in the face of the rigid positions of the two sides. Unlike Dag Hammarskjöld, Thant did not choose to go to the Middle East for personal consultations with Israeli and Arab leaders. He did talk with them at United Nations Headquarters on numerous occasions, but he preferred in the main to deal through Jarring. Thant also placed much hope in the private peace efforts of the big four powers, who kept him fully informed on their meetings at Headquarters. Up to the time he left office, however, there was never any real sign of a breakthrough. Instead, there were repeated incidents along the borders, there were threats and counterthreats, and tension never relaxed. After almost twenty-five years of effort by the United Nations, peace in the Middle East appeared to be as remote as ever.

III

The deadlock on the Cyprus problem was also stubborn. Since the United Nations intervention in 1964, Thant had been deeply involved both personally and through mediators and special representatives appointed by him. Although the outlook for a settlement between the Greek and Turkish communities brightened temporarily on several occasions, the situation never improved enough to permit the withdrawal of the United Nations Force in Cyprus. There was a brief moment of optimism, for example, in 1968 when the Secretary-General's special representative succeeded in opening a direct channel of communication between the two communities for the first time in four and a half years. Thant referred to this development in the Introduction to his final annual report in 1971, noting that "expectations were high" at that time. By 1971, however, the negotiations had broken down completely and the attitudes of both sides had hardened perceptibly. As in the Middle East, Thant blamed the impasse on the unwillingness of the leaders to accept necessary compromises and accommodations. Before leaving office, Thant urged the Security Council to take a new look at the Cyprus problem, especially the financial aspects of it. He had often expressed his unhappiness over the Council's insistence that the United Nations operation in Cyprus be financed by voluntary contributions and he did so once more in the Introduction to his 1971 annual report. Since 1964 it had been his responsibility to obtain the necessary contributions and this was becoming increasingly difficult. The result was a steadily growing deficit. Thant felt that the costs of such an operation should be shared by all Member states, not borne by a few. In his final report on Cyprus, he noted that the mandate of the United Nations Force had been extended twenty times—sometimes for three months and sometimes for six—and declared, "It is obvious that this situation cannot continue indefinitely. . . ."

IV

Although the United Nations was not directly involved in the Vietnam war, Thant continued the personal initiatives he had begun in 1964. He was especially active during the months preceding the 1968 agreement of the United States and North Vietnam to open preliminary peace talks. In fact, two meetings he had with representatives of the Hanoi government in February 1968 may have provided the basis for the partial United States bombing halt, which led to the preliminary talks in Paris. Thant had expressed the view numerous times that a cessation of bombing would be followed by peace negotiations, but he acknowledged that he had no official authorization from Hanoi to make such a commitment. On February 8, however, he was told by North Vietnam's consul-general in New Delhi, Nguyen Hoa, that Hanoi would discuss "all relevant matters" with Washington after an unconditional cessation of bombing. In an effort to pin the commitment down further, Thant had Nguyen Hoa transmit a list of questions to Hanoi. On February 14, the Secretary-General got the answers through the North Vietnamese representative in Paris, Mai Van Bo. The official word was that Hanoi was ready to begin talks just as soon as the bombing halt became effective. Mai Van Bo said further that either side could bring up any matter, including a reduction in the fighting in South Vietnam and the reconvening of the Geneva Conference of 1954. On February 21, Thant gave a full account of these conversations to President Lyndon B. Johnson in Washington. Johnson told Thant he sincerely desired a peaceful settlement. He reaffirmed the readiness of the United States to stand by the so-called San Antonio formula and halt all "aerial and naval bombardment when this will lead to productive discussions."

The breakthrough came on March 31 when Johnson announced that United States bombing of North Vietnam would cease "except in the area north of the demilitarized zone where the continued enemy build-up directly threatens allied forward positions and where the movement of their troops and supplies are closely related to that threat." This fell far short of the complete and unconditional bombing halt demanded by North Vietnam, but it proved to be enough to open the door to negotiations. On April 3 Hanoi radio declared that North Vietnam was ready to meet with United States representatives to begin preliminary talks. The next step was to determine the time and place. Thant again intervened by proposing four potential sites: Geneva, Paris, Phnom Penh, and Warsaw. It was not until May 10, however, that the talks finally got under way in Paris. There were still further delays over arrangements and procedure.

The talks continued month after month without progress. During this period, Thant had followed a hands-off policy for fear any intervention by him might complicate the negotiations, but he had become convinced that the continued United States bombing north of the demilitarized zone was the major cause of the delay and that he must do his best to get the United States to agree to a complete and unconditional cessation of the bombing. He consequently launched a series of appeals in September for a total bombing halt. By so doing, he once more annoyed the Johnson administration. George Ball, the permanent representative of the United States at the United Nations, accused the Secretary-General of placing too much emphasis on the bombing issue and of blowing it "way out of life-size." Thant replied that his view was shared by many governments, including some North Atlantic Treaty Organization (NATO) members, and that he did not regret being associated with governments "who feel, as I do, that essential first steps be taken to generate further processes which could eventually lead to a peaceful solution." Thant later suggested that if the question of the bombing halt were to be put before the General Assembly, a majority would back his position. This led to charges in the United States press that Thant in effect was inviting delegations to put such an item on the agenda. This he denied, however, declaring that he was merely wondering whether this might not be one means of finding out what the international attitude was.

Finally, on October 31, President Johnson announced his decision to halt all air, naval, and military bombardment of North Vietnam. Some additional bickering over seating arrangements and other procedural questions caused further delays, but the substantive talks, expanded to include representatives of South Vietnam and the National Liberation Front, began at last on January 16, 1969.

Thant had little to say about the Vietnam war during 1969, but by the spring of 1970 he felt he must make a new effort to help break the Paris stalemate. He was especially concerned about the extension of the war into Cambodia and Laos and the resumption of United States bombing of North Vietnam. In a public statement on May 5, he proposed the convening of an international gathering, similar to the Geneva Conferences of 1954 and 1962, which would include the parties involved in the fighting, the five big powers (including the People's Republic of China), and the three members of the International Control Commission (Canada, India, and Poland). His proposal found little support and nothing came of it. This was his last major initiative in the search for peace in Indo-China, which had been one of his chief preoccupations through most of his two terms in office. Although he was distressed by the failure of his own efforts and those of others to bring peace in the area, he was convinced that he had played a significant role despite the fact that his initiatives were not always welcomed by some of the parties. From the very beginning, he had insisted that the conflict would not be settled by military victory. He had urged a cessation of United States bombing as the first step toward negotiations and he had insisted that peace talks must include all the parties directly involved, including the National Liberation Front. Acceptance of these principles was implicit in the agreement that led to the Paris peace talks. Thant himself claimed no credit for getting the talks started, saying it was up to future historians to evaluate his role.

V

The tragic civil war in Nigeria, as an internal matter, was not within the competence of the United Nations but it nevertheless triggered another wave of public criticism in which Thant was accused of apathy and callousness and the Organization was denounced as indifferent to the human suffering in the newly proclaimed Republic of Biafra. Although Member states understood and accepted the legal limitations that barred United Nations intervention, the public did not. Coming as it did at a time when the Organization was sitting on the sidelines in the Vietnam war and was making little or no progress in bringing peace to the Middle East and Cyprus, the Nigerian conflict undermined still further the prestige of the United Nations.

When the conflict began on May 30, 1967, Thant wrote to General Yakubu Gowon, head of the military government in Nigeria, offering his good offices. Gowon declined the offer on the ground that the secession of the Eastern Region (Biafra) was an internal matter, but Thant kept in close touch with Gowon and made it clear that the offer still stood. Thant was disappointed at his inability as Secretary-General "to help directly in forestalling the horrors of the war in Nigeria," but he accepted from the beginning the position of the Organization of African Unity (OAU) that this was not a matter for the United Nations. Like the OAU, Thant recognized the federal government as the only legitimate government in Nigeria, but he repeatedly communicated with the Biafran authorities in his efforts to send food, medicine, and other relief supplies to the civilian population of the Eastern Region.

Throughout the war, which ended suddenly on January 15, 1970, Thant sought to convince the public that its criticism was based on a misunderstanding of the reasons for United Nations inaction. He pointed out that not a single Member state had seen fit to bring the question before either the Security Council or the General Assembly, adding that if any state had raised the question neither body would have inscribed it on the agenda because of its internal character. He was especially disturbed by the personal attacks on him that suggested that his cooperation with the OAU stemmed from his Burmese origin. Referring to these attacks at a press conference on February 17, 1970, Thant said, "The functioning of the Secretary-General in this particular situation or in similar types of situations is not concerned with the nationality of the Secretary-General, whether he is an Afro-Asian, a European or a Latin American. What is important is his attitude toward the problem." Thant's Asian background had been raised once before, it may be recalled, by Lord George Brown, former British foreign secretary, who suggested that this may have influenced his decision to bow to Egypt's demand for the withdrawal of the United Nations Emergency Force (UNEF) in 1967 (see volume VII of this series, pp. 15–16).

VI

The United Nations received another setback in August 1968, when military forces of the USSR, Poland, Hungary, Bulgaria, and East Germany invaded Czechoslovakia to squelch Alexander Dubček's program to liberalize communist controls over the press and public expression. In this case, the situation was brought before the Security Council, but a Soviet veto killed a resolution condemning the military intervention and calling for an immediate withdrawal of foreign military forces. Thant was seriously concerned over the invasion partly because it was another clear-cut instance of one of the superpowers openly violating the United Nations Charter. In a statement to the press, he called it "a serious blow to the concepts of international order and morality" and "a grave set-back to the East-West détente which seemed to be re-emerging in recent months." One of his main fears was that the invasion, like the United States intervention in Vietnam, would rekindle the cold war and thereby place new obstacles in the way of important United Nations efforts. In the Introduction to his 1968 annual report, he appealed directly to both superpowers to abandon the "strong-arm methods common to the thirties." Some diplomats were disturbed about a new concept advanced by the Soviet Union in opposing Security Council action. The Soviet position, in brief, was that any question arising between socialist states could and must be settled by those states without "foreign interference." The Charter does provide for regional arrangements for the maintenance of international peace and security. But does it go so far as to authorize enforcement action by regional organizations? In the case of the dispatching of a military force to the Dominican Republic by the Organization of American States (OAS), the USSR challenged the right of the OAS or any other regional organization to take enforcement action. The United States agreed, but contended that the inter-American force was not on enforcement action, but was there simply to guarantee the security of the public and to create an atmosphere of conciliation. The Security Council gave up its attempts to act because of the opposition of the new Czechoslovak government which replaced Dubček after the invasion. Although numerous delegates condemned the intervention of the Warsaw Pact members during the twenty-third session of the General Assembly, which opened a few weeks later, no move was made by any Member state to place the question formally on the Assembly's agenda. This was another case, like the Soviet invasion of Hungary in 1956, which added to the public disillusionment with the United Nations.

VII

Equally frustrating was the 1971 crisis on the Indian subcontinent, which began as an internal political conflict in Pakistan, grew into a rebellion of the predominantly Bengali population of East Pakistan, and wound up as a devastating war between India and Pakistan. Thant watched the escalation of the conflict with growing concern, especially because the United Nations found itself once more sitting on the sidelines—except for its humanitarian role. Neither Pakistan nor India wanted political intervention by the United Nations during the months preceding the large-scale fighting that began in late November 1971. Although the Secretary-General recognized a clear threat to international peace and urged the Security Council to act, members of the Council were reluctant to intervene partly because of the attitude of the parties to the dispute and partly because they knew that the permanent members of the Council were divided so sharply that a meeting was not likely to produce constructive results. For the same reason, Thant decided against using his prerogative to call a meeting under Article 99 of the Charter.

Thant's concern was reflected in a confidential *aide-mémoire* circulated to Security Council members on July 20 and made public on August 2 after distorted versions of the communication appeared in the press. He made these points: (1) the time had come when the international community could not continue to stand by, hoping that humanitarian efforts and "good intentions will be enough to turn the tide of human misery and potential disaster"; (2) the political aspects of the problem were too important for the Secretary-General to make substantive proposals without prior consideration of the situation by the Security Council; (3) the Council could and should reach agreed conclusions on possible measures to head off open hostilities. The Council, however, continued to ignore the threat. In the absence of action by the Council, Thant tried again a few months later to assist in a settlement. In identical communications to the Indian and Pakistani governments on October 20, he declared, "My good offices are entirely at your disposal if you believe they could be helpful at any time." Unfortunately, his offer was not accepted.

United Nations intervention came only after India and Pakistan were locked in a bloody conflict. And even then it was ineffectual. In the Security Council, the big powers were divided, as predicted, with the Soviet Union backing India and the United States and the People's Republic of China supporting Pakistan. Soviet vetoes blocked efforts by the majority to issue a cease-fire appeal. When the question was shifted to the General Assembly, a cease-fire resolution was adopted but it failed to halt the fighting. The war finally came to an end on December 16 when the Pakistani defense collapsed in East Pakistan, clearing the way for the establishment of the state of Bangladesh.

VIII

During his final years as Secretary-General, Thant reflected with increasing frequency on the plus and minus performances of the United Nations, its strengths and weaknesses, and the reasons for its disappointing record in the political field. He acknowledged on many occasions that the Organization had recorded more failures than successes on political problems—and this was what the public judged it by—but he firmly challenged those who belittled the United Nations, those who talked of abandoning it, and those who called for radical structural changes. Even if he sometimes spoke of the need for more clout to enforce United Nations decisions, he was convinced after ten years in office that the Organization was structurally sound and that any desirable changes could be achieved through evolution within the Charter. The paramount problem, he felt, was not with the Charter but with the attitudes of the Member states, their unwillingness to rise above their suspicions, their ideologies, their nationalism and their reluctance to stop relying on the unilateral use of force to settle disputes.

Thant's assessment of the United Nations is presented in detail in a number of documents in this and earlier volumes of this series. Those interested in his evaluation will be rewarded by reading the introductions to his ten annual reports, particularly his 1971 report (see pp. 605–71), in which he takes a comprehensive look backward and concludes that, despite its disappointing performance in the political field, "the institution itself is sound." "I have never been so convinced as now," he said, "of the usefulness, the potential and the absolute necessity of the United Nations." Thant took stock of the Organization's status in several speeches during the observance of its twenty-fifth anniversary in 1970, notably one at a dinner in San Francisco on June 26 and one in Ottawa on August 23 before the World Federation of World Federalists.

Apart from his general conclusions, Thant held firm views on specific questions relating to the evolution of the Organization. He was a strong believer, for example, in the importance of developing the influence of the General Assembly by expanding its role even in the field of peace-keeping, which is the primary responsibility of the Security Council. He acknowledged that the real power lay in the Security Council, where the five permanent members could exercise the veto, but said the Assembly was the place where the small and medium powers had an opportunity to influence the course of events. Without mentioning any specific case, he warned against the trend of the majority to misuse its power by sup-pressing opposition points of view and by adopting unrealistic resolu-tions. It may be recalled that the powerful Afro-Asian group had on one occasion sought to expunge from the record a speech by the foreign minister of South Africa. Thant's reference to "realistic" decisions apparently was directed at the tendency to deal with problems by threats of sanctions or other measures that could not be carried out. "It would be a grave pity," he said in the Introduction to his 1971 annual report, "if the smaller and medium powers throw away their opportunity and fail to establish some collective credibility through a more realistic approach to what they can or cannot do. Such failure would strengthen the criticisms of the United Nations which are increasingly heard and which could, in the long run, destroy the Organization. On the contrary, if the opportu-nity is grasped by those concerned, the Organization can look forward to a future bright with hope and success." In this connection he left no doubt that he was unalterably opposed to any form of weighted voting. Throughout his decade in office he endorsed repeatedly the principle of "one state, one vote." "To have the right to vote as such cannot be harmful," he said, "although the irresponsible exercise of that right—as of any other right—is bound, in the long run, to have undesirable consequences."

Summing up his overall view of the United Nations, Thant had this to say in the Introduction to his final annual report:

At this stage the United Nations system provides the best available and workable method by which nationalism and national sovereignty can evolve in order to keep pace with the vast changes that have made the nations of the world interdependent. If this evolution can succeed we may achieve a world concert of nations which preserves the best elements of nationalism. In a concert of nations where each plays its rightful part, the relations between states should at last be based on reality and fact, rather than on conflicting ideology, prejudice and xenophobia. This simple hope may be said to be naïve and unrealistic, but how immensely productive and practical its realization would be in terms of the better use of our resources, our talents and our brief span of life on this planet!

IX

Like Dag Hammarskjöld, Thant was convinced that the Secretary-General of the United Nations must not limit his activities to a purely technical role as chief administrative officer and servant of the deliberative organs, but must play a political role as well. During his ten years in office, Thant sought continuously to win acceptance of this concept and—despite a challenge now and then—he repeatedly put it to the test by taking political initiatives. Of course, the principal objective of these initiatives was not to strengthen the office of Secretary-General, but rather, to help settle disputes. He believed, however, that the office must not be static. "The office is, of necessity, developed through trial and error," he said on one occasion, "and in response to the demands and challenges of the passing years. Each Secretary-General must build as best he can on the office as he inherited it" (see pp. 590–91).

Thant talked about this subject frequently, but his views were presented in detail in his speech at a luncheon of the Dag Hammarskjöld Memorial Scholarship Fund of the United Nations Correspondents Association (see pp. 587–600) and in the Introduction to his 1971 annual report (see pp. 605–71). In these expositions, he went to some pains to outline the legal principles dealing with the functions and responsibilities of the Secretary-General, spelled out mainly in Articles 33, 97, 98, and 99 of the Charter. The one most often referred to in connection with the responsibilities of the Secretary-General is Article 99, which authorizes him to "bring to the attention of the Security Council any matter which in his opinion may threaten the maintenance of international peace and security." Under this article the Secretary-General may go so far as to call a meeting of the Security Council if, in his opinion, international peace and security are threatened. His options are not limited, however, to calling a meeting. He may—and, in fact, Thant and his predecessors frequently did—simply express his views to the Council either orally or by means of a written memorandum. Only once did any of the first three Secretaries-General invoke Article 99 to summon the Council into session. This was done by Hammarskjöld in the Congo situation in 1960. But in this case the circumstances were unusual in that the Congolese government had requested United Nations intervention. Lie, Hammarskjöld, and Thant were in agreement that there would be little to be gained by calling a Council meeting if the members themselves were opposed to a meeting. Thant preferred to act privately and informally, either through the use of his good offices or through consultations with members of the Council. He also felt that the Secretary-General should have a free hand in expressing his views on international developments, whether or not they posed a threat to peace. One of the reasons for his reluctance to accept a second term was the pressure being exerted by some Member states to curb his public statements. Before accepting reappointment in 1966, Thant insisted on a clear statement of his rights in this respect. The result was a declaration by the Council members that they would respect "the Secretary-General's position and his action in bringing basic issues confronting the Organization and disturbing developments to their notice." This was important in the strengthening of the Secretary-General's role, since it specifically recognized a right not spelled out in Article 99.

Thant was fully convinced that he had authority to use his good offices not only in compliance with resolutions of the Security Council and the General Assembly, but in response to requests of Member states and even on his own initiative. In his speech of September 16, 1971, he said his own idea of the office of Secretary-General was best described by the word "moderator," which had been suggested by President Franklin D. Roosevelt as the title for the Organization's chief officer. "I have always felt," he said, "that the most important political duty of the Secretary-General was to concentrate on the harmonizing functions of the United Nations as set out in Article 1, paragraph 4, of the Charter. I have tried to use the office, with all the discretion that the importance of the task requires, to allay unnecessary fears and suspicions, to establish communication between conflicting parties and to do whatever I could to bridge the gulf between East and West." He understood the necessity of remaining absolutely impartial in dealing with disputing parties, of maintaining his independence despite the inevitable pressures, of upholding decisions of United Nations organs even when he did not think them correct or realistic, and occasionally of accepting the role of scapegoat in dangerous situations where no solution could be found.

Despite his conviction that the Secretary-General could and should play an active political role, Thant had no illusions that the powers of the Secretary-General were unlimited or that they even compared to those of the head of a government. He often pointed out that he had no power other than that which the Member states were willing to delegate to him, that he could not intervene in the domestic affairs of states, and that he was useful in settling disputes only so long as he could maintain the confidence of the parties involved. Whenever the Secretary-General decided that the public interest demanded that he pronounce a moral judgment, such as he sometimes did, he was aware that he might alienate some Member states and bring public criticism upon himself. On the other hand, if he decided to withhold moral judgment, there was a chance that he would be accused of callousness and insensibility to human suffering.

Thant did not accept Trygve Lie's pronouncement that the Secretary-Generalship was the "most impossible job in the world." He himself acknowledged that it was difficult, but he also found it "an absorbing, a thrilling and a deeply frustrating task" (see p. 599). He concluded that two considerations must always be taken into account by the Secretary-General in determining the possibilities of effective action in matters relating to peace and security:

First, the Secretary-General must always be prepared to take an initiative, no matter what the consequences to his office or to him personally may be, if he sincerely believes that it might mean the difference between peace and war. In such a situation, the personal prestige of a Secretary-General—and even the position of his office—must be considered to be expendable. The second cardinal consideration must be the maintenance of the Secretary-General's independent position, as set out in Article 100 of the Charter, which alone can give him the freedom to act, without fear or favor, in the interests of world peace. Such an independence does not imply any disrespect for the wishes or opinions of Member governments. On the contrary, his independence is an insurance that the Secretary-General will be able to serve, in full accordance with his oath of office, the long-term interest in peace of all the Members of the Organization.

X

Much has been said in this introduction about the failures and disappointments experienced by the United Nations during the 1961–1971 decade. It must be remembered, however, that the Organization was already in the midst of a grave financial and political crisis when Thant took office on November 3, 1961, and the atmosphere was one of gloom. The office of Secretary-General itself was still faced with the threat that the Soviet Union would press for adoption of its troika plan. The Congo operation was adding new strains daily and the end was not in sight. The world situation generally was tense and uncertain, as was soon to be reflected in the Cuban missile crisis. And, with the escalation of the Vietnam war after 1964, both the international atmosphere and the functioning of the United Nations were to receive still further setbacks.

When Thant left office on December 31, 1971, was the situation better than when he took office? Or worse? Certainly, the international political climate had improved with the growing détente between the United States and the USSR and with the trend toward a European détente. The Congo conflict had long since ended. The Vietnam war was still in progress, but peace negotiations were continuing. The United States and the People's Republic of China were showing signs of patching up their differences. Peking had finally taken its place in the United Nations, ending the long conflict over Chinese representation. Whether the position of the United Nations itself was better in 1971 than in 1961 is difficult to say. Its prestige had suffered from its inability to take an active role in the Vietnam peace efforts, the Nigerian civil war, and the conflict between India and Pakistan, as well as its failure to settle such problems as the Middle East and Cyprus. Although the Organization could boast of its achievements in the economic and social field, it could not dispel the widespread public belief that it was impotent to deal with the big political problems of the day.

In a large measure, the Secretary-General was included in this public assessment. His standing among the Member governments, however, was another matter. One evidence of this was the fact that he was under strong pressure to accept an unprecedented third term. He achieved the difficult feat of remaining on excellent terms with all the big powers—and all of them, including the People's Republic of China, wanted him to stay on. This is all the more remarkable in view of his outspoken views on such questions as the United States bombing of North Vietnam and the Soviet military invasion of Czechoslovakia. One of his main regrets was not being able to solve the financial problems he had inherited. There is little doubt but that he contributed substantially to the development of the office of Secretary-General as a political organ of the United Nations. That he would maintain the independence of the office became apparent when, in 1961, he rejected Soviet attempts to make his decisions subject to consultations with certain under-secretaries, including those from the United States and the USSR.

Thant, like Hammarskjöld, was an ardent practioner of "quiet diplomacy." Much of his time, in fact, was occupied in the exercise of his good offices—often secretly and without any directive from any United Nations organ. "This quiet method of forestalling conflict," he said, "seems to me to be a part of the Secretary-General's role which should be continuously developed as an alternative to the specific—and much more dramatic—invocation of Article 99. There are good reasons why Article 99 has been specifically invoked only once. Nothing could be more divisive and useless than for the Secretary-General to bring a situation publicly to the Security Council when there is no practical possibility of the Council agreeing on effective or useful action. On the other hand, a quiet approach which avoids a public confrontation may often hold out some hope of success" (see pp. 595–96). Thant's best-known initiatives into the political field were his private intervention in the Cuban missile crisis and his frequent peace efforts in the Vietnam conflict. In the Cuban missile crisis, he was formally thanked by President John F. Kennedy and Chairman Nikita Khrushchev for his assistance. His intervention in the Vietnam conflict was also credited frequently with helping open the way for the peace talks. Thant himself was convinced that the exercise of his good offices constituted one of his most significant contributions to peace during his two terms as Secretary-General.

April 1977   MAX HARRELSON

⚜ *1968* ⚜

THE SITUATION IN THE MIDDLE EAST

JANUARY 1968

By JANUARY 1968 the six-day Middle East war had been over more than six months. The atmosphere, however, remained tense and little progress had been made toward implementing resolution 242 (1967), adopted by the Security Council on November 22, 1967, laying down principles on which it was hoped a permanent peace could be based. Border incidents continued on the cease-fire lines between Israel and Egypt and between Israel and Jordan. Shuttling between his headquarters in Nicosia and Jerusalem, Cairo, Amman and Beirut, the Secretary-General's special representative, Gunnar Jarring, had begun substantive discussions with Israeli and Arab leaders in an effort to implement the November 22 resolution. Jarring had made a preliminary round of visits between December 10 and 20 mainly for the purpose of getting acquainted. As reported by U Thant on December 22, Jarring had been received cordially and "all the governments visited welcomed the prospect of his early return to continue the conversations." Jarring's second round of visits began on December 26. By January 17, when the Secretary-General made his second progress report, Jarring had made a total of four visits to Jerusalem and three to Cairo. He had also made a second trip to both Amman and Beirut. Thant disclosed that Jarring had taken up a number of "secondary" questions including the possible release of the fifteen ships stranded in the Suez Canal and the exchange of prisoners of war, two factors in the continued tension.

Although Thant did not mention it in his January 17 report, Jarring's efforts played a major role in the exchange of prisoners between Israel and Egypt, which was announced by the International Committee of the Red Cross on January 11. On the other hand, his efforts on the clearance of the Suez became bogged down in an Israeli-Egyptian dispute over the procedure for removing the ships. Israel insisted that the clearance operations should be limited in the beginning to the southern part of the canal and that the movement of the stranded vessels should be southward. A serious incident occurred on January 30 when Egypt, ignoring Israel's objections, sought to extend its survey into the northern portion of the canal by sending two Suez Canal Authority launches into that area.

The launches were fired upon by Israeli forces. Foreseeing such a possibility, Thant had urged Egypt to limit its survey to the southern part pending the outcome of an appeal he had made to Israel on January 28. In his letter to Israel, the Secretary-General had pointed out that the survey was a technical undertaking and stated that he did not consider it a security risk for Israel. Israel's reply to Thant, delivered after the incident, said Israel still favored and would facilitate the southward release of the stranded vessels, but that any northward evacuation would have to be considered as a separate question. As a result of the incident and Israel's attitude, Egypt halted the whole operation, thereby leaving the canal blocked indefinitely.

Both Thant and Jarring had decided on a policy of silence with regard to the discussions on resolution 242 (1967). In his January 17 report, the Secretary-General said the talks had "not reached the stage at which any conclusions can be drawn" and that it would be premature to disclose the substance of the conversations. The one positive aspect was the readiness of all the parties to continue the Jarring mission.

Report on the Efforts of the Special Representative

NEW YORK　　　JANUARY 17, 1968

---

1. On December 22, 1967, in pursuance of paragraph 4 of Security Council resolution 242 (1967) of November 22, 1967, I submitted to the Security Council a report (S/8309) on the progress of the efforts of the special representative to the Middle East, Mr. Gunnar Jarring. The purpose of the present report is to cover his activities since December 22, 1967.

2. On December 26, 1967, Mr. Jarring left his headquarters in Nicosia for Jerusalem, from where he went to Cairo on December 27, returning to Nicosia on December 30. On January 3, 1968, he visited Jerusalem again, returning to Nicosia on January 4. On January 7 he went back to Jerusalem and on the same day to Amman. After returning to Nicosia on January 10, Mr. Jarring paid a one-day visit to Beirut on the following day. On January 16, he went again to Jerusalem and on the same day to

SOURCE: Security Council Official Records, Twenty-third Year, Supplement for January, February and March 1968, document S/8309/Add.1.

Cairo, from where he intends to return to Nicosia on the afternoon of January 18.

3. It would be premature at this time for me to report to the Council on the substance of Mr. Jarring's talks thus far with the governments concerned, since these talks are continuing at the wish of the parties and have not reached the stage at which any conclusions can be drawn. It may, however, be stated in general that the talks have covered two types of questions. The first of these is concerned with the large and fundamental problems, which are of course the most difficult ones and which are referred to in Security Council resolution 242 (1967) of November 22, 1967. The second type of questions are the kind of secondary problems, the solution of which would contribute to an improvement of the general atmosphere by relieving certain unnecessary hardships which have essentially resulted from the hostilities in June 1967. Such questions include the release of the ships stranded in the Suez Canal, the exchange of prisoners of war, and certain measures of a humanitarian character.

4. Mr. Jarring has been in regular communication with me throughout the talks and keeps me fully informed. He sees no need to return to New York for consultations at this stage of his mission, nor do I.

5. It is pertinent to note that the courtesy and willingness to cooperate on the part of all the governments visited, which was reported in my first report (S/8309), have continued to prevail. Mr. Jarring also reports that all of the governments visited have expressed positive reactions concerning the desirability of continued steps to improve the general atmosphere while at the same time searching for solutions to the fundamental problems. The governments visited have also expressed the wish that the round of talks with Mr. Jarring should continue, and he and I both take the same position. At the same time we are mindful of the time factor.

DISARMAMENT

THE EIGHTEEN-NATION COMMITTEE on Disarmament met in Geneva on January 18 in an atmosphere of optimism. After months of intensive negotiations inside and outside the United Nations, it appeared that a breakthrough was near on a treaty to prevent the further spread of nuclear weapons. In fact, the twenty-second session of the General Assembly was standing in recess ready to reconvene to consider the draft as soon as the expected agreement was reached. On December 19, 1967, the Assembly had asked the Committee to give top priority to completion of the treaty and to report back by March 15. In a message to the Committee on January 17, U Thant appealed to the delegates to "make every possible effort to achieve a mutually acceptable agreement within the time limit set for the submission of the report to the General Assembly." He called this the "immediate overriding task" and declared: "I regard the successful conclusion of a treaty for the non-proliferation of nuclear weapons as an indispensable first step towards further progress on disarmament." It was generally agreed that this would be the most significant international treaty in the disarmament field since the partial nuclear weapons test-ban treaty in 1963. The breakthrough had been virtually assured when the United States and the USSR submitted identical drafts of the proposed treaty on August 24, 1967. It became even more certain when they presented revised identical texts on January 18, taking into account many suggestions made during the Committee discussions. The new drafts by no means met all the objections of the non-nuclear states. The United States and the Soviet Union made more changes. New texts were presented to the Committee on March 11 and on March 14, one day ahead of the deadline set by the General Assembly, the Committee approved its report and forwarded it together with the draft treaty to the Assembly.

It was discussed by the resumed session of the Assembly from April 22 to June 12. After voting several additional amendments, the Assembly finally gave its approval to the draft and requested the depository governments to open the treaty for signature and ratification at the earliest possible date. Many non-nuclear countries remained unhappy with the treaty because of what they described as loopholes. One criticism was that the pact did not contain adequate provisions for the security of non-nuclear countries against possible nuclear attack. To meet this objection, the United States, the United Kingdom, and the USSR agreed to provide guarantees both individually and collectively through the Security Council. In a joint declaration they asserted that they would seek immediate Security Council action to assist any country that was attacked with nuclear weapons. The Council approved a resolution along these lines, sponsored by the three powers, reaffirming the right of individual and collective self-defense pending action by the Security Council.

---

1. Message to the Eighteen-Nation Committee on Disarmament

GENEVA   JANUARY 17, 1968

THE CONFERENCE of the Eighteen-Nation Committee is reconvening for a new session whose work may be crucial for the prospects of further progress on disarmament in the immediate future.

The Conference is resuming its task after a very brief recess, with a compelling sense of urgency. You have before you a number of resolutions adopted by the General Assembly at its twenty-second session. Once more they entrust important responsibilities to the Eighteen-Nation Committee.

The question of non-proliferation of nuclear weapons is at the top of the disarmament agenda. Resolution 2346 A (XXII) calls upon the Eighteen-Nation Committee urgently to continue its work on a draft non-proliferation treaty, and requests it to submit to the General Assembly on or before March 15, 1968, a full report on the treaty negotiations. I have often in the past referred to the real and grave dangers of nuclear proliferation and expressed the hope that a treaty on non-proliferation would be agreed upon and implemented at the earliest possible date. I regard the successful conclusion of a treaty for the non-proliferation of nuclear weapons as an indispensable first step toward further progress on disarmament. I wish on this occasion to appeal to the Committee to make every possible effort to achieve a mutually acceptable agreement within the time limit set for the submission of the report to the General Assembly.

SOURCE: UN Press Release SG/SM/891.

It is universally accepted that the ultimate goal is general and complete disarmament. On that question as well as on the questions of a comprehensive nuclear test ban and of the elimination of foreign military bases in the countries of Asia, Africa and Latin America, some guidelines have been provided by the General Assembly in the resolutions now before the Conference. These resolutions request the Eighteen-Nation Committee to report on the progress achieved to the Assembly at its twenty-third session. In another resolution the Assembly has referred to the possibility of negotiations by the Committee on the conclusion of a convention on the prohibition of the use of nuclear weapons. I am confident that the Conference will devote all due attention to these matters.

The immediate overriding task is, however, that of reaching agreement on a draft non-proliferation treaty. The years of patient negotiation by the parties to narrow and remove their differences on the treaty must now be brought to fruition. All the participants in the Conference will, I feel sure, exert their best efforts and utilize their full resources to achieve the right solution.

In extending to the Eighteen-Nation Committee on Disarmament my good wishes for success in its endeavors, I want to assure its members that I will follow their work with close interest and earnest hope.

---

2. Statement in the First Committee

NEW YORK   APRIL 26, 1968

EVER SINCE the General Assembly unanimously adopted resolution 1665 (XVI) on December 4, 1961, the prevention of the further spread of nuclear weapons has been one of the most important goals of the United Nations. The General Assembly has repeatedly called for the conclusion of a treaty on the non-proliferation of nuclear weapons as a matter of

SOURCE: UN Press Release SG/SM/937. The summary record is given in General Assembly Official Records, Resumed Twenty-second Session, First Committee, 1556th meeting.

urgent priority. During the intervening years, very great efforts have been made to achieve a generally acceptable treaty.

It is hardly necessary for me to stress in this forum the grave dangers that would confront the nations and peoples of the world if the proliferation of nuclear weapons is not halted. If these dreaded weapons were to spread, it might set off a "chain reaction" of proliferation with dire consequences for the security of all states—large and small, nuclear and non-nuclear.

As the distinguished delegates know, I have long regarded disarmament as the most important problem facing mankind. The report requested of me by the General Assembly on the effects and implications of nuclear weapons, which was prepared and agreed upon unanimously by a panel of international experts, sets forth very clearly and very starkly the threat of nuclear weapons. Among other things, it points to the high probability that "any further increase in the number of nuclear weapons states or any further elaboration of existing arsenals would lead to greater tension and greater instability in the world at large."

In the Introduction to my annual report to this twenty-second session of the General Assembly, I stated:

I regard the successful conclusion of a treaty for the non-proliferation of nuclear weapons as an indispensable first step toward further progress on disarmament. In fact, it is difficult to conceive of any agreement in the foreseeable future on any other measure of disarmament if it is not possible to reach agreement on a treaty to prevent the spread of nuclear weapons.

The presentation on March 11, 1968, to the Conference of the Eighteen-Nation Committee on Disarmament by the Union of Soviet Socialist Republics and the United States of America of a jointly agreed draft text of a treaty on non-proliferation of nuclear weapons was an event which marked the culmination of years of efforts toward reconciliation to achieve a mutually acceptable compromise. I am sure that the fact of this compromise agreement by these great powers will be welcomed as an important landmark in the field of disarmament.

The members of the General Assembly will, of course, understand that I am not commenting on the provisions of the draft treaty, which is a matter for them to consider, but am expressing my appreciation to the Co-Chairmen of that Conference for their success in having produced an agreed draft treaty, and to all the members of the Conference for their perseverance and most valuable contributions to the work on non-proliferation.

All the Members of the United Nations now have an opportunity to express their views and opinions on the draft treaty which has been submitted in the report of the Conference of the Eighteen-Nation Committee on Disarmament. I realize that there are some serious questions, including those concerning security assurances, which will require thorough consideration during the resumed session. In approaching these questions, the members of the First Committee will, I am confident, discharge their responsibilities with full consciousness of their interests and their obligations and those of the world community.

I should like to express the hope that all outstanding issues will soon be resolved, so that an agreed treaty on non-proliferation of nuclear weapons will come into force at the earliest possible date. Thus, the way will be open to achievement of the cessation of the nuclear arms race, to the dedication of nuclear energy exclusively for the benefit and not for the destruction of mankind, and to general and complete disarmament.

I extend to all of you my most earnest wishes for success in your work.

THE SITUATION IN VIETNAM

JANUARY TO MAY 1968

SIGNS BEGAN to appear during the first weeks of 1968 that the Vietnam problem might at last be headed toward the conference table. The harsh words from Washington and Hanoi were suddenly being replaced by conciliatory statements. U Thant told a press conference on January 18 that a recent statement by the foreign minister of North Vietnam had reinforced his own conviction that meaningful talks could take place within three or four weeks if the United States halted its bombing of North Vietnamese territory. He said the first step after a cessation of the bombing should be preliminary talks between Washington and Hanoi to create conditions congenial for further and wider discussions. Shortly afterward Thant resumed his own peace efforts, which had been in suspension since the spring of 1967. His new round of consultations began on February 8 when he conferred with Nguyen Hoa, Hanoi's consul-general in New Delhi, who affirmed that his government would "hold talks with Washington on all relevant matters at an appropriate time after the unconditional cessation of bombing and of all other acts of war" against North Vietnam. Thant handed him a list of questions that he promised to transmit to Hanoi. Thant, in New Delhi for a session of the United Nations Conference on Trade and Development, also held a long discussion with Prime Minister Indira Gandhi on the Vietnam problem, and during stopovers in Moscow and London en route back to New York he talked with top Soviet and British officials.

While the Secretary-General was in London, he received word that the North Vietnamese representative in France, Mai Van Bo, had received a message for transmittal to him. He flew to Paris immediately. The message was a reply to the questions he had submitted to Nguyen Hoa in New Delhi. In a meeting with Mai Van Bo on February 14, Thant was told that talks between Washington and Hanoi could begin just as soon as the bombing halt became effective and that either side could bring up any matter. Mai Van Bo mentioned specifically two subjects, a reduction of the fighting in South Vietnam and the reconvening of the Geneva Conference of 1954. The Secretary-General then returned to New York, where he gave a full report to the permanent United States representative, Ambassador Arthur J. Goldberg, and to Saigon's United Nations observer, Huu Chi. Thant also gave his report to President Johnson and Secretary of State Dean Rusk on February 21 during a brief trip to Washington. Johnson told the Secretary-General he sincerely desired a peaceful settlement. He affirmed the continued validity of the San Antonio formula, which he had presented in a speech the previous September 29 at San Antonio, Texas. The two-sentence formula read as follows: "The United States is willing to stop all aerial and naval bombardment of North Vietnam when this will lead to productive discussions. We, of course, assume that while discussions proceed, North Vietnam will not take advantage of the bombing cessation or limitation."

This was the prelude to a breakthrough. The President announced on March 31 that United States bombing of North Vietnam would cease "except in the area north of the demilitarized zone where the continued enemy buildup directly threatens allied forward positions and where the movements of their troops and supplies are clearly related to that threat." It was not clear immediately whether Hanoi would be satisfied with the United States move, since the North Vietnamese had been insisting upon a complete and unconditional cessation of the bombing. However, on April 3 Radio Hanoi stated that North Vietnam was ready to meet with United States representatives to consider an end to the fighting. On the following day, Johnson paid a surprise visit to Thant at United Nations Headquarters in New York. All seemed to be settled except the time and place of the talks between Hanoi and Washington. This proved more difficult than it had initially appeared. Thant told reporters in Geneva on April 8 that he had suggested Geneva as a possible site and had mentioned "one or two other capitals." The problem was still unresolved on April 23 when he stopped over in Paris on his return from the International Conference on Human Rights in Teheran. At that time he disclosed that the sites he had suggested in addition to Geneva were Warsaw, Paris, and Phnom Penh. Thant ackowledged that he had been in touch with Hanoi and Washington continuously on the question of a site, but he made it clear that he did not expect to take part in the preliminary peace talks, once they got under way. "Only the two sides—Washington and Hanoi—will be involved," he told Paris reporters. The talks finally began in Paris on May 10, opening a new and trying phase of the problem, a phase of talking while the fighting continued.

---

1. From Transcript of Press Conference

NEW YORK   JANUARY 18, 1968

. . . MR. FOELL[1] (President, United Nations Correspondents Association): . . . Last night, in his State of the Union message, President

SOURCE: *UN Monthly Chronicle,* Vol. V, February 1968, pp. 47–58.

[1]Earl Foell, *Christian Science Monitor.*

Johnson said that he was still exploring North Vietnam's latest peace talk statements. In the past, you have often played a central role in this so far abortive exploration process. Are you aware of the extent of the current exploration? Are you satisfied that they are sincere? And are you hopeful that they will lead to concrete results?

THE SECRETARY-GENERAL: I am sure all of you will agree with me that it would be very improper on the part of the Secretary-General of the United Nations to comment on the public statement of any head of state or head of government, particularly the head of state of a big power. Therefore, in this context, I do not want to make any observations. But, in the particular case of Vietnam I want to make a few observations, not necessarily in the context of the President's State of the Union message last night.

I have been saying all along that I was convinced—and I am still convinced—that once the bombing of North Vietnam is ceased, is ended, there will be meaningful talks in the course of three to four weeks. As you will recall, this conviction was reiterated by some heads of government and by some statesmen and diplomats who had close relations with Hanoi. You will also recall that Hanoi had never publicly refuted these statements. The statement of the foreign minister of Hanoi on December 29 last reinforced my conviction that meaningful talks would take place once the bombing of North Vietnam was ceased, in the course of three to four weeks.

QUESTION: Mr. Secretary-General, in connection with what you have just said, Hanoi is now claiming that it will talk if the bombing is stopped, and the President has indicated that the bombing will stop if there is some indication from Hanoi that North Vietnam would not take advantage of our military position. Do you consider this a narrowing of the gap between the two stands, or a widening of the gap, and is there anything that you can do to help narrow it still further?

THE SECRETARY-GENERAL: I think the positions of the two sides are well known. I would not attempt to interpret these new stands as narrowing or widening, but everybody is aware of the position of the United States government. It obviously wanted some sign of reciprocity. If the bombing of North Vietnam is to be stopped, the other side's point of view, as I have explained to you on a previous occasion, is completely different. Although they did not admit, and they have not admitted the presence of North Vietnamese regular forces in South Vietnam, it is, of course, common knowledge that quite a sizable force of North Vietnamese regulars have been operating in South Vietnam for some time.

According to official statements, emanating from Washington, there are at present 50,000 to 55,000 North Vietnamese regulars in the South, and, of course, it is public knowledge that there are about 500,000 United States and allied troops in South Vietnam, apart from the fact that there are over 200,000 South Vietnamese indigenous Vietcong troops operating in the South and over 200,000 government troops under the authority of the government in Saigon, also operating in the South.

So, in terms of figures in the view of Hanoi, if Hanoi has to reciprocate it will be militarily in a very disadvantageous position. This is one of the factors, and of course there are other factors too, which motivated Hanoi in not coming out with any definitive statement on this question of reciprocity.

QUESTION: Have you had any private reassurances, either directly or indirectly, from Hanoi on this recent situation on these statements by the leading Hanoi figures?

THE SECRETARY-GENERAL: Apart from the published statement, I have no other private source of information emanating from Hanoi.

QUESTION: Sir, you have been one of those who have agreed that, because neither of the two Vietnams, the principal parties, are Members, this Organization cannot be directly involved in Vietnam. But the situation is fast developing in that area where a neighboring state, Cambodia, is being threatened with being invaded by a big power in hot pursuit. What should the United Nations do and what does it plan to do?

THE SECRETARY-GENERAL: As far as Cambodia is concerned, you will remember that the Geneva Conference of 1954 had categorically declared Cambodia to be a neutral state. I have followed the developments in and around Cambodia for some time with very close interest. On this question I should like to make a brief statement.

First of all, Cambodia is a Member of the United Nations and, according to the principles of the Charter, all Members of the United Nations have undertaken to respect Cambodia's sovereignty and territorial integrity. In addition, when Cambodia joined the United Nations in 1955, it already enjoyed the status of neutrality, which was internationally recognized by the Geneva agreements of 1954 and confirmed in the same year, in July 1954, in the declaration of the Royal Government of Cambodia. It follows that, from the point of view of the Geneva agreements, as well as of the United Nations, the status of neutrality of Cambodia is particularly significant. Therefore, it is my conviction that it would be in the interests of peace for all states and all authorities, in particular the members of the Geneva Conference, to continue to respect the status of neutrality of the Kingdom of Cambodia. I am convinced that Cambodia is making all efforts to preserve its neutrality and independence in a very difficult situation. In this difficult task, I hope Cambodia will succeed, convinced as I am that the preservation of its neutrality is in the general interest of Southeast Asia and of the world at large.

QUESTION: To go back to reciprocity, is it your understanding that if the bombing were to cease and talks were to begin, the North Vietnamese would continue to supply their troops and the Vietcong, but would not send in new forces to increase their forces already in South Vietnam?

THE SECRETARY-GENERAL: On this I do not know; I really do not know. But, as I have said on a previous occasion, once the bombing is stopped, there will be talks between Washington and Hanoi. I am afraid that the fighting will still go on in the South. That is the indication I have received from all sources, as in the case of the 1954 Geneva agreements; while the Geneva Conference was going on, the fighting was still going on also in Vietnam. First of all, a cease-fire in the present circumstances is a very difficult and delicate issue. I do not believe that Hanoi will agree to any suggestion of a cease-fire, because Hanoi's position, as you know, is that it has not been primarily involved in the South. The fighting is being done by the South Vietnamese themselves. If Hanoi were to come out with an agreement on a cease-fire, it would be an open admission of Hanoi's predominant role in South Vietnam. That is one aspect, in my view, which will render any statement from Hanoi very difficult, if not impossible.

As I have also said on a previous occasion, once the bombing stops there will be talks between Hanoi and Washington. The meeting between Hanoi and Washington will not solve the problem of South Vietnam. But such a meeting will create conditions congenial for the next step to be taken.

So what are the next steps to be taken? I think it is very necessary for all of us to be clear in our minds what should be the next steps. In my view, the next steps should be a meeting between Washington and Hanoi that will deal with relevant questions pertaining to the United States and North Vietnam. At the same time, these talks should generate further and wider discussions, with a view to the reconvening of the Geneva Conference—of course, after appropriate and necessary consultations.

This is a "must." I think negotiations must lead to the reconvening of the Geneva Conference.

What should this reconvened Geneva Conference do? In my view, the reconvened Geneva Conference must focus its attention on the modalities of the implementation of the agreements arrived at in 1954. This, in my view, is the most sensible line of approach. The reconvened Geneva Conference should not involve itself with other extraneous activities and issues. It should concentrate its attention on the modalities, on the implementation of the Geneva agreements of 1954.

The basic issues are connected primarily with the agreements arrived at thirteen years ago, and of course there is some difference between the implementation of the Geneva agreements of 1954 and coming to some sort of agreement on the basis of the Geneva agreements of 1954. There is some difference. I am afraid that the better alternative, the most sensible alternative, is to concentrate attention on the full implementation of the Geneva agreements of 1954. . . .

QUESTION: Mr. Secretary-General, you have shown us the road to peace in Vietnam, but I think you have also made it obvious that nobody now is of a mind to take that road. What can be done now to get peace in Vietnam?

THE SECRETARY-GENERAL: Well, Mr. Grant,[2] I have defined priorities regarding steps to be taken leading toward peace. The first priority is the cessation of the bombing of North Vietnam. So long as that priority is not met, I do not see any way how the conflict can be shifted from the battlefield to the conference table. I think this is concerned with the understanding of the basic issues involved in the war in Vietnam. To make my point clear, let me say this. If you really believe that all the trouble in South Vietnam was caused exclusively by the so-called communist aggression from the North, and have no other causes, then you have to agree that the bombing of North Vietnam is necessary, because the government in Saigon has the legitimate right to request its allies to come to its aid and bomb North Vietnam—and, even more, they must do something against those countries which have been providing the sinews of war to North Vietnam. That is the logical conclusion on the premise that you agree that all the troubles in South Vietnam were caused exclusively by the so-called communist aggression from the North. Then you have to agree that bombing is justified, and that even

[2]Donald Grant, *St. Louis Post-Dispatch.*

further steps beyond North Vietnam are justified—if you agree with that premise. But, as you all know, I do not subscribe to that view.

On the other hand, there is a school of thought which maintains that all the trouble in South Vietnam is caused by the so-called United States aggression. If you agree that all the trouble in South Vietnam is caused by the so-called United States aggression against the people of Vietnam, then you have to agree that the United States must leave Vietnam tomorrow. As I have explained on a previous occasion, I do not subscribe to that view either.

The causes leading to the conflict in Vietnam are so complex and so involved, and pertain to many issues, including the struggle of a long-suffering people for a quarter of a century for national independence and national identity—social upheavals, a struggle against economic disparities, a struggle against economic discrimination. There are so many factors involved which culminated in the Geneva Conference of 1954. I think we have to pick up the threads from the Geneva Conference of 1954.

As you know, the Geneva Conference took place and very important decisions were adopted. I do not suppose that the signatories to the Geneva agreements of 1954 were so naïve as to be unaware of the political implications of their action. They did what they did with the full knowledge of the implication of this action. I have been supporting the Geneva agreements of 1954 from their very inception. Therefore, the basic issues are: Why were those Geneva agreements not implemented? Who were responsible for the nonimplementation of those Geneva agreements, and why? These "whys" and "hows" and "whos" must be answered if you want to assess the situation in its proper perspective.

QUESTION: Mr. Secretary-General, the Canadian government early this week, on the occasion of Prime Minister Levi Eshkol's visit, expressed the view that the Middle East situation, like other world problems, is linked in some way to the situation in Vietnam, that the problem in the Middle East cannot be solved until the problem of Vietnam is solved. Would you care to comment? Do you hold a similar view, Mr. Secretary-General?

THE SECRETARY-GENERAL: I would not go that far. I would not go so far as to say that the Middle Eastern crisis cannot be solved unless and until the crisis in Vietnam is solved. But I agree with the assessment that the Vietnam war poisoned the atmosphere and caused a very serious setback in East-West détente. It was even reflected in the General

Assembly and the Security Council, as you are aware. So the Vietnam war has definite and direct impacts on any crisis situations anywhere. But I would not go so far as to say that the solution of the Middle Eastern problem rests or is predicated upon the settlement of the Vietnam war.

QUESTION: Mr. Secretary-General, do you believe that the International Control Commission for Cambodia should be strengthened, so as to inspect any border violations from Vietnam by either side?

THE SECRETARY-GENERAL: Well, Mr. Estabrook,[3] it is primarily a question for the International Control Commission to consider and decide. I think the International Control Commission is quite competent within the framework of its functions to enlarge its activities or to enlarge its powers. . . .

QUESTION: Mr. Secretary-General, how do you interpret the insistence on the part of President Nguyen Van Thieu of South Vietnam that they shall have something to do about making the peace terms? Do you consider this a delaying tactic on the part of President Thieu and his Vice-President, General Nguyen Cao Ky?

THE SECRETARY-GENERAL: Well, I do not suppose you would really expect an answer to this question. But you will recall that early last year, the Prime Minister of Ceylon made a proposal—I think a very ingenious proposal. It was to the effect that the problem of Vietnam must be settled by the Vietnamese people themselves. With a view to achieving this result, he suggested that a meeting between the government in Hanoi and the government in Saigon and the National Liberal Front should be held to discuss the whole problem. I was asked about this at a press conference in Colombo in the course of my visit there, and I said that there was merit in this proposal, because it conforms to the generally recognized principle of the people of Vietnam settling their problems themselves. Apart from that, I do not want to make any observations on the attitude or motivations of the government in Vietnam.

QUESTION: Since the appointment of Ambassador Gunnar Jarring as mediator in the Middle East, do you have any enlightening pronouncements to make at this time pertaining to finding a solution to the Middle East crisis involving the principles listed in the Security Council resolution and including the withdrawal of Israeli forces from all occupied territories?

[3]Robert Estabrook, *Washington Post*.

THE SECRETARY-GENERAL: As you all know, I have submitted two reports to the Security Council on this question. The second report was circulated only yesterday. Since Ambassador Jarring is very actively involved in discussions and consultations with the parties primarily concerned, I do not think it would be in the public interest—and I think it would be even harmful—if I projected myself into the picture and made some substantive announcements. I am sure you will agree with me that Ambassador Jarring has been doing a magnificent job, and from time to time I have had occasion to congratulate him on the progress of his efforts.

QUESTION: Mr. Secretary-General, in the light of the political decisions coming out of London, and of course the United States, which cripple aid and restrict trade possibilities for developing countries, what can these developing countries hope to get from the upcoming New Delhi meeting of UNCTAD [United Nations Conference on Trade and Development]?

THE SECRETARY-GENERAL: Well, you will remember the Algiers Declaration which is a prelude to the New Delhi conference. The Algiers conference very clearly defined the issues, and it is for the New Delhi conference to devise ways and means of acting on this definition of issues.

I think we have passed the stage of defining the issues and outlining the theories. We have come to the stage of action. I think the New Delhi conference should focus its attention on the practical measures to be taken, not only on the question of trade, but also on the question of aid. As you know, the gap between the rich countries and the poor countries is still getting wider, in spite of multifarious efforts that have been made in and outside the United Nations. The first session of UNCTAD which took place in 1964 in Geneva outlined priorities and steps to be taken. But still, the gulf is widening. It is, in my view, much more basic and much more fundamental to the future of the world, the future of the peace and security of the world, than the gulf between East and West.

I think it is worth reiterating that we are apt to focus our attention on the widening gulf or the narrowing gulf between East and West. What is much more fundamental and what is much more significant, and in the long run what is much more explosive, is the widening gulf between the North and the South. Unless and until leaders of men and leaders of thought realize this aspect, I am afraid to think of the future. This is one hope I have for the forthcoming second UNCTAD Conference in New Delhi.

QUESTION: Mr. Secretary-General, a moment ago you said that you disagreed with both schools of thought on Vietnam: one saying it is a communist aggression; the other saying it is a United States aggression. On the first school, by your asking for a bombing cessation by the United States, you clearly express your opinion on United States behavior in this context. Would you care to address yourself to the Soviet Union in the context of the second school?

THE SECRETARY-GENERAL: No, I do not want to refer to any big power in the context of the subscription to these two theories or concepts, but I am convinced that any simplistic explanation or any, if I may say so, juvenile approach to the war in Vietnam as aggression from this, or aggression from that, quarter is very misleading. I think you have to understand the background to the whole conflict, the circumstances leading to the Geneva Conference, as I have said, the circumstances leading to the nonimplementation of the Geneva Conference, and further complications. I think these are very relevant to a proper assessment of the whole situation. Let me say again that this aggression, from this or that side, is an oversimplication and therefore misleading.

QUESTION: Mr. Secretary-General, one year ago intensive diplomatic efforts were focused on the Tet truce in February, offering an unusual opportunity for getting talks started. Do you believe the forthcoming Tet truce offers such an opportunity this year?

THE SECRETARY-GENERAL: Well, I do not know what is going on behind the scenes. But I expressed the opinion only last week that any truce, however short or however long, is desirable, because it will create an atmosphere congenial for more desirable talks in more desirable contexts. So in this context I have always supported any move from any quarter for a truce—of one day, or one week, or one month. I am always in favor of it. But I do not know what are the real negotiations or discussions behind the scenes regarding the extension of this truce.

QUESTION: Mr. Secretary-General, how would you interpret the fact that President Johnson, in his message last night to the Congress, did not mention the United Nations once? Is it an ominous sign?

THE SECRETARY-GENERAL: If I remember correctly, President Johnson did mention Ambassador Jarring's activities in the Middle East. And if I remember correctly, he even endorsed Ambassador Jarring's effort for peace. And for this I am grateful.

QUESTION: Mr. Secretary-General, do you see anything that the United Nations will or can do in Nigeria, in Biafra?

THE SECRETARY-GENERAL: The question of Nigeria and Biafra is before the Organization of African Unity. I attended the last session of the OAU Conference in Kinshasa last September. The matter was brought to the attention of the OAU by the members themselves. The OAU has taken certain steps toward the settlement of that problem. The OAU has formed a committee. The committee is actively involved with this question. And since the regional organization is actively involved in the problem, I do not think it will be useful or even desirable for the United Nations to be involved. . . .

2. *Statement to the Press*

NEW YORK   FEBRUARY 24, 1968

VARIOUS QUESTIONS have been raised, and different interpretations have been given, following my recent talks in certain capitals. Indeed, it is for me a great advantage in the discharge of my responsibilities as Secretary-General of the United Nations to be able to meet at intervals with leaders of governments and to exchange views with them. Obviously, in the present circumstances, the war in Vietnam has taken precedence over all other subjects in the discussions, simply as a result of the increasing concern that this war causes the world over. Although it is for the parties directly involved, ultimately—and, I hope, soon—to take the steps and establish the contacts necessary for negotiations, which they know must take place if this war is ever to be brought to an end, the Vietnam conflict has repercussions which extend far beyond the parties themselves. That is why I feel it would be useful to present this account of what happened during these recent meetings.

Some of the details of my travel have already been made public on a day-to-day basis by the United Nations Headquarters. Nevertheless, as

SOURCE: *UN Monthly Chronicle,* Vol. V, March 1968, pp. 15–17.

I feel it relevant to what I wish to state today, I will record them again in the order in which they took place. As is known, I took the opportunity during a brief visit to New Delhi in connection with the second session of the United Nations Conference on Trade and Development to meet the Consul General of the Democratic Republic of Vietnam (North Vietnam), Mr. Nguyen Hoa, on February 8, and to discuss with him the question of Vietnam. The Consul General affirmed that his government "would hold talks with Washington on all relevant matters at an appropriate time after the unconditional cessation of bombing and of all other acts of war against the Democratic Republic of Vietnam." He drew my attention to the statement that had been made on this subject the day before (February 7) by the Foreign Minister of the Democratic Republic of Vietnam (North Vietnam) in an interview with a press agency, which said, in particular, that talks will begin as soon as the United States has proved that it has really unconditionally stopped the bombing. I then put to him some questions which he promised to transmit to his government, assuring me that it would reply to these questions as soon as possible.

While in New Delhi, I called on the President of India, Dr. Zakir Husain, and had several meetings with the Prime Minister of India, Mrs. Indira Gandhi. From there, I flew to Moscow where I was received by the Secretary-General of the Communist Party, Mr. Leonid Brezhnev, the Chairman of the Council of Ministers, Premier Aleksei Kosygin, President Nikolai V. Podgorny, and Foreign Minister Andrei A. Gromyko. In London, I was received by Prime Minister Harold Wilson and had discussions with him, Foreign Secretary George Brown, Commonwealth Secretary George Thomson, the Minister of State Lord Chalfont, and the Leader of the Opposition, Mr. Edward Heath.

While in London on February 13 I was informed that the Delegate General of the Democratic Republic of Vietnam (North Vietnam) in France, Mr. Mai Van Bo, had just received a message from his government for transmittal to me. This was the reply to the questions I had submitted in New Delhi. I left for Paris on the 14th and saw Mr. Mai Van Bo, who conveyed to me the reply from his government, dated February 13, to my questions. In this message, there was a further clarification of Hanoi's position concerning discussions with Washington. I was told that the Democratic Republic of Vietnam (North Vietnam) would hold talks with the United States at the appropriate time, that is, as soon as the unconditional cessation of bombing and of all other acts of war against the Democratic Republic of Vietnam (North Vietnam) became effective. I was further informed that, at the talks, the United States could bring up any matter for discussion in the same way as the Democratic Republic of Vietnam (North Vietnam) could bring up any matter. In reply to my query, Mr. Mai Van Bo stated that the question of the reduction in the fighting in South Vietnam, the question of the reconvening of the Geneva Conference, and any other question could be brought up at the talks.

On the same day, I was received by President Charles de Gaulle and Foreign Minister Maurice Couve de Murville. Upon my return to New York on February 15, I informed Ambassador Arthur Goldberg of the substance of my discussions on Vietnam during my visit to various countries. On February 16, I conferred with the permanent observer of the Republic of Vietnam (South Vietnam), Mr. Nguyen Huu Chi. On February 21, I was received by President Lyndon B. Johnson and Secretary of State Dean Rusk in Washington. The President reaffirmed his continued desire to achieve a peaceful settlement and the continued validity of the San Antonio formula. Both the President and the Secretary of State stressed the nonmilitary advantage provision of that formula.

My talks in various capitals have reinforced my conviction which I have repeatedly expressed in my public statements on the issue of Vietnam for the past three years, namely, that the question is essentially a political problem which cannot be solved through the application of military force. In the light of my talks, I reaffirm all that I have said in the past concerning my assessment of the Vietnam problem and my approach to it. If the Vietnam question is seen as a contest of unyielding will, there can be no solution. In the broader context it appears, indeed, that both the United States and the Soviet Union are firmly determined to prevent the defeat of the side which each supports. If such a trend continues, the conclusion is inescapable that there will be continued intensification and escalation of the conflict, resulting in unforeseeable developments with dire consequences.

On the other hand, my recent contacts have confirmed my view that, if essential steps are taken, they will lead to a chain of events which, in the end, can bring about a just solution to the problem, and which will save both South Vietnam and North Vietnam from devastation and virtual destruction and will offer a chance for the people of Vietnam to regain a sense of national identity and to reconstruct their wartorn country. Everywhere I found a genuine desire to bring this tragic conflict to an end. The increased intensity of the hostilities during the past few weeks should not lead to the conclusion that the door is closed for negotiations. In my view, the indispensable first step of ending all bombing and other acts of war against the Democratic Republic of Vietnam (North Vietnam) should be taken and could be taken without too great a military risk. If such a step were to be taken, I am more than ever convinced that meaningful talks will take place much earlier than is generally supposed, even perhaps within a matter of a few days. As for the questions concerning the conduct of the fighting after the unconditional cessation of the bombing, particularly in the demilitarized zone and across the frontiers, it can reasonably be assumed that these will be dealt with in good faith. The parties themselves should solve this problem in order to allow for the larger negotiations to take place, with the participation of all parties concerned, including the government of the Republic of Vietnam (South Vietnam) and the National Liberation Front of South Vietnam.

The Vietnam war has already poisoned the atmosphere and strained international relations. This strain is keenly felt in the United Nations, whose effective functioning has been impaired as a result. We are witnessing more and more the unfortunate and undesirable repercussions of this war in other parts of the world.

Inasmuch as the United Nations remains humanity's main hope for peace, it is my duty, regardless of all criticisms, to try to reflect the consensus of international public opinion and the deep concern which has expressed itself through the forum of the General Assembly.

Indeed, the world is anguished and sickened by the continued intensity and savagery of the war. It is heartrending to witness the agony of the innocent civilians who cannot possibly know what it is all about. Also the military casualties steadily mount. The ugliness of the war is matched only by its futility. There can be no victory, no defeat, only more suffering, more death, and more destruction. The very survival of Vietnam is at stake. It is time to call a halt.

3. Statement Recorded for Television and Radio

NEW YORK   APRIL 3, 1968

THIS MORNING at about 10:00 o'clock, I received the following news dispatch by Reuters. It reads: "Hanoi Radio said tonight that North Vietnam was ready to meet with American representatives to consider an end to the fighting."

Based on this news dispatch I issued the following message at noon today. The message is as follows:

I have read with gratification news reports that the government of North Vietnam is ready to send representatives to meet with United States representatives to consider an end to the fighting.

I very much hope that such talks will constitute a positive first step toward ending the tragic conflict in Vietnam.

In this context, I am happy to note that the initiative taken by President Johnson in de-escalating the war has led to this promising development.

Finally, I wish to reiterate my long-held conviction that meaningful talks will take place even perhaps within a matter of a few days once all bombing and other acts of war against North Vietnam are ended.

SOURCE: UN Press Release SG/SM/923/Rev.1.

4. Statement to the Press

NEW YORK   APRIL 13, 1968

IN THE COURSE of my visit to Geneva, Paris, and the Benelux countries, I had opportunities of contact with both Washington and Hanoi. I feel

SOURCE: UN Press Release SG/SM/928.

very strongly the urgent need for agreement on the venue for preliminary talks which both sides have agreed to undertake.

Any further delay in the agreement on the venue would be most unfortunate in view of the fact that massive destruction of life and property is still going on. I would fervently appeal to both sides to come to a prompt agreement on the choice of the venue.

---

5. Statement to the Press

NEW YORK　　　　APRIL 24, 1968

THREE WEEKS have elapsed since agreement has been reached between the United States and the Democratic Republic of Vietnam to hold preliminary talks. Taking into account the considerations publicly advanced by both sides regarding the selection of a venue for such talks, it seems to me that the range of choice has now narrowed down to a few cities. Among these, in my view, Warsaw and Paris could be regarded as suitable sites.

While I am not aware of any new developments in this regard, it is distressingly clear to me that meanwhile the war in Vietnam has been raging unabated. Bombing raids above the 17th parallel in the past weeks were reported to be more intensive than ever before, although the area of bombing is more limited. There are signs that fighting in the South will increase in intensity. Such a situation is far from propitious for meaningful preliminary talks, and I would fervently appeal to all parties directly involved in the war to endeavor to create a more favorable atmosphere. I also appeal to Washington and Hanoi to agree without further delay on a venue for the preliminary talks.

SOURCE:　UN Press Release SG/SM/934.

6. *Statement to the Press*

NEW YORK   MAY 3, 1968

THE AGREEMENT of the Democratic Republic of Vietnam and the United States to hold preliminary talks in Paris beginning on May 10 will be hailed with satisfaction throughout the world. I am very happy at this encouraging development which, while only a first step, is a vital and indispensable one. I most earnestly hope that the preliminary talks will be amicable and fruitful.

The parties may be assured that the international community heartily applauds their decision to go to the conference table and will readily extend its cooperation and assistance whenever required. I am also confident that the government of France will afford every help and make all necessary arrangements for the proper conduct of these talks.

SOURCE: UN Press Release SG/SM/940.

7. *Excerpts from Speech at the University of Alberta*

EDMONTON, ALBERTA   MAY 13, 1968

DURING THE PAST four years or so, we have seen an escalation and intensification of the fighting in Vietnam to such an extent that this has become a major threat to the maintenance of international peace and security. For a variety of reasons, both historical and political, the United Nations as an organization has been powerless to intervene or to

SOURCE: *UN Monthly Chronicle,* Vol. V, June 1968, pp. 112–114.

promote in any way either a de-escalation of the fighting or a peaceful solution to the conflict. Meanwhile the Vietnam war has adversely affected not only the relations between the major powers but also the entire atmosphere in the United Nations. I believe that, but for the Vietnam war, there are many areas where international cooperation may have resulted in producing solutions to long-standing problems.

It is for this reason, among others, that I have been involved in my personal capacity in the past four years in trying to contribute to a just and peaceful solution of this tragic war. In the course of 1964, I attempted, without success, to bring about a dialogue between Washington and Hanoi. Since 1965, I have, in my private capacity, offered several formulas to the parties directly concerned with a view to shifting the quest for a solution from the field of battle to the conference table, and creating a favorable atmosphere for fruitful negotiations.

I have always held the view, which I reiterate today, that there are certain essential first steps that need to be taken in this context, and that the first and most important step is the unconditional cessation of the bombing of North Vietnam. Many experts and even responsible officials in the United States have testified that the bombing has had little or no effect on the rate of movement of North Vietnamese to the South. On the other hand, the continuation of the bombing has only hardened the determination of the North to prosecute the war, and not to negotiate under duress. I also regard such bombing as of questionable morality and doubtful legality.

At long last, Washington and Hanoi have agreed to hold preliminary talks in Paris and the first order of business is reported to be the discussion of the unconditional cessation of bombing and other acts of war against the Democratic Republic of Vietnam. I believe that once agreement has been reached on this issue, all other matters can be brought up by either side.

I have all along held the view that all wars are evil and basically alike. All wars have brought about immense destruction of property and priceless human lives. In modern war, more powerful weapons are used, which can kill more people and bring about wholesale destruction of both life and property. At the present time, and in this nuclear age, wars have become obsolete as instruments of national policy. Further, it is difficult to contain a war in view of the ever-present risk of its spreading and of the involvement of the major powers in it. This is indeed a most serious state of affairs.

It seems to me that the real issue of the Vietnam war has gradually become, not so much the political rightness or wrongness of one side or the other, as the savage conduct of the war itself. I find it difficult to express adequately the strong sense of repugnance to all established standards and norms of civilized society that the continuance of this savage war evokes. I do not see how one can build a democratic government or a stable society over huge graveyards and with the participation of enormous refugee camps. I know that advocates of escalation prescribe more drastic and large-scale destruction, but such senseless escalation would only produce a cure that is infinitely worse than the disease; in the words of an eminent theologian, "The operation might be successful but the patient would certainly be buried and the hospital buried with him."

The savagery of the fighting in Vietnam has been the subject of serious discussion by deeply concerned leaders everywhere. I am very much afraid that the violence that we are witnessing in Vietnam is bound to have its repercussions elsewhere. In fact, I regard the prevailing mood of violence in the United States and elsewhere as a consequence of the psychological climate created by the Vietnam war. I fear that if this trend is not reversed, and if the principle of the sanctity of human life is not re-established, the future for international peace and security itself is indeed a very dark one.

The experience of the last four years must surely have convinced all parties that only by a direct dialogue will they be able to bring this conflict to an end. All along, I have been urging that the problem be solved by negotiation because no durable result could be achieved by the mere application of military force. I fail to see how, in the circumstances prevailing, the war could bring about a clear-cut victory or defeat for one side or the other. The terrain is such and the nature of the fighting is so organized that there can be no end to the guerrilla warfare, as the record of the past twenty years has shown. There is no doubt that the guerrilla activity has resulted in considerable loss of life and destruction. On the other side, huge flying machines have been used to rain down death and destruction in the form of bombs, napalm, and rockets, but this has not brought about any conclusive military victory, even if it is claimed that a particular operation is successful or is the largest strike up to date.

It is also commonly held that all the problems in Vietnam can be resolved once the people of Vietnam are given the right to cast their votes. I simply fail to see how free and fair elections can be conducted in a war situation while arms are lying all around. There is a Burmese saying, "One has to fear the nearest sword." When fear is the motivating force in casting one's ballot, how can one expect free and fair elections?

The Vietnam war has often been represented as a "holy war" against communism. I regard this concept as entirely erroneous. I personally feel and have always felt that nationalism is a main motivating force in Vietnam. Nationalism is a force which is much more potent than political ideology. In the face of the adversity which has befallen Vietnam, nationalism has offered its people a new faith in their ability to maintain their identity and renewed their confidence in their own destiny. In spite of the grave divisions—territorial, political, and religious—in Vietnam, I believe that nationalism still remains the strongest motivation for the people of Vietnam.

Once peace is restored, could we not expect that all the energies and talents of the people of Vietnam would be turned toward healing their divisions and toward the reconstruction and modernization of both parts of the country? Indeed, one may expect that Vietnam, given its natural resources and the intellectual capacity and vigor of its people, would at some future date become the moving spirit of a new cooperative effort among the countries of the region, irrespective of their overall political systems.

In this connection, let me remind you that on July 21, 1954, at the closing session of the Geneva Conference, British Foreign Secretary Anthony Eden read what became known as "The Final Declaration of the Geneva Conference." The Final Declaration was intended to set forth the principles of a future political settlement for what had been French Indo-China. One of the clauses of that Declaration was of special significance. Item 6 stated that the conferees recognized that "the military demarcation line" which the conferees had drawn at the 17th parallel "is provisional and should not in any way be interpreted as constituting a political or territorial boundary." The important point to remember is that the 17th parallel was never intended to be a permanent demarcation line, cutting up Vietnam into two parts.

We are all aware, of course, that the projected elections did not take place in July 1956. Since that date, the Democratic Republic of Vietnam has believed that it has been cheated and that what was won on the battlefield by blood and sweat was lost at the conference table. It is also important to remember that many leaders in Hanoi were born in the South and many leaders in the South, including Vice-President Ky, were born in the North. President Ho Chi Minh himself had his education in the city of Hue, which has recently been the scene of such wholesale destruction.

However, it is my understanding, based on the programs presented by the interested parties, including the National Liberation Front of South Vietnam, that the unification of the two Vietnams is not an immediate problem; it is a matter which can be decided upon in due course when the overall situation is much more settled.

I believe that the Paris talks should start an irreversible trend toward the normalization of the situation in Vietnam. No pretext should be offered and no excuse accepted by either side to halt the movement toward gradual normalization. It may be inevitable that the talks should be protracted and that meanwhile both sides should seek to improve their military situation so as to be able to negotiate from a position of strength. But I do hope that the preliminary talks which began in Paris at the end of the last week will not only prove fruitful but also lead without interruption to substantial talks involving all interested parties and leading eventually to a peaceful solution.

As part of such a settlement of the overall problem of Vietnam, I believe that it would be useful to envisage a neutralization of the entire area that was known as French Indo-China, including both North and South Vietnam, Laos, and Cambodia. It would also be a source of stability in the area if the neutrality of the region could be guaranteed by all the big powers.

The talks in Paris have just begun. All the world over the progress of these talks will be watched with keenest interest. Men of good will everywhere will certainly share my wish that these preliminary talks should be the beginning of the long road toward an enduring peace.

UNITED NATIONS CONFERENCE ON
TRADE AND DEVELOPMENT

THE UNITED NATIONS CONFERENCE on Trade and Development (UNCTAD) held its second session in New Delhi from February 1 to March 29, 1968, four years after its original session. The intervening period was one of frustrated hopes, partly because of the international atmosphere and partly because of the gap between the thinking of the developed and the developing countries. In fact, the second session had been delayed for two years in the hope that the situation might improve. U Thant frankly acknowledged that he found the progress since 1964 disappointing. On January 18, before leaving for New Delhi to address the opening of the second UNCTAD session, he told a press conference: "I think we have passed the stage of defining the issues and outlining the theories. We have come to the stage of action. I think the New Delhi conference should focus its attention on the practical measures to be taken, not only on the question of trade, but also on the question of aid" (see p. 33). He noted that the gap between the rich countries and the poor countries was continuing to become wider despite all efforts inside and outside the United Nations. This, he stated, was potentially more explosive than the gulf between East and West. "Unless and until leaders of men and leaders of thought realize this aspect," he declared, "I am afraid to think of the future. This is one hope I have for the forthcoming second UNCTAD conference in New Delhi."

The New Delhi conference did focus its attention on the relationship of trade and aid and their role in economic development, but the results again fell far short of expectations. In the words of Dr. Raúl Prebisch, Secretary-General of UNCTAD, "Only very limited positive results were obtained." Thant described the outcome as "a matter of grave concern." In an address before the Economic and Social Council on July 8, Thant asked: "What went wrong in New Delhi?" and then, replying to his own question, he placed the blame on both the developed countries and the developing countries. The main ingredient that was lacking in New Delhi, he said, "was the readiness of industrial countries to enter into commitments in regard to trade and aid, commitments which, of course, if they are to have the desired effect, should be matched by commitments on the part of the developing countries."

1. From Statement at the Second Session of UNCTAD

NEW DELHI   FEBRUARY 9, 1968

. . . OVER THE PAST few months, one has heard it said that the timing of the Conference is unfortunate. The war in Vietnam continues, and is not only a tragedy in itself, but limits the freedom of action of some governments, and even their ability and will to attend to other matters.

It has also been said that the Conference comes at a bad time, inasmuch as governments faced with pressures on their balances of payments or budgetary resources would find it difficult to enter into new international commitments whether on trade or aid. Indeed the recent past has witnessed a number of setbacks in international economic relations, and there is evidence of serious uncertainty about the future of the world's trade and payments system.

Excuses for delay can, of course, always be found if one is disposed to do so. On the other hand, it can scarcely be suggested that we have been unduly hasty in calling this Conference. Indeed, the Final Act of the First Conference provided that the second session should be held early in 1966. The two additional years that have elapsed have been used fruitfully to prepare the ground, and as a result there are a number of issues which are ripe for action. If there are difficulties and dangers ahead, let them be brought forward and frankly discussed here at this Conference. If we face the possibility of retrogression, the need for the Conference is surely even greater, not less.

Above all, we cannot continue indefinitely to postpone the consideration of action in the hope of better times in the political arena. The political and economic strains in the world are interdependent and we must move forward on both fronts together if we are to achieve satisfactory results in either.

The intimate relationship between the political and economic aspects of world problems was the subject of a remarkable statement by the

SOURCE: UN Press Release SG/SM/904.

president-designate of the International Bank for Reconstruction and Development at Montreal nearly two years ago. As he pointed out at that time, there is a direct and constant relationship between the incidence of violence and the economic situation of the countries afflicted, and he drew attention to the danger of assuming that problems of security could be dealt with by purely military means. The most important ingredient of international security is economic and social development, and not the armaments and armed forces, however powerful the latter may seem to be.

What can we say about progress since the first Conference in 1964 in creating the conditions for economic and social development? It must be admitted that to a large extent it has been a period of frustrated hopes. The countries that agreed in 1964 to the establishment of UNCTAD are well aware that the building of a new institution, however necessary and important, cannot be a substitute for substantive measures. Nevertheless, the setting up of UNCTAD has unfortunately not yet led to the adoption of the measures which the situation patently requires.

The failure in this respect is particularly difficult to accept in the light of the notable success which has attended the negotiations connected with the Kennedy Round and the question of international monetary reform, even though more recent events may have cast a shadow on the latter. Unfavorable as the circumstances have been, it was found possible by the major trading nations to agree on an unparalleled program of tariff disarmament in the middle of last year. This was quickly followed by agreement at the annual meeting of the International Monetary Fund at Rio de Janeiro on an outline scheme for international monetary reform. What is it that made it possible for success to be achieved in these two major areas at a time when it was considered impossible to expand the efforts being made in the much more basic problem of world economic development?

If we are frank with ourselves, I think we may identify two main reasons for the difference. The first is that, although both the Kennedy Round and the outline scheme for international monetary reform will tend to benefit the developing countries to some extent, their main significance is in regard to the economic relations among the developed countries. And it is simply a fact of life that the developed countries have a larger volume of trade and monetary exchanges with one another than with the developing world.

But there is a second and perhaps even more significant reason for the difference. While the new developments in trade and monetary relationships among the developed countries involve an exchange of reciprocal obligations, the developed world continues to regard its economic relationships with the less developed countries as a one-sided affair in which concessions are granted but not received. Human nature being what it is, countries are much more willing to consider concessions for which there is some *quid pro quo* than those which are, or at least appear to be, unilateral.

One could, of course point out that world economic development is a matter of cooperative action to secure objectives that are common ground among us all, and which have been repeatedly accepted and endorsed by the General Assembly of the United Nations, by UNCTAD, and by other global and regional institutions. But the acceptance of high-minded principles is not the same thing as securing effective action for their implementation. I do not in any way underrate the importance of moral principle as a guide to national and international action. Indeed, I continue to believe in the disinterestedness of all those in the advanced countries who have helped to support the idea of commitments by the developed countries to assist in accelerating world development. We can, I think, take particular satisfaction in the small but increasing group of developed countries which have not only accepted the assistance targets of the General Assembly and of UNCTAD but which have either already implemented them or have publicly stated their intention of doing so within a fixed period of time. Enlightened acts of economic statesmanship of this kind will, I am sure, be of growing importance in the years ahead, and one must hope that the time is not far distant when all the developed countries will feel able to emulate the achievements of those among them—by no means the largest or richest—which have already assumed precise commitments of this sort.

There is a danger of viewing the problem of reciprocity in too narrow a context. It is true that developing countries are not in a position to match the tariff concessions granted by the developed countries in the Kennedy Round, and this fact was fully recognized in the negotiations. But that does not mean that the opening up of markets for the exports of developing countries would benefit only these countries. People are apt to forget that the developed countries stand to gain no less than the developing countries from a rationalization of the trade relations between them. The developed countries find themselves short of labor and even of capital, and yet they are protecting the inefficient use of both these resources in sectors of agriculture and industry which could be much more efficiently supplied from developing countries. One could understand this protectionism if there were large-scale chronic unemployment in the developed countries, but this, of course, is very far from the situation that prevails. Nor would anyone expect the developed countries to lower their trade barriers in a manner which would create serious disturbance to their economic life. A gradual approach to the problem would surely be acceptable to all so long as we are moving in the right direction. What is happening at present, however, is that restrictions are maintained and even intensified because of the fear of short-term difficulties. Thus the long-term benefits tend to be sacrificed to short-term expediency. But what I want to emphasize is that it is not simply the developing countries that suffer from all this, but the developed countries as well. One cannot therefore accept the proposition that the restructuring of world trade on a more rational basis is something which is exclusively in the interests of the developing countries.

Even when we come to the area of aid, it should not be assumed that the benefits accrue entirely to the developing countries. I am not here concerned with aid given from the narrow standpoint of political or military security. Nor, once again, an I in any way downgrading the importance of aid as an expression of international solidarity. I fully subscribe to the remark once made by the distinguished minister leading the United Kingdom delegation that: "If one seeks to abolish poverty at home, one should seek to abolish it abroad. If one wants a Welfare State, one should untimately want a Welfare World."

But aid brings much more direct advantage to those who give it. In the short run it creates additional purchasing power for the exports of the donor countries. More importantly, in the long run it helps to accelerate the growth of the developing countries and thus builds markets for the future—markets which will be able to pay their own way. Aid is thus an investment in the future which will be of direct benefit to developed and developing countries alike.

I would therefore suggest that the questions of trade and aid before this Conference do not involve as one-sided an approach to the problem of development as is sometimes suggested.

Even so, we must go beyond this. We must try and envisage ways in which the assumption of concrete commitments by developed countries could be accompanied by corresponding commitments in developing countries. As I mentioned earlier, it is now common ground among us all that equivalence of concessions in the narrow sense should be required only of countries of comparable economic strength and not of countries with vastly different economic potentials. The matching of commitments by developed and developing countries should therefore be viewed from the very different situations of each as well as from the very different responsibilities which they bear in relation to the development problem.

The developing countries have accepted that the fundamental responsibility for solving their own development problems rests with them and the commitments which they can and should undertake flow naturally from this recognition. I will not attempt in this brief statement to spell out the details of such commitments any more than I intend to dwell upon the undertakings which the developed countries may wish to consider. It does seem to me, however, that UNCTAD provides a forum in which this matter could be fruitfully discussed, negotiated, and resolved.

UNCTAD could be particularly effective in this sense because it includes representation from all the main groups of countries—developed market economy, socialist, and developing. I am particularly struck by the opportunities which exist for joint approaches by socialist and private-enterprise countries to the problems of development. Naturally there are bound to be differences of view between them as to the broad strategy of development, and these matters will continue to be discussed during the years ahead. But I believe there is some basis for saying that the ideological content of the debate over the development problem need no longer deter us from entering into specific schemes of cooperation across political frontiers. It has already been found possible for private enterprise to cooperate with socialist enterprise in projects of mutual interest in Europe, and it is, perhaps, not unrealistic to foresee that such cooperation could be extended to projects in the less developed parts of the world.

I believe that there are many other ways in which the trade and aid policies of the private enterprise and socialist parts of the world could be brought together. The time is, perhaps, approaching when socialist participation in multilateral aid could be considered as a logical step forward from their present participation in multilateral technical assistance and a useful complement to their bilateral endeavors. But one must recognize that a number of other conditions would have to be fulfilled, notably a solution of a number of difficulties now besetting East-West trade and payments. For it is an inevitable consequence of growing international interdependence that the constriction of any one channel of economic relationships tends to react adversely upon other channels as well.

These are challenging problems and I am sure that every effort will be made on all sides to go beyond the routine expression of entrenched positions in discussing them here, with a view to reaching negotiable solutions. There is no spirit of confrontation but, rather, of earnest endeavor to seek workable and mutually acceptable solutions. I think it will be recognized on all sides that the Algiers Charter represents a serious effort by one of the groups participating at this Conference to state the problems that the Conference faces without rancor or bitterness. It is, I am sure, to be viewed not as a statement of demands but as a basis for discussion—a discussion in which give and take is to be expected on all sides.

My own view is that developing countries will in any case find their own way toward the solution of the economic problems that now confront them and that in the long run they will overcome the obstacles which they face, with or without a better framework for world trade, and with or without more external financial resouces.

The real question is not whether development will occur, but how it will occur and within what international framework. Do we envisage a framework of international cooperation or a framework in which the developing countries are forced back largely upon their own resources and are compelled to take the political and economic steps required for an autarchic pattern of development? No responsible person will expect the problem of centuries of economic backwardness to be solved overnight. The world is, however, entitled to expect a clearer definition of the objectives to be achieved in the longer run and an indication of the steps which each country and group of countries intends to take for the realization of those objectives.

That is the issue before the New Delhi conference. That is the question to which the world expects an answer.

2. *From Statement at the Conference of Non-Governmental Organizations*

NEW YORK   MAY 22, 1968

. . . SINCE THE THEME of this year's Conference is "Trade, Aid and People in an Interdependent World," I hope it will be relevant if I make some brief observations on the Development Decade, which will soon come to a close, and on the endeavors and arrangements being made by the United Nations and its sister agencies to launch a second Development Decade.

I want to draw your attention to the report submitted to the entire membership by the Secretary-General of UNCTAD, Dr. Raúl Prebisch, on the Second UNCTAD Conference which took place in New Delhi earlier this year. I would commend that report to your consideration. I am sure you will agree with me that it would not be proper for me to assess the results of UNCTAD II, held in New Delhi, inasmuch as the Secretary-General of that agency has himself done so. I would, however, wish to give you a brief idea of my thinking on the subject of the Development Decade.

The first Development Decade, launched in 1961, has given us an inspirational impetus, has defined the issues clearly and set the priorities. Opinions may differ about the success or lack of success of the first Development Decade, but in my view it has set humanity on the right path and has cleared the ground for launching the second Development Decade. In order to launch the second Development Decade successfully, some basic principles and guidelines must be borne in mind.

First, the second Development Decade must be based on the concept of a global strategy, a strategy which recognizes that this small planet of ours—despite its divisions into North and South, into developed and developing, into rich and poor—is in fact an indivisible entity. That fact must be recognized. This global strategy must also recognize that

SOURCE: UN Press Release SG/SM/952.

humanity, despite its divisions on the basis of race, creed or religion, is an indivisible whole. I think it is essential for all of us to recognize that basic fact.

Second, we have to remember that the national interest of any country cannot remain within the boundaries of its own territory. I repeat: the national interest cannot remain tightly inside the national boundaries. The future of every nation depends primarily on international security, international peace, and the development of international resources. In my view, that is a very important principle which all of us must bear in mind.

Third, humanity has now reached the crossroads of human history. This is a time when both the developed and the developing countries have to make a choice: either to come together to plan for a prosperous future to their mutual benefit, or to lead humanity to an unplanned society and to a chaotic future. That is the choice before both the developed and the developing countries. If common sense prevails, the choice of both the developed and the developing countries will, I am sure, be to plan collectively for mutual prosperity. . . .

---

3. *From Statement in the Economic and Social Council*

GENEVA   JULY 8, 1968

THERE HAVE unquestionably been better times for international cooperation in the economic and social field. Looking back on this period of some fifteen to twenty years, when the concept of collective responsibility for economic development began to take roots in international life and to find its way into the national policies of governments, we cannot but ask ourselves whether there has not been somehow a retreat from the high ideals of the postwar years. These ideals were strongly

SOURCE: UN Press Release SG/SM/971. The summary record is given in Economic and Social Council Official Records, Forty-fifth Session, 1531st meeting.

expressed in the rapid emergence of a complex institutional system, the acceptance of international aid as a durable factor in the functioning of the world economy, the spontaneous and spectacular growth of public capital transfers during the 1950s. Moreover, at the threshold of the present decade, targets were set for the transfer of resources to poor countries, and for the minimum annual rate of growth to be reached by each of the developing countries—something surely without precedent in history.

It was only five years ago that the historic decision was made to question and re-examine the basic structure of trade relations among nations, a decision which led to the convening of the First United Nations Conference on Trade and Development. But now we must ask whether this decision, reached, it is true, after some hesitation, was merely a ritual concession, made in the knowledge that no international conference, however broad and spectacular, no new elaborate machinery could really alter the balance of forces and induce new policies, against the will of those who are the repositories of economic power. At that time, the growth of international aid had already begun to falter; a climate of fatigue and disenchantment was gradually setting in. And by the time the Second Conference on Trade and Development was convened, people were talking of a "decade of frustration."

In this Council, which is devoted to balanced and sober judgment, it would be wrong to focus our attention solely on the more negative aspects, unless we thought that such a process might yield political dividends by once more impressing on reluctant governments the urgency of the development problem. But we have reasons to believe that this is not so. At this stage, if we want to inspire new courage, we need, at least as urgently, to highlight some of the more encouraging trends. In this respect, I am inclined to follow the lead so eloquently given by Mr. George Woods, the former president of the World Bank, to whom the cause of development is so indebted, when, in his Stockholm speech, he stated that development is possible but requires exceptional efforts.

For all has not been a failure in these years of admittedly disappointing results. The current *World Economic Survey* reminds us, on the basis of a thorough analysis, that progress is taking place, that the foundation for future improvements is being laid, and that the capacity for development is today greater, considerably greater, than it was at the beginning of the decade. Industrial countries, on whose behavior so much depends, have learned something of the art of economic management. They have adopted the habit of far closer consultations with one another. They have, thereby, been able to guard successfully against the transmission of deflationary tendencies, in spite of a precarious international monetary system. They have made great strides in liberalizing international trade between themselves, releasing its great potentialities as an engine of growth. They have shown more readiness to take into account the impact of their domestic policies on the rest of the world and have avoided the "every-man-for-himself" attitudes that precipitated the great depression of the interwar period. The majority of the developing countries have succeeded in raising, sometimes quite remarkably, their savings ratios. They have significantly—at times, perhaps excessively—expanded their infrastructure. They have strengthened their educational systems, their health services. They have begun to lay the foundation of good economic management and planning, and to adapt their administrative structure to its requirements.

When all these factors are taken together, it is not at all sure that progress in the 1960s has been slower than it was in the 1950s, as is frequently surmised. What is certain is that, although remarkable by historical standards, growth has not been as fast as it could have been, and that the main reason for this would appear to be the lack of adequate international action.

As so much hope in this respect had been placed in UNCTAD, it is with the results of the New Delhi conference that our annual exercise of self-examination should begin. In my address to that conference, I stated that the world was entitled to expect a clearer definition of the longer-run objectives of economic development and an indication of the practical steps that each country and group intended to take to realize these objectives.

In neither case, I regret to say, was there a full and satisfactory response. The world is still waiting for an answer.

It is not my intention here to go into much detail concerning the achievements, or lack of achievements, in New Delhi. Dr. Raúl Prebisch, the Secretary-General of UNCTAD, in his report on the significance of the second session, has already provided a concise and cogent view of what was attempted and what was attained. His report is not encouraging. "Only very limited positive results were obtained," he says, "that are not commensurate with the dimensions and urgency of the development problem."

This is a situation on which we may reflect, as such an outcome affects not only UNCTAD but also your work here in the Economic and Social Council, and indeed the whole pattern of relationships between members of the United Nations family of nations.

If we indefinitely defer action to implement our own decisions in the vitally important field of trade and development, we are threatening the viability of our belief in solving international problems peacefully, by consultation, negotiation, and concerted action. At both the national and the international levels, the poor are increasingly aware of the gap that separates them from the rich, increasingly impatient at the denial of adequate help for them to bridge this gap. Failure to act is an invitation to violence. In this context, the outcome of the Second UNCTAD is a matter for grave concern.

What went wrong in New Delhi? As is known, this was a most carefully prepared conference. Considerable progress had been made since the first session in 1964 in defining the problems and in pointing the way for governments to agree on a concerted and integrated attack on them. The secretariat of UNCTAD, in close cooperation with the Department of Economic and Social Affairs, the secretariats of the regional commissions, and other agencies, had prepared a valuable documentation to assist the delegates in their work. Governments, themselves assembled in Algiers, and within the Organization for Economic Cooperation and Development, had conscientiously worked to pave the way to fruitful negotiations. Hence the expectation was widespread that the second session of UNCTAD would inject a new sense of purpose into the first Development Decade as well as the preparation of the second, and revive the faith of people everywhere in the possibilities offered by the United Nations for joint planning and action in a common cause: mutual prosperity. This was the challenge and the opportunity offered at New Delhi.

One of the dangers of taking an overall view of the results of the conference, of course, is that the positive achievements may be overlooked or minimized. Although relatively few, they are by no means negligible. Agreement on the principle of a system of tariff preferences to benefit the exports of developing countries, even though the elements of the scheme have yet to be agreed, is a noteworthy step forward, as is the acceptance by developed countries of a higher assistance target which increases by some 25 percent the potential resources they are urged to transfer to developing countries. The declaration on trade expansion and economic integration among developing countries, the decisions dealing with trade with socialist countries, shipping matters, least-developed and land-locked countries—these are, to varying degrees, grounds for satisfaction.

Were the requests of the developing countries so extreme as to deserve the fate that befell them? Was it for instance too much to ask of the developed countries, as they grow richer and their consumption increases, that they reserve a proportion of this increase for the exports of developing countries? Was it too much to ask that, having just achieved a major lowering of trade barriers among each other in the Kennedy Round, they do something similar for the products of developing countries? Was it too much to ask that aid should be less strictly tied than it has become? And that the terms on which it is offered be softened?

I do not think it was expecting too much. And yet, in each case, the response was largely negative.

I do not consider that the blame should rest solely on the developed countries. Developing countries, too, often exhibit a lack of farsightedness in their policies and in the positions they adopt vis-à-vis the developed countries. They too tend at times to follow policies of self-delusion, in which long-term benefits are continually sacrificed to short-term expediency, and national interest is considered as ending at the frontier.

And yet, considering that the conference was dealing with international problems and policies, I am forced to the conclusion that the main ingredient for success that was lacking in New Delhi was the readiness of industrial countries to enter into commitments in regard to trade and aid, commitments which, of course, if they are to have the desired effect, should be matched by commitments on the part of the developing countries.

Let us not delude ourselves that this absence of political will can be laid at the door of short-sighted governments. Governments are merely the instruments of the will of the people of a country; the problem is more fundamental. The Secretary-General of UNCTAD goes to the heart of the matter in his report. I would like to quote his words: "It seems that prosperity, in people as well as in nations, tends to form an attitude of detachment, if not indifference, to the well-being of others." I, myself, not so long ago, spoke of the danger in international life of "prosperous provincialism." One of the most important lessons to be learned from the Second UNCTAD Conference is the need to persuade people in the developed countries that their future prosperity and security, and that of their children and grandchildren, is inextricably linked with the well-being of people in the developing countries. Now that the turmoil affecting so many of the richer countries is revealing and creating new claims on their resources, it is more important than ever to do everything within our power and our means to help create that receptivity to United Nations objectives and policies which is as yet so seriously lacking. In this connection may I stress the importance I attach to the establishment, within the framework of the Office of Public Information, of a centre for economic and social information. I hope that governments as well as non-governmental organizations will assist it in its tasks.

That our joint planning during the first Development Decade has not fulfilled all the hopes we had placed in it does not indicate that we should abandon it. As the *World Economic Survey* indicates, events may have cast doubts on the adequacy of our targets, in their simple but ambiguous arithmetic. But as tangible expressions of need and intention, they represent unprecedented landmarks in international economic policy. Though their impact and significance have differed considerably from one country to another, there can be little doubt that their total effect has been stimulating. We, therefore, firmly believe that the approach is valid, and we are now actively seeking ways of improving upon it. It is true that the averages or aggregates which we use fail to do justice to the essential diversity. Should we now perhaps pay more attention to appropriate subregional groupings? What information do we really need to keep track of progress and to catch the early symptoms of disequilibrium or faulty development strategy?

I raise these questions not because I have any ready-made answers but because we are now turning our attention to the preparation of the next Development Decade. We shall be discussing the question of development strategies, of interaction of international and national policies, and of the desirability of setting policy objectives and quantitative targets. This debate will continue when we have had the benefit of the advice of the Development Planning Committee laid before us next year. But there is no reason why serious thought should not be given to it as soon as possible and by as many instances as possible.

I should add that a discussion of the next Development Decade, its aims and character, and some aspects at least of the preparations involved, some problems it poses and the conditions for its success, has just taken place at the joint meetings of the Administrative Committee on Coordination, the Committee for Programme and Cooperation, and the officers of the Council at Bucharest. These discussions on which the chairman of the CPC and I will shortly be submitting a report to the Council will certainly prove to have been of value in facilitating the task that faces us and in strengthening cooperation between the ACC and the Council. . . .

Address at the International Conference on Human Rights

TEHERAN APRIL 22, 1968

LOOKING AHEAD to the twentieth anniversary of the adoption of the Universal Declaration of Human Rights, the General Assembly, in its resolution of December 12, 1963, designated 1968 as International Year for Human Rights. This was part of a comprehensive program to focus world attention on human rights and to promote observance and respect for fundamental freedoms. As one of the highlights of the celebration, the Assembly decided on December 20, 1965, to convene an International Conference on Human Rights. The Conference was held in Teheran, Iran, from April 22 to May 13, 1968, with representatives of eighty-four countries attending. The following address by U Thant, opening the Teheran conference, takes stock of the progress made in the field of human rights and raises questions as to new programs for "carrying out the continuing struggle for the recognition and enjoyment of human rights, which is so closely linked to the struggle for peace, for prosperity and for all the other basic aims and objectives of the United Nations."

I SHOULD LIKE to begin by expressing my sincere gratitude to His Imperial Majesty and to the Government of Iran for their generosity in offering to act as host to this very important International Conference on Human Rights, by which we commemorate the twentieth anniversary of the adoption of the Universal Declaration of Human Rights. It is very fitting that we should commemorate such an anniversary in a land whose culture and civilization are among the oldest in the world.

May I express the warmest appreciation of all of us for the excellent arrangements that have been made by our hosts for the holding of this Conference. We are well aware of the magnitude of the task involved and cannot fail to be impressed by all that has been done for us.

SOURCE: *UN Monthly Chronicle,* Vol. V, May 1968, pp. 65–72.

When toward midnight on December 10, 1948, the General Assembly of the United Nations, meeting in Paris for its third regular session, formally approved the Universal Declaration of Human Rights, the president of the session, Dr. Herbert Evatt of Australia, declared that the adoption of the Declaration was "a step forward in a great evolutionary process." He added:

It is the first occasion on which the organized community of nations has made a declaration of human rights and fundamental freedoms. That document was backed by the authority of the body of opinion of the United Nations as a whole, and millions of people, men, women and children all over the world, will turn to it for help, guidance and inspiration."

Since that memorable date United Nations organs have given consistent and unreserved support to the Universal Declaration. Its initial provisions boldly proclaim as its philosophical basis and an article of faith that "All human beings are born free and equal in dignity and rights. They are endowed with reason and conscience and should act towards one another in a spirit of brotherhood." Consequently, everyone is entitled to all rights and freedoms set forth in the Declaration "without distinction of any kind, such as race, colour, sex, language, religion, political or other opinion, national or social origin, property, birth or other status," and no distinction is allowed as to the political status of the territories to which the Declaration applies.

These basic principles of freedom and dignity for all, of nondiscrimination and tolerance embodied in the Universal Declaration, are as relevant today as when, in the wake of the horrors of the Second World War, they were initially enunciated.

As an expression of the conscience of the United Nations on the rights of the individual in society, it has often been used as a yardstick to measure the degree of respect for human rights and as a basis of exhortation and action by various organs of the United Nations itself, by international conferences, as well as by national governments. A significant point was reached when, in 1960, twelve years after its adoption, the General Assembly itself proclaimed in another Declaration, namely, the Declaration on the Granting of Independence to Colonial Countries and Peoples, that "all States shall observe faithfully and strictly the provisions of the Charter of the United Nations, the Universal Declaration of Human Rights," as well as the new Declaration which was then being adopted.

Within the United Nations family, specialized agencies such as the International Labour Organisation and the United Nations Educational, Scientific and Cultural Organization have found inspiration for specific actions of special importance in the Universal Declaration of Human Rights.

Outside the United Nations, it may be recalled that, among many other international instruments, the European Convention for the Protection of Human Rights and Fundamental Freedoms signed in Rome in 1950 lists the Universal Declaration as the international instrument which led the signatory governments to conclude the European Convention. The Universal Declaration was invoked in the Declaration of the Caracas Conference of American States of 1954, as well as in the pronouncements of the Bandung Conference of Asian-African States of 1955, and the purposes of the Organization of African Unity include that of promoting international cooperation "with due regard for the United Nations Charter and the Universal Declaration of Human Rights."

The impact of the Declaration on national constitutions, on legislation and, in some instances, on court decisions, is another area of the effective influence exercised by the Universal Declaration of Human Rights. No fewer than forty-three recently enacted constitutions are clearly inspired by the provisions of the Universal Declaration and very often reproduce its phraseology. The examples of legislation enactments expressly quoting or manifestly reproducing provisions of the Declaration are very numerous and can be found in the law of countries of all continents.

It may safely be said therefore that the Declaration has guided and inspired many statesmen and legislators. It has undoubtedly also helped the men, women, and children for whom it had been proclaimed. Those who suffered from inequities, from prejudices, from humiliations, from fear and insecurity, found in it a justification for their complaints and protests and additional grounds for their claims for redress. Those who defended the victims of violations demanded its universal and effective recognition and observance. Governmental as well as non-governmental institutions greatly helped in spreading its knowledge by teaching and the use of educational and information media.

As regards the United Nations, "the great evolutionary process," to which the President of the third regular session of the General Assembly referred, continued through the years. The adoption of the Universal Declaration was followed by the approval of a number of other United

Nations declarations and conventions, which found their inspiration and guidelines in the Declaration and progressively led to the building of a body of principles and legal rules for the conduct of those whose responsibility it is to ensure respect for human dignity. These principles and rules constitute now a rapidly developing branch of international law which the United Nations elaborates for all states of the world and all communities.

In recent years, this movement of setting worldwide standards continued at an accelerated pace. The more pressing concern of the Members of the United Nations for the respect of human rights everywhere found its expression in a rapid succession of significant international instruments. The Declaration on the Elimination of All Forms of Racial Discrimination, which was approved by the General Assembly in 1963, was followed in 1965 by the adoption of the International Convention on the Elimination of All Forms of Racial Discrimination. Nineteen states have now ratified or acceded to that convention; eight other ratifications are needed to bring it into force.

In 1966, the International Covenants on Human Rights and an Optional Protocol were adopted after many years of consideration and study. The vote of all 106 participating Member states was unanimous, and it underlined the gradually emerging common philosophy within the United Nations regarding the right of every individual, without distinction, to secure respect for his dignity as a human being—whether in the political and civil or the economic, social, and cultural fields—and of the right of peoples to self-determination.

The principles proclaimed in the Universal Declaration and the right of self-determination of all peoples were placed in an incontestable legal context. The International Bill of Rights, for the enactment of which fervent hopes had been expressed in the early years of the United Nations and which was to consist of the Universal Declaration, the Human Rights Covenants and the measures for their implementation, was thus completed.

At its last session, the General Assembly adopted two other important declarations, the Declaration on the Elimination of Discrimination against Women and a Declaration on Territorial Asylum. By a unanimous vote of 112 Members, it also called for the acceleration of the process of ratification of the Human Rights Covenants by all eligible states. Their coming into force will be a great moment in the history of mankind.

The inclusion of measures of implementation in recent human rights instruments corresponds to what I believe is a discernible and largely held hope that the United Nations role should be strengthened in promoting, assisting, and reviewing national and local efforts to apply the standards which the United Nations has itself proclaimed and defined. Without awaiting the coming into force of these instruments, significant initiatives were taken under directives of the General Assembly to permit consideration by the Commission on Human Rights and the Economic and Social Council of certain persistent situations involving gross violations of human rights, the principal example of which is the policy of *apartheid* practiced by the government of the Republic of South Africa.

The ultimate objective of United Nations efforts must obviously be the implementation of the standards at the levels where they can be enjoyed and exercised by the people concerned.

In the light of these developments and the increasing world concern, the time seems to have come for taking stock of United Nations programs and activities for the promotion of human rights. On the one hand, there is the remarkable effort by the international community to define common aspirations on a worldwide and on a regional basis. On the other hand, it is clear that, in spite of the greater awareness and demand for the respect of the individual, serious violations of human rights, including resort to violence and terror, continue to occur in a number of places and these are made known and publicized more than ever before.

Practices of discrimination prevail in many territories and, in large parts of the world, economic imbalances prevent in fact the enjoyment of economic and social rights, a situation which also has adverse consequences in the area of civil and political rights. The inadequacy of the international community's institutions to help in correcting these deplorable situations and in effectively encouraging desirable levels of compliance with United Nations standards is often pointed out.

Four and a half years ago, at the time of the fifteenth anniversary of the adoption of the Universal Declaration, the General Assembly declared that the whole of 1968, the twentieth anniversary year of the adoption of the Universal Declaration, should be devoted to intensified national and international efforts and undertakings in the field of human rights, and designated 1968 as the International Year for Human Rights.

This International Conference was convened by the General Assembly because it was felt that an extraordinary event of such importance could most effectively assist in furthering the purposes of the International Year.

It was undoubtedly useful to depart from the routine succession of United Nations meetings on human rights for the purpose of a detached stock-taking and long-term planning. It was important to call on governments to send specially qualified persons, including some of those who have participated in United Nations activities, as well as many who were active in the field of human rights outside the United Nations framework, in a great confrontation of cultures, historical traditions, political conceptions, religious and philosophical outlooks.

A review of the situation as regards human rights in the world, if conducted in a constructive spirit designed to lead to future international cooperation, may undoubtedly contribute to a better understanding of the tasks ahead. The Preparatory Committee for the Conference has stressed the need for moderation, restraint, and objectivity and of an atmosphere as free as possible from political recrimination in order to achieve the desirable results from such a review.

An examination of the degree of effectiveness of the methods used by the United Nations, its family of organizations, and possibly of the role of existing regional organizations can lead to conclusions as to the strengthening and better functioning of competent United Nations organs, their present status within the Organization, and their future needs.

But it is the programming of future action by the United Nations which will in all likelihood retain the most active attention of the Conference.

One of the provisions of the Universal Declaration may perhaps be usefully recalled. Article 28 states that "Everyone is entitled to a social and international order in which the rights and freedoms set forth in this Declaration can be fully realized." This far-reaching assertion by the United Nations has many implications. The experience of the last twenty years has abundantly shown that the international order which it is the purpose of the United Nations to promote and finally to establish is very closely linked with adequate respect for the rights of all human beings.

It was said in the first paragraph both of the Universal Declaration and of each of the International Covenants that recognition of the inherent dignity and of the equal and inalienable rights of all members of the human family is the foundation, not only of freedom and justice, but also of peace in the world. It has also been repeatedly stated that, in the absence of international or internal peace, chances of genuine respect for human rights are slight.

The pattern of history before the establishment of the United Nations, and unfortunately also since the establishment of our Organization, has shown the extent to which preoccupations for the life and well-being of the individual give way to requirements of military imperatives. Violence breeds violence. Fear breeds fear. Restraints of those who possess force disappear in situations where the use of force is openly encouraged.

Independently of international and internal conflicts, any observer of present-day realities can hardly fail to be alarmed by the persistance or even the increase of violence and brutality in today's world. Massacres, tortures, arbitrary arrests, including cruel detentions of those who are already victims of various forms of discrimination, and summary executions are reported by information media so frequently that the natural human reaction of horror tends to be dulled. The necessity of better compliance with Article 5 of the Universal Declaration, which refers to torture and cruel, inhuman, or degrading treatment or punishment, needs particular stress.

In addition, violence seems to have been consecrated in many parts of the world as an essential element of the entertainment media, featuring prominently, for example, in television, movies, and popular literature, to the point that it becomes a daily ingredient in people's lives. Such saturation of violence cannot but have grave consequences in the behavior of communities and nations.

Economic development, which should permit the achievement of essential economic and social rights—those to adequate nourishment, to medical services, to education, to work, to social security, and hence to political and civil rights and fundamental freedoms—requires mutual understanding and cooperation between nations. The common philosophy which has emerged within the United Nations regarding what are no longer mere aspirations, but rights, of every individual without distinction to secure respect for his dignity and essential needs as a human being, is an important factor of harmonious world economic and social development.

In the work of the United Nations in the field of human rights and particularly in the preparation for this Conference and the listing of its objectives, special stress was rightly given to the importance and urgency of the United Nations struggle against racial discrimination and to the persistent and intense efforts which must be made to secure its eradication, and in particular the abandonment of the policy of *apartheid* which, in the words of the General Assembly, constitutes one of the most flagrant abuses of human rights and fundamental freedoms.

It is indeed essential that the principles laid down in the Charter of the United Nations, the Universal Declaration of Human Rights, the Declaration on the Granting of Independence to Colonial Countries and Peoples, the United Nations Declaration on the Elimination of All Forms of Racial Discrimination, and the International Convention on the Elimination of All Forms of Racial Discrimination, as well as in the related conventions of the specialized agencies, be put into practice, not at some future time but in our own generation.

The impact of inferior status, of lack of opportunity to attain adequate standards of living, of permanent humiliation of the individuals concerned, is clear to all. The consequences for humanity as a whole are no less obvious. In an address to the Algerian House of Assembly which I made four years ago (see volume VI of this series), I said: "There is the clear prospect that racial conflict, if we cannot curb and finally eliminate it, will grow into a destructive monster compared to which the religious or ideological conflicts of the past and present will seem like small family quarrels. Such a conflict will eat away the possibilities of good of all that mankind has hitherto achieved and reduce men to the lowest and most bestial levels of intolerance and hatred. This, for the sake of all our children, whatever their race and color, must not be permitted to happen."

I hope that in proposing programs for the future you will reflect on these and other sad remnants of the past which, most regrettably, are also current ills.

You may also wish to project your thoughts into the future. Careful attention must be paid to certain rapid developments of our societies which contain certain ominous warnings. I shall only refer to a few of these signs of danger.

Everywhere in the world, the family constitutes a natural and fundamental unit, and both parents as well as the children and adolescents must benefit from measures designed to allow them to live their full life. Considerable thought and concern were expressed in the last few years regarding the problem of the size of families and that of the effects of the rapid increase in world population.

On Human Rights Day, 1967, heads of state or prime ministers of thirty countries transmitted to me a "Declaration on Population." These world leaders stated their belief that a great majority of parents desire to have the knowledge and means to plan their families and that the opportunity to decide the number and spacing of children is a fundamental human right.

The unprecedented technological development of the last two or three generations has already had, and will increasingly have, effects on the status and self-respect of the individual. The promise which science offers is understandably high but, having invented and perfected the machine, is man going to become himself the slave of the machine or of those few in number who will be in the position to manipulate it? Can man and his essential right to a minimum of privacy be protected against the ever-present listening and seeing electronic or other devices? How can we escape being led on the road to anonymity and emptiness so strikingly predicted by some well-known contemporary authors? Will science fiction in its degrading aspects become reality? How will democracy and the right to self-determination of peoples be preserved in a world of advanced and domineering technical development?

But, of course, science and technology, although posing problems which need to be identified and tackled in time, offer as well stirring possibilities for a decisive attack on poverty, disease, and ignorance, which still continue to afflict such a large part of humanity. It is to the ways and means of turning science and technology from destruction to the enhancement of life that we should devote our urgent efforts.

The importance of this Conference, therefore, hardly needs to be underlined. Having examined past achievements and failures, having assessed the effectiveness of the United Nations machinery, it will have to point the way ahead. It must find the means to make the principles which guide the United Nations in the field of human rights more than simply words. It must examine the soundness of those principles and of the programs built upon them as a lever for the promotion and protection of the rights and freedoms of all peoples everywhere. It must reaffirm the determination of the world community to put an end to serious violations of human rights. And it must evaluate the methods followed by the United Nations up to the present time, in the light of both the tremendous needs and difficulties and the amazing possibilities that can be foreseen for the future.

In short, the Conference must find new means of carrying out the continuing struggle for the recognition and enjoyment of human rights, which is so closely linked to the struggle for peace, for prosperity, and for all the other basic aims and objectives of the United Nations. If it succeeds in this task, it will succeed in contributing to the improvement of the conditions of mankind. For it may be, if sufficient dedication is shown and a sufficient effort is made, that it will be the historic privilege of our generation to bring about conditions in which human beings would be assured of life in the kind of dignity which our civilization can, perhaps for the first time, afford to provide and which men, women, and children everywhere so richly deserve.

In order to be effective, these noblest of efforts must in our time be international and cooperative in character.

Last summer, in a speech I made in the United States, I expressed my profound belief that real and effective international cooperation can only be achieved if there is an awareness at all levels that no man can save himself or his country or his people unless he consciously identifies himself with and deliberately works for the whole of mankind.

The magnitude of our task is obvious. Its importance is paramount. I invite the Teheran conference to seize the opportunity of a unique worldwide gathering to make a decisive contribution. I convey to those in government and official positions, in universities and schools, in workers' and employers' organizations, the lawyers, the women, the young, all the humanitarians who have accepted the challenge of the International Year for Human Rights, my appreciation for the work they are doing and my high expectations of the results which they will achieve for their fellowmen.

This is my message for the International Year for Human Rights.

Statement on the Observance of Africa Day

NEW YORK   MAY 27, 1968

U THANT had been deeply involved in African problems since the days when he was Burma's permanent representative to the United Nations. One of his first major problems upon assuming the office of Secretary-General was the United Nations operation in the Congo. After this trying and costly operation was over other African problems continued to be a major preoccupation of the United Nations and of Thant personally. There were questions like South Africa's policy of *apartheid,* the question of Namibia, Portuguese territories, and Ian Smith's white minority government in Southern Rhodesia, as well as pressing general problems such as economic development. Thant had made it a practice to attend the periodic meetings of the Organization of African Unity and had spoken out bluntly on African problems. On May 27, 1968, the Secretary-General joined in the observance of Africa Day by urging "renewed dedication and redoubled determination to remove the last traces of colonialism from Africa and the rest of the globe with the least possible delay."

WHEN, AT THEIR historic Conference in Addis Ababa during May 1963, the heads of state and government of the independent African states decided that this day of the year should thenceforth be observed as Africa Day, their purpose was not merely to initiate an annual celebration of the emergence to independence of a sizable number of dependent territories in Africa. Rather, their principal intention was that the observance of this anniversary should be a continuing reminder to all African peoples and to the international community of—and I quote from the relevant resolution of that Conference—"the urgent necessity . . . to accelerate the unconditional attainment of national independence by all African territories still under foreign domination."

It is therefore fitting on the occasion of Africa Day this year to reflect, with serious disquiet, that the right of colonial peoples to self-determina-

SOURCE: UN Press Release SG/SM/954.

tion, freedom, and independence has yet to be universally recognized. Indeed, the extent to which decolonization has progressed in the last few years serves only to underline the anomaly of the fact that several million people are still subject to colonial rule—and, worse still, that most of them live under régimes which offer them no hope of an early or peaceful emancipation.

The United Nations has of course given its consistent support for the principle of self-determination and has done a great deal to encourage and to assist the emergence of dependent peoples. The adoption in 1960 of the Declaration on the Granting of Independence to Colonial Countries and Peoples was generally regarded as a most constructive achievement. The majority of Member states considered it a landmark in the efforts of the United Nations toward the realization of the purposes and objectives of the Charter as regards dependent peoples.

Since that time, the General Assembly has, as is well known, taken a number of decisions which represent a notable development of the principles embodied in that Declaration. It has extended the concept of the inalienable right of colonial peoples to self-determination and independence to include a recognition of their endeavors to achieve the effective exercise and enjoyment of those rights. Proceeding from this recognition, the General Assembly has repeatedly appealed to all states to give to the colonial peoples the support necessary for the restoration of their inalienable rights.

With the same objectives in view, the General Assembly has given attention to the study of such economic and other factors as may constitute impediments to the progress of colonial peoples toward the attainment of freedom, or militate against the preservation of their independence when it is attained.

Moreover, there has developed a growing conviction—which has been exemplified in a number of territories—that the United Nations, in seeking to play an increasingly large role in the process of decolonization, should actively participate in the processes involved in the exercise by colonial peoples of their right to self-determination and independence.

Nevertheless, the United Nations has so far been unable to provide or facilitate effective solutions to the several difficult and serious colonial problems which remain. The reason for this state of affairs lies not in lack of concern or effort on the part of the United Nations, but principally in the noncompliance by the powers directly concerned, and in the reluctance of some others, to lend their full cooperation to the Organization in the application of effective solutions to outstanding colonial problems.

Of these problems, those currently affecting the southern part of Africa are in a class by themselves, for they constitute the most conspicuous mass violation of human rights and freedoms. As I stated in my address to the Assembly of Heads of State and Government of the Organization of African Unity during September 1967, the determination of the United Nations to bring the story of colonialism to an end seems to have met a solid wall of defiance in that part of the world.

Regarding South West Africa, the government of South Africa has refused to comply with the resolutions by which the General Assembly terminated the Mandate, brought the territory under the direct responsibility of the United Nations and set up a Council to administer the territory until its independence. That government has further refused to relinquish its control over the territory and has frustrated the efforts of the United Nations Council to fulfill the tasks assigned to it. The government is also proceeding with measures which will impair the territorial integrity and international status of South West Africa and which have been interpreted as a step toward the progressive integration of the territory within the *apartheid* system of South Africa. The disregard of that government for the pertinent United Nations resolutions as well as of world public opinion is further illustrated by its recent illegal arrest, trial, and conviction of a group of South West Africans.

Where Angola, Mozambique, and Guinea, called Portuguese Guinea, are concerned, no progress can be recorded in the implementation of the considerable number of relevant United Nations resolutions. The government of Portugal has persisted in its refusal to give effect to the principle of self-determination as defined in those resolutions and has refused to reverse its policy of political and economic integration of those territories with Portugal. Further, its reported intensification of military operations in those territories has aggravated a situation which, as was affirmed by the Security Council during 1965, was even at that time seriously disturbing international peace and security.

Furthermore, the question of Southern Rhodesia, which remains a source of general concern, has not shown the speedy movement toward peaceful resolution which the international community had been encouraged to expect. The recent introduction by the illegal minority régime of more systematic policies of separate racial development, as well as of increasingly repressive measures, has again underlined the responsibility of the United Kingdom as the adminstering power to restore constitutional rule. At the same time, the economic and other sanctions which governments have in varying degrees applied in response to the United Nations resolutions on the subject have yet to produce discernible signs of progress toward the goal of majority rule in accordance with the Declaration.

It is not my intention to comment on the colonial problems afflicting other parts of Africa, which are different in dimension, if not in kind, from those I have mentioned. Even so, the continued delay in the speedy implementation of the Declaration in all these and other dependent territories in Africa cannot but be a source of mounting concern to the international community and particularly to the states members of the Organization of African Unity, whose charter, I need scarcely recall, commits them to the eradication of all forms of colonialism in Africa. It is therefore to be expected that these states members and the world community at large should refuse to accept this situation as a *fait accompli*. Consequently, it is right and appropriate that Africa Day should once again provide an occasion for renewed dedication and redoubled determination to remove the last traces of colonialism from Africa and the rest of the globe with the least possible delay.

Of this noble endeavor, the United Nations will undoubtedly remain a major focal point. Yet I would be lacking in realism were I not to remark that a number of developments on the international scene have cast their shadow on, and have tended to impede progress in, most areas of international cooperation, including the field of decolonization. As I have said on a previous occasion, the interest of a nation or of a region is often affected by developments outside its own frontiers. Every country's and every region's future depends, to a large extent, on international peace, international security, and international prosperity. Therefore, the war in Vietnam and the situation in the Middle East have a certain relevancy to the peace, security, and prosperity of Africa and the whole process of decolonization.

In this dynamic process of decolonization, progress depends largely on the acceptance by the governments concerned of international decisions and machinery, and on their realization that the wider interests of international peace may also coincide with their own best interests. To the task of resolving these and other crucial issues which impair the chances of fruitful international cooperation, the African governments will continue, I am confident, to contribute the qualities of maturity and restraint which they have so often displayed.

At the same time, the African states are fully entitled to expect the international community to share their strongly held conviction that, to use the words of the Declaration, "the subjection of peoples to alien subjugation, domination and exploitation constitutes a denial of fundamental human rights, is contrary to the Charter, and is an impediment to world peace and cooperation." The African states, as are dependent peoples everywhere, are equally entitled to expect the international community to ensure that "immediate steps will be taken in . . . all . . . territories which have not yet attained independence to transfer all powers to the peoples of those territories without any conditions or reservations, in accordance with their freely expressed will and desire, without any distinction . . . in order to enable them to enjoy complete independence and freedom."

From Report to the Security Council
on the Situation in Cyprus

NEW YORK   JUNE 11, 1968

IN MARCH 1968 the United Nations Force in Cyprus (UNFICYP) had been in existence for four years, but the political differences between the Greek and Turkish communities remained as wide as ever. In fact, a new crisis was precipitated in the last days of 1967 with the announcement that a "provisional Cyprus Turkish administration" had been set up. The president of Cyprus, Archbishop Makarios, replied by declaring the Turkish move "flagrantly unlawful." In a special report to the Security Council on January 3, U Thant expressed fears that "this development might well have a damaging effect both on the use of my good offices and on further steps toward normalization in Cyprus." He urged both sides to show moderation and restraint. By the time the Secretary-General made the following periodic report to the Council on June 11, proposing a further six-month extension of UNFICYP's mandate, not only had the situation calmed down, but a direct channel of communication between the two communities had been opened for the first time in four and a half years. Thant found this "most encouraging."

---

91. . . . THE RELAXATION of tension in Cyprus which set in at the beginning of the year has continued during the period under review. There have been increasing contacts between the Greek and Turkish Cypriots with but few incidents having intercommunal implications. What is more, there have been no military clashes and the number of shooting incidents is low considering that there are still thousands of men under arms in Cyprus.

92. There are recent indications that both Greek and Turkish Cypriots have at last begun to realize that they cannot solve their dispute by force

SOURCE: Security Council Official Records, Supplement for April, May and June 1968, document S/8622.

and that any further attempt to do so not only would be costly in terms of human life and property but also might unleash an unpredictable chain of events. On the other hand, the basic issues dividing the two communities have remained unresolved.

93. In my last report to the Security Council I gave an outline of the initiatives which in my view should be taken without delay in the search for a solution to the Cyprus problem. Some of these initiatives have yet to materialize.

94. Little progress has been made during the last three months in the matter of military disengagement. Although the opposing armed forces have shown commendable discipline and restraint, their proximity to one another continues to constitute a latent danger both to the present improved atmosphere in Cyprus and to future progress toward a solution.

95. Moreover, despite the government's normalization measures and their beneficial effects on the Turkish Cypriot population, their leadership has not yet found it possible to respond with measures of its own so as to further a steady movement toward normality. However, my special representative has been given to understand by the Turkish Cypriot leadership that the matter is under active consideration and I am hopeful that positive developments in this regard will be forthcoming shortly.

96. On the other hand, the efforts of my special representative in arranging for intercommunal talks have been successful. Two prominent leaders of the two communities, Mr. Glafcos Clerides and Mr. Raul Denktash, after preliminary talks in Nicosia, met in Beirut from June 2 to 5. They have agreed to resume their talks in Nicosia as from June 24 and their first meeting there will be opened by my special representative. This establishment of a direct channel of communication between the two communities for the first time in four and a half years is most encouraging. I attach very great importance to these intercommunal talks. Apart from the basic issues that must be solved if a lasting settlement is to be achieved, there are many current internal problems which have to be overcome. I am deeply conscious of the difficulty and complexity of the task that lies ahead and it is my earnest hope that, in the interest of the country as a whole, both communities will find it possible to make those concessions and accommodations without which no agreement can be attained. The will to compromise and adjust their differences would be a historic demonstration of statesmanship which the leaders in Cyprus could offer toward a just and lasting peace in their

country. I hope that the talks will be fruitful and will constitute an important step toward a settlement of the Cyprus problem.

97. It is obvious that continued peace is an essential condition for the success of the intercommunal talks which have just begun and that, despite the relaxation of tension and the improved relations between the two communities, the situation remains unstable in the island. Therefore, I consider it unavoidable that the mandate of UNFICYP should be extended for another period. Because the intercommunal talks have to deal with very complex problems and are likely to be protracted, I feel that the period of extension should be of six months. Consequently, I recommend that the Security Council extend the stationing of UNFICYP for a further period of six months until December 26, 1968.

98. In this connection, I must draw the Security Council's attention to the growing deficit of the UNFICYP budget. This deficit, due to inadequate and now decreasing contributions, has reached alarming proportions and if this is allowed to continue it could make unavoidable a premature withdrawal of the Force. I therefore appeal to the members of the Security Council to give most serious and urgent attention to this matter.

99. In concluding this report, I wish once again to express my deep appreciation to the governments of those countries providing contingents to UNFICYP and to those which have made financial contributions to its budget. Without their generous support it would not be possible to maintain this important peace-keeping operation of the United Nations.

THE SITUATION IN VIETNAM

JUNE AND JULY 1968

IT SOON BECAME apparent that the preliminary talks between the United States and North Vietnam in Paris were not making the progress many had hoped for. To make matters worse, the fighting had become more intense instead of less. In a press conference on June 18, U Thant noted that even though the United States had restricted the area it was bombing in North Vietnam it had increased the number of attacks during May. On the other hand, he said the Vietcong had increased the number of its "barbarous raids . . . causing the death of many innocent civilians." "This mutual escalation by one side and then by the other is most deplorable," the Secretary-General said. At the same press conference, Thant said: " . . . in my view the Paris talks will be deadlocked for a long time to come. I think there is an assumption on both sides that military victory or military defeat is still possible. You are fully aware of my views on that subject. I have been saying for the past three and a half years that in a unique situation like that in Vietnam there can be no such thing as military victory or military defeat; there can only be more destruction, more devastation and more death."

As Thant prepared to go to Geneva for the summer session of the Economic and Social Council, scheduled to open July 8, the discussions in Paris were still deadlocked. He decided to stop over in the French capital to see if he could help. On July 6, he held separate meetings with the American negotiators, Averell Harriman and Cyrus Vance, and with the North Vietnamese representative, Xuan Thuy. At a press conference in Geneva on July 10, he described his contacts as "just exploratory—to get a final assessment of the two parties on the progress or lack of progress of the discussions and their analysis and assessment of the overall situation in Vietnam." He said that although there had been no progress in substance the fact that the parties were going on with their dialogue was a hopeful sign. "It is going to be a long and delicate process," he said. He stressed the preliminary nature of the Paris talks. "I do not believe for a moment," he declared, "that Washington and Hanoi will be able to solve the whole question of Vietnam. Other parties . . . have to be brought in at some stage. Of course, I have no means of knowing when that stage will come. . . ."

1. From Transcript of Press Conference at Luncheon
of United Nations Correspondents Association

NEW YORK   JUNE 18, 1968

. . . . THE SECRETARY-GENERAL: Mr. President and friends: I am very happy indeed to be with you once again after a lapse of many weeks caused by the resumed session of the General Assembly. I think we have rightly observed the long-established tradition of not having press conferences during sessions of the General Assembly.

I am grateful to all of you for this kind hospitality, which has developed into an annual event. I am particularly grateful to you, Mr. Foell,[1] for your generous introduction. I am aware of the feeling among the public that I have been unusually candid in my public utterances. Of course I have never shared that view. I do not think that I have been unusually candid. Perhaps I have been candid on occasions when I have felt that candid expressions of opinion would help.

While on this subject, I should like to elaborate somewhat on a point about which I feel very strongly. From time to time there are accusations in certain quarters that I am not neutral on this or that subject. I do not know what they mean by "neutral." As I understand the nature of my functions, I do not believe that the Secretary-General should be neutral on every issue. If he feels that a particular development is likely to disturb international peace and security, he has to come out with what he considers to be an appropriate statement or observation in order to focus public attention on that issue which is likely to endanger international peace and security. You are all familiar with the famous article 99 of the Charter, which empowers the Secretary-General even to bring to the Security Council's attention certain types of international developments.

SOURCE: *UN Monthly Chronicle,* Vol. V, July 1968, pp. 64-72.

[1]Earl Foell, *Christian Science Monitor.*

Therefore, I do not think that the Secretary-General must necessarily be neutral or keep quiet on every issue.

Another factor in my thinking is that the Secretary-General must try to understand the mood or the conscience of international public opinion on many issues. I think he must try to reflect international public opinion. That is one of his functions.

Most of you will remember that before I assumed my present functions I made a distinction between "neutral" and "impartial." I do not think the Secretary-General should be neutral, but I think he should be impartial. I think that if he feels there is a certain consensus of international public opinion on a particular subject or a particular question, he should try to reflect that consensus.

I do not wish to make a long introductory statement. I shall be very glad now to answer questions.

QUESTION: What do you think would happen to the talks in Paris and the fighting in South Vietnam if the United States stopped all bombing and other acts of war against North Vietnam?

THE SECRETARY-GENERAL: I have no means of knowing what would happen in Vietnam if certain action were taken as a prerequisite. However, I maintain that my two-year-old three-point formula is still valid. I am sure that all of you remember that my plan stipulates three steps, all of which constitute a means to an end. They are not the solution to the problem; they constitute only a means toward the achievement of certain objectives. The three points are: first, the cessation of the bombing of North Vietnam; second, the de-escalation of fighting by all parties in South Vietnam; and third, the willingness to talk to all those who are directly involved in the fighting. You will remember that the first step was not acceptable to Washington; the second step was not acceptable to Hanoi, because, in its view, I should not have equated the "aggressors" with "the victims of aggression." So my three-point formula was not acceptable, generally speaking, to the parties directly involved. But I still think that this two-year-old formula is valid today.

QUESTION: Should North Vietnam take some action now to match the limitation of United States bombing of the North?

THE SECRETARY-GENERAL: First, I wish to say the following regarding this "limitation" of the bombing of North Vietnam. It is clear to me from published accounts that the area of bombing was limited, after President Johnson's very gracious statement of March 31, to the 17th parallel and the 20th parallel. Later, it was further reduced—to the 19th parallel. But all the information available to me indicates that, although the area of bombing was drastically reduced or limited, the number of bombing sorties was increased.

I shall illustrate my point. It appears from all published accounts that the number of bombing sorties over the whole of Vietnam before the limitation was about 2,000; that was in March 1968. With effect from April 1, the area was reduced very much. But, in spite of the reduced area, the number of bombing sorties over that reduced area was more than 2,000 in April 1968. During the first week of May 1968 the bombing was still more intense and the number of sorties still larger. According to my information, during the first week of May the number of raids over the restricted area was much larger than the number of bombing raids in the corresponding week of April 1968—that was before I went to Alberta University.

From all accounts, the number of bombing raids over this restricted area in North Vietnam for May was a record.

Then of course, as you all know, in May the National Liberation Front and its military arm, the Vietcong, escalated their raids—I would even say their barbarous raids—on many cities, causing the death of many innocent civilians.

This mutual escalation by one side and then by the other is most deplorable. You all know my position. I am against escalation by either side; I am for de-escalation. I am even for cessation of all hostilities—but for practical purposes that is not, I know, a realistic assumption. I feel very strongly that if the essential first steps—according to my conviction of the last two years—were taken, the logical and rational steps would follow. That is why I have been trying in the past few years to bring about a dialogue between the two parties concerned. A dialogue is now taking place, and while it goes on I do not propose to make any observations on any aspect of the war, for obvious reasons.

I have made the foregoing observations just to project myself in an area that is not very well understood. Let me repeat: I am against all escalation of the war by either side. The death of a soldier is bad enough; the death of an innocent civilian is much more distressing, much more deplorable, much more heart-rending.

QUESTION: Would you expect that the bombarding of the civilian population in the North and the bombarding of civilians with rockets in the South should cease simultaneously?

THE SECRETARY-GENERAL: Of course, that is my wish, and I am sure it is the wish of every one of us. But for practical purposes there must be some sort of international machinery to supervise this type of cessation of hostilities. I am sure that will be one of the subjects discussed once the essential first step is taken.

QUESTION: The Paris talks on Vietnam seem to be deadlocked because, first, the United States is trying to use the talks to secure for the Saigon régime and its United States supporters the security that the United States military has been unable to provide through three years of military escalation; and, second, Hanoi seems to be waiting for the erosion and collapse of the Saigon régime and the choosing of candidates in the United States presidential elections. Do you agree with that assessment, and have you any views on making the Paris talks more fruitful than they now are?

THE SECRETARY-GENERAL: For obvious reasons I would not wish to comment directly on the substance of that question. But, in my view, the Paris talks will be deadlocked for a long time to come. I think there is an assumption on both sides that military victory or military defeat is still possible. You are fully aware of my views on that subject. I have been saying for the past three and a half years that in a unique situation like that in Vietnam there can be no such thing as military victory or military defeat; there can only be more destruction, more devastation, and more death.

In my view, there are two important factors that contribute toward the military stalemate in Vietnam. First, the United States, the most powerful nation in the world—or in any case one of the two most powerful nations on earth—cannot be militarily defeated or dislodged from Vietnam if it decides to keep on fighting and if there is the political will to stay there. Second, the United States, with its very sophisticated weaponry, its very powerful arms, cannot subdue the National Liberation Front and its military arm so long as the National Liberation Front and its military arm are determined to go on with their struggle for what they consider to be their legitimate national aspirations. That is also one lesson of history.

That is why I have been saying that in strictly military terms, in the classical sense, the United States will never be defeated in Vietnam and the National Liberation Front and its military arm can never be subdued in the sense that, for example, Nazi Germany was defeated in 1944–1945 by the allied forces. I think the situations are completely different. You cannot expect a repetition of the First World War or the Second World War situation in the Vietnam war.

The nearest parallel, in my view, is the Algerian war, which came to a conclusion about ten years ago and resulted in the victory of both sides. Of course, what happened in Algeria in the late 1950s and what is happening in Vietnam today are not identical. There are many features in the two situations that are very dissimilar—for instance, the historical background, the nature and development of the war, and the character of the fighting. But the Algerian war approximates more closely the Vietnam war than does the classical First World War or the Second World War, where one side capitulated and the other side dictated terms. I do not think this will be the case in Vietnam. I think we should draw a lesson from the Algerian war, at the end of which, as you all know, the two sides were on the friendliest terms. France and Algeria have maintained the friendliest relations since the termination of that tragic war in Algeria. I think the Algerian war can provide some guidance in the solution of the Vietnam war—although, as I have said, the two wars are not identical in all respects.

QUESTION: What can you, or anyone else, do to help Ambassador [Gunnar] Jarring get serious negotiations under way for peace in the Middle East?

Do you consider that his mission still has a chance of success or would you recommend that it be terminated?

THE SECRETARY-GENERAL: Since the arrival in New York of Ambassador Jarring, I have been in constant touch with him. According to our latest conversation, he expects to submit a report to me before the end of July. Of course, I in turn have to transmit this to the Security Council for whatever action the Council might deem fit to take. Of course, I have no means of knowing whether Ambassador Jarring's report to me will indicate some progress or lack of progress. But his expectation is to submit a report before the end of July. At that time, of course, it is up to the Security Council members to decide whether to meet or not to meet on the basis of that report.

QUESTION: How long a leave does Ambassador Jarring have from his government?

THE SECRETARY-GENERAL: In the first instance, at my request the government of Sweden very kindly granted Ambassador Jarring a six-month leave, which expired, of course, at the end of May. At my request again, the government of Sweden very kindly extended his leave for another three months—June, July, and August. Therefore, for the moment his leave will expire at the end of August.

QUESTION: You have given strong endorsement to the concept of direct talks between the Greek Cypriot and Turkish Cypriot communities. Do you see any possibility of bringing about similar direct talks between the Arab states and Israel in connection with the Jarring mission, and do you intend to make such a recommendation?

Now that you have had the benefit of discussions with Ambassador Jarring and General [Odd] Bull, do you still believe that direct negotiations in the Middle East of a kind similar to that which you favor between the parties in Vietnam are not possible?

THE SECRETARY-GENERAL: I do not want to project myself, for the moment in any case, into such very controversial issues, which is one of the bones of contention, if I may say so, between the parties directly involved in the Middle Eastern crisis. But in my view they are situations which are not identical, and because of their differences in the background, differences in the political and geographical factors, I think we have to assess the situations differently.

I remember having made a similar observation at one of the press conferences in the past. I even brought in the example of somebody projecting an idea of direct talks between President Johnson and Premier Fidel Castro. I do not know whether I said that at a press conference or on another occasion. But my point for the moment is this: I do not wish to project myself on this very contentious issue, which is primarily the concern of the Secretary-General's special representative, Ambassador Jarring, who has been trying his very best to achieve some progress in the context of the Security Council resolution of November 22, 1967. . . .

QUESTION: On March 27, the government of the Republic of South Africa agreed conditionally to receive a personal representative of the Secretary-General in connection with the question of South West Africa. Is this proposal still active and, if so, what arrangements are being made to dispatch a representative to the area?

THE SECRETARY-GENERAL: Yes, the government of South Africa replied to my letter a few months ago. But in the debate in the plenary session of the General Assembly on the question of South West Africa, many of you will recall that some representatives mentioned the possibility and even the necessity of the Secretary-General sending a representative to South Africa to discuss this question of South West Africa along with other matters.

But, although such a view was expressed by a few Member governments in the debate, this particular aspect did not feature in the resolution. So I do not think I can proceed on that basis without an appropriate mandate by the General Assembly.

QUESTION: Do you think the United Nations can now play a useful role in the Nigerian civil war with the collapse of the talks in Kampala [in Uganda] sponsored by the Commonwealth Secretariat?

THE SECRETARY-GENERAL: I do not believe that the United Nations will be in a position to play a useful role in the very tragic situation in the Federal Republic of Nigeria. But I have been in correspondence with the head of state, General [Yakubu] Gowon, for some time, and General Gowon has very kindly kept me posted on the developments. On this occasion I can only express my very deep concern about the situation in Nigeria resulting in death and destruction, and I would very much hope that the parties concerned will get together and discuss their common problems in a mutual spirit of cooperation and accommodation, so that these talks can lead to an enduring peace in that unfortunate country.

QUESTION: What do you consider the essential factor in achieving a successful outcome of the talks on Cyprus—to which you attach very great importance—on the Middle East talks under the auspices of Ambassador Jarring, and on the Paris talks on Vietnam? Do you have any common factor in achieving a successful outcome for those sets of talks?

THE SECRETARY-GENERAL: Regarding the Middle East and Vietnam, I had made a few observations a moment ago. Regarding Cyprus, as you all know, I submitted my report to the Security Council only last week. This report will be considered by the Security Council this afternoon. As I indicated in my report to the Security Council last March, I have been asking my special representative, Mr. Osorio Tafall, to encourage the two communities to get together. Due to his strenuous efforts, the leaders of the two communities got together in Beirut from the second to the fifth of this month. Mr. Glafkos Clerides, the Greek Cypriot president of the House of Representatives, and Mr. Denktash, the president of the Turkish Communal Chamber, got together in Beirut and, according to their joint communiqué, the talks were conducted in a very cordial atmosphere. The next talks are scheduled to take place in Cyprus on the twenty-fourth of this month in the presence of the Secretary-General's special representative, Mr. Osorio Tafall, who will then remain at the disposal of the two parties for consultations as and when necessary. So far as the situation in Cyprus is concerned, the atmosphere has improved, the political climate has improved, the psychological climate has improved and, with a spirit of cooperation and understanding, I hope the two communities will achieve their common aspirations. . . .

THE PRESIDENT OF UNCA: If I may ask one question on my own behalf, Mr. Secretary-General. You mentioned earlier that you thought the Paris talks would be going on for some long time still. Do you maintain either daily or nearly daily contact, through some means or another, with the parties involved in the Paris talks?

THE SECRETARY-GENERAL: Since the talks started on May 10, I have not attempted to establish contact with either side. Since one of the primary objectives of my endeavors in the past few years was to bring about a meeting of the two parties, and since a meeting is taking place, I have not felt and I still do not feel that my contacts would serve any useful purpose. Of course, if and when necessary, I may have to resume my contacts with both parties. But, until now, I have no contacts with either of the parties.

THE PRESIDENT OF UNCA: Thank you very much, Mr. Secretary-General. I think we will remain with our differences over whether or not you are candid. I maintain that you have been very candid with us today once more, and we all thank you for it.

---

2. From Transcript of Press Conference

GENEVA   JULY 10, 1968

. . .

THE SECRETARY-GENERAL: As most of you are aware, when my office announced my projected departure from New York on this present trip, the Foreign Minister of France very kindly invited me to lunch with him on Saturday—last Saturday. I accepted that kind invitation and I

SOURCE: Note to Correspondents No. 43.

decided to take the opportunity of my brief visit to Paris by establishing contacts with the negotiators of both sides. I made the request to both parties—both parties very kindly complied with my request and I saw, as you know, both the American negotiators, Ambassadors [Averell] Harriman and [Cyrus] Vance, and the North Vietnamese negotiator— Mr. Xuan Thuy.

As I made this very clear in my brief statement in Paris, I had no new ideas or proposals to present to the parties at this stage, since one of my endeavors in the past four years had been to bring about the dialogue between Washington and Hanoi and since that objective was achieved I do not believe that any useful purpose will be served, at least at this stage, to come out with any new proposals or ideas on the substance of the Vietnam problem.

As I said in Paris, my visit was just exploratory—to get the final assessments of the two parties on the progress or lack of progress of the discussions and their analysis and assessment of the overall situation in Vietnam. Although there was no progress in substance, the very fact that both parties agreed to carry on with the conversations is a hopeful sign, in my view. My assessment is that these negotiations or conversations will take some time. It is going to be a long and delicate process, but, of course, the international community is very anxious to see a breakthrough. As far as the Vietnam problem is concerned, as you all know, I have stated my position on many previous occasions and I do not think it will be in the public interest for me to reiterate these views at this time.

. . .

QUESTION: Sir, do you have the impression that the Vietnam talks in Paris will lead to the convening of the new Vietnam conference in which all interested parties will participate?

THE SECRETARY-GENERAL: It is very difficult at this stage to antici- pate what will be the outcome of the talks currently taking place in Paris. Of course, at some stage the talks shall involve other parties too. In my view, Washington and Hanoi alone cannot solve the problem of Viet- nam. Washington and Hanoi can deal with matters of common interest to both and nothing more. I do not believe for a moment that Washington and Hanoi will be able to solve the whole question of Vietnam. Other parties directly involved have to be brought in at some stage. Of course, I have no means of knowing when that stage will come but as I have said, the present phase of discussions will be a long process.

QUESTION: Could you say what you have been doing about the situation in Nigeria while you have been in Geneva and whether you have any views on the attitude of the Biafran authorities toward letting relief operations operate there?

THE SECRETARY-GENERAL: Well, regarding the Nigerian situation, particularly the situation in the Eastern Region which is known as Biafra, I first had the opportunity of discussing the matter with General Gowon, head of the Federal Government, in Lagos last September on my way to attend the African summit conference which took place in Kinshasa, Congo. I had a very useful exchange of views with him, and at the African summit conference, as you will remember, it was decided unanimously by all heads of African states to constitute a small committee under the distinguished leadership of the Emperor of Ethiopia to go to Nigeria to contact the parties concerned and to bring about a peaceful solution of this tragic problem. The committee did go there. I have been advised at the Kinshasa summit meeting that the Organization of African Unity would be seized of this matter and I believe OAU is still seized of it. Of course on the basis of later developments the Commonwealth Secretariat was very deeply involved; its able Secretary-General, Mr. Arnold Smith, was personally involved and he was able to bring about a meeting of the two parties in Uganda, but in the meantime the United Nations was not staying quiet.

I have been in constant touch with General Gowon since September and in the meantime the United Nations and its agencies have been involved, although there was not much publicity in the public media. To cite one example, UNICEF has been offering very substantial aid to the unfortunate people in the Eastern Region of Nigeria, through the good offices of the International Committee of the Red Cross. In my view ICRC should be the only channel for the transmission of international aid to those stricken people in the Eastern Region. As far as the UNICEF assistance is concerned I just want to say that so far, with the very full cooperation of ICRC, it has been able to send to the stricken people of the Eastern Region, which is called Biafra, two hundred tons of skimmed milk powder, ten million vitamin capsules, and quantities of medical supplies and quantities of salt, and a variety of transport equipment. I want to take this opportunity of stating that only yesterday I had a very useful exchange of views with Dr. Gonard, head of ICRC, and I have assured him of my fullest cooperation in his endeavors in the discharge of his responsibilities by ICRC. They estimate that the requirements of the population in distress amount to at least two hundred tons daily of supplementary food supplies. This is a huge quantity as you will recognize, but there are now no channels of communication to that region. The dispute, according to reports available to me, has been still going on between the federal government on the one hand and the dissidents on the other.

In my view, the federal government is desirous of facilitating all international aid and assistance to the people in distress in the Eastern Region. Only last night my attention was drawn to a letter from the permanent mission of Nigeria to the United Nations, addressed to UNICEF, on July 3. It says in effect "that the head of the government has agreed that relief supplies for the Eastern Region areas can be airlifted to Enogu, Port Harcourt, or any other airports under federal control, and from thence transported by road to agreed points in the rebel-held territory." He further offered to supply vehicles and escorts and to render every possible assistance and facilities desired by the Red Cross to ensure that the relief supplies reach their destination.

I think this is a very welcome move on the part of the federal government. Yesterday I had very useful discussions with some heads of the specialized agencies which were involved in this humanitarian work. As soon as I get back to New York I will take it up immediately. Of course actions of the United Nations and the family of agencies will be purely humanitarian. I want to make this very clear.

As far as the constitutional aspect of the problem is concerned the United Nations has to regard this situation as purely within Article 2, paragraph 7, of the Charter, but the federal Nigerian government has very kindly agreed to accept and facilitate the transmission of all aid on humanitarian grounds. I will take this opportunity of appealing to the leaders of the Eastern Region, or Biafra, to take advantage of this offer and to cooperate more fully with the international community in its genuine endeavor to ameliorate the miserable plight of the peoples in that region.

. . .

QUESTION: I would like to return to the question of Nigeria. I noted that you personally and heads of other organizations of the United Nations family have done much to help these people from the humanitarian point of view. However, I am preoccupied and anxious about another matter. Is it not really so that the United Nations is in a position politically and otherwise in order to intervene in this genocide—I stress this genocide—in a more effective way? I would recall in this connection that there is in existence a convention on genocide approved by the General Assembly on December 9, 1948. I do not believe that this convention had ever been applied or implemented—from all information that is available here in Switzerland. I am correspondent of a Swiss newspaper. I would say that public opinion is most occupied by the events in Biafra. According to information that is available it is a case of genocide. You, Sir, have said that this is an internal matter affecting Nigeria. I would like to recall in this connection that the United Nations did take up the question of South Africa, the question of Rhodesia; in other words they take up matters that are internal in character. Mr. Secretary-General, may I ask you whether there does exist a legal or political basis as a result of which the United Nations could intervene to put an end to this most unfortunate series of events in Biafra. You have taken up the Congo matter and others as well. I apologize for my length, Mr. Secretary-General.

THE SECRETARY-GENERAL: Well, I think we have to recognize some home truths regarding the United Nations. It is a gathering of organizations of 124 sovereign independent states. If one Member says that this is genocide, another Member will say that this is not genocide. If one Member says that the Security Council must take action, another Member will say that the Security Council must not take action. These are problems connected with all human organizations. Whatever my distinguished friend may think, there are many others here who do not share his view. Even in this room I am sure my friend's assessment is not shared totally by the rest. The same applies to international organizations.

As far as the functioning of the United Nations is concerned there are principal deliberative organs, the General Assembly and the Security Council. The Security Council has to deal principally with political matters—matters affecting peace and security. The Security Council has not taken any initiative or any action in this matter. There is no one of us which can force the United Nations to act, nobody.

You cited the question of the Congo and this and that. These actions were taken on the basis of the decisions of deliberative organs. In some cases the decisions were made by the General Assembly, in other cases decisions were made by the Security Council.

In the present case if a Member state or Member states feel that the United Nations should be involved, of course it is up to any one of the

124 Member states to take the initiative either in the General Assembly or in the Security Council to present a case and get a decision. I don't see any other mechanism or any other procedure by which the United Nations can be involved. When you say that many people in the world consider the situation in the Eastern Region of Nigeria as genocide, I want to recall, without in any way associating myself or identifying myself with these accusations, the volume of correspondence in the past six years from many quarters alleging that a particular situation in a particular country is genocide. Why was the United Nations inactive?

For instance, during the past several years I received scores of complaints alleging that the Vietnam war is genocide. About two years ago I got many complaints regarding what was alleged to be genocide in Indonesia. According to those allegations, almost one million people were killed. Why was the United Nations inactive? Many allegations have been made but who is to determine whether a particular case is a case of genocide in terms of the resolution? I am not competent to determine this. I am sure my distinguished friend is not competent to determine whether a particular situation is genocide or not genocide. It is only the competent organ of the United Nations which can determine whether a particular situation is a genocide or not a genocide. So my conclusion is that it is not some individuals or some newspapers or some radio stations or some television stations which can pass judgment regarding genocide. I don't think it will be a fair or reliable assessment. A fair and reliable assessment must be made only by the Member states themselves in an appropriate organ of the United Nations.

QUESTION: Mr. Secretary-General, do you see any prospect in the near future for a concerted big-power move to a decent settlement in the Middle East?

THE SECRETARY-GENERAL: In all similar situations like the Middle East a concerted action by the big powers will contribute very significantly toward a solution. I have no doubt about it. In my view in all situations of a grave character, involving the disturbance of international peace and security the concerted action of the big powers will be the most potent instrument for the solution of these problems. You will recall that General [Charles] de Gaulle proposed it first but the general feeling in the Security Council was that it should be the Security Council which should be involved at least for the moment.

QUESTION: It seems to me that your representative in the Middle East is in a state of impasse. What further action do you propose to undertake in order to help resolve the problem of the Middle East and do you think that it might be useful to send Blue Helmets[1] into that region?

THE SECRETARY-GENERAL: Ambassador Gunnar Jarring, the Secretary-General's special representative in the Middle East, has been engaged in the last few weeks with direct contacts with the parties directly involved and, for your information, he is coming to Geneva perhaps before lunch today and I will have the benefit of his views and assessment. For the moment I do not think it will be in the public interest for me to comment on the situation. As you all know, Ambassador Jarring told me before he left New York that it was his intention to submit a report on his assessment of the situation by the end of this month. Beyond that I am sorry I cannot say. . . .

[1]The term "Blue Helmets" was originally used to describe the personnel of UNEF.

From Address to the International Bar Association

DUBLIN   JULY 11, 1968

. . . THE EXISTING SYSTEM of modern international law was built around the concepts of sovereignty and of independence. Yet while these may be called the roots of modern international law, they are also a hindrance in an age when we are moving from independence to interdependence. In national law the existence of and necessity for legislative, judicial, and law-enforcement organs are self-evident. In international law, because of the barrier of sovereignty, they have existed scarcely at all or only on an *ad hoc* basis. In the twentieth century, through custom, practice, treaty, and judicial decision, the rules of international law have proliferated, but the development of means of truly enforcing those rules through compulsory adjudication and through collective action has been painfully slow. The horrors of two world wars, and the death and suffering of countless millions were the price mankind was forced to pay before that barrier of sovereignty was lowered sufficiently to permit international law, both on a regional and on a universal plane, to create or strengthen organizations designed to keep the peace and to settle disputes through both diplomacy and impartial adjudication. As a result we have today the Charter of the United Nations, the Statute of the International Court of Justice, and the regional organizations such as the Council of Europe, the Organization of American States, the League of Arab States, and the Organization of African Unity.

Given this machinery and the principles upon which it is based— including, specifically, the principles of international law—what role does law play in keeping the peace today? At best it can be said that it can be likened to the candles which light the darkness. The Rann of Kutch dispute, which was a contributing factor leading to the war between India and Pakistan, has recently been settled by arbitration. A territorial dispute between Argentina and Chile has likewise been settled

SOURCE: *UN Monthly Chronicle,* Vol. V, August-September 1968, pp. 114-120.

by the same means. The dispute between the Republic of Indonesia and the Kingdom of the Netherlands regarding West Irian, which had already broken out into armed clashes, was solved by an agreement negotiated by the parties in 1962. The more these examples are followed, the sooner the darkness will be dispelled.

Hope also lies along the road which has recently been followed in Antarctica and in outer space. A few years ago Antarctica was a possible source of friction and hostility by virtue of the numerous competing territorial claims by various states. With the conclusion of the Antarctic Treaty in Washington, on December 1, 1959, this potential source of strife and conflict was converted into an area of peace and cooperation. Principles were established for Antarctica, moreover, which were utilized as the foundation for the provisions which now govern man's exploration of the limitless realm of outer space. Through the instrumentality of the Legal Sub-Committee of the United Nations Committee on the Peaceful Uses of Outer Space, the Treaty on Principles Governing the Activities of States in the Exploration and Use of Outer Space, including the Moon and Other Celestial Bodies, was concluded in 1966. This treaty affirms that the exploration and use of outer space shall be carried out for the benefit of all countries. It proclaims the freedom of outer space. It affirms that outer space and celestial bodies are not subject to national appropriation, and provides that outer space and celestial bodies shall not be used for any military purpose. It therefore establishes a broad and forward-looking régime for an area which might have become a source of strife and conflict. The process of law has neutralized this possible source of conflict, and has converted it into an area of peace and cooperation.

Within the framework of the régime established by the Outer Space Treaty, the United Nations continues work on more detailed aspects of the law of outer space. Only last December, the General Assembly commended to governments the Agreement on the Rescue of Astronauts, the Return of Astronauts and the Return of Objects Launched into Outer Space. This constituted the culmination of five years of work by the Legal Sub-Committee of the United Nations Committee on the Peaceful Uses of Outer Space and yet another significant step in the development of international law relating to outer space. The text of the agreement reflects a carefully designed balance between the legitimate interests of the party on whose territory search and rescue operations are conducted and those of the launching authority, and seeks to secure

the safe and prompt return of astronauts and space objects to the
launching authority. It is my hope that this agreement will shortly be
supplemented by an agreement on liability for damage caused by objects
launched into outer space, which was the principal item discussed by the
Legal Committee of the United Nations Committee on the Peaceful Uses
of Outer Space during a session in Geneva which ended a few days ago.

The law of outer space is therefore developing fast and along lines
which promise much for the furtherance of peace and cooperation.
There remains one other area for which a new régime may have to be
created, and for which outer space should provide many fruitful analo-
gies. This area is one of potentially vast significance in bettering the life
of man in the generations immediately ahead, as it will, with improved
technology, provide an almost limitless source of food and minerals. I
speak of the seabed and ocean floor in areas now considered beyond the
limits of national jurisdiction. On the initiative of Malta, the General
Assembly, at its session last year, took up an item entitled ''Examination
of the question of the reservation exclusively for peaceful purposes of
the sea-bed and the ocean floor, and the subsoil thereof, underlying the
high seas beyond the limits of present national jurisdiction, and the use
of their resources in the interests of mankind.'' The Assembly decided to
establish a thirty-five member *Ad Hoc* Committee to Study the Peaceful
Uses of the Sea-Bed and the Ocean Floor beyond the Limits of National
Jurisdiction. This committee has established a Working Group to consider the legal aspects of the item. Its task will not be either easy or
short, in view of the many varying interests which are involved. However, if it proves to be as successful as the Legal Sub-Committee of the
Committee on the Peaceful Uses of Outer Space we can rest assured that
another potential area of friction between states will be converted,
through law, into an area of peace and cooperation.

The role of international law is, of course, not confined to providing
new régimes for new areas of man's endeavor. It also regulates existing
relations between states. A very significant step was taken only a few
weeks ago by the General Assembly of the United Nations, when it
commended to states the Treaty on the Non-Proliferation of Nuclear
Weapons. This treaty, taken together with the Moscow test-ban treaty of
1963, is the first really significant breakthrough in the field of global
disarmament since the end of the Second World War. The nations of
Latin America, on a regional plane, took a further significant step last

year when, in Mexico, twenty-one of them signed the Treaty for the Prohibition of Nuclear Weapons in Latin America. This treaty was welcomed with special satisfaction by the General Assembly of the United Nations last December as an event of historic significance in the efforts to prevent the proliferation of nuclear weapons and to promote international peace and security. If the treaties I have just mentioned can only serve as an inspiration and example for other measures of disarmament, we may be able to look forward to the end of the armaments race, and the release of enormous amounts of wealth and experience for peaceful development.

These, then, are some of the bright places, where law has constituted the cornerstone of peace. However, there are still great areas of darkness and of strife in this world where force and power politics rule to the detriment of law and peace. In the ultimate analysis, law cannot prevail over force and power politics until mankind comes to regard the impartial adjudication of international law in disputes among states as the rule, not the exception.

If the record of the law in the history of keeping the peace is still a modest one, its record in the history of long-term interational cooperation is a more brilliant one, less often discussed, perhaps, only because it relates to fields less spectacular than breaches of the peace. Here it may be said, at least in certain parts of the world, that through legal processes states are moving from independence to integration, particularly in the economic sphere. Indeed, there is already a fast-growing body of international norms which is beginning to be referred to as the "law of integration."

When we view the global picture of cooperation in economic and social questions, we see a world closely tied by thousands of treaties regulating matters as diverse as narcotics and commodity prices, slavery and atomic energy, road transportation and maintenance obligations. This cooperation is not limited to the economic and social needs of the day, but has also extended to the fabric of the law itself. In the twenty-two years of its existence, through codification in treaty form of the law of the sea, and of diplomatic and consular relations, the United Nations has achieved more progress in this field than was achieved in the previous three hundred years. The success earlier this year of the first part of the United Nations Conference on the Law of Treaties, has brought us to the threshold of a convention, to be completed in Vienna next year, which progressively develops and codifies the entire law of treaties and which will, I hope, become one of the fundamentals of the constitutional law of the entire society of nations.

With the great success it has achieved in codifying and developing public international law in mind, the United Nations now seeks to achieve similar results in the field of private international law. An important step in this direction was the recent creation of the United Nations Commission on International Trade Law (UNCITRAL), which was established by the General Assembly in December 1966 and held its first session early this year.

The object of UNCITRAL is to deal with a concrete and practical problem.

Lawyers and persons engaged in international commerce are aware that conflicts and divergences among the laws of different countries often constitute an obstacle to the flow of trade. The purpose of this new commission is to help remove those obstacles by promoting the harmonization and unification of the law of international trade.

The different legal systems of the world and all stages of economic development are represented among the twenty-nine states elected by the General Assembly to membership in UNCITRAL. In addition to being spokesmen for their governments the delegates are also eminent jurists. The combination of these elements gives me confidence that this new commission will make a significant contribution to removing legal barriers to international trade.

It is true that the conclusion of international agreements on particular aspects of economic, social, and legal matters is not as spectacular as the conclusion of agreements in the political field. However, through their sheer numbers and scope, and through their ultimate objectives of eliminating poverty and ignorance, the agreements themselves contribute to the stabilization and development of national societies, and thus contribute to the maintenance of international peace. The world will never be truly safe for peace until mankind has eradicated poverty, ignorance, and injustice. The processes of international cooperation are simply the processes of ridding the world of these ancient evils.

As we look to the future we must realize that peace and cooperation are impossible without legal regulation. While international law does not yet carry the force or conviction of national law, even today it is the cornerstone of peace and cooperation on the international plane. As modern discoveries and technological progress bring growing interdependence, that interdependence must accelerate the further development of international law. The ultimate goal must be that fortunate day when international law will enjoy, in the society of nations, a place as important and as compelling as law in our present national societies. But to do so, it must be responsive to the realities of the world, to the needs of society, and to the temper of mankind. It cannot afford, any more than can national law, to refuse to meet the challenges with which it is confronted, or allow itself to become static. In the end, it is the confidence of peoples and of nations in the rule of law that can bring to international law its greatest strength, and to win this confidence it must be as dynamic as are the lives of peoples and nations themselves. Through international organizations means now exist for developing the law at an unprecedented rate, and, potentially at least, the means for enforcing that law also exists through those organizations. The cause of international law is a noble and a compelling one. It is a cause in which you all, as lawyers, have a part to play, and in which I wish you every success. We all live for the day when justice may be established in the hearts not only of men, but also of nations.

NIGERIA–BIAFRA

ONE OF THE MOST tragic events during U Thant's decade as Secretary-General was the civil war in Nigeria, which erupted on May 30, 1967, when the Eastern Region seceded from the former British territory and proclaimed itself the Republic of Biafra. Despite the incredible human suffering, the international community could play only a limited role because of the internal character of the conflict. In the Congo, the central government had requested United Nations intervention to prevent the secession of Katanga Province on the ground that the secession was being inspired and supported from the outside. In the case of Nigeria, the Lagos government not only did not seek United Nations assistance; it rejected such help except for humanitarian aid. At the outset of the war, Thant wrote to General Yakubu Gowon, head of the military government of Nigeria, offering his good offices for the purpose of negotiating a settlement, but the offer was not accepted. The offer was repeated later on, as were similar offers from other international figures, with the same result. The Secretary-General discussed the problem personally with General Gowon during a brief visit to Lagos in September 1967, while en route to Kinshasa for a meeting of the heads of state and government of the Organization of African Unity (OAU). As he was to say later, he "deeply regretted" his inability "as Secretary-General to help directly in forestalling the horrors of the war in Nigeria." He kept in close touch with General Gowon, however, especially on the humanitarian aspects of the war and was represented in Nigeria by a personal representative, at first by Nils-Goran Gussing of Sweden and later by Said-Uddin Khan of Pakistan. These representatives served a twofold purpose: (1) to assist in the distribution of relief supplies, which by agreement were being channeled through the International Committee of the Red Cross and (2) to keep the Secretary-General informed.

As for the international community's role in seeking a settlement of the conflict, the main effort was in the hands of a six-nation committee, established by the OAU and headed by Emperor Haile Selassie of Ethiopia. The committee did go to Nigeria after the Kinshasa meeting but left empty-handed. Another unsuccessful attempt was made by the Secretary-General of the British Commonwealth, Arnold Smith. He was able to bring about a meeting of the two parties in Uganda, but this too ended without positive results. At the Kinshasa meeting, the OAU formally recognized the situation in Nigeria as an internal affair, which under Article 2, paragraph 7 of the United Nations Charter would place it outside the jurisdiction of the organization. The African heads of state and government also recognized "the sovereign and territorial integrity of Nigeria" and pledged "faith in the federal government." Thant agreed with this position. As he said in a press conference on September 23, 1968: "My approach to the problem and my policy toward it are guided primarily, if not exclusively, by the decision of the Organization of African Unity, which was arrived at last year in Kinshasa. I shall continue to be guided by the decisions of the OAU which, in my view, should be the main machinery for the settlement of this dispute."

At a press conference on January 18, 1968, the Secretary-General was asked a question which was being raised with increasing frequency in the press, just as the press and the public were asking about Vietnam: "Do you see anything that the United Nations will or can do in Nigeria, in Biafra?" Thant replied: "The question of Nigeria and Biafra is before the Organization of African Unity. I attended the last session of the OAU conference in Kinshasa last September. The matter was brought to the attention of the OAU by the members themselves. The OAU has taken certain steps toward the settlement of that problem. The OAU has formed a committee. The committee is actively involved with this question. And since the regional organization is actively involved in the problem, I do not think it will be useful or even desirable for the United Nations to be involved." At a luncheon of the United Nations Correspondents Association on June 18 he was asked again, after the collapse of Arnold Smith's efforts at the Uganda meeting, whether the United Nations might now play a useful role. Once more he replied: "I do not believe that the United Nations will be in a position to play a useful role in the very tragic situation in the Federal Republic of Nigeria. But I have been in correspondence with the head of state, General Gowon, for some time, and General Gowon has very kindly kept me posted on the developments. On this occasion I can only express my very deep concern about the situation in Nigeria resulting in death and destruction, and I would very much hope that the parties concerned will get together and discuss their common problems in a mutual spirit of cooperation and accommodation, so that these talks can lead to an enduring peace in that unfortunate country."

During this period the UN effort was concentrated on trying to get food and medicines to the civilian victims of the war, especially in Biafra which was feeling the effect of the blockade imposed at the beginning of the conflict by the Lagos government. General Gowon notified the United Nations Children's Fund (UNICEF) on July 3 that he would permit relief supplies for Biafra to be "airlifted to Enugu, Port Harcourt, or any other airports under federal control, and from thence transported by road to agreed points in the rebel-held territory." He further offered to supply vehicles and escorts and to render every possible assistance desired by the International Committee of the Red Cross to ensure that the relief supplies reached their destination. The Secretary-General commended the federal government on its attitude and in a press conference on July 11 he appealed to the Biafran leader, Colonel Odumegwu Ojukwu, "to take advantage of this offer and to cooperate more fully with the international community in this genuine endeavor to ameliorate the miserable plight of the peoples in that region." In a message, dated July 13, Thant told General Gowon, "I am receiving numerous messages from many quarters, drawing my attention to the seriousness of this problem." Noting Gowon's offer to cooperate in getting relief supplies to Biafra, he said he was "encouraged to hope that this offer will help solve" the problem. Starvation and suffering continued, however, as Biafran officials raised one impediment after another, while the international community—including the United Nations—was blamed by the public for failure to act.

---

1. Message to General Yakubu Gowon, Head of the Military Government of Nigeria

NEW YORK   JULY 13, 1968

YOUR EXCELLENCY will understand that I am increasingly concerned by the urgency and magnitude of the needs of civilian victims of the hostilities in Nigeria. I am receiving numerous messages from many quarters, drawing my attention to the seriousness of this problem. The humanitarian organs of the United Nations as well as other relief agencies are making strenuous efforts to help meet this tragic situation. One agency of the United Nations, namely UNICEF, acting on understandings reached with your government last winter, has already provided some vital assistance. It hopes to do more and to this end the Executive Director of UNICEF issued an appeal on July 11 on behalf of all Nigerian children. The distribution of UNICEF supplies in Nigeria would continue to be channeled through the International Committee of the Red Cross.

The humanitarian organs of the United Nations are ready to make their contribution, with the concurrence of your government, and also to channel their supplies directly through the International Committee of the Red Cross. I know that Your Excellency is making appropriate arrangements to facilitate the transport and distribution of relief supplies to those urgently in need in the areas under effective federal control. The movement of supplies to those in need in the Central Eastern Region, on

SOURCE: UN Press Release SG/SM/998.

the other hand, has so far presented serious logistical problems. Your Excellency has confirmed to UNICEF, in communications of July 3 and 10 from your chargé d'affaires at the United Nations, your agreement to ensure access corridors via airports or seaports in federal-controlled territory, which would permit overland transport of relief supplies to the Central Eastern Region and to provide necessary vehicles and escorts. I am encouraged to hope that this offer will help solve the above-mentioned problems. May I also express my hope that everything possible will be done by your government to enable the Red Cross, the United Nations, and the voluntary agencies concerned to carry out their humanitarian task.

In a statement I made earlier this week in Geneva, I appealed to those in charge in the Central Eastern Region to take advantage of the present opportunity and to cooperate fully with the current efforts to relieve the desperate plight of the peoples in that area. I am confident that Your Excellency and your government share the concern of the United Nations and the whole world that this tragic situation should not be allowed to deteriorate further. I would be glad to send a representative to Lagos immediately to discuss the modalities of this humanitarian task if Your Excellency agrees.

---

2. From Statement to Heads of State and Government
of the Organization of African Unity

ALGIERS   SEPTEMBER 13, 1968

. . . IF I AM UNABLE to conceal my concern about developments stemming from the persistence of colonial and racial policies in Africa, even less can I refrain from expressing my distress and dismay at the mounting toll of destruction, starvation, and loss of life resulting from the tragic

SOURCE: UN Press Release SG/SM976.

fratricidal strife in Nigeria over the past year. As has been verified from impartial sources, a very large number of people, combatants and non-combatants alike, are either dying or undergoing acute suffering; many, particularly children, are dying from, or are on the verge of, starvation. In the name of humanity, it is essential that everything be done to help relieve the impact of this tragic conflict.

It will be recalled that I had the privilege of attending the fourth session of the Assembly of Heads of State and Government of OAU in Kinshasa last year when this issue was discussed. The Assembly adopted a resolution which recognized the "soverign and territorial integrity of Nigeria" and pledged "faith in the Federal Government." It further recognized the Nigerian crisis as an internal affair and expressed "concern at the tragic and serious situation in Nigeria." This resolution is a basis for my attitude and approach to this problem, and I believe that the OAU should be the most appropriate instrument for the promotion of peace in Nigeria. In order to coordinate efforts and thus undertake the most effective action, it has been agreed by a number of organizations, both governmental and private, that all the humanitarian aid to the victims of the Nigerian conflict should be channeled through the International Committee of the Red Cross and this arrangement still stands.

In addition, deeply disturbed by the extent of human suffering involved in the present conflict, and wishing to determine in what way I might contribute toward a solution of the relief problems, I appointed a representative who proceeded to Nigeria over a month ago in order to assist in the relief and humanitarian activities for the civilian victims of the hostilities. Similarly, in coordination with the International Committee of the Red Cross, other organs within the United Nations family have been active in sending supplies and in trying to speed up their distribution to the distressed areas. However, it would appear that, apart from the need for larger shipments of relief supplies, there is an urgent need for greater efforts and fuller cooperation on the part of those bearing responsibility in the areas of the conflict as regards facilities for the movement and distribution of supplies.

Even so, it goes without saying that there can be no quick end to the present plight of the people in the areas affected by the conflict unless concrete measures are taken with a view to bringing about the cessation of hostilities and the negotiation of arrangements for a permanent settlement. In this connection, I wish to pay tribute to the efforts of the OAU and in particular to its six-member Consultative Committee under whose auspices useful preliminary talks recently took place at Niamey [Niger] and Addis Ababa [Ethiopia]. It is my earnest hope that, pursuant to the practical steps and procedures thus far agreed upon, fruitful negotiations will take place leading to a just solution which would guarantee the security of all the people of Nigeria.

In expressing this hope I am also taking into account the possibility that situations of this type can be easily—as indeed the present situation has been in some circles—misrepresented or exaggerated to the disadvantage of Africa as a whole. Already the Nigerian conflict has created difficulties in relations between African states, and its continuance is bound to affect badly needed cooperation and unity among African countries. As I have said elsewhere, the many problems that the African peoples are facing are by no means all of their own making. Nevertheless, few, if not all of them, can be solved except by the African countries themselves showing the qualities of maturity and restraint which they have often displayed, and using these qualities to engender the greatest spirit of cooperation and willingness to work together, which is essential to the fulfillment of Africa's destiny. This task is so important that governments and peoples must agree to put aside their differences in the higher interests of Africa and of the world as a whole. . . .

Statement by a Spokesman for the Secretary-General on Soviet Military Intervention in Czechoslovakia

NEW YORK   AUGUST 21, 1968

THE CZECHOSLOVAK CRISIS of August 1968 had no clear-cut starting point. The people had long been restive. Many resented efforts to break their cultural ties with the West. Others were angered by communist repressions, bureaucratic ineptness, and a deteriorating economy. The unrest assumed the proportions of a political upheaval in mid-1967 when students began demonstrating against poor housing and other inadequate facilities at the universities, and the police retaliated with harsh measures. Up to the end of 1967 the difficulties were internal, but Moscow was beginning to show signs of nervousness.

Czechoslovakia's strained relations with the Soviet Union and the other Warsaw Pact allies took a critical turn with the decision of the Czechoslovak Communist Party leadership on January 5, 1968, to replace Antonin Novotny with Alexander Dubček as first secretary. It soon became apparent that Dubček's "action program" to liberalize the orthodox communist controls over the press and public expression had placed Czechoslovakia on a collision course with the USSR. During the following months tension mounted as Dubček refused to bow to pressure, including such transparent threats as the Warsaw Pact military maneuvers, first along Czechoslovakia's borders early in May and then actually inside Czechoslovakia. On July 14–15, the USSR, Poland, Hungary, Bulgaria, and East Germany met in Warsaw and signed a letter to Czechoslovakia asserting that the liberalization program of Dubček had created an "absolutely unacceptable" situation. The letter included a number of demands, among them the banning of all noncommunist political groups, the reinstatement of tight controls over the press, and the strengthening of the Czechoslovak army. In a nationwide television statement, Dubček told his people: "We do not wish to yield anything at all on our principles." On August 20, the troops of the Soviet Union and the four allies that had participated in the July 14–15 meeting invaded Czechoslovakia and seized control of the country.

The situation was brought before the United Nations on August 21, when the representatives of Canada, Denmark, France, Paraguay, and the United States requested an immediate meeting of the Security Council to consider the military invasion of Czechoslovakia. Without waiting for the Council meeting, which took place later that day, U Thant appealed to the USSR and the other invading countries "to exercise the utmost restraint." Through a press spokesman, the Secretary-General called the invasion "another serious blow to the concepts of international order and morality" and a "grave setback to the East-West détente which seemed to be re-emerging in recent months." The Security Council held five meetings on the question between August 21 and August 24. The opening meeting produced a dramatic clash between the representative of the Soviet Union and the representative of Czechoslovakia, the USSR claiming that the invasion took place at the request of the Prague government and the Czechoslovak representative asserting that the foreign troops entered his country without the knowledge or consent of his government. The Soviet representative strongly opposed any United Nations discussion on the ground that the events in Czechoslovakia were exclusively a matter of concern for the Czechoslovak people and the states in the socialist community. The Soviet position, later explained in more explicit terms, was that any question arising between socialist states could and must be settled by those states without "foreign interference." This, the Soviet Union contended, was within the provisions of the United Nations Charter concerning individual and collective self-defense and the provisions on regional arrangements for the maintenance of international peace and security.

The majority of the Council rejected this argument and pressed for a vote on a draft resolution condemning the "armed intervention" in Czechoslovakia and calling for the immediate withdrawal of all foreign military forces from Czechoslovak territory. The vote on this was 10 in favor, 2 against (Hungary and the USSR), with 3 abstentions (Algeria, India, and Pakistan). The Soviet vote, of course, killed the resolution. Consideration of the question by the United Nations formally ended when the Czechoslovak government, once more firmly under Moscow's control, requested the withdrawal of the item from the Security Council's agenda. Thant, however, continued to voice his concern over the use of force against Czechoslovakia and its possible effects on East-West relations. He told correspondents at a luncheon of the Dag Hammarskjöld Memorial Scholarship Fund on September 19: "I am very much afraid that there will be an intensification of the cold war during the coming months as a result of these developments in Czechoslovakia. Whatever the motives might have been for the action taken by the Soviet Union and its Warsaw Pact allies, I cannot help observing that the action has produced a feeling of disquiet and insecurity in the world at large which, I am afraid, will continue for quite some time."

In the Introduction to his 1968 annual report, dated September 24, the Secretary-General discussed the Czechoslovak events at some length. While speaking out against the Soviet action, he took the occasion to condemn unilateral military intervention generally and to appeal to both superpowers to abandon what he referred to as the outmoded and dangerous "strong-arm methods common to the thirties."

He said in part: "It is certainly a frightening commentary on the ominous state of world affairs that one superstate or the other can become exercised to the point of resorting to military action because of the liberalization of a régime in a small country like Czechoslovakia or because of an internal upheaval in another small state, such as the Dominican Republic. In both cases, the action taken was regarded by those who took it as necessary self-protection without any thought of territorial acquisition. . . . It is, however, a dismal outlook for the small and militarily weak states of the world—as the overwhelming majority of states are— if they can hope to control their own affairs only in so far as they do nothing to displease a powerful neighbor. . . . The major powers should realize that it is as much in their interest as it is in the interest of the smaller powers for all Member states to abide faithfully by the provisions of the Charter, and to use the United Nations as their chosen instrument to maintain peace and to achieve a just and stable world order. . . ."

THIS MORNING, the Secretary-General has had meetings with the heads of missions directly concerned with the events in Czechoslovakia and with the President of the Security Council.

The Secretary-General does not yet have full official information in regard to the most recent developments and the circumstances which led to them. It is well known, however, that the Secretary-General deplores any resort to force to settle international problems, wherever it may occur, in contravention of the Charter of the United Nations.

In the present case, the Secretary-General regards the developments in Czechoslovakia as yet another serious blow to the concepts of international order and morality which form the basis of the Charter of the United Nations and for which the United Nations has been striving all these years. It is also a grave set-back to the East-West détente which seemed to be re-emerging in recent months, and to which the Secretary-General attaches the greatest importance. He has appealed to the government of the Union of Soviet Socialist Republics to exercise the utmost restraint in its relations with the government and people of Czechoslovakia, and strongly hopes that this appeal will be heeded by the government of the Union of Soviet Socialist Republics and its Warsaw Pact allies.

In the circumstances, the Secretary-General has canceled his entire European program, including the visits to Vienna and Geneva in connection with the Outer Space Conference and the Conference of Non-Nuclear Powers.

SOURCE: *UN Monthly Chronicle*, Vol. V, August-September 1968, p. 105.

Message to Pope Paul VI on the Occasion of the International Eucharistic Congress

BOGOTÁ   AUGUST 21, 1968

THE FOLLOWING MESSAGE to Pope Paul VI is one of many U Thant sent Pope John XXIII and Pope Paul VI reflecting his close relationship with the two Roman Catholic leaders beginning immediately after he became Secretary-General. He visited the Vatican a number of times for private talks with both pontiffs. The high point, of course, was Pope Paul's visit to the United Nations in 1965.

THE INTERNATIONAL EUCHARISTIC CONGRESS now convening in Bogotá is one of the outstanding events of the world this year. The fraternity of man is indeed at the center of its deliberations. It is because of the enlightened concern of Your Holiness with the fate of mankind, with the solidarity and friendship between peoples and nations, that I am permitting myself to refer to those aspirations and preoccupations, those aims and goals, which are as basic for the International Eucharistic Congress as for the United Nations.

We are living in a momentous period in history. We are going through—and we ourselves are forging—a great revolution of ever-growing impetus. It is in our hands to channel the profound changes which are being brought about in our times toward the most fruitful directions, away from suffering, violence, and enmity. We can see, when we pause in our pursuits to reflect on this rapid transformation, many reasons for which to be grateful and hopeful despite so much misery, intolerance, and discrimination. Man has reached a threshold of knowledge that could permit him to build on this earth a society more in keeping with his inherent dignity, more adequate to his needs and hopes.

SOURCE: UN Press Release SG/SM/989.

With this knowledge and this power, new dangers and increased inequities have also appeared, so ominous and on such a scale as heretofore unknown. We witness progress and we witness destruction. But, as Your Holiness said on the occasion of your visit to the United Nations, the peril comes neither from progress nor from science: "The real peril is in man, who has at hand ever more powerful instruments, suited as much to destruction as to the highest conquests."

All of us believe and know that, in our times, peace is paramount. But peace is not only the absence of organized violence by men against men. Peace is also the assertion of the dignity of all human beings. It is freedom from ignorance, hunger, and conquerable disease. Peace is also the sense of fulfillment and the stability which result when parents are able to provide for both the spiritual and material needs of their children. It is likewise the sharing of bread and leisure, the solidarity in efforts and sufferings. Peace is caring for our neighbor as much as for ourselves.

Peace is not easy to attain; it does not depend only on governments, on the observance of treaties, or on good will among nations. True, all this is essential. But peace equally depends on individual endeavor and understanding, on personal generosity and compassion. Peace cannot be strengthened or maintained without bridging the abyss between rich and poor countries, or between rich and poor persons. Peace is the respect for the rights of individuals and the rights of states. Peace is social justice as much as economic development.

Our common goal in the great revolution of our times is to promote and attain speedily those changes for which mankind has hoped throughout centuries and that are now within reach. Many religions and ideologies share those aspirations. Our collective task is the deliberate elimination of injustice and of poverty, as much among men as among nations, and the many changes that this requires begin in the heart of man.

In closing, may I express to Your Holiness, on this occasion, my most respectful regards, together with my best wishes for the success of the Congress.

Staff Day Address

NEW YORK   SEPTEMBER 20, 1968

I AM VERY GLAD to welcome you in this Hall of the General Assembly today. It is only right and proper that the voice of the staff should be heard in this Hall on Staff Day, literally and as a matter of tradition. That it is heard on other days, figuratively speaking, is a theme to which I would like to refer separately. But before I do, I would like to share with you a few reflections on matters of concern to the Secretariat.

Let me begin by reassuring you that I am quite aware of some of your current preoccupations. I know that fluctuations in the impact which the United Nations has upon the world situation profoundly affect anyone who seeks to relate his own individual effort to the ideals and objectives set out in the Charter. A sense of personal satisfaction on the job is normally associated with periods of progress and discernible attainments. Standstills and setbacks are not, as a rule, conducive to that kind of feeling, although it is true that, on occasion, reverses do spur individuals to renewed and more vigorous endeavors.

Such an occasion is, I believe, the present moment in the life of the United Nations. However disappointing some of the recent events, particularly in the field of international peace and security, there is no escape from the stubborn reality of a world committed to a joint undertaking to improve the human condition, for its ills transcend national boundaries, its needs are widespread, while the means of assistance are unevenly distributed. The task of matching the world's needs against its resources is clearly beyond the capacity of any but a universal institution.

Viewed from this broader perspective, the ups and downs in the fortunes of the Organization are no more than phases in its evolution, stages on the road to a more orderly world which one ardently believes is bound to come.

SOURCE: UN Press Release SG/SM/1008.

It is to pave the way for such a world, to serve its needs for today and tomorrow, that our international civil service must be maintained and steadily improved, and it remains my firm intention, under the powers conferred upon me by the Charter, to ensure that this will be done.

I need not elaborate before you on the extent to which the function of building the Secretariat and making it equal to the demands placed upon it is determined by the General Assembly. In the exercise of its authority to establish regulations for the appointment of the staff, the Assembly lays down the fundamental conditions of service. In addition, the Assembly has recently taken a series of actions in the field of budgetary and financial management which are not without relevance to the administration of the staff.

These actions reflect a concern on the part of Member governments that whatever resources are made available for carrying to fruition approved programs are spent wisely and efficiently. And since the budget of the United Nations contains a relatively high proportion of expenditures for the employment of the professional, technical, and ancillary personnel required for the activities of the Organization, measures designed to extend the scope of scrutiny over the various stages of planning through budgeting significantly influence the conduct of our administrative business as a whole.

Let me cite just two examples. Last year, the Economic and Social Council reconstituted its Committee for Programme and Coordination in pursuance of the recommendations of the *Ad Hoc* Committee of Experts to Examine the Finances of the United Nations and the Specialized Agencies, which the General Assembly had endorsed previously. Later in the year, the General Assembly established the Enlarged Committee for Programme and Coordination.

The mandate of these two bodies called for the preparation of several comprehensive reports on the functions, procedures, and practices of the United Nations and its related agencies in the field of economic and social development. In volume alone, the staff work involved is quite considerable. Most of the reports are the result of a good deal of interagency consultation and cooperation at several levels.

In January of this year, we put into operation yet another instrument of administrative and financial control: the Joint Inspection Unit. The Unit, which has been established for an initial period of four years, consists of inspectors appointed from among candidates nominated by the Member states which have been designated by the president of the

General Assembly. The inspectors have broad powers of investigation in all matters relating to the efficiency of the services of the United Nations family of organizations and to the proper use of the funds administered by them.

These new organs of inquiry in no way diminish the functions and responsibilities of existing bodies of administrative review. Indeed, the current trend of putting under close scrutiny the procedures evolved in the domain of international cooperation is similarly evident in the work of such long-established bodies as the Advisory Committee on Administrative and Budgetary Questions, the Board of Auditors, and the International Civil Service Advisory Board.

I refer to this development to drive home the fact that, because so much of our work in the Secretariat is done through complex machinery which has been built up over a period of years, whatever we do is subject to rather special restraints. If, therefore, we are to make the fullest use of the Secretariat as the administrative arm of the United Nations, it is vitally important that we bear in mind the somewhat unique set of circumstances in which we operate.

It is against this background of governmental attitudes that we must set our staff administration policy, and I think it is right to define it as being fair to the staff and fair to the Member states.

I mentioned a while ago some of the procedures we have recently instituted to ensure fairness to the governments which foot the bill. In the next few days I expect to receive the report of the Committee of Experts on the Reorganization of the Secretariat, which I established earlier this year. On the basis of the recommendations made by this Committee, I intend to take additional measures designed to streamline and expedite our working arrangements. I shall also complete the changes in the structure of the Secretariat which I began in January. As part of these changes, both the financial and the personnel management functions of the Secretariat will be placed under a single direction. I will shortly announce the appointment of the Under-Secretary-General for Administration and Management.

At the coming session of the General Assembly, I shall seek approval for a number of measures of immediate interest to the staff.

First, I will put before the Assembly several proposals relating to the composition of the Secretariat. One of these proposals will deal with the question of linguistic proficiencies of the staff. Our position on this matter has been worked out in consultation with the other organizations of the United Nations system. The proposal will, I hope, reflect an awareness which we all share of the importance attached by Member governments to the introduction of a reasonable balance between the various languages of the Organization. It also takes account of the special problems facing our multinational staff, as well as of the diversity of linguistic practices of the specialized agencies. Underlying the proposal is our earnest desire to reconcile the need for control of the resources devoted to administration with the need to secure equitable treatment of the staff.

I know that the debate on languages has somehow affected staff attitudes and given rise to new apprehensions. It was perhaps unavoidable that many a staff member should now feel a little more conscious of his linguistic shortcomings, whether because the language in which he works does not happen to be his mother tongue, or because the language in which he works does not enjoy the same currency as that used by other staff members. Superimposed on the traditional debates regarding the nationality composition of the Secretariat, the emphasis on the differences which characterize the staff may have sharpened the sensitivity about the weight of merit in relation to the principle of geographical distribution.

I had occasion earlier this year, when the subject was raised with me by the representatives of the Staff Council, to state my position on this subject. I should like now to amplify it by saying that, in consonance with the letter and spirit of the Charter, it is my intention to ensure that the principle of geographical distribution remains relevant only to staff recruitment. It cannot and will not play any role in the processes of promotion or placement.

In the last two calendar years, a total of 597 staff members were promoted to the professional and higher-level posts of the Secretariat, including 53 to the senior level of Principal Officer and Director. During the same period, there were 632 appointments of new staff members to such posts, 33 of which were to the two senior levels. In the first eight months of this year, the corresponding number of promotions was 173, including 21 to the senior posts, as against 159 appointments, of which four were to the senior posts. I am sure you will agree that these figures amply illustrate our desire to enable each staff member to rise to the limits of his capacity.

The second proposal which I will shortly put before the Assembly concerns salaries. Last year I indicated to you that, at the end of our thoroughgoing study of the principles underlying the United Nations salary system, I expected to see pay adjustments at more regular intervals than had been the case previously. The record will show that this has already been applied in respect of the large number of staff in the Field Service, General Service, Security Service, and Manual Workers categories, whose rates of pay are fixed by the Secretary-General.

Insofar as the professional and higher-level categories are concerned, we are still engaged in the elaboration of the new principles. It is not, you will appreciate, an easy exercise. It was in 1965 that the issue of reviewing the principles of our salary system for the professional and higher-level staff was first raised by the International Civil Service Advisory Board and endorsed by the General Assembly. In the next two and a half years we directed our efforts toward the examination of possible alternatives. The scope of the material required for the study, the diversity of the elements entering into the concept of an equitable pay system for the international civil service, and the need to work out agreed positions between all the organizations of the United Nations family—these are some of the reasons for the extensive consultations and numerous man-hours which have gone into the exercise. The end result of the study is yet to come. It is not expected for another two years. But some progress has been made and, on the basis of our findings so far, we shall be able to propose interim salary adjustments.

I said at the beginning of my remarks that the voice of the staff is heard in the General Assembly, not only on Staff Day. Your elected representatives are certainly familiar with the procedure we have followed in arriving at the proposals I have just mentioned. We in this house need no reminder, such as has so manifestly been provided by recent events in various parts of the world, that people everywhere are ill disposed to accept decisions affecting their rights and well-being which are imposed upon them. Our system of administration has thus built up a process of staff participation which is unequaled in national administrations. Although we hear on occasion that some phases of this process are unduly time-consuming, we have good reason to think that time spent on them is well spent.

For my part, I shall continue the policy of the closest contact with the staff representatives in the interests of an effective Secretariat. It is in line with this approach that last year, for the first time in the history of the Secretariat, I recommended that representatives of the staff of our Office at Geneva should be granted a hearing by the Advisory Committee on Administrative and Budgetary Questions. This is also why, in the spring of this year, I recommended that representatives of the staff at Headquarters should be invited to state their views before the Committee of Experts on the Reorganization of the Secretariat, even though the Committee's terms of reference only indirectly concern staff conditions of service.

It is with these thoughts in mind that I invite you all to take time out of your daily pursuits in the Secretariat and enjoy this Staff Day, and then to turn back to your work in the Secretariat inspired by the promise which the United Nations holds for all of us and confident that, as its servants, you can expect to be treated with fairness and justice.

THE SITUATION IN VIETNAM

SEPTEMBER TO NOVEMBER 1968

As THE PRELIMINARY peace talks in Paris dragged through the summer without any visible progress and without any let-up in the intensity of the military action in Vietnam, U Thant became increasingly concerned over the possibility of a breakdown in the negotiations. As he said in the Introduction to his 1968 annual report, issued on September 24, the initial promise of the talks appeared to be fading away. He decided it was time for him to speak out once more. He felt, as he had felt since he made his first peace moves, that a complete and unconditional cessation of United States bombing in North Vietnam was an essential first step toward peace. When a spokesman for the North Vietnamese delegation in Paris urged him to use his influence, as an Asian statesman, to get such a bombing halt, he responded by making an appeal on September 17 during a meeting with correspondents in Paris. "Without this step," he said, "I don't see how the conflict can be moved from the battlefield to the conference table." Back at United Nations Headquarters, he told a press conference on September 23 that he did not know whether he had the influence and prestige referred to by the North Vietnamese representative, but he pressed again for a total bombing halt. In taking such a stand, he said he believed he was voicing the general feeling of the international community. In fact, he suggested that if a resolution requesting a bombing halt were put before the General Assembly it would receive a majority vote.

His renewed appeal for a cessation of the bombing was not well received in Washington. The Johnson administration's reaction was reflected in a most unusual and blunt statement by U.S. Representative George Ball on September 28 as he left United Nations Headquarters after a meeting with Thant. Ball called Thant's appeal "naïve" and said the Secretary-General's emphasis on the cessation of bombing was "enormously distorted" and had been "blown way out of life-size" by him. Thant replied: "I have never claimed that once the bombing of North Vietnam ceases there will be heaven on earth the next day. As you know, my view is shared by many governments around the world, including some NATO members. I do not regret being associated with that group of governments who feel, as I do, that essential first steps must be taken and should be taken to generate further processes which could eventually lead to a peaceful solution."

The Secretary-General was severely criticized by the American press for his reference to the possible outcome of a vote on a hypothetical resolution on a bombing halt. In the September 23 press conference, one correspondent asked whether he was "in effect inviting delegations to put such an item on the agenda and put in this draft resolution in fact." He replied that he was not inviting such action. "In order to allay any misunderstanding or confusion regarding my consistent advocacy of the cessation of the bombing of North Vietnam," he said, "I was just citing one reason, one of the many reasons, why I have been saying this. This reason is that I am trying to reflect international public opinion; I am trying to reflect the conscience of humanity. Just to put it to the test, I was wondering whether it might not be one means of finding out what the attitude of the international community is on this particular item." Because of widespread reports in the press, despite this statement, a United Nations spokesman on September 24 said the Secretary-General had made it clear that this was not "a realistic idea in the present circumstances," and he went on: "The Secretary-General wishes it to be clearly understood that he has no intention of proposing himself, nor of suggesting to any delegation, to inscribe an item on Vietnam on the agenda of the twenty-third session."

Thant dealt with the Vietnam problem comprehensively in the Introduction to his annual report. Among other things he said: "Even though it was clear from the beginning that these [Paris] talks would be difficult and that meanwhile the fighting would continue, both parties must be aware that the usefulness of the Paris talks might be jeopardized if attention were to be concentrated on the conduct of military operations. One would at least hope that, by opening these first direct contacts, the interested governments have clearly signified that they know peace will not be brought about by military means or military escalation. . . . In my view it would be a fatal error to underestimate the unique opportunity which the Paris talks represent in themselves, an opportunity which should be fully utilized by the parties concerned in taking the decisions that are required to move ahead."

On October 31, President Johnson took the step which Thant had been urging since 1965: a decision to halt all air, naval, and military bombardment of North Vietnam. Thant was immensely pleased by the announcement and by the reported agreement that the government of South Vietnam and the National Liberation Front would join the United States and North Vietnam in the Paris talks. "In the light of these encouraging developments," Thant said, "it seems to me that the prospects for peace in Vietnam are brighter today than at any time in the past three years."

1. From Transcript of Press Conference

NEW YORK   SEPTEMBER 23, 1968

. . .

THE SECRETARY-GENERAL: It is very difficult to anticipate the outcome of the forthcoming session of the General Assembly. In my view, the atmosphere will not be as congenial as we would wish it to be.

In any case, my assumption is that in the political field Member states will attach special importance to questions of disarmament, and particularly to the report of the Eighteen-Nation Committee on Disarmament, which, as you all know, is before the Assembly. I believe that the report of the Conference of Non-Nuclear-Weapon States will also be here, although so far there is no specific item on this subject on the Assembly's agenda. The Conference of Non-Nuclear-Weapon States in Geneva is tackling three very important disarmament issues: the question of security guarantees; further disarmament measures; and the peaceful uses of nuclear energy. I believe that those are very important questions and that, at the conclusion of the Conference this coming Friday, a report will be submitted.

Those, in my view, are some of the important questions to be discussed. I hope that perceptible progress will be made on disarmament measures.

In the economic and social field, the report of the Economic and Social Council will receive very close attention. In my view, an earnest attempt should be made to lay solid foundations for the launching of the Second Development Decade.

Due attention will also be given by Member states to the perennial colonial questions.

Last but not least, the question of China should, I believe, receive greater attention from Member states than in the past.

QUESTION: I am often asked why the United Nations has not been able to deal successfully and directly with problems such as Vietnam, Czechoslovakia, and Biafra. Could you comment on that?

SOURCE: *UN Monthly Chronicle,* Vol. V, October 1968, pp. 101-111.

THE SECRETARY-GENERAL: You know as well as I do that there are technical and political difficulties involved in bringing these items before the General Assembly.

With regard to Vietnam, among other reasons for this, as I have been saying for the past four years, is that, of the participants directly involved in the war, only one—the United States of America—is a Member of the United Nations. As I have also said in the past, I would be the happiest person in the world if the question of Vietnam were to be taken before one of the deliberative organs of the United Nations. But you are aware of the difficulties.

In the case of Czechoslovakia, there are other reasons, of which you are aware. The government of Czechoslovakia has requested even the deletion of the item from the agenda of the Security Council.

Although the United Nations is not directly involved in these questions, I am sure that the vast majority of the Member states are very much concerned at the developments, and I am also sure that this concern will be reflected in the general debate that is to begin early in October.

QUESTION: I also mentioned the question of Biafra.

THE SECRETARY-GENERAL: The situation in Nigeria is very tragic. My attitude toward the question of the Nigerian internecine strife is well known. My approach to the problem and my policy toward it are guided primarily, if not exclusively, by the decision of the Organization of African Unity, which was arrived at last year in Kinshasa. I shall continue to be guided by the decisions of the OAU, which, in my view, should be the main machinery for the settlement of this dispute. As you all know, the OAU has repeatedly—last year as well as this year—adopted resolutions recognizing the sovereignty and territorial integrity of Nigeria. On the other hand, the OAU has expressed very deep concern at the disastrous and calamitous fate of these unfortunate people in the Eastern Central Region of Nigeria.

The United Nations and the specialized agencies, particularly the United Nations Children's Fund (UNICEF), have been very much involved in giving aid, and particularly food, milk, and medicine, to the victims of the civil war. I want to take this opportunity of expressing my thanks to the International Committee of the Red Cross for the splendid job it has been doing.

. . .

QUESTION: With relation to the United States and Vietnam, you said once again on Thursday that the essential first step—and I quote you—

"should be taken by the side which is the militarily more powerful and is therefore in a position to show magnanimity." I ask you, Sir, would you also apply that language, with its moral implications, to the Soviet Union's invasion and occupation of Czechoslovakia?

THE SECRETARY-GENERAL: In the case of Vietnam, as you know, I have been advocating the cessation of the bombing of North Vietnam for the last three years and more. I have given many reasons, but for the moment I would confine myself to one particular reason; that is, that I have been trying to reflect the collective conscience of the international community on this issue. I believe that the international community is deeply concerned over the war in Vietnam; and I also believe, on the basis of my discussions with government representatives and even heads of state and heads of government of many countries, that the general feeling among the international community is that essential first steps should be taken—and must be taken—to move the conflict from the battlefield to the conference table.

Just to put this to the test—of course, this is not a very realistic proposal—I was wondering whether, at a session of the General Assembly, if a resolution on such lines were to be tabled and put to the vote, it would not receive a majority endorsement. The resolution would be phrased somewhat on these lines:

The General Assembly,
   Deeply concerned at the war in Vietnam,
   Convinced that essential first steps should be taken to move the conflict from the battlefield to the conference table, so as to lead to meaningful and positive steps toward a peaceful settlement of the problem,
   Requests that the bombing of North Vietnam—that is, the Democratic Republic of Vietnam—should cease.

I was wondering whether, if such a resolution were tabled, it would not receive the majority vote. Of course, it is, as I have said, not a very practical proposition, since the item is not before the Assembly and not on the agenda. But what I am trying to explain is that I have been all along trying to reflect the conscience of humanity from this vantage point of the international Organization.

As regards Czechoslovakia, I do not want to add anything to what I have been saying in the past. First of all, I would draw your attention to my statement of August 21 and to the statement that I made in the course of my speech before the United Nations Correspondents Association lunch last week. In both cases, of course, arguments have been adduced against the withdrawal of the foreign troops. In one case, the argument put forth is that there is a kind of implicit contractual relationship among the Warsaw Pact countries for collective security. In another case, the argument is that the United States forces are in Vietnam at the request of the government of South Vietnam, that is, at the request of the Republic of Vietnam—that is, at the request of the nine successive governments in the last four years in Saigon. I do not want to be involved in a discussion of these arguments. But, in any case, I must say that the developments in Czechoslovakia in the past few weeks constitute a very deplorable episode in the history of international relations.

QUESTION: You referred to that in your statement last week and you expressed the fear that it might open up the cold war. The cold war lasted twenty-three years. I want to ask you, in connection with the problems that you mentioned—Czechoslovakia, Nigeria, the Middle East, and Vietnam—how the statesmen who might open up this cold war think it would help to solve those problems. Or would it not be a triumph of the folly of statesmen to use this House to open up a cold war that for twenty-three years brought us to nothing but the edge of nuclear destruction? How is it even possible for anyone to envisage such a throwback to the stone age in the nuclear age? I ask you to comment on that question.

THE SECRETARY-GENERAL: I agree with you that the cold war went on for twenty-three years. But, according to my assessment, there were ups and downs. In my view, the cold war was at its height in the early fifties. Then, I think it started to thaw in the late fifties and the early sixties. Recently, there were even signs of East-West détente resulting in the agreement on the non-nuclear treaty and other manifestations of a rapprochement. But I must say that the developments in Czechoslovakia in late August were a serious setback to this détente. It poisoned the atmosphere all over the world, and this poisoned atmosphere, I am afraid, will be particularly reflected in this big Hall. That is why I have stated in the past, on two occasions, my views on these problems, and I am also elaborating on these ideas in my Introduction to the annual report, which I hope to submit in the course of this week, perhaps on Wednesday or Thursday.

QUESTION: It would seem clear now that the United States contribution to the United Nations Development Programme (UNDP) is either going to be drastically cut or, if the Senate does not take final action on the foreign aid bill, there may even be no United States contribution to UNDP this year. What will be the effect on other countries' contributions and what will happen to the program itself if the United States withdraws aid?

THE SECRETARY-GENERAL: I am not aware of the decision in Washington regarding contributions to UNDP, but my information some time ago was that there is a strong possibility that the United States might contribute the same figure as it did last year. Of course, I am not aware of the latest developments, so I do not want to answer this question on a hypothetical basis.

QUESTION: I should like to ask you another question concerning the Charter. The Soviet ambassador in the Security Council developed a new doctrine that relations between states that are grouped ideologically or regionally are not subject to discussion in the United Nations bodies, including the Security Council. Now, is it your opinion that Article 2, paragraph 7, or any other article of the Charter prohibits discussions of events in the regional or ideological groupings and that those groupings do away with the national sovereignty of the respective states?

THE SECRETARY-GENERAL: That is a very complex and delicate question, with legal and political implications. All I want to say at this moment is that different interpretations are put on specific articles of the Charter vis-à-vis the constitutions and functions of the regional groups. I recall, for instance, the example of the Dominican Republic. When certain developments took place, the Organization of American States (OAS) felt that the matter should be dealt with by the OAS only, as far as peace-keeping functions were concerned; that the United Nations should not be involved in that particular problem because of certain specific provisions in the Charter of the OAS.

Thus, if we assess certain developments in a certain country which is a member of a military group or a politically aligned group, then we have to think of the precedents and the circumstances arising out of certain political or military considerations. That is why, in the course of my statement last week, I brought up the question of the necessity for a vocal and articulate third force or third world in the cold war. When I used the term "third world" or "third force" I was not thinking primarily in a geographical or regional context or of militarily or politically nonaligned countries; I was thinking of those countries which do not want to see the world in tightly knit groups or spheres of influence or spheres of domination.

You will recall the history of the 1930s, just before the outbreak of the Second World War, when the idea of spheres of influence or spheres of domination developed. At that time, Europe was meant for Hitler; Africa was meant for Mussolini; and Asia was meant for Tojo.

With these objectives they tried to develop the military technology, the military might, and it all resulted in the Second World War. At that time, the motivation was the creation of spheres of domination. After the Second World War, we saw some signs of similar developments in certain areas. But now the groupings are not necessarily spheres of domination but, in my view, spheres of influence.

I think that if you really believe in the United Nations, if you are really dedicated to the principles of the Charter of the United Nations, then you and I must do our utmost to see the reverse trend, the trend away from polarization. In other words, we should do our utmost to achieve a reverse trend of depolarization—that is, a trend of loosening the tightly knit groups. I think that those who really believe in this concept—those who really believe in the future of the United Nations, those who really believe in the principles of the Charter for the sake of our security and for the sake of the security of our children and grandchildren—should grow in numbers; and for those countries I use the words "third force" or "third world." I am sure that you will agree with me that the trend toward polarization into spheres of domination or influence will be a disaster for the world.

QUESTION: Mr. Secretary-General, since Hanoi has been perfectly well aware of the fact all along that you have made a considerable effort to get a complete bombing halt over a period of more than three years, as you have now pointed out, would it not be reasonable to assume that when their delegation in Paris made a rather interesting public appeal to you to use your prestige and influence in order to get a bombing halt, this may have been their way of saying that they are now more interested in mediation efforts such as yours, now more in harmony with your approach to the question than they may have been at some times in the past?

THE SECRETARY-GENERAL: I have been involved in the search for a solution regarding the Vietnam problem for the past three years or more. As regards the statement by the North Vietnamese spokesman in Paris last week that the Secretary-General has influence and prestige, I am not sure whether I have both or either. But, so long as the war in Vietnam goes on, it will be my constant endeavor to try to contribute toward a peaceful solution of the problem. I still feel very strongly that in this very tragic war, essential first steps are necessary and, without these essential first steps, I do not see how the stalemate can be broken. As a matter of fact, I must confess that I do not see the light at the end of the tunnel for another year or so.

QUESTION: The Security Council, on November 22, 1967, adopted the resolution which created the mission of Mr. [Gunnar] Jarring. Nearly a year has passed and nothing has happened. Arab states have said that they accept the principles and the resolution. In your opinion, what are the major reasons for this resolution not being implemented, and what is the future of Mr. Jarring's mission?

THE SECRETARY-GENERAL: As you know, the Secretary-General's special representative, Ambassador Jarring, has been involved in a search for peace within the framework of the Security Council resolution of November 22 of last year, and he is still continuing with his efforts. He is due to arrive in New York tonight and, of course, he will continue with his consultations and discussions with the parties primarily concerned, along with others.

One gratifying aspect of his functions or involvement is the fact that all the parties directly involved in the conflict want him to carry on, and even the Security Council last week gave him a big boost with a resolution endorsing his mission. Apart from this, I do not wish to give a reason or reasons for the stalemate. At the appropriate time, of course, Ambassador Jarring will be in a position to report his assessment and findings.

QUESTION: Apparently, you do not wish to acquiesce in the matter of spheres of influence, and you have made a comparison between the Soviet excuse for occupying Czechoslovakia and the American excuse for occupying South Vietnam. Could you extend that comparison further by adding to your draft resolution on Vietnam a draft resolution on withdrawal from Czechoslovakia?

THE SECRETARY-GENERAL: I think you do not understand the import of my answer. I am not equating the two situations. I am just saying that arguments are adduced against withdrawal in both cases. In one case, the argument is that there is some sort of implicit contractual relationship among the Warsaw Pact countries for collective security. In the other case, there are some other arguments. But I am not trying to equate the two. Of course, if the Russians were to bomb and napalm the people of Czechoslovakia and the towns and villages in Czechoslovakia, please wait to hear what I would have to say.

QUESTION: Do you think that, in the present circumstances, a new summit meeting between the leaders of the United States and the Soviet Union might be a useful thing?

THE SECRETARY-GENERAL: On this particular subject I am making a few observations in the Introduction to my annual report, which you will see in the course of this week.

QUESTION: May I ask you, in the light of the continuing occupation of Czechoslovakia and the reactions to that from the United States Congress and from many non-nuclear powers, how much hope do you hold for the ratification of the non-proliferation treaty at this time, or for the success of the non-nuclear-powers conference?

THE SECRETARY-GENERAL: The events in Czechoslovakia last month, in my view, have very much damaged the prospects for the wide acceptance of the treaty by the international community; but of course, I have no means of knowing now what the actual results will be. But I still feel that it will damage a great deal not only the ratification of the non-proliferation treaty, but also many other areas of joint activity in the international sphere.

QUESTION: Would the supply of American jets to Israel affect the peace efforts in any way?

THE SECRETARY-GENERAL: Regarding the situation in the Middle East in general and, in particular, the introduction of massive armaments in the area, I am still working on the Introduction to my annual report and I would request you to wait for the publication of this report in the course of this week.

QUESTION: Have you had any reaction from any governments to your statements on the intervention in Czechoslovakia? If so, which governments were they, and what was their reaction?

THE SECRETARY-GENERAL: My talks with the accredited representatives of governments to the United Nations are privileged. So, I do not want to divulge the nature of those talks.

QUESTION: Is it the position that you have had reactions, but you do not want to say what they are now?

THE SECRETARY-GENERAL: No, for the moment I do not want to reveal what the positions of the governments are.

QUESTION: You have outlined the agenda for this Assembly session and you say the question of China will receive greater attention this time than in the past. Can we draw from this that it is your feeling that Red China may have a greater opportunity of gaining membership in the United Nations now?

THE SECRETARY-GENERAL: Well, I am not saying that. What I have been saying is that the question of China is a very important question, a vital question, not only for the United Nations but for the whole world, and so my idea is that the international community should give greater attention to this question than in the past.

QUESTION: You read out what sounds like the draft of a resolution. Are you in effect inviting delegations to put an item on the agenda and put in this draft resolution in fact?

THE SECRETARY-GENERAL: No, I am not inviting any resolution or any inscription of the item on the agenda. What I am trying to say is that there has been a very large volume of criticism of my consistent advocacy of the cessation of bombing of North Vietnam, particularly from knowledgeable and perceptive journalists like Dr. Louis Halasz. So, in order to allay any misunderstanding or confusion regarding my consistent advocacy of the cessation of the bombing of North Vietnam, I was just citing one reason, one of the many reasons, why I have been saying this. This reason is that I am trying to reflect international public opinion; I am trying to reflect the conscience of humanity. Just to put it to the test, I was wondering whether it might not be one means of finding out what the attitude of the international community is on this particular item. That was my only idea. I was not inviting the inscription of an item on the agenda, nor was I inviting the tabling of a draft resolution on the lines I stated earlier.

. . .

QUESTION: I wonder, Sir, whether, in the light of comments you made on a number of situations, you might clarify a little bit more the relationship that you think the United Nations has to the regional organizations. You have indicated that the OAS properly handled the Dominican Republic problem and that the OAU should handle the Nigeria problem. You have not said, but you have raised the argument, that the Warsaw Pact powers are dealing with Czechoslovakia and that the South East Asia Treaty Organization (SEATO) is dealing with Vietnam. But is it not true that the United Nations Charter, in itself and accordingly all of the charters of those organizations and military pacts, is overriding, and that if any of those regional organizations or military pacts, is doing anything that is a violation of the Charter, the United Nations should be properly seized of it?

THE SECRETARY-GENERAL: I agree with the substance of your question: the United Nations Charter should override all other charters and constitutions of regional organizations. What I have been saying is that there are certain provisions in the charters of some regional organizations which maintain that certain developments in the particular region are the prerogative of that regional organization. I am not saying that this is right or that it is wrong; I am just stating the facts.

As far as the OAU is concerned, you will recall the General Assembly resolution that was adopted two years ago professing closer cooperation between the United Nations and the Organization of African Unity. The question of the Nigerian civil war came up. I went to the Congo last year, in September. I attended a meeting of the heads of state and heads of government of the OAU. They adopted a resolution recognizing the sovereignty and territorial integrity of Nigeria and they advised me that the United Nations should comply with the decisions of the OAU, particularly in cases like the Nigerian civil conflict. So I reported to the OAU summit conference only the week before last that my approach to the problem of the Nigerian civil war and my policy regarding that situation have been and are primarily guided by the decisions of the OAU. I am not saying that this is the right course or the wrong course, but it is a fact.

Speaking of Nigeria, of course I am fully conscious of the humanitarian problems involved in the Eastern Region, now sometimes called Biafra. That is why I have been endeavoring to the best of my ability, in cooperation with the specialized agencies, particularly UNICEF, to facilitate the transshipment of food, medicine, milk-powder, etc., to the stricken people. And the International Committee of the Red Cross has been doing a magnificent job. I believe the problem will be settled very soon.

---

2. Statement to the Press

NEW YORK   NOVEMBER 1, 1968

ALONG WITH so many who believe in peace, I am happy and gratified at the announcement by President Johnson last night, October 31, of his government's decision to cease all air, naval, and artillery bombardment

SOURCE: UN Press Release SG/SM/1030.

of North Vietnam, effective this morning, November 1. This is a first and essential step toward peace which I and many others have been urging for nearly three years in the conviction that it could lead to further steps toward achievement of a just and peaceful settlement of the prolonged and increasingly tragic and dangerous war in Vietnam. The reported agreement on the participation in the Paris peace talks of representatives of both the government of South Vietnam and of the National Liberation Front, together with those of North Vietnam and the United States, is also a most welcome and practical development, since peace talks can be most effective only when all of those engaged in the fighting are enabled to participate. In the light of these encouraging developments, it seems to me that the prospects for peace in Vietnam are brighter today than at any time in the past three years. I would appeal with great earnestness to all of the parties in the Vietnam war to approach this new phase in the talks with a determination to exert their utmost effort to avoid any action likely to impede progress toward an early and peaceful settlement of the war.

Introduction to the Twenty-Third Annual Report

NEW YORK   SEPTEMBER 24, 1968

IN THE INTRODUCTION to the twenty-third annual report of the Secretary-General, U Thant noted that the deterioration of the international situation had continued and had actually been accelerated by the Soviet military intervention in Czechoslovakia. He took a long look at this problem, as well as the situation in Vietnam and the Middle East, the civil war in Nigeria, and other major questions commented on elsewhere in this volume. "In the final analysis," he said, "there can be no solid foundation for peace in the world so long as the superpowers insist on taking unilateral military action whenever they claim to see a threat to their security. Why should they not bring their fears and complaints about threats to their security to the Security Council, as they regularly demand that less powerful states do?" He concluded by saying he was well aware that the Introduction made gloomy reading, but that he did not believe "a facile optimism would be justified under present international conditions."

I. General

1. I noted in the Introduction to the annual report last year that the international situation at that time had not only not improved, but had in fact deteriorated considerably. In general, the deterioration has continued throughout the past year. There has been no progress toward peace in Vietnam and the military conflict is continuing with unabated ferocity, while every passing day reinforces my conviction that this problem cannot be solved by military means. The initial promise of the Paris talks between the representatives of the Democratic People's Republic of Vietnam and the United States of America is fading away. In the Middle East, the year has been one of continuing tension and frustration. The most recent developments in Czechoslovakia have cast a long shadow and created a feeling of uneasiness and insecurity which will take determination and sustained effort to overcome.

SOURCE: General Assembly Official Records, Twenty-third Session, Supplement No. 1A (A/7201/Add. 1).

2. Some limited progress has been made in disarmament, where the outstanding event during the year was the conclusion of the Treaty on the Non-Proliferation of Nuclear Weapons. The Conference of Non-Nuclear-Weapon States is still in session at the time of writing and one can only hope that it may lead to some positive results. In the field of outer space and human rights, two major international conferences have been held during the past year and their deliberations are reviewed elsewhere. In the field of economic and social development, the second session of the United Nations Conference on Trade and Development has not lived up to the high hopes and great expectations that the participants, especially from the developing countries, brought to it.

3. The frustrations to which I have referred every year in respect of the chronic problems in the field of decolonization, *apartheid,* and other problems which have so long persisted in Africa south of the equator, in defiance of the United Nations, have continued and deepened. These problems are also dealt with in greater detail elsewhere in this Introduction.

4. I referred last year to the progress made in regard to the discharge of the responsibilities of the United Nations in West Irian. As I noted then, the Indonesian government had given me assurances that it would comply fully with the remaining responsibilities concerning West Irian deriving from the Agreement signed on August 15, 1962, by the Republic of Indonesia and the Kingdom of the Netherlands. Pursuant to these assurances, I appointed Mr. Fernando Ortiz-Sanz as my representative for the "act of free choice" by the inhabitants of West Irian. Mr. Ortiz-Sanz, together with his initial staff, arrived in Djakarta on August 12, 1968, for consultations with the Indonesian government on the arrangements and modalities regarding the act of free choice, including the fixing of the date of the consultations, which will be held some time in 1969. On August 23, he traveled to West Irian and has now completed a tour of the territory to acquaint himself with conditions there. According to the provisions of article 17 of the Agreement of August 15, 1962, my representative "will carry out the Secretary-General's responsibilities to advise, assist, and participate in arrangements which are the responsibility of Indonesia for the act of free choice". Thus, with the cooperation of the Indonesian government, the remaining provisions of the Agreement which brought to an end the dispute between the Republic of Indonesia and the Kingdom of the Netherlands concerning West Irian will, I hope, be fulfilled within the time specified in the Agreement. I shall, of course,

report to the General Assembly at the conclusion of my representative's mission to West Irian.

5. Within the Organization itself, once again I find it necessary to report with regret that the financial difficulties are no nearer solution. In fact, the Organization's financial position deteriorated during the past year in that net liquid assets—cash and investments plus current accounts receivable less current accounts payable—decreased by $15.3 million between June 30, 1967, and June 30, 1968. Unpaid contributions assessed on Member states in respect of the regular budget increased during the period by $20.5 million, while there was a decrease of $2 million in respect of the Special Account for the United Nations Emergency Force, and the amount in respect of the *Ad Hoc* Account for the United Nations Operation in the Congo remained unchanged. The unpaid assessments for the three accounts as of June 30, 1968, totaled $260.7 million, an increase of $18.5 million over the previous year.

6. Moreover, the amount of cash on hand plus short-term investments which could be readily converted to cash decreased during the twelve-month period from $15.8 million to $7.6 million, the latter figure representing less than one month's cash requirements for regular budget activities.

7. No additional pledges of voluntary contributions were made during this period to assist the Organization out of its financial difficulties, although a payment of approximately $1.5 million was received from one government with regard to an earlier pledge.

8. As of June 30, 1968, the Working Capital Fund had been depleted principally because of the necessity to make advances of $27.3 million to finance regular budgetary expenditures pending the receipt of assessed contributions and advances of $11.9 million to the United Nations Emergency Force Special Account.

9. The figures given above relate only to the regular budget and to peace-keeping operations financed in whole or in part by assessed contributions. They do not take into account an estimated deficit of about $8.7 million as of June 26, 1968, in respect of the United Nations Peace-keeping Force in Cyprus. In the circumstances, I cannot but be concerned about the unfavorable prospects in the near future of being able to honor the Organization's commitments to reimburse the Member states for the extra and extraordinary costs they incurred in providing men and *matériel* for the various peace-keeping operations of the United Nations. The cumulative shortfall in the payment of assessments in

respect of the regular budget is likewise a matter of continuing serious concern.

10. I trust the General Assembly will give renewed attention to the problem of finding prompt and effective means for restoring the financial integrity and solvency of the Organization.

11. The question of peace-keeping operations continues to pose serious and difficult problems. It is increasingly obvious that the system of voluntary contributions, on which the financing of the peace-keeping operations in Cyprus is based, is unsatisfactory from several points of view. As I have noted above, no new voluntary contributions have been made since my last report, and there has been no progress, either toward a solution of the problem of indebtedness for past operations or toward agreement on means of financing present and possible future activities in this field.

12. However, there have been some welcome indications of possible movement in regard to other aspects of the question. The consensus reached on May 28 by the working group of the Special Committee on Peace-keeping Operations, under which it will study, as a first model in its program of work, the military observer operations established or authorized by the Security Council, represents a hopeful sign of willingness on all sides to consider new departures as a means of moving toward a solution. It is noteworthy that the decision was taken by a working group comprising, among others, representatives of four permanent members of the Security Council. There appears to be a growing recognition that what is involved in the notion of peace-keeping operations is closely related to the whole range of functions of the Organization in respect of the maintenance of international peace and security and in regard to methods for the pacific settlement of disputes. It is to be hoped that the study launched by the working group will lead to a realistic examination of this most important of its responsibilities.

13. During the past year, I put forward proposals for the first major change in the structure of the top echelon of the Secretariat in over a decade. These proposals were unanimously approved by the General Assembly at its twenty-second session. At that time, I had announced my intention of appointing a committee of seven members to review the organization of the Secretariat. This committee was appointed early this year and has been working continuously since April. It has undertaken field trips to the major United Nations offices away from Headquarters, at Geneva, Rome, Vienna, Beirut, Addis Ababa, Bangkok, and San-

tiago. The committee is now engaged in finalizing its report, and I look forward to receiving its recommendations with the greatest interest. I have no doubt that they will prove of practical value in my continuing efforts to improve the structure as well as the functioning of the Secretariat.

II. Disarmament

14. The past year has been a year of achievement in the field of disarmament. The successful conclusion of the Treaty on the Non-Proliferation of Nuclear Weapons is the culmination of ten years of efforts in the United Nations and in the Conference of the Eighteen-Nation Committee on Disarmament. After a year of intensive negotiations in the Eighteen-Nation Committee the draft treaty was also subjected to a most thorough and detailed consideration at the resumed twenty-second session of the General Assembly this year. As a result of that consideration, a number of important improvements were introduced into the text and the revised draft treaty was commended by an overwhelming vote on June 12, 1968. The Treaty was opened for signature on July 1, 1968, and more than seventy states have already signed it. The General Assembly, in resolution 2373 (XXII), called for the widest possible adherence to the Treaty; I am hopeful that the necessary ratifications will shortly be forthcoming so that the Treaty may enter into force at the earliest possible date.

15. The Treaty, which has been acclaimed as "the most important international agreement in the field of disarmament since the nuclear age began" and as "a major success for the cause of peace" is important on several accounts. First, the purpose of the Treaty is to prevent the further spread of nuclear weapons among countries which do not possess them and establishes a safeguards system for the purpose of verifying the fulfillment of the obligations assumed under the Treaty. If this international agreement is duly implemented, it will help to limit and contain the threat of nuclear war.

16. Second, the Treaty not only reaffirms the inalienable right of non-nuclear-weapon states to develop research and the production and use of nuclear energy for peaceful purposes without discrimination; it also provides that all parties to the Treaty are to facilitate, and have the right to participate in, the fullest possible exchange of equipment, materials, and scientific and technological information for the peaceful uses of

nuclear energy. In particular, the Treaty provides that, under appropriate international observation and through appropriate international procedures, potential benefits from any peaceful applications of nuclear explosions will be made available to non-nuclear-weapon states parties to the Treaty on a nondiscriminatory basis, and that the charge to such parties for the explosive devices used will be as low as possible and will exclude any charge for research and development.

17. Third, since the Treaty is not an end in itself but a step toward disarmament, each of the parties to the Treaty undertakes to pursue negotiations in good faith on effective measures relating to the cessation of the nuclear arms race at an early date and to nuclear disarmament, and also on a treaty on general and complete disarmament under strict and effective international control.

18. Agreement on these provisions, let us not forget, was reached only after several years of long and patient negotiations and even a longer period of preparatory work extending as far back as 1958, when the first draft resolution on preventing the spread of nuclear weapons was introduced in the General Assembly. Many adjustments and mutual concessions had to be made along the way by the parties concerned, both nuclear and non-nuclear. As a result, the final outcome necessarily represents a compromise solution. Yet, I am confident that, if this Treaty is accepted by the great majority of states and is faithfully implemented, it will play an essential role in the continuing pursuit of security, disarmament, and peace.

19. Indeed, the question of the non-proliferation of nuclear weapons has provided additional evidence of how closely security and the regulation of armaments are linked together. It is enough to mention, in this connection, the debate in the Security Council, following the conclusion of the Treaty, which led, first, to declarations of intentions by the USSR, the United Kingdom, and the United States that they would provide or support immediate assistance, in accordance with the Charter, to any non-nuclear-weapon state party to the Treaty that was a victim of an act or an object of threat of aggression in which nuclear weapons were used, and, second, to the adoption of Security Council resolution 255 (1968) on the question of the security of non-nuclear-weapon states.

20. Further evidence of how much the international community is concerned with the security of states which have forsworn nuclear weapons is provided by the program of work of the Conference of Non-Nuclear-Weapon States, which was convened at Geneva on August 29,

1968, in accordance with General Assembly resolution 2346 B (XXII). Two main questions before the Conference are programs for cooperation in the field of peaceful uses of nuclear energy, and measures to assure the security of non-nuclear-weapon states. In dealing with the latter question, the Conference may be expected to give consideration to feasible measures of disarmament which can best contribute to security.

21. Owing to the fact that for a number of years the efforts toward disarmament have been concentrated on the isse of non-proliferation, less attention has been given to other important aspects of the disarmament question. Therefore, it will be desirable for the Conference of the Eighteen-Nation Committee on Disarmament and the General Assembly to review the situation and take up, with firmness of purpose, those questions which are more urgent and more amenable to early agreement.

22. One such question is a comprehensive test-ban treaty. Undoubtedly, a treaty banning nuclear weapon tests in all environments would be a most desirable step following the conclusion of the treaty on the Non-Proliferation of Nuclear Weapons. Very appropriately, the preamble of the Treaty recalls the determination expressed by the parties to the 1963 Treaty banning nuclear weapon tests in the atmosphere, in outer space, and under water to seek to achieve the discontinuance of all test explosions of nuclear weapons for all time. Moreover, progress in the identification of seismic events has reduced to manageable proportions the issue of verification of a comprehensive ban. It is, indeed, to be hoped that improved instrumentation, international cooperation in the exchange of seismic data, and the use of statistical methods can provide a control system sufficiently reliable to deter parties to an agreement from violating such an agreement.

23. "A comprehensive test-ban treaty, prohibiting the underground testing of nuclear devices, would . . . contribute to the objectives of non-proliferation and would clearly help to slow down the nuclear arms race." This was one of the conclusions in my report to the twenty-second session of the General Assembly, transmitting the study of the consultant group on the effects of the possible use of nuclear weapons and the security and economic implications for states of the acquisiton and further development of these weapons. I believe it is fitting to recall this unanimous statement of a group of highly qualified experts from all parts of the world.

24. The group further noted that the objectives of non-proliferation would be served also by other effective measures safeguarding the

security of non-nuclear-weapon countries. In its words, "nuclear-weapon-free zones additional to those of Antarctica and Latin America, covering the maximum geographical extent possible and taking into account other measures of arms control and disarmament, would equally be of major assistance." At the twenty-second session of the General Assembly, the Treaty for the Prohibition of Nuclear Weapons in Latin America received considerable attention. The Assembly, in resolution 2286 (XXII), welcomed the Treaty with special satisfaction, as an event of historic significance in the efforts to prevent the proliferation of nuclear weapons and to promote international peace and security.

25. The Assembly also commended the Treaty as having established the right of Latin American countries to use nuclear energy for demonstrated peaceful purposes in order to accelerate the economic and social development of their peoples. It is, indeed, in the interest of all countries to see that the Treaty enjoys universal observance and that its entry into force is not in any way delayed.

26. "Whatever the path to national and international security in the future," the report concluded, "it is certainly not to be found in the further spread and elaboration of nuclear weapons." At this stage, after the conclusion of the Treaty on non-proliferation, I believe that the closest attention must be given to the situation in the entire nuclear sector, including the development of new weapons.

27. In spite of the limited successes which have been achieved in the field of arms control during the last ten years, the situation is still fraught with dangers. The stockpiles of nuclear weapons possessed by the great powers are still increasing. The development and deployment of antimissile systems are spurring accelerated changes in offensive missile technology. The possible military uses of the seabed and the ocean floor beyond the limits of present national jurisdiction are causing growing concern. New biological and chemical weapons are developed and tested in scientific laboratories.

28. As regards nuclear delivery vehicles, the willingness on the part of the United States and the Soviet Union to open talks aimed at limiting and reducing both offensive nuclear weapons and defensive antimissile systems is an encouraging step forward. It would not be realistic, however, to underestimate the difficulties that will have to be overcome before agreement is reached on this very complicated question. Having this in mind, I strongly feel that the testing and development of new nuclear weapon systems should be halted while the talks are going on.

This would, in my opinion, facilitate the difficult task that the two major nuclear powers will have to face.

29. The unanimous adoption of resolution 2340 (XXII) on the question of the reservation exclusively for peaceful purposes of the seabed and the ocean floor, and the subsoil thereof, and the uses of their resources in the interests of mankind was a positive achievement of the General Assembly at its twenty-second session. It is necessary, however, that the initial steps envisaged by the resolution be followed soon by further measures of international cooperation aimed at preventing actions and uses which might be detrimental to the common interests of mankind.

30. While progress is being made in the field of nuclear disarmament, there is another aspect of the disarmament problem to which I feel too little attention has been devoted in recent years. The question of chemical and biological weapons has been overshadowed by the question of nuclear weapons, which have a destructive power several orders of magnitude greater than that of chemical and biological weapons. Nevertheless, these too are weapons of mass destruction regarded with universal horror. In some respects they may be even more dangerous than nuclear weapons because they do not require the enormous expenditure of financial and scientific resources that are required for nuclear weapons. Almost all countries, including small ones and developing ones, may have access to these weapons, which can be manufactured quite cheaply, quickly, and secretly in small laboratories or factories. This fact in itself makes the problem of control and inspection much more difficult. Moreover, since the adoption on June 17, 1925, of the Geneva Protocol for the Prohibition of the Use in War of Asphyxiating, Poisonous or Other Gases and of Bacteriological Methods of Warfare, there have been many scientific and technical developments and numerous improvements, if that is the right word, in chemical and biological weapons, which have created new situations and new problems. On the one hand, there has been a great increase in the capability of these weapons to inflict unimaginable suffering, disease, and death to ever larger numbers of human beings; on the other hand, there has been a growing tendency to use some chemical agents for civilian riot control and a dangerous trend to accept their use in some form in conventional warfare.

31. Two years ago, by resolution 2162 B (XXI), the General Assembly called for the strict observance by all states of the principles and

objectives of the Geneva Protocol of 1925, condemned all actions contrary to those objectives and invited all states to accede to the Protocol. Once again I would like to add my voice to those of others in urging the early and complete implementation of this resolution. However, in my opinion, much more is needed.

32. During the twenty-three years of the existence of the United Nations, there has never been a thorough discussion in any United Nations organ of the problems posed by chemical and biological weapons, nor has there been a detailed study of them. Recently the matter has been receiving more attention and it is felt that the time has come to deal with it more fully. I therefore welcome the recommendation of the Conference of the Eighteen-Nation Committee on Disarmament to the General Assembly that the Secretary-General appoint a group of experts to study the effects of the possible use of chemical and bacteriological means of warfare. I believe that such a study which would explore and weigh the dangers of chemical and biological weapons, would prove to be a most useful undertaking at the present time. It could attract attention to an area of multiplying dangers and of diminishing public appreciation of them. It could also serve to clarify the issues in an area which has become increasingly complex. Certainly a wider and deeper understanding of the dangers posed by these weapons could be an important element in knowing how best to deal with them. . . .

IV. Peace-keeping

42. The year since the war of early June 1967 has been one of high tension and great frustration in the Middle East. The war came quickly to an end, but the cease-fire demanded by the Security Council has often been broken by a succession of incidents of fighting varying in seriousness. This was especially the case in the Israel-Jordan and the Suez Canal sectors. The machinery of the United Nations Truce Supervision Organization in Palestine, although truncated and dislocated by the events of June 1967, has been an important factor in preventing an escalation of the fighting, especially by limiting the scope of incidents and by securing on-the-spot cease-fires through the cease-fire arrangements in the Syrian and the Suez Canal sectors made after the June war. In the Israel-Jordan cease-fire sector, where because of the lack of agreement by the parties it has not been possible to station United Nations observers, incidents of fighting have tended to be more frequent

and serious. Indeed, the Security Council has had to meet on several occasions as a result of such incidents. I have repeatedly urged that observers be stationed in all cease-fire sectors and have stressed that such arrangements of a practical nature, which need not prejudice the claims and positions of the parties, would be in the interest both of the parties and of the United Nations.

43. It must be borne in mind, in considering the background for the many and regrettable breaches of the cease-fire, that on one side the cease-fire sectors in the Middle East are almost entirely areas under military occupation. History shows that such situations tend to give rise to a more than ordinary incidence of acts of violence.

44. In the light of the situation in the area of the conflict of June 1967 and especially in the occupied territories, I felt that there was a great need for—and had proposed—a second humanitarian mission to the Middle East, in particular for the purpose of meeting my reporting obligations under Security Council resolution 237 (1967) and General Assembly resolution 2252 (ES-V) concerning humanitarian questions. It was with great disappointment, therefore, that I had to report on July 31, 1968, to the Security Council and the General Assembly that my efforts in this regard had thus far been unavailing.

45. The situation of the refugees since the June war has further deteriorated, and the task of the United Nations Relief and Works Agency for Palestine Refugees in the Near East has become correspondingly more difficult. In particular the shortage of funds, food, supplies, and equipment to meet the emergency conditions has on occasion been acute. With this in mind, I addressed two appeals to governments for special contributions, one on March 2, 1968, for funds and additional tents, and the other for food aid made jointly with the Director-General of the Food and Agriculture Organization of the United Nations on April 30, 1968. The response to both these appeals has been disappointingly limited.

46. Hopes for progress toward easing tensions in the Middle East and avoiding conflict through solution of the major issues between the Arab states and Israel have centered on the efforts of my special representative to the Middle East, Ambassador Gunnar Jarring. By their very nature, these efforts must be confidential and discreet. It has been Ambassador Jarring's policy to make no public pronouncements or even substantive reports while his efforts continue. It would be equally

inadvisable for me at this time to discuss substantive questions relating to the Jarring mission. It may, however, be useful to make some general comments at this stage on that mission in the context of the Middle East situation and also in the larger context of the United Nations involvement in it.

47. Resolution 242 (1967) adopted unanimously by the Security Council on November 22, 1967, was in itself a considerable achievement and provided a basis for a constructive and peaceful approach both by the parties and by the international community to the bitter problems of the Middle East. The resolution provided for a special representative "to establish and maintain contacts with the states concerned in order to promote agreement and assist efforts to achieve a peaceful and accepted settlement." This was a heavy responsibility for one man to undertake, but in a practical sense it was the wisest of the obviously limited alternatives.

48. The tireless, persistent, and understanding efforts of Ambassador Jarring over the past nine months have more than justified the confidence placed in him by me and by the Security Council. No one has ever doubted the extreme difficulty and complexity of the problems with which he has had to grapple, and certainly no reasonable person could have expected quick or miraculous solutions. I do not find it surprising, although it is disappointing, that despite Ambassador Jarring's unceasing efforts the promise of the November 22 resolution has not yet been fulfilled in any significant degree. The basic situation in the Middle East in relation even to the beginnings of a settlement remains much the same as it was eight months ago. Until now, the one clear point of agreement among all concerned has been that Ambassador Jarring should continue his efforts.

49. This, certainly, is a personal tribute to Ambassador Jarring, and it may be hoped that it is also an expression of a genuine desire of the parties to find a peaceful solution. There is implicit in the Middle East situation, of course, a very great urgency about achieving a peaceful settlement. No one is more sensitive to this than Ambassador Jarring himself. In the interest of peace, the United Nations cannot tolerate an indefinite lack of progress toward a peaceful settlement in the Middle East.

50. Ambassador Jarring's efforts to promote agreement among the parties to the Middle East dispute have been impeded by the disagree-

ment among them thus far on the procedure to be employed in taking up the substantive questions. One party has insisted upon "direct negotiations" by which is meant, apparently, a face-to-face confrontation of the two sides; the other side has rejected, initially at any rate, the direct procedure, but has been willing to carry on substantive talks concerning the implementation of the resolution indirectly, with Ambassador Jarring as the intermediary. All of his efforts will be unavailing unless he is able to carry on some form of dialogue with the two sides involving matters of substance. Such a dialogue cannot be fruitful if it is substantive on one side but only procedural on the other.

51. The key to a peaceful settlement of issues dividing states and peoples which lead to armed conflict, or threaten to do so, is negotiation. It is often difficult, owing to political and other circumstances, to bring the parties involved in a conflict to the negotiating table, and there is no certainty that, once they are there, agreement can be reached within any reasonable period of time.

52. Negotiations may be undertaken in different ways. There is no fixed formula controlling them. A workable procedure in one set of circumstances may be quite impractical and unsuitable in another. The right road, obviously, is that which will lead to fruitful negotiations, whether direct or indirect. It would seem to me that as a general rule the emphasis should be on the results rather than on the procedure.

53. As this text is being written, three different sets of peace negotiations are under way, each differing from the others in the procedure being followed. These are the preliminary talks in Paris on Vietnam, the talks between leaders of the Greek and Turkish Cypriot communities in Cyprus, and the talks on the Middle East being undertaken by Ambassador Jarring.

54. These talks differ from each other in the extent of the initiatives taken by the parties involved, or by a third party, in bringing them about, in their direct or indirect nature, and in the extent of assistance given to the parties by a third party as the negotiations proceed. It will be recalled that the successful talks between India and Pakistan at Tashkent in January 1966 were arranged through the good offices of the Soviet Union, whose representatives assisted the two parties in the talks. In this regard, it may also be recalled that the negotiations at Rhodes in 1949, which led to the general armistice agreements between the four Arab states and Israel, were arranged by the United Nations. At Rhodes negotiations as such were basically indirect, the respective parties being

brought together in meetings under the chairmanship of the Acting Mediator to formalize agreements reached by indirect talks through him.

55. It is often said, in the Security Council and elsewhere, by parties to conflicts that, while the United Nations has achieved a measure of success in keeping the peace in areas of conflict, it has failed or is failing in its duty to resolve the political problems at the root of these conflicts. Those who hold such views tend to overlook the simple fact that the primary responsibility for peaceful settlement of conflicts must inevitably rest with the parties themselves and that without their cooperation and effort no peace mission of the United Nations, however skillfully conducted or strongly supported, can hope to succeed. On the other hand, given that cooperation the United Nations can be of inestimable assistance. This is nowhere truer than in the Middle East.

56. After four years of tension and conflict, during which the situation in Cyprus was kept under control in no small measure by the efforts of the United Nations Peace-keeping Force, a number of developments of unusual significance and promise have occurred on the island during the past several months. The armed clashes at Ayios Theodhoros and Kophinou in November 1967 had brought the intercommunal confrontation to an explosive state and had for a time even threatened to disrupt international peace in the eastern Mediterranean. Wiser counsels prevailed, however, and as a result of intensive diplomatic efforts, including three appeals that I addressed to the parties, the danger of war receded and an accommodation was arrived at whereby Greek and Turkish armed personnel in excess of the respective national contingents would be withdrawn from Cyprus.

57. There has ensued, since the beginning of 1968, a steady relaxation of tension marked by increasing contacts between Greek and Turkish Cypriots, a very significant reduction in shooting and other intercommunal incidents, and a large-scale effort by the government to return the country to normality by eliminating economic restrictions and granting full freedom of movement to the Turkish Cypriots.

58. In this improved atmosphere, my special representative has been able to arrange for direct intercommunal talks, the first serious contacts of this kind in four and a half years. These talks, which began in early June of this year, have so far been encouraging. Of course, many difficulties remain to be overcome and the participants in the talks and other leaders in both communities will have to continue to display statemanship, forbearance, and mutual understanding of the highest

order if lasting and sound results are to be achieved. In full realization of the difficulties, however, it is possible to say that in Cyprus there would now seem to be some real promise of progress toward a settlement.

59. The United Nations Peace-keeping Force will, of course, do everything possible within its terms of reference to assist the parties in promoting a return to full normality, and the good offices of the Secretary-General, either directly or through my special representative, continue to be available to the parties in the effort to achieve a peaceful settlement of the Cyprus problem.

60. I feel obliged, nevertheless, to warn the parties involved in the Cyprus dispute of the need to move with speed toward a solution of the problem, for the financial situation in connection with the Force has continued to deteriorate and the deficit for this operation now stands at a figure of approximately $13,586,000. In my periodic reports to the Security Council on the operation in Cyprus, I have repeatedly underscored the unsatisfactory method decided upon by the Security Council for the financing of the Force, but no remedial action has yet been taken. I feel bound, therefore, again to give warning, and particularly to the parties to the Cyprus dispute, that the United Nations Peace-keeping Force cannot, in these circumstances, be maintained much longer on the island, and that the time is fast approaching when drastic action—even including the withdrawal of the Force—may have to be taken.

VIII. Decolonization

146. In the Introduction to my last annual report, I recalled the continued endeavors of the United Nations in the field of decolonization and outlined the serious and difficult problems which called for the close and urgent attention of the competent organs of the Organization.

147. During the intervening period, Southern Yemen, the territory formerly known as Aden, followed by Nauru, Mauritius, and Swaziland, acceded to independence; Equatorial Guinea is expected to attain the same status within the next few months. Furthermore, constitutional advance has taken place in certain of the smaller dependent territories. Even so, it is a matter of deep regret that nearly eight years after the adoption of the historic Declaration on the Granting of Independence to Colonial Countries and Peoples, there has been no significant movement toward peaceful resolution, in accordance with the Charter, of the remaining major colonial questions. The reason for this state of affairs is

to be found not in a lack of concern or effort on the part of the United Nations, but principally in the noncompliance by certain administering powers with the relevant United Nations resolutions and in the reluctance of some other powers to extend their full cooperation to the Organization in the application of effective solutions to the outstanding problems.

148. Of these problems, those currently plaguing the southern part of Africa are in a class by themselves, for they represent the most conspicuous mass violation of human rights and fundamental freedoms. As I have observed elsewhere, the collective determination of the United Nations to put an end to colonialism seems to have met a solid wall of defiance in that part of the world.

149. With regard to Namibia, the government of South Africa has continued its refusal to give effect to the resolutions by which the General Assembly terminated the Mandate, brought the territory under the direct responsibility of the United Nations, and established the United Nations Council for Namibia to administer the territory until its independence. South Africa has also refused to relinquish its control over the territory and has frustrated the efforts of the Council to carry out the tasks assigned to it. That government's disregard of United Nations decisions relating to the territory as well as of world public opinion was further illustrated by its arrest, trial, and conviction, under retroactive legislation, of a considerable number of Namibians. The negative and intransigent attitude of the South African government was again demonstrated by its obstruction of the Council's efforts in April of this year to proceed to Namibia in order to take up the functions assigned to it in the territory by the General Assembly. In pursuit of its policies of *apartheid,* the South African government, on June 6, 1968, enacted legislation designed to further the setting up of Bantustans in South West Africa. It has also initiated repressive measures of forcible settlement in segregated areas.

150. As the General Assembly has pointed out in its appeals to the states concerned, a measure of responsibility for the present serious situation must be borne by those states whose continued political, military, and economic collaboration with the South African government has had the effect of encouraging that government to defy the authority of the United Nations and to impede the attainment of independence by Namibia. It is obvious, nevertheless, that meaningful progress toward the objectives laid down in the relevant United Nations decisions

depends essentially upon the willingness and ability of the Security Council to bring effective pressure to bear on the South African government to abandon its present course and abide by the relevant resolutions so as to enable the Council to perform its functions.

151. The question of Southern Rhodesia has also given cause for increasing concern. Two and a half years have passed since the unilateral declaration of independence by the illegal minority régime in Southern Rhodesia, and over eighteen months have elapsed since the Security Council determined that the situation in the territory constituted a threat to international peace and security. Yet neither the action taken by the government of the United Kingdom nor the diplomatic and other sanctions applied in varying degrees by other governments in response to the relevant United Nations resolutions have led to the speedy amelioration which the international community had been encouraged to expect. Not content with flouting the authority of the United Kingdom government by proceeding with the execution of a number of African nationalists, the illegal régime has, with South Africa's assistance, resorted to suppressive military operations and has pursued the application of policies of separate racial development, including plans for creating a façade of African participation in its activities. These developments represent a further challenge to the general desire for rapid advance in the territory toward majority rule and a just society free of discrimination. While the Security Council's decision in May 1968 to impose extensive mandatory sanctions against the illegal régime by no means detracts from the responsibility of the United Kingdom government, as the administering power, to restore constitutional rule in the territory, it is imperative that all governments, including in particular the governments of Portugal and South Africa, should comply with that decision so as to pave the way for the attainment of the Declaration's objectives.

152. As regards the territories under Portuguese administration, it is a matter of deep regret that yet another year has passed without progress in the implementation of the pertinent United Nations resolutions. In violation of the principles of the Charter, the Portuguese government has continued to deny the people of these territories the right to self-determination and independence and has maintained its policy of political and economic integration of the territories with Portugal. The intensification of military operations by that government in Angola, Mozambique, and Guinea, called Portuguese Guinea, has aggravated a situation

which in 1965 the Security Council considered a serious disturbance to international peace and security. Concerted international action has been limited mainly to efforts at withholding assistance which would enable the Portuguese government to continue its suppression of the people of the territories and at providing humanitarian assistance to refugees therefrom. Not only is there a need to increase these efforts, but further international measures are required, in my view, to assist the peoples of these territories to attain their goal of freedom and independence and to make the Portuguese government a willing partner in this undertaking.

153. The colonial problems to which I have referred are different in magnitude, if not in kind, from those affecting most of the other remaining dependent territories. With regard to these territories, the administering powers, far from forswearing their obligations under the Charter, have agreed and undertaken to give effect to the principle of self-determination as well as to their pledge to ensure the political, economic, social, and educational advancement of the people. Yet there is considerable misgiving among the majority of Member states as to the modalities, emphasis, and pace adopted by the administering powers concerned in the decolonization of these territories. Furthermore, as I have previously indicated, their compliance with specific recommendations on these territories by the General Assembly and the Special Committee on the Situation with regard to the Implementation of the Declaration on the Granting of Independence to Colonial Countries and Peoples has, on the whole, been less than full.

154. Equally, their attitudes for the most part have been either negative or qualified when the question has arisen of permitting access to the territories by United Nations visiting groups. These attitudes, by denying to the United Nations a most important source of information on the political, economic, and social situation in these territories and on the views, wishes, and aspirations of the peoples, serve to impede the search for concrete solutions to the problems of the territories in question; many of them are, indeed, afflicted by peculiar difficulties arising from their small size and population, their limited natural resources, and sometimes their geographical isolation. It is my belief that the development by the administering powers of a positive approach to the question of visiting groups would contribute as much to the adoption of decisions which would take full account of their demand for realism and balance as

to the attainment of the objectives laid down in the Charter and the Declaration, to which administering and nonadministering powers alike subscribe.

155. The emphasis which the competent United Nations bodies place on the value of visiting groups reflects the conviction widely held among Member states that the Organization, including, as appropriate, international institutions associated with it, should play an increasingly active role in assisting the emergence of colonial peoples from dependence to independence. It was in this spirit that the General Assembly, at its twenty-second session, requested me, in consultation with the administering power and the Special Committee, to ensure the presence of the United Nations in Equatorial Guinea for the supervision of the forthcoming general elections and to participate in all other measures leading toward the independence of the territory. I am confident that the mission which, in consultation with the government of Spain and the Special Committee, I was able to appoint and dispatch to Equatorial Guinea in August of this year will play a constructive part in enabling the territory to accede to independence as a single entity in conditions of peace and harmony.

156. Another category of problems deserving careful attention relates to territories which are the subject either of conflicting claims to sovereignty or of special interest to some governments by reason of geographical, historical, or other circumstances. While the General Assembly and the Special Committee have affirmed that the Declaration is fully applicable to such territories, their recommendations have taken into consideration the special features of each, with a view to facilitating the resolution of the divergent claims or interests through mutual accommodation and goodwill. I am certain that these bodies will consider and make further recommendations which help the governments concerned in resolving the problems to which I have alluded within the context of the Declaration.

157. In a year that has been proclaimed as International Year for Human Rights, I think it is appropriate to recall that, in the Declaration on the Granting of Independence to Colonial Countries and Peoples, the General Assembly declared:

The subjection of peoples to alien subjugation, domination, and exploitation constitutes a denial of fundamental human rights, is contrary to the Charter of the United Nations, and is an impediment to the promotion of world peace and cooperation.

It also declared:

Immediate steps shall be taken . . . in all . . . territories which have not yet attained independence, to transfer all powers to the peoples . . . without any conditions or reservations, in accordance with their freely expressed will and desire, without any distinction as to race, creed, or color, in order to enable them to enjoy complete independence and freedom.

158. It is my earnest hope that, aware of the hope and inspiration that dependent peoples everywhere derived from the adoption of the Declaration, all Member states, in particular the administering powers, will in a spirit of constructive cooperation do their utmost to assist those peoples to realize their legitimate aspirations to freedom and emancipation.

X. Other Questions

168. In my concluding observations last year I drew attention to "the urgent need for states to have wider recourse, in their relations with other states, to the various means for the pacific settlement of disputes." In this context I drew attention to the availability of the International Court of Justice, as a principal organ of the United Nations, for the settlement of legal disputes. This year the Court has, for the first time, presented a report to the General Assembly. I believe that it would be to the common interest of the United Nations if the General Assembly and the other principal organs of the United Nations, in addition to the Member states, were to utilize more fully the machinery of the Court in dealing with problems which are capable of solution by legal and judicial processes.

169. In the same context, I recommended last year that a modest beginning might be made to test the value of holding periodic meetings of the Security Council at which its members might be represented by a member of the government or by some specially designated representative. So far, there has been no follow-up on this suggestion. I would like to suggest that, as an alternative, it would be useful to take advantage of the presence of the foreign ministers of France, the Soviet Union, the United Kingdom, and the United States during the coming session of the General Assembly to arrange for them to meet and discuss common problems. So far as the agenda for such a meeting is concerned, this could be left to the foreign ministers, or a provisional agenda could be

prepared by the Secretary-General. Hopefully a meeting of the foreign ministers could lead to a meeting of the heads of state and government of the four major powers. I feel that some such initiative is needed at the present time to counteract the serious setback to the détente in East-West relations that has resulted from recent events. A special effort of this kind may also prove useful in identifying some major issues with regard to which, despite present adverse circumstances, big-power agreement may be possible.

170. Situations continue to arise in which governments find it useful to request the good offices of the Secretary-General in seeking to resolve outstanding problems between them. One such example was the recent hijacking of an Israeli airliner, which was taken to Algiers on July 23. For many weeks, I exercised my good offices in an attempt to secure the release of those passengers and members of the crew of the aircraft still detained in Algiers, and of the aircraft itself. In doing so, I was mindful of the recent increase in hijacking incidents and of the danger that this trend, if not checked, could easily lead to widespread disruption of international air travel with all the attendant risks involved. If this disturbing trend is to be discouraged, as it must be, it is essential that two principles be universally observed, namely, that international law and order, as an essential condition of the freedom and safety of air travel, must be preserved, and, second, that no one may derive gain or advantage from the lawless act of hijacking an aircraft. It is a matter for gratification that the governments of Israel and Algeria heeded my appeal for restraint during this most trying period. It is also appreciated that in the interest of international law and morality the Algerian authorities finally resolved the problem by the release of the aircraft and its occupants.

171. I should like to reiterate that it is desirable and, indeed, necessary for the United Nations to achieve universality of membership as soon as possible and I regret that there has not been a greater interest in solving this problem. It is obvious to me that inasmuch as one of the members of the "nuclear club" stands outside the world Organization it is difficult to make progress on major issues of disarmament, for example, without achieving this universality. The problem of the divided countries is also one that requires attention. In regard to some of these countries, at any rate, the political obstacles may not be insuperable, while there will be obvious advantages in admitting them to membership

and enabling them to take part in the work of the Organization and in making a contribution to the solution of outstanding problems.

172. I drew attention last year to the problem of the "micro-states." I can well understand the reluctance of the principal organs of the United Nations to grapple with this problem, but I believe it is a problem that does require urgent attention. The question has been considered by many scholars and also by the United Nations Institute for Training and Research. It seems to me that several of the objectives which micro-states hope to achieve by membership in the United Nations could be gained by some other form of association with the Organization, such as the status of observers. In this connection, I should like to reiterate the suggestion that I made last year that the question of observer status in general, and the criteria for such status, require consideration by the General Assembly so that the present institutional arrangements, which are based solely on practice, could be put on a firm legal footing.

173. In 1969, the International Labour Organisation will be completing its first half-century of continuous effort to build the foundation of peace in social justice for the common man throughout the world. In the tradition of the International Labour Organisation, its commemoration of the event will look to the future rather than to the past, with the major immediate emphasis being placed on a world employment program designed in the spirit of the Second Development Decade to mobilize human resources to meet human need. The Director-General of the International Labour Organisation has informed me of his desire, which I endorse, to mark the half-centenary of that organization's cooperation with the League of Nations and the United Nations by forging an ever-closer partnership in the building of peace through social justice. I am confident that in the course of the anniversary year all of the appropriate organs of the United Nations will welcome full discussion of how this can best be achieved.

XI. Concluding Observations

174. In the period under review, I regret to have to report that little progress, if any, has been recorded toward the growth of international order based on law and justice. On the contrary, there has been a serious decline in the standards of international ethics and morality, with states relying increasingly on force and violence as a means of resolving their

international differences. This tendency to return to force as a means of national policy strikes at the very basis of the United Nations; just settlement is sacrificed to superior might, and international tensions are consequently heightened. If this trend is not reversed, and if the principle of nonintervention in the free destiny of nations is not re-established, the future of international peace and security itself is indeed a very dark one.

175. The prevailing pessimism concerning the international situation, and the recent serious and distressing developments in Europe should not be used as reasons for delaying the search for peace in Vietnam. Indeed, the problem of Vietnam, complex enough in itself, has often been made more intractable by the impact of the conflicting interests of the major world powers.

176. For example, there are many people who see the Vietnam war as an ideological struggle. But is it not true that such a concept is only concealing the reality of a nationalist struggle which has somehow become the stake in a worldwide strategic rivalry? Only the powerful motivation of nationalism could explain the extraordinary resilience of the Vietnamese on all sides during this agonizing war. For the larger powers interested in the conflict, various particular interests may be affected by its outcome. But, for the Vietnamese, their own identity, their own survival as a nation is threatened by the prolongation of the fighting. I submit that the time is overdue for a political de-escalation regarding Vietnam. All should strive now to isolate this conflict from adverse international influences which in the past have caused so many opportunities to pass, and to let the Vietnamese themselves deal with their own problems. I am convinced that after all the sufferings which their own past differences have caused, all Vietnamese must realize that their energies and their great talents should now be turned toward healing their divisions and toward the reconstruction and modernization of both North and South Vietnam. The people of Vietnam, in conditions of peace, have a great role to play in Southeast Asia as a stabilizing influence in a new cooperative effort among countries of the region, irrespective of their political systems.

177. Again and again, I have consistently advocated a military de-escalation by all sides, starting with a complete cessation of the bombing and all other acts of war against North Vietnam. I am fully aware of the objections which are raised against this essential first step. Undoubtedly, there are risks for all sides which engage in such a difficult negotiation. In

my view, it is for the side which is militarily more powerful to take the initiative. I reiterate my personal conviction that a cessation of the bombing would set in motion positive steps which can eventually lead to a peaceful settlement in Southeast Asia in accordance with the Geneva agreements of 1954.

178. In this connection, I would recall one or two important aspects of these agreements. In the Final Declaration of the Geneva Conference, the powers agreed on a number of principles for a future political settlement for what had been French Indo-China. Among such principles, article 6 clearly stipulated that "the military demarcation line is provisional and should not in any way be interpreted as constituting a political or territorial boundary." However, the political machinery for the reunification, namely, the elections projected for July 1956, failed to materialize. This is one of the main problems which will no doubt receive the attention of the negotiators, even though it appears from the programs of all the interested parties, including the National Front for the Liberation of South Vietnam, that the unification of the two parts will involve a long process of adjustment to be decided by degrees when the situation is more settled.

179. There is another principle included in the 1954 declaration which now should clearly constitute the basis of a settlement. This is the neutralization of the entire Indo-Chinese peninsula, including all of Vietnam. To become a source of stability in the whole region, this neutrality should be accepted and, preferably, guaranteed by all the larger powers.

180. There is widespread disappointment at the apparent lack of progress of the preliminary conversations between the North Vietnamese and United States delegations which have been taking place in Paris since early May. Even though it was clear from the beginning that these talks would be difficult and that meanwhile the fighting would continue, both parties must be aware that the usefulness of the Paris talks might be jeopardized if attention were to be concentrated on the conduct of military operations. One would at least hope that, by opening these first direct contacts, the interested governments have clearly signified that they know peace will not be brought about by military means or military escalation. Indeed, I hope I am right in thinking that, by persevering in these peace discussions, the interested governments are showing their desire to cling to the only serious sign of common will and hope for peace that exists. If this is true, then, despite the discouraging develop-

ments of this ominous year, all will not have been lost. In my view, it would be a fatal error to underestimate the unique opportunity which the Paris talks represent in themselves, an opportunity which should be fully utilized by the parties concerned in taking the decisions that are required to move ahead.

181. As Secretary-General of the United Nations, I have consistently—indeed, necessarily—deplored any and every resort to force as a means of settling international differences since such action is in contravention of the Charter of the United Nations and results in a setback to the establishment of a world order based on the rule of law rather than military power. It follows therefore that I deplored the action of the Soviet Union and four of its Warsaw Pact allies in sending their armed forces into Czechoslovakia in late August 1968. Even though at the time only unofficial information about events in Czechoslovakia was available to me, I issued a statement to the effect that I deplored the use of force anywhere to settle international problems, as contravening the United Nations Charter. I characterized the developments in Czechoslovakia as another serious blow to those concepts of international order and morality which constitute the very basis of the entire structure of the United Nations and which are at the same time the prime objectives which the United Nations has been persistently striving to achieve throughout the more than twenty-two years of its existence. The same morning I also strongly appealed to the government of the Union of Soviet Socialist Republics, through its permanent representative to the United Nations, to exercise the utmost restraint in its relations with the government and people of Czechoslovakia, who have been showing for some time a genuine desire to fashion their own future without outside interference from any quarter.

182. I feared at the time of this action, and my fear continues, that there would be a number of consequences which could have a seriously adverse effect upon international relations. Of these, I may mention a few.

183. The East-West détente, which seemed to me to be showing signs of reinvigoration in recent months and to which I had attached very great importance, would suffer a severe reversal similar to that which has resulted from the Vietnam war.

184. There would be a renewed intensification of the cold war, taking the world back to the worst days of the cold war in the early fifties.

185. Regional defense alliances would find new justification and support, with greater reliance being placed on the outmoded and dangerous concept of international stability through military blocs.

186. The "hard liners" and the "hawks" in many countries would derive from the experience of Czechoslovakia encouragement and nourishment for their position that there should be no attempt at coexistence or accommodation with the socialist countries; and the voices of liberalism and progressive thought in many parts of the world would be muted.

187. The action in Czechoslovakia was one of overwhelming military force undertaken by one of the two superpowers, assisted by four of its allies, in respect of a small state which was, in fact, a loyal member of its own bloc. The repercussions of this act of sheer military power were felt around the world and engendered a feeling of dismay, uneasiness, and insecurity.

188. In the situation in which Czechoslovakia found itself, the United Nations afforded a unique opportunity to its government to present its case to the world in the forum of the Security Council. Subsequently, as is known, the government of Czechoslovakia requested that this matter should no longer be considered by the Security Council and should be removed from its agenda.

189. It is, certainly, a frightening commentary on the ominous state of world affairs that one superstate or the other can become exercised to the point of resorting to military action because of the liberalization of a régime in a small country like Czechoslovakia or because of an internal upheaval in another small state, such as the Dominican Republic. In both cases, the action taken was regarded by those who took it as necessary self-protection without any thought of territorial acquisition. In the case of Czechoslovakia, the parties directly concerned seem to have reached an agreement on the phased withdrawal of the foreign troops. I would very much hope that this agreement would be implemented as expeditiously as possible. Such action would be in the interest of mutual good will and also of international peace and security.

190. It is, however, a dismal outlook for the small and militarily weak states of the world—as the overwhelming majority of states are—if they can hope to control their own affairs only insofar as they do nothing to displease a powerful neighbor.

191. It seems to me that now, more than ever, there is need for that will for peace and the matching strength and courage in action which

alone can enable governments to exercise the restraint in word, policy, and deed necessary to prevent a mounting spiral of fear and danger.

192. In this regard, I have in mind certain attitudes and policies which, I think, could prevent an irreparable rupture in East-West relations and thus revive hope among men.

193. There should be an avoidance of the all too obvious temptation to use the events in Czechoslovakia as grounds for an intensified build-up of nuclear and thermonuclear weapons. Such a course would only compound the madness of the existing nuclear arms race. The only reason which could induce either the Soviet Union and its allies, or the Western powers, to attack the other would be a pervading fear by one side of a pre-emptive strike by the other. This fear is fed by, and grows proportionately with, the increase in the offensive military power of the two superstates. It is, clearly, the build-up of excessive military power beyond any reasonable demands of defense which has become the most ominous threat to world peace.

194. I also believe that it would help to reduce tension if both the NATO and Warsaw Pact powers would refrain from using Czechoslovakia as a reason for a military build-up to the point that it becomes a positive, offensive threat rather than a strictly defensive posture.

195. A constructive and most helpful action in these perilous times would be the strengthening of the peace-building and peace-keeping capability of the United Nations system. Conversely, military alliances must gradually give way to a global concept of international security and international progress. This will require an intensified effort to reach the minds and hearts of all men with the irrefutable message that war is not only folly and madness, but that mankind's future depends upon its aboliton abolition. There is a need, now more imperative than ever before, for worldwide education toward international understanding and peaceful coexistence.

196. The world badly needs an end to the outmoded but dangerous tactic of trying to cope with the problem of the sixties by the strong-arm methods common to the thirties. It is high time for the great military powers to realize that the present superior military force on which they rely so heavily and are prone to use so freely, is in itself a grave and ever-present danger. Used injudiciously, it also saps the most valuable asset of any nation, its moral authority. Instead of maintaining the policy of reliance on their own military power and the unceasing build-up of arms for their national security, they should take those steps which they alone

can effectively take to reduce international tension through progressive disarmament in regard to both nuclear and conventional weapons. At the same time, the major powers should realize that it is as much in their interest as it is in the interest of the smaller powers for all Member states to abide faithfully by the provisions of the Charter, and to use the United Nations as their chosen instrument to maintain peace and to achieve a just and stable world order.

197. In reality, the two superpowers hold the master-key to peace in the world. Little wars, or wars by little states, can be contained so long as the superpowers do not pose a threat of the big, the nuclear, the ultimate war.

198. In the final analysis, there can be no solid foundation for peace in the world so long as the superpowers insist on taking unilateral military action whenever they claim to see a threat to their security. Why should they also not bring their fears and complaints about threats to their security to the Security Council, as they regularly demand that less powerful states do? In the Cuban missile crisis this course proved helpful, and it could prove equally useful in other cases where big-power interests and peace are both directly involved.

199. As I had occasion to state on September 13, 1968, to the Assembly of Heads of State and Government of the Organization of African Unity meeting in Algiers, the resolutions adopted by that organization concerning the conflict in Nigeria are the basis for my attitude and approach to this problem. I also expressed to that Assembly my earnest hope that, pursuant to the efforts of the Organization of African Unity, in particular its six-member Consultative Committee under whose auspices useful preliminary talks recently took place at Niamey and Addis Ababa, fruitful negotiations may take place leading to a just solution which would guarantee the security of all the people of Nigeria.

200. In the resolution approved in Algiers by the Assembly of Heads of State and Government, the Organization of African Unity took note of the report on Nigeria submitted by the Consultative Committee, called upon the secessionist leaders to cooperate with the federal authority with a view to restoring peace and unity in Nigeria, recommended to the Federal Military Government in Nigeria, if preceding conditions are fulfilled, to proclaim a general amnesty and to cooperate with the Organization of African Unity with a view to ensuring the personal security of all Nigerians without distinction until mutual confidence is restored, and called again upon all parties concerned to cooperate with

a view to ensuring the rapid delivery of humanitarian relief aid to all those who are in need of it. It also called upon all states Members of the United Nations and members of the Organization of African Unity to abstain from any action which might jeopardize the unity, territorial integrity, and peace of Nigeria. It further invited the Consultative Committee, in which it renewed its confidence, to pursue its efforts with a view to implementing the resolutions adopted at Kinshasa and Algiers. I sincerely trust that this resolution may serve as a framework to bring about the restoration of peace and with it the end to this tragic fratricidal conflict.

201. The activities of the United Nations family regarding the conflict in Nigeria have been of an exclusively humanitarian nature. Deeply disturbed about the plight of the population in the war-affected areas of Nigeria, I indicated on July 13, 1968, to General Yakubu Gowon, Head of the Federal Military Government of Nigeria, that the humanitarian organs of the United Nations were ready to make their contribution to meet the urgent needs of civilian victims of the hostilities and I also state my willingness to send a representative to Lagos immediately to discuss the modalities of this humanitarian task. On July 29 General Gowon confirmed his acceptance of my offer to send a representative and, consequently, on August 1 I appointed Mr. Nils-Goran Gussing as my representative to assist in the relief and humanitarian activities for the civilian victims of the hostilities. After consultations in New York and Geneva, Mr. Gussing arrived in Lagos on August 17. In the meantime, Mr. Henry R. Labouisse, Executive-Director of the United Nations Children's Fund, had been in Nigeria, had traveled extensively in many of the areas where the population, especially children, were in dire need of supplies, and had made arrangements for the assistance which the Fund has been providing to the affected population.

202. For the purpose of coordinating efforts and thus undertaking the most effective action, it was agreed by a number of organizations, both governmental and private, that all the humanitarian aid to the victims of the Nigerian conflict would be channeled through the International Committee of the Red Cross. This arrangement, which includes the relief activities of the United Nations, mainly those of the United Nations Children's Fund, still stands.

203. More recently, in response to a request from the federal government that I appoint an observer to visit the war-affected areas in Nigeria, on September 18 I designated Mr. Gussing for this purpose. This addi-

tional responsibility will be undertaken by Mr. Gussing within the framework of his mandate as my representative on humanitarian activities in Nigeria. His task is to see for himself the situation of the population in those areas, to make an assessment of the relief needs there, to recommend ways and means of expediting the distribution of relief supplies, and to report directly to me.

204. It is regrettable that the efforts to speed up the distribution of supplies to the distressed areas have been hampered by difficulties arising from the conduct of the military operations by both sides. There is no question that there is great need for larger shipments of relief supplies, but the immediate and greater problem is to secure a fuller cooperation on the part of those bearing responsibility in the areas of the conflict as regards facilities for the movement and distribution of supplies.

205. I am well aware that this document must make gloomy reading. I do not believe, however, that a facile optimism would be justified under present international conditions. At the same time, I feel that it is not enough to bemoan the past; we must also renew our efforts to promote the cause of international understanding and rededicate ourselves to the principles of international order and morality set out in the Charter. It seems to me that such an occasion for rededication will present itself to all Member states as we approach the twenty-fifth anniversary of the founding of the United Nations. I believe that Member states would wish to celebrate this occasion with due solemnity and I should like to suggest that, very early in the twenty-third session, the President of the General Assembly may, after due consultations, appoint a committee of Member states with a request to them to submit their report for consideration by the Assembly before the close of the present session. I hope that the Assembly will be able to adopt recommendations which will make it possible to celebrate, in a most fitting manner, the twenty-fifth anniversary of the United Nations.

U THANT
Secretary-General

September 24, 1968

Text of Identical Letters to the Foreign Ministers of France, the United Kingdom, the United States, and the USSR Proposing a Big Four Meeting

NEW YORK   OCTOBER 7, 1968

U THANT on numerous occasions proposed high-level meetings, especially among representatives of the big powers, as a possible approach to common problems which had defied solution by conventional negotiations. In the Introduction to his 1967 annual report, for example, he renewed the suggestions of his predecessors, Trygve Lie and Dag Hammarskjöld, for a periodic meeting of the Security Council as provided by Article 28, paragraph 2, of the Charter. Under this provision Member states might be represented by members of their governments or by specially designated representatives, who could discuss world problems at informal closed meetings. Thant offered to draw up a tentative agenda for such a meeting if the Member governments approved the idea. The Secretary-General reported a year later that the Members had failed to follow up his suggestion.

In the Introduction to his 1968 annual report, Thant proposed that "as an alternative, it would be useful to take advantage of the presence of the foreign ministers of France, the Soviet Union, the United Kingdom and the United States during the coming session of the General Assembly to arrange for them to meet and discuss common problems." He suggested further that the proposed meeting might lead to a meeting of the heads of government of the four major powers. "I feel," he said, "that some such initiative is needed at the present time to counteract the serious setback to the détente in East-West relations that has resulted from recent events." On September 28, four days after circulation of the Introduction, a United Nations spokesman told correspondents that there had been no official reaction to his suggestions regarding a four-power meeting.

On October 7 Thant followed up the suggestions with a letter to the big four foreign ministers spelling out his idea in more detail. He mentioned a number of subjects that could be usefully discussed, including the financial problems of the United Nations, peace-keeping, disarmament, and the Middle East. He mentioned specifically his hope that such a meeting might give helpful "guidance and support" for the Middle East peace mission of his special representative, Gunnar Jarring. The letter produced no immediate results except for another informal

SOURCE: UN Press Release SG/SM/1021, October 15, 1968.

dinner of the four foreign ministers with Thant, similar to one held during the 1967 session of the General Assembly. There was no summit meeting. A few months later, however, on April 3, 1969, the foreign ministers of France, the Soviet Union, the United Kingdom, and the United States began a series of private meetings on the Middle East which were to continue throughout the remainder of 1969 and 1970.

YOU WILL PERHAPS recall that in my Introduction to the annual report on the work of the Organization last year I advanced a suggestion that an attempt might be made to assess the value of holding periodic meetings of the Security Council at which its members might be represented by a member of the government or by some specially designated representative. It was actually my hope that such a meeting would be attended by the foreign ministers of the Member states concerned and that this would give an opportunity for a free-ranging discussion of major problems which have a bearing on international peace and security.

It may also be recalled that, at an informal dinner I gave for the foreign ministers of the four major powers last year, I discussed some of the ideas which were at the back of my mind when I made this suggestion. Since I put forth this possibility last year the international situation has further deteriorated and the hopes for an East-West détente have been seriously set back. I feel that some special effort should now be made in spite of the present unfavorable atmosphere—or, indeed, because of it—to identify some important issues where a community of interest may facilitate big-power agreement irrespective of the adverse circumstances.

It is with this thought in mind that, in my latest Introduction to the annual report, which was issued last month, I proposed that it might be useful to take advantage of the presence of the foreign ministers of France, the Soviet Union, the United Kingdom, and the United States during the current session of the General Assembly so that they might meet and discuss some common problems. I felt that such a meeting would help to halt the growing feeling of insecurity in the world and provide some antidote to the feeling of pessimism about the future of international peace and security that is now so widespread.

Let me state that I am well aware of some of the risks involved in organizing such a meeting. Among these may be mentioned the real risk that hopes may be raised which may not be realized. However, I believe that some concrete results might be achieved if an agenda could be agreed upon which would be realistic and not over-ambitious.

If the idea of such a meeting is acceptable, I shall be happy, if so desired, to prepare a draft agenda. I realize that at the present time spectacular results in regard to the serious developments in many parts of the world may not be achieved. However, I believe that a modest start could and should be made in an attempt to deal with the basic problem facing the Organization, namely how can the United Nations be enabled to develop into a really effective instrument for peace and progress as envisaged in the Charter. This, of course, is my main concern; but one cannot ignore the existence of other problems which also have a bearing on the effectiveness of the world Organization. I may mention among these the financial solvency of the United Nations, and its peace-keeping and peace-building functions. These problems can be solved only if, to start with, the big powers could agree among themselves either on the general principles of their solution, or on a pragmatic approach which, without prejudice to the respective positions of principle, may allow the Organization to function effectively. Another thought I have is the need to reaffirm the Charter principles and the accepted rules of international conduct. One could hope also that such a meeting might give attention to ways of more helpful collective guidance and support for Ambassador Jarring's vital mission. It may also be opportune to discuss certain aspects of disarmament at such a meeting.

In the Introduction to the annual report I had stated that hopefully a meeting of the foreign ministers could lead to a meeting of the heads of state and government of the four major powers. I know it requires most careful preparation to arrange such a meeting. I also recognize that, in view of the current political situation in individual countries, such a summit meeting could hardly be envisaged until some time in 1969. I cannot help feeling very strongly that the mere fact of agreement in principle to hold such a summit meeting would shine as a ray of hope in the presently clouded sky and bring a sense of relief to human beings all over the world who are deeply concerned about the trend of international developments today.

Let me add that in my thinking it is not necessary that the four foreign ministers should meet as a group. It would be equally effective if they were to meet individually with each other, taking advantage of their presence at the current session of the General Assembly, Preliminary discussions now initiated could be followed up by subsequent meetings at a time and place which would be mutually convenient. In all such efforts I shall of course be happy to be of help, if so desired.

I feel that the ideas I had expressed, perhaps too tersely, in my Introduction to the annual report, needed to be spelt out a little. It is with this thought in mind that I address this letter to you. I have no doubt that you will wish to give this suggestion your most earnest consideration.

United Nations Day Message

NEW YORK   OCTOBER 24, 1968

ON OCTOBER 24, 1968, the twenty-third anniversary of the establishment of the United Nations, U Thant took the occasion to express his full confidence in the ideals of the Charter and in the structural capability of the Organization to perform the tasks assigned to it. He blamed the disappointing performance of the United Nations mainly upon the "short-sighted self-interests" of the Member states. "The machinery for international cooperation," he said, "is as yet largely untested and untried."

WE COME TO the observance of this United Nations Day, the twenty-third anniversary of the establishment of the world Organization, in the somber realization that the ideals and goals set out in the Charter are not being realized as we expected; nor have some of our fondest hopes and aspirations come to fruition.

Despite our determination "to save succeeding generations from the scourge of war," we continue to live under the threat of a possible nuclear annihilation.

In Asia, Africa, the Middle East, Europe, and elsewhere, policies are pursued and courses of action set in motion which seem to go completely contrary to the Charter principle that we should "practice tolerance and live together with one another as good neighbors."

In this International Year for Human Rights, commemorating the twentieth anniversary of the adoption of the Universal Declaration, millions of our fellow human beings still suffer from want, from discrimination, and from the lack of opportunity to guide their own destinies.

Despite two decades of technological progress—years which have seen the beginning of the conquest of space—there are vast areas of our

SOURCE: *UN Monthly Chronicle,* Vol. V, pp. iii-iv.

planet where the war against poverty, hunger, ignorance, and disease is still far from being won.

It is, therefore, hardly surprising that people may sometimes question whether the aims and purposes of the United Nations can ever be realized, whether the machinery for international cooperation can ever be made fully effective.

My message to you this United Nations Day is simply this. The goals established by the founding fathers of the world Organization are as valid today as they were in 1945.

We must continue to strive "to unite our strength to maintain international peace and security." We must continue to "reaffirm our faith in fundamental human rights" and to promote the economic and social advancement of all peoples.

The alternatives to these goals are unthinkable. They are injustice, suffering, and mass destruction.

Nor is the structure of our world Organization, although admittedly imperfect, incapable of performing the tasks assigned to it. Indeed the machinery for international cooperation is as yet largely untested and untried.

What is lacking at this critical hour in human history in our efforts to build the world envisaged by the Charter is the moral strength which will be required to overcome our short-sighted self-interests, the moral strength needed to enable us to combine our efforts toward the common goal.

A renewed will to peace on behalf of peoples and governments, a renewed dedication to the ideals of the Charter—these alone can enable us to face the coming months and years with hope and confidence.

THE SITUATION IN THE MIDDLE EAST

NOVEMBER

U THANT'S special representative to the Middle East, Gunnar Jarring, pursued his peace mission tenaciously during 1968 but without substantial results. After shuttling from capital to capital for some eight months, Jarring flew to New York in September to consult with the Secretary-General and to be on hand for talks with Middle East foreign ministers attending the opening weeks of the twenty-third session of the General Assembly. Thant acknowledged his disappointment at the lack of progress, but expressed confidence in the worth of the Jarring mission and his gratification at the willingness of the Middle East governments to continue it. In the Introduction to his 1968 annual report, Thant said. "The basic situation in the Middle East in relation even to the beginnings of a settlement remains much the same as it was eight months ago." Much of Jarring's effort had been directed at breaking an impasse over procedure. Israel was insisting on direct negotiations, while the Arabs wanted to carry on negotiations indirectly with Jarring as intermediary, "All of his efforts will be unavailing," Thant said, "unless he is able to carry on some form of dialogue with the two sides involving matters of substance. Such a dialogue cannot be fruitful if it is substantive on one side and procedural on the other." Thant's view, as expressed previously (see volume VII of this series, p. 50), was that direct negotiations were the ideal where possible but that they were not practical under existing circumstances in the Middle East.

While the Secretary-General's main preoccupation was with the peace efforts in the Middle East, he was also deeply concerned over the plight of the million Palestine refugees left homeless after the 1948 war and the thousands of additional Arabs who fled their homes during the Six-Day War. His concern was reflected in his decision to appear in person before the Special Political Committee of the General Assembly to stress the need for a just settlement of the twenty-year-old refugee problem and for continued assistance through the United Nations Relief and Works Agency for Palestine Refugees in the Near East.

Statement in the Special Political Committee

NEW YORK   NOVEMBER 11, 1968

THIS IS THE first time, I understand, that a Secretary-General has addressed this Committee during its consideration of the subject of the United Nations Relief and Works Agency for Palestine Refugees in the Near East (UNRWA) and the Palestine refugees. I do so now only because I consider it to be my duty to call for special attention of the members of this Committee to certain acute situations requiring urgent action. My purpose here, therefore, is to point out and underscore certain vital needs which are, in my view, an international responsibility.

Before doing so, I may be permitted to make one general remark. For twenty years the Palestine refugees—well over one million of them—have had no homeland, no future, and not even a detectable glimmer of hope on their horizon.

We should remind ourselves, I think, that in all of these twenty years, the General Assembly has not found it possible to take any significant step toward a real solution of this great and tragic human problem. It has found it possible mainly to discuss each year, at length, the arrangements to be made through UNRWA for the relief of the refugees in their present plight, without touching upon measures which might achieve a fundamental solution for them.

This fact reflects upon us all and certainly upon the United Nations, and we should not allow ourselves to forget it in the debate which is ahead of us in this Committee. Having said that I will proceed to the three main points to which I wish to call attention.

In the first place, it is, in my view, clearly imperative that UNRWA be in a position to meet adequately the increased demands that have been placed on the Agency since June of last year. The report of the Commissioner-General is before you and provides much detailed information

SOURCE: UN Press Release SG/SM/1033. The summary record is given in General Assembly Official Records, Twenty-third Session, Special Political Committee, 612th meeting.

about the current conditions of the refugees and the problems facing the Agency. The Commissioner-General himself will be giving the Committee further information and clarifications. I do not propose, therefore, to go into detail in my statement today. I do wish, however, to draw the attention of the Committee, at the opening of its discussion on these matters, to the urgent necessity of meeting the responsibilities of the United Nations for the care of the refugees and displaced persons.

At the outset, I may point to the basic question which faces this Committee under the item now being considered, namely, the renewal of the mandate of UNRWA. It must be renewed, of course. Not to continue UNRWA after next June would be, in my view, unthinkable. The international community which the United Nations represents cannot abandon this very large group of people for whose plight the United Nations must bear a considerable measure of responsibility without dealing a harsh blow to international morality and to the conscience of humanity which the United Nations must always seek to reflect.

All Members know of the efforts being made by Ambassador Jarring under the terms of the Security Council resolution of November 22, 1967, to promote, among other objectives, the achievement of a just settlement of the refugee problem. I should like to take this opportunity to appeal to governments to afford Ambassador Jarring all possible cooperation and assistance in finding a solution. Whatever success may ultimately attend these efforts, they are unavoidably directed toward a long-term solution which could not, by its very nature, immediately be put into effect.

Pending the implementation of a just settlement of the refugee problem, some agency, obviously, must continue to perform the functions and supply the services which for so long now have been the responsibility of UNRWA—providing shelter, food, health services, education, and training facilities for the refugees. Certainly, the elimination of these services would make far more difficult the long-term settlement of the refugee problem which is being sought and which must be achieved.

It seems to me, therefore, that the renewal of UNRWA's mandate is by far the most practicable, if not the only, method of continuing the main task of caring for the refugees until a final settlement of the refugee problem is achieved. I strongly urge that the Committee decide positively—and, I would hope, unanimously—on the renewal of the mandate of UNRWA for a suitable and reasonable period.

Second, I wish to refer to a problem which will immediately arise if, as

I hope, it is decided to continue UNRWA. I have in mind the necessity of providing UNRWA with the means for carrying out its task adequately and well.

The General Assembly, in its resolution 2252 (ES-V) of July 4, 1967, on humanitarian questions, made an urgent appeal to all governments to make special contributions to UNRWA. It also appealed to other intergovernmental and non-governmental organizations for the purpose of obtaining the means to meet the new demands of the refugee situation. The General Assembly last December repeated in resolution 2341 (XXII) of December 19, 1967, its appeal to governments to consider increasing their contributions to UNRWA, as well as to governments, organizations, and individuals to make special contributions to UNRWA or to other intergovernmental and non-governmental organizations concerned. I myself have made various appeals, including one made jointly with the Director-General of the Food and Agriculture Organization on April 29, 1968.

Although some governments have responded generously to the appeals for additional contributions for UNRWA, the total received has fallen short of what is required to meet its responsibilities. In 1968, the Agency will again have to draw on its working capital to finance its operations. For 1969, to maintain the present program of UNRWA activities will require some $42.5 million—about $5 million above the level of expenditure before the June 1967 hostilities. Income is again likely to be inadequate—on present indications, by as much as $5 million. This would be very serious—almost catastrophic.

The consequences in human suffering, as well as in complicating the efforts for a solution of the problems of the area, lead me to appeal once again, and this time most urgently, to all governments to make contributions as generous as they possibly can in order that UNRWA will be enabled to meet this great humanitarian challenge to and responsibility of the United Nations.

I must emphasize that the increased requirements of UNRWA are not only to meet the special hardships of newly displaced persons and refugees, but also to make it possible for UNRWA to continue the services which it is already performing and which are vital both to the present and future well-being of the refugees.

As the Commissioner-General has pointed out in his report, the hostilities of June 1967 created a situation which has resulted in increased hardships for many of the existing refugees and the displacement of large numbers of other persons as well. This situation has, in turn, greatly increased the task of UNRWA and has also put an additional burden on the governments in the area, in particular on the governments of Jordan, Syria, and the United Arab Republic. Since June 1967, further violent incidents, especially in the Jordan-Israel sector, have created a new displacement of refugees and other persons in Jordan, many of whom, having fled from the valleys, will be facing an even harder winter this year than they did last year, for they will be in tented camps on the hills, where climatic conditions are severe.

As Secretary-General, I would be derelict in my duty if I did not recall to the Special Political Committee the resolutions of the Security Council and of the General Asssembly relating to humanitarian questions, and in particular to Security Council resolution 237 (1967) of June 14, 1967, which, among other things, asked that the return of those inhabitants who have fled the areas since the outbreak of hostilities be facilitated. A similar appeal was made by the General Assembly in its resolution 2252 (ES-V) of July 4, 1967, a resolution which also endorses the efforts of the Commissioner-General of UNRWA to provide humanitarian assistance, as far as practicable, on an emergency basis and as a temporary measure, to persons other than refugees in the area who were displaced and were in serious need of immediate assistance as a result of the hostilities. This resolution was reaffirmed by the General Assembly, on the basis of the report of this Committee, in Assembly resolution 2341B (XXII) of December 19, 1967.

It cannot be questioned that the plight of many of the refugees could best be relieved immediately by their return to their homes and to the camps which they formerly occupied. For the displaced persons, the only remedy that would appear to be at once acceptable and practical is their early return to their former places of residence. Although efforts have been made to secure such a return for both the refugees and the displaced persons, the results in terms of the numbers who have actually returned have been relatively small, I think it is necessary to state that if the camps on the West Bank could again serve their original purpose, and if the displaced persons could return to their former homes, a long step would have been taken toward reducing the hardships faced by a large number of the refugees and displaced persons in Jordan. At the same time, it would reduce the financial burdens on the Agency.

I realize, however, that a major factor and a possible obstacle to such a development from the standpoint of the displaced persons and refugees themselves, and conceivably of the government of Israel as well, is the continuing occupation by Israel forces of the area concerned and the lack of any present indication as to when that occupation will be terminated and peaceful conditions prevail.

May I conclude with a general comment. Of all the humanitarian situations with which the United Nations is concerned, the plight of the Palestine refugees should arouse the most active compassion of all the governments and peoples of the United Nations, for we are dealing here with nothing less than a twenty-year-old tragedy for a group of people who considerably outnumber the whole population of a number of the states which are members of the United Nations.

Members may differ on the rights and wrongs of the situation in the Middle East, of which the Palestine refugees are the innocent and long-suffering victims. Efforts may be exerted through the United Nations, or outside it, to find solutions to the problems of the Middle East, of which the refugee problem is a major one.

I believe, however, that everyone will agree that the tragedy of the Palestine refugees, who three times in twenty years have known at first-hand the cruel blast of war, demands that the United Nations should live up generously, and without hesitation, to its humanitarian duty toward them. I earnestly hope the action of this Committee collectively, and of its members individually, will alow the United Nations to meet this responsibility to the fullest possible extent.

From Report to the Security Council on the Situation in Cyprus

NEW YORK   DECEMBER 4, 1968

AS 1968 drew to a close the situation in Cyprus seemed to be improving at last. In the following report, U Thant noted the continued relaxation of tension and saw reason for encouragement because of the patience and good will shown in the negotiations between representatives of the Greek and Turkish communities. Unfortunately, the parties were unable to produce a breakthrough on fundamental questions and, as far as the United Nations Force was concerned, the end was not in sight. Another six-month extension was voted.

. . .

87. IT IS MOST gratifying for me to be able to report to the Council that relaxation of tension in Cyprus has continued and that at last the emphasis seems to be shifting from military confrontation to negotiation. The last six months have been good for peace in Cyprus. Not only has there been no bloodshed but not one serious intercommunal incident has occurred to mar the atmosphere of calm and expectancy surrounding the important talks taking place between leading members of the two communities. The talks are proceeding in all earnestness and I take this opportunity to pay a warm tribute to the patience, good will, and statesmanship being displayed by the two negotiators and their principals. Nevertheless, in spite of some rapprochement on certain questions, no breakthrough on fundamental issues has yet been announced and the conversations are bound to continue for some time. This is not surprising, in view of the complexity and difficulties of the Cyprus problem.

88. What is significant and promising in these talks is that the parties

SOURCE: Security Council Official Records, Supplement for October, November and December 1968, document S/8914.

in Cyprus are now engaged in a determined effort to emerge from the deadlock resulting from the rigid positions adopted in the past. This is an encouraging indication of their willingness to move forward from those positions and to entertain other policies which, while still maintaining principles which they regard as vital, are capable of being harmonized to the benefit of all the people of Cyprus.

89. As I have often stated, no peace mission of the United Nations can hope to succeed without the cooperation and effort of the parties themselves, but once such cooperation and effort are present, the United Nations can be of great assistance. Since its establishment in March 1964, the United Nations Peace-keeping Force in Cyprus (UNFICYP) has labored diligently—sometimes by direct intervention but more often by using the moral authority of the United Nations—to prevent the recurrence of fighting and to contribute to a return to normal conditions insofar as that is possible short of a final political settlement. At this stage, it may be said that the presence of UNFICYP in the island constitutes an assurance to both communities that no unforeseen accident will be allowed to initiate a chain of events that might bring back the tragic conditions of the past and disrupt the efforts being undertaken by the Greek and Turkish Cypriot leaders to overcome their differences.

90. It would be most unfortunate in my view if the promising efforts of the parties in Cyprus to reach a peaceful settlement of their differences were to be in any way jeopardized by the uncertainties that might arise if the United Nations presence in Cyprus were to be withdrawn or radically changed at this most constructive and crucial stage. Therefore, I consider it essential that the mandate of UNFICYP should be extended for yet another period. Since, from all available information, the inter-communal talks will require some time before tangible results can be realistically expected, I strongly recommend that the Security Council extend the stationing of UNFICYP for a further period of six months until June 15, 1969. The government of Cyprus, as well as the governments of Greece and Turkey have informed me of their agreement for the proposed extension.

91. As indicated above, the improved conditions in the island have made it possible recently to reduce the strength of the Force by about 25 percent. But despite this reduction the deficit of the UNFICYP budget continues to be of alarming proportions. I feel obliged to raise this matter once again with the Security Council and to appeal to the members of the Council to give it their most serious and urgent attention. . . .

❧ *1969* ❧

TRYGVE LIE

DURING HIS DECADE in office, U Thant lauded his predecessor, Dag Hammarskjöld, on many occasions and acknowledged his contribution to the strengthening of the United Nations and of the office of Secretary-General. The death of Trygve Lie in the final hours of 1968 provided an opportunity for acknowledging the role of the first Secretary-General as "a fighter for peace, a defender of the Charter and a tireless builder of the new world Organization." He praised Lie in the following message of condolences to the prime minister of Norway, Per Borten, and much more in detail in a speech at St. Bernard's School, attended by Lie's two grandsons. Noting that Lie was sometimes criticized for trying to do too much, he said the first Secretary-General "laid the foundations of the United Nations as we know it today." Thant was a firm believer, as Lie and Hammarskjöld were, that the role of the Secretary-General should be much broader than that of an administrator. It was Lie who first fought to ensure that the Secretary-General would have political functions as well as administrative. "As the third Secretary-General of the United Nations," Thant said, "I often have cause to be grateful to Trygve Lie for the fine work he did in setting up the world Organization. I can also understand, perhaps better than anyone, what a difficult and exhausting job he had to do as first Secretary-General, and how well he did it."

1. Message of Condolence to Per Borten, Prime Minister of Norway

NEW YORK   DECEMBER 30, 1968

I EXPRESS to you and to the government and people of Norway my profound sorrow and condolences on the death of Trygve Lie. As its first Secretary-General, Trygve Lie holds a unique place in the history of the United Nations. After a distinguished career as a wartime leader of his embattled country he was given the herculean task of putting into operation the new world Organization, of recruiting its Secretariat, of finding its permanent home after several years in temporary quarters, of building the New York Headquarters, and of installing the Organization in it. The execution of these highly complex administrative tasks ran parallel with the infinitely difficult duty of seeing the United Nations through its first, and halting, steps toward making a reality of the purposes and principles of the Charter. Trygve Lie's tenure of office, from February 1946 to April 1953, was beset by many crises and was afflicted by the increasing rigors of the cold war. Despite the unceasing problems of those years—Palestine, Berlin, Kashmir, and Korea, to name only four—Trygve Lie continued as he had started out, a fighter for peace, a defender of the Charter, and a tireless builder of the new world Organization. Like anyone who occupies an exposed position of world importance, he was frequently criticized from many sources, as often for doing too much as for doing too little. No one was more aware than he of the contrast between his great responsibilities for peace and the stringent limitations on his authority and on his possibilities for effective action. It was he more than anyone else who was responsible for building from nothing the physical structure and administration of the United Nations. Thus the Headquarters in New York is in a sense his most enduring monument.

SOURCE: *UN Monthly Chronicle,* Vol. VI, January 1969, p. 109.

My sympathy goes to his family and to the people of Norway in their great loss, which is shared by all the Members of the United Nations.

2. *Address at St. Bernard's School*

NEW YORK   JANUARY 24, 1969

I AM VERY GLAD to be with you this morning to pay a tribute to the first Secretary-General of the United Nations, Trygve Lie. Although two of his grandsons[1] are here with us today, most of you were not born when Trygve Lie completed his service as Secretary-General of the United Nations. I feel, therefore, that I should try, in the next few minutes, to give you some idea of what Trygve Lie was like and what he achieved.

Trygve Lie was in every sense a large man. He was big, jovial, and tough-minded. He often spoke out bluntly in his strong Norwegian accent against things he thought wrong. He loved life and especially sport of all kinds. He was a keen hunter, a good skier, and an excellent tennis player. He gave a lot to life and he got a lot out of it.

The Second World War brought horror and disaster to millions of people all over the world. After the German army took Norway in 1940, Trygve Lie escaped in a British destroyer, with the King of Norway and other like-minded members of the government, to carry on in exile in England their resistance to the Nazis, who were finally defeated in 1945.

At the end of the war, the United Nations was set up by the nations of the world to ensure, if possible, that the disasters and horrors of the Second World War would never be repeated.

The United Nations was, and is, a great experiment by the nations of the world. The aim of this experiment is to make the world better and more peaceful for all its peoples. The United Nations is now an enormous Organization working in almost every branch of human activity, although you hear most about the political conflicts with which it tries to

SOURCE: UN Press Release SG/SM/1060.

[1]William and Arthur Zeckendorf, ages 11 and 10, sons of Mrs. Guri Lie Zeckendorf.

deal. But when Trygve Lie was appointed as the first Secretary-General of the United Nations in 1946, the Organization was little more than an idea. It had no home and no staff to run it. No one really knew how it would work. It had plenty of problems and plenty of trouble to deal with, but not much else. Trygve Lie was chosen because he represented a small country which had fought gallantly against Nazi tyranny. This made him acceptable to both East and West,

Trygve Lie established the United Nations in New York, recruited its staff and supervised the building of the United Nations Headquarters, the big glass skyscraper by the East River which you all know well. This would have been enough work for most people, but besides all that, he had to guide the new Organization in its first efforts to deal with all sorts of difficult problems—the Middle East, for example, and the Berlin problem, and Kashmir and Korea, to name only a few.

Trygve Lie was a fighter for peace, an active man of strong views and great courage. People often criticized him for saying and seeking to do too much. His own feeling was that if he was being criticized from all sides at once he must be somewhere near the right course. It would have been much easier, of course, for him to play safe and not try to do anything about the troubles of the world. But he did not think that that was good enough for the Secretary-General, however small his authority was and however much opposition he was sure to arouse.

The United Nations was set up to deal with trouble and to prevent war. It is not always successful, any more than a police force is always successful in preventing crime. But the world would be a much more dangerous and disorderly place without it, and we must all work to make it more successful in keeping the peace and improving the lives of the peoples of the world. It will be a long job, and neither I, nor even you, will see the end of it. But at least we have made a beginning. Trygve Lie was a pioneer in this effort, and he laid the foundations of the United Nations as we know it today.

As the third Secretary-General of the United Nations, I often have cause to be grateful to Trygve Lie for the fine work he did in setting up the world Organization. I can also understand, perhaps better than anyone, what a difficult and exhausting job he had to do as first Secretary-General, and how well he did it. His name will live on in the memory of people all over the world for his work in getting the United Nations going as a real force for peace.

THE SITUATION IN THE MIDDLE EAST

U THANT dealt with a number of questions in his first press conference of 1969, but the predominant subject was the continued tension in the Middle East and the frustration experienced by his special representative, Gunnar Jarring, In response to a question, he said he shared President Richard Nixon's fear that the next explosion in the Middle East could lead to a nuclear confrontation between the big powers. He strongly urged greater involvement of the four big powers in the search for peace in the Middle East, insisting, however, that they must act within the context of the United Nations. What he had in mind was that any agreement reached by the big four would be brought back to the Security Council for approval by that body. "Such a procedure," he said, "would facilitate the work of the Secretary-General's representative, Ambassador Jarring, and I am confident would contribute to a just and lasting peace in the area." Elaborating still further, Thant agreed that Israel and the Arab countries would have to be consulted and that some sort of pressures probably would be necessary to obtain their acquiescence in any agreement by the big powers. The Secretary-General was convinced that there could be no imposed solution. "Imposition," he said, "is a very debatable concept and a contentious word." Thant said Jarring would be available for consultations, if big power talks were held, but both he and Jarring agreed that the special representative should not participate directly in big-power meetings.

The already difficult Middle East situation was complicated by an attack on an El Al passenger plane in Zurich on February 18 by members of the Palestine Liberation Front. Thant himself became involved in an exchange of letters with Israeli Foreign Minister Abba Eban. Although the Secretary-General condemned the attack and took it up with the International Civil Aviation Organization and the International Air Transport Association, he angered Israeli authorities by turning down a request that he transmit two Israeli questions to the governments of Iraq, Jordan, Lebanon, Syria, and Egypt. The essence of the questions was whether these governments dissociated themselves from such acts of violence and whether they were prepared to take steps against the organizers and perpetrators of the attacks. Thant said he had explained to Israeli Ambassador Yosef Tekoah that he was considering steps to prevent a recurrence of airport attacks and that he believed such steps were likely to be more productive if taken on his own initiative. He suggested that Israel could bring the two questions to the attention of those concerned by sending a communication to the Security Council.

The Secretary-General, in the exchange of letters, took the opportunity to appeal for a peaceful settlement of the Middle East conflict on the basis of the Security Council resolution of November 22, 1967. This, he said, is the only sure way to end the acts of terrorism.

1. From Transcript of Press Conference

NEW YORK   JANUARY 28, 1969

THE SECRETARY-GENERAL: Mr. President and friends, since this is the first formal press conference of the year, I should like to start with a very sincere expression of good wishes to all of you for the coming year. I should also like to reiterate my congratulations to you, Mr. Littlejohns,[1] on your very well-deserved election as president of the United Nations Correspondents Association. I have known you for a good number of years and have come to respect you not only for your obvious competence as a journalist, but also for your objectivity and perception.

It has been a pleasure for me to have had the friendship and cooperation of all of you in the past years, and I look forward to still closer cooperation and friendship in the year ahead.

In accordance with tradition, I now give the floor to the president of the United Nations Correspondents Association, Mr. Littlejohns.

MR. LITTLEJOHNS: Thank you, Mr. Secretary-General, for your very kind words, which I am sure we in the United Nations Correspondents Association heartily reciprocate. We wish you and all the members of the Secretariat at all levels, from the third basement to the thirty-eighth floor, a very happy and peaceful New Year. This is the first opportunity we have had—although the year is now almost a month old—to express these sentiments to you, though we did have an opportunity of greeting you on your recent birthday.

SOURCE: *UN Monthly Chronicle*, Vol. VI, February 1969, pp. 32–42.

[1]Michael Littlejohns, Reuters.

May I begin the questioning with a question about the Middle East situation, which is currently preoccupying governments and peoples in many parts of the world. Will you give us your evaluation of the Middle East situation and the current prospects for a political settlement?

THE SECRETARY-GENERAL: My attitude toward the Middle East question and my approach to the problem are, I belive, well known.

First of all, I feel that the United Nations must be involved actively in the search for a just and lasting peace in the area. I feel very strongly that in order to enable the United Nations to contribute significantly toward the creation of justice and peace in the area, big-power cooperation is essential. Past experience has shown that, without big-power cooperation in this particular situation, the United Nations is not able to contribute significantly toward a just and peaceful solution of this problem. That explains why I have been advocating for some time that the big powers must be actively involved in the search for peace, either collectively or separately.

But what is very important from my point of view is that the actions of the big powers must be solely within the context of the United Nations. In other words, for the moment their activities must be confined solely within the framework of the Security Council resolution of November 22, 1967. Once there is a measure of agreement among the big powers on the fundamentals—after meetings, collectively or individually, as I said a moment ago—then the matter should be brought back to the Security Council. Such a procedure would facilitate the work of the Secretary-General's representative, Ambassador [Gunnar] Jarring, and I am confident would contribute to a just and lasting peace in the area. I do not see any other sensible and realistic alternative.

QUESTION: Would it be your idea that, under that procedure, the big powers would work out an arrangement for peace which it would be expected that the parties would accept; or would the parties themselves—the Israelis and the Arabs—be included in the discussions among the big powers on an arrangement?

THE SECRETARY-GENERAL: Of course, in the process of consultations and discussions among the big powers, the parties primarily concerned in the conflict must be involved at some stages. They cannot be left out of the picture; they must be put in the picture.

I must say in parenthesis that, so far as Security Council involvement is concerned, some sort of pressure is necessary. With regard to almost all the resolutions adopted by the Security Council in the past, in any crisis situations, some degree of pressure has been necessary—and I believe that some degree of pressure in all directions is necessary in the present case. . . .

QUESTION: What are your impressions—if you have formed any—of the way the new administration in Washington is moving into the whole area of war and peace, and particularly into such current areas as Vietnam, the Middle East, the question of the new weapons, and perhaps a détente with the Soviet Union?

THE SECRETARY-GENERAL: I do not think that in my position I should attempt to assess or evaluate the attitudes, policies, and activities of any Member state, particularly a big power, a permanent member of the Security Council.

But I must say that I watched President Nixon's press conference on television yesterday and I was impressed by his sincere desire to create conditions of peace and progress in the world. . . .

QUESTION: Mr. Secretary-General, when the Soviet Union invaded the land of Czechoslovakia, you spoke strongly urging an early withdrawal of the invading troops. Many months have passed since then and Czechoslovak protests have been manifested in demonstrations and recently in sad and unwarranted immolations. How would you express your feelings today about withdrawal?

THE SECRETARY-GENERAL: My attitude toward the developments in Czechoslovakia was made known in my public statements and they are on record. Let me say that I stand by every word of what I have said in the past regarding Czechoslovakia. But as you all know, the government of Czechoslovakia itself has requested the Security Council to drop the item of Czechoslovakia from the agenda of the Security Council. Of course the Council, as a master of its own procedures, has refused to comply with the request of the government of Czechoslovakia. The implication of that request by the government of Czechoslovakia is very plain. As far as I am concerned, the government of Czechoslovakia does not wish any principal organ of the United Nations to come out with any public pronouncements on the situation there. To the best of my knowledge, the government of Czechoslovakia has not brought to the attention of any principal organ of the United Nations the situation in that country, and so I do not want to say anything more than what I have said in the past. My attitude remains the same.

QUESTION: Mr. Secretary-General, have you had any recent encouragement to believe that a four-power meeting on the Middle East, such as you have suggested, is now likely?

THE SECRETARY-GENERAL: All my meetings with the permanent representatives of the United Nations are privileged, and I do not want to disclose any of those privileged discussions publicly, at least for the moment. But I very much hope that the four powers will work together, as I stated earlier, collectively or singly, toward a practical, realistic, and just settlement of the problem of the Middle East within the framework of the Security Council.

QUESTION: Will Ambassador Jarring be available here for such a meeting?

THE SECRETARY-GENERAL: I do not think it would be in the public interest for Ambassador Jarring to participate in such a meeting. Of course he will be available to all the big powers and to all the parties primarily involved in the conflict, as he has been in the past. But I do not think—and he agrees with me—that he should actively participate in the discussions which are contemplated among the big powers.

QUESTION: Mr. Secretary-General, what is your assessment of the various recent indications that China is about to reactivate her role in international affairs?

THE SECRETARY-GENERAL: It is very difficult to assess the situation in mainland China or to evaluate the public statements of the leaders in Peking. In the past two years or so, as you all know, the happenings in China and the statements by the Chinese leaders in Peking have been very baffling, to say the least. But it seems to me, from all available accounts, that China is opening up. Peking's intention to discuss seriously with Washington on the 20th of next month is one indication of the degree of self-assurance, if I may put it that way, on the part of the Chinese leaders.

I must say that, whatever our views may be regarding China, I feel very strongly that China is going to be a big power in the next decade. I remember having made a similar observation in the course of one of my press conferences about three years ago. I still maintain that view. China is definitely developing into a big power, and I believe she will be a big power in the next decade—perhaps even a superpower. So this fact should be borne in mind by all those governments that are revising and reformulating their policies on a long-term basis with a view to creating conditions for peace and progress in the world.

QUESTION: In this context, Mr. Secretary-General, will you welcome initiatives which are being attributed to the Italian and Canadian governments to establish some relations with Peking as a positive step toward a more general inclusion of China in the family of nations?

THE SECRETARY-GENERAL: I do not want to comment directly on the actions of Member states, but my views on the involvement of China in the international community are well known. And, of course, my private views have been expressed from time to time whenever I had to speak of China's involvement in the international community. I remember having told you in one of the press conferences that there are two U Thants: U Thant as a private individual and U Thant as the Secretary-General of the United Nations. Sometimes, I cannot say things which I want to say because of my position. But I believe very strongly in the concept of contact and communication and discussion, and the United Nations must really be universal in the true conception as envisaged in the Charter. So my private view is that the decision of some Member states to open up to China or of China to open up to the international community should be welcomed.

QUESTION: Mr. Secretary-General, when you speak of big-power initiative on the Middle East, are you speaking exclusively of the four powers or do you include talks between the Soviet Union and the United States?

THE SECRETARY-GENERAL: No, my public statements to that effect always involve four powers. . . .

QUESTION: At your last press conference, which was before the Assembly, you expressed some pessimism about the talks in Paris, and since then we have had a cessation of the bombing and now the beginning of the substantive talks. Would you care to revise your earlier feelings of pessimism, or do you still feel we are a long way from the end of the tunnel?

THE SECRETARY-GENERAL: Since then, some encouraging developments have taken place, as you know, Out of my three proposals, two points have been met, at least technically. From all available accounts, there is now a cessation of the bombing of North Vietnam, and, second, discussions have started involving all the parties involved in the fighting. So, I must say that the prospects for peace in Vietnam today are brighter than at any time in the past. Of course, it is going to be a long and difficult process, but I am now more hopeful of prospects for peace than in the past. . . .

QUESTION: You spoke earlier today of Security Council pressures on the parties in the Arab-Israel dispute following an agreement among the four powers. But Israel has frequently said in the Council that it cannot get justice in that organ. Why do you think Israel will decide that Security Council pressures following a four-power meeting will be less inimical to it?

THE SECRETARY-GENERAL: This involves a certain basic principle regarding our attitude to the United Nations. Like all human organizations, like a club or a society or an association, the United Nations has certain rules and regulations to guide its actions and to conduct business. I think for an orderly and civilized functioning of this Organization it is necessary, and, in my view it is even essential, that all Members abide by the rules. In other words, all Members give particular attention to the decisions and resolutions of the principal deliberative organs of the United Nations. To be frank, in my view, if only all the resolutions and decisions of the principal deliberative organs of the United Nations were heeded by the parties primarily concerned in the area, there would be no Middle Eastern problem today. That is my firm conviction. So what is the United Nations here for? The United Nations is here to function and to operate and to act in crisis situations. Any of us who wants to see the United Nations develop into a really effective instrument for peace, a really effective instrument for the creation of conditions for peace, must also favor the concept I have outlined earlier: that this international Organization is guided by certain rules and regulations, and that these rules and regulations require Member states to comply with the decisions and resolutions of the deliberative organs of this Organization.

In the past twenty-one years, the deliberative organs of the United Nations have adopted numerous resolutions regarding the situation in the Middle East, the crisis in the Middle East, wars in the Middle East, but the plain fact is that most of those resolutions went unheeded. My point is that, as in all international organizations, if only the members in a club or a society or an association were to comply with the decisions of that organization, through the executive committee, for instance, then that would result in the orderly and smooth functioning of that particular organization. I would apply the same analogy to the United Nations. The United Nations is here precisely to perform the functions envisaged in the Charter vis-à-vis the crisis situation in the Middle East. I do not see any alternative way of dealing with this crisis situation outside the United Nations. So my point is that, if only the parties primarily concerned in the conflict were to pay heed to the previous resolutions of the deliberative organs of the United Nations, then I am confident there would have been peace in the area long ago.

QUESTION: Do you share the fear of President Nixon that the Middle East is in such a state at the moment that the next explosion could lead to a nuclear confrontation between the big powers?

THE SECRETARY-GENERAL: I must say that I agree with the President's assessment on this question.

QUESTION: Are you suggesting that the big four initially and afterward the Security Council should work out the details and fill up the ambiguities in the November 22 resolution and ensure that it is implemented?

THE SECRETARY-GENERAL: I do not want to suggest to or advise the big four how they should proceed. I think it should be left to them to define the procedures and modalities of formulating a common attitude toward this problem within the framework of the United Nations. . . .

QUESTION: Contrary to some predictions, the Nigerian civil war has not drawn to an early conclusion. Can you give us your assessment of the present state of affairs in the region from both the political and the humanitarian points of view?

THE SECRETARY-GENERAL: I believe that I have made my attitude and position on the civil conflict in Nigeria well known. I am guided in may attitude to this problem primarily by the decisions of the Organization of African Unity. You will recall that the heads of state and government of African states met in Kinshasa in September 1967. I attended that summit conference. Then, in September 1968, the heads of state and government of African states attended the summit conference in Algiers. I also attended that conference. It is useful to recall the decisions of those African heads of state.

It was made very plain by the heads of African states that the problem in Nigeria is an internal affair. At both summit conferences, the Organization of African Unity requested all the Members of the United Nations and all the members of the OAU to refrain from any action likely to impede the peace, unity, and territorial integrity of Nigeria. To me that is a very important guideline. If the heads of African states have asked all the Members of the United Nations and all the members of the Organization of African Unity to refrain from any action likely to endanger the peace, unity, and territorial integrity of Nigeria, I do not see how a Member state, or for that matter the Secretary-General, can be actively involved.

That is only one aspect of the problem. Another aspect is, of course, the humanitarian problem. As you all know, I have been engaged in facilitating the shipment of relief commodities to the civilian victims of the conflict in Nigeria. The United Nations Children's Fund and the World Food Programme have been and continue to be very actively engaged in this great humanitarian task. To the best of my knowledge, the Federal Military Government in Lagos has not impeded the flow of relief goods to the civilian victims of the war. To the best of my knowledge, the Federal Miliary Government in Lagos is willing to cooperate with the international community and relief agencies in order to transship the necessary supplies and foodstuffs to the afflicted people in the area.

Thus, my assessment of the problem is that impediments have not come from Lagos. That is my conclusion, based on the conclusion of my special representative, Mr. Gussing, who has been there for some time, as you all know.

Another important principle from the United Nations point of view, and for that matter from my point of view, is that the United Nations as such cannot endorse or support any action or any movement for the secession of a particular part of a Member state. You will recall that the United Nations spent over $500 million and many precious lives in the Congo to perform certain functions. As things developed the United Nations was instrumental in preventing the threatened secession of Katanga from the Congo. That is the attitude—and I think the right attitude—for the United Nations to take.

As you know, there are secessionist movements in many parts of the world. I would say that more than half of the Member states of the United Nations are beset with that problem. Of course, it is a purely internal problem. If the United Nations were to give endorsement to the principle of secession, there would be no end to the problems besetting many Member states.

That was, therefore, one primary consideration in the minds of the heads of state of Africa when they adopted the two resolutions to which I referred earlier. As far as the humanitarian aspects are concerned, as I said, the United Nations as such and the Secretary-General as such will do all they can, in their power, to alleviate the suffering of the people who are the civilian victims of the conflict.

QUESTION: Archbishop [Helder] Camara of Brazil has asked for an end to the isolation and excommunication of Cuba. Archbishop Camara made that suggestion during a meeting here in New York of the Conference of the Catholic Inter-American Co-operation Programme. He said specifically that Cuba must be integrated into our community with due respect for its political options and the acceptance of its autonomy as a sovereign nation. Would you care to comment on that statement?

THE SECRETARY-GENERAL: Generally speaking, my attitude is well known. I am always for the termination of the isolation or segregation of any member of the international community. I am always for the revival of contacts and communications and exposure, as I have said. So I must say that I agree with the observations of the Archbishop on this point.

QUESTION: Sir, you talked a moment ago about the importance of abiding by the rules of the United Nations. Were you disturbed by some of the moves during the recent session of the General Assembly which were of rather doubtful legality? I have in mind the effort, even though it was unsuccessful, to expel South Africa from the United Nations Conference on Trade and Development (UNCTAD).

THE SECRETARY-GENERAL: I do not think that the Secretary-General should attempt to challenge the decisions of a principal deliberative organ. Of course, from time to time the decisions of the deliberative organs make some of the Member states unhappy, to say the least, and from time to time the decisions of the principal deliberative organs of the United Nations even offend some Member states. But, from the point of view of the Secretary-General, if my understanding of my functions is correct, I have to stand by every resolution or decision of any principal deliberative organ of the United Nations.

QUESTION: How do you envisage a piece of paper that might come from big-four consultations, an imposed peace endorsed by the Security Council or a peace freely arrived at by the parties concerned?

THE SECRETARY-GENERAL: I am of the opinion that any imposition on any area, on any country, is likely to generate further problems in the years to come. So I would not use the word "imposition" in the context of big-power action or prospective Security Council action. "Imposition" is a very debatable conception and a contentious word. You will recall that many Member states have even accused the United Nations of having imposed the State of Israel on the Middle East against the wishes of many people in the area. So I do not want to enter into a discussion on this conception of imposition. But, in my view, some sort of moral pressure by the big powers in all directions, through the machinery of the Security Council, and of course as far as possible by promoting agreement by the powers particularly involved would be very desirable. I would prefer to use the word "pressure" and not "imposition."

QUESTION: Mr. Secretary-General, in your earlier comments you spoke about the parties concerned. Did you have in mind the people of Palestine and their liberation movements?

THE SECRETARY-GENERAL: Well, there is a very wide recognition of the fact that the question of the Palestine refugees is the crux of the problem. I believe that was the essence of some of the resolutions of the principal deliberative organs also. Without trying to tackle this very tragic problem in right earnest, I am afraid the move toward a just and peaceful settlement will be very slow. Of course the situation in the Middle East cannot remain static forever. Time is not on the side of peace. In all crisis situations like this, they either deteriorate or improve. To improve the situation, of course, it is very urgent for the Security Council, and particularly the big powers, to be actively involved in the search for a settlement.

---

2. Letter to the Foreign Minister of Israel

NEW YORK   FEBRUARY 26, 1969

I HAVE THE HONOR to acknowledge receipt of your letter to me of February 20, 1969, relating to the attack upon an El Al aircraft at Zurich on February 18. In pursuance of your request your letter was transmitted to all Members of the United Nations in the customary form of a *note verbale*. In response to a subsequent request by the permanent representative of Israel to the United Nations it has also been circulated as an official document of the General Assembly and the Security Council.

You have inquired as to what constructive international action is envisaged to prevent such acts of violence against international civil

SOURCE: Security Council Official Records, Twenty-fourth Year, Supplement for January, February and March 1969, document S/9030.

aviation in the future. Even before your letter was received I was in contact with the International Civil Aviation Organization (ICAO) and the International Air Transport Association, regarding the Zurich incident, and I have kept in close touch with ICAO since. I am also consulting with certain Members of the United Nations specially concerned, with a view to finding means to prevent such acts of violence.

There is no question that every effort should be made to put an end to attacks on civilian carriers which endanger innocent passengers and jeopardize international travel, from whatever quarter they may come. As I said through my spokesman on February 18, 1969, after the Zurich incident:

Such attacks, involving as they do a great risk to innocent persons and the disruption of an important branch of international communication, are a matter of urgent concern to all governments and peoples. If the hitherto peaceful world of civil aviation is to be saved from chaos and anarchy, governments and peoples, regardless of their political views, must condemn acts of this kind and take all possible measures to prevent them.

In this connection, improved methods of international police cooperation and regulations of a national as well as an international character may contribute toward the prevention of those acts of terrorism and violence. However, I believe that the only sure way to bring an end to terrorist acts would be some substantial movement toward a peaceful settlement of the major issues underlying the Middle East conflict. In the circumstances, I hope you will agree that, although there may be some scope for positive action by the Secretary-General in a matter of this kind, the most natural and proper recourse, and that which should hold the best promise for constructive international action, is clearly the Security Council.

It is my firm conviction that the Security Council resolution of November 22, 1967, offers the only practical basis for the promotion of a just and lasting peace in the area. I also remain convinced that progress toward this goal can be made through the dedicated efforts of Ambassador Jarring to assist and promote agreement between the parties with the active cooperation especially of the major powers. An essential first step toward this end, in my view, would be a declared readiness by the parties to implement the Security Council resolution of November 22, 1967.

In this connection let me recall what I have stated on another occasion, that "if only all the resolutions and decisions of the principal deliberative organs of the United Nations were heeded by the parties primarily concerned in the area, there would be no Middle East problem today.''

In spite of the apparent lack of progress in the search for a just and lasting peace in the Middle East, my abiding faith in the United Nations as the instrument for obtaining ultimate success remains unshaken. Indeed I can see no practical alternative to the active continuation of this search.

Since your letter under reference has been circulated as an official document of the General Assembly and the Security Council I have arranged that this letter be circulated similarly. I am also arranging for my spokesman's statement of February 18, to which you have referred in your letter, to be circulated as a document of the General Assembly and the Security Council.

---

3. *Letter to the Foreign Minister of Israel*

NEW YORK   MARCH 10, 1969

I HAVE THE HONOR to acknowledge receipt of your letter of March 5, 1969, in reply to my letter of February 26, 1969, concerning the attack on an E1 A1 aircraft on February 18, 1969, at Zurich. One point in your letter requires some clarification, and I feel that the episode to which it refers should be described in more detail, since no record of it was made public at the time.

You refer to the request conveyed to me through the permanent representative of Israel to the United Nations to put two questions to certain Arab governments and you state that you regret that these questions were not conveyed. Ambassador Tekoah transmitted to me on February 19, by an informal *aide-mémoire,* the request of the government of Israel that two questions should be transmitted through the good offices of the Secretary-General to the governments of Iraq, Jordan,

SOURCE: Security Council Official Records, Twenty-fourth Year, Supplement for January, February and March 1969, document S/9064.

Lebanon, Syria, and the United Arab Republic, The questions were as follows:

1. The Government of Israel desires to be advised whether the Secretary-General can assume that the above governments, Members of the United Nations and signatories to the international conventions on aviation, firmly dissociate themselves from the acts of violence of the kind that have been committed at airports of countries that are not involved in the Middle East conflict.

2. The Palestine Liberation Front has announced its responsibility for the acts committed in Rome, Athens, and Zurich. It is known that this organization maintains contact with the above-mentioned governments and enjoys their material and moral support. The government of Israel desires to know whether these governments are prepared to take steps against the organizers and perpetrators of the acts referred to above, so as to ensure the cessation of such acts.

I gave my reaction to this request to Ambassador Tekoah at the same meeting on February 19, and this reaction was embodied in an informal *aide-mémoire* which I gave to Ambassador Tekoah on February 20. The text of that *aide-mémoire* was as follows:

The Secretary-General has already expressed his deep concern over the Zurich incident and previous incidents of a similar nature. He is giving serious and urgent consideration to the matter and to the steps that may be effective in helping to prevent a recurrence of such incidents in the future. He believes that such steps are more likely to be productive if taken on his own initiative.

Recourse to the good offices of the Secretary-General is available to all Member governments, and the Secretary-General will be glad to respond to such a request whenever he feels, in his discretion and judgment, that such action would be helpful. In general, it would not be helpful if the Secretary-General were to transmit questions or messages of a political or controversial nature from one government to another unless the parties concerned have previously agreed to such a procedure.

Therefore, the Secretary-General considers that it would not be helpful if he were to act on the request of the government of Israel that he should transmit certain questions to Arab governments. The Secretary-General has suggested, however, that a communication from the government of Israel to the Security Council might be an appropriate method of bringing these questions to the attention of those concerned.

You will understand, I am sure, my desire to have the full background of this matter on record.

I note your view that the need is "to break out of the semantic and declaratory phase," but I must reiterate my conviction that an essential first step toward a just and lasting peace in the area would be a declared readiness by the parties to implement the Security Council resolution of November 22, 1967. I certainly would not regard such a declaration as a semantic exercise.

Since your letter under reference has been circulated as a document of the General Assembly and the Security Council, I have arranged that this letter be circulated similarly.

Letter to the Emperor of Ethiopia
Regarding the Situation in Equatorial Guinea

NEW YORK   MARCH 10, 1969

IN FEBRUARY 1969 U Thant received a number of messages from Macias Nquema, President of Equitorial Guinea, a former Spanish territory that had achieved independence in 1968. The President charged that Spain had violated the sovereignty of his country by deploying armed forces on its territory and he required that a United Nations peace force be dispatched to the area.

Spain acknowledged that it had sent a limited number of police units to Equatorial Guinea to guarantee the safety of Spaniards there and asked the Secretary-General to designate one or more personal representatives to make an on-the-spot inquiry and help resolve the dispute. Equitorial Guinea agreed and the Secretary-General appointed a senior member of the United Nations Secretariat, Marcial Tamayo, who left New York on March 10 with a small staff. By April 5, through the efforts of Tamayo, agreement had been reached and the last of the Spanish forces had been withdrawn along with all Spanish civilians who wanted to leave.

Your Imperial Majesty,

I am most grateful to you for the message which you addressed to me on March 8, 1969, concerning the situation in the Republic of Equatorial Guinea.

As Your Imperial Majesty is no doubt aware, the President of Equatorial Guinea addressed to me several cables, which I brought to the attention of the Security Council, requesting the dispatch of a United Nations peace force to his country. In my replies to President Macias Nguema, I underlined that the dispatch of a peace force would require authorization by the Security Council, which had to be convened for the purpose, but I nevertheless offered to President Macias Nguema the

SOURCE: UN Press Release SG/SM/1073.

sending of a representative to assist Equatorial Guinea in the solution of its differences with Spain. For this purpose, I designated as my representative Mr. Marcial Tamayo, a senior official of the Organization who, accompanied by a small staff, left New York on March 8 and was scheduled to arrive this morning in Santa Isabel.

It is my earnest hope that the presence of Mr. Tamayo will help the parties in settling their difficulties peacefully and will also assist in lessening the tension in Equatorial Guinea. I am much heartened to know of Your Imperial Majesty's willingness to help in any way possible to bring about such peaceful settlement, and I shall not fail to communicate with Your Imperial Majesty regarding developments in Equatorial Guinea.

I wish Your Imperial Majesty to know that I am keeping the Organization of African Unity informed concerning the United Nations action in Equatorial Guinea.

DISARMAMENT

IN THE DISARMAMENT field the most spectacular development in 1968 had been the conclusion of the Treaty on the Non-proliferation of Nuclear Weapons, but another event of importance took place in July of that year. This was the agreement between the United States and the USSR to open bilateral discussions on the limitation of strategic arms, later to become known as SALT. In the Introduction to his 1968 annual report, U Thant touched briefly on this agreement, describing it as "an encouraging step forward." It was generally recognized, however, that the proposed discussions could not begin immediately because of the United States presidential election coming up in November. President Johnson was not a candidate for re-election and much depended upon the views of his successor. Quite apart from this obvious reason for delay, the whole question of limiting the delivery systems of offensive strategic nuclear weapons and systems of defense against ballistic missiles was a highly technical and complicated one. Thant warned that it would not be realistic to underestimate these difficulties. Foreseeing the possibility of protracted discussions, he suggested a freeze on the testing and development of new nuclear weapons systems while the talks were going on.

Richard M. Nixon was elected president of the United States in November, but was not to take office until January. As the General Assembly approached the end of its twenty-third session, nothing had been done to implement the July agreement. The Assembly, however, recognized the importance of getting the talks started without undue delay. In its resolution 2456D (XXIII) of December 20, 1968, it urged the two superpowers to enter into the agreed discussions "at an early date." Thant added his own appeal in a message to the Eighteen-Nation Committee on Disarmament on March 18, 1969. Noting the Assembly resolution, he said this was a recognition "that it was in the world's interest to encourage bilateral negotiations on this question in order to prevent the dangers and enormous expense of a new spiral in the nuclear missile race." Thant was gratified by a number of developments during the next few weeks, especially statements from Chairman Aleksei Kosygin and President Richard Nixon stressing the importance of reaching agreement on the limitation of strategic arms. Apparently the only thing delaying the opening of the talks was the time needed by the Nixon administration to make the necessary preparations. On April 7, 1969, Secretary of State William Rogers said " . . . there is nothing that stands in the way and they [the discussions] can go forward very soon. We are in the process of preparing for them now and we expect they will begin in the late spring or early summer."

1. From Message to the Eighteen-Nation Committee on Disarmament

NEW YORK   MARCH 18, 1969

. . . THE COMMITTEE is certainly aware that its task is becoming increasingly urgent in view of new developments in the arms race. As I have pointed out on many recent occasions, in spite of the arms control achievements in the last few years, there has been no reversal or even slowing down of the nuclear arms race. On the contrary, global expenditures for military purposes have reached new record-high levels. It is estimated that since 1962, when I submitted the *Report on the Economic and Social Consequences of Disarmament,* the yearly world military outlay has increased from about $120 billion to more than $180 billion. The rate of increase in military expenditures in recent years has been even more rapid than the growth of world gross national product. Moreover, as everyone knows, if plans currently under discussion for the development of new offensive and defensive weapon systems should be implemented, they could lead to a massive new escalation both in military expenditures and nuclear weaponry.

I would therefore wish to draw attention to resolution 2456 D (XXIII), one of the four resolutions adopted by the General Assembly in connection with its review of the results of the Conference of Non-Nuclear-Weapon States. By that resolution, which was adopted with 108 affirmative votes, including those of all the participants in the work of the Eighteen-Nation Committee, the General Assembly urged the governments of the Soviet Union and the United States to enter at an early data into the projected bilateral discussions on the limitation of offensive strategic nuclear-weapon delivery systems and systems of defense against ballistic missiles. The General Assembly thus recognized that it was in the world's interest to encourage bilateral negotiations on this question in order to prevent the dangers and enormous expense of a new

SOURCE: UN Press Release SG/SM/1077.

spiral in the nuclear missile race. It is my fervent hope that it will be possible for the two great powers to begin their talks at an early date. . . .

---

2. *From Transcript of Remarks to Non-Government Organizations*

NEW YORK   MAY 27, 1969

YOU ALL KNOW that in spite of repeated resolutions and decisions of the deliberative organs of the United Nations on the need to disarm, or, more realistically, on the need to reduce armaments, the arms race has been going on at a terrific speed. Now just think for a moment of the super-sophisticated means of mass destruction manufactured and deployed by both superpowers, the United States and the Soviet Union. It is common knowledge that both the United States and the Soviet Union have now the means to eliminate each other as viable societies, because of the intercontinental ballistic missiles, which cannot be destroyed in a first strike. Even if the United States or the Soviet Union strikes first, the ICBMs, which cannot be destroyed in the first strike, will be—or at least some of them will be—still in operation. It is common knowledge that this is the most serious problem facing mankind today.

Apart from these facts, it is also common knowledge that both the United States and the Soviet Union are in effect defenseless, as far as the population and industry are concerned. As a matter of fact, the insecurity of these two superpowers is at present at a new high and still growing. Then there are, of course, other factors, financial and human. Just think of the tremendous sacrifices that both the United States and the Soviet Union would have to make in order to manufacture and deploy these weapons of mass destruction, at a tremendous cost in money, skilled

SOURCE: UN Press Release SG/SM/1116.

manpower, and resources. This is a most serious problem. I would classify it as the problem of the seventies.

You will recall that the General Assembly at its last session adopted a very important resolution, urging "the governments of the Union of Soviet Socialist Republics and the United States of America to enter, at an early date, into bilateral discussions on the limitation of offensive strategic nuclear weapons delivery systems and systems of defense against ballistic missiles." A similar appeal to the governments of the United States and the Soviet Union was also contained in the Final Document of the Conference of Non-Nuclear-Weapon States in Geneva.

As many of you are aware, in January this year, I transmitted to the governments of all states Members of the United Nations and members of specialized agencies and of the International Atomic Energy Agency the text of the aforementioned resolution, as well as the declaration of the Conference of Non-Nuclear-Weapon States. I also transmitted a copy of the Final Document of the Conference of Non-Nuclear-Weapon States.

In February this year, I sent a letter to the Co-Chairmen of the Conference of the Eighteen-Nation Committee on Disarmament in Geneva, transmitting, *inter alia,* the aforementioned resolutions.

In my message sent in March this year to the Conference of the Eighteen-Nation Committee on Disarmament in Geneva, I again drew the attention of the participants to that resolution. It was pointed out in that message that the General Assembly, by adopting that resolution, thus recognized that it was in the world's interest to encourage bilateral negotiations on this question, in order to prevent the dangers and enormous expense of a new spiral in the nuclear missile race.

I expressed my fervent hope that it would be possible "for the two great powers to begin their talks at an early date." Then some heartening developments took place, as all of you are aware.

On March 18, 1969, in his message to the Eighteen-Nation Committee on Disarmament, the Chairman of the Council of Ministers of the Soviet Union, Mr. Kosygin, pointed out that solutions should be found "to the vitally important problems of cessation of manufacture of nuclear weapons, the reduction and destruction of their stockpiles, the limitation and subsequent reduction of means of delivery of strategic weapons."

Then, on March 15, 1969, in the letter of instructions which was given by the President of the United States, Mr. Nixon, to Ambassador Gerard C. Smith, who as you all know is the representative of the United States in the Disarmament Committee in Geneva, it was pointed out that "regarding the question of talks between the United States and the Soviet Union on the limitation of strategic arms, the United States hoped that the international political situation will evolve in a way which will permit such talks to begin in the near future."

Then, the representative of the United States in the Disarmament Committee, referring to this subject, indicated that "the passage of some time was needed for the new administration to make the necessary preparations" for such talks, and that "the timing should be favorable in a political sense."

In his testimony before the Senate Foreign Relations Committee on March 27, 1969, the Secretary of State, Mr. William Rogers, referring to the talks with the Soviet Union on limiting strategic armaments, stated: "Preparations for possible talks with the Soviet Union on limiting strategic armaments are also under way. The President's consultations with our allies on this subject during our European trip found them very favorable to the idea. We hope such talks can begin within the next few months."

Then, during the news conference on April 7, 1969, the Secretary of State, Mr. William Rogers, answering the question whether there is anything that stands in the way of strategic arms limitation talks with the Soviet Union, answered that " . . . there is nothing that stands in the way and they can go forward very soon. We are in the process of preparing for them now and we expect they will begin in the late spring or early summer."

These, ladies and gentlemen, are some encouraging trends in line with the General Assembly resolution adopted last year. And with this note of guarded optimism, may I extend to all of you once again my very sincere thanks and I wish you all a very successful conference.

From Transcript of Press Conference at Luncheon of the United Nations Correspondents Association

NEW YORK   APRIL 17, 1969

IMPORTANT DEVELOPMENTS were taking place in the spring of 1969 on a number of major problems, including the Middle East, Nigeria, and Vietnam. At his press conference, following the April 17 luncheon of the United Nations Correspondents Association, U Thant had something to say on all these questions and others.

The Middle East peace efforts of Thant's special representative, Gunnar Jarring, had virtually ground to a halt by April 3, 1969, when the representatives of France, the United States, the United Kingdom, and the USSR began their private meetings at United Nations Headquarters to seek a way out of the stalemate. It was public knowledge that Jarring was discouraged and felt that continuation of his mission would be futile unless his efforts got some sort of boost, perhaps through big four pressure on the Middle East countries. His return to Moscow early in April, to resume his duties as Swedish ambassador, gave rise to rumors that he had quit his Middle East mission or was about to quit. Thant told the April 17 luncheon that Jarring's return to Moscow was a routine visit to take care of his embassy duties, but he did acknowledge that Jarring was not prepared to go on indefinitely with the Middle East assignment unless his efforts produced some progress. "I do not believe Ambassador Jarring would like to repeat this more or less futile exercise for the next one and a half years," he said.

Thant welcomed the entry of the big four into the Middle East peace efforts. In fact, he had been urging a more active participation by the big powers for some time. He said: "Since the stated objective of the four permanent members of the Security Council is to help Ambassador Jarring in the performance of his functions on the basis of the Security Council resolution of November 1967, I welcome this and I have begun to pin my very great hopes on the success of their discussions and deliberations, and I believe that this viewpoint is shared by the majority of the delegates here."

As the Nigerian civil-war continued into 1969, Thant was acutely sensitive to the criticism directed at the United Nations for alleged inaction, but he was more

SOURCE: *UN Monthly Chronicle,* Vol. VI, May 1969, pp. 73–83.

than ever convinced that the conflict was an internal affair and was not within the competence of the United Nations. In a press conference on January 28, he said: "If the heads of African states have asked all the Members of the United Nations and all the members of the Organization of African Unity to refrain from any action likely to endanger the peace, unity, and territorial integrity of Nigeria, I do not see how a Member state, or for that matter the Secretary-General, can be actively involved." In the same press conference, the Secretary-General raised another question which was troubling many Member states—the general question of secession. He pointed out that there were secessionist movements in many parts of the world, possibly in as many as half the countries in the United Nations. "If the United Nations were to give endorsement to the principle of secession," he said, "there would be no end to the problems besetting many Member states."

One of the major criticisms of the world community, including the United Nations, was that it did not find a way to alleviate the starvation and suffering of innocent women and children caught up in the civil war. Despite all the efforts of the United Nations Children's Fund (UNICEF) and the World Food Programme, acting through the International Committee of the Red Cross, the world was flooded with pictures of emaciated children. Although much of the public sympathy was with Biafra, Thant spoke out frankly in blaming the Biafran leaders for the lack of food in the areas controlled by the Biafrans. In his January 28 press conference, he asserted that the Federal Military Government was not responsible for the starvation conditions in Biafra, but on the contrary had been willing to cooperate fully with relief agencies. "My assessment of the problem," he said, "is that impediments have not come from Lagos," He went further by stating that his conclusions were based on the assessments of his special representative, who had examined the situation on the scene.

Despite his repeated explanatory statements, criticism continued to mount. At the April 17 press conference, a correspondent called his attention to the criticism and asked the Secretary-General why he could not, in view of the failure of the Organization of African Unity (OAU) to find a solution, call a meeting of the Security Council to deal with the problem. Thant replied that he was aware of the criticism but that the majority of the Member states as well as the OAU held that the Nigerian conflict was an internal matter. He added that he did not believe the question would be inscribed on the agenda of the Security Council or the General Assembly even if the Secretary-General or any Member state requested such action. "From a realistic point of view," he said, "any such attempt would not succeed because of the knowledge that the Organization of African Unity is against such a course. . . . " Thant noted that he was keeping in close touch with the six-nation committee appointed by the OAU to seek peace in Nigeria and was doing all he could in the humanitarian field, but beyond that, he said, "I do not see any early prospect of a deeper involvement by the United Nations and its family of agencies."

When Thant met correspondents on January 28 in his first press conference of 1969, Soviet military forces still had not withdrawn from Czechoslovakia. The question of the Soviet intervention still remained on the list of items which the

Security Council had considered but had not formally dropped. Because of the opposition of the Czechoslovak government, which had replaced the Dubček régime, the Council had not discussed the problem since August 24, 1968. No move had been made to take it up at the twenty-third session of the General Assembly. Thant had vigorously condemned the Soviet intervention when it took place and had urged the immediate withdrawal of the invading troops. At the January 28 press conference, Thant made it clear that he still stood by his statement of the previous August, but was not prepared to pursue the matter in view of the attitude of the Czechoslovak government. "As far as I am concerned." he said, "the government of Czechoslovakia does not wish any principal organ of the United Nations to come out with any public pronouncements on the situation there. To the best of my knowledge, the government of Czechoslovakia has not brought to the attention of any principal organ of the United Nations the situation in that country, and so I do not want to say anything more than what I have said in the past. My attitude remains the same." The question was raised again at the April 17 luncheon. Once more he declined comment. "I said in one of the previous press conferences," he replied, "that I stood by every word I had said in the past, and I do not think that there is any new basis now for me to add anything more to what I have said."

. . .

QUESTION: Mr. Secretary-General, the Vietnam war, the *Pueblo* and the latest United States spy aircraft incidents, the debates relating to the non-proliferation treaty here, and a host of other troubles around the world, all seem to indicate that in this the sixties, the small and medium powers are no longer prepared to be cowed by the superior might of the big powers or to accept their tutelage, individual or collective. Since the United Nations was founded in 1945 on the basis of great-power tutelage, what is the future outlook?

THE SECRETARY-GENERAL: Well, I do not necessarily agree with the assumptions in this question. To my way of thinking, for the future of humanity, the future of peace and progress, what is of the utmost importance to all of us is the growth of the United Nations and the strengthening of the United Nations as a really effective instrument for peace. I think this is basic to all issues. Those of us who believe in the concept that the United Nations must develop into a really effective instrument for peace and progress must exert our utmost to see that it functions in the manner in which it was designed to function by the founding fathers twenty-three years ago.

Now, speaking of the big powers, I must say that the permanent members of the Security Council have a special responsibility because of their special status in the Security Council under the Charter. So to enable this world Organization to function effectively, I am convinced, the active cooperation and participation of the permanent members of the Security Council is not only necessary, but essential. Without their cooperation and participation I am afraid that the United Nations will not function in the way it was meant to function and the international scene will be as messy as ever.

I think that to contribute toward the improvement of the international situation, the first prerequisite is the strengthening of the United Nations as an instrument for peace and progress.

QUESTION: Mr. Secretary-General, are there reasons to believe—I would like to add, to hope—that your idea of developing a "third moral force" has been making progress in the world community since you first suggested it?

THE SECRETARY-GENERAL: I am afraid I have to answer in the negative. Among the third world, as all of you are aware, there have cropped up problems involving one another, not only in the political field but also in the economic and social fields, The problems faced by the members of the third world have multiplied, if I may say so, in the last decade. If we assess the international situation in the context of the performance of the third world in 1955 and 1965, I must say that the picture is one of deterioration insofar as the cohesiveness of the third world is concerned.

I have been thinking primarily of the situation during the time of the Bandung Conference and the situation which was prevalent three or four years ago. But, of course, it is up to the members of the third world, the leaders of the third world, statesmen, who must have vision and imagination, to get together, to strive together to build a better world—within the context of the United Nations. That is why I believe very strongly that the United Nations must be universal in character and concept. This is one of the prerequisites not only for the development of the United Nations as an instrument for peace, but also for the proper functioning of the third world within the context of the United Nations system.

QUESTION: Do you have any comment on the shooting down of the American plane by North Korean fighters?

Do you see a way in which incidents such as the shooting down of a United States military plane off the coast of North Korea can be avoided by two states, one of which is not a Member of the United Nations?

THE SECRETARY-GENERAL: Regarding this particular incident, the information available is very fragmentary. So I do not think it would be appropriate on my part to assess the incident on an inadequate basis. By the way, the *New York Times,* in its editorial yesterday, I believe, had a wise observation on this particular subject. If I remember correctly, it said that the urgent need of today is to prevent the mood of national hysteria. I am also encouraged by the wise and cautious statement made by the Secretary of State, Mr. Rogers, in Washington yesterday.

As far as the second part of the question is concerned, I do not believe, personally, that the matter can be usefully brought to the United Nations. As you, Mr. President [President of UNCA], have rightly pointed out, as Mr. MacVane[1] has stated in his question, one of the principal parties involved is not a Member of the United Nations.

QUESTION: In the light of recent developments in the Middle East crisis, would you kindly give us you own assessment of the chances of establishing a just peace?

THE SECRETARY-GENERAL: Regarding the situation in the Middle East, I believe my views are well known. To clarify my position, I would say, first of all, that the United Nations must be actively involved in the search for a solution. I feel very strongly that it is the responsibility of the international community to try to contribute toward the establishment of a just and lasting peace in the area, and to enable the United Nations to perform this function effectively, as I said a moment ago, the active involvement and participation of the permanent members of the Security Council is essential. Without this involvement and participation, I do not see how we can have any progress in the direction of peace and justice.

As you all know, the Secretary-General's representative, Ambassador Jarring, has been involved in the search for peace, within the framework of the Security Council resolution of November 22, 1967, for the last one and a half years, with patience, tact, and wisdom. But so far, if I may say so, there has been no perceptible progress in our common search for peace. I do not believe that Ambassador Jarring would like to repeat this more or less futile exercise for the next one and a half years or so. So, that is why I believe that the permanent members of the Security Council must be more actively involved in our joint search for peace. Since the stated objective of the four permanent members of the Security Council is to help Ambassador Jarring in the performance of his functions on the basis of the Security Council resolution of November

[1]John McVane, American Broadcasting Company.

1967, I welcome this and I have begun to pin my very great hopes on the success of their discussions and deliberations, and I believe that this viewpoint is shared by the majority of the delegates here.

QUESTION: There appears to be some difference of opinion about the state of acceptance of the Security Council's resolution of November 22, 1967. Could you tell us which countries, parties to the Middle East dispute, have in your judgment accepted the resolution, and which have rejected it?

Can you tell us if, in your view, Israel has accepted the resolution? A flat yes or no would suffice.

THE SECRETARY-GENERAL: It is very difficult, of course, for me to attempt to enumerate the countries which have accepted the Security Council resolution of November 1967. Some of the countries are on record, as far as this question is concerned. Some of them have accepted the resolution and even expressed their readiness to implement the terms of the resolution, and some countries have not gone that far. So I do not want to give a catalogue of the countries and enumerate their positions accurately. These are all on the record. I believe, as far as Israel's position is concerned, from the public statements of the Israeli leaders, that Israel has also accepted the resolution. But, of course, Israel has not come out with a categorical statement that it is willing to implement it. Of course, the formulation used by the leaders of Israel, as you all know, is that they are ready to implement it by agreement. That is the position.

QUESTION: Do you find any points of agreement in the United States and Soviet proposals and in the Israeli and Arab answers to Ambassador Jarring regarding a political settlement in the Middle East? If so, in what regard? How soon would you expect some announcement of progress or agreement?

THE SECRETARY-GENERAL: I do not think it would be proper on my part to disclose the substance of the replies given to Ambassador Jarring by the parties primarily involved in the conflict, and even the official papers of some of the big powers are supposed to be confidential. But as far as my assessment is concerned, the replies to Ambassador Jarring's questions do not reveal any new elements or new positions. That is why I said earlier that Ambassador Jarring, in my view, would not like to repeat a more or less futile exercise for the next one and a half years or so.

QUESTION: May we have your comments on the appeal of the states participants of the Warsaw Pact to convene an all-European conference to discuss the problems of European security? What is your opinion on the reaction of the NATO states to this suggestion?

THE SECRETARY-GENERAL: I have studied the Budapest Declaration published by the Warsaw Pact countries and the Washington Declaration published by NATO countries relating to that Budapest Declaration, and all I can say for the moment is that from my point of view, from the point of view of the United Nations, we have to assess the merits or lack of merits of a particular communiqué or statement against the background of a relevant resolution or decision of a principal deliberative organ.

As far as this matter is concerned, we have the General Assembly resolutions which were adopted in the past few years pertaining to an item which I believe is called "The principles of international law concerning friendly relations and cooperation among states in accordance with the Charter of the United Nations." From those resolutions adopted in the last few years, there seems to be a general consensus in the United Nations that contacts and communications between different groups, professing different ideologies, are necessary and desirable.

So, in this context, I would very much hope that both parties, both the Warsaw Pact countries and the NATO countries, will find a way to establish closer contacts with a view to coming out with substantive discussions and negotiations which, as you all know, are in strict conformity with the Charter of the United Nations.

QUESTION: You are probably aware that both the United Nations and your personal position on Biafra are being strongly criticized by some organs of the world press and by some groups of individuals concerned with the matter. In view of the fact that the civil war is continuing, that the number of refugees and victims is increasing, that the OAU has proved unable to do anything about it, why cannot you call a meeting of the Security Council with a view to establishing an *ad hoc* agency whose only task would be to save the several million people who, according to many accounts, are going to die in the next few months in Biafra and in Nigeria?

THE SECRETARY-GENERAL: I am aware of the fact that my attitude toward the civil conflict in Nigeria has come under criticism in a section of the world press, which is understandable. I think that the Secretary-General of the United Nations also came under severe criticism in a section of the world press in 1960 for the United Nations involvement in the Congo, particularly in relation to the United Nations attitude toward

Mr. [Moïse] Tshombé. We have to take into consideration the human factors, the emotional factors involved.

As far as the civil conflict in Nigeria is concerned, I believe that I have made my position very clear. As you all know, the government of Nigeria has proclaimed that this is an internal affair. The Organization of African Unity, attended by heads of government and heads of state of Africa, considered this question twice in two successive years, the first time in September 1967 and the second time in September 1968, both of which sessions I attended. The heads of African states and heads of government decided unanimously in 1967, and almost unanimously in 1968, that the civil conflict in Nigeria is an internal affair and that the Organization of African Unity recognizes the unity and territorial integrity of Nigeria; that the Organization of African Unity has already set up a Special Committee of Six, headed by His Imperial Majesty the Emperor of Ethiopia. This Special Committee of Six will continue to deal with this question.

Then, any international organization outside the Organization of African Unity should not get itself involved in this question. These are more or less my paraphrase of the essence of the declarations of the Organization of African Unity.

So in my view, as I stated earlier, the United Nations should be and must be involved in all crisis situations everywhere which are likely to threaten international peace and security. That is my belief of how the United Nations should function. But there are of course one or two exceptions to this thesis. The first exception is that the United Nations cannot be involved in a crisis situation involving non-Member states. That is obvious to all of you. Second, the United Nations cannot be involved in a crisis situation which is declared by the Member state concerned to be an internal matter under Article 2, paragraph 7. This point of view is endorsed and supported by the whole Organization of African Unity.

So, in the face of this attitude by the Organization of African Unity, I do not believe that any Member of the United Nations has any desire to inscribe the item "The situation in Nigeria" before a principal organ of the United Nations.

If I may anticipate something, if any Member state were to bring this item, "The situation in Nigeria," before the Security Council or the General Assembly, I am sure that the item would not be inscribed on the agenda. So it does not make any difference whether any Member state tries to inscribe this on the agenda or the Secretary-General tries to inscribe it on the agenda. From a realistic point of view, any such attempt would not succeed because of the knowledge that the Organization of African Unity is against such a course as the inscription of an item on the agenda of either the Security Council or the General Assembly.

But as regards the humanitarian aspects of the problem, as you all know, the United Nations and its family of sister organizations have been involved very deeply in trying to alleviate the suffering of the peoples who are the victims of the civil conflict. The United Nations Children's Fund has been involved, the Food and Agriculture Organization has been involved, the World Food Programme has been involved. Of course their involvement was through the good offices of the International Committee of the Red Cross.

I have been in constant touch with His Imperial Majesty, the Chairman of the Special Committee of Six. I have also been in constant touch with the Administrative Secretary-General of the OAU in Addis Ababa.

Beyond that, I do not see any early prospect of a deeper involvement by the United Nations and its family of agencies. But speaking of the humanitarian aspects, I think that I should add one more word. In my view, the government in Lagos has been very understanding of the need to transship foodstuffs, medicines, milk powder, etc., to the victims of the civil strife in both parts of the country. So the government in Lagos has agreed to open land corridors. The government in Lagos has agreed to permit flights only in the daytime because of the obvious reason that night flights might get confused with the shipment of arms. I feel that these are reasonable attitudes, opening land corridors and permitting day flights. Of course, you know as well as I do what the impediments to these proposals are. Now the government in Lagos has even agreed to night flights also under certain conditions.

QUESTION: The USSR has increased the number of its occupation troops in Czechoslovakia. Earlier on, you expressed the hope that the troops would leave quietly. Do you have any comment on the continuing and growing aggression?

THE SECRETARY-GENERAL: On this question of Czechoslovakia, I have made public statements in the past. I said in one of the previous press conferences that I stood by every word I had said in the past, and I do not think that there is any new basis now for me to add anything more to what I have said.

QUESTION: What can the United Nations or any other body do about the problems of southern Africa apart from passing resolutions which do not appear to be leading to a solution?

THE SECRETARY-GENERAL: I do not believe in this hypothesis that the Security Council resolutions do not lead to a solution. I believe that the Security Council resolutions will lead to something. Indeed, my assessment is that even now the Security Council resolutions have some impact, although not a very perceptible impact, on the situation, and I still feel that, with the active cooperation again of the permanent members of the Security Council, much more perceptible progress can be expected in this field. . . .

QUESTION: Are you satisfied with the progress of the Paris peace talks, and what in your opinion can be done to produce more progress?

THE SECRETARY-GENERAL: I understand that the negotiations or talks in Paris have reached a very delicate stage, and I understand also that there is a genuine desire on the part of some of the participants to end the war as quickly as possible. So in my view this is a very important element, the will to end the war. I consider this to be more important than any other factor. So in this delicate stage of talks and in this changing psychological and emotional climate, I do not believe that it would be of public interest for me to make any substantive statement or observation.

QUESTION: What is your evaluation of some recent tendencies in seeking improvement of East-West relations, and do you see in particular any encouraging signs and possibilities of better multilateral European understanding and security?

THE SECRETARY-GENERAL: There are definite indications that both East and West are now eager to understand each other more, which is different from the attitudes of the two groups in the last decade or so. I think that this shift of policies to negotiations is a very welcome and encouraging sign. From the point of view of the United Nations this attitude or this policy is in line with the provisions of the Charter and should be welcomed. I believe that we should welcome not only this new climate prevailing between East and West, but we should also try our best to bring about a more congenial climate between China and the rest of the world. As I have said on previous occasions, I am one who believes in the concept of exposure, contact, and communication, and I believe in the universality of the United Nations as an effective instrument. So we should not content ourselves with merely endorsing this trend toward East-West détente, but should also strive in the direction of détente in other fields and in other areas and other regions.

QUESTION: From your repeated observations on Ambassador Jarring's mission, may we justifiably conclude that it—that is, the mission—is shelved pending developments in the big-four Middle East talks?

THE SECRETARY-GENERAL: No, Ambassador Jarring's mission is not shelved or suspended, as I made clear in one of my statements about ten days ago, I believe. As you know, Ambassador Jarring never resigned from his foreign diplomatic service when he accepted my offer to serve as my special representative within the framework of the Security Council resolution. From time to time, he went back to Moscow to join his family. He did this during Christmastime and he did it last week. It was nothing unusual.

But I may say that he has been involved in a very patient search for peace and a search for the conditions for the promotion of peace and the promotion of agreement. No perceptible progress has been made in the past one and a half years in which he was involved, and I do not believe that he would like to repeat this same performance for the next one year or so. I believe I know Ambassador Jarring's thinking on this subject more than anybody else, and so whatever I say on the subject is designed not to contradict his thinking. You can conclude that what I have been saying in the past regarding the situation in the Middle East reflects his thinking also.

QUESTION: Would you equate the role of the National Liberation Front and the role of the Palestine liberation movements? And if so, since the Paris talks became meaningful with the presence of the NLF at the negotiating table, do you consider essential a Palestine liberation movement's presence in any meaningful Middle East peace talks?

THE SECRETARY-GENERAL: All I want to say in response to this question is that, as I have said on some previous occasions, when a solution to a serious crisis situation is too long delayed, then extreme forces come to the surface and dominate the scene. That is one great lesson of history. At that time the voices of moderation will be stilled. So this applies to all situations in all circumstances. That is my conviction.

QUESTION: Mr. Secretary-General, in recent cases of Secretariat officials who have published magazine articles or given public speeches without specific clearance, have you decided on any corrective action?

What are the applicable United Nations regulations, and what do you regard as the proper course for international civil servants to follow?

How do you go about transforming a group of nationals working for an international organization into a true international civil service where officials talk publicly and operate internally solely from the point of view of the good of the organization itself? Should the United Nations institute its own training program to achieve this?

THE SECRETARY-GENERAL: My attention was drawn to a published article written by a member of the Secretariat staff who happens to be a Soviet citizen. I read the article a couple of days ago and I have asked the appropriate heads of departments to look into the matter from the point of view of staff regulations and to report to me. So far I have not received a report.

In this particular instance, the article is captioned, if I remember correctly, "The Soviet Scholars' Viewpoint of the United Nations." It seems to me that, apart from the applicability or nonapplicability of the staff regulations to this particular case, it is just plain common sense to realize that such articles written by members of the Secretariat are very undesirable. For instance, if an American member of the Secretariat staff was to publish an article, "The American Scholars' Viewpoint of the United Nations," if a French member of the Secretariat published another article, "The French Scholars' Viewpoint of the United Nations," if a British member of the Secretariat staff published an article, "The British Scholars' Viewpoint of the United Nations," if an Israeli member of the Secretariat staff published an article, "The Israeli Scholars' Viewpoint of the Situation in the Middle East," and if an Arab member of the Secretariat staff published an article, "The Arab Scholars' Viewpoint of the Situation in the Middle East," I think it would come to the stage where the very concept of the international civil servant would collapse completely. That is my reaction, of course.

I have not received the considered opinion of my colleagues as far as the application of the staff regulations is concerned, and I have to study the case very carefully on the basis of the advice offered to me.

QUESTION: Have you noted any movement in Latin America and in the United States to allow the return of Cuba to the inter-American community?

THE SECRETARY-GENERAL: So far, I have not seen any indication.

QUESTION: How does the Sino-Soviet conflict affect the long-standing issue of Chinese representation in the United Nations?

THE SECRETARY-GENERAL: It is difficult to assess the significance of the recent clashes between China and the Soviet Union because no adequate data are available except of course from the newspapers, television, and radio. But I believe that the current session of the Party Congress which is still meeting in Peking will be important from the point of view not only of Soviet-Chinese relations, but also of the wider context of relations between China and the outside world. . . .

From Speech to the United Nations Association of Great Britain

LONDON   APRIL 25, 1969

THE UNITED NATIONS Association of Great Britain on more than one occasion was chosen by U Thant as the medium for launching an important speech. Like the United Nations Association of the United States, it provided him a select audience of United Nations supporters representing a wide range of interests. In addressing the United Nations Association of Great Britain on April 25, 1969, he dealt with basic problems such as the sources of world tensions, the weaknesses of the United Nations structure and the future outlook for a world of security and freedom.

. . .

THE MAIN SOURCES of tension in the world are all too easy to identify. They arise from three main sets of issues which may be broadly described as the East-West problem, the North-South problem, and the general problem of the relation between the strong and the weak. Politically, the East-West problem still commands a great deal of attention, although its nature has changed greatly over the past twenty-three years, and there are encouraging signs of constructive and positive developments in the relation between East and West. In the East-West issue, which is fundamentally a problem between great powers and differing ideologies, the United Nations has of necessity played a secondary role. It seems to me, however, that it has been a secondary role of the greatest importance, for on numerous occasions the Organization has provided the middle ground for the meetings of East and West and the framework within which many complex and long-term problems can be thrashed out without either side losing face or making concessions which might, if made elsewhere, be interpreted as signs of weakness. I

SOURCE: *UN Monthly Chronicle*, Vol. VI, May 1969, pp. 58–64.

am thinking, for example, of a large general problem such as disarmament at one end of the scale and of a particular and immediate crisis like the Cuban missile crisis at the other. In cases of both kinds the great powers have made constructive use of the intermediary possibilities of the United Nations.

The fact that the great powers have been able and anxious, in recent years, to reach agreement or consensus in the Security Council on a number of extremely critical issues, as, for example, the Middle East or the question of Southern Rhodesia, is another example of the usefulness of the United Nations system in great-power relations. I might add that the leading role played by the United Kingdom and by its permanent representative, Lord Caradon, in working out the resolutions on both these issues is a good example of the vital contribution which the United Kingdom makes to the United Nations. The current four-power talks on the Middle East, which are taking place in an effort to provide support for the United Nations search for a peaceful solution in that area, are another and current example of the same hopeful trend toward the cooperation of the great powers in facing world problems.

By the North-South issue I refer to the whole range of problems which arise from the contrast between the situation and prospects of developed countries and those of the developing countries. The rapid process of decolonization, which has been one of the most striking features of the first twenty-three years of the United Nations, has, of course, brought this problem into a much sharper focus. The new Member states of the United Nations created by the decolonization process are for the most part those who have the greatest difficulties in catching up with the more highly developed states and thus taking their rightful place in the potentially bountiful works of the twentieth century. In my view this is, and seems likely to remain for a long time, the most fundamental and difficult problem with which the world community has to deal. Although some 85 percent of the effort of the United Nations in terms of personnel and resources is employed in tackling various aspects of this problem, the effort is utterly inadequate in relation to the magnitude and importance of the problem itself. Within their limits, however, the United Nations Development Programme and the work of the United Nations and the specialized agencies are designed to make the best possible use of the limited resources available. As you know, the United Kingdom is one of the major contributors in the United Nations Development Programme and provides the largest number of experts employed in all parts of the world in that Programme. It is fitting that a country with the historic traditions of the United Kingdom should take such a major part in this new venture under international auspices.

There is another aspect of the North-South problem which has an importance out of all proportion to the actual number of people directly involved. I refer to the problem of racial discrimination and in particular to the persistence of the dogma of white supremacy, in Southern Rhodesia and South Africa. There are, of course, racial problems in many countries of the world, but the two I have mentioned are especially of international significance because the United Nations has not been able till now to carry out effectively its own decisions. The historic process of decolonization, in which the United Kingdom has taken a lead and set a fine example, is by no means complete. I very much fear the consequences, if this residue of colonialism in its most unenlightened form in allowed to persist.

The third issue I mentioned—the problem of the strong and the weak—is as old as human history, but in our time we have seen some novel changes in the normal historical relationship between the strong and the weak. It is, of course, still true that a few nations with immense resources are incomparably stronger both militarily and economically than the vast majority. But this classic situation has been mitigated in our world in two different ways. On the military side the scale and appalling potential of the nuclear deterrent has induced a new spirit in the most powerful countries, a spirit which shies away from war or involvement in situations which may lead to a global war. War as an instrument of policy for great powers is, for both practical and moral reasons, increasingly unacceptable. On the economic side, again for both moral and practical reasons, the notion of the responsibility of the rich for the poor has to a surprising extent in the past twenty-three years extended itself to the relationship between nations. We now see a general acceptance of the idea that the more fortunate nations have a duty, as well as a practical interest, in assisting the less fortunate, not only because it is, in the long run, in their interest to do so, but also because of a genuine feeling of moral responsibility.

It seems to me, therefore, that in the relation between the strong and the weak, we can register some advance in our time, in spite of occasional and sharp reminders that neither the spirit of domination nor military adventurism is by any means dead. This change is already reflected to some extent in the way the United Nations is used by its

Members. In spite of its inability to act in some critical situations, the Member governments of the United Nations, especially through the tireless, devoted, and often unnoticed service of their permanent representatives in New York, have already begun to make a reality of one of the quieter objectives of the United Nations, which is to provide a center for harmonizing the actions of nations in attaining peace and in facing great international problems. It is also encouraging that such issues as the peaceful uses of outer space, the exploitation of the seabed, and more recently the global problem of environmental pollution have all been brought to the United Nations in an effort to apply the experience of the past to the better ordering of the future.

No one accustomed to public life is likely to believe in miraculous solutions or sudden conversions. I believe, however, that the nations of the world have already come a long way toward learning to use the machinery of the United Nations to deal with some of their most intractable problems. The long hours of debate and exchange of views in the United Nations on a vast range of subjects have made, over the years, a very real contribution to tolerance and understanding. That does not, of course, mean that the ideals of the Charter have become a reality, but it is an important step in the right direction.

The Member governments acting through the various organs of the United Nations have tried especially to build bridges between antagonists, conflicting interests, and different parts of the world. In fact, there have been a number of critical situations in which the United Nations has provided the only surviving bridge between conflicting parties. As Secretary-General, my view of the world is essentially a view seen from these bridges between antagonists provided by the United Nations framework. They are often flimsy structures which threaten to be swept away by the currents of conflict and antagonism, but they have provided, and do provide as long as we can maintain them, that contact between conflicting parties without which all hope of a peaceful solution would be lost.

I hasten, however, to add that these first steps toward international order are nothing like enough, and there is no cause whatsoever for complacency about the present state of international relations. A world of security and freedom is still very far in the future.

It is not only that international effort seems incapable at present of mastering such intractable problems as the Middle East or Vietnam. It is not only that the expressed intention and authority of the large majority of the international community seems unable to make itself felt even on numerically quite small groups such as the white minorities in Southern Rhodesia or, for that matter, in South Africa. The lack of any contact with the People's Republic of China is also a shortcoming with obvious and serious disadvantages for the Organization. These are signs of a very grave weakness in the structure and reality of world order. But such failures reflect a more basic failing. The world community as represented in the United Nations has been painfully slow, it seems to me, to react to some of the most pressing realities of our time. Thus governments and the United Nations are still operating in a political context of almost unqualified national sovereignty which has long since been rendered anachronistic by the scientific, technological, social, and economic changes of the past century.

It is our dilemma that, short of some fearsome and imminent threat of disaster, a dramatic change in the attitude of governments to international order is unlikely, especially where their own interests or sovereignty are vitally concerned. In the present state of affairs governments tend to cite the attitude of others as a good reason for making no concessions themselves. To that extent sectional interests continue to dominate over the common good. It is a dangerous fact, which should never be forgotten, that on the international scene we still live in a state of perpetual insecurity comparable to the condition of a country where no central authority, no police force, and no enforceable code of law are yet consistently functioning. Instead, we improvise at the last minute, within the broad framework of the United Nations Charter. United Nations peace-keeping operations, for example—successful though most of them have been in their limited objectives—are essentially *ad hoc* and voluntary improvisations to meet a particular danger. Although they are a fine example of international cooperation in pioneering new methods of keeping the peace, they are no substitute for a system which by its regular existence and acceptance could create confidence and understanding among nations. The tension, suspicion, and fear which now bedevil and endanger our society and demand vast expenditures in armaments and defense will not be dispersed until we begin to develop such a system. In this context idealism is also realism.

Any progress in this direction will require a number of conditions. One is that all states will abide by the notion of international conduct indicated in the United Nations Charter. This includes giving due attention and respect to the decisions and resolutions of the principal organs of the

United Nations. Such respect would be a practical indication of the subordination of sectional interests to the common good, however much the wisdom of some majority decisions of the United Nations are, on occasion, questioned by some of the Member states. It might also lead to the liquidation of some of the great problems which now appear insoluble.

Another condition of progress is the existence of a strong and effective international civil service. Although the last twenty-three years have seen a great growth in the scope and activity of international secretariats, the resources and authority of secretariats are often quite inadequate to the tasks assigned to them by governments. That, however, is not the basic problem. The basic problem is twofold. First we must have international civil servants of the highest quality whose objectivity and judgment are beyond question. Here I may say that I think we have advanced a long way in the last twenty-three years, and I pay tribute to my colleagues in the United Nations and the specialized agencies all over the world who are the pioneers of the international civil service of the future. But the existence of a body of skilled, loyal, and devoted international civil servants is not enough. International civil servants must also be accepted as such by governments, and their objectivity and freedom from national bias must be generally believed in, especially when, as is often the case, their duty requires them to take actions or decisions which are unpopular with one government or another. Here we have made less progress, and it is clear that the effective acceptance of an impartial international civil service is going to be a slow process. Without such acceptance and confidence the international civil service can never function as fully or as effectively as it should.

In this age of all ages we must, in every sphere, try to adjust our policies and aims to new concepts and new possibilities as well as to new dangers. Leaders and peoples must lift their eyes from time to time from their present problems to contemplate the shape and the hopes of the future. Only thus can we fulfill the promise of a decent life for all, preserve and enhance the quality of that life and turn our prodigious technological progress into humanly desirable channels. With all our day-to-day preoccupations, this requires a tremendous effort, and yet it is an effort which we cannot afford not to make. Perhaps this is basically what, all over the world, people under twenty-five are trying to tell those over thirty. The so-called generation gap, which has existed throughout the ages in one form or another, seems to me to be especially concerned today with the revolution in the human condition made possible by technology and the very valid concern that this revolution should lead to freedom and to the general good rather than to a new bondage and the advantage of the few. It is vital that this message is received and acted on at all the many levels of our now incredibly complex society.

Institutions, by their very nature, tend to be a little out of date. This is no less true of the United Nations than of many other institutions. To compensate for this tendency, those whose job it is to make institutions work must always be on the lookout for the reforms and adjustments of policies and attitudes which can make their institutions respond to the urgent realities of the time. In the international sphere certainly we shall face a future which will be at best insecure and disagreeable, and at worst fatally self-destructive, if we do not come to grips with realities. Another essential factor is confidence—confidence in ourselves, in the basic good will and common sense of others, and in the goals we have set ourselves. An increase in confidence is especially vital if the United Nations machinery is to be made to work in a reliable way.

The United Nations has some considerable advantages over the League of Nations, which was predominantly a European organization. What the United Nations lacks in orderliness it gains in the breadth of its base and the wide spectrum of interests represented in its work and deliberations. But that fact does not mean that the European countries, who have pioneered so much in the field of international cooperation, have a less vital or valuable role to play in the United Nations than in the League. On the contrary, the United Nations gives them possibilities of influence and effective action in a far wider sphere. That sphere includes man's creative potential to shape his destiny on this earth and to explore with new vigor his capacity to live in peace and justice. The lifeblood of this great new expedition can only be the concern, the understanding, and the will of the peoples of the United Nations to solve their problems and make use of their opportunities. Their involvement is vital. That is why I am very glad to have had the chance to be with you here this evening.

Address at Unveiling of League of Nations
Fiftieth Anniversary Plaque

GENEVA   APRIL 30, 1969

This is an occasion, I feel, when one comes not to bury Caesar, but to praise him. We have come not to mark the passing of the League but to celebrate the fiftieth anniversary of its foundation. We have come to try and recapture some of the spirit and faith of those early days of 1919 when "the war to end all wars" had finally come to a halt, and the exhausted nations were determined to put into operations a new and highly original idea in order to prevent the outbreak of another holocaust.

In view of its structure and the self-imposed limitation of its functions, the lack of success of the League in its almost revolutionary conception of international peace-keeping is not surprising. What is of significance to us is that the courage and inspiration of those who launched this frail vessel of hope should still remain with us in spite of the setbacks and disasters which have overtaken mankind in the course of the last half-century.

The League has been described as the first organism of international morality—not a coalition against those nations outside the League, but a coalition against the wrong-doing of its own members.

This was in itself a tremendous advance in international relationships. In comparison with its predecessor, the Hague Conference, there was all the difference between a giant and a pigmy, despite the essentially European character of the League which deprived it of much of the moral authority of a truly global organization.

For the first time in history there was a permanent organization designed to safeguard the interests of peace. There was a rallying point, a clearing house which enabled the nations who desired peace to mobi-

SOURCE: UN Press Release SG/SM/1102.

lize and concentrate their forces. And to remind humanity of its common interests, there was a Labour Office, a Health Service, and a Committee on Intellectual Cooperation. Lastly, there was a new sounding board for world opinion.

We owe a great debt to the framers of the Covenant who, in the space of a few weeks, in an atmosphere of emotion and prejudice engendered by war, succeeded in laying the foundations of an imposing edifice. It represented one of the most positive and constructive acts of the peace conference.

It was upon these foundations that the United Nations was later erected to continue the pioneering aspirations of Woodrow Wilson, Viscount Cecil, Aristide Briand, and Vittorio Orlando.

But until the Assembly met in Geneva there was no League. Up to then it had only been a paper organization with an embryo council meeting in London to give it some shape and body. It was in Geneva that the League took roots and grew.

The choice of Geneva was not a decision which was taken lightly—the cradle of Calvinism and the Reformation was indeed thought to be a fitting place for the political reformer of the twentieth century, but other cities had also pressed their claims.

The chief anxiety of the founders of the League was to ensure that the task of building a peaceful world should take place in a setting which was not associated with bitter memories and national tensions, and which would be more likely to promote good will than to poison international relations.

While any part of Switzerland would have satisfied these conditions, Geneva seemed especially suitable because of its historic, intellectual, and humanitarian past.

In the last fifty years Geneva has given even further proof of its international character and attitude of neutrality, and the Palais Wilson has given way to the Palais des Nations and the other headquarters of the many organizations, both governmental and non-governmental, which have sought its hospitality to such an extent that Geneva has now come to have a symbolic significance in the international world. A peaceful milieu and an atmosphere of good will are indeed indispensable as a basis for positive international action.

Amid this austere and tranquil spirit of freedom, matched by respect for law and order, battle was joined against man's common enemies—war, poverty, disease, and ignorance. And not only Geneva but the whole of Switzerland became involved in this new crusade.

Speaking at the first Assembly of the League, in the Salle de la Réformation of the Hotel de Ville, the then President of the Swiss Conferation, Mr. Guiseppe Motta, said, "If I make no attempt to conceal the emotion which I feel, it is because I am trying to realize the unprecedented greatness and the significance of the event now taking place upon my native soil."

Since that day, nearly fifty years ago, much has happened in a world which is still seeking peace, justice, and prosperity and fighting famine, ignorance, and disease for its ever-growing millions.

Progress there has been, although the international community has not yet realized its cherished ideals. Much still remains to be done. It is also worth remembering that international conditions have changed radically since the end of the Second World War, and it requires the highest degree of statesmanship and vision to realize that the political landmarks most prominent in the late forties and early fifties have disappeared or are disappearing.

It is therefore for us today to rededicate ourselves with new vigor and vision to the unfinished work which they who labored here tried so arduously to advance.

I am sure that in the years to come this plaque will serve as a constant reminder of man's indomitable spirit in his struggle for peace and progress with justice.

Statement to the Press
on the Situation in Vietnam

NEW YORK   MAY 17, 1969

U THANT had been happy to see a complete halt of United States bombing in North Vietnam and even happier to see substantive peace talks begin in Paris in which the National Liberation Front, South Vietnam, North Vietnam, and the United States were participating. Two points of his three-point peace plan had been met. The third point—a reduction of military activities by both sides—still remained to be fulfilled. He was plainly optimistic at his press conference on January 28. The prospects for peace, he said "are brighter than at any time in the past." He pointed out, however, that "it is going to be a long and difficult process." As the talks continued in Paris, Thant followed a hands-off policy, carefully avoiding any comment that might be considered as interference. On April 17, he told a luncheon of the United Nations Correspondents Association that there seemed to be a genuine desire on the part of some of the participants to end the war quickly and "in this delicate stage of the talks and in this changing psychological and emotional climate, I do not believe that it would be of public interest for me to make any substantive statement or observation." A month later he did break his silence to welcome new sets of peace proposals presented in Paris by the United States and the National Liberation Front. "It is clear from these proposals," he said, "that there is an acknowledgment that military methods have failed to provide a solution."

I WELCOME the diplomatic initiatives regarding the Vietnam war taken by the National Liberation Front and President Nixon. The stated desire of both sides to bring the war to an end and their willingness to take new initiatives in order to move the Paris talks forward are also to be welcomed. There will now be on the table at Paris, among others, two new sets of proposals: the ten points from the N.L.F. and President Nixon's eight points. It is clear from these proposals that there is an

SOURCE: *UN Monthly Chronicle*, Vol. VII, June 1969, p. 36.

acknowledgment that military methods have failed to provide a solution. I can only hope that these proposals would provide a basis for meaningful discussions in order to reach a just and peaceful settlement of the very tragic war in Vietnam. They should also help to clarify the character of the international involvement envisaged in both proposals.

THE SITUATION IN CYPRUS

In both his June 3 and December 3 reports to the Security Council on the situation in Cyprus, U Thant was able to present a picture of continued improvement. He stated frankly, however, that solutions of the basic problems dividing the Greek and Turkish communities were still not in sight and that the continued presence of the United Nations Force was necessary after nearly six years of peace-keeping. In the Introduction to his 1969 annual report, the Secretary-General warned once more that "the passage of too much time may hamper rather than facilitate a settlement." He urged the parties to make the concessions necessary for a lasting peace even though these would be painful. He reminded the parties that his good offices continued to be available.

1. From Report to the Security Council

NEW YORK   JUNE 3, 1969

. . .

78. The improvement of the situation in Cyprus, to which I referred in my last report, has been maintained during the period under review. The island has remained generally quiet; there have been no major breaches of the cease-fire and there has been a substantial decrease in the number of shooting incidents. At the same time, tension persists, especially in the areas of direct confrontation between the government forces and the Turkish Cypriot fighters, requiring constant watchfulness and, as necessary, intervention by the United Nations Force in Cyprus (UNFICYP) to maintain calm.

79. Similarly, a great deal remains to be done to bring about real progress toward a return to normal conditions in civilian life. There have, nevertheless, been some improvements in the social and economic

Source: Security Council Official Records, Twenty-fourth Year, Supplement for April, May and June 1969, document S/9233.

fields. With the assistance of UNFICYP, members of the two communities have been brought closer together, especially by participation in joint projects such as soil conservation and water development. I note with satisfaction the increased participation of Turkish Cypriots in such joint activities, as well as the marked increase in other contacts between members of the two communities. On the other hand, some major anomalies persist, including the policy of the Turkish Cypriot leadership—instituted at the time of the disturbances of 1963–1964—of denying to Greek Cypriot civilians access to a number of public roads. I express again the hope that this policy may now be reconsidered, particularly in view of the fact that Turkish Cypriots have for more than a year enjoyed full freedom of movement over the whole island except in a few militarily restricted areas.

80. Hopes for a lasting settlement, as distinct from the present arrangement, are centered on the intercommunal talks in Nicosia between two prominent leaders of the Greek Cypriot and Turkish Cypriot communities. Limited agreement has been reached in these talks on certain important but secondary points, including the establishment of two subcommittees. These should significantly contribute to the widening of contacts between leading Greek Cypriot and Turkish Cypriot personalities and thus help to narrow the communications gap which has plagued Cyprus for many years. For the time being, however, no substantive results on the basic issues which separate the two sides have as yet emerged.

81. In this connection, I should mention that on March 26 and 28, 1969, I conveyed to the parties directly involved in Cyprus, as well as to the governments of Turkey and Greece, my deep concern at the slow rate of progress in the intercommunal talks, and my earnest hope that a determined effort would be made by the parties to expedite those talks. While fully aware of the difficulties involved and of the fact that time and caution were needed, I pointed out that the passage of too much time might hamper rather than facilitate a settlement, and, moreover, might make it increasingly difficult to maintain the United Nations Force in the island. The replies received from the parties made it clear that they shared my concern, although their analyses of the causes of the present situation differed widely.

82. I strongly hope that the parties will not allow a deadlock to develop over such admittedly difficult issues as local government. With good will and statesmanship, it should be possible to find common

ground that would safeguard the fundamental interests of both communities.

83. I am convinced that in the present circumstances the peace-keeping work of the United Nations Force represents an indispensable element in maintaining and further improving the calm atmosphere in the island and in promoting the steps toward normalization, which constitute as before the two major prerequisites for substantive progress in the intercommunal talks. Therefore, I consider a further extension of the stationing of the United Nations Force to be imperative. All the parties concerned, moreover, have made it clear to me that they support the continued presence of the Force in Cyprus.

84. Taking account of all the circumstances and in the light of the positions of the parties and of the situation relating to the intercommunal talks, I recommend a six-month extension of the mandate, for a period ending December 15, 1969. In this connection, I might mention that the governments contributing contingents to UNFICYP have indicated their readiness to maintain their contingents for such a period.

85. The substantial deficit in the UNFICYP budget continues to be a cause for serious concern. Constant attention has been given to the possibility of reducing the operating expenditures of UNFICYP without impairing its effectiveness, but it should be borne in mind that the United Nations as such has only limited control over the amounts of these expenditures, since approximately 90 percent of them are certified by contributing governments as extra costs incurred by them in providing contingents and/or logistic support for UNFICYP. The main cause of the deficit, of course, is the insufficiency of voluntary contributions to meet current expenditures and to reimburse governments contributing contingents for their extra costs. In this connection I must repeat the misgivings I have expressed on previous occasions concerning the method of financing UNFICYP by voluntary contributions, which continue to come from a disappointingly limited number of governments.

86. I wish once again to place on record my deep appreciation to the governments providing contingents to UNFICYP, several of which have absorbed some or all of their extra costs at their own expense, and to those governments which have generously made voluntary contributions for the maintenance of the United Nations Peace-keeping Force in Cyprus. I wish also to take this opportunity to express my appreciation to my special representative, the commander of the Force and its officers and men, as well as the civilian staff, for the exemplary manner in which they have carried out their important and difficult tasks.

2. *From Report to the Security Council*

NEW YORK   DECEMBER 3, 1969

. . .

73. THE IMPROVEMENT in the situation in Cyprus, which began in December 1967, has continued during the period under review. There were few intercommunal incidents and no major breaches of the cease-fire. The atmosphere of mutual restraint and the prevailing quiet have helped to create a climate of progressively better understanding between Greek and Turkish Cypriots in certain areas, which has greatly facilitated the solution of numerous day-to-day problems, in particular those affecting farmers and the business community; it has also improved prospects for the employment of an increasing number of Turkish Cypriots through government labor exchanges. Another encouraging development has been the joint participation of Greek and Turkish Cypriots at several international conferences held recently in Nicosia.

74. Despite this improvement, however, solutions of the basic problems dividing the two communities are still not in sight. The National Guard and the Turkish Cypriot fighters continue to stand in direct confrontation in sensitive areas and to maintain a high degree of military preparedness and vigilance. After nearly eighteen months, the intercommunal talks have yet to achieve any meaningful agreement on the fundamental political issues.

75. I have expressed on several occasions and most recently in the Introduction to my annual report to the General Assembly, my concern over the slow progress in the intercommunal talks. I have pointed out to the parties that the passage of too much time might hamper rather than facilitate the settlement. While I realize that the issues involved are too complex and too deep-seated for a solution to be easily found, I remain convinced that the Cyprus problem can be settled peacefully if the conflicting parties have the will and the determination to achieve agreement. The understanding which led to the intercommunal talks in June 1968 was a great step forward in the search for a settlement of the

SOURCE: Security Council Official Records, Twenty-fourth Year, Supplement for October, November and December 1969, document S/9521.

Cyprus problem. It was achieved because the parties, in the interest of peace in the area, were able to overcome some of the suspicion and mistrust which affected their relations. Now that the intercommunal talks have resumed after an interval of nearly two months, it is my earnest hope that the parties will find it possible to exert a determined effort and to make the mutual concessions and accommodations necessary to expedite the progress of the talks and achieve agreement on substantive issues.

76. While the intercommunal talks continue, a number of measures could be usefully taken further to improve the situation in the island, particularly as regards military disengagement and a return to normal conditions. UNFICYP's (United Nations Force in Cyprus) efforts to persuade the parties to agree to military disengagement have so far achieved no tangible result. Both government and Turkish Cypriot security forces are still being maintained at high levels of strength. At a time when the parties seem agreed that their problems cannot be solved by further resort to violence, it is not unreasonable to expect them to reconsider their policy of keeping a large number of young men under arms who would otherwise be engaged in economically productive activities.

77. It is also to be hoped that the Turkish Cypriot leadership will give renewed consideration to UNFICYP's proposals, to which the government has already agreed, for replacing military sentries by police along the entire Nicosia Green Line. There is no doubt that as long as the present close military confrontation persists, tension will inevitably remain high, and with it the risk of accidental armed clashes. This, despite the policy of restraint of the government and of the Turkish Cypriot leadership, can only hinder improvement in the political atmosphere.

78. Nearly six years of patient and persistent efforts, in which UNFICYP has played a vital role, have resulted in a great improvement in the situation in Cyprus. Nevertheless, in view of the undoubted fact that the situation remains basically unsatble and uncertain, I see no reasonable alternative to recommending a further extension of the stationing of the United Nations Force in Cyprus. Since it is unrealistic in the present circumstances to expect that an agreement can be quickly reached in the intercommunal talks, I am definitely of the view that the period of extension should again be for six months. All the parties concerned have informed me of their agreement to this proposed extension.

79. In making this recommendation, I must once again draw attention to the financial difficulties facing UNFICYP. While the deficit of the UNFICYP budget has recently been somewhat reduced, the voluntary contributions still fall far short of the requirements. As I have stated earlier in this report, in view of my deepening concern over the continuing deficit, I appointed in August 1969 a Secretariat Survey Team to look thoroughly into the financial situation of UNFICYP with particular attention to the possibility of reducing its cost. The members of the Security Council will observe that the survey team has indicated certain courses of action which might over a period of time result in reductions in the cost of UNFICYP to the United Nations. These suggestions seem to me to be generally sound, and I intend, if the Council should decide to extend the mandate of UNFICYP beyond December 15, 1969, to put them into effect in consultation with the governments concerned and with my special representative in Cyprus and the Force commander. However, it must be borne in mind that the above measures can only alleviate the financial problem of UNFICYP, not solve it. The solution of this problem can be achieved only by devising a more adequate method of financing, or by a substantial increase in voluntary contributions, both as regards the level of contributions and the number of contributing countries. It is to be noted that little more than one third of the Members of the United Nations have contributed to the UNFICYP Special Account. I consider it my duty to bring this problem once again to the urgent attention of the members of the Security Council.

80. In concluding this report, I wish once more to place on record my deep appreciation to the governments providing contingents to UNFICYP and to those governments which have generously made voluntary contributions for its maintenance. I wish also to take this opportunity to express my appreciation to my special representative, the commander of the Force, and its officers and men, as well as the UNFICYP civilian staff, for the exemplary manner in which they are carrying out their important and difficult tasks. To the Force commander, Lieutenant-General A. E. Martola, who is about to relinquish his command at his own request after three and one-half years of devoted and distinguished service, I would wish to pay a special tribute for the outstanding contribution which he has made to the United Nations effort in Cyprus.

Address at the Fiftieth Anniversary Conference of the International Labour Organisation

GENEVA   JUNE 18, 1969

As I JOIN with you today to celebrate and to reflect upon the fiftieth anniversary of the International Labour Organisation, my thoughts go back to the year 1919, which also gave birth to the League of Nations— that first noble attempt to establish an "organized common peace." The ILO, dedicated to peace through the pursuit of social justice and welfare, has been a steadfast, active, growing partner, first to the League, then to the United Nations which followed it, as mankind's agent for achieving a stable international order.

The United Nations has always valued this partnership with the ILO and keenly desires—as I know the ILO does—that this partnership should become ever closer and more fruitful in the years to come. We both know that we cannot achieve social justice without peace, or peace without social justice. Together, and in concert with our sister agencies of the United Nations family, we must try to achieve both. It is no exaggeration to say that the future of mankind depends on whether, during the immediate years ahead, the international organizations, our member governments, and the peoples of the world, can muster the necessary imagination, disinterestedness, determination, and courage for this task.

I have come to Geneva, not only to praise the substantial and admirable achievements of the ILO, nor merely to express admiration for its vigorous growth during the last half-century. I have also come to stress the vital and continuing role of the ILO and our United Nations system in the years ahead of us.

The efforts of these past fifty years have given birth to the beginning of a world system of orderly government, based on the unity of mankind

SOURCE: *UN Monthly Chronicle,* Vol. VI, July 1969, pp. 96–101.

and the equality of all men, respecting national and personal individuality and cultural diversity, and seeking peace, freedom, and welfare for all. Next year the United Nations will reach its first quarter-century mark as a world organization which serves mankind on a scale unparalleled in history. As we approach a new era, with man about to go forth into the vast unknown of the universe, we can be grateful to have survived a half century of cataclysmic change that has irreversibly transformed the political, economic, and social order of the early years of this century.

Our generation of workers for peace, inadequate though the results of our efforts may be, strove to the best of our ability to begin the laborious task of building an international community of nations in which the next generation and those to follow may live full lives in peace and dignity. I believe that we have made a tangible and lasting contribution toward that end, much as we may have stumbled on the way. We have defined the goals, and created the basic international machinery necessary to reach those goals. This is no small achievement.

Today, the great majority of mankind recognizes and agrees in principle, at least, that ours is an interdependent world, the security of which can only be assured through mutual assistance and concerted effort to improve the quality of life for all mankind. The principles so clearly enunciated in the Charter of the United Nations remain fully valid today and are worthy of our most strenuous efforts to translate them into a living reality.

But that reality continues to escape us. The gap between dire poverty and vast riches in different parts of the world continues to grow despite the incredible technological innovations and the vast resources that could now provide us with the means to conquer hunger, disease, and illiteracy throughout the world. The prospects of lasting peace are at best precarious, the balance of terror continues to hold sway, and the possibilities of nuclear annihilation are still ever present. What hope is there and what can now be done?

I believe that our work has not been in vain, that lasting peace and progress can still be secured, and that our system of international institutions has an absolutely crucial role in securing it. If we are to succeed, it seems to me that there are three broad conditions that will need to be fulfilled.

The first is that we find bold, imaginative leadership, and mobilize the active support of organized labor and management. Let me say at this point what a profound source of satisfaction it is to me to be able to address an appeal for such support through you today and to be assured of your positive response. We must at the same time look to the younger generation and do all in our power to ensure that it is increasingly involved in the process of development and in the quest for peace, a peace of which the young people of today will be the main beneficiaries. How can their cooperation be more fully enlisted? Peace-building may seem to them a long, slow, continuing process, yet those who work at it can testify what a challenging and rewarding adventure it can be. Our international institutions must never be considered, in the jargon of today, part of the "establishment." The active participation of youth, moreover, should ensure that our international institutions, built on the firm foundations of experience, constantly adapt themselves to changing needs. One thought that was expressed by your great first director, Albert Thomas, exactly fifty years ago seems to me to be particularly relevant. Noting that a lasting peace must draw on the deeply felt desires of a whole century and on the good will released by past generations, he said, "It is up to the present generation to make the effort, an effort which entails both ardent faith and clear thinking, in order to finish the work started by its predecessors." I am glad to say that the United Nations system of organizations has been developing its programs for the participation of youth in economic and social development, and that the ILO has been playing a significant pioneering role with its special employment and training schemes for youth for development purposes and its special emphasis on the training and protection of young people in its world employment plan.

The second condition is that the United Nations, the ILO and all our United Nations institutions should conceive of development and promote it in terms not just of material progress but of moral and spiritual growth. As I have said many times in different contexts, mankind must match its material progress with moral and spiritual growth. His Holiness, Pope Paul VI, to whom you had the privilege of listening only last week, emphasized this point in his *Encyclical Letter on the Development of Peoples* when he wrote:

If further development calls for the work of more and more technicians, even more necessary is the deep thought and reflection of wise men in search of a new humanism which will enable modern man to find himself anew by embracing the higher values of love and friendship, of prayer and contemplation.

I join with him in expressing the hope that our generation, and succeeding generations, may have the maturity and wisdom to pursue the path of full and integrated human development.

The third condition is that the resources of the United Nations family of organizations should be maintained at an adequate level, and used in a purposeful and integrated manner. In this context, we all recognize the coordinating role of the Economic and Social Council under the authority of the General Assembly as an essential element in the effective functioning of our decentralized system of autonomous specialized agencies, of which the ILO was the prototype. At the inter-agency level, the Administrative Committee on Co-ordination, which brings together the executive heads of all the organizations in the United Nations system, has a key role, and indeed a growing role, to play in planning and ensuring the best use of international resources, especially for the benefit of the developing countries. The ILO has always cooperated wholeheartedly in this partnership and I wish to pay a special tribute to your Director-General and my esteemed colleague, Mr. David Morse, for the constant support he has afforded me in my dual capacity of Secretary-General of the United Nations and Chairman of the Administrative Committee on Co-ordination.

The United Nations system embraces within its preoccupations virtually the whole life of man and covers all areas of concern to the modern state. To discharge this formidable range of responsibities the United Nations system must make possible a constant interplay of international and national action where it can be most effective. This requires continuous worldwide cooperation with all the major departments of government with substantive responsibility for important international matters. It must also operate in a manner which permits and ensures firm priorities, proper coordination and concerted action, both nationally and internationally.

The United Nations system as a whole draws immense strength from having direct and natural links throughout the complex structure of contemporary government. Only if a strong United Nations family loyalty gives us all a common vocation to pursue the common good by common action will the system work. We appreciate the part which the ILO has played in developing a sense of common vocation and we count on your continued cooperation in tackling the ever more complex challenges of the future.

Your unique tripartite composition enables you to make a special contribution to the process of bringing society as a whole into the momentum of organized international cooperation. The impact of your work on economic growth has been, and remains, manifold, but certain aspects of it are of exceptional immediate importance.

The United Nations is embarking on the Second Development Decade. Unless we pay far more attention than we have done hitherto to the human factor, the Second Development Decade may fail. Without human skills, tools rust and resources are squandered. The skills required to reach our development goals are so varied that virtually all of the member organizations of the United Nations family will have some part to play in providing them. The World Employment Programme, which you are launching at this fiftieth anniversary session of the conference, is a bold and far-reaching contribution to the full development and wise deployment of human resources.

No less important than the human factor in development are the human purposes of development. Economic development is not an end in itself. The ILO shares with the United Nations family as a whole the major concern of translating the broad objectives of development into policies and programs which can be of maximum assistance to member countries and which take into account the close interrelationship between economic and social factors in development.

Technological achievements also are not an end in themselves. Of what avail will be our splendid scientific and technological advances unless we are able to translate them into human satisfaction for all? Unless wisely applied and disseminated, technology can be a source of disruption in a society. By stressing the social objectives of development, the ILO can do much to ensure that the progress of science and technology meet modern man's rising expectations for a fuller life.

The definition of social objectives can also, in my view, be a key factor in securing political backing in advanced and developing countries alike for the Second Development Decade. For without political cooperation and public support, the Second Development Decade cannot hope to enjoy the general, consistent, and continuous support vital for its success. On the other hand, neither economic growth nor social justice can be achieved by the action of governments alone; both require the continuous cooperation of the state with those engaged in production. Economic growth requires the vitality of the whole economy just as social justice requires involvement of the whole community. Both require public spirit and discipline. The ILO exists to make continuous cooperation of the partners in production with the state a habit and to make almost instinctive the discipline and public spirit necessary, domestically and internationally, to secure social justice with economic growth throughout the world.

No less valuable than the ILO's contribution to economic growth is its contribution to the cause of human freedom. Your unique composition gives you relative immunity from some of the political inhibitions which have tended to weaken effective action for the international protection of human rights. You have been prompt to exploit this advantage, but wise to use it with judgment and restraint. It has been a source of strength to the whole United Nations system. It has enabled you to pioneer in formulating human rights, including such fundamental rights as freedom from forced labor, freedom of association, and freedom from discrimination. These freedoms have been set forth in widely ratified international conventions. You have devised new procedures for the protection of fundamental human rights. You have pledged your full cooperation in the implementation of the United Nations Convenants on Human Rights. We welcome this pledge and accept your offer of full cooperation, which we believe will make an important contribution to the effective implementation of the Covenants.

There will be no secure peace until the membership and effective influence of the United Nations embrace the whole world, and the purposes and principles of the Charter are recognized and accepted everywhere. The absence from our councils of any member of the world community of nations weakens our structure and places limitations on the effectiveness of our efforts. You in the ILO have always aspired to universality, you have made great strides in that direction. Universality poses problems of various kinds for international organizations, each of which has its own charter or constitution. Universality requires tolerance, good neighborliness, and fairness while maintaining your unswerving pursuit of the freedom and dignity of man. Universality implies the capacity to transcend divergences of ideology and national interest. I have every hope that the ILO will do its part in helping to consolidate and expand the universality of the whole United Nations system.

A universal ILO, strong in the confidence of labor and management throughout the world, contributing its strength to the common effort of the whole United Nations family to promote social justice by economic growth and expand human freedom, is a most valuable political asset of the United Nations system. Not only will universal membership reflect the political reality of the world, but it will also enhance the influence and wholehearted acceptance of the ideals of the United Nations. We live in one world, and the United Nations looks to the ILO to mirror the whole of that world in our common pursuit of peace through social justice, and social justice through peace. In pursuit of this goal, let us continue to move forward together with faith, determination, and courage.

Statement to the Press on Southern Rhodesia

NEW YORK   JUNE 21, 1969

THE QUESTION of Southern Rhodesia had been before the United Nations, in one form or another, since 1962 when the General Assembly declared it a Non-Self-Governing Territory as defined in Chapter XI of the Charter. The issue became critical on November 11, 1965, with the unilateral declaration of independence by the white minority régime of Ian Smith. Both the United Nations and the United Kingdom, the administering power, condemned the act. The British government described it as "an open act of defiance and rebellion." The United Nations Security Council called on the United Kingdom to quell the rebellion. It also called on all states to desist from supplying arms and to impose economic restrictions, including an embargo on oil and petroleum products, in an effort to force the fall of the Smith régime. In 1966 the Security Council voted to impose selective mandatory sanctions against the Southern Rhodesian government. It was the first time in United Nations history that such sanctions had been invoked. This too failed to bring down the Smith régime, as did broader sanctions in 1968. The failure of the sanctions was due mainly to the open defiance of the trade embargoes by two of Southern Rhodesia's leading trading partners—South Africa and Portugal—and to large-scale clandestine trade by other countries. Despite the United Nations pressure, the Smith régime submitted to the white minority voters in 1969 a new constitution providing for racially separated electoral rolls, allowing only a small number of African representatives in the legislature. The constitutional proposals were approved in a referendum on June 20 along with a plan to end all ties with the British Commonwealth and establish a republic. In a statement on June 21 U Thant condemned the referendum as a "deplorable step in the wrong direction."

Thant had been an outspoken critic of the Southern Rhodesian government on many occasions. He discussed the question extensively in the Introduction to his 1969 annual report, denouncing the new constitution as one of a series of "ominous developments" aggravating the existing threat to peace. The constitution, he said, "can have no validity whatsoever." The Secretary-General expressed his deep regret that the United Nations sanctions had failed to bring down the Smith régime. He placed the primary responsibility directly on the governments of South Africa and Portugal and at the same time urged them to abandon their opposition to the sanctions. Thant further appealed to all to exercise greater vigilance to interrupt the flow of covert trade.

SOURCE: UN Press Release SG/SM/1121.

THE RESULT of the so-called referendum on the new constitution for Southern Rhodesia, though not unexpected, is a further and deplorable step in the wrong direction for Southern Rhodesia, for Africa, and for the world. This result is, needless to say, in complete defiance and contravention of United Nations resolutions on this subject as well as being in absolute conflict with the principles of the United Nations Charter. Both the method and the result of the "referendum" are the product of the kind of racism which is abhorrent to the vast majority of mankind. The persistence and strengthening of racist attitudes and acts in Southern Rhodesia, as exemplified by the result of the "referendum," are a threat to peace which cannot and must not be ignored.

NIGERIA–BIAFRA

DESPITE THE failure of the Organization of African Unity (OAU) to find a formula for ending the civil war in Nigeria, U Thant continued to maintain his position that the peace efforts should be left in the hands of a six-nation consultative committee set up by the OAU. He was active, however, in seeking ways to bring relief to the thousands of civilian victims of the war. The Secretary-General was deeply concerned over the suspension of the main flow of supplies by air to the war-stricken areas during the summer of 1969. Huge stockpiles of food and medicine had been assembled by the International Committee of the Red Cross in nearby depots, but because of impediments raised by one or the other side they could not be delivered to the starving women and children. In a statement on July 30, Thant appealed to both the federal government and the Biafran authorities to grant the necessary facilities so that emergency airlifts could be resumed at once "even if concessions are required from both sides." He also urged the two sides to give immediate consideration to the opening of land and river corridors to ensure continued distribution of supplies to the war-affected areas. As in previous instances, his appeals went unheeded.

In a speech before the heads of government and state of the OAU in Addis Ababa on September 7, Thant said: "The dreaded cycle of starvation, disease, and death engulfing the population in the areas of the conflict has yet to be broken." The urgent problem, he said, "is to elicit the full and whole-hearted cooperation of those bearing responsibility for the afflicted areas as regards facilities for the movement and distribution of supplies." On September 12 the Secretary-General told a luncheon of the United Nations Correspondents Association that "owing mainly to political developments and conditions, it has not been possible to maintain without interruption the flow of supplies to the stricken areas." In the Introduction to his 1969 annual report, issued on September 15, Thant again expressed his concern over political difficulties which were blocking the distribution of supplies to the civilian victims of the war. He stressed that his own activities had been limited to the humanitarian aspects of the conflict. "On the political side," he said, "I continue to feel that the right course is to leave the political aspects of the Nigerian problem to the Organization of African Unity for solution." An overwhelming majority of the Members of the United Nations agreed with Thant's position. As a result there was no move to bring the Nigerian civil war before the Security Council or the General Assembly. A large segment of the press, however, continued to brush aside the argument that United Nations intervention would amount to interference in the internal affairs of a Member state. Both the United Nations and the Secretary-General were widely criticized for not taking an active role in peace efforts and even for the failure to get relief supplies to the war victims.

1. Statement on Relief to Civilian Victims

NEW YORK   JULY 30, 1969

THE SITUATION regarding humanitarian relief to the civilian victims of the conflict in Nigeria is a matter of deep and universal concern. For several weeks now, the main flow of supplies by air to the war-stricken areas has been suspended, and there is the risk that the population in the area of the conflict will again be plunged into the dreaded cycle of starvation, disease, and death.

My position concerning the civil war in Nigeria is well known. I support the decisions taken by the Organization of African Unity at Kinshasa in 1967 and at Algiers in 1968. These decisions provide the framework for the settlement of the civil war by peaceful means, which is the objective ardently hoped for by people all over the world who have, with grief, watched this tragedy unfold in Nigeria. I am addressing myself at this time, however, to the humanitarian effort which, under the auspices of the International Committee of the Red Cross, has been instrumental in bringing relief to untold thousands of civilian victims of the war. Thanks in great part to this effort to which the United Nations family has contributed significantly, in particular through the United Nations Children's Fund (UNICEF), it had been possible to stem the tide of an even greater disaster. This effort is now in jeopardy.

It has long been recognized that the most satisfactory method for the distribution of supplies in the war-affected area of Nigeria would be the establishment of land and river corridors, and I urge both sides to give immediate consideration to the opening of such corridors. However, until the flow of supplies by land and river corridors is established and operative, some arrangement must be urgently made for the resumption of emergency flights even if concessions are required from both sides. The first question is to move immediately the stocks which have accumulated in various locations from which aircraft of the International Committee of the Red Cross can transport them by day to their destina-

SOURCE: UN Press Release SG/SM/1139.

tion. I appeal to both sides, based on the most fundamental humanitarian principles, to grant the necessary facilities for the movement of these supplies without delay.

Notwithstanding the passions and bitterness inherent in every war, and most particularly civil war, there must be shown by those directly concerned the degree of magnanimity and humanity which is required to ensure that the civilian population is spared the misery of hunger and the ravages that come in its wake.

---

2. Address to the Organization of African Unity

ADDIS ABABA   SEPTEMBER 7, 1969

IT IS INDEED an honor for me to be invited once again to address the Assembly of heads of state and government of the Organization of African Unity. It also gives me great satisfaction to be present in person at this very distinguished gathering. Chief among the reasons for my satisfaction is that the present session follows closely in the wake of the commemoration of the Tenth Anniversary of the United Nations Economic Commission for Africa in which I was privileged to participate and which was such an important landmark in the efforts of the African countries to achieve higher levels of economic and social advancement. Another reason for my satisfaction is the opportunity that my presence here affords me to make amends, in some small measure, for my inability, owing to sudden ill health, to undertake my projected visit to a number of African capitals earlier this year—a visit which, all being well, I hope to be able to pay in a few months' time.

It is appropriate, if I may say so, that the principal preoccupations of the present conference include the very grave problems arising from the persistence of colonialism in large parts of the African continent. For it cannot be denied that the expectations aroused by the adoption, nearly nine years ago, of the United Nations Declaration on the Granting of

SOURCE: UN Press Release SG/SM/1151.

Independence to Colonial Countries and Peoples have very largely failed of fulfillment in southern Africa. Indeed, there are disquieting signs that those expectations may soon be turning into skepticism, if not disillusion, about the willingness of the international community effectively to assist the dependent peoples in that part of the world in their efforts to realize their legitimate rights to freedom and independence.

In Namibia, the government of South Africa has maintained its totally negative attitude to the United Nations resolutions which terminated the mandate for South West Africa, brought the territory under the direct responsibility of the United Nations, established a United Nations Council to administer the territory pending its accession to independence, and to that end, called upon the South African government to withdraw its administration therefrom. With regard to Angola, Mozambique, and Guinea, called Portuguese Guinea, the government of Portugal, in stubborn disregard of the pertinent United Nations resolutions, has continued to deny to the people the right to self-determination on the pretext that these territories are overseas provinces of Portugal. In Southern Rhodesia, neither the actions initiated by the United Kingdom as the administering power nor the economic and other sanctions applied by the majority of Member states in response to the decisions of the Security Council have yet succeeded in bringing down the illegal régime as a prelude to the transfer of power to the majority. Furthermore, in their resolve to stifle the endeavor of the people to achieve emancipation, the authorities in those territories, acting in collaboration with one another and with the assistance of certain foreign interests, have had recourse to increasingly harsh methods and have not failed, indeed, to threaten the security and territorial integrity of neighboring African states.

If the United Nations has not yet succeeded in applying effective solutions to these serious colonial problems, it is not for want of deep concern or close study or constructive effort. Since the adoption of the historic Declaration, the United Nations, which has been in the forefront of support for the principle of self-determination, has done a great deal to encourage and assist the dependent peoples in Africa in their progress toward freedom from colonial rule. This is reflected in the emergence since 1960 of some fifteen African countries from dependence to independence. Further, in the course of its work in the field of decolonization, the United Nations has extended the concept of the inalienable right of the colonial peoples in Africa to self-determination and independence to include a recognition of the legitimacy of their struggle to achieve the effective exercise and enjoyment of those rights. Proceeding from that recognition, the Organization has repeatedly appealed to all states to give to those peoples the moral and material support necessary for the restoration of their inalienable rights.

Furthermore, the United Nations family has made a significant contribution to the provision of assistance to African peoples suffering from the ravages of colonial rule. The United Nations has also given attention to the study of such economic and other factors as may constitute impediments to the progress of colonial peoples toward freedom and independence. In addition, it has sought, by stimulating the dissemination of information on existing colonial problems and the efforts of the Organization to promote their resolution, to mobilize world opinion in the cause of decolonization. What is more, the efforts made over the past few years by Member states, including in particular the African countries, to enlist the active support and involvement of the Security Council in the task of decolonization have recently met with a modest measure of success, although, as must be recognized, the decisions actually taken by that organ have not yet brought about the desired results.

Where the situation in South Africa is concerned, the problems resulting from the continued enforcement of the policies of *apartheid* have likewise shown no movement toward peaceful solution. Indeed, the South African government appears more determined than ever to consolidate the application of racial separation and segregation and ruthlessly to eliminate all opposition to these policies. It would seem from some of the legislation that the government has recently enacted that it is aiming to exclude any possibility of peaceful evolution toward a society based on justice and equality. Furthermore, it is attempting to extend the influence of its philosophy of racial discrimination and segregation to Southern Rhodesia and has proceeded to impose its abhorrent policies in Namibia in flagrant violation of the relevant United Nations decisions. Meanwhile, the fairly extensive humanitarian, educational, and other programs of the United Nations and its family of agencies designed to alleviate the consequences of the above-mentioned situation have continued, with the support of Member states. Nevertheless, there has been understandably widespread dissatisfaction at the failure of the United Nations to effect any change in the situation itself, despite the grave dangers which it poses of violent conflict in that part of the world. The ability of the international community to ward off these dangers depends not only on the determination of governments to shoulder their responsibilities under the Charter and the relevant United Nations resolutions, but no less importantly on the willingness of some great powers and the major trading partners of South Africa to take effective measures to turn that country off its present course.

The frustrations of the majority of Member states in respect to the chronic problems of colonialism, *apartheid*, and racial discrimination afford no basis for optimism regarding the future. Yet the picture I have sketched would be incomplete were I to omit reference to one or two of the more encouraging developments which have been increasingly discernible in the work of the United Nations over the past year or so. I have in mind, for instance, the broad agreement which has emerged to the effect that in the important task of eliminating colonialism and racialism in southern Africa, the United Nations should play an increasingly large role and that progress toward the desired objectives depends mainly on the acceptance by governments of the relevant international decisions and machinery, as also on their realization that the wider interests of international peace may also coincide with their own best interests. No less significant is the growing awareness among Member states of the wide consensus that has developed with regard to the colonial and racial problems afflicting southern Africa. Equally, there appears to be a general recognition of the importance of giving full and meaningful expression to that consensus through consultations and mutual accommodation, together with the acknowledgment that collaboration and concerted effort are essential for the translation of the resulting decisions into effective action.

Bearing in mind that the coming year will mark the twenty-fifth anniversary of the United Nations and the tenth anniversary of the Declaration, as well as the tenth anniversary of the tragic incident at Sharpeville, South Africa, I would venture to commend the foregoing considerations to the notice of the present Assembly, as it prepares to dedicate itself anew to the eradication of the vestiges of colonialism, *apartheid*, and racial discrimination from the continent.

When I addressed the last session of this Assembly in September 1968, I stated that if I was unable to conceal my concern about the persistence of colonial and racial policies in Africa, even less could I refrain from expressing my distress and dismay at the mounting toll of destruction, starvation, and loss of life resulting from the tragic fratricidal strife in Nigeria. Since that time, I have more than once expressed my belief that the decisions taken by the Organization of African Unity at Kinshasa in 1967 and at Algiers in 1968 provide the framework for a just settlement of the civil war by peaceful means. It is a matter of universal distress that this objective has not yet been attained. If anything, events have served only to intensify the general feeling of concern at the continuance of the conflict. The dreaded cycle of starvation, disease, and death engulfing the population in the areas of the conflict has yet to be broken.

In this situation, the exclusively humanitarian activities of the United Nations family, particularly through the United Nations Children's Fund (UNICEF) and the World Food Programme and in coordination with the International Committee of the Red Cross, have constituted a valuable contribution to the effort to provide and distribute relief to the civilian victims of the hostilities. Within the same context, the representative whom I had appointed for the purpose in August 1968 has continued his work of assisting in these relief and humanitarian activities, of assessing relief needs and of recommending ways and means of expediting the distribution of relief supplies. Even so, it is to be deeply regretted that it has not been possible to maintain without interruption the flow of supplies to the war-stricken areas. I should therefore like to take this opportunity to stress once again in the name of the most fundamental humanitarian principles that while there is still a great need for larger shipments of relief supplies the urgent problem is to elicit the full and whole-hearted cooperation of those bearing responsibility for the afflicted areas as regards facilities for the movement and distribution of supplies.

At the same time it is self-evident that in the long run only the acceptance of the OAU recommendations, which should lead to the cessation of hostilities and the successful negotiation of arrangements for a permanent settlement, would put an end to the present plight of the war-stricken population. For that reason, I must once again express the earnest hope that notwithstanding the passions and the bitterness engendered by the hostilities, fruitful negotiations pursuant to the initiatives which have recently been undertaken under the aegis of the Consultative Committee will be carried out, with a view to bringing the strife to an end and to assure the security of all the people of that country.

In the economic and social field I am well aware that, beset with enormous problems, Africa suffers like the rest of the world from the ever-growing intensity of unfulfilled expectations of nations and peoples. Hampered by a colonial legacy which excluded many of the prerequisites for modernization, the African countries have yet to shed the bonds of underdevelopment and break through to the goal of self-sustaining growth. The outlook, however, is not one of unrelieved gloom. The groundwork for the achievement of economic and social progress has largely been laid thanks to the efforts of the African countries themselves since their accession to independence and to the instrumentality of the Economic Commission for Africa. The seeds of purposeful cooperation and teamwork have been sown, and the pace as well as pattern of economic growth during the past decade stands in sharp contrast to the relative stagnation of the preceding period. With this in mind, I am gratified to note the growing cooperation between the Organization of African Unity and the United Nations Economic Commission for Africa in economic and social matters. For it is my conviction that a further strengthening of their relationship would enhance their capacity to serve the interests of the African countries at all levels and, with the cooperation of the United Nations family of organizations and programs, assist in generating greater momentum to the process of economic and social advancement in Africa during the Second United Nations Development Decade.

I wish this Assembly every success in its deliberations!

AERIAL HIJACKING AND TERRORISM

U THANT was seriously concerned during his second term as Secretary-General over the increase in aerial hijacking, the kidnapping of diplomats and acts of terrorism employed as a political weapon. In May 1967 he had denounced what he called "the El Fatah type of incidents" which were causing new tensions in the Middle East. He told a press conference, "That type of activity is insidious, is contrary to the letter and spirit of the armistice agreements and menaces the peace of the area." He further called on all governments concerned to take every possible measure to end such activities. Thant played an important role in resolving an international hijacking incident in July 1968. The case involved an Israeli El Al airliner that was seized and taken to Algiers. The Secretary-General, through the use of his good offices, was able to obtain the release of the passengers and crew. Commenting on the incident in the Introduction to his 1968 annual report, Thant warned that the trend toward increased hijacking, if not checked, could have a disastrous effect on international air travel. "If this disturbing trend is to be discouraged, as it must be," he said, "it is essential that two principles be universally observed, namely, that international law and order, as an essential condition of the freedom and safety of air travel, must be preserved, and, second, that no one may derive gain or advantage from the lawless act of hijacking an aircraft." As recounted elsewhere in this volume (see pp. 189–193). Thant became involved in a controversy with Israel over an attack on an El Al passenger plane at the Zurich airport on February 18, 1969.

The Secretary-General condemned the attack and took the matter up with the International Civil Aviation Organization and the Air Transport Association, but he refused to transmit two Israeli questions to Arab states. He suggested that because of the political nature of the questions, they should have been sent to the Security Council. He was considering steps to prevent future incidents of this type, he said, and he felt it would be better if he acted on his own initiative. Thant was brought actively into the hijack problem again following the hijacking of a Trans World Airlines plane to Damascus, Syria, on Agust 28. In a cable to the Secretary-General on September 1, the president of the International Federation of Air Line Pilots Associations (IFALPA) requested a meeting with Thant to consider the "alarming growth" of the hijack problem. He called on the United Nations to take such measures as were necessary to obtain the release of two passengers being detained in Syria and to see that the hijackers were punished. The IFALPA threatened a worldwide cessation of airline flights for twenty-four hours if the United Nations failed to act. Thant did not agree with the approach proposed by IFALPA, but he met its president, O. Forsberg, and three other officers in Geneva on September 6. Thant agreed with the pilots that the problem had advanced from the question of air safety into the political field and suggested that the pilots' organization might urge some governments to bring the question before either the Security Council or the General Assembly, which was expected to meet shortly. Thant made these other points: (1) Acts of hijacking "in the past have generated worldwide revulsion against the political causes which the perpetrators hope to promote"; (2) a worldwide cessation of flight operations for twenty-four hours, as proposed by the IFALPA, "would not produce the desired results" but would "only cause serious inconvenience to airline passengers throughout the world."

The hijacking question was brought before the General Assembly a few weeks later by Argentina, Australia, Belgium, Brazil, Canada, the Dominican Republic, Ecuador, Lesotho, Luxembourg, Madagascar, the Netherlands, and New Zealand. Although the International Civil Aviation Organization, a specialized agency of the United Nations, had been actively concerned with the problem, this was the first time it had come before the Assembly. On December 12 that body adopted a resolution, by 67 votes to 1 (Cuba), with 17 abstentions, calling upon all states to take appropriate measures to ensure the prosecution of persons who seize or wrongfully exercise control of civil aircraft in flight. The resolution also urged states that had not done so to accede to the 1963 Tokyo Convention on hijacking and to support efforts of the International Civil Aviation Organization to prepare a new convention providing for the punishment of hijackers.

Another problem involving the employment of terrorism and sabotage for political reasons was giving United Nations diplomats trouble during this period. This was the wave of attacks on permanent missions of Member states in New York. Most of the attacks were carried out by Jewish extremists against Arab missions, but there were also threats and attacks on the missions of the USSR, Cuba, and others by political foes. The Security Council requested the Secretary-General on September 11 to take up the matter with the United States, the host country, and attempt to work out measures to protect the missions in the future. Thant reported back on September 15 that he had been assured that police protection would be provided to threatened missions on a round-the-clock basis and that special protection would be provided on request. The attacks continued, however, despite police precautions. About forty members of the *Ad Hoc* Committee for the Jewish Defense League staged a "sit-in" on December 3 at the Permanent Mission of Syria and remained an hour and a half. Representatives of the Arab countries joined in a request that the Secretary-General convey their protest to the United States delegation in the strongest terms and again call for improved protection.

1. Statement after Meeting with Representatives of the International Federation of Air Pilots Associations

GENEVA   SEPTEMBER 6, 1969

TODAY I MET with the following representatives of the International Federation of Air Line Pilots Associations at the United Nations Office at Geneva: O. Forsberg (president), V. Nicolaeff (deputy-president), J. Ogrady (vice-president), C. Jackson (executive secretary).

Georges Palthey, deputy director-general of the United Nations Office at Geneva, was also present at the meeting.

The meeting was conducted in a very cordial atmosphere and I found the exchange of views very useful.

I expressed my appreciation to the representatives of IFALPA for their keen and legitimate concern regarding the serious problem of hijacking and I agreed with them that the problem had projected beyond the question of air safety into the political field. I also reiterated my view that no advantage should be taken by anyone of the criminal act of hijacking, for to do so could only encourage such reprehensible acts. It is my firm conviction that all such acts in the past have generated world-wide revulsion against the political causes which the perpetrators hope to promote. In fact, acts of hijacking only damage the cause which the perpetrators espouse.

I noted with appreciation the measures already taken by ICAO (International Civil Aviation Organization) to prevent the occurrence of any acts of unlawful interference with international civil aviation and welcomed the decision of the Council of ICAO in establishing a committee of eleven to recommend specific preventive measures or procedures.

I also noted with appreciation that, only yesterday, the United States deposited with ICAO the instrument of ratification of the Tokyo Convention on Offences and Certain Other Acts Committed on Board

SOURCE: UN Press Release SG/SM/1152.

Aircrafts. This convention will consequently enter into force on December 4, 1969. More ratifications can probably be anticipated in the near future.

I also informed the representatives of IFALPA that I had been in constant communication with the International Air Transport Association through its director general, Knut Hammarskjöld, on the problems of hijacking and possible measures of preventing them.

I expressed my appreciation to the representatives of IFALPA for their motive in suggesting that the solution to the problem of hijacking "lies with the United Nations Security Council rather than with technical organizations."

They explained the historical background of the problem of hijacking, and they believed that the situation has now come to such a stage that it is threatening international peace and security. They felt very strongly that because of this political and security aspect, the Security Council should urgently take up this question with a view to arriving at certain decisions. For instance, requiring Member states to make a statement of intent to ratify the Tokyo Convention and the punitive clauses recommended by the Council of ICAO.

However, I pointed out that for the matter to be dealt with by the Security Council it would be necessary for some Member states to request the inclusion of the item on the Council's agenda. It is always open to a Member state to make such a request at any time, and the members of IFALPA can always urge the governments of the states of which they are nationals to do so.

As an alternative to a discussion of the matter in the Security Council, it could be brought before the General Assembly at its forthcoming session as an additional item of an urgent and important character under rule 15 of the Assembly's rules of procedure, by either one or more Member states.

Regarding the projected worldwide cessation of flight operations for twenty-four hours or a series of such operations, which the president of IFALPA mentioned in his cable dated September 1, 1969, addressed to me, I expressed, as my personal opinion, that such a step would not produce the desired result and that it would only cause serious inconvenience to airline passengers throughout the world.

I also informed the representatives of IFALPA that since the recent hijacking of a TWA Boeing 707 to Syria and the detention of two of its passengers, I have been in touch with the government of Syria on that matter.

2. Statement in the Security Council

NEW YORK   SEPTEMBER 15, 1969

AT THE 1509th meeting of the Security Council, on September 11, the president of the Security Council drew my attention to terrorist threats against permanent representatives of Member states of the United Nations, and asked me to study the matter, together with the representative of the United States, so that the necessary measures could be taken.

I wish to inform the Security Council that I have been in contact with the permanent representative of the United States. I have been assured that police protection is being provided to the delegations concerned on a round-the-clock basis. Should further protection be required, I am advised that the United States Mission would arrange for it upon request, as it has always been prepared to do in the past. I have also been assured that the United States authorities are examining appropriate steps to prevent the occurrence of similar threats. It is my intention to keep up my contacts with the permanent representative, and I shall keep the Council informed of developments.

SOURCE: Security Council Official Records, Twenty-fourth Year, 1512th meeting.

THE SECRETARIAT

DESPITE HIS preoccupation with political problems, much of the Secretary-General's time was spent on administrative matters. It was his responsibility not only to see to the recruitment, training, and efficient use of the staff, but also to satisfy the demands of the General Assembly for the utmost economy in operating costs. The following two documents deal with some of the staff problems with which he was concerned during 1969. One important decision taken by U Thant was the creation of a new Administrative Management Service to be headed by an Under-Secretary-General. Among other things, this department was given the task of conducting a continuing review of the deployment and utilization of secretariat manpower—the first such survey in fifteen years. By September 12, when he addressed the Secretariat on Staff Day, survey teams were at work studying ways to improve operations in the Office of Conference Services, the Office of Public Information, and in the secretariat of the United Nations Conference on Trade and Development. Similar surveys were planned for each unit in the Organization.

1. From Staff Day Address

NEW YORK   SEPTEMBER 12, 1969

. . . As REQUESTED by the Assembly, I shall soon be placing before it certain projections on the growth of the Secretariat during the next two decades and the disposition of its staff in relation to available and potential office space in New York and elsewhere. Since the authority to approve programs and to provide the means to carry them out is vested in the General Assembly, our projections are necessarily based on past experience.

SOURCE: UN Press Release SG/SM/1154.

Although the rate of growth over a given period is a legitimate criterion for planning future needs, the actual rate of growth in the years to come will not be decided on the strength of this indicator alone. What is ultimately decided will be of great significance because it will reflect the collective judgment of Member states as to the extent to which they wish to use the Secretariat as an instrument by which to achieve the Charter goals of peace and progress.

That the perils common to mankind call for common efforts to meet them is as evident today—perhaps more so—than it was twenty-four years ago.

Is it not evident that many local conflicts which have erupted during this past quarter of a century have been contained, and helped toward settlement, by international assistance?

Can there by any doubt as to the mutual advantage to all members of the community of nations that arises from the cooperative effort to facilitate the flow of knowledge, skills, and resources so that the gap between the abundance of the few and the poverty of the many may be narrowed?

And is it not obvious that a steadily expanding population on the one hand, and a progressively declining quality of the human environment on the other, carry with them hazards which are of universal concern?

In face of such patent facts, one cannot escape the conclusion that effective international machinery, capable of adjusting to the changing demands placed upon it, is a vital element of world order. How effectively this conclusion is to be translated into political action will be answered, in part, by the General Assembly when it decides on the desirable growth rate of the Secretariat during the next twenty years.

The answer to the question of the Secretariat's role in the future has another important facet which is very much within our competence to provide. It is given by each and every one of you.

This qualitative answer lies first in the degree to which you feel able to commit your intellectual talents and technical skills to the work to be done. Not all of you stay long enough on the job to allow for its complete mastery. Many jobs are too complex to be performed well in a relatively short period. That there is a need to create the conditions which would make longer-term appointments more prevalent is generally recognized. But over and above these conditions, there must be a feeling of involvement in the work you are doing and a sense of identification with the ideals you are serving.

Second, it is up to the Secretariat itself to make the best use of its available resources. This is what the current staff utilization survey is all about.

It is understandable that changing priorities established by the Organization should have affected the various sectors of the Secretariat unevenly. A systematic review of work as it is now apportioned, initially to be carried out in the larger areas of activity, and then in the remaining ones, will certainly enable us to smooth out whatever disparities may exist in the allocation of functions and staffing arrangements.

Three survey teams are already at work in the Office of Conference Services and the Office of Public Information at Headquarters, and in the secretariat of the United Nations Conference on Trade and Development in Geneva. As soon as the review of these units has been completed, work will begin in the Department of Economic and Social Affairs at Headquarters, in the secretariats of the regional economic commissions and of the United Nations Industrial Development Organization in Vienna. The other units of the Secretariat will be surveyed thereafter.

On the basis of this comprehensive internal study of the relation between the tasks assigned to the Secretariat, the resources placed at its disposal, and its methods of work—the first such undertaking in fifteen years—it is my intention to make whatever adjustments are necessary to ensure both efficient operation and equitable treatment for the staff. This survey has not been designed as a temporary measure. It is merely the first phase of what I regard as a permanent function of the administration of the Secretariat, to ensure that our multifarious activities, conducted in nearly three hundred offices scattered in 142 localities around the world, are subject to the same test of relevancy to the objectives of the United Nations.

Third, it is important that every member of the Secretariat should have ample opportunity to develop his capacity to reach higher standards of performance and to assume greater responsibilities. I was therefore very pleased to note the emphasis placed on staff training by the Committee on the Reorganization of the Secretariat, which submitted its recommendations to me last year. I propose to follow up on the recommendations of this Committee and gradually to broaden the present scope of training both at Headquarters and at the other major duty stations.

Development of training will of course eventually have budgetary implications and will consequently require Assembly approval. I will shortly submit my report to the Assembly on the recommendations of the Committee on the Reorganization of the Secretariat. It will contain an endorsement of the Committee's view that a systematic plan of staff training should be instituted in the Secretariat, a plan which would take account of the advantages, as well as the limitations, of post-entry schooling in the subjects and techniques of international civil service work.

In line with the policy which I have laid down for the preparation of the next annual budget, I am not seeking any additional provision for staff training at this time. It is, however, my intention that, on the firm foundations which have already been established, a good training program should be built into the administration of the Secretariat.

And lastly, let me say a word about staff relations. I think it is by now widely acknowledged that the United Nations tradition in regard to staff participation in matters affecting conditions of work and general welfare compare favorably with that of any international organization. To my mind, good management means good staff relations. It does not mean that management can abdicate its responsibility or subordinate its own best judgment to the pursuit of agreement as an end in itself. What it does mean is an honest and patient effort to make decisions affecting the staff which take as much account as possible of the views of its representatives. It further means an unprejudiced approach to the facts at hand, an open mind in assessing their significance and a mutual respect for differing opinions. All this presupposes, of course, the willing acceptance by all of us of the unique obligations resting upon us as members of an international civil service. . . .

---

2. From Statement in the Fifth Committee

NEW YORK   OCTOBER 2, 1969

. . .

THE COMMITTEE [Committee on Administrative and Budgetary Questions] will recall that the staff utilization survey was requested in the

SOURCE: UN Press Release SG/SM/1163.

context of its examination of the budget estimate for 1969 and was based on the suggestion which the Advisory Committee made in its report. The endorsement of this suggestion by the Committee on the Reorganization of the Secretariat was somewhat broader in scope in that it was linked to the need for more effective management services within the Secretariat. Bearing in mind these proposals and after careful consideration of the various possible approaches, I decided to create on a permanent basis a new Administrative Management Service directly responsible to the Under-Secretary-General for Administration and Management.

The immediate task of the Administrative Management Service, and one which must have undisputed first claim on its resources, is to conduct the comprehensive review of the deployment and utilization of the manpower authorized by the General Assembly on the recommendation of this Committee, a task which inevitably involves the close scrutiny of management practices. The subsequent follow-up, detailed advisory and assistance activities, will be undertaken as a continuing function of the Service.

I am glad to report that the organization of the new Service, which I announced in June, has been completed. The review of three of the major segments of the Secretariat, namely, the Office of Conference Services, the Office of Public Information, and the secretariat of the United Nations Conference on Trade and Development, is already in progress. The plans for 1970, which involve the review of the Secretariat units engaged in work related to other programs in the economic and social fields, and those for 1971 which cover the rest of the Secretariat, will be prepared in the near future taking into account the experiences of the surveys now under way.

It is my expectation that this Service, besides conducting the first comprehensive study in fifteen years of the relation between the tasks assigned to the Secretariat, the staff resources made available to it, and the methods of work employed by it, will constitute a valuable mechanism for achieving continuing improvements in the administration of the Secretariat, through management studies, manpower reviews, and assistance to departments in the examination of their work practices.

Improvements in administration have taken place in yet another way. Although it is too soon to draw conclusions, I am sure the Committee will be pleased to hear of the initial response of the staff to the call for a more equitable use of language in the Secretariat.

The language training program has been expanded both at Headquarters and at other major offices. The accelerated courses at Headquarters have been extended to include Russian and Spanish along with English and French. The number of courses has been substantially increased and additional accommodation has been provided for them. But above all, it is the attitude of the staff that is noteworthy, the recognition that linguistic proficiency is an asset to the Secretariat as well as to its individual members. Hence the impressive enrollment of staff members of all levels in the language classes and the even more remarkable persistence with which they pursue the effort of acquiring a second or third official language.

As authorized by the General Assembly, arrangements have been made for the temporary accommodation of staff in rented offices outside the Headquarters buildings, and an architectural firm has been employed to develop detailed plans and cost estimates for a general expansion of Headquarters facilities, including new construction. Studies have also been made of the needs of the economic commissions and will be submitted to this Committee in the course of the next few weeks. It is clear to me that the expedients which have been used for years at Headquarters and at some of the other offices of the United Nations can no longer be reconciled with the overall drive to ensure efficiency and economy.

Let me now turn to yet another area of work where the capacity of the Secretariat to discharge its responsibility is largely determined by decisions of other principal organs. I have in mind the problem of documentation.

In line with my basic approach to the 1970 budget estimates, which is intended not to prejudge the outcome of the current staff survey, I have refrained from requesting new posts for the officially approved manning table of the Office of Conference Services. Instead, it is proposed to meet the immediate staffing requirements on a provisional basis.

That this is no more than a temporary measure may be illustrated by the following facts. Backlogs in translation of documents, which had been greatly reduced in the past years, are again accumulating. To date, the total volume of untranslated documents and publications is of the order of 85,000 pages despite recourse to contractual translation and a high proportion of internal production. In 1968, for instance, 172,000 pages have been translated internally and 37,300 by outside translators. External translation in turn creates problems of its own since texts must, in most cases, be checked for accuracy and typed before publication.

Much has been done recently to ensure timely distribution of documents in all languages for meetings held at Headquarters and other locations. Successful efforts have been made to fill vacancies with qualified translators, to undertake careful planning, and to raise the average output of translation notwithstanding the highly technical character of a major part of the texts. But a good deal remains to be done, and if the trend of the past decade continues—a trend which is marked by the addition since 1960 of some fifty new subsidiary organs still active in 1969 and the holding of even more seminars all year round in various parts of the world—I shall have no alternative but to ask for a substantial increase in the number of language staff next year. . . .

VIEWS ON THE SITUATION IN VIETNAM, THE MIDDLE EAST, AND OTHER PROBLEMS DURING THE AUTUMN OF 1969

U THANT always used the Introduction to his annual report as a vehicle for communicating his views to the Member states and to the public on issues facing the United Nations and on world problems generally. His frequent meetings with the press served the same purpose, but on a more informal basis. He reviewed the developments of 1969 in a statement on September 12 at a luncheon of the Hammarskjöld Memorial Scholarship Fund, at a press conference on September 15, and in the Introduction to his annual report, issued on the same day. The text of his statement, together with the partial text of the Introduction and the partial transcript of the press conference, are reproduced below.

Despite his known inclination to refrain from comment on the Vietnam problem while peace talks were in progress in Paris, Thant invariably was asked for his views wherever he met with news correspondents. Most of his comments during 1969 were brief and cautiously worded. He told the luncheon on September 12 that he had purposely kept silent because he felt that "direct talks between the parties involved in the war is the right step for working out a solution to the problem." He went on to say, however, that further de-escalation of the fighting would create conditions "whereby the Vietnamese people themselves will be able to resolve their own differences without outside interference." At his press conference three days later he noted that there had been a number of missed opportunities in the past five years, but "on the whole, I must say that I am optimistic about the outcome in regard to Vietnam." One questioner asked whether Thant would consider calling for a Vietnam cease-fire, a proposal that had been suggested to him on several occasions in the past. Once more he ruled out such an initiative on his part. "The next step," he said, "which is essential for the creation of conditions for peace is de-escalation and not a cease-fire right now. In my view, a cease-fire is not realistic in the prevailing circumstances." In the Introduction to his annual report, he said again that he saw some signs of improvement in the outlook for Vietnam peace, the main factor being the willingness of the parties to continue their talks in Paris. Here his comments were also brief. The main point he made was that every effort should be made to bring about a further de-escalation of the fighting.

After almost two years of peace efforts by the Secretary-General's special representative, Gunnar Jarring, supplemented by six months of discussions by representatives of the big four, the Middle East situation remained as dangerous as ever, if not more so. Thant said in his September 12 statement that the situation in the Suez Canal area amounted to "open warfare." He urged "even more sustained and concentrated effort" on the part of the big four and expressed hope that the presence of the foreign ministers of the four powers at the opening of the twenty-fourth session of the General Assembly might provide an opportunity for speeding up peace efforts. At the time he spoke, the four-power meetings were in suspension pending the outcome of bilateral talks between Washington and Moscow. Thant told his press conference that he would like to see the Middle East problem taken up at a big four summit meeting, but that he had been informed that the time was "not very congenial" for talks at the summit level. Asked about his views on direct talks between Israel and the Arab countries, the Secretary-General said that because of psychological, emotional, and political factors it was "not realistic to insist on direct talks between the parties in the Middle East just now." He added that if there were "a sufficient basis for talks, for agreement, for the reconciliation of positions, then I do not think direct contacts can be ruled out." This is what happened, he said, when Ralph Bunche as United Nations mediator was conducting negotiations on the island of Rhodes, which ended in the 1949 armistice agreements.

In the Introduction Thant said the preceding six months had seen the highest level of armed conflict in the Middle East since the 1967 war. He commented further: "It is no exaggeration to say that, failing some early progress toward a settlement, there is a very real danger that this great and historic region, the cradle of civilization and of three world religions, will recede steadily into a new dark age of violence, disruption, and destruction." He was especially concerned by the growing employment of terrorism and the hijacking of commercial passenger aircraft as a political weapon. "This trend, if unchecked," he said, "could introduce the conditions of the jungle in considerable and important areas of human activity."

From the time he became Secretary-General, Thant had never concealed the fact that he believed the People's Republic of China should be represented in the United Nations. Sometimes he had spoken in terms of universality of membership. At other times he had sought to make a distinction between what he called the "two U Thants." As Secretary-General of the United Nations, he said, he could not take a position on the China representation problem, but as a Burmese he had advocated the seating of the Peking régime and this was still his private view. Quite apart from the question of representation in the United Nations, he had frequently urged that the People's Republic be brought into United Nations disarmament negotiations and that more strenuous efforts be made to draw Peking away from its isolationist position. At a press conference on January 28, a questioner noted that Canada and Italy were moving to establish closer relations with Peking. The Secretary-General replied that because of his position he could not always say what he wanted to, but that he believed strongly in the concept of contact and discussion and felt that the United Nations must be universal. "So my private view," he said, "is that the decision of some Member states to open up to China or of China to open up to the international community should be welcomed." At his press conference on September 15, Thant said he still held the opinion that for some years to come the nature of the relationship between mainland China and the two superpowers would dominate the international scene. "In my view," he said, "the present impasse in the relationship between [mainland] China and the rest of the world is a tragedy."

The association of the People's Republic with the other nuclear powers in disarmament negotiations, he said, would be "the indispensable step to fashion a world free from fear." He welcomed a recently held meeting between Soviet Premier Aleksei Kosygin and Premier Chou En-lai at the Peking airport and— somewhat prophetically—expressed the hope that relations between Peking and Washington would "become normal, if not cordial." At that time the United States was preparing to lead another round of diplomatic maneuvers to keep the Peking régime out of the United Nations. It would have seemed unrealistic to speculate that President Richard Nixon would visit Peking less than two years later.

In the Introduction below, Thant noted with regret that very little progress had been made in the field of disarmament during the year and said that "some of the momentum and promise of previous years seems to have been lost." He was especially disappointed that the Treaty on the Non-Proliferation of Nuclear Weapons remained unsigned by a number of potential nuclear powers and by less than half the number of states required to bring it into force. He also expressed regret that the United States and the USSR still had not agreed on a date for beginning the bilateral talks on the limitation of strategic arms announced on July 1, 1968. He appealed to Moscow and Washington to begin the talks immediately and, meanwhile, order a freeze on the development and deployment of new nuclear weapons systems, pending the outcome of the proposed discussions. It was in this Introduction that Thant proposed that the 1970s be designated as the Disarmament Decade with the purpose of spurring a concerted and concentrated effort to achieve "measurable progress toward general and complete disarmament by the end of the decade of the seventies." His proposal was approved by the General Assembly on December 16.

1. Statement at Luncheon for the Hammarskjöld Memorial Scholarship Fund

NEW YORK   SEPTEMBER 12, 1969

ONCE AGAIN I am glad to attend the annual luncheon which is being held every year by the United Nations Correspondents Association (UNCA) on the occasion of the award of the Hammarskjöld Memorial Scholarship. I wish to reiterate my conviction that this is a most constructive initiative on the part of UNCA. I would like again to express the hope that the Scholarship Fund, established in memory of my illustrious predecessor, may continue to receive the widest support in the years to come.

As in previous years, this luncheon precedes only by a few days the publication of my Introduction to the annual report. I do not, therefore, wish to make any attempt to depict a picture of the world scene. However, I cannot let this occasion pass without referring to three or four major problems facing us today.

The world at large, and the peoples of the world, in whose name the United Nations claims to speak, tend to regard the United Nations as a kind of supranational authority, and to blame the United Nations for every failure of the system of collective international security which is envisaged in the Charter. In actual fact, the United Nations is not a supranational authority, and while the General Assembly, which is due to meet next week, is in a sense the parliament of mankind, it does not have the legislative authority with which national parliaments are endowed. For the Organization to become more effective, the crucial issue, however, is not the fact that the United Nations is not a supranational authority. The real issue is the willingness of the Member states to uphold the Charter principles and abide by them.

However, this fact is not wholly understood by the common man, and sometimes even by highly educated and sophisticated people. The letters

SOURCE: *UN Monthly Chronicle*, Vol. VI, October 1969, pp. 54–57.

that pour into my office whenever a crisis situation erupts in any part of the world show that, so far as the public opinion of the world is concerned—and you, ladies and gentlemen, have a big role in molding that public opinion—the United Nations is held accountable if, in any of these crises, the United Nations does not exert every effort to resolve the situation and to restore normalcy. Take for example the situation in Vietnam. The mail that comes into my office on this subject has gone down considerably in volume since the Paris talks began. But before that, despite every effort which was made to explain the historical and political reasons why the United Nations as such was not actively involved in the quest for a solution to the Vietnam problem, the public at large and, as I said, even some very well-informed and sophisticated people, could not understand this noninvolvement of the United Nations. I have purposely refrained from commenting publicly on the Vietnam situation since the Paris talks began, as I feel that after the cessation of bombing of North Vietnam, direct talks between the parties directly involved in the war is the right step for working out a solution to this problem. With further de-escalation of fighting and creation of conditions whereby the Vietnamese people themselves will be able to resolve their own differences without outside interference, the solution of this tragic problem may be in sight. But there is also no doubt that in the past, both relatively remote and recent, many opportunities for significant steps toward a peaceful solution were missed.

In the case of the Middle East, you are all aware that the situation has deteriorated since we last met. The tension and frustration to which I referred when I addressed you last year—the tension in the area and the frustration on the part of the peace-makers—have heightened during this period. In fact, in a recent report I described the situation especially in the Suez Canal area as a resumption of "open warfare." While the active involvement of the four permanent members of the Security Council in the quest for a solution to the Middle East situation is to be welcomed, and any success that they may achieve will greatly help the efforts of the mission of my special representative, Ambassador Jarring, it seems to me that there is need for even more sustained and concentrated effort on the part of the four permanent members in the months ahead if we are to save the situation. I am convinced that the Security Council as the principal organ of the United Nations for the maintenance of international peace and security must have a definite role to play in the solution of the Middle Eastern problem. The permanent members of the

Security Council, because of their special status under the Charter, have equally a special responsibility in contributing to the effective functioning of the Security Council. I hope that the presence of the foreign ministers of these four permanent members in connection with the General Assembly may give an opportunity for them to meet and take necessary steps to redouble their efforts to contribute toward a solution.

It is needless for me to point out to you, ladies and gentlemen, that in the case of the Middle East the United Nations as an organization has even less of an alibi than in the case of Vietnam. Here all the parties involved are Members of the United Nations. There is a unanimous resolution approved by the Security Council almost twenty-two months ago which lays down a well-conceived framework for moving toward a peaceful solution. And yet, during these twenty-two months the situation has deteriorated considerably, while we should have expected significant improvement.

The reason for this state of affairs is not far to seek; it is simply the failure of the Member states concerned to abide by their Charter obligations. I have observed on different occasions that when it comes to any country's national interest, it seems to forget its obligations under the Charter. This is particularly true of the Middle East situation. Mutual recrimination will not get us anywhere in a situation like this. It is only when all Member states, and especially those affected by the resolutions and decisions of competent principal organs, particularly the decisions of the Security Council, decide to honor their Charter obligations and to implement these resolutions and decisions, that we can move forward, not only in the Middle East but on the whole front of international peace and security.

I could not let this occasion pass without repeating my personal distress at what I called recently "the mounting toll of destruction, starvation, and loss of life resulting from the tragic fratricidal strife in Nigeria." For over two years now most of us in the United Nations have felt that the right course to follow is to leave the political aspects of the Nigerian problem to the Organization of African Unity so that, through its efforts, a just settlement of the civil war can be achieved by peaceful means. It is a matter of universal distress that this objective remains to be attained, though there have been some hopeful developments as a result of the statesmanlike and imaginative initiatives taken by the Conference of the Organization of African Unity, which met at Addis Ababa earlier this week and which I was privileged to attend. Meanwhile, the exclusively humanitarian activities of the United Nations family have continued but it is regrettable that, owing mainly to political developments and conditions, it has not been possible to maintain without interruption the flow of supplies to the stricken areas. As I said in Addis Ababa last Sunday, I would like to stress once again, "in the name of the most fundamental humanitarian principles," that the urgent need is not only for larger shipments of relief supplies but also the enlisting of the full and whole-hearted cooperation of those in positions of responsibility and authority in regard to the facilities for the movement and distribution of supplies.

Soon the United Nations will be twenty-five years old. Every passing year underlines the importance of all Member states adhering to the principles and purposes of the Charter in the conduct of international relations. I have said repeatedly that I recognize nationalism as a fact of contemporary life and the binding force of that advanced form of political and social organization, the nation-state. The United Nations is made up of these nation-states, and it is entirely legitimate for the representatives of these nation-states to pursue their national interest in and through the United Nations. But when the larger interests of the international community are involved it is essential that the Member states should give up the concept of absolute sovereignty and try to harmonize the pursuit of national interest with the larger interest of the international community. And that interest is primarily the maintenance of international peace and security, because the other goals of the Charter would, in fact, be even more difficult to reach if this prime goal of peace and stability is not achieved.

---

2. From Transcript of Press Conference

NEW YORK   SEPTEMBER 15, 1969

MR. LITTLEJOHNS (President of the United Nations Correspondents Association): . . . Since your recent meeting with the representatives of the airline pilots, there have been further hijacking incidents. These are

SOURCE: *UN Monthly Chronicle*, Vol. VI, October 1969, pp. 58–66.

now so common that there are reports of plane-loads of passengers applauding with relief when they are delivered safely to their destinations. Do you not feel that the United Nations—perhaps even the Assembly—might appropriately consider this world problem and recommend measures for dealing with it, possibly by trying to make sure that hijackers pay a severe penalty for their folly?

THE SECRETARY-GENERAL: As you all know, I have expressed my views on this subject, particularly in my statement released in Geneva on September 6, after my meeting with the representatives of the International Federation of Air Line Pilots Associations. I have condemned all these criminal acts of hijacking; I have drawn their attention to some possibilities of bringing this issue before the United Nations—either the Security Council or the General Assembly—and I have pointed out to them the procedures and modalities of bringing this matter before the principal deliberative organs of the United Nations.

As some of you are no doubt aware, ICAO—the International Civil Aviation Organization—has appointed a committee of eleven to go into this matter, as well as other aspects of international civil aviation, and I understand that the Council of ICAO is scheduled to meet on September 23. I hope very much that very positive steps and measures will be taken at that meeting. Failing that, of course, it is up to any Member state to bring this matter before the General Assembly or the Security Council.

As I indicated in my statement issued in Geneva on September 6, there are one or two things that the United Nations may be able to accomplish, that is, requiring all Member states to come out with a statement of intent, to ratify the Tokyo Convention of 1963 and accept the punitive measures which are before ICAO. If these two steps can be taken, I believe that there will be a tremendous step forward in preventing these criminal and lawless acts.

QUESTION: Mr. Secretary-General, on Friday you urged the permanent members of the Security Council to take a more active role to facilitate a Middle East solution. Do you see advantage in four-power talks in New York that have not obtained in the Soviet-American bilateral talks that have been taking place in Washington and Moscow?

THE SECRETARY-GENERAL: As you know, the four permanent members of the Security Council have been seized of this matter for several months. I understand that their talks were suspended pending the outcome of bilateral talks between Washington and Moscow. Late in July, I was informed of the latest proposals of the United States to the Soviet Union. Late in August, I was informed also of the reactions of the Soviet

Government to Washington. If there is a basis for the resumption of the four-power talks in New York, I believe that these talks will be resumed immediately. So the arrangement, as I understand it, is that the four powers have suspended their deliberations awaiting the outcome of the bilateral talks going on between Moscow and Washington. The two sets of discussions do not conflict. I hope very much that the four powers will resume their talks at the United Nations while the foreign ministers are here in connection with the General Assembly.

QUESTION: Mr. Secretary-General, would a summit meeting between the United States and the Soviet Union, or possibly the big four, help to promote some sort of progress toward peace in the Middle East, as well as possibly a settlement of the Vietnam war?

THE SECRETARY-GENERAL: You will no doubt recall that this was one of my proposals last year. But I understand that the big four would prefer to have comprehensive and practical preliminaries before they think of having a summit meeting. I have been informed by some of the big-power representatives that the time is not very congenial for the conduct of big-four talks at the summit level, but I very much hope that serious efforts will be made to create conditions for the conduct of a summit meeting of the big powers. . . .

QUESTION: Mr. Secretary-General, on Friday, in your remarkable address at the Hammarskjöld luncheon, you said, and I quote in part: ". . . direct talks between the parties directly involved in the war is the right step for working out a solution. . . ." Then you said that the parties will "resolve their own differences without outside interference." That was, of course, on Vietnam. Do you also think that the application of these principles of international conduct would be a step in the right direction in the Middle East?

THE SECRETARY-GENERAL: As far as the question of direct talks is concerned, I believe that my attitude is well known. I am always for exposure, contact, and communication by all disputants in any crisis situation. I think that it would be ideal if direct talks could take place between President Nixon and Chairman Mao Tse-tung, and Chairman Mao Tse-tung and President Chiang Kai-shek, and Premier Fidel Castro and President Nixon, but the question is whether such proposals are realistic, at least for some time, because of the psychological factors, the emotional factors, the political situation, and domestic considerations.

As far as the Middle Eastern situation is concerned, as the Secretary-General I have to be guided necessarily by the relevant resolutions of the General Assembly and the Security Council. The most comprehensive and, in my view, the most important resolution adopted by the Security Council regarding the situation in the Middle East is the one adopted on November 22, 1967. I do not think there was any mention of direct talks in that resolution. But there was mention of the Secretary-General's representative promoting agreement between the parties directly involved. So Ambassador Jarring, as you all know, has been trying his very best in the last two years to promote agreement. In order to promote agreement there must be some basis for him to come up with some ideas or suggestions.

The most important thing is for the parties directly concerned to tell him their respective positions, definitively. Only then will he be in a position to bring about the situation desired by the Security Council. In this connection, I am reminded of a precedent which took place on the island of Rhodes in February and March of 1949, when Dr. Ralph Bunche was the United Nations mediator for the Middle East. The discussions were going on between Dr. Bunche and the parties concerned without involving direct talks. But when there was a basis for agreement, Dr. Bunche was able to bring about direct talks—at last.

So, in my view, it is not realistic to insist on direct talks between the parties in the Middle East just now. If there is a sufficient basis for talks, for agreement, for the reconciliation of positions, then I do not think direct contacts can be ruled out.

QUESTION: Mr. Secretary-General, recently you said that the most important factor in international affairs in the next few years will be the relations among the Soviet Union, the United States, and Communist China. The question of Chinese representation is coming up in the Assembly. Can you elaborate on that situation a bit?

THE SECRETARY-GENERAL: Some time ago, in response to questions, I stated, through a United Nations spokesman, that for some years to come the nature of the relationship between mainland China and the two superpowers will dominate the international political scene. I still hold that opinion. In my view, the present impasse in the relationship between China and the rest of the world is a tragedy. As you all know, the threat of nuclear war is increasing every day with the mounting escalation of nuclear stockpiles and armaments. I am elaborating on the question of disarmament in the Introduction to my annual report. It seems to me that it is now time for every government to make serious efforts to associate all the five nuclear powers in all negotiations for disarmament in one way or another. The association of all the five nuclear powers in disarmament negotiations will be the indispensable step to fashion a world free from fear. In this context, I am very glad to note that Premier Kosygin and Premier Chou En-lai the other day had a meeting at the Peking airport and exchanged views on matters of mutual interest. I very much hope that the relations between Peking and Moscow, and, for that matter, Peking and Washington, will become normal, if not cordial.

QUESTION: Mr. Secretary-General, since Mr. Jarring will be here at the very time the foreign ministers of the big four will be here, do you think that there might be an opportunity for coordinating the desires of the big four for a Middle East settlement with the work of Mr. Jarring?

THE SECRETARY-GENERAL: Yes, Ambassador Jarring is arriving in New York tonight. Of course, as in the past, he will be available for discussion with the representatives of the parties directly involved, as well as the members of the Security Council, particularly the four permanent members of the Security Council. I am sure Ambassador Jarring, with his great diplomatic ability and patience, will be able to contribute materially to the progress of the talks that are likely to go on, particularly among the representatives of the big four here, during the presence in New York of the foreign ministers.

QUESTION: Some observers feel that perhaps a chance was lost a few days ago in moving toward peace in Vietnam. What, in your view, might have been the progress had the three-day cease-fire called at the time of Ho Chi Minh's funeral been extended?

THE SECRETARY-GENERAL: To my knowledge there have been several missed opportunities in the past, in the course of the last five years or so. But the situation in Vietnam, as I see it, is as I stated it at your luncheon last Friday. You will recall my original three-point proposal: the cessation of bombing of North Vietnam, the discussion by the parties directly involved in the conflict, and de-escalation of fighting. I believe two essential steps have been taken by the parties concerned; I very much hope that the fighting will be de-escalated so that a situation will be created whereby the peoples of Vietnam themselves will be able to fashion their own future without outside interference. But there are indications that the people of Vietnam themselves will play an increasing role in fashioning their own future. So, on the whole, I must say that I am optimistic about the outcome in regard to Vietnam.

QUESTION: Both today and in your spokesman's response on the China question, you have spoken of "mainland China," a concept which has been used in the West to denote the two-China theory. Are you accepting that theory? And do you seriously think there is any hope of reconciliation with China on the basis of a two-China concept?

THE SECRETARY-GENERAL: No, I am not very much concerned with the nuances and nomenclatures. I do not mind calling it the "People's Republic of China" or "mainland China" or "continental China" or "government in Peking." What I mean is, I am sure, known to everybody. When I say "mainland China" I mean the People's Republic of China, of course—continental China, the China with its seat of government in Peking. . . .

QUESTION: Would you be at liberty to tell us anything about how the decision by Mr. Nixon came about to come to the United Nations General Assembly, and how you see the significance of this visit—or whatever you want to say about it?

THE SECRETARY-GENERAL: President Nixon's decision to address the General Assembly this coming Thursday has received universal approbation and appreciation, to my knowledge. The fact that the President has decided to come and address the General Assembly is an indication of his active interest in the work of this Organization and I believe it is an indication of his trust in the United Nations, and his desire to see that this Organization develops into a really effective instrument for peace and progress. I very much hope that the President's address will be very constructive and important. I want to take this opportunity to express my very sincere thanks to the President for his decision to come to the Assembly and address it on Thursday.

QUESTION: Earlier you were asked a question relating to Vietnam in which the name of Ho Chi Minh was mentioned. Would you give us your thoughts on the meaning of the passing of Ho Chi Minh and what can now be expected from the North Vietnamese side? You are very familiar with those people.

THE SECRETARY-GENERAL: Well, personally speaking, I do not think the policy patterns of North Vietnam will change after President Ho Chi Minh's death. In such societies as the one prevailing in North Vietnam, there is prevalent the concept of collective leadership. So the death of one leader normally does not effect a change in policy patterns. Personally speaking therefore, I do not see any radical change in the foreign policy or military policies of Hanoi after the death of President Ho Chi Minh.

QUESTION: Mr. Secretary-General, on Vietnam you in the past made various suggestions on how to stop the fighting, the ceasing of the bombing, and so forth. Would you now consider asking for a cease-fire by all the parties concerned?

THE SECRETARY-GENERAL: I remember having made some observations on the question of a cease-fire in South Vietnam. To be effective, cease-fire proposals must meet with certain requirements. In my view, there must be a certain definite demarcation of lines, where the opposing sides can be clearly identified. At the same time, in a civil war situation like that prevailing in South Vietnam, where one village is occupied by the government forces and another village two miles away is occupied by the forces of the National Liberation Front, it is practically impossible in my view to supervise a cease-fire, even if there is a general willingness to observe a cease-fire. I do not see any means of supervising breaches of the cease-fire, because of the nature of the war there. Therefore, the next step which is essential for the creation of conditions for peace is de-escalation and not a cease-fire right now. In my view, a cease-fire is not realistic in the prevailing circumstances. . . .

QUESTION: I think you have pointed out—and many representatives and members of the press have pointed out—a recent tendency for Member states to treat the adopted resolutions—some of which have even been adopted unanimously—rather lightly, with a little less respect than might have been expected. Sometimes they are bypassed; the United Nations is sometimes defied and insulted. This is a tendency that undermines the very hope of the only institution in the world to which people can turn. It is perhaps the most fatal thing that could happen to the United Nations; and everything else will fall by the wayside— disarmament and everything else—if people cannot be certain that when their governments vote for a draft resolution—or when the majority votes for a draft resolution—that something will result other than a mineographed piece of paper. I know you have expressed yourself once on this subject; I would like to ask you how you feel about this on the eve of this Assembly.

THE SECRETARY-GENERAL: I agree with the premise of your question. There is an increasing tendency among some Member states to disregard the decisions of the principal organs of the United Nations. You know as well as I do that the resolutions or decisions of the Security Council are mandatory. They are different in many respects from the resolutions of the General Assembly. When the Security Council decides on a certain line of action, particularly when its decision is unanimous, I feel that it is very necessary that all the provisions of such a resolution be implemented.

As you all know, for the implementation of a Security Council resolution, the most essential element is the unanimity of the big powers, a spirit of cooperation among the big powers, and a willingness on the part of the big powers to see that the resolutions are implemented. That is why I have been stressing this aspect of the Security Council's functioning from time to time. I very much hope that, with the greater cooperation of the permanent members of the Security Council, in future, the effectiveness of the Security Council will be increased. . . .

3. From Introduction to the Twenty-Fourth Annual Report

NEW YORK   SEPTEMBER 15, 1969

I. General

1. During the past twelve months, the deterioration of the international situation, which I noted in the Introduction to the annual report last year, has continued. In the Middle East, the year has been marked by rising tension, and the level of conflict in the area has never been higher since June 1967. So far as the tragic situation in Nigeria is concerned, while the most recent developments have given rise to a feeling of hope, the tremendous suffering of the civilian population and the loss of life and property have evoked universal concern. In regard to Vietnam I can, however, see signs of some improvement. It is true that the Paris talks have not produced any conclusive results so far, but the very fact that all the parties involved in the conflict are engaged in these discus-

SOURCE: General Assembly Official Records, Twenty-fourth Session, Supplement No. 1A (A/7601/Add. 1), sections I, II, IV, VII, VIII, IX, X.

sions is a most important step in the right direction. The situation in Cyprus has improved steadily in terms of a return to normal conditions of civilian life and the leaders of the two communities are continuing their talks. Basic issues, however, still await solution.

2. In the field of disarmament, progress is indeed very limited; further, there is the frightening prospect of a new arms race in the field of nuclear weapons, involving antimissile defense systems and missiles with multiple warheads. The recent report prepared with the assistance of consultant experts on chemical and bacteriological (biological) weapons and the effects of their possible use, and the attention given to this problem by the Conference of the Committee on Disarmament, lead me to hope that at the forthcoming session of the General Assembly some consensus may be reached on the future approach of the international community to this question. I am also gratified by the interest being displayed at the same Conference on the question of ensuring that the seabed and the ocean floor should be used exclusively for peaceful purposes.

3. I have referred in past years to the chronic problems of colonialism and *apartheid,* which have persisted in southern Africa in defiance of the United Nations. These problems have continued and there is no evidence of the political will to solve them on the part of those in a position to make such a contribution. The same is true of the difficult questions of Rhodesia and Namibia.

4. In recent years I have on a number of occasions touched upon the question of public information activity in support of the various aims and functions of the United Nations. I have noted the increasing importance placed by individual United Nations organs and bodies upon securing stronger information support for their particular areas of concern. As I have said before, this increased interest in, and appreciation of, public information as an essential component of the substantive activities of the United Nations—be they political, economic, social, or humanitarian—is most welcome.

5. In response to various requests originating with diverse United Nations organs and bodies, a series of assessments and reports on information problems and possibilities, such as those presented to the Advisory Committee on Administrative and Budgetary Questions, the Preparatory Committee for the Second United Nations Development Decade, and the Trade and Development Board, have recently been issued. I am both hopeful and confident that these related reports will

provide an opportunity for a major rethinking of the problem of United Nations information activities as a whole and of the organizational structure as well as the material and manpower resources required for the pursuit of such activities in the context of present-day needs and possibilities. I hope that this rethinking and reinvigorating of the information activity will not be long delayed. For my part, I have already taken a number of steps in the direction of strengthening United Nations information activities and increasing the output in all fields. Thus, for example, I have authorized the establishment of a Centre for Economic and Social Information within the United Nations Office of Public Information, made up of a group of professionals with specialized training in the economic and social fields and in the techniques of information relating to these needs. This Centre, which is presently financed for the most part through voluntary funds, will, I hope, play an important part in providing the necessary information support for the Second United Nations Development Decade.

6. Similarly, arrangements have been made for increased coordination between the Office of Public Information and the relevant substantive departments with respect to information relating to the political fields of United Nations endeavor. Consequently, an increased effort and better directed information policy can be anticipated in endeavors such as the elimination of *apartheid* and racism, decolonization, and the promotion of human rights.

7. In offering these general remarks, I think it useful to restate and reaffirm two basic propositions which have guided and inspired all United Nations information activity since it was first organized under the authority of General Assembly resolution 13 (I) of 1946: United Nations information activity must be as universal, factual, and objective as possible on all matters—political as well as economic and social; further, the formulation and execution of information policy must be vested, subject to the general authority of the principal organs of the United Nations, in the Secretary-General and, under him, in the Assistant Secretary-General in charge of the Office of Public Information.

8. As is evident, each of these two basic principles derives from and supports the other. By its very nature and purpose, United Nations information activity has, in terms of subject-matter, to encompass all the diverse and yet interrelated fields of United Nations endeavor and, in terms of dissemination, it must comprehend all geographical regions of the world. This requirement, in turn, makes the centralization of policy

direction and operational control established by the General Assembly twenty-three years ago in the interest, at once, of ensuring economy in operations and uniformity in policy.

9. The Organization's financial situation remains precarious and its ability to meet the payroll and other current expenses rests on borrowings from trust and special accounts in the custody and control of the Secretary-General. In respect of the regular budget as at June 30, 1969, current liabilities (accounts payable, sundry credits and amounts due to trust, special accounts, and surplus account) exceeded current assets (cash, investments, deferred charges, accounts receivable, and amounts due from trust funds) by $5.8 million. At the same date, $39.5 million had been advanced from the Working Capital Fund, and $14.3 million of the voluntary contributions in the United Nations Special Account had been utilized, to finance regular budgetary expenditures. There was, therefore, a cumulative shortfall of $59.6 million in contributions received in relation to expenditures incurred as of June 30, 1969. Unliquidated obligations at the same date totaled $13.3 million.

10. While there was some temporary improvement in the situation in July, as the result of the receipt during that month of some $28 million of assessed contributions to the regular budget, it may be anticipated that the situation will deteriorate during the balance of the year and again become critical before the end of 1969.

11. Unpaid assessed contributions to the regular budget totaled some $130 million as of June 30, 1969. Of this amount, $26.7 million is attributable to the position taken by some Members of not paying for the parts of the regular budget assessments covering the cost of servicing United Nations bonds and the cost of certain activities which they consider illegally included in the regular budget; the balance of $103.3 million represents delayed payments by Members. On the basis of the pattern of past payments, it is estimated that $22.3 million of the balance of $103.3 million is likely to remain unpaid at the end of 1969.

12. The financial situation in respect of the Special Account for the United Nations Emergency Force and the *Ad Hoc* Account for the United Nations Operation in the Congo remains a matter of serious concern. As at June 30, 1969, unpaid assessments to these accounts, which must be considered as virtually uncollectable, totaled $132.7 million, of which $50.6 million related to the United Nations Emergency Force and $82.1 million to the United Nations Operation in the Congo. Amounts owed to governments which provided contingents and logisti-

cal support to the two peace-keeping forces at the same date totaled, respectively, $20.1 million and $10.0 million, although $5.9 and $0.2 million of the voluntary contributions in the United Nations Special Account had been utilized to reduce the indebtedness in the accounts. Additional net liabilities and unliquidated obligations in the two accounts amounted, respectively, to $5.5 million and $3.2 million. As there are no cash balances or investments in these accounts at this time, except for the equivalent of $1.8 million in unconvertible Congolese zaires, it is not possible to pay any of the balances due governments which so generously responded to the Organization's request that they provide contingents and logistical support to the peace-keeping forces.

13. Voluntary contributions and interest credited thereon to the United Nations Special Account increased by $0.4 million during the first half of 1969, thus bringing the total amount credited to this account to $20.4 million. There is no indication that additional substantial pledges and payments may be forthcoming in the near future to help the Organization out of its present financial difficulties.

14. The financial situation in respect of the United Nations Peace-keeping Force in Cyprus is also of most serious concern for, unless additional pledges are received, it is estimated that the deficit in that account as of December 15, 1969, will be approximately $10.8 million.

15. In the field of economic and social development, considerable effort is being devoted to the formulation of the goals and targets of the Second United Nations Development Decade. This is a natural preoccupation not only of the Economic and Social Council, but also of the United Nations Conference on Trade and Development. I believe that we are now well organized to take up the tasks of the Second United Nations Development Decade with the family of institutions developed within the United Nations, such as the United Nations Development Programme, the United Nations Conference on Trade and Development, the United Nations Industrial Development Organization, the United Nations Children's Fund, and the United Nations Institute for Training and Research and also, of course, the family of agencies constituting the United Nations system.

16. The beginning of the Second United Nations Development Decade coincides with the twenty-fifth year of the Organization. As the General Assembly considers questions related to the objectives and strategies for the Second Development Decade, it would be encouraging if there were a greater degree of optimism and enthusiasm consistent

with the signal successes that have attended the efforts of the Organization, particularly as a multinational instrument for promoting economic
and social development. While the developing countries increasingly
turn to the United Nations for assistance in their development efforts,
we have witnessed, in recent years, a growing reluctance on the part of
the more affluent Members to provide financial support to the Organization on a scale in keeping with the increased magnitude and complexity
of its tasks, especially those in the economic, social, and human rights
fields.

17. Recognition of the ever-increasing divergence between decisions
taken by program-formulating bodies and the resources voted for implementing these decisions has not been lacking. Starting with General
Assembly resolution 1797 (XVII) on an integrated program and budget
policy, several recommendations on this subject have been made by the
Economic and Social Council, the Advisory Committee on Administrative and Budgetary Questions, and the General Assembly itself. Following the recommendations of the *Ad Hoc* Committee of Experts to
Examine the Finances of the United Nations and the Specialized Agencies, the Economic and Social Council has called upon its subsidiary
bodies to draw up ''long-range programs of work containing clear indications of priority among the various projects,'' and entrusted its Committee for Programme and Co-ordination with program review and coordination functions covering the full range of activities in the economic,
social, and human rights fields. Furthermore, the General Assembly
requested the Secretary-General to draw up a planning estimate for the
second succeeding budget year, for consideration at the time it takes
decisions on the level of appropriations for the first budget year.

18. Side by side, improvements in the process of budget preparations
have been introduced through the work of the internal budget review
groups, and a survey of manpower utilization and deployment aimed at
improving the efficiency and effectiveness of the Secretariat has been
started, pursuant to the recommendations of the Advisory Committee on
Administrative and Budgetary Questions.

19. While these various measures, designed, on the one hand, to
secure improvements in program formulation and budget preparation
and, on the other, to enhance the efficiency of the Secretariat, are to be
welcomed, it is essential that the review and reorganization processes
should not impede the necessary growth of the Organization, in keeping
with its responsibilities. Nor should they imperil ongoing programs of

proved value or the initiation of new programs which could be of direct benefit in areas which call for international action.

20. Inasmuch as the preparation of the budget is no more than an attempt to reflect in financial terms the level of resources regarded as necessary to undertake the tasks entrusted to the Organization, it would seem inappropriate to try to control growth in programs through limitations on the level of the budget. The emphasis should rather be on improving the program formulations processes, on establishing concrete objectives for United Nations action, and on translating these into long-term and medium-term programs for which, in turn, budgetary provisions can be made.

21. In raising these broad policy issues, I am aware of the fact that, for the immediate future, my attitude toward the budget cannot ignore the concern voiced by some Member governments at its growth in recent years (a growth which in large part is attributable to the creation of new machinery in the fields of trade and industry) and the call for a survey of manpower utilization and deployment. In drawing up my budget proposals for 1970, I have, therefore, limited myself to seeking a lump-sum credit to permit me to augment resources in critical areas so that proved priority programs might not be adversely affected. I have imposed this discipline on the Secretariat in the expectation that the survey of manpower utilization and deployment currently under way would have covered the major part of the Secretariat by the end of 1970, and that I would then have a better basis for presenting to the General Assembly at its twenty-fifth session any necessary revisions in the budget of 1971, or for reflecting the results of the survey in the initial budget for 1972. I am confident that the General Assembly will view with favor any requests for increased resources that I might be constrained to present in order to undertake in the interval new and urgent programs that may be called for by decisions taken by the competent organs. I have in mind, in this connection, the new areas for international action that have emerged in recent years, such as questions related to the peaceful uses of the seabed and the ocean floor, cooperation in outer space, chemical and bacteriological warfare, problems of the human environment and population.

22. Elsewhere in this Introduction reference is made to the global problems of economic and social development in the context of the Second United Nations Development Decade. The problems of the human environment and population have just been mentioned. I am particularly gratified at the attention that has been paid, during recent

years, to the problems of human environment—the earth we tread, the air we breathe, the water we drink. I hope that prospective international action in this field may result in the improvement of the human environment in those countries where pollution has already become a serious problem. I hope that the developing countries may benefit from the experience of the advanced countries and learn to take preventive action when developing their own resources.

23. I have been greatly encouraged by the increasing attention being paid to problems of population growth in recent years by the competent bodies. I am also deeply gratified by the response to my appeal for contributions to a trust fund, established under the auspices of the United Nations, to finance an enlarged program of population activities. I have every hope that this fund, which will be administered on my behalf by the administrator of the United Nations Development Programme, will receive vastly augmented resources on a continuing basis in the years ahead. If this hope is realized, the United Nations and its family of institutions and agencies can make a significant contribution to the alleviation of the problems caused by the rapid growth of population, and help interested countries in developing programs which may contribute to the reduction of their rates of growth and thus bring about an improvement of the quality of life of individuals and families.

24. In the Introduction to the annual report last year, I referred to the consensus reached by the Working Group of the Special Committee on Peace-keeping Operations to study, as a first model in its program of work, the military observer operations established or authorized by the Security Council, and noted that it represented a hopeful sign of willingness on all sides to consider new departures as a means of moving toward a solution of the various aspects of the question of peace-keeping operations.

25. The Working Group, which has met almost continuously since the end of March this year, has devoted its efforts to drawing up comprehensive guidelines for United Nations military observer operations established or authorized by the Security Council. Although the Working Group has made considerable progress in its task, there are still differing views on some important issues. This is not surprising, of course, if we realize that positions which have been maintained and defended over a period of several years cannot be expected to be changed overnight. In view, however, of the expressed desire on all sides to reach agreement on the remaining issues, it it my hope that a consensus would soon be

reached on workable arrangements concerning military observer operations established or authorized by the Security Council, including questions of management and financing. It is also to be hoped that progress would be made in due course on the second model dealing with military contingents.

II. Disarmament

26. In the field of disarmament the past year has seen little progress. Indeed, some of the momentum and promise of previous years seems to have been lost. The world is standing at what may be regarded in the perspective of history as one of the decisive moments in the grim challenge of the nuclear arms race. It is accordingly most disquieting to see that the solution of the problems of preventing the proliferation of nuclear weapons, both horizontally and vertically, is still hanging in the balance. The testing of nuclear weapons continues apace. Global military expenditures continue to mount at an alarming rate. Most dangerous of all, the world seems threatened by an uncontrollable escalation of the nuclear arms race.

27. Hopes for progress toward halting the nuclear arms race were raised when, on July 1, 1968, the Treaty on the Non-Proliferation of Nuclear Weapons was opened for signature, and, on the same day, it was announced that the governments of the Union of Soviet Socialist Republics and the United States of America had agreed "to enter in the nearest future into bilateral discussions on the limitation and reduction of both offensive strategic nuclear weapons delivery systems and systems of defense against ballistic missiles." Since then, however, only very limited progress has been made. The Treaty on the Non-Proliferation of Nuclear Weapons, designed to prevent the spread of nuclear weapons to non-nuclear states, remains unsigned by a number of states which are potential nuclear powers; it has been ratified by one of the three nuclear signatories (the other two have not yet finished their procedures of ratification) and by less than one half of the other forty states required for its entry into force. As regards the interrelated problem of preventing the further qualitative and quantitative proliferation of nuclear weapons and delivery systems among the nuclear powers themselves, the continuing negotiations have not brought any concrete results so far. Despite resolution D of the Conference of Non-Nuclear-Weapon States, which was convened on August 29, 1968, in Geneva and General Assembly resolution 2456 D (XXIII) of December 20, 1968,

calling for the early commencement of the bilateral talks for the limitation and reduction of strategic nuclear arms, at the time of writing the parties had not yet found it possible to announce the date for the opening of the talks.

28. Far from making progress toward limiting and reducing the threat of nuclear weapons, the world seems poised on the verge of a massive new escalation in the field of nuclear weaponry. Plans being discussed at present for antimissile defensive systems and for missiles with multiple warheads generate a renewed sense of fear, insecurity, and frustration. The product of the awful alphabet and arithmetic of ABMs (anti-ballistic missiles) and MIRVs (multiple independently targetable re-entry vehicles) can only be the acceleration of what has been described as the "mad momentum" of the nuclear arms race. The development of such new weapons would greatly magnify and complicate the problems of verification and control of any measures to halt the nuclear arms race. The notion of "superiority" in such a race is an illusion, as that notion can only lead to an endless competition in which each side steps up its nuclear capabilities in an effort to match, or exceed, the other side until the race ends in unmitigated disaster for all. As the spiral of the nuclear arms race goes up, the spiral of security goes down.

29. On the other hand, the opportunities, as well as the need, for halting the nuclear arms race have never been greater than at the present time. There now exists a rough balance between the Soviet Union and the United States where each is capable of virtually destroying the other and neither is capable, if nuclear war should ever break out, of preventing or escaping the holocaust. The present situation of relative stability could disappear, even if only temporarily, if new generations of nuclear weapons systems were developed and deployed. This upsetting of the balance, or "destabilization," would create unknown temptations and pressures and greatly increase the danger of possible miscalculation. Hence there may never be a better time to put a stop to the nuclear arms race, nor a more favorable opportunity to take advantage of the possibilities. I have never been able to understand why, given this rough balance, the major nuclear powers could not assume the calculable and manageable risks of freezing that balance and then reducing it to lower and safer levels, rather than assume the incalculable and unmanageable risks of pursuing a race which may end in disaster for all mankind. Surely, every conceivable national security interest would be protected and even enhanced by agreeing to preserve the balance at progressively reduced levels.

30. I accordingly appeal to the Union of Soviet Socialist Republics and the United States of America to begin immediately their bilateral talks to limit and reduce offensive and defensive strategic nuclear weapons. In the meantime, pending progress in these talks, it would be helpful if they stopped all further work on the development of new offensive and defensive strategic systems, whether by agreement or by a unilateral moratorium declared by both sides. Little or nothing would be lost by postponing decisions to embark on the development and deployment of new nuclear weapon systems in order to explore thoroughly the possibilities of agreement: a very great deal might be lost by failure or refusal to do so. I am sure that the peoples of the world would breathe a sigh of relief if the governments of these two states were to avoid taking any decisions which might prove to be irreversible and which might further escalate the nuclear arms race. Such a pause for reflection and the exercise of restraint while the bilateral talks were being undertaken might well become a historic decision which would be a blessing for all mankind.

31. Inseparably linked to the question of a freeze or limitation of strategic nuclear weapons development is the ending of underground nuclear weapon tests. As long ago as November 1962, the General Assembly, in resolution 1762 A (XVII), explicitly condemned all nuclear weapon tests and asked that they cease immediately and not later than January 1, 1963. The partial test-ban treaty of August 5, 1963, which prohibited tests in the atmosphere, in outer space and under water, contained a promise to seek the ending also of underground tests. Thus far, that promise remains unfulfilled.

32. A number of constructive proposals have been put forward to halt or limit underground nuclear tests. A draft of a comprehensive test-ban treaty that would ban all underground nuclear tests has been submitted to the Conference of the Eighteen-Nation Committee on Disarmament. A proposal has been put forward for a treaty to ban underground tests beginning with a threshold ban of explosions above 4.75 on the seismic scale, which would be progressively lowered as the technology and instrumentation for the detection and identification of tests continue to improve. Still another proposal suggests a ban on underground explosions above the 4.75 magnitude, with a moratorium on explosions below this threshold. Proposals have also been made for encouraging, improving, and better organizing international cooperation for the exchange of seismic data and information as a means of reducing the problems of

verification and thus facilitating an underground test ban. In order to avoid the long-standing difficulties of on-site inspection, proposals have also been made for verification-by-challenge which would seem to provide a relatively easy system for handling suspicions or complaints of possible evasions. All these proposals merit the most careful consideration in order to make some advance from the present impasse.

33. Additional testing of nuclear weapons can be required only for the further sophistication of existing nuclear weapons or for the development of new weapon systems in the nuclear arms race. The several proposals made for controlling or stopping these tests would seem to provide ample possibilities for doing so in safety. The non-nuclear powers would appear to regard the attitude of the nuclear powers to the halting of nuclear tests as an earnest indication of their good intentions to abide by article VI of the Treaty on the Non-Proliferation of Nuclear Weapons, whereby they undertook "to pursue negotiations in good faith on effective measures relating to cessation of the nuclear arms race at an early date and to nuclear disarmament."

34. I would venture to address a renewed appeal to the nuclear powers, in the spirit of the General Assembly resolution of 1962, to end all nuclear tests. I would hope that they would once again review their positions with a view to suspending underground tests, pending progress in the bilateral missile talks.

35. At the same time, I would appeal to all countries to sign and ratify the Treaty on the Non-Proliferation of Nuclear Weapons at the earliest possible date.

36. In September 1968, the non-nuclear powers, imbued with a desire to improve their security by preventing both the horizontal and vertical proliferation of nuclear weapons and to improve their economies by the fullest utilization of nuclear energy for peaceful purposes, held the Conference of Non-Nuclear Weapon States in Geneva. That Conference adopted a number of resolutions which were considered by the General Assembly at its twenty-third session. The Assembly, in its turn, adopted resolutions 2456 A and C (XXIII) requesting the Secretary-General to prepare three reports in regard to these matters for the consideration of the Assembly at its twenty-fourth session—first, a comprehensive report on the progress achieved in implementing resolution 2456 A (XXIII) on the Conference of Non-Nuclear-Weapon States; second, a report prepared by a group of experts on all possible contributions of nuclear technology to the economic and scientific advancement of the develop-

ing countries; and third, a report on the establishment, within the framework of the International Atomic Energy Agency, of an international service for nuclear explosions for peaceful purposes, under appropriate international control. I am hopeful that these reports will help to promote the fulfillment of some of the aspirations of the non-nuclear-weapon states.

37. In pursuance of General Assembly resolution 2454 A (XXIII) of December 20, 1968, I have also prepared a report, with the assistance of consultant experts, entitled *Chemical and Bacteriological (Biological) Weapons and the Effects of Their Possible Use,* which has been submitted to the Conference of the Eighteen-Nation Committee on Disarmament, to the Security Council, as well as to the General Assembly. The report has already been the subject of considerable discussion, and a number of proposals have been made in the Eighteen-Nation Committee for dealing further with the threat posed by chemical and bacteriological (biological) weapons, including an appeal to all states to sign and ratify the Protocol for the Prohibition of the Use in War of Asphyxiating, Poisonous or Other Gases, and of Bacteriological Methods of Warfare, signed at Geneva on June 17, 1925, and a draft convention to prevent the development, production, and stockpiling of biological weapons. I am confident that the report and the various proposals on this important subject will lead to specific decisions at the forthcoming session of the General Assembly that will facilitate political and legal action to eliminate these inhuman and barbarous weapons of war.

38. The Eighteen-Nation Committee on Disarmament has also devoted considerable attention to the prevention of an arms race on the seabed and the ocean floor. Separate draft treaties were presented by the USSR for the demilitarization of that environment and, by the United States, for its denuclearization and the banning of weapons of mass destruction. A number of proposals were made by other countries for finding compromises between the positions set forth in the two draft treaties. At the time of writing, the Committee is continuing its intensive efforts to produce an agreed draft treaty. The forthcoming session of the General Assembly will no doubt wish to give full attention to this problem in an attempt to agree on a text acceptable to all. A treaty that would prevent the spread of the arms race to the seabed and ocean floor would mark another important step forward in this field.

39. In what has been on the whole a less productive year for disarmament, there has been one ray of light. The treaty of Tlatelolco has been

ratified by the requisite number of countries and the Agency for the Prohibition of Nuclear Weapons in Latin America has now been established. I was glad to be able to address, on September 2 in Mexico City, the first session of the General Conference of the Agency. It is a matter of profound satisfaction that the structure of this project, to which the General Assembly first gave its support in 1963 by resolution 1911 (XVIII), has now been formally constituted. It is my hope that, pursuant to the General Assembly resolutions in that regard, additional signatures and ratifications of the Treaty and of its Additional Protocol II will soon be forthcoming to ensure that none of the states of that area will manufacture or acquire nuclear weapons and that the nuclear-weapon powers will not station, deploy, use, or threaten to use such weapons against any of the states in the nuclear-weapon-free zone. The continuing efforts and the steady progress made by the states of Latin America, which have now come to fruition, are deserving of the highest admiration and praise. They have given an exemplary demonstration of what can be achieved, given the moral commitment, careful planning, and persistence. They have successfully taken a first important step toward disarmament and the expansion of peaceful uses of nuclear energy, and have given the world some novel ideas in the field of control. I am hopeful that the system established by the Treaty of Tlatelolco will provide a model for other nuclear-weapon-free zones as well as for additional measures of global disarmament.

40. In a report which I presented to the General Assembly in 1962 on the economic and social consequences of disarmament, it was estimated by a group of experts that the total of world expenditures for military purposes had reached the astronomical figure of about $120,000 million per year. That report was made in the same year that the Eighteen-Nation Committee on Disarmament began its work. Now, seven years later, despite the continuing and very great efforts of the members of the Committee, it is estimated that the world expenditure for armaments is almost $200,000 million per year. Even allowing for the increase in the price level, this inflation of military expenditure is both startling and depressing. During the same period, a number of important successes were achieved by the Committee or were influenced by its efforts. These include the partial test-ban treaty of August 5, 1963, the Treaty on Principles Governing the Activities of States in the Exploration and Use of Outer Space, including the Moon and Other Celestial Bodies of 1967, and the Treaty on the Non-Proliferation of Nuclear Weapons of 1968. It

is true that all these treaties were related to "nonarmaments" or to "preventive disarmament" rather than to disarmament in the sense of the actual reduction of armaments. Nevertheless, each of these treaties was rightly considered as an outstanding achievement in its time. At the same time, however, stockpiles of both nuclear and conventional armaments were steadily increasing both in numbers and in death-dealing capacity. Thus, despite the successes achieved in the decade of the sixties, the armaments race and military expenditures have mounted at an accelerated rate. The diversion of enormous resources and energy, both human and physical, from peaceful economic and social pursuits to unproductive and uneconomic military purposes was an important factor in the failure to make greater progress in the advancement of the developing countries during the First United Nations Development Decade.

41. The world now stands at a most critical crossroads. It can pursue the arms race at a terrible price to the security and progress of the peoples of the world, or it can move ahead toward the goal of general and complete disarmament, a goal that was set in 1959 by a unanimous decision of the General Assembly on the eve of the decade of the 1960s. If it should choose the latter road, the security, the economic well-being, and the progress not only of the developing countries, but also of the developed countries and of the entire world, would be tremendously enhanced.

42. I would accordingly propose that the Members of the United Nations decide to dedicate the decade of the 1970s, which has already been designated as the Second United Nations Development Decade, as a Disarmament Decade. I would hope that the members of the General Assembly could establish a specific program and timetable for dealing with all aspects of the problem of arms control and disarmament. Useful guidelines already exist in the provisional agenda, adopted on August 15, 1968, by the Eighteen-Nation Committee on Disarmament, and in resolution C adopted by the Conference of Non-Nuclear-Weapon States in September 1968.

43. A concerted and concentrated effort during this Disarmament Decade to limit and reduce nuclear and other weapons of mass destruction, to reduce conventional weapons, and to deal with all the related problems of disarmament and security could produce concrete, measurable progress toward general and complete disarmament by the end of the decade of the seventies.

44. In the new decade, an enlarged Conference of the Eighteen-Nation Committee on Disarmament, which henceforth will be known as the Conference of the Committee on Disarmament, will be grappling with the problems of arms limitation and disarmament with the benefit of the fresh approaches brought by the new members. It is hoped that the bilateral missile talks will be under way and that their early success will open new vistas for progress.

45. In this connection, I would regard it of the highest importance that serious attempts be made to associate in one way or another all five nuclear powers with the negotiations for disarmament. The full participation of all the nuclear powers in all efforts to contain the nuclear arms race and to reduce and eliminate armaments would be not only beneficial, but indeed indispensable for a full measure of success.

46. The nations of the world have what may be a last opportunity to mobilize their energies and resources, supported by the public opinion of all the peoples of the world, and to tackle anew the complicated but not insuperable problems of disarmament. I am confident that, given sufficient dedication, the political will and the requisite planning of specific objectives, they can succeed. . . .

IV. *The Middle East and Cyprus*

62. During the past six months there has been a marked deterioration of the situation in the Middle East. This period has seen the highest level of armed conflict in the area since the June 1967 war. Although the extent of such violence has been greater in the Suez Canal sector, in the sense of the frequency of exchanges of heavy fire by both sides, there have been various kinds of recurrent breaches of the cease-fire in all sectors of the Middle East conflict. War actually is being waged throughout the area, short only of battles between large bodies of troops. Patrol and guerrilla activity have become common, as have raids and counter-raids by land and at times by air or sea, bombardments of suspected centers of guerrilla activity, and explosive charges on roads and in civilian structures. This is a pattern of activity which recently, in part at least, has extended to the Israel-Lebanon sector—an area that had been relatively quiet. In the Suez Canal sector, in particular, the increased use of armed force has taken place despite the cease-fire called for by the Security Council, repeated warnings by the Secretary-General, and the ceaseless efforts of United Nations military observers to maintain the

cease-fire. Indeed, I have twice in recent months taken the unusual step of submitting special reports to the Security Council (on April 21 and July 5, 1969) warning the Council of the almost complete breakdown of its cease-fire in the Suez Canal sector and the virtual resumption of war there, despite the unceasing and valiant efforts of the United Nations military observers, who are exposed to great danger, to maintain the cease-fire.

63. There can be no doubt that this constant resort to force is to a considerable extent connected with the present impasse in the search for a peaceful settlement and the absence of an early prospect for the implementation of Security Council resolution 242 (1967) of November 22, 1967. The hopes for such a settlement, which were widely prevalent after the unanimous adoption by the Security Council of this resolution, have thus far been unfulfilled in spite of nearly two years of effort by the United Nations and other parties.

64. This continuing situation is, first of all, a disaster for the Middle Eastern countries directly involved. It is a grim reflection of the state of affairs in the Middle East that, despite all the activities of governments, of the United Nations, and of various individuals, the prospect of even a first step toward a peaceful settlement now still seems remote, and the emotional climate for progress toward peace is no more favorable than ever.

65. This situation also creates, to a considerable extent, a crisis of effectiveness for the United Nations and for its Members. Developments in the Middle East, particularly since June 1967, have posed acutely the challenging problem of how states Members of the United Nations can fulfill the obligation to ensure that decisions of the Security Council and the General Assembly will be respected and given due effect. In the ultimate sense, this can be achieved only by the sovereign Members themselves.

66. For twenty-two years, the Middle East has presented the United Nations with its greatest opportunity as well as its sternest challenge. It is noteworthy that, within the United Nations at least, all the parties to the conflict have stated on numerous occasions that they seek peace. The Security Council's unanimous resolution of November 22, 1967, provided a possible basis upon which this desire for peace could have begun to be realized, although it soon became all too clear that widely divergent interpretations of its meaning and practical applications prevailed among the parties who had accepted it.

67. Ambassador Gunnar Jarring, my special representative in the Middle East, is universally respected and trusted and he has made, and continues to make, persistent efforts to achieve at least a first step toward a settlement. However, experience has painfully demonstrated that in these efforts Ambassador Jarring has found himself acting largely on his own with little or no effective support from other sources in the sense of helpful guidance and backing on the resolution of specific issues. I do not accept the narrow interpretation of the role of Ambassador Jarring, as my special representative in the Middle East, as being exclusively or even primarily to bring the parties together around a common negotiating table. There can be no question that this would be highly desirable, if it could be done. On the other hand, it cannot be said positively at this juncture that it can be done. If, however, it cannot be done immediately, it is not be be concluded that there is nothing else for Ambassador Jarring to do. There is more than one procedural route to peace. Ambassador Jarring has also the function of seeking to bring the positions of the parties together by such means and efforts as he may find possible. In my view, the parties have the duty to cooperate with him in this respect and to provide him with all information concerning their positions and demands necessary for the conduct of fruitful discussions, exchanges, and negotiations.

68. In addition to the efforts of the Security Council and of Ambassador Jarring, in recent months four permanent members of the Security Council, on the initiative of their governments, have engaged in consultation in an attempt to strengthen Ambassador Jarring's hand in his quest for a solution to the problem. This is a development which should have been greeted universally as an encouraging and auspicious step.

69. Despite all these efforts, the rising tide of violence in the Middle East creates still further bitterness and hatred and widens the gulf between Arab and Jew. The severe damage by fire on August 21 to the Al Aqsa Mosque in Jerusalem, whatever may have been its origin, has also served to increase bitterness and tension in the area. Deep emotions, as well as vital interests, are factors to be reckoned with in dealing with the Middle East problem. In some other conflict situations, however, where such emotions and interests have been heavily involved, the international community has been able to assist in restoring quiet and moving along the road to peaceful settlement when the parties to the conflict have been willing to cooperate with it in some degree toward this end. A will to attain peace by the parties themselves is the decisive

factor. In the Middle East, regrettably, international assistance in finding a settlement has thus far not met with an adequate response of this kind. Instead, violent exchanges, the building up of armaments of all kinds, propaganda, and a constant exchange of recriminations prevail.

70. In a situation as grave as this, attempts to assign blame or responsibility to this or that party or the exchange of recriminations for past actions or present policies can only be counter-productive. If a way out of the existing impasse and this deeply ominous state of affairs is to be found, the crux of the problem must be attacked. It is, certainly, the right of every state to exercise control over its own territory, free from alien occupation. Every state is equally entitled to enjoy the right to exist within recognized boundaries which are secure from attack or threat of attack. But, before it is possible to have fruitful discussions on this and related problems, it is indispensable to have some idea of the location of the future boundaries. This relates most directly to the question of the termination of occupation and how these boundaries are to be made secure. It seems to me that the only hope of breaking out of the present impasse must lie in a determined effort to overcome these basic obstacles.

71. What is now at stake is the future of the whole Middle East area and everyone in it. This somber fact alone should discourage any tendency toward either too much bargaining over substance or bickering over procedure. The issues, admittedly, are extremely vital to the parties. But, given the alternative, can any issue be more vital than peace? It is no exaggeration to say that, failing some early progress toward a settlement, there is a very real danger that this great and historic region, the cradle of civilization and of three world religions, will recede steadily into a new dark age of violence, disruption, and destruction. The words of my predecessor, in the context of another international crisis, are relevant to the present Middle East situation. On October 24, 1960, Dag Hammarskjöld said, " . . . no matter how deep the shadows may be, how sharp the conflicts, how tense the mistrust reflected in what is said and done in our world of today as reflected in this Hall and in this house, we are not permitted to forget that we have too much in common, too great a sharing of interests and too much that we might lose together, for ourselves and for succeeding generations, ever to weaken in our efforts to surmount the difficulties and not to turn the simple human values, which are our common heritage, into the firm foundation on which we may unite our strength and live together in

peace.'' It seems clear enough to me that no one of the parties to the Middle East conflict, no matter what temporary military or other superiority it may enjoy at any given time, can hope in the long run to emerge as the victor from the struggle now under way.

72. Moreover, the Middle East conflict is now being extended far beyond the area itself in some ways that are irresponsible and indefensible. No political end, however worthy it may seem to its proponents, can justify means such as the hijacking of commercial passenger aircraft or terrorism against civilians. This trend, if unchecked, could introduce the conditions of the jungle in considerable and important areas of human activity. All governments have an overriding, long-term, common interest in protecting and preserving the framework of peaceful international communications and the simple rules of responsible behavior on which human society is necessarily based. Only sovereign governments can take the indispensable measures to this end.

73. There are many innocent and helpless victims of the situation in the Middle East. I feel impelled to mention in particular one very large group for which the United Nations has specific responsibility and concerning which it has taken firm decisions in principle—the Palestine refugees and the persons displaced by the 1967 hostilities. The reports of the Commissioner-General of the United Nations Relief and Works Agency for Palestine Refugees in the Near East and some of my own recent communications to Member states give a comprehensive view of the task which faces the Agency and of its critically meager resources in dealing with this huge task. Until there is some new and more hopeful turn of events in the Middle East, it is essential that the General Assembly take urgent and effective action to reinforce the Agency and to give it the resources needed to provide for even the minimum requirements of the refugees and the persons displaced by the 1967 war. It bears emphasis and reiteration that the problem of the Palestine refugees, which has persisted now for a score of years, should be regarded as one of the most pressing and urgent of all international problems demanding solution.

74. I share the widely held concern for the plight of another, smaller group of helpless persons. Although I have no direct means of knowing exactly the conditons of life of the small Jewish minorities in certain Arab states, it is clear that, in some cases at least, these minorities would be better off elsewhere and that the countries in which they now live would also be better off, given the prevailing circumstances, if the

departure of those who would wish to leave could be sanctioned and arranged, since their continued presence is a source of both internal and international tension. I hope very much, therefore, that it may soon be possible to find sensible ways of solving this largely humanitarian problem. The approach to the situation can be based only on humanitarian considerations and the lessening of tension in the area, since these Jewish people, being citizens of the countries in which they live, are under the exclusive jurisdiction of the governments of those countries.

75. For all these reasons, therefore, the continuation of the struggle in the Middle East is a prospect which all of the Members of the United Nations should contemplate with the utmost concern and for which the United Nations itself inescapably bears a heavy responsibility. It is imperative and urgent that some way be found to reverse the present trend toward catastrophe.

76. The situation in Cyprus has continued to improve slowly but steadily from the point of view of the return to normal conditions of civilian life. This is in good measure attributable to the tireless efforts of the United Nations Peace-keeping Operation, now in its sixth year on the island.

77. Hopes for a lasting settlement continue to be centered on the intercommunal talks which have been going on for well over a year between two prominent leaders of the Greek Cypriot and Turkish Cypriot communities, Mr. G. Clerides and Mr. R. Denktash. The limited extent of the progress achieved so far in these talks is a cause for growing concern. In March 1969, I expressed to the parties directly involved in Cyprus, as well as to the governments of Turkey and Greece, my hope that a determined effort would be made by the parties to expedite the talks. There has, however, been no indication so far of significant progress on the fundamental issues which separate the two sides, particularly the problem of local government. This is not to imply that an impasse has been reached, which would be very serious indeed, since the talks constitute the only hope, at present, for progress in the search for a solution.

78. It is obvious that a solution of the basic issues requires more than a willingness to engage in talks or even to agree on procedural points, though these are, of course, indispensable prerequisites. The clear precondition for progress on the basic issues is a willingness on the part of both parties to make the concessions necessary for a lasting peace.

79. I pointed out in my *aide-mémoire* of March 26, 1969, that the

passage of too much time may hamper rather than facilitate a settlement. Time, in my opinion, is not on the side of a successful resolution of the problems of the island. More than five and a half years have now passed since the violent disturbances which abruptly and almost completely cut off communications between the two communities in Cyprus. In those five and a half years, a new generation of Greek and Turkish Cypriots has been growing up who hardly know each other at all except in hostility. It stands to reason that members of this generation will have far greater difficulty in finding a basis for living in peace with each other than those of the older generation now searching for a solution. I must therefore again urge the parties to consider earnestly and with a broad concern for the future the difficult and perhaps even painful decisions that are now urgently required of them. The good offices of the Secretary-General, directly or through my special representative, continue of course to be available to the parties.

80. The lack of substantial progress in the intercommunal talks inevitably raises the question of the future of the United Nations Peace-keeping Force in Cyprus. The strength of the Force has been considerably reduced in the past year. At present, its numerical strength is only slightly more than half its original size of five years ago. Recently the question of further reduction in the strength of the Force, and particularly in its cost, has been raised in some quarters. I am naturally concerned with the continuing costs of the Force, especially since, in the nature of the financing arrangements prescribed by the Security Council, the financial burden is most unequally and inequitably distributed among governments.

81. Obviously, the most desirable solution would be a degree of progress in the intercommunal talks which would make the presence of the Force in the island no longer necessary. Meanwhile a major factor in considering further reductions in the strength of the Force is the continued existence of direct armed confrontations between the two communities in Cyprus, particularly in Nicosia. I am taking all possible measures to ensure that the costs of the Force are reduced to as low a level as possible commensurate with maintaining its minimum essential effectiveness. To that end, I have appointed a Secretariat team which, in consultation with my special representative and the Force commander, will make an on-the-spot review of the organization and operation of the United Nations Peace-keeping Force and submit to me its report, with recommendations, later this year.

. . .

VII. Apartheid

145. In the tenth year since the tragic event at Sharpeville led the Security Council to recognize the danger to peace resulting from the policies of *apartheid* of the government of the Republic of South Africa and to call for an abandonment of that policy, there has again been little progress toward a solution.

146. United Nations organs have continued to give active consideration to the question. The General Assembly, which again emphasized the need for a solution of the situation, in order to eliminate the grave threat to peace in southern Africa as a whole, requested the Security Council to consider effective measures and adopted various recommendations to promote international action against *apartheid*. The Special Committee on the Policies of *Apartheid* of the Government of the Republic of South Africa has continued its efforts to publicize the situation and promote an international campaign against *apartheid*. The Economic and Social Council and the Commission on Human Rights and its subsidiary bodies have dealt with gross violations of human rights in South Africa.

147. The government of South Africa, however, has remained intransigent and has in fact intensified its efforts to entrench the system of racial discrimination, in defiance of appeals by the international community that it abandon its racial policy and seek a new course consistent with its obligations under the United Nations Charter. Further discriminatory measures have been enacted during the past year. Harassment of opponents of *apartheid,* in violation of the principles of the rule of law, has continued. United Nations organs have expressed grave concern over reports of ill treatment of political prisoners and the deaths of persons detained under arbitrary laws.

148. Moreover, the South African government has proceeded with the imposition of *apartheid* in Namibia in defiance of resolutions of the General Assembly and the Security Council. It has been the main source of support for the illegal régime in Southern Rhodesia and a source of encouragement to the government of Portugal in their defiance of the resolutions of competent United Nations bodies. These aspects will be dealt with in greater detail in the section on decolonization. It is clear that the policies and actions of the South African government have increasingly become the crucial element in the grave situation in southern Africa as a whole.

149. Earnest consideration should be given to ways and means of improving the effectiveness of the United Nations in concerting international efforts toward a solution of this situation so as to avert the incalculable dangers inherent in its continuation.

150. On the one hand, during the many years that the United Nations has considered this matter, there has emerged a wide consensus that the policies of *apartheid* are abhorrent and that they are inconsistent with the obligations of a Member state under the Charter; that the situation resulting from these policies constitutes a grave danger to international peace and security; that a solution must be sought by securing the abandonment of the policies of *apartheid* and the release of the opponents of *apartheid* from imprisonment and arbitrary repressive measures, and the holding of consultations among all the people of South Africa to determine a new course which would ensure human rights and fundamental freedoms to all, irrespective of race, color or creed; and that the people of South Africa deserve sympathy and appropriate assistance in their legitimate struggle for the achievement of human rights and fundamental freedoms. On the basis of this wide consensus, United Nations organs have made numerous decisions and recommendations.

151. On the other hand, there remains a lack of agreement on further effective measures which require, in particular, the full cooperation of the main trading partners of South Africa, including some permanent members of the Security Council.

152. I reiterate my earnest hope that progress, under United Nations auspices, will soon be made toward meaningful and effective measures to persuade the South African government to abandon its policy of racial discrimination and to satisfy the yearning of the people of South Africa for equality and justice. I also consider it essential to secure the full and effective implementation of measures already decided upon by the competent United Nations organs.

153. In this connection, I wish first to draw attention to the solemn appeals by the Security Council in 1963 and 1964 that all states cease the sale and shipment to South Africa of arms, ammunition of all types, military vehicles, and equipment and materials for the manufacture and maintenance of arms and ammunition.

154. Member states and world public opinion will need to exert more vigorous efforts in pursuance of resolutions, adopted by unanimous or overwhelming votes, for the liberation of all persons subjected to repres-

sion for their opposition to *apartheid*. The enactment of increasingly arbitrary legislation to suppress the legitimate protest against racial discrimination and the ruthless and vengeful actions against the leaders of movements opposed to *apartheid* have been a source of increasing concern to United Nations organs. Such measures are not only unjust and deplorable, but aggravate tension and tend to exclude the possibility of peaceful change in South Africa.

155. The United Nations has been providing humanitarian and educational assistance to the prisoners and their families and to other victims of the policies of *apartheid* under two programs financed by voluntary contributions from states and the public—the United Nations Trust Fund for South Africa and the United Nations Educational and Training Programme for Southern Africa. While these programs have received substantial contributions, the number of contributing states has remained rather small. I very much hope that a larger number of states will consider generous contributions to these programs, and thereby demonstrate the growing concern of the international community for the plight of the victims of racial discrimination.

156. In order to promote more energetic international action, the General Assembly and other organs have stressed increasingly the need for wider dissemination of information to the people of South Africa and to the people of the world on the situation in South Africa, its wider dangers, and the efforts of the United Nations toward a peaceful solution. In this connection, I wish to emphasize, as I did last year, that an effective program of information must derive from and depend upon an effective program of substantive action. Moreover, while information activity of the United Nations on this matter should be purposeful and imaginative, it is essential that it must be based on objective and authoritative information on the situation resulting from the policies of *apartheid* in South Africa, the deliberations and decisions of all United Nations organs concerned and the consensus in the Organization.

157. Pursuant to decisions of the organs concerned, the United Nations Secretariat has already taken a number of steps in this respect, and further steps toward sustained activity are under consideration. I trust that, in this effort to create an accurately informed world public opinion, the indispensable cooperation of Member states, information media and non-governmental organizations will be forthcoming.

158. Finally, I would point to the need for greater coordination and concentration in the activities of United Nations organs and specialized

agencies with regard to this question. The Economic and Social Council has decided to consider this matter further at its forty-eighth session. It is to be hoped that consideration will be given by the various organs concerned and by Member states to appropriate means of ensuring that United Nations activities will be better coordinated in order to provide maximum assistance to the people of South Africa in their legitimate strivings and to promote sustained and vigorous international action toward a just and peaceful solution.

VIII. Decolonization

159. The past year has been mainly one of continuing disappointment and frustration in the field of decolonization. There has been some progress, notably the accession to independence of Equatorial Guinea following a referendum and election under United Nations supervision, and the conclusion of an agreement between Spain and Morocco which terminated the colonial status of Ifni. It is, nonetheless, a matter of deep regret that, despite nearly nine years of continuing endeavor on the part of the United Nations, the goals set forth in the Declaration on the Granting of Independence to Colonial Countries and Peoples are still far from early realization.

160. While there were limited constitutional advances during the year in a number of smaller dependent territories, the fact remains that, apart from the two instances mentioned, there has been no significant movement toward the peaceful resolution, in accordance with the Charter of the United Nations, of the remaining major problems of decolonization.

161. In the Introduction to my last annual report, I referred to the colonial situation in southern Africa as representing the most conspicuous mass violation of human rights and fundamental freedoms and observed that the collective determination of the United Nations to put an end to colonialism in that part of the world seemed to have met a solid wall of defiance. I must regretfully add that events during the past year have reinforced my views. Indeed in southern Africa millions of dependent peoples are still denied their most fundamental rights. The authorities in power in this region continue to pursue repressive and retrogressive policies in conflict with the basic objectives of the Charter, the principles enshrined in the Universal Declaration of Human Rights, and the numerous decisions of the Security Council and the General Assembly. Such a situation presents a most serious challenge to the collective

will and, indeed, to the very authority of the United Nations. The close and urgent attention which the competent organs of the United Nations, including the Security Council, have given to the colonial problems in southern Africa during the past year emphasizes the increasing gravity of the situation resulting from the frustration of the legitimate aspirations of those peoples. To meet this challenge effectively requires a full and cooperative effort on the part of all Member states.

162. With regard to Namibia, a territory and people for which the United Nations has assumed a direct responsibility, the government of South Africa remains adamant in its refusal to recognize or give effect to the resolutions whereby the General Assembly terminated the Mandate and established the United Nations Council for Namibia to administer the territory until independence. That government has continued not only to reject these and subsequent resolutions of the General Assembly concerning Namibia, but it has also refused to comply with Security Council resolutions calling for its immediate withdrawal from the territory and for the release and repatriation of Namibians illegally tried and convicted under retroactive legislation.

163. Maintaining its intransigent attitude, the government of South Africa has persisted in frustrating the efforts of the United Nations Council for Namibia to carry out the principal tasks assigned to it, and, in further defiance of the decisions of the United Nations, as well as of world public opinion, it has enacted new legislation aimed at destroying the unity and territorial integrity of Namibia and applying to that territory its own policies of *apartheid,* including the creation of separate racial "homelands." More recently, the government of South Africa has placed on trial a fresh group of Namibians on charges under the retroactive "Terrorism Act" despite the condemnation of such action voiced earlier by the Security Council, the General Assembly, and the overwhelming majority of states Members of the United Nations.

164. In Southern Rhodesia, the illegal régime which usurped power in November 1965 has continued to defy the administering power and the international community. It has engaged in further provocative acts of suppression aimed at consolidating its racist policies, including the introduction of a so-called new constitution designed to perpetuate the domination of the African majority by the white settler minority. These ominous developments in the territory further aggravate the existing threat to international peace and security in southern Africa and call for a positive response from both the administering power and the United Nations. As far as the United Nations is concerned, the so-called new

constitution can have no validity whatsoever and can in no way affect the responsibility of the administering power for the territory.

165. It is a matter of deep regret that the sanctions imposed on the illegal régime in Southern Rhodesia by the Security Council have not as yet had the desired result of bringing down that régime. Now, as before, the primary responsibility for this impasse rests with the governments of South Africa and Portugal which, in defiance of the decisions of the Security Council, have continued to maintain close economic, trade, and other relations with the illegal régime and to accord transit and other facilities through territories under their control for trade between Southern Rhodesia and its overseas principals, I should like to express the hope that the governments of both South Africa and Portugal would be persuaded to abandon their present policies and cooperate with the United Nations in the implementation of the relevant resolutions on Southern Rhodesia. Pending further action by the administering power and the United Nations with a view to finding a solution to the problem which would enable the people of Southern Rhodesia to exercise their inalienable right to self-determination and independence, I also wish to appeal to all states that are complying with the sanctions to exercise greater vigilance to interrupt the flow of covert trade, as well as to states concerned to take more stringent measures to prevent their nationals and their registered ships and aircraft from engaging in activities in contravention of resolutions of the Security Council. In this connection, I would like to commend the fine work of the Security Council's Committee on Sanctions against Southern Rhodesia.

166. When the question of territories under Portuguese administration was discussed by the General Assembly at its twenty-third session, it was hoped by many that the new government in Portugal might reconsider its policy toward those territories and recognize the right of the inhabitants to self-determination and independence. Regrettably, the ensuing months have brought no change in this direction. Continuing military operations by the Portuguese government in Angola, Mozambique, and Guinea, called Portuguese Guinea, once more led to a violation of the territorial integrity of an African state. In July 1969, the Security Council, gravely concerned that incidents of this nature were endangering international peace and security, once again called upon Portugal to desist from such acts.

167. It is clearly not sufficient that the government of Portugal should be working, as it claims, toward increasing autonomy for the territories under its administration within the constitutional framework of the

Portuguese state and seeking to improve the peoples' welfare. Its contin-
ual denial to those peoples of their fundamental right to self-determination and independence in accordance with the principles of the United
Nations Charter remains the crucial obstacle to peace in southern Africa
and exacerbates the grave situation prevailing in that region. It is to be
hoped that, during the year ahead, the international community will
make a concerted, clear, and unequivocal effort to persuade the government of Portugal to take the historic step which will open the door to
freedom and independence to the peoples of the territories under its
administration.

168. In the meantime, I have been encouraged to note that further
international measures have been taken to increase humanitarian assistance to refugees from territories under Portuguese administration. I
trust that such measures will be continued and intensified.

169. Different in magnitude, although not in kind, the problems of the
remaining dependent territories have continued to occupy the General
Assembly and, particularly, the Special Committee on the Situation with
regard to the Implementation of the Declaration on the Granting of
Independence to Colonial Countries and Peoples. That there are still,
nearly nine years after the adoption of that historic Declaration, a large
number of territories whose peoples have not yet attained the prescribed
goals is due not so much to the refusal of the administering powers to
accept their responsibilities under the Charter as to a lack of that
cooperation which would hasten the pace of decolonization. As many
Member states pointed out during the twenty-third session of the General Assembly, the remaining problems of decolonization are precisely
those which are most difficult to solve; many of the territories which are
still dependent present peculiar difficulties owing to their small size, their
paucity of human and natural resources and, in some cases, their
geographical isolation. As a result, differences of opinion have arisen
between the competent United Nations organs and the admistering
powers concerning the measures, modalities, and timing to be applied in
each particular case.

170. It is not surprising that the administering powers, in view of their
intimate knowledge of problems peculiar to each of the territories which
they administer, attach great importance to realism and balance in the
decisions of the United Nations concerning those territories. It is equally
understandable that other Member states, sharing the general desire to
hasten the process of decolonization, view this attitude with impatience.

Yet it is my belief that the two concerns are not mutually exclusive. If the competent organs of the United Nations had access to more adequate and first-hand information regarding conditions in those dependent territories as well as the views and aspirations of their peoples, both of these concerns could undoubtedly be met to a greater degree. It is with that objective in mind that the Special Committee has consistently and continuously urged the development of a more positive approach by the administering powers to the sending of visiting missions.

171. It is precisely because the problems of many of the remaining dependent territories are complex and difficult that it is desirable that the United Nations and, where appropriate, the international institutions associated with it, should play a more active role in helping to solve those problems. An example of what can be achieved through close cooperation between the administering powers and the United Nations was the fruitful operation conducted last year, at the request of the government of Spain, by a United Nations mission in Equatorial Guinea, which enabled that territory to accede to independence as a single entity, and later to full membership in the United Nations.

172. There remains, as I mentioned last year, a special category of problems relating to territories which are the subject of conflicting claims to sovereignty or which are of particular interest to some governments by reason of geographical, historical, or other circumstances. In respect of such territories, the General Assembly and the Special Committee have sought, within the framework of the Declaration on the Granting of Independence to Colonial Countries and Peoples, to make recommendations which would help to reconcile divergent claims and interests. Here, too, the United Nations can play an important role in helping to achieve the objectives laid down in the Declaration, but only if it receives the full cooperation of the governments concerned.

173. In view of the magnitude and difficulty of the tasks which remain, it is my earnest hope that all Member states, and especially those directly concerned, will redouble their endeavors in a final concerted effort to achieve the goals set out in the Declaration.

IX. Other Questions

174. One of the most important steps forward in the codification and progressive development of international law by the United Nations was taken this year at the second session of the United Nations Conference

on the Law of Treaties, held in Vienna from April 9 to May 22, 1969. The Conference, at which 110 states were represented, adopted the Vienna Convention on the Law of Treaties, consisting of eighty-five articles covering such topics as the conclusion and entry into force of treaties, reservations, application and interpretation, and invalidity and termination. The opening of the Convention for signature and ratification was the culmination of twenty years of work on the subject in the International Law Commission, the General Assembly, and the Conference, which held its first session in 1968. Though the Convention provides that it applies only to treaties concluded by states parties to it after its entry into force, many representatives at the Conference said that the provisions, most of which were adopted unanimously or by very large majorities, embodied existing law. It therefore seems likely that the formulations laid down will be widely accepted in practice even before the entry into force of the Convention. As treaties now provide most of the legal framework of international relations, and as the customary rules governing them are frequently unclear and subject to dispute, the clarification of those rules in a convention is a contribution to the aim laid down in the United Nations Charter "to establish conditions under which justice and respect for the obligations arising from treaties . . . can be maintained."

175. At the time of the writing of this Introduction, the fifth session of the Special Committee on Principles of International Law concerning Friendly Relations and Co-operation among States is being held at United Nations Headquarters. Since 1964, the Committee has been engaged in elaborating upon seven of the basic principles of international law enshrined in the Charter. These principles relate to the prohibition of the threat or use of force, the pacific settlement of disputes, nonintervention, sovereign equality, equal rights and self-determination, and the duties of states to cooperate with one another and to fulfill in good faith the obligations assumed by them in accordance with the Charter. From their mere enumeration, it is clear that these principles lie at the very heart of present-day international relations and their elaboration in a generally acceptable form will be a great step forward in the growth and progressive development of international law. Given their vital character, it is only natural that the elucidation of the principles is a difficult and time-consuming task. Since 1964, however, progress has been made on reaching points of agreement on nearly every principle, and I very much hope that, as a result of the endeavors of the Special Committee, it will

be possible for the General Assembly, at its twenty-fifth anniversary session next year, to adopt unanimously a declaration on the principles. This anniversary would be a particularly fitting occasion for the Assembly to adopt such an important declaration in discharge of its responsibilities under Article 13, paragraph 1, of the Charter for encouraging the progressive development of international law and its codification.

176. One aspect of the work of the Secretary-General perhaps merits special comment in this disturbed period when both governments and the United Nations are frequently frustrated in their efforts to find solutions to difficult problems. I refer to the wide range of informal and confidential activity sometimes covered by the broad term "good offices." This activity covers a great variety of subject-matter and constitutes a considerable part of the workload of the Secretary-General, but it is my impression that its nature and possibilities are sometimes not very well understood. In fact, very often there is no public knowledge at all of specific activities of this kind.

177. It is natural that governments, when faced with delicate problems which urgently demand solution, should ask the Secretary-General for such help as he personally may be able to give through discreet approaches to the other party or parties concerned. The Secretary-General himself, in the very nature of his position and responsibilities, on occasion also takes initiatives in an attempt to promote a satisfactory solution to a difficult or dangerous problem, which, unless solved, might deteriorate to the point where peace and security would be threatened or which, while not involving issues of peace and security, might prevent the maintenance of good relations between states.

178. The nature of the Secretary-General's good offices, their limitations, and the conditions in which he may hope to achieve results are perhaps less well understood. The kind of problem involved is invariably delicate and difficult, and usually involves the prestige and public position of the governments concerned. If a way out is to be found, it must, therefore, be through mutual confidence, mutual respect, and absolute discretion. Any hint that an action of the Secretary-General might serve to score political points for one party or another, or, indeed that credit might be claimed publicly on his behalf for this or that development, would almost invariably and instantly render his efforts useless. Any public pressure on him would usually have the same result, and any publicity at all for what he is doing is likely to have a severely adverse effect on his efforts. Thus, it is often the case that while the Secretary-

General is working privately with the parties in an attempt to resolve a delicate situation, he is criticized publicly for inaction or even for lack of interest.

179. I mention this particular aspect of the matter solely with the thought in mind that a better general understanding of the good-offices function may serve to enhance its effectiveness in the future.

180. In this connection, I should also mention a separate question which has been raised in regard to the competence of the Secretary-General to use his good offices without in each case specific authorization from an organ of the United Nations.

181. My own views on the role of the Secretary-General in matters affecting peace and security and on the existing practice concerning good offices were reflected in my statement to the Security Council prior to its adoption on December 2, 1966, of resolution 229 (1966) recommending my appointment for a second term of office. On that occasion I said:

The Secretary-General takes note of the observations made by the Security Council and recognizes the validity of the reasons it has advanced in requesting him to continue to serve the Organization for another full term. He notes with particular appreciation that, for its part, the Security Council respects his position and his action in bringing to the notice of the Organization basic issues confronting it, and disturbing developments in many parts of the world. He hopes that the close attention being given to these issues and developments will serve to strengthen the Organization by the cooperative effort of the entire membership, and promote the cause of world peace and progress. It is in this hope that the Secretary-General accedes to the appeal addressed to him by the Security Council.

182. It is a matter of course that the Secretary-General will keep the Security Council informed, as appropriate, of developments in questions of which it is seized, and that these may on occasion include questions in which he is exercising his good offices either at the request of the Council itself or of the parties concerned.

183. The Charter, unlike the Covenant of the League of Nations, foresaw, in Article 99, that the Secretary-General would have a political role to play. This was recognized, and elaborated upon by the Preparatory Commission which stated in section 2, chapter 8, of its report:

The Secretary-General may have an important role to play as a mediator and as an informal adviser of many governments, and will undoubtedly be called upon from time to time, in the exercise of his administrative duties, to take decisions which may justly be called political. Under Article 99 of the Charter, moreover, he has been given a quite special right which goes beyond any power previously accorded to the head of an international organization, viz: to bring to the attention of the Security Council any matter (not merely any dispute or situation) which, in his opinion, may threaten the maintenance of international peace and security. It is impossible to foresee how this Article will be applied; but the responsibility it confers upon the Secretary-General will require the exercise of the highest qualities of political judgement, tact, and integrity.

By its resolution 13 (I), adopted unanimously on February 13, 1946, the General Assembly transmitted the foregoing section to the Secretary-General for his guidance.

184. It should also be recalled that, under Article 33, paragraph 1, of the Charter, the parties to any dispute, the continuance of which is likely to endanger the maintenance of international peace and security, have a duty first of all to seek a solution by negotiation, inquiry, or mediation. If the parties request or agree to receive the help of the Secretary-General in performing their duty under the Charter to seek a solution, the Secretary-General is clearly competent to assist them.

185. Against this background, I have come to the clear conclusion that I am competent, under the Charter, to use my good offices.

186. I may add that my views regarding my competence in this matter, and the practice followed in this regard, must have been generally accepted by the Members of the United Nations, since many of them, when the occasion has arisen, have availed themselves of my good offices. In each such case, the Secretary-General's decision on whether to exercise his good offices must, of course, depend upon his own judgment as to whether his action would be appropriate, useful and, above all, not counterproductive.

187. Both in 1967 and last year, in the Introduction to the annual report, I drew attention to the problem of "micro-states." I am very glad that the question was discussed at length in the Security Council toward the end of August and that the Council decided to refer this question to a Committee of Experts comprising all the members of the Council, for further consideration. I shall await the Committee's conclusion with the greatest interest.

188. In recent months, I have been greatly distressed at the number of incidents involving hijacking of planes and their diversion to unauthorized destinations. In the Introduction to the annual report last year, I referred to this problem with regard to one specific example and I

expressed the fear that if hijacking incidents were not checked they could easily lead to widespread disruption of air travel.

189. I have been in close contact with the International Civil Aviation Organization, and also the International Air Transport Association, in connection with this problem. I am glad that the Council of the International Civil Aviation Organization has established a committee of eleven member states to recommend specific preventive measures or procedures to stop hijacking. I believe it is a most important principle that no state or person should derive any advantage from the criminal act of hijacking; otherwise there would be only encouragement for this reprehensible act. I sincerely hope that the committee of the International Civil Aviation Organization will be able to come forward with concrete recommendations and that these recommendations will be universally accepted.

190. Hijacking is serious enough when it is conducted for the benefit of individuals; but when it projects itself into the political field and is perpetrated as an instrument of political action or reprisal, it becomes even more reprehensible. It would therefore be extremely desirable if, even before the Committee produces its recommendations, all Member states could take action to ensure that the safety of international air travel is not jeopardized by the irresponsible acts of misguided individuals or organizations.

191. The news of the outbreak of hostilities between El Salvador and Honduras on July 14, 1969, was received at the United Nations with shock and disbelief. Two states, in a region where international peace had not been disturbed for a long time, had taken the fateful step of trying to resolve, by military means, the difference existing between them. Both governments had brought the dispute to the Organization of American States while keeping the Security Council informed of developments.

192. The Organization of American States, acting with speed and determination, made every effort to bring the conflict to an end, first through the Council of the Organization, acting as an organ of consultation and then through the Meeting of Consultation of Ministers of Foreign Affairs under the Inter-American Treaty of Reciprocal Assistance. Important resolutions were adopted by these two organs, and through their implementation it was possible to stop the fighting and restore the military situation to that which had prevailed prior to the hostilities.

193. On July 15, 1969, I addressed separate and identical messages to the ministers for foreign affairs of El Salvador and Honduras, appealing urgently for the immediate cessation of acts of force and the initiation of negotiations without delay.

194. It is a matter of gratification that the governments of El Salvador and Honduras complied with the decisions of the Organization of American States, thus bringing to a quick end the hostilities which, although brief, left in their wake a grievous toll in loss of life and property. While the fighting has been halted, there are underlying problems between the two countries which should also be tackled with a sense of urgency in order to avoid a recurrence of conflict in the future. It is my earnest hope that the governments of the two countries will show the statesmanship demanded by the circumstances and move toward a peaceful and lasting solution to their difficulties. In particular, I call upon them to avoid any damage to the promising structure of the Central American Common Market, in which we all place great hope for the progress of the region.

195. Year after year, I have drawn attention to the need for the United Nations to make progress toward universality of membership as soon as possible. I cannot help feeling that—to give only one example—more successful efforts toward the solution of the difficult problem of Vietnam could have been made within the Organization if all the parties concerned had been represented in it. The same is true of the problem of disarmament and especially non-proliferation of nuclear weapons: so long as one member of the "nuclear club" is not represented in the Organization, it is unrealistic to expect progress in this field. Some international incidents in the Far East might have been defused more effectively if a dialogue could have been initiated at United Nations Headquarters with the representatives of those who are now absent for one reason or another. The same remarks would apply in the case of the divided countries, as I pointed out in the Introduction to the annual report last year. I feel that somehow this problem should be resolved in the near future in the interest of the greater effectiveness of the United Nations.

196. In recent months I have given much thought to the establishment of an international university. The idea occurred to me because my attention was drawn to the work being done by individuals to establish institutions of learning with an international character. I also have in mind some institutions of research and training which were established under international auspices and which have had considerable success in

promoting economic development. I feel that the time has come when serious thought may be given to the establishment of a United Nations university, truly international in character and devoted to the Charter objectives of peace and progress. Such an institution may be staffed with professors coming from many countries and may include in its student body young men and women from many nations and cultures. Working and living together in an international atmosphere, these students from various parts of the world would be better able to understand one another. Even in their formative years they would be able to break down the barriers between nations and cultures, which create only misunderstanding and mistrust.

197. The primary objective of the international university would thus be to promote international understanding at both the political and the cultural levels. I feel that such a scheme could be the legitimate concern of the United Nations Educational, Scientific and Cultural Organization, which would be responsible for working out the details, selecting a board of trustees for the university, and appointing as its head a scholar of international renown. The location of the university should be in a country noted for its spirit of tolerance and freedom of thought. I very much hope that the United Nations Educational, Scientific and Cultural Organization might find it possible to develop this idea further and eventually bring it to fruition.

X. Concluding Observations

198. It is clear to me that in the light of the above observations, I can report very little progress in the world at large toward the goals of the United Nations Charter—to maintain international peace and security, develop friendly relations among nations, and achieve international cooperation. Furthermore I have a strong feeling that time is running out. This is true as much in regard to international peace and security, including disarmament, as it is true for economic and social development. I hope that in the coming months, when the United Nations will celebrate the twenty-fifth anniversary of the establishment of the Organization, there will be some progress in these fields, because I believe that this would be the most fitting manner in which to celebrate the anniversary.

199. In the period under review, I have already noted some encouraging signs in regard to the problem of Vietnam. I do not believe it would be useful for me to comment on the situation in Vietnam, since the

parties are in contact with each other in Paris. I believe that such talks between the parties involved is essential for working out a solution to this problem. I must also point out that, despite these contacts, the war is continuing with consequent loss of life and property, although reportedly at a reduced level. I would very much hope that before long there might be a further de-escalation of the fighting and that the people of Vietnam might be enabled to resolve their differences by themselves without outside interference. It is also important, in view of the many lost opportunities of the past, that every opening that might present itself in the future should be seized and the fullest advantage derived from it in moving toward de-escalation and a final settlement.

200. I commented at length on the situation in Czechoslovakia in the Introduction to the annual report last year. I have followed subsequent developments with close attention and have also been in touch with the government. I refrain from public comment on the question at this stage, as I believe it will not serve any useful purpose.

201. So far as West Irian is concerned, it is a matter of public knowledge that the "act of free choice" was recently completed. The eight regional assemblies, whose membership was enlarged for the purpose, were consulted from July 14 to August 2, 1969, and decided in favor of West Irian remaining with the Republic of Indonesia. I have already proposed this item for inclusion in the agenda of the twenty-fourth session of the General Assembly. The Assembly will also have before it my report on this question, as well as those of the government of Indonesia and my representative, Mr. Fernando Ortiz-Sanz.

202. As a result of the difficulties which arose between the governments of Equatorial Guinea and Spain at the beginning of this year, I designated Mr. Marcial Tamayo, a senior official of the Organization, as my representative in Equatorial Guinea. His task was to assist in the solution of the problems between Equatorial Guinea and Spain, and to cooperate with the parties in order to reduce the tension which had already developed in the relations between the two countries. Accompanied by a small staff, my representative arrived in Equatorial Guinea on March 10, 1969.

203. By April 9, when my representative left Equatorial Guinea, the situation had improved considerably and the two countries had agreed on a number of important points affecting their relations.

204. This was an instance when it was possible to assist a newly independent country in settling, before it was too late, some of its pressing international problems with the former administering power.

205. I am deeply distressed that the fratricidal and tragic conflict in Nigeria is continuing, with its mounting toll of death, destruction, and starvation. My concern has been exclusively with the humanitarian aspects of this conflict, for reasons which I have explained publicly on several occasions. I strongly feel that it should be possible, notwithstanding all the political and other difficulties, for the humanitarian activities of the United Nations family to continue and for the flow of supplies to the stricken areas to be maintained. Only a few days ago, addressing the Assembly of Heads of State and Government of the Organization of African Unity in Addis Ababa, I invoked "the most fundamental humanitarian principles" to this end. I do hope that larger shipments of relief supplies will be made available, and that those persons in positions of responsibility and authority will facilitate the movement of these supplies. On the political side, I continue to feel that the right course is to leave the political aspects of the Nigerian problem to the Organization of African Unity for solution. As I observed recently, I have been impressed by the statesmanlike and imaginative initiatives taken at the recent conference in Addis Ababa. I hope that these initiatives will be followed by wise and conciliatory action on the part of both parties so that a just and fair settlement of the issues which have occasioned this tragic war may be achieved by peaceful means.

206. "The situation in the North of Ireland" was brought to my attention by the foreign minister of the Republic of Ireland at the same time that the matter was brought before the Security Council. I have also been in contact with the government of the United Kingdom in connection with this matter. However, as the question appears as an item on the draft agenda of the twenty-fourth session of the General Assembly, I do not wish to comment further on it.

207. In the Introduction to my annual report last year, I suggested that the twenty-fifth anniversary of the founding of the United Nations might be celebrated in 1970 "with due solemnity," and I am very glad indeed that this suggestion was found acceptable by the General Assembly which, at its twenty-third session, established a Preparatory Committee for this purpose. I have been keeping in close touch with the deliberations of the Preparatory Committee and its officers, and I wish to express my appreciation to them for the many forward-looking initiatives which, I understand, the Committee will be recommending to the General Assembly at its twenty-fourth session. I feel very strongly that the celebration of the twenty-fifth anniversary should not be ceremonial,

but substantive. All organs of the United Nations should, in my view, make a special effort to reach specific agreement on such major issues before the world Organization as development, peace-keeping, disarmament, decolonization, and friendly relations among nations.

208. As I have noted elsewhere, the twenty-fifth anniversary will coincide with the inauguration of the Second United Nations Development Decade. The beginning of the decade is also being celebrated as International Education Year, and I am very glad that the United Nations Educational, Scientific and Cultural Organization will mount a special effort in 1970 for an attack on the problem of mass illiteracy and ignorance. I have suggested elsewhere that the 1970s might also be declared the Disarmament Decade. The year 1970 is also the tenth anniversary of the adoption by the General Assembly of the Declaration on the Granting of Independence to Colonial Countries and Peoples. With so many constructive avenues open to it, I hope that in the coming months the Organization may make great strides toward the agreed theme of the twenty-fifth anniversary—Peace and Progress.

U THANT
Secretary-General

September 15, 1969

Address to the Navy League

NEW YORK OCTOBER 28, 1969

IN THE FOLLOWING speech to the Navy League, U Thant spoke frankly of the public disillusion with the United Nations and enumerated some of the shortcomings of the Organization. This, of course, was not the first time he had discussed this subject, but it is of interest as an exposition of his thinking after eight years as Secretary-General. Some of the disillusion, he said, was due to ignorance of politics and history in general and the history of the United Nations in particular, but he conceded that the state of the United Nations after twenty-four years "leaves a great deal to be desired." "The trouble," he asserted, "is not fundamentally with the concept of the United Nations, but with the state of the world in relation to that concept." It is not necessary to go into detail in this commentary, but, to summarize briefly, the main obstacle in his opinion was the unwillingness of the Member states to put larger loyalties ahead of self-interest. "Too often," he said, "I have the feeling at the United Nations that the Members are more preoccupied with nationalism or saving themselves from the predictable results of their own policies than with pressing on to that international order and degree of mutual confidence which alone can begin to remove the threat of war, bring disarmament, promote a more just and equitable world, and allow us to save ourselves from some of the social and economic disasters which threaten us ever more ominously as we approach the last quarter of the twentieth century." One of the results of this sort of thinking, he declared, was "a disturbing tendency toward willful disregard and defiance" of even unanimous and repeated decisions of the Security Council. He added that unless the Council used the means at its disposal to enforce its decisions its authority would be eroded and "the fabric of international peace will be seriously weakened."

I AM HAPPY to participate in this fine gathering by which the Navy League has chosen to honor the United Nations tonight. I hope you will bear with me if I take this opportunity to look back to some of the fundamentals of the Charter and to examine with you their relevance to the demands and challenges which we must face today.

SOURCE: *UN Monthly Chronicle*, Vol. VI, November 1969, pp. 84–88.

It has been said fairly regularly for the past twenty years or so that the United Nations is declining. Annually, at this time of the year, many people at the General Assembly tell each other that the life has gone out of the United Nations, that things aren't what they used to be and so on, ignoring the fact that people, both within and outside the United Nations, have said this every year since about 1948 when the United Nations was two years old. I would be the first to admit that the state of the United Nations, which reflects the state of the world, leaves a great deal to be desired, as it always has done. But having said that, it would be wise to search for the real reasons for this shortcoming rather than to escape from the problem by the easy course of blaming the world organization as if it were some independent all-powerful body. The trouble, of course, is not fundamentally with the concept of the United Nations but with the state of the world in relation to that concept. If the world and the world organization are to do better, they must tackle the problem at its roots. We all must ask ourselves why sovereign nations find it so hard to coexist and cooperate sensibly except under the imminent threat of disaster or extinction, and what changes of attitude might begin to liberate us from this highly dangerous dilemma.

For the continuing frustration of the world organization is highly dangerous, and time is not on humanity's side. It is not only the threat of war which must deeply concern all responsible people, but also some of the other major problems of our age which can only be tackled and solved by real international cooperation and action, and whose solution is indispensable to secure an enduring peace.

There are now few serious and responsible people who do not agree with the objectives of the Charter—international peace and security, justice, equal rights and self-determination of peoples, economic and social progress, the elimination of racism in all its forms, and human rights. The problem is to reconcile these objectives with national policies and with the concept of national sovereignty. It is also true that some of the means provided by the Charter to secure these ends have not worked out in the manner that was envisaged by the founding fathers. Of these, perhaps the most significant are the arrangements in Chapter VII of the Charter for the use by the Security Council of military force, including naval and air units, to maintain or restore international peace and security—provisions which, in their time, were considered to be among the most radical innovations of the Charter. These provisions have never been used. This is the result of two unforeseen events, the change in the nature of war caused by the development of atomic weapons, and the cold war, which have somewhat belied the notion that the Security Council, with the great powers in total agreement, would keep the peace of the world, if necessary by force.

But even supposing it had proved possible for the great powers to agree to constitute United Nations forces under the Security Council, would such an arrangement really have been of much assistance in the context of the last twenty-four years? The Chapter VII arrangement had been designed with Manchuria and the nazi and fascist aggressions of the 1930s especially in mind, for situations where aggressors could be easily identified and where the "good guys" of the international world would have no moral doubts about collectively fighting the "bad guys." But the situation that has prevailed since the Second World War defied such simplifications. It is worth remembering that United Nations enforcement measures were actually suggested as early as 1948 when war broke out in the Middle East. But this suggestion quickly lapsed when it was found impossible to answer even the simplest questions about such a United Nations force. Which way, by what criteria, and at whom would it shoot, and who would give the command to shoot? On what ground would the force take its stand? What countries, indeed, would be prepared to lend their soldiers to such a force in such a situation?

And so one of the greatest innovations in the Charter has up till now remained a virtually dead letter. The idea of collective security which these arrangements were supposed to provide has broken down and has to some extent been replaced by regional defense pacts outside the United Nations.

Meanwhile the United Nations has faced some of the novel challenges of the last twenty-four years by improvising the quite unforeseen mechanism which has come to be called peace-keeping. It has pioneered the use of military personnel and units in a nonviolent role, acting as peace-keepers rather than soldiers, and relying for their success on the voluntary cooperation of the parties to a conflict, on the moral authority of the United Nations, and on their own skill as pacifiers, negotiators, and guardians of the peace. Peace-keeping on a voluntary basis has been undertaken in the Middle East, Kashmir, Lebanon, the Congo, Cyprus, and the Dominican Republic, for example, with considerable success in situations where an enforcement operation would have been out of the question. Although United Nations peace-keeping is still the subject of some international controversy, it has, I believe, provided in the political sphere one of the most encouraging examples of what internationalism, acting in the light of Charter principles and aims, can at its best achieve.

The United Nations Security Council itself provides an interesting example of a gradual return to Charter fundamentals after long years of frustration and paralysis. The Council, which has under the Charter primary responsibility for the maintenance of international peace and security, was originally intended to act on behalf of all the Members of the United Nations and, with the unanimity of the great powers, to deal with threats to world peace in an Olympian manner which would far transcend considerations of purely national interest. We know all too well how in the years of the cold war this dream was largely shattered, but it is encouraging to note that in the past few years the Security Council has taken on a new life by beginning to return to something like the original Charter concept. Where the Security Council used to specialize in acrimonious public disagreement, its members now strive laboriously for consensus and make a particular effort to avoid public displays of complete disagreement and deadlock. It now tends to pass important resolutions unanimously and has in the past two years succeeded in agreeing on resolutions upon some uniquely difficult subjects, such as the Middle East and Southern Rhodesia. The next essential step is to improve the effectiveness of and respect for the Council's decisions, but at least a first step in the right direction has been made—a step in the direction of international responsibility. There is a pressing need, however, to achieve for the Security Council and its decisions the sort of authority and influence envisaged for them in the Charter. There is a disturbing tendency toward willful disregard and defiance of even the unanimous and repeated decisions of the Council, a tendency which erodes its authority.

The Council itself, and especially its permanent members, can best combat this tendency by following up, with all the various means at their disposal, the decisions of the Council, and by trying, through vigilance and persistence, to ensure that its decisions take real effect within a reasonable limit of time. If the world becomes accustomed to the decisions of the highest United Nations organ for peace and security going by default or being ignored, we shall have taken a very dangerous step backwards toward anarchy. The fabric of international peace will be seriously weakened, and bad situations will grow worse. I think especially of the Middle East, a problem for which the Council in November 1967 unanimously agreed on a resolution which was a major step toward a solution. Despite this considerable achievement, and after two years of effort, a peaceful solution seems as far away as ever, and an almost daily outbreak of violent events makes it ever more possible that we may be witnessing in the Middle East something like the early stages of a new Hundred Years' War. There has never been a situation in which all of the Security Council's prestige, resources, and persistence, and the support of other Member states as well, were so vitally needed to reverse a disastrous trend.

We are still far from the spirit, or the realization, of the internationalism which the horrors of the Second World War inspired the authors of the Charter to strive for—and even to expect. Too often I have the feeling at the United Nations that the Members are more preoccupied with making nationalism safe or saving themselves from the predictable results of their own policies than with pressing on to that international order and degree of mutual confidence which alone can begin to remove the threat of war, bring disarmament, promote a more just and equitable world, and allow us to save ourselves from some of the social and economic disasters which threaten us ever more ominously as we approach the last quarter of the twentieth century. National sovereignty and patriotism are fine concepts and have a vital place in the world. But already in other major fields of human activity they have taken their place in a larger order of loyalties and objectives with excellent results— I think, for instance, of the fields of science, of art, of communications, of commerce and, by no means least, of the world of youth.

It has become almost obligatory nowadays for public speakers to mention youth. I do so this evening not out of any sense of fashionable compulsion, but because I believe that the United Nations and the young people of the world have a lot to learn from each other and that we may all be missing a great opportunity through a failure, due to misunderstanding or ignorance, to identify the basic interest we have in common. It is often said that young people now show little interest in the work of the United Nations. Insofar as this may be true, I think there is a good reason for it. Intelligent young people since time immemorial have tended to be critical of, or even to be against, the *status quo* as embodied in what has come to be known as the "Establishment." Sovereign governments are certainly "Establishments," and the fact that 126 governments constitute the United Nations makes the United Nations a super-Establishment, and therefore of limited concern to the progressive young. It is not surprising that a generation which takes the atom bomb, the computer, space exploration, and supersonic earth travel for granted should not be duly impressed by the concept of national sovereignty as the controlling influence in world politics. Many of the most intelligent young people all over the world are less and less interested in nationalism and increasingly regard themselves as an international entity with common interests, ideals, and goals, which are not always sympathetic or understandable to their elders in the "Establishment."

But disillusion with the United Nations should not be a logical consequence of this state of mind—in fact, quite the contrary. Public disillusion with the United Nations is often based on ignorance of politics and history in general and of the history of the United Nations in particular. In fact, the tendency in some young progressive circles to write off the world organization as just another instrument of the "Establishment" echoes the similar, and equally badly informed, sentiments which we have heard over the last twenty years from a diminishing chorus of isolationists and supernationalists—a coincidence which would not, I believe, be welcome to either party. Let us bear in mind that although the United Nations is an organization of sovereign governments, the collective will of the Organization, inspired by the Charter, has worked solidly, and often effectively, for change in many vitally important areas of human activity. I think, for example, of the process of decolonization, which has liberated nearly a billion people in less than a quarter of a century—a development on a scale which was inconceivable in 1945 and in which the United Nations has played a central role. I think of the concept of international assistance for economic development, which has in twenty short years become an accepted fact, so that the obligation of the rich nations to assist the poor ones is now widely regarded as a normal feature of life and a new moral precept in the international community. I think of the Universal Declaration of Human Rights, the effort to make it increasingly applicable and the endless struggle against racism and discrimination in all their different forms which has been and is being waged in the United Nations. In all of these developments we must recognize that progress is slow and that certain major obstacles have so far remained. But the spirit and the aims are there, as well as enough practical results to point the way. It is this kind of activity that makes the United Nations greater than the sum of its parts, the 126 sovereign Member nations. The United Nations has set, and will, I am sure, continue to set, high standards and to urge nations, whose individual policies on such matters may often be weak or indecisive, to cooperate for their achievement. Quite apart from the peace-keeping and peace-making achievements of the organization, this is by no means an inconsiderable or insignificant record.

I hope, therefore, that people, whatever age group they may belong to, will sometimes take the time, and make the effort, to go back to the fundamentals of the Charter, and to find out how they have been developed and put into effect over the first twenty-four years of the United Nations; and to ask themselves what can be done now to make a better and more fruitful world on the basis of these fundamental principles. Older people may well find unexpected progress in many areas which have been forgotten, and the young may realize that many of the things they seek and to which they attach importance have all along been very much at the heart of the United Nations effort.

Of all human activities, the relations between states seem to have been left stranded in the old pattern of rigid nationalism, while in most other important fields of activity men have stepped forward into a more contemporary and more international setting. Nothing could do more to increase the effectiveness of the United Nations than a modification of the concept of national sovereignty in harmony with the intellectual and technological realities of our time, and here I believe that artists, scientists, businessmen, those who deal with communications of all kinds, and the young people can help us in a decisive way. I have confidence that the new internationalism of the young and a reassertion of the spirit of internationalism which inspired the Charter will help us to make this crucial step forward before it is too late.

⚘ 1970 ⚘

NIGERIA–BIAFRA

THE CIVIL WAR in Nigeria came to a sudden end on January 15, 1970, and the Republic of Biafra ceased to exist. At the time U Thant was in Africa paying visits to a number of states. As late as January 4, the Secretary-General was asked at a press conference in Dakar whether or not there was any way he could contribute to a settlement of the conflict. He explained, as he had done many times, that he believed the best approach was to leave the matter in the hands of the Organization of African Unity (OAU), which had only recently sent new peace proposals to both sides. He appealed to the Biafran leader, Colonel Odumegwu Ojukwu, to accept the proposals "for the sake of a greater Nigeria, a more prosperous Nigeria and for the sake of African unity and for the sake of a more disciplined international organization." The question of the civil war was again the major topic of a press conference in Accra on January 9. Thant went to great pains to explain once more that the hands-off policy of the United Nations was not due to any indifference but to the fact that almost all Member states considered the Nigerian conflict an internal matter which did not fall within the competence of the United Nations. He told the Accra press conference that, although certain individuals and certain newspapers had been advocating United Nations intervention for more than two years, not a single Member state had seen fit to bring the Nigerian question before either the Security Council or the General Assembly. If any state had raised the question, he said, neither body would have inscribed it on its agenda. By the time he reached Lomé, Togo, on January 12, it had become apparent that the end was near. The Biafran headquarters at Owerri was taken by federal forces on January 10.

Ojukwu fled to the Ivory Coast, one of the few states recognizing Biafra. Major General Philip Effiong was left behind to negotiate the surrender. In a statement at Lomé, Thant said he had sent an appeal to General Yakubu Gowon, head of the Nigerian military government, to exercise restraint in dealing with the civilian population in Biafra. "I believe," he said, "that the federal government of Nigeria will, with the international community, ameliorate the plight and sufferings of the peoples of Nigeria, since peace is now in sight after a long and tragic conflict."

Although Lagos had not been on Thant's African itinerary, he quickly revised it to accept an invitation from General Gowon. The Secretary-General was pleased to have an opportunity to talk with Gowon and with his personal representative, Said-Uddin Khan, as well as Henry R. Labouisse, executive director of the United Nations Children's Fund, and Henrik Beer, Secretary-General of the League of Red Cross Societies, who were involved in the distribution of relief supplies. He decided, however, to stay only one day in Lagos rather than cancel a scheduled meeting with French President Georges Pompidou in Paris. This added fuel to the criticism which the supporters of Biafra had already been directing at him. His critics were accusing him of being callous and indifferent to the civilian suffering and of being biased in favor of the federal government. They now said he should have taken the time to make a personal inspection visit to the war-ravaged areas of Eastern Nigeria. To make matters worse, the mass media distributed throughout the world garbled versions of a statement he issued before his departure from Lagos on January 19. In this statement, he quoted Dr. Beer as saying that during a tour of the afflicted areas he saw no evidence of violence or ill treatment of the civilian population by federal troops. The widely published version omitted the reference to Dr. Beer and attributed the assessment of the situation to Thant himself. On the basis of these reports, Thant was severely attacked in the press—especially in Europe. It was one of his most trying experiences, compared by him to the ordeal which Dag Hammarskjöld went through as a result of the United Nations military operations against Moïse Tshombé in the Congo. He was particularly upset because many newspapers brought up the question of his Burmese origin, asserting that a European would have acted differently. The Secretary-General discussed this incident at a press conference at United Nations Headquarters on February 17. It was clear that he was not only angry but puzzled as to the reasons for what he called the distortions of his statements. Without drawing any conclusions, he said he had learned during his African tour that the same public relations firm that had worked for Tshombé during the attacks on Hammarskjöld had later worked for the Biafran régime. Part of the blame he placed on a syndicated column by *New York Times* correspondent Anthony Lewis, in which, he said, Lewis "made a very bitter attack on me based on this false and distorted news." Referring to remarks about his origin, he said: "I must say that the functioning of the Secretary-General in this particular situation or in similar types of situations is not concerned with the nationality of the Secretary-General, whether he is an Afro-Asian, a European, or a Latin American. What is important is his attitude toward the problem. If his attitude happened to be contrary to the attitude of the Organization of African Unity and contrary to the attitude of the government of Nigeria, then I am afraid he would not have been invited to visit Lagos. . . .

1. From Transcript of Press Conference

DAKAR, SENEGAL   JANUARY 4, 1970

. . .

QUESTION: Mr. Secretary-General, isn't there a deep contradiction between the people's right to self-determination—a right recognized by the United Nations—and the attitude of the Federal Government of Nigeria toward Biafra? Moreover, do you think that, while touring Africa, you could contribute to a fair solution of this delicate problem?

THE SECRETARY-GENERAL: Regarding the civil conflict in Nigeria, my views, I believe, are well known. It is necessary to bear in mind the two aspects of the problem. One aspect is constitutional or political and the other aspect is humanitarian. As far as the constitutional aspect is concerned, you all know that when a state applies for membership in the United Nations, and when the United Nations accepts the membership of that applicant, all the Members tacitly accept the principle that that particular state has an entity or unity. In other words, when a Member state is admitted to the United Nations, there is the implied acceptance by the entire membership of the principle of territorial integrity, independence, and sovereignty of that particular State.

This has been the tradition since the establishment of the United Nations. You will recall that the United Nations spent over $500 million in the Congo primarily to prevent the secession of Katanga from the Congo. So, as far as the question of secession of a particular section of a Member state is concerned, the United Nations attitude is unequivocable. As an international organization, the United Nations has never accepted and does not accept and I do not believe it will ever accept the principle of secession of a part of its Member state. That is my first observation.

My second observation is, this question has been discussed at the Organization of African Unity (OAU) summit conferences, as you all know, in Kinshasa, in Algiers, and in Addis Ababa. In all these OAU summit conferences, the heads of African states and African govern-

SOURCE: *UN Monthly Chronicle,* Vol. VII, February 1970, pp. 34–38.

ments considered this very tragic civil conflict in Nigeria, and they had come to the conclusion that, both for political and constitutional reasons, and for humanitarian reasons, there is only one means to adopt. There is no need for me to reiterate the resolutions. I attended all these OAU summit conferences, and I will refer only to the last summit conference of the OAU in Addis Ababa.

The resolution was adopted almost unanimously, without any opposition, as you know. African heads of state and heads of government believe very strongly that, to put an end to this tragic human suffering and agony and death and destruction in areas of civil conflict in Nigeria, the only course open to the parties concerned is to agree to certain principles, certain lines of action. These lines of action were clearly defined in the resolution. The African heads of state and heads of government believe very strongly that if the parties directly concerned in the conflict were to comply with these resolutions, then there will be not only peace and justice, but there will be an end to the human suffering and misery and hunger and starvation and destruction and death in the areas of civil conflict.

I agree entirely with the assessment of the African heads of state and heads of government. Not only because of the need for the United Nations to cooperate very closely with the OAU, but also because of my conviction that the steps outlined by the African heads of state and heads of government are the only means to end this very tragic situation.

I just want to take this opportunity of appealing to Colonel Ojukwu, who has shown remarkable qualities of leadership, to show also magnanimity and vision for the sake of a greater Nigeria, a more prosperous Nigeria, and for the sake of African unity and for the sake of a more disciplined international organization, to please comply with the proposals of the OAU. In my view, such a compliance, only, will end the indescribable human misery in the areas of civil conflict in Nigeria. . . .

2. From Transcript of Press Conference

ACCRA, GHANA   JANUARY 9, 1970

. . .

QUESTION: Mr. Secretary-General, as a follow-up of the Nigerian issue, it has been reported that the United Nations does not support secession, as you have just indicated. But, by necessary implication, you realize that certain states which are Members of the United Nations have recognized Biafra as a sovereign state. Is the United Nations going to take any action in this matter?

THE SECRETARY-GENERAL: The United Nations, as you all know, is an organization of independent sovereign states. It is up to the United Nations as a body to take action or not to take action on any particular issue. The question is that the issue must be brought to the attention of the United Nations. So far, not one single Member state out of 126 has brought the question of the civil conflict in Nigeria to the United Nations, not one government. Of course, under the Charter, under the established rules of procedure, any one of the 126 Member states has the right to bring this question before the principal organs of the United Nations at any time. Now, since the eruption of this crisis, not one single Member state has brought up this question, although individuals, Mr. A, Mr. B, Mr. C, and newspaper A, newspaper B, newspaper C have been advocating for the last two years that the United Nations should take some action. Of course, the United Nations cannot take action on the basis of Mr. A's views or newspaper B's views. The United Nations can take action only on the initiative of the government of a Member state. So far, not one single Member state out of 126 has brought this to the attention of the Security Council or the General Assembly. The reason why not one single Member state has brought this to the United Nations is very simple; because every government of a Member state knows full well that, if it attempts to bring this question to the United Nations, the United Nations will simply refuse to discuss it. It is as simple as that. The United Nations attitude on this question, in my view, is very plain.

SOURCE: *Ibid.,* pp. 38–44.

The question must be brought to the United Nations by the government of a particular Member state. Of course, if the federal government in Lagos brings this matter to the United Nations, I am sure the United Nations will take it up very promptly. But, if any other Member state or states attempts to inscribe this particular item on the agenda of the Security Council or the General Assembly, the chances are that such an attempt will be rejected, because the attitude of the Member states is well known in the United Nations, and all the governments are fully aware of this fact. That explains why not one single government has taken the initiative to bring this item before the United Nations. . . .

---

3. Statement to the Press

LOMÉ, TOGO   JANUARY 12, 1970

. . . When I heard about the new developments in the Nigerian conflict, I sent an appeal to General Gowon to exercise restraint and some degree of humanity towards the civilian population. I believe that the Federal Government of Nigeria will, with the international community, ameliorate the plight and sufferings of the peoples of Nigeria, since peace is now in sight after a long and tragic conflict. The international community should cooperate with the government of Nigeria in facilitating the resumption of peace and calm in the area.

During my trip in the African countries, I had the opportunity to state my views on the question of Nigeria's civilian population. Besides the leaders of the countries, I met with representatives of several other governments, including France, the United Kingdom, the United States, Ethiopia and, of course, Nigeria and the Secretary-General of the Organization of African Unity, and discussed the question of the conflict in Nigeria. The talks were useful.

I take this opportunity to appeal to those governments, who in the past cooperated with the federal government, to redouble their efforts, with

SOURCE: UN Press Release SG/T/277.

the agreement of the federal government, to observe the new developments and trends of events, in particular, the United Kingdom, Canada, Sweden, Poland, and the international agencies and the Red Cross to cooperate for the restoration of peace and calm.

In conclusion, I express my best wishes for the people and government of Nigeria and its dynamic chief.

---

4. Statement to the Press

LAGOS, NIGERIA   JANUARY 19, 1970

. . . I AM CONVINCED that the process of national reconciliation has started auspiciously. I had talks with General Gowon on the situation in Nigeria and also with General Khan, Mr. Labouisse, and the heads of United Nations agencies here. I saw Dr. Beer this morning, who has just returned from visiting the afflicted areas, and he reported that there was no hint of the slightest evidence of violence or ill treatment of the civilian population in the area by federal troops.

Outside assistance can only be given to Nigeria with the consent and agreement of the federal government. The cooperation of the government is essential for the flow of outside assistance into Nigeria.

I am taking with me very pleasant memories of my trip to Lagos and want to express my very best wishes to the government and people of Nigeria, and I wish them success in their noble endeavor for unity and progress.

SOURCE: UN Press Release SG/T/284.

5. *Statement to the Press*

PARIS   JANUARY 19, 1970

. . . I MADE STATEMENTS at every stop during my African tour. My position is clear and well-known. Unfortunately, I discovered later on in the course of the trip that some of my statements made in Dakar, for instance, or in Accra, had been distorted. I do not know by whom or why. When I arrived in Abidjan, I was informed that the press reports in Abidjan of my earlier press conference in Dakar were so much distorted that there was widespread misunderstanding of my position, and so I had to instruct the United Nations people in Abidjan to release to the press and the public the full texts of that press conference. When released then, it was clear that some press reports had been distorted. I do not know the motivation, but, anyhow, if you study the press conference statements I made, you will understand my position. I yield to no one in my abhorrence and condemnation of violence and hatred and war in all their forms.

About my quick trip to Lagos—I had talks with General Gowon, as well as with my special representative, Mr. Khan, with Mr. Labouisse and with Mr. Henrik Beer, Secretary-General of the League of Red Cross Societies, who had just returned from the afflicted areas and who told me that the situation in the areas of conflict is peaceful. There was even fraternization between the federal troops and the local population, including the Ibos, and the psychological climate in those areas was congenial for national reconciliation. There was peace and quiet in these areas, and over sixty journalists in Lagos, including foreign correspondents, left Lagos today to visit the areas. Of course, you had better wait to hear their evaluation when they return to Lagos. . . .

SOURCE: UN Press Release SG/T/285.

6. *Transcript of Press Conference*

NEW YORK   FEBRUARY 17, 1970

THE SECRETARY-GENERAL: Mr. Oatis[1] and friends, since this is my first press conference for the year at Headquarters and since this is the first time that Mr. William Oatis has headed the United Nations Press Corps in a formal meeting, I want to offer my very sincere congratulations to you, Mr. Oatis, on your election as the President of the United Nations Correspondents Association (UNCA) for the year. I have known you for more than twelve years, and I know your dedication to your work and your rare ability to sift the important from the ordinary and your omnipresence at the right spot at the right time for the gathering of news and, last but not least, your very great human qualities of charm, understanding, compassion, friendliness, and warmth which have won the respect and affection of all those who have met you. I just want to extend my very best wishes to you for a very fruitful year. At the same time, I want to express my very best wishes to all the members of UNCA in 1970.

MR. OATIS: Mr. Secretary-General, I am much obliged to you for your gracious congratulations to me, and I am sure that we will have a year of productive cooperation between you and the Executive Committee of UNCA, since you have always been so helpful to newsmen and to me personally on those occasions when I was "omnipresent," as you say. I should like to wish you a Happy New Year and a successful and productive trip. Although I have not taken a poll, I dare say, judging from the crowd here this morning, that something like 250 percent of the correspondents who work here every day are grateful to you for coming down here to answer our questions.

Before I ask the first question, I must remind every correspondent here that whatever he gets is embargoed for release a half hour after the news conference is over.

SOURCE: *UN Monthly Chronicle,* Vol. VII, March 1970, pp. 26–36.

[1]William N. Oatis, Associated Press.

My first question is: Do you see progress in the big four talks, Mr. Secretary-General, toward agreement on the guidelines for Ambassador [Gunnar] Jarring, and are there any circumstances in which, even without such guidelines, you would ask Ambassador Jarring to resume his contacts with the Arabs and Israelis in the Middle East?

THE SECRETARY-GENERAL: My assessment of the progress or lack of progress of the big four talks in New York can be summarized in a few words. I have studied the three proposals very carefully—the United States proposal, the Soviet proposal, and the French proposal—and it seems to me that a common denominator can be found in these three proposals on one or two basic issues of the problem. Since my return from Africa, I have been in constant contact with the permanent representatives of the big four. I have discussed with them the possibility of formulating something on these common denominators. Of course, it will be very difficult, at least for some time, to agree on all the basic issues of the problem as provided for in Security Council resolution 242 (1967), but in my view there are certain basic issues on which the big four can come to an agreement leading to a formulation of the guidelines to enable Ambassador Jarring to reactivate his mission. Of course, as I have said on a previous occasion, the reactivation of Ambassador Jarring's mission will depend primarily on the agreement of the permanent members of the Security Council on certain guidelines—but not exclusively. That is one reason why I look forward to my discussion with Ambassador Jarring tomorrow, with a view to ascertaining whether the time has come for him to give some thought to the reactivation of his functions.

QUESTION: Mr. Secretary-General, is the search for peace in the Middle East affected in any way by offers of offensive weapons to the opposing sides by both the United States and the Soviet Union?

THE SECRETARY-GENERAL: I believe that I expressed my views on this subject through a United Nations spokesman some time ago. Just to refresh your memory, perhaps I should elaborate on this a little bit.

I am in principle in favor of arms limitation—particularly limitation of highly sophisticated arms—when a situation such as that in the Middle East develops. But it would be misleading to leave the matter there. No restriction of this kind is ever self-executing. The measure of the justification for arms limitation and its utility is its effectiveness, its impartial application. This comes down to a question of the willingness and readiness of all states concerned to observe the limitation strictly.

Otherwise, the results of the declared limitation or embargo could defeat its own ends and could even give a military advantage to one side or the other.

QUESTION: Mr. Secretary-General, in December, in answer to a question about whether the big four were considering an embargo on arms and whether they were considering a guarantee to all parties on the boundaries on which the parties might agree, you told us that you would transmit these views to the big four. Would you kindly tell us what specific reaction you might have had from the big four on these two suggestions, and also on the proposals that have been made that the big four adopt a move for restoration of the cease-fire in the Middle East?

THE SECRETARY-GENERAL: This has been the prime preoccupation of the big four at the last several meetings. They have kindly briefed me on the results of their deliberations. As you all know, whenever the big four met, the permanent representative who happened to preside over that particular meeting came to report to me about the results of the deliberations.

As regards the cease-fire, one of the big four has presented certain ideas to the rest and I understand that that matter, among others, will come up for disucssion at the next meeting, scheduled for the 19th of this month. The cease-fire, of course, has been a matter which has occupied the attention of the big four in the last several meetings and I have been giving a lot of thought to that. As you all know, the Middle East situation is again heating up most dangerously. It becomes apparent that only some very strong measures can avert a new catastrophe. At the moment, at any rate, one must still look principally to the four-power talks for the necessary effort. As I said some time ago in special reports to the Security Council—you will recall that I have submitted at least four reports to the Security Council on this subject—the Middle East cease-fire demanded by the Council at the time of the June 1967 war has broken down and is now totally ineffective, especially in the Suez sector. Breaches of the cease-fire committed by both sides have been daily occurrences for a long time and recently have increased in number and in intensity.

For almost a year now I have been making daily reports to the Council on breaches of the cease-fire in the Suez Canal sector. Indeed, as regards the Suez sector, both sides in the conflict now frequently make public announcements of breaches committed by themselves on their own military initiative. This is an unprecedented situation in United Nations peace-keeping experience. It is really alarming. It is my duty as Secretary-General, of course, to do all that I can to have the cease-fire observed. I have been doing all that I can toward that end, but admittedly with little success in recent months.

I also have a deepening concern for the safety of the United Nations military observers in the Suez sector, who recently have been exposed to fire from both sides with disturbing frequency, particularly as regards small-arms fire from the West Bank of the Canal. The inescapable conclusion from this only United Nations attempt to maintain a cease-fire over an extended period, concurrently with military occupation by one of the conflicting parties, is that it has become increasingly unsuccessful.

As you know, I asked General [Odd] Bull, who is here with us this morning, to come here urgently. My request was sent to him on February 11 and we have been conferring on what more, if anything, can be done at this time of a helpful nature by the United Nations Truce Supervision Organization as well as by the United Nations Headquarters. I had very fruitful meetings with General Bull on Sunday and again yesterday. I hope to wind up the discussions with the General today. Of course, I am sure you will understand that at least for the moment it will not be in the public interest to divulge any details of those discussions and consultations.

QUESTION: Mr. Secretary-General, the war in Vietnam continues and the talks in Paris seem to be bogged down. Do you feel that there may be any other formula than the one of an accommodation between the warring parties within South Vietnam which may put an end to the war?

THE SECRETARY-GENERAL: You will notice that I have not made any substantive observations on the Vietnam war for some time. As a matter of fact, once the negotiations in Paris started, I decided not to make any evaluation of the situation or assessment of the problem. For the moment I would prefer not to make any substantive statements. In my view, such statements will not help. But at the appropriate time I intend to make some statements on the war in Vietnam.

QUESTION: Mr. Secretary-General, in the light of what you have just said about the breakdown of the cease-fire, further, in the light of the fact that Mr. [Ralph] Bunche, speaking to the press not long ago, said that this was a state of active war and had been since April and that the observers were military observers, no longer cease-fire observers, that they were reporting on the war; and in the light also of the fact that only the other day official spokesmen for the Egyptian government denounced the cease-fire once more and spoke in terms of denigrating and canceling out the November 22 resolution, do you not think that the time has arrived to take new initiatives, entirely aside from the resolution, aside from the old cease-fire, which has now admittedly gone into the rubbish heap?

THE SECRETARY-GENERAL: In answering your question, it does not necessarily follow that I accept the hypothesis or the premise of your question. But I must say that I have been reporting to the Security Council almost every day on the breaches of the cease-fire. General Bull has very kindly kept me posted with information every day—indeed, many times a day. The full facts are before the Security Council. So it is up to the Security Council to take new initiatives if it considers that necessary. For the moment, I do not want to venture an opinion on what the Security Council can do and should do at this time. I have submitted all the facts available to me to the Security Council almost every day and, for the moment at least, I do not propose to take any initiatives anticipating any possible Security Council action.

QUESTION: Do you have any time table in mind for when the big four must act, or when the point of no-return will have been reached in this situation? Are you thinking of any deadline for action by you or by the big four in the next few weeks or the next few months?

THE SECRETARY-GENERAL: You know that I have no time table or deadline in mind, but as I stated a moment ago, I still believe that a political solution is possible. I still believe that the big four can come up with a formulation of guidelines on certain basic issues, not necessarily a comprehensive agreement on all issues provided for in the Security Council resolution of November 22, 1967. I have been exchanging views with the permanent representatives of the big four, as I have said, since my return from Africa.

I believe that a kind of formulation by the big four on the basic issues—at least one or two basic issues—of the problem is still possible. I believe that they are striving toward that end. So I must say that I am not pessimistic about the outcome of the deliberations of the big four. I do not think it would be realistic to set a time table or a deadline.

QUESTION: Mr. Secretary-General, yesterday United Nations spokesmen announced that you would review with Ambassador Jarring tomorrow in Geneva the roles of the Secretary-General and his special representative. We know the role of Ambassador Jarring and the Security Council resolution, but did you have in mind in addition the role of the Secretary-General and his powers under Article 99?

THE SECRETARY-GENERAL: I am looking forward to discussing with Ambassador Jarring tomorrow in Geneva many aspects of the problem of the Middle East, particularly in the context of Security Council resolution 242 (1967). I have some ideas to present to him and I am sure that he must have some ideas to present to me. Of course, his reactivation, as I said earlier, does not necessarily depend on the agreed formulation of guidelines by the big four, but primarily, of course, he cannot function in the way in which he had been functioning for one year, and I do not believe that he would wish to repeat the futile exercise which he had been carrying out during the last year or so.

Regarding the invocation of Article 99, it would be interesting to recall that, in the history of the United Nations during the last twenty-four years, the Secretary-General only once invoked Article 99. That was in the case of the Congo. At that time Mr. Hammarskjöld had the full support of all African states, and also the full support of all the permanent members of the Security Council. So, when he invoked Article 99 to call a meeting of the Security Council he was on very firm ground. Nobody objected to that. That explains why Article 99 was invoked only once in the history of the United Nations in the past twenty-four years.

In the present situation—as, of course, you all know—if I were to invoke Article 99 and call a meeting of the Security Council, we have to think in terms of the results. Not one member of the Council has indicated to me that the Council should meet now and discuss the situation, because every member of the Council realizes that, at this time at any rate, a meeting of the Council to discuss the Middle Eastern problem would not be productive. So, since not one single member of the Council has hinted to me, or even whispered to me, that the Council should meet, I do not think it would be appropriate on my part to invoke Article 99 at this stage.

QUESTION: Mr. Secretary-General, a moment ago you said that only very strong measures can prevent a catastrophe in the Middle East. Would you be kind enough to enumerate some of the prime measures that you have in mind.

THE SECRETARY-GENERAL: As I said, the measures are the legitimate concern of the Security Council and, for that matter, the permanent members of the Security Council.

QUESTION: Can you indicate what measures you are thinking of?

THE SECRETARY-GENERAL: Not publicly.

QUESTION: Sir, you have said twice today that it is possible for the big four to have some common denominator of guidelines on one or two basic issues. Could you tell us what are, in your view, those basic issues in the Security Council resolution on which they could now formulate guidelines?

THE SECRETARY-GENERAL: I have mentioned those basic issues to the big four, and since those discussions and consultations are of a privileged character, I do not think I can divulge them publicly now.

QUESTION: Mr. Secretary-General, in another area, if I may. Now that the ice is slowly melting between Washington and Peking, there is perhaps a chance that the United Nations deadlock on the China issue might also ease. Now what do you think of the suggestion of some of your Asian colleagues that perhaps an interim solution for both Peking and Taipei may be found in multiple United Nations membership for China, for which there is a precedent in the three Soviet votes?

THE SECRETARY-GENERAL: I believe in the greater association of China with the rest of the international community. I believe in the advantages of improved relations between China and the outside world, particularly the superpowers. As I said on a previous occasion, the character of the relationship between China and the outside world will dominate the history of the seventies. So, I am all for greater contacts and greater communication between China and the rest of the international community.

As regards your specific question, I think it is right and proper for the competent organs of the United Nations to consider, debate, discuss, and decide. I do not think it is within the proper jurisdiction of the Secretary-General to venture any opinion.

QUESTION: Sir, at your last press conference in this room you welcomed the efforts for détente in the heart of Europe and in Europe as a whole. One of the proposals put forward recently in the framework of those efforts was that both German states apply for membership in the United Nations. What is your assessment of this problem today?

THE SECRETARY-GENERAL: You are right in assuming that I am for détente. I am for understanding; I am for increased cooperation between all Member states and all states. That is why I welcomed the projected meeting of European nations, both East and West; and I believe it will come about sooner or later. There is a growing consensus even in Europe that such a meeting is desirable and timely.

As regards your second question about my attitude toward the projected membership of two Germanys, first of all I must say that I am all for universality. I am for the principle of universality of membership of the United Nations. That is the premise. As regards divided countries, whether in Korea or Vietnam or Germany, I believe in their greater participation with the international community in our collective activities. As regards the specific question of joining the United Nations as members, that is a matter, of course, for the Security Council to discuss and make recommendations to the Assembly. For the moment I do not want to venture any opinion on that question.

QUESTION: To return to the China issue, is it not conceivable that some totally new initiative could be undertaken in order to increase the effectiveness of the United Nations and get China into the United Nations. Have you ever considered whether or not there is any possibility that you yourself might play some private role to that end?

THE SECRETARY-GENERAL: I am afraid that my role in such an enterprise would be very minimal. I think it is for the Member states, with full consciousness of the implications of such a step, to be more interested and more active in giving very close consideration to that problem.

QUESTION: Mr. Secretary-General, during the Nigerian civil war there were many efforts to involve the United Nations on one side or the other. Have you, on the basis of your own experience in Africa during that war, concluded any lessons from the experience as it applies to the United Nations in any such situations in the future?

THE SECRETARY-GENERAL: My attitude to the Nigerian civil conflict is well known. Let me say that I stand by every word of what I have said regarding the Nigerian civil conflict in the last two and a half years. It is interesting to note the divergence of attitude and the divergence of approach to this problem by the African leaders and by a substantial section of the European press. As you all know, I was in Africa in January and I had the opportunities for discussions with many heads of state and heads of government. Their one preoccupation at that time was the Nigerian civil war. I found that their attitude to the problem of the Nigerian civil war was completely different from the attitude of a very substantial section of the European press and mass media.

First of all, let me say that many African leaders told me that the Organization of African Unity (OAU) charter itself had very explicit provisions regarding the territorial integrity of all member states of OAU. They pointed out to me the charter. I think it would be useful to you to recall the actual phraseology of the OAU charter:

We, the Heads of African States and Governments assembled in the City of Addis Ababa, Ethiopia. . . .

Determined to safeguard and consolidate the hard-won independence as well
as the sovereignty and territorial integrity of our States . . .

and so on. One of the purposes of the organization is also defined as
follows: "to defend their sovereignty, their territorial integrity and independence." This to them is their Bible. So, they do not understand that,
in spite of the repeated resolutions of OAU at the summit conferences to
recognize the territorial integrity of all states of Africa—not only
Nigeria—a very substantial section of the mass media in Europe looks at
the situation in a different light. Many African leaders told me that they
reviewed the situation very comprehensively. They wanted to end the
agony and misery and starvation and death and destruction. They
outlined certain steps, very concrete steps, in their resolutions, particularly in the last resolution, adopted almost unanimously in Addis Ababa,
with only five abstentions and with no opposition. They proposed a
three-step plan to end the starvation and misery and death and destruction. Then they were amazed to find that a very substantial section of the
European press and mass media blamed the side which accepted these
proposals and praised the side which rejected them. This was beyond
them.

Another fact I gathered was this. African leaders put the blame for the
civil war on Colonel Ojukwu—most African leaders I talked to. One
African leader even went to the extent of saying that Colonel Ojukwu
had gambled with hundreds of thousands of African lives to serve his
political ends. But a substantial section of the European press and mass
media put the blame on the Federal Military Government of Nigeria.

I am just trying to outline the differences between the attitudes.
African heads of state and heads of government believe that the United
Nations was quite right to respect the wishes of the government of a
Member state. If the government of Nigeria were to request United
Nations involvement, as in the case of the Congo or Cyprus, of course
the United Nations would be involved, but without such a request the
United Nations was not involved except in humanitarian activities. As
you all know, the United Nations Children's Fund (UNICEF) is the
main humanitarian arm of the United Nations. UNICEF, under the
distinguished leadership of Henry Labouisse, has been involved very
heavily in ameliorating the plight of the long-suffering people in the areas
of conflict in Nigeria. As for the specialized agencies, as you know, they
are governed by certain rules and regulations. Specialized agencies
cannot function in a state without the invitation and agreement and
cooperation of the government of that state. So, the United Nations has

been involved in a humanitarian manner. But what the African leaders do not understand is the attitude of a very substantial section of the European press. It seems to me that what they resent most is what they regard as the patronizing or paternalistic attitude from outside toward them. Many African leaders feel that a very important section of the international community looks upon the African leaders as children who do not know how to run their affairs. That is most resented by African heads of state and heads of government.

I knew for the first time in the course of my trip that—according to one African leader—the public relations firm which worked for Colonel Ojukwu is the same firm as that which worked for Mr. Tshombé ten years ago. You know the volume of criticism leveled at the United Nations and the then Secretary-General, Mr. Dag Hammarskjöld, ten years ago because of the United Nations military involvement in the Congo. This was, to my knowledge, more or less the same as the volume of criticism leveled at the United Nations and myself by a very substantial section of the Western European press—and of course a substantial section of the press in this country also. It is very interesting to compare the two. At that time also a very substantial section of the Western European mass media and the mass media in this country was solidly with Tshombé, and a similar situation has prevailed in the past two and a half years. I do not know why a very substantial section of the Western European mass media seems to be solidly with Colonel Ojukwu. It is a very interesting phenomenon, but I must say that it has something to do with false assumptions or distorted facts. My experience, I think, is worth repeating here.

Before my departure from Lagos on January 19, I made a statement to the press at the Lagos airport. I said at that time that, according to those who had been to the areas of the conflict, the situation was reported to be so and so. The full text of my statement was released to the press at the same time in Lagos and in New York. A section of the mass media came out next morning with statements like: "The Secretary-General, without going to Biafra, said that the situation was so and so"—without any reference to my attribution to those who had been to the area. Based on those distorted news dispatches, some correspondents came out with a blistering attack on me. You will recall that Mr. Anthony Lewis made a very bitter attack on me based on this false and distorted news, and of course his article was syndicated not only in this country but all over Europe. After the publication of his article—I believe, on January 26— the European press from Oslo to Vienna came out with a full blast. I still have cuttings with me. For one week or more the European press, or a very substantial section of the European press—I must repeat, from Oslo to Vienna—said that a European would not have done this or a European would not have said that, and so on and so forth.

I must say that the functioning of the Secretary-General in this particular situation or in similar types of situation is not concerned with the nationality of the Secretary-General, whether he is an Afro-Asian, a European, or a Latin American. What is important in such matters is his attitude toward the problem. If his attitude happened to be contrary to the attitude of the Organization of African Unity and contrary to the attitude of the government of Nigeria, then I am afraid he would not even have been invited to visit Lagos, whether he is an Afro-Asian or a European or a Latin American—nationality does not count.

Then, a section of the European press referred to what I had done in May 1967 in regard to the United Nations Emergency Force. There were articles saying that it had been a mistake on my part not to proceed with my projected trip to Czechoslovakia in August 1968, and so on.

I have been at pains to answer those charges for the past two and a half years. My reports to the General Assembly and the Security Council are on record. So far, not a single government has questioned any of the facts presented in my report.

You will recall that when I issued instruction for the withdrawal of the United Nations Emergency Force on May 18, 1967, I submitted my report to the General Assembly on the very same day, and within twenty-four hours I submitted my report to the Security Council, drawing the Council's attention to the very menacing character of the developments. Not one Member from among the then 125 Member states advised me, even privately, to call a meeting of the Security Council to deal with the matter. I repeat that I submitted my report to the Assembly on the same day and my report to the Security Council within twenty-four hours, and that not one Member state out of the then 125 even whispered to me that I should call a meeting of the Security Council. The governments know the basis of the stationing of the United Nations Emergency Force. The baiss is completely different from that of the stationing of the United Nations Force in Cyprus (UNFICYP) in Cyprus, for instance. If the government of Cyprus were to ask me to withdraw UNFICYP today, I should have to tell the government of Cyprus: I am sorry, I cannot do anything about it; I have to refer this to the Security Council. The two bases are completely different.

As you know, the big four are discussing, among other things, the possibility of stationing United Nations troops in the area. However, some doubts have been expressed in certain quarters: the United Nations has done that before; would the United Nations be all right again? But my feeling is that the Security Council is the master of its own procedures and the master of its own lines of action. It can decide on anything. For instance—for the sake of argument—the Security Council can decide to station a United Nations force in the area for five years or ten years or twenty years, unless reversed earlier by a vote of the Council. Many such formulations are possible.

As I have said, there were other statements in the European press raking up the past: I should have gone to Czechoslovakia in August 1968. You know the facts. Two days before my projected departure from New York, the developments with which you are all familiar took place in Czechoslovakia. The acting permanent representative of Czechoslovakia in New York came to me and told me that his government had requested me to postpone the visit because of the developments. So I had to cancel that trip. The government of Czechoslovakia had invited me to make the visit. I had accepted the invitation. Then the government of Czechoslovakia requested me to cancel the trip because of the developments. I had to respect its wishes. Anybody who still maintains that I should have gone ahead with the trip to Prague despite the government's wish to the contrary needs to have his head examined.

QUESTION: You are going to talk to the Disarmament Committee tommorow. What agreements do you expect to emerge from the new session of the Disarmament Committee in such a form as to be capable of being adopted and approved by the General Assembly next autumn?

THE SECRETARY-GENERAL: It is very difficult to anticipate the outcome of the Conference of the Committee on Disarmament. As you all know, I intend to address tomorrow the new session of that Conference. My speech will be released to you in a few moments, with an embargo for tomorrow. In that speech, I make some observations on the question you have raised, and I am sure you will find in it an answer to that question.

DISARMAMENT

THE TREATY on the Non-Proliferation of Nuclear Weapons entered into force on March 5, 1970. Although a number of potential nuclear countries as well as two nuclear powers—France and the People's Republic of China—still had not signed it, the treaty was nevertheless a major step forward in disarmament. U Thant expressed deep satisfaction and at the same time pointed to the need for universal support to bring about full implementation of the treaty. In a statement to the Conference on the politics of disarmament on May 22, Thant noted that the Disarmament Decade, proposed by him the previous September, had begun but he saw difficulties ahead. Progress during the Disarmament Decade, he said, would depend partly on the full implementation of the Treaty on the Non-Proliferation of Nuclear Weapons and partly on the outcome of the bilateral talks between the United States and the USSR on the limitation of strategic weapons systems. "Unless success is achieved in both these fields," he said, "it is difficult to conceive of much real progress in other significant disarmament or arms control measures." He was equally concerned about finding ways to bring France and the People's Republic of China into the arms negotiations. This, he said, was one of the conditions for the achievement of any significant progress during the decade.

1. Statement on the Occasion of the Entry into Force of the Treaty on the Non-Proliferation of Nuclear Weapons

NEW YORK   MARCH 5, 1970

IT IS WITH deep satisfaction that I welcome the entry into force of the Treaty on the Non-Proliferation of Nuclear Weapons. Thus, many years

SOURCE: *UN Monthly Chronicle,* Vol. VII, April 1970, pp. 55–56.

of persistent efforts and intensive negotiations in the United Nations and in the Conference of the Eighteen-Nation Committee on Disarmament are finally coming to fruition.

It is hardly necessary for me to stress the importance of the non-proliferation Treaty, which has been widely acclaimed as the most important international agreement in the field of disarmament since the nuclear age began. In preventing the further spread of nuclear weapons and in establishing a safeguards system for verifying the faithful implementation of its obligations, the Treaty cannot fail to play a very significant role in containing the nuclear arms race.

At the same time, the Treaty promotes the peaceful uses of nuclear energy and creates most favorable conditions for the development of a wide international cooperation in this field. In this regard, the Treaty not only reaffirms the inalienable right of all parties to develop research and the production and use of nuclear energy for peaceful purposes, it also provides that all the parties will facilitate and have the right to participate in the fullest possible exchange of equipment, materials, and scientific and technological information for this purpose.

It should also be stressed that the Treaty is not an end in itself but a step toward disarmament and that the Treaty imposes on all parties a solemn obligation to pursue negotiations of effective measures relating to the cessation of the nuclear arms race, to nuclear disarmament, and to general and complete disarmament. This is a most pressing task for the future—and the parties to the Treaty, and especially the nuclear-weapon powers, have a great responsibility in fulfilling the obligation they have accepted under the terms of the Treaty.

I note with great satisfaction that as of today almost one hundred states have already signed the non-proliferation Treaty. Now that the Treaty has entered into force, those states which have not yet signed or ratified it will undoubtedly be encouraged to take positive action to contribute to the universality of the Treaty, so that it may fully achieve its objectives. It is my firm belief that it is in the best interests of the world community that the non-proliferation Treaty should command universal support.

2. From Statement to the Conference on Politics of Disarmament, Sponsored by the Institute on Man and Science

NEW YORK   MAY 22, 1970

. . . PROGRESS IN ALL fields of human endeavor, but particularly in the field of disarmament because of its complex nature and the still existing suspicion and mistrust between nations, can be achieved only if there is a strong political will on all sides to undertake the policies and measures that could lead to agreements and if discussions and negotiations are conducted with determination to achieve specific objectives. If we are to make real progress toward disarmament, governments must approach this subject in a new spirit. They must stop questioning the seriousness of purpose of others and think how they can demonstrate their own.

It was with these considerations in mind that I proposed last September that the United Nations dedicate the decade of the 1970s as a Disarmament Decade. I was gratified that the General Assembly accepted this idea. Without a single dissenting vote, the General Assembly declared the 1970s as a Disarmament Decade and requested the Conference of the Committee on Disarmament in Geneva to work out "a comprehensive program dealing with all aspects of the problem of the cessation of the arms race and general and complete disarmament under effective international control, which would provide the Conference with a guideline to chart the course of its further work and its negotiations." The Geneva Disarmament Conference is discussing the question of the comprehensive program and will be making a report thereon to the next session of the General Assembly.

While not presuming to go into detail as to the possible contents of the comprehensive program, there are certain considerations which come to mind and which I believe it worthwhile to share with the participants in this conference.

SOURCE: UN Press Release SG/SM/1261.

It is of course axiomatic that any comprehensive program for disarmament must begin with a halt or "freeze" or limitation of the armaments race, above all the nuclear arms race; thereafter, measures must be taken to turn the spiral downward by reducing and finally eliminating nuclear and other weapons of mass destruction. A comprehensive program must of course be balanced and flexible rather than rigid. It must also provide for the limitation and reduction of military budgets and of conventional armaments. At the Geneva Conference a number of delegations have called on the Soviet Union and the United States to revise and bring up to date the draft treaties for general and complete disarmament which each of them tabled in 1962. While this may pose difficult problems for each of these powers, the efforts to bring their draft treaties up to date could prove a most useful endeavor, which might reveal many new areas for early progress.

It seems clear that progress during the Disarmament Decade will, to a very large extent, depend upon two developments—first, the full implementation of the non-proliferation Treaty to halt the horizontal proliferation of nuclear weapons, and second, the making of substantial headway in limiting the offensive and defensive strategic nuclear armaments, that is, in halting the vertical proliferation of nuclear weapons. Unless success is achieved in both these fields, it is difficult to conceive of much real progress in other significant disarmament or arms control measures.

It would also seem to me to be equally clear that a condition for the achievement of far-reaching measures of disarmament during the decade is the finding of ways and means of associating all nuclear powers, including France and the People's Republic of China, with the negotiations. . . .

THE HUMAN ENVIRONMENT

THE GENERAL ASSEMBLY in 1968 approved a Swedish proposal for an international conference on the human environment to be held in Stockholm in 1972, but preparations did not begin in earnest until the spring of 1970 when the Preparatory Committee on the Human Environment held its first meeting at United Nations Headquarters. U Thant issued a comprehensive report in 1969 outlining the main problems, such as air and water pollution, soil erosion, waste of natural resources, many of which he said must be dealt with at the international as well as the national and local levels. In a statement at the opening session of the Preparatory Committee on March 9, 1970, the Secretary-General declared that "never in the twenty-five-year history of the United Nations has there been a problem of more relevance to all nations than the present environmental crisis." From the beginning he was heartily in accord with the Assembly's view that the Stockholm Conference must be action-oriented rather than a mere forum for speeches. On May 14, Thant delivered an address at the University of Texas on the international role in protecting the environment. He suggested the creation of a global authority with broad powers to police and enforce its decisions on matters affecting the environment. The immediate question, he said was whether "the sovereign nations of the world have the courage and the vision to set up and support such an agency now, and thus, in the interest of future generations of life on earth, depart radically from the hitherto sacred paths of national sovereignty." He added, "The crisis of the environment could be the challenge which might show us the way forward to a responsible and a just world society—a path which, for all the efforts of the United Nations in the political crises of our time, has so far eluded us."

1. Statement at Opening of the Preparatory Committee for the United Nations Conference on the Human Environment

NEW YORK   MARCH 9, 1970

I WISH TO WELCOME you to this first session of the Preparatory Committee for the United Nations Conference on the Human Environment. Never in the twenty-five-year history of the United Nations has there been a problem of more relevance to all nations than the present environmental crisis. The time has come for the United Nations, in the spirit and the letter of the Charter, to be a center for harmonizing the actions of nations in solving the problems of the human environment.

The work which you are about to undertake is symptomatic of new trends which are emerging in contemporary events and which seem to me to mark the beginning of a new era in human history. The mastering of energy and the transformation of natural resources into innumerable instruments and goods at the service of man, brought about by the industrial revolution, have provided one of the most astounding pages of human history. It would seem, however, that the aims and methods of the industrial revolution, which has brought such immense prosperity to some areas of the earth, must come under review before it has even reached the entirety of the globe. A new civilization characterized by more human beings, with longer lives and a better quality of life, has flowered in the last two centuries, and is spreading slowly over the entire world. Justice in the worldwide distribution of these benefits so far has not been ensured. Indeed, it has been one of the major preoccupations of the world community during the last twenty-five years to enhance the share of the poorer countries in these benefits and to help in their development.

The realization of a new and very disturbing aspect of the spreading and growing industrial civilization has now arisen: man has suddenly

SOURCE: UN Press Release SG/SM/1220.

awakened to the dimensions, to the rapidity, and to the mass effects of productive processes on the physical endowment and configuration of this planet and on its basic biological balances. To produce at any cost, without due consideration to effects on the environment, can no longer be the central preoccupation of man. Control of the effects of productive processes will require new economic thinking, new legal instruments, new administrative measures, and new governmental priorities. I am convinced that men and institutions will be able to solve this problem in time, for under the pressure of necessity, man is quite capable of adapting to new conditions. The new challenge posed to industry can be solved by industry itself, once the minds of our best scientists and engineers are bent on devising clean processes of production and proper means of waste disposal.

Mankind is also coming to the realization that a new dimension of time, reaching substantially into the future, must be added to its thinking, planning, and endeavors. For never before has the future been so decisively engendered and molded by present-day decisions. Historically, man has been preoccupied with a time range of scarcely a few years ahead. Life spans were short. The rate of change was slow. Anyone who dealt with forecasts was labeled a utopian, a visionary, or a dreamer. In our time it is the utopians who have become realists, and even their forecasts often fall short of reality. The seeds of future benefits and levels of life on our planet are being planted now and are already beginning to germinate. We must carefully weigh the effects of present behavior on the future if we do not wish to be considered by later generations as having failed in our foresight. It is consequently of paramount importance that the youth of the world be fully involved in our planning. I think that their current unrest and revolt against many of the values of the past arise in part from their uneasiness with the deterioration of the human environment and human situation. Seldom has any century or any generation been faced with such serious responsibilities.

The United Nations and its specialized agencies pioneered in dealing with prospective problems. We possess today sound long-term projections for a great variety of economic and social phenomena such as population, urbanization, education, food requirements, international trade, rates of growth in national income, and so forth. But much remains to be done: we need similar long-term forecasts for the consumption of our natural resources such as water, minerals, and energy, which will increase prodigiously in the decades ahead. We will need statistics and projections on the total effects of consumption, production, and transportation processes on the human environment.

We are thus necessarily on the threshold of a new era of international cooperation. Whatever the political stalemates may be and however long they may last, it seems clear that most economic, social, and physical world indicators will change by at least 100 percent every twenty-five years: world population will double and so will world consumption of water, of energy, of minerals, of transportation, and so forth. Under the impact of rapid scientific and technological changes, nations are being brought closer together and problems are progressively becoming the same in all countries. The total effects of changes within all countries, added together, will require joint international surveillance, consultations, and actions if human life on this planet is to be preserved and enriched.

It is urgent that we rapidly fill the gaps in our knowledge. While immense resources are being devoted by many towns, states, and national governments in order to obtain better knowledge of their territorial areas, not enough is being done to improve our collective knowledge and to monitor what is happening to·our atmosphere and our oceans. Little is being done, for example, to calculate the totality of wastes and deleterious material which are being introduced by nations and by international transports into our common resources through rivers and oceans, combustion and radiation. As noted in my report on problems of the human environment issued in May 1969, only a few regional efforts had been made toward the development of systematic air-pollution sample networks.

I sincerely hope that the international community will decide to make the necessary arrangements so that all nations will be informed year by year of the changes occurring in vital elements of the human environment. The time has come when we must establish an appropriate worldwide network of environmental statistics and forecasts as we have done in other major economic and social areas of collective concern. The time has come when nations must realize that each of them has responsibilities toward the state of the natural endowment of the earth as a whole and that its individual actions added to individual actions of other nations may have collective deleterious effects. Concerted preventive action now is far less costly than to repair the damage after it has occurred.

At this first session of your Preparatory Committee, I would like to make one remark on the orientation of your work. When the Conference was proposed by the government of Sweden—to which we must be so grateful—one of the major preoccupations was to arouse worldwide attention to human environment problems. We are living in a world of extremely rapid communications and of a great sensitivity to new emerging problems, and it would seem that this original objective of the Conference has already been largely achieved. The human environment is now a matter for almost daily discussion in governments, in the press, in non-governmental organizations, in the schools, and in the municipalities of industrialized societies. Two years will pass before the Conference takes place. You must be alert to the rapid changes which are likely to take place during this period. The Conference must be in step with whatever developments may occur during this interval. It must live up to the expectations which will prevail two years hence. Knowledge about the human environment is likely to improve considerably in that time as well as public awareness to the problem. It would seem to me, therefore, that the Conference should be planned in a predominantly action-oriented manner.

The 1972 Conference on the Human Environment can provide a unique opportunity for the United Nations family to provide leadership in dealing with a complex of problems which endanger the most fundamental well-being of mankind. I would like to make a passing reference to the considerable efforts already made by the United Nations institutional system in the environmental field as well as to the first international agreements concluded by major governments. Let me remind you that the universality of the concern with human environment was dramatically recognized in 1963 with the entry into force of the tripartite treaty banning nuclear weapon tests in the atmosphere, in outer space, and under water. This was one of the most enlightened acts of statesmanship witnessed in recent years. May I express the hope that the wisdom of nations inspired by the vision of a world united around the human objectives of peace, justice, and prosperity will soon enrich human life with a renewed respect for the earth's resources, and reward us with a hostility-free and weapon-free human environment. Perhaps it is the collective menaces, arising from the world's scientific and technological strides and from their mass consequences, which will bind together nations, enhance peaceful cooperation and surmount, in the face of physical danger, the political obstacles to mankind's unity.

I wish you every success in your important deliberations.

2. *From Address at the University of Texas*

AUSTIN, TEXAS   MAY 14, 1970

. . . IF EFFECTIVE MEASURES are to be taken in time, we need something new—and we need it speedily—a global authority with the support and agreement of governments and of other powerful interests, which can pull together all the piecemeal efforts now being made and which can fill in the gaps where something needs to be done. This authority must embark expeditiously, with the good of all men in mind, on the delicate process of reaching a workable compromise among governments and interests on matters affecting the environment. It should be able, if necessary, to police and enforce its decisions. Apart from the general support of governments, such an agency will have to rely, as Mr. George Kennan has rightly observed, on experts, scientists, and scholars who will be "true international servants, bound by no national or political mandate, by nothing, in fact, other than dedication to the work in hand." The immediate question is this: Do the sovereign nations of the world have the courage and the vision to set up and support such an agency now, and thus, in the interest of future generations of life on earth, depart radically from the hitherto sacred paths of national sovereignty? I sincerely hope that they do have this courage and wisdom, for I increasingly doubt whether any lesser measures will suffice to meet the challenge which faces us. Certainly the clouds and currents of pollution ceased to respect national sovereignty long ago.

There is a secondary question which relates to the nature of this new global agency. Mr. Kennan has suggested, for reasons which he considers cogent and practical, that, to begin with at any rate, it should be constituted by a small group of leading industrial and maritime nations, whose economies are largely responsible for the environmental problem in the first place. With all respect for Mr. Kennan's judgment, I profoundly disagree with this idea. It has always seemed to me ironical that the powers who had created, or who owned, nuclear weapons were

SOURCE: *UN Monthly Chronicle,* Vol. VII, June 1970, pp. 69–77

precisely those who were so insistent that others should forswear them, although, from a practical point of view, they were unquestionably right in seeking to curb the spread of nuclear weapons. But in the matter of environmental pollution it seems to me to be absolutely essential that all countries and peoples should be associated from the outset with the effort to face what may well prove to be the gravest threat that mankind as a whole has ever encountered. As I said earlier, a balance has to be reached between economic development and human and social needs, and between population, development, and environmental control. The developing countries are intimately concerned in these problems, which are crucial both to their own future and to the future of the environment. Their voices must be heard, and listened to, even if at the outset their technical contribution may be relatively small. Their confidence and their cooperation, as representing the largest part of the world's population, are vital. Otherwise we shall once again increase the gap between advanced and developing nations which is already one of the major sources of tension in the world.

I further venture to say that I believe that a global authority for the protection of the environment should be closely associated with the United Nations. I hasten to add that in saying this I am motivated by no impulse for empire-building. The United Nations has no shortage of great and difficult problems on its agenda. But the United Nations, for all its shortcomings, is the nearest thing we have to a world organization, and it suffers from all the difficulties of a world organization. If the United Nations has so far failed to develop the degree of world order and the kind of international authority and responsibility which many of us believe the present state of the world demands, it is perhaps because the challenges it has faced hitherto have not seemed compelling enough to persuade its sovereign Members to advance sufficiently fast from self-centered nationalism to internationalism. The fact remains, however, that the United Nations is still the only forum where the development of world order is continuously discussed and actively striven for. For the task of saving the environment, nothing less than a new step toward world order will do. Any new and separate universal agency set up for this purpose will have to face the same hard facts of international life which the United Nations faces, without the advantages of the accrued experience and existing organization of the United Nations.

One of the standard plots of science-fiction is the overwhelming and mysterious threat from outer space which unites all men on earth to defend their planet and which makes them forget at last their petty, earthbound differences. If much of what we now hear about environmental problems is true, we may well, on our own, have provided the overriding incentive to unite and to cooperate, and we shall not be needing help from outer space. If that is so, I can only hope that we have the imagination and the strength to react in time and in a fitting manner. If we do, our present near-disaster could be turned, like the flight of Apollo 13, into a triumph of the human spirit and of human ingenuity. Every cloud, even if it consists of smog, may have a silver lining. The crisis of the environment could be the challenge which might show us the way forward to a responsible and a just world society—a path which, for all the efforts of the United Nations in the political crises of our time, has so far eluded us.

Is it wholly fantastic and utopian to ask that some of the ingenuity and the vast sums of money now spent on armaments might be diverted to the saving of our native earth? Is it silly to believe that man can find within himself the generosity and the imagination to put the common good before self-interest? Is it naïve to hope that ideological struggles might give way to the struggle for survival and for a decent future? Is it unrealistic to suggest that the undoubted global challenge we now face might become the basis for a new start in world order and a more civilized and generous way of life for the peoples of the earth?

A great American public servant recently observed that "invariably the right things get done for the wrong reasons, so the organizer looks for the wrong reasons to get the right things done." While this dictum may err on the side of skepticism, there is a great deal of wisdom in it. As Secretary-General of the United Nations, I am deeply concerned with the threat to the environment, but I cannot let this concern overshadow all of the other objectives for which the United Nations has striven and will strive. All of these aims—peace, disarmament, justice, human rights, world order, improved conditions for all peoples, the development of international law—are interrelated, and an advance in one area benefits all the others. If the threat to our environment proves to be as great and as imminent as many experts now say it is, and as I believe it to be, and if the concern now being expressed all over the world is sincere, I would hope with all my heart that the lessons we can learn from this bitter experience may also find a wider application. I would hope that in saving ourselves by preserving our environment, we might also find a new solidarity and a new spirit among the governments and peoples of the earth, and so look to the future with greater courage and confidence.

THE SITUATION IN VIETNAM

U THANT had become increasingly disturbed as the Vietnam peace talks in Paris dragged on into 1970 with no signs of agreement. All during 1969, he had refrained from making substantative statements which might appear to be an intrusion in the delicate private negotiations. He broke his silence on May 5, 1970, with a public statement urging the convening of an international gathering which would include representatives of all parties interested in Indo-China, along the lines of the Geneva Conferences of 1954 and 1962. The Secretary-General felt that not only had the Paris talks bogged down but that the war had moved into a new and dangerous stage. His main concern was the extension of the conflict to Cambodia and Laos and the resumption of United States bombing of North Vietnam. "If the parties involved do not take urgent, decisive, and courageous measures toward peace," he said, "it will become increasingly difficult to end a war which constitutes a threat not only for the peoples of Indo-China but for the whole of mankind." He noted that for reasons often stated, the United Nations was not in a position to play a decisive part in the peace efforts, but he added that it was incumbent upon the Secretary-General "to express the anxiety and keenly felt apprehension of an increasing number of people in the world who are deeply disturbed by the grave risks created by the recent aggravation of the situation." He described the proposed new international gathering as "an indispensable step of the utmost urgency." Despite the absence of any positive response, Thant continued pressing for a broadened international discussion which would deal with the entire Indo-China situation, not just the Vietnam war. He told a luncheon of the United Nations Correspondents Association on June 11 that the only realistic course is international pressure. "That is why I believe," he said, "that there could be an intensive concentration on achieving an international parley or conference, in which all parties to the conflict would be participants, along the Geneva model, in a determined attempt to terminate this spreading war. It is utterly unacceptable, on both moral and humanitarian grounds, for that barbarous war to continue, for whatever reason, whether on a limited or unlimited scale." Since he first made his proposal on May 5, he had discussed it with a number of governments, including the United Kingdom and the USSR, co-chairmen of the Geneva Conference, and the United States and France. At the time of his June 11 statement he was preparing to visit London and Moscow where he planned to take up the Indo-China conflict again. He said the two co-chairmen already were aware of his thinking on the composition of a new conference, which he felt should include fifteen "elements." These would be all those participating in the fighting (seven), the five big powers (including the People's Republic of China) and the three members of the International Control

Commission (Canada, India, and Poland). At a press conference in Geneva on July 7, after his visits to London and Moscow, Thant acknowledged that his proposal had been blocked by the opposition of some key parties, just as a similar proposal by him in 1965 had been turned down. He insisted, however, that "this is the only means of bringing about a just and lasting solution to the very tragic situation in Indo-China."

---

1. Statement to the Press

NEW YORK   MAY 5, 1970

FOR MANY YEARS I have expressed my belief that military methods would not bring about a peaceful solution to the Vietnam problem, and I have always stated that the only sensible objective was to return to the provisions of the 1954 Geneva agreements.

Since the inception of the Paris talks, I have refrained from public statements in order to avoid any risk of creating unnecessary difficulties for those talks. The decision to break that silence at this time is not to be interpreted as signalling the collapse of the Paris talks or that they are moribund, although thus far they have been disappointingly unproductive.

In truth, the Paris talks and every other opportunity for a peaceful solution of the Vietnam war should be exploited to the fullest, for efforts toward peace in Vietnam are more imperative and more vital now than ever before. This is because, as becomes alarmingly clear, a new and critical stage in the development of that war is being reached. It is for this reason, seeing a widening and escalation of the war in Vietnam, which could have fateful consequences, that I have decided to make the present statement.

I had been saying for several years that there was an ever-present danger that the war in Vietnam might spread and even spill over the frontiers of that country. It is now clear that this is occurring before our eyes, and we are viewing a situation even more dangerous than the one created by the conflict which ravaged Indo-China before 1954.

I cannot conceal my deep concern regarding the recent involvement of Cambodia in the war. One country which had been trying very hard to

SOURCE: *UN Monthly Chronicle,* Vol. VII, June 1970, p. 44.

keep itself neutral seems now to have been drawn into the conflict. Recent reports of a resumption of the bombing of North Vietnam have given further cause for grave anxiety. I would also like to make public the concern I have felt in recent months regarding the intensification of the fighting in Laos. I fear that, if the parties involved do not take urgent, decisive, and courageous measures toward peace, it will become increasingly difficult to end a war which constitutes a threat not only for the peoples of Indo-China but for the whole of mankind.

Although there seems to be a broad consensus among all parties concerned to use the Geneva agreements as a point of convergence, the chances of peace still appear remote. In fact, as long as the Vietnam question is seen as a contest of unyielding wills, there will be no solution. The present extension and intensification of the war can only result in increasing the traditional racial animosities among the peoples of this area, as we have seen recently, and in an aggravation of the suffering, death, and destruction. In a civil conflict situation as that prevailing in Southeast Asia, it is the innocent civilian population who always suffer most. Only with the spirit of give and take, mutual restraint, and determination to take the necessary risks, can we escape the tragic developments which will inevitably result. This hideous war must be brought to an end.

In this context, I have expressed my interest in the suggestion made by France on April 1 that "the extension of a war which is tending to become indivisible can only be avoided by negotiation among all the interested parties with a view to seeking out and guaranteeing the basis for peace—itself indivisible." I regret that this suggestion did not receive the approval of some of the parties concerned. I still believe strongly that the solution to the conflict and the restoration of peace to this part of Asia reside in the Geneva agreements of 1954 and 1962 and that the only means of returning to these agreements is for all parties concerned to undertake urgent negotiations, whatever their form.

In view of the fact that several of the parties concerned are not Members of the United Nations, and that many of its Members, including some permanent members of the Security Council, are not in favor of United Nations involvement, the Organization has not been in a position so far to play a decisive part in bringing an end to the conflict. However, it is incumbent upon its Secretary-General to express the anxiety and keenly felt apprehension of an increasing number of people in the world who are deeply disturbed by the grave risks created by the recent aggravation of the situation. In my view, therefore, an international gathering of the nature described above, to cope with the old war in South Vietnam and the new war in Cambodia, is an indispensable step of the utmost urgency. All who seek peace and justice should support such a move.

---

2. Statement to the Press

NEW YORK   JUNE 8, 1970

THE EXTENSION of the Vietnam war to Cambodia has resulted in more death, more destruction, and more devastation. The Vietnam war has already become an Indo-China war.

The latest news dispatches indicate that one of the most sacred and renowned religious and cultural monuments of man—Angkor Wat in Cambodia—is in danger of following the fate of Hue, another cultural and religious center revered by all Vietnamese people. Angkor Wat must be saved.

I earnestly appeal to all concerned to respect, and to take every possible precaution to preserve, the many historic religious and cultural edifices in the fighting zone and elsewhere in Indo-China.

SOURCE: UN Press Release SG/SM/1272.

3. From Transcript of Remarks at Luncheon of United Nations Correspondents Association

NEW YORK   JUNE 11, 1970

. . .

THE SECRETARY-GENERAL: . . . I am gratified and delighted that the United Nation's Correspondents Association (UNCA) has been doing

SOURCE: *UN Monthly Chronicle,* Vol. VII, July 1970, pp. 108ff.

me the honor of offering luncheons every year like the one we are having today; I have always regarded these luncheons as among the most memorable and moving moments in my career.

We are now living in a time of crisis; all of us are deeply concerned about certain developments in some parts of the world. My foremost concerns, naturally and inescapably, continue to be the intensifying *de facto* war in the Middle East and the prolonged and broadening war in Indo-China. Both of these war situations are agonizing, and seriously threaten the peace of the world.

As to the Middle East, the situation steadily deteriorates with an increase in daily incidents of violence and fighting, and dimming prospects for a restoration of peace. The will for an end to fighting, which led to the discussions and compromises that made possible the armistice agreements twenty-one years ago, is tragically lacking today. Progress toward peace in situations of this kind can be made only when there is a give-and-take attitude on the part of the parties involved with regard to their own positions. There is not likely to be a breakthrough to a fruitful peace effort in the Middle East until that stage is reached; and, in all frankness, I see no sign at the moment of reaching it. It would appear, as a matter of fact, that in recent months the positions of the parties may have hardened.

Looking at the Middle East conflict realistically today, it is obvious that its international aspects and concerns are greater than ever before. The firmer alignments of the two superstates on opposite sides have become a vital factor. The political and other repercussions from the conflict extend far beyond the area. International efforts to resolve the conflict have been the greatest ever—the Security Council and General Assembly actions, Ambassador Jarring's determined efforts, the four-power talks, and the bilateral talks—but all have been unavailing thus far.

During the three years following the 1967 war there has been no evidence that the issues of the Middle East conflict can be settled by the parties through their own efforts. Therefore, international assistance should be increased and intensified.

On the international side, the four powers will have to do much more than they have been able to do thus far in support of and in carrying out resolution 242 (1967) of November 1967, and in helping Ambassador Gunnar Jarring's efforts. There would seem to be no other road to a just and peaceful long-term settlement. Both sides have indicated their acceptance of resolution 242 (1967), but this has little meaning in the absence of a clear and unequivocal indication from both sides of a readiness to carry out the provisions of the resolution in full.

That indication has not been forthcoming thus far from one of the parties.

As I read the resolution, its stated principles and objectives are not to be the subject of negotiation, but the means of attaining them are negotiable.

In my thinking, the essential condition for the restoration of peace in the Middle East has now come to be an international consensus on the vital issues which, to be effective, requires agreement among the four powers, which, in turn, could be possible only if agreement could be reached between the two biggest powers.

To this end, if any real progress is to be made, the four powers themselves also will have to adopt a give-and-take attitude and seek and accept compromises on their positions. It is evident that in the four- and two-power talks this process has not gone far enough thus far to produce significant agreement.

Security Council resolution 242 (1967) sets forth the vital issues requiring solution, and defines applicable principles and steps to be taken in resolving them. They are difficult and complex, but they are not beyond the pale of agreement.

I cannot believe, for example, that the two most basic of those issues are irreconcilable—the inherent right of a state to be free of military occupation of its territory, on the one hand, and the entirely legitimate demands for the right of a state to exist behind secure boundaries, on the other.

It merits repetition and emphasis that the provision of arms to the fighting parties in the Middle East, and particularly the provision of arms which are clearly and primarily for use in offensive actions, can serve only to intensify the war and impede progress toward peace.

My position on the Vietnam war—a war now widened to include Cambodia—remains unchanged: I deplore that war, which I have always regarded as needless, senseless, and barbaric, inflicting untold suffering and misery upon countless millions of innocent people. I hold firmly to the conviction that it is unrealistic and short-sighted for any party to seek or hope for military victory as the outcome of the war in Indo-China.

Therefore, I can regard only with dismay what, in my view, seems to be the recent tendency to stress military operations and success in military effort in that war. I personally see such a course as illusory and as one which ultimately can lead only to complete disaster.

It follows, of course, that I view with deep concern and anxiety the extension of the Vietnam war into Cambodia. I strongly hope that the Cambodian adventure will be quickly ended, as promised—the sooner the better—and that thereafter the independence and neutrality of that country will be fully respected by all parties.

It is not likely that the Vietnam war will be ended through a unilateral act of disengagement by either side, although I do not doubt that the party which would have the wisdom and courage to take such a step would be widely applauded throughout the world and win the plaudits of history.

The only realistic recourse, therefore, is international action and international pressure.

That is why I believe that there could be an intensive concentration on achieving an international parley or conference, in which all parties to the conflict would be participants, along the Geneva model, in a determined attempt to terminate this spreading war. It is utterly unacceptable, on both moral and humanitarian grounds, for that barbarous war to continue, for whatever reason, whether on a limited or unlimited scale.

Now I am ready to take on the questions. . . .

QUESTION: This question concerns Article 99 of the Charter, which, as we know, says that: "The Secretary-General may bring to the attention of the Security Council any matter which in his opinion may threaten the maintenance of international peace and security." Former United States Under Secretary of State Elliot Richardson, in a speech on April 19, said that the full potential of the Secretary-General's role under Article 99 had been neglected.

Could you comment on this?

THE SECRETARY-GENERAL: I believe I commented on that question at one of my previous press conferences. You will recall that in the course of the last twenty-five years the Secretary-General of the United Nations invoked Article 99 only once: in the case of the Congo. At that time, all the African states wanted the Secretary-General to invoke that Article. All the big powers, permanent members of the Security Council, wanted him to invoke that Article. There was no opposition whatever from any quarter, so he was on firmer ground when he invoked Article 99 and summoned a meeting of the Security Council.

That explains why there has been only one instance of the Secretary-

General invoking Article 99 in the course of the history of the United Nations. In this respect, I want to make one very brief observation. In asking for a meeting of the Security Council, the Secretary-General has the same right, the same power, the same influence, as any one of the 126 Member states. The Secretary-General can request a meeting of the Security Council on any situation involving threats to international peace and security; any one of the 126 Member states has the same right. So the question is: If any one of the 126 Member states is reluctant to ask for a Security Council meeting on a particular issue, why should the Secretary-General rush into the whole thing and face disaster?

For the sake of argument, to illustrate my point concretely, let us say I invoke Article 99 today and ask for a meeting of the Security Council on the situation in Southeast Asia. Does anyone of you really believe that that item would even be inscribed on the agenda? I doubt that the proposed item would be inscribed on the agenda.

Supposing, however, for the sake of argument, that the item is inscribed on the agenda, in the face of the opposition of some members of the Security Council—including two permanent members. Does anyone really believe that any substantive, positive, concrete resolution would come out of that? I do not think so.

Those are some of the considerations I want to present as to why I have not so far invoked Article 99.

QUESTION: In pursuance of the General Assembly resolution adopted unanimously on December 16, 1969, you have asked Member states to inform you of their recommendations and proposals on the strengthening of international security. In view of the present situation, and according to the communications you have already received, what is your evaluation of the importance of the consideration of measures for the strengthening of international security at the coming session of the General Assembly?

THE SECRETARY-GENERAL: As you know, some Member states have responded to my request to reply to my queries on the basis of that particular resolution of the General Assembly. I released all the answers to the Member states only last week. If I remember correctly, only a very small percentage of the Member states have responded to my request. Of course, I have studied them very closely. It is for the Members of the United Nations to consider these answers and take any step they may deem necessary at the coming session of the General Assembly.

QUESTION: You have frequently spoken out about humanitarianism.

Can you say a few words about the clubbing of baby seals in Canada by fur traders?

THE SECRETARY-GENERAL: I have seen some of the scenes of this particular type of activity in Canada on television. Of course, as a Buddhist, I regard all life as sacred, and the taking of life as a sin. Beyond that, I do not wish to comment.

QUESTION: News dispatches in the last few days have reported heavy fighting in and around refugee camps between commando groups and the Jordanian army, indicating that the commandos maintain headquarters in some of those UNRWA (United Nations Relief and Works Agency for Palestine Refugees in the Near East) camps in Jordan. Do you have any reports on that situation from Mr. Michelmore?[1] What is UNRWA's position in those camps in Jordan where the commandos seem to operate openly? Are there any further reports about the camps in Lebanon recently occupied by the commandos?

Also, is it true that UNRWA camps in Jordan have come under fire from Jordanian troops? What is the general situation in Jordan now, and what steps is the United Nations taking to deal with it?

THE SECRETARY-GENERAL: As far as the current developments in Jordan—particularly in the city of Amman—are concerned, as you all know the United Nations has had no presence in the form of observers, since the stationing of observers between Jordan and Israel was rejected. But, of course, we do have an UNRWA branch in Amman, and a liaison officer in Amman for the chief of staff of the United Nations Truce Supervision Organization. I have been in touch with both of them.

I must say that I am very much concerned about the developments there, and before I receive a considered assessment and reports from my people in the area, I do not wish to comment on the situation at this moment.

QUESTION: Since the Arabs will not observe the cease-fire as long as Israel occupies their land, and Israel will not withdraw unless the cease-fire is observed, how can the United Nations, or anyone, resolve this dilemma?

THE SECRETARY-GENERAL: Regarding the question of a cease-fire, you all know the positions of the parties concerned; you all know the reasons given by both sides in explanation of their attitudes.

It is worth recalling that a cease-fire was ordered by the Security

---

[1]Laurence Michelmore, commissioner-general of the United Nations Relief and Works Agency for Palestine Refugees in the Near East.

Council, and that my primary function is to send observers to the affected areas, particularly, as you know, to the Suez Canal sector; and their function is to observe and report—to observe whether there are any breaches of the cease-fire and to report to me, through the chief of staff; and I, in turn, have to report to the Security Council, which I have been doing almost every day.

So beyond that, I do not wish to comment. It is primarily the responsibility of the Security Council to give consideration to this aspect; but you all are aware of one fact: that there is a growing body of opinion in this house, to my knowledge, that the question of a cease-fire cannot be considered separately from the consideration of the overall question of peace and stability in the area. That is the general feeling of many representatives with whom I have discussed this question.

QUESTION: You have said that resumption of Ambassador Jarring's mission depended primarily, but not exclusively, on the big four talks. Do you believe that relaunching Ambassador Jarring on his mission—or renewed efforts to reactivate his mission—might soon follow or result from your talk with him in Moscow?

THE SECRETARY-GENERAL: My assessment of the situation in the Middle East, particularly with respect to the reactivation of Ambassador Jarring's mission, I believe is well known. As you all know, the four permanent members of the Security Council have been meeting here almost regularly for some time; they have been in constant touch with me.

It seems to me that the picture is now clearer than before. As I have said on previous occasions, there is still a possibility for a political solution. There are two very good bases on which to start: the first basis is Security Council resolution 242 (1967), as I indicated in my opening remarks. The second basis is the statement issued by the four foreign ministers of the permanent members of the Security Council on the night of September 20, 1969, immediately after my dinner on the thirty-eighth floor. I believed at that time—and I still believe—that those two documents can serve as a sensible, suitable basis for launching the next efforts.

You will recall that the four foreign ministers, in their statement on September 20 last year, made a categorical commitment along the following lines: they reaffirmed that Security Council resolution 242 (1967) of November 22, 1967, should be supported and carried out. That is the language used by the four foreign ministers of the permanent members.

In my view, the next logical step is for the four permanent members of the Security Council to ask the parties concerned to accept that resolution and carry it out.

I am afraid they have not done that.

Of course, as I said earlier, I have been in contact with the four permanent members; I have presented these ideas to all of them. Personally speaking, I believe the next step is for the four permanent members of the Security Council to draw the logical conclusion from that statement and ask the parties involved not only to accept resolution 242 (1967) but to carry it out—to implement it, in other words.

Then, in my view, whatever else they want to put in their statement they should put in, and then submit that statement to the Security Council for distribution as an official document of the Council. So it would be official as the expression of the combined will of the four permanent members of the Security Council. At such time I might take it that that was the consensus of the Security Council. Then I could request Ambassador Jarring, my special representative, to reactivate the mission and go into the area to discuss the methods and modalities of carrying out that resolution, including the setting of a timetable. That would be a very good basis for the reactivation of Ambassador Jarring's mission. For the moment, I do not see any other alternative. . . .

QUESTION: You spoke in your statement of the increasing involvement of the two big powers in the Middle East. However, the United States has not positioned troops or advisers in Israel, but the USSR has done just this in Egypt. Do you have a comment on this apparent one-sided acceleration?

THE SECRETARY-GENERAL: When I spoke in my introductory statement regarding the increasing involvement of the two superstates, I was not thinking in terms of the concrete help and assistance given to the parties involved. I was not thinking of the degree or the equality or the balance of the kind of aid rendered. But I am sure you will agree with me that both superstates are still involved in the conflict in the Middle East, and there are indications of greater involvement in the future. That is why I have to sound this note of warning.

QUESTION: I have a few questions about Indo-China, Cambodia, and your trip to London and Moscow. Will you take the occasion of your visit to Moscow to advocate convening a Geneva-type conference on Cambodia? I should like to know if you have in mind some new initiative when you are in London and Moscow to get under way an international conference to settle the war in Indo-China? Can you tell us whether you have any hope that your visit to Moscow might facilitate a convocation of the Geneva Conference or an international conference of any kind on Indo-China?

THE SECRETARY-GENERAL: First of all, I must say that I have no set agenda of items to be discussed with the leaders of both the United Kingdom and the Soviet Union in the course of my projected trip next week. Inevitably the question of the Indo-China war will come up in both places. You will recall that I made an appeal on May 5. Primarily I aimed at the consideration of convening an international gathering or conference to settle the whole Indo-China war. After that I elaborated on these ideas to the two co-chairmen of the Geneva Conference—the United Kingdom and the Soviet Union—and the chairman of the International Control Commission (ICC), India. Later on I also informed other big powers and two other members of the ICC on how I should like to develop those ideas. These can be outlined in broad terms.

You will recall that in 1965 I advocated a convening of a Geneva-type conference to consider the Vietnam situation, with the participation of all those who were actually fighting. That was my first proposal.

At that time both sides rejected my proposal; you know the reasons why. It took two and a half years for both sides to agree to this formulation—that is, participation of all those who were actually fighting in Vietnam, in any conference to discuss the question of the Vietnam war. They met in Paris, as you know. Even the choice of a location took from two to three months. You will recall that I proposed four convenient venues: Phnom Penh, Warsaw, Geneva, and Paris. At last they selected Paris. So the meetings have been going on for some time.

So my point is: the fact is that all the parties to the conflict accepted the principle of participation in any future conference by all those who are actually fighting. This is a very important point. It is a principle of primary significance. If the parties to that conflict have agreed to this principle, why not extend this principle logically to the whole of Indo-China? That is my argument.

So since they have accepted the principle of participation by all those who are fighting, for the purpose of discussing the Vietnam question, why not enlarge this principle to cover all of Indo-China? So my proposal—I think I should better describe these as my ideas—could be described as follows: a future conference on Indo-China should be participated in by fifteen elements: I would prefer to use the word "elements," not states. In the first category, on the basis of my previous statement, all those who are fighting in Indo-China must be permitted to participate in that conference. That means seven: the government in Hanoi; the government in Saigon; the government in Phnom Penh; the government in Vientiane; the National Liberation Front, now called the PRG—the Provisional Revolutionary Government of South Vietnam; and those elements in Cambodia which are supporting Prince Sihanouk, and those elements in Laos who are supporting Prince Souphanouvong. There will be seven elements that are actually fighting in the area.

Then the five big powers which participated in the Geneva conferences: the United States, the United Kingdom, France, the Soviet Union, and the People's Republic of China. They were all there in Geneva; they should be there again in future conferences. Then all the three members of the ICC, which is a creation of the Geneva Conference—India, Canada, and Poland—also must participate.

So that is my elaboration of the ideas which were presented publicly on May 5. Now the two co-chairmen of the Geneva Conference and the chairman of the International Control Commission are fully aware of my thinking. But I must say that an agreement on the composition is only half the problem; as a matter of fact it is less than half of the problem. The more important problem is: What are they going to discuss? That is much more important than agreement on composition.

You will recall that in 1954, when the first Geneva Conference met, the situation was completely different from the situation prevailing today in Vietnam, or for that matter, in Southeast Asia. At that time, after Dien Bien Phu, the French publicly declared that they were withdrawing. The French made their position known, that they were leaving the scene. I must say that the French government decided on this line of action with wisdom and vision. So when the Geneva Conference met in 1954 there was no question of discussing the problem of French withdrawal. It was a *fait accompli*.

The focus of the Conference was on other factors: what to do with Vietnam after the French left? What would be the future set-up of Vietnam? What would be the political, social and economic alignment or non-alignment of Vietnam, looking at the future? The participants were not obsessed with the question of French withdrawal; it was a *fait accompli*. So the primary outcome of the Geneva conference of 1954 was to define the objectives for the State of Vietnam.

As you know, those objectives can be summarized in three words: independence, neutrality and non-intervention from outside. Of course, those objectives were not fulfilled for reasons which we know, but we do not all agree with reasons given by this side or that side. I do not want to go into that aspect fot the moment.

My point is that in 1954 it was much easier to define the issues to be discussed—because there was no question of discussing French withdrawal when the French had very wisely stated that they would withdraw.

But the situation today is completely different. I do not want to suggest for the moment what should be the items on the agenda for the next conference. Naturally, I would leave it to the prospective participants to discuss. In my view, this is an aspect that is much more important than agreement on the composition of the participants. That explains why the Paris talks are still stalled. They agreed on the nature of the participants, but up to now there is no agreement on the items to be discussed. One side has some items, the other side has a different set of items. So there must be agreement on the items to be discussed before they convene any international conference.

These represent the elaboration of my ideas to the powers directly involved in the conflict, which I conveyed early last month.

QUESTION: Here are two questions about your appeal for a Geneva conference. Are you encouraged by any moves for such a conference? In line with what you were just saying, what would be your suggestion for the agenda?

Recalling the Asian conference in Djakarta which endorsed your appeal, I should like to know what are the obstacles that have prevented the materialization of the conference and how one could cope with these obstacles.

THE SECRETARY-GENERAL: I think that for the greater part these questions have been dealt with in my previous answer.

Regarding my ideas on the agenda, as I have stated I do not propose, at least for the moment, to present my own ideas on the nature of the items on the agenda.

As regards my contact with the Asian nations, which are also very rightly involved with this question of Indo-China, you will be interested to know that the eleven-nation conference in Djakarta designated three emissaries to contact me: emissaries from Japan, Malaysia, and Indonesia. I have an appointment to see them tomorrow morning. I believe that the exchanges of views with them will be very helpful.

QUESTION: I have two final questions on Cambodia. On the "Meet the Press" program on June 4 last, Secretary of Defense [Melvin] Laird and General [Earle G.] Wheeler reiterated what seems to be a new recipe in the Vietnam conflict, that is, the so-called air interdiction strategy in Cambodia and, if necessary, in Laos "in order to save American lives in Vietnam." I should like to know if you consider this a proof of expansion of the Indo-China war or if you care to make any comment on it.

My final question is: At what point do you feel Cambodia became involved in the war? Was it when the "sanctuaries" were first created, when Prince Sihanouk sought unsuccessfully to dislodge them, when the North Vietnamese attacked the Cambodian army in April, or when the United States and South Vietnam moved in force across the border?

THE SECRETARY-GENERAL: Regarding the question relating to the words used about "air interdiction," I think it would be of interest for you to know that during the Second World War, Rothenburg in Germany, which was set as a target for air attack, was saved on the ground that it was a seat of religious and cultural heritage in Germany for a very long time. So Rothenburg was preserved.

Then again, in the same war—the Second World War—Kyoto, the religious heart of Japan, was originally marked for air attack. But due to the intervention at the last moment by the Secretary of War, Mr. Henry Stimson, Kyoto was saved. Mr. Stimson happened to be in Kyoto before the war. He was so impressed with the religious and cultural edifices and buildings in that city that, according to historians, he was mainly responsible for saving Kyoto and preserving it. Unfortunately, in the case of Hue in Vietnam, there was no Mr. Stimson, so you know what the fate of Hue was.

With that in mind I appealed recently to all the parties in the conflict to try to preserve the religious and cultural edifices which are the most treasured legacy of man. I had in mind particularly Angkor Wat in Cambodia, and of course there are many other edifices and monuments in Cambodia.

I have been assured by the United States government that it has issued standing instructions to all the armed forces to respect the religious and cultural edifices in areas of fighting.

About the question of Cambodia's involvement in the war, it is a very puzzling phenomenon, if I may say so. You will recall that in the last five years or so the government of Cambodia lodged over one hundred official complaints to the Secretary-General and to the Security Council alleging that A and B were the aggressors against Cambodia. Then in the last three months, with the change of government, the government of Cambodia made four or five official complaints to the Security Council alleging that C and D were the aggressors against Cambodia. There was no mention of A and B, so you can draw your own conclusions. I do not think that it would be in the public interest for me to draw my own conclusion. So when Cambodia was involved in this conflict is a very difficult question to answer.

QUESTION: I have two final questions. Do you as Secretary-General feel that the disagreement of the two superpowers on major problems like Indo-China and the Middle East has impaired or crippled the ability of the United Nations to deal with future problems involving world peace and security?

The second question is: Have you reached a decision regarding a third term as Secretary-General? Would you be prepared to accept a third term if this were clearly the wish of the membership, including the permanent members of the Security Council?

THE SECRETARY-GENERAL: In answer to the first question about the future of the United Nations vis-à-vis the present international crisis situations, I have explained my position and attitude on many previous occasions. With the very brief space of time at our disposal, I do not want to elaborate on this. But on one thing I am clear: the United Nations so far, although it has accomplished many things in many areas of activities, has not come up with a very satisfactory response to the challenges of our times—I mean a response with courage and initiative. In this respect I want to say that in a way it is the failure of the old generation to meet the extraordinary and great challenges of our times, challenges involving questions of war and peace, development, social justice, and so on. I feel that I am increasingly aware of this conscious-ness that the old generation has failed in meeting courageously the great challenges of our times. That is why I want to give the benefit of the doubt to the new generation. Let them try to face these challenges with greater courage, greater vision, and greater imagination, particularly the United Nations generation who were born after 1945.

On the question of the third term, you all know my feelings. In 1966, before the expiry of my first term, I had been saying at that time and before that time that no one should aspire to be the Secretary-General of the United Nations for more than one term. Of course I still have this feeling, but I do not want to make any dramatic announcements on this occasion. I do not think it is the time or the occasion to make any categorical announcement about my future plans. As you are no doubt aware, for the last six years or so my one preoccupation has been the war in Vietnam. I might say that it is an obsession with me, because I regard this war as a colossal horror story, a thousand times grimmer than the grimmest of the horror stories written by man. Of course, people speak of atrocities in this village or that village or that town or this town. In my view these reported atrocities here and there represent a very small part in this total horror. Therefore, this war must be stopped.

With these few words, ladies and gentlemen, I want to thank you for your very patient attention. I thank you also, Mr. President, for this most enjoyable lunch. . . .

4. From Transcript of Press Conference

GENEVA   JULY 7, 1970

. . .

QUESTION: In your speech yesterday to the Economic and Social Council you admitted the failure to pacify the Middle East and Southeast Asia. Does that mean that you have given up the hope and the optimism that you had two weeks ago when you came back from Moscow?

THE SECRETARY-GENERAL: No, I have not given up hope, as far as the Middle East situation is concerned. As most of you are no doubt aware, during my stay in Moscow last month the Soviet leaders briefed me very fully about their latest proposals on the Middle East—that is, the proposals which the Soviet government submitted to the big four meeting in New York on the 24th of last month, after I had returned from Moscow.

During my stay in Moscow, the United States government also briefed me fully about their latest proposals on the Middle East. As a matter of

SOURCE: *UN Monthly Chronicle, Vol. VII, August-September 1970, pp. 93–101.*

fact, I received the briefing about the Soviet proposals on June 18 and the briefing about the United States proposals on June 20.

I had occasion to have a discussion with Ambassador Gunnar Jarring in Moscow; as you know, Ambassador Jarring is the Secretary-General's special representative to the Middle East.

As soon as I returned to New York, I got in touch with the permanent representatives of the big four. They met on June 24, and again on July 1.

Ambassador [Yakov] Malik of the Soviet Union, who happened to preside over the big four meeting on July 1, reported to me on the results of the deliberations. He did that the next morning; that is, on Thursday morning. Hence, I could leave New York only on Thursday evening, July 2.

If I am to assess the latest proposals, I must say that the Soviet proposals have some interesting and concrete elements as regards the establishment of a just and lasting peace in the Middle East. I am still hopeful that a peaceful solution, a political solution, is possible as regards the Middle East situation.

QUESTION: Do you think that the Soviet plan is more interesting and concrete than the United States plan?

THE SECRETARY-GENERAL: I do not want to venture any opinion by way of comparing the two proposals. But, as I said a moment ago, so far as the question of establishing a just and lasting peace in the Middle East is concerned, the new Soviet proposals have certain new and concrete elements.

QUESTION: Were you informed in Moscow about the installation of the Soviet missiles in Egypt, and what was your reaction? Also, what is your reaction to the direct involvement of Soviet military forces in the Middle East war?

THE SECRETARY-GENERAL: During my recent visit to Moscow, the question of Soviet missiles, reported to have been installed on United Arab Republic territory, was not brought up. Of course, I have not been officially informed of these missiles; I have learned of them only from newspaper reports.

QUESTION: Would you be kind enough to comment on this matter?

THE SECRETARY-GENERAL: I have made observations on the question of arms shipments to the Middle East on many previous occasions. I have made a distinction between offensive weapons and defensive weapons. I think that to be fair we have to make a distinction between those two types of weapons. My views on this matter are well known.

QUESTION: Is it envisaged that a United Nations force should ultimately be sent to the Middle East and, if so, would there be Soviet participation this time and would there be any proviso to prevent the precipitate withdrawal of the force, as happened in 1967?

THE SECRETARY-GENERAL: I regret to note that there still seems to be a misunderstanding or misconception regarding the withdrawal of the United Nation's Emergency Force (UNEF) in 1967. My reports to the Security Council and the General Assembly are on record. Not one single Member questioned the correctness of my decision to withdraw UNEF. Of course, there have been from time to time comments in newspapers and on radio and television.

Just to set the record straight, I want to take this opportunity of explaining certain aspects of the withdrawal of UNEF. As soon as I got the request from the United Arab Republic government to withdraw UNEF, I discussed it with the Advisory Committee on UNEF. I then reported to the General Assembly, on the same day. I reported to the Security Council within twenty-four hours. Not one single Member suggested to me that I should not comply with the request. As a matter of fact, when the request reached me the United Arab Republic forces were already on the lines in front of UNEF, so I had no alternative but to give instructions to withdraw. That was agreed upon by the Force commander, of course, General [Indar] Rikhye. The withdrawal was not effected in a few days; it took five weeks. During that period of five weeks, fourteen soldiers of peace, serving with UNEF, were killed.

Those are some of the aspects of the problem which are not properly understood.

As far as the future involvement of the United Nations in the Middle East is concerned, I feel very strongly that the United Nations has a responsibility to maintain law and order and peace and security in the area. I understand that the permanent members of the Security Council have been giving a great deal of consideration to the stationing of a United Nations force in the area. Of course, the proper and effective functioning of a United Nations force in the area requires Security Council action—not General Assembly action, as was the case with UNEF. The Security Council must take the necessary steps, in my view, to station a United Nations military presence in the area, to maintain peace and security. As I have said on many occasions in the past, United Nations involvement in the search for peace is essential, and the United Nations should continue to be interested in the maintenance of peace and justice in the area. Security Council action—not General Assembly action—is essential.

QUESTION: When you were in Geneva in February you mentioned the fact that you felt that the impact made by the gas centrifuge should be a study of the United Nations Disarmament Commission. After you left there was very vehement objection to your suggestion by the EURA-TOM[1] people in the Disarmament Commission. Do you still feel that your suggestion about the impact of the gas centrifuge on nuclear proliferation is valid?

THE SECRETARY-GENERAL: I still maintain my position. It was far from my intention when I made that statement to have a particular Member state in mind. I was speaking in the context of the relevant resolutions and decisions. I still maintain my position and I do not think there were many protests to my statement. Even the delegate who made the statement explained to me that his protest was not vehement; he was just stating his government's position. I explained to him that I had no particular Member state in mind when I made the statement. I made the statement just in the context of the decisions, in the context of progress of the disarmament talks—just in the context of the progress of the human community as a whole.

QUESTION: First, in the context of the United Nations resolutions on South Africa, what would be your reaction if the British government decided to resume arms supplies to South Africa? Second, to return to the Middle East, what are your views on the presence of Soviet pilots in the Middle East and particularly on what is coming from the White House, that the United States may feel obliged to send United States military personnel into the Middle East if the pilots are not removed, and the comparison being made with the missile confrontation over Cuba?

THE SECRETARY-GENERAL: As regards the first question, it is, of course, a hypothetical situation. I have no official information from the British government that it is about to reverse its position regarding the sale of arms to South Africa, so I do not wish to comment on a hypothetical question.

As regards the second question, no organ of the United Nations has any official information regarding the presence or the nature of the functions of the Soviet pilots alleged to have been involved in the United Arab Republic. Of course, from time to time I have read press accounts

[1]European Atomic Energy Community.

of their presence and according to unofficial information they were involved in training programs only and not in operations. Of course it is difficult to comment on these aspects of the problem without any concrete evidence to base any comments upon.

QUESTION: Is there any possibility of Dr. Jarring's mission being reactivated during the course of this month? Second, with regard to the United Nations Observers, in view of the escalation of hostilities along the Suez Canal, apart from their providing a symbolic United Nations presence, do they have any other function, and is it your intention to leave them in that rather exposed position?

THE SECRETARY-GENERAL: Regarding the question of the reactivation of Ambassador Jarring's mission, since my arrival in Geneva I have been in contact with him and, in the present context, both Ambassador Jarring and I agree that, at least for the moment, there is no basis for the reactivation of his mission. Of course, as I explained earlier, the big four have been meeting and I understand they are meeting again on July 15. By that time, if there is a real basis for the reactivation of Ambassador Jarring's mission, I am sure he will be very glad to go to the area or to stay at the Headquarters of the United Nations to resume his activities.

Regarding the functions of the United Nations Observers in the Suez Canal sector, it is worth recalling that they are stationed there on the basis of a Security Council resolution. That relevant resolution of the Security Council defined their functions and, therefore, it is not within the competence of the Secretary-General to revise their functions or review their functions. They are performing their functions in the context of the relevant resolution of the Security Council.

QUESTION: But did that resolution not refer to a truce, to truce observers?

THE SECRETARY-GENERAL: No, the resolution referred to the presence or the stationing of United Nations Observers in the Suez Canal sector.

QUESTION: You said that you were not going to compare the Soviet and American proposals, but you said that the Soviet proposal was very interesting for lasting peace. By implication, one would say that the American proposal is not.

THE SECRETARY-GENERAL: No; I am just pinpointing one aspect of the problem. You will recall that the big powers seemed to agree that there remain three basic issues in the Middle East: withdrawal, peace, and boundaries. As far as the question of peace is concerned, in my view the Soviet proposal has concrete elements. I am not saying that the United States proposal has no concrete elements, but the United States proposal deals with other aspects of the problem. The United States position on peace is also well known. The United States is very desirous of the restoration of peace in the area, as is well known. But what I am saying is that the new Soviet proposal contains some new elements regarding the establishment of a just and lasting peace in the area. I am just stressing the fact that the Soviet Union—for the first time, to my knowledge—has come out with concrete and positive elements regarding this particular aspect of the problem, that is, the establishment of a just and lasting peace in the area.

QUESTION: Could you identify these concrete elements that you find interesting in the new Soviet proposal?

THE SECRETARY-GENERAL: I do not think I am in a position to disclose the substance of the proposals; but they are, of course, in the possession of all the big powers.

QUESTION: On Southeast Asia again, do you feel that the appointment of Ambassador [David] Bruce to Paris is a helpful element, and do you feel he can achieve something? Do you feel the other side may react to this? And what other elements are required to try and move toward a political settlement now?

THE SECRETARY-GENERAL: I believe President [Richard] Nixon's decision to send Ambassador Bruce to Paris is a very positive step, a step in the right direction. As far as the whole question of the Vietnam war is concerned—as you know, the Vietnam war has developed into an Indo-China war—I have expressed my views from time to time on many previous occasions.

You will recall that in 1965 I proposed for the first time that all those who were fighting should participate in a conference to discuss and decide on the future of Vietnam. When I suggested that, the parties directly involved in the fighting rejected my proposal. It took more than two years, you will recall, for the parties to accept that proposal, and the Paris peace talks started only in 1968. By that time, of course, the United States, North Vietnam, South Vietnam, and the National Liberation Front had agreed that all of them should participate in the discussions. So I am just projecting this idea to cover the whole of Indo-China.

Early last May, I proposed to the parties directly concerned a formulation which was an extension of the previous one—that all those who were fighting in the area should participate in a conference. I made those proposals to the two co-chairmen of the Geneva Conference—the United Kingdom and the Soviet Union—and the chairman of the International Control Commission, India; and, later on, I informed all the other participants. My proposals, in essence, are the following: if this principle of participation by all those who are fighting is accepted by the parties, the number of participants in the next Geneva-type conference will be fifteen. In the first category there are seven elements: the government of North Vietnam, the government of South Vietnam, the government of Laos, the government of Cambodia; then the National Liberation Front of South Vietnam—which is now called the Provisional Revolutionary Government, as you know—and those elements which are supporting Prince Souphanouvong in Laos and those which are supporting Prince Sihanouk in Cambodia. Those seven elements constitute the first category.

In the second category come the five big powers which participated in the Geneva Conferences of 1954 and 1962—that is, the United States, the United Kingdom, France, the Soviet Union, and the People's Republic of China.

In the third category there are three elements—the chairman and two members of the International Control Commission; that means India, Canada, and Poland.

So my proposal is not a new concept; it is just an extension of my previous proposal, which I made in 1965 and which was accepted by the parties two years later. So I was not surprised that my new proposals were rejected, for understandable reasons, but I believe very strongly that this is the only means of bringing about a just and lasting solution to the very tragic situation in Indo-China.

QUESTION: You have mentioned several times recently China and the necessity for the People's Republic of China to participate in the United Nations and in international cooperation. Is there any direct contact between your office and the People's Republic of China? Have you had any direct reply from Peking?

THE SECRETARY-GENERAL: To answer your second question first, I have no direct contact or communication with Peking. From time to time, if there are important matters to be transmitted, I use third parties which are Members of the United Nations, but I have no direct contact with Peking.

Regarding my advocacy of more involvement of the People's Republic of China in international affairs, I must say that I believe very strongly that, while the question of the representation of China in the United Nations is being debated and discussed year after year, some sort of arrangment should be devised by means of which Peking can be involved in the discussion of basic international issues involving war and peace. I believe very strongly that some sort of involvement of Peking in such deliberations is essential if we are to achieve results.

As I have said on one or two previous occasions, the nature of Peking's relationship with the outside world and particularly with the two superpowers will dominate the international scene in this decade. This will be the primary factor in international relationships in the seventies. So I have been trying to alert the membership to the discussions, particularly on matters of war and peace.

QUESTION: It has been reported that the Irish government intends to put the Ulster question before the United Nations. What is your reaction to that?

THE SECRETARY-GENERAL: The government of Ireland has not decided, to my knowledge, to put the question of Ulster before the United Nations; so I do not wish to comment on that.

QUESTION: I have two questions. First, I want to ask your opinion of the use in the United Arab Republic of the surface-to-air missiles, apparently with some Russian supervision. Do you regard this as justified as a means of self-defense and do you or do you not consider it to be an obstacle to the acceptance of a Soviet peace plan? Second, at what stage do you think the United Nations should send a military force to the United Arab Republic to separate the combatants? Do you think that should be done only after the acceptance of a broader plan from the Soviet Union or the United States, or do you think it should be done now?

THE SECRETARY-GENERAL: Regarding the reported presence of SAMs on United Arab Republic territory, I have never said that is a good thing and I have never specified any category of arms as being involved in the area. What I have been saying is that, from the United Nations point of view, a distinction should be made between two types of weapons, weapons which are of a purely offensive character and weapons which are of a purely defensive character. That is my only point of view.

Regarding the second question, on the stationing of United Nations forces in some areas of the Middle East, that is possible and desirable only with the endorsement of the Security Council. I feel very strongly that the Security Council has the responsibility of restoring peace in the area, of restoring justice in the area, and, in this context, the permanent members of the Security Council have a special responsibility to contribute to the successful outcome of the Security Council deliberations.

When I say that the permanent members of the Security Council have a special responsibility, I am conscious of their special status under the Charter. So I have been advocating the closer collaboration of the permanent members of the Security Council in seeking a just and peaceful solution to the problem. You will recall that I was the first to endorse the French proposal more than two years ago to the effect that the four permanent members of the Security Council must be actively involved in the search for a solution. I see no other alternative.

I do not think that a solution is possible outside the framework of the United Nations. A solution is possible and desirable only within the framework of the United Nations. If the four permanent members agree on the basic issues of the Middle East problem, that will facilitate the task of the Security Council in adopting worthwhile, concrete, and realistic resolutions. By that time, in my view, the United Nations should station a peace-keeping force which could not be withdrawn immediately—unlike the case of 1967. On that point, I wish to call your attention to the presence of the United Nations Force in Cyprus. You will recall that the United Nations Force in Cyprus was stationed there as a result of a Security Council resolution. For the sake of argument, let us suppose that the government of Cyprus were to ask me today to withdraw the United Nations Force from Cyprus, I would have to reply to the government of Cyprus by saying: I am sorry; that is beyond my competence. It is for the Security Council to meet and to debate and to discuss and decide. That is a different basis altogether from the basis of the stationing of a United Nations Emergency Force in the Middle East. I want to make very clear the difference between Security Council action and General Assembly action, particularly in the context of a United Nations Emergency Force.

QUESTION: Do you intend to ask for a renewal of your mandate?

THE SECRETARY-GENERAL: I am sure that all of you are aware of my feelings in 1966, when my first mandate was about to expire. I felt at that time, and I still feel today, that nobody should aspire to serve as Secretary-General of the United Nations for more than one term. I think that one term is more than enough. I have the same feeling today, of course.

However, I do not think that this is the time or the occasion to make a categorical declaration of my intentions. Personally speaking, from a purely selfish point of view, I would be happier if I could leave my post even before the expiry of my present term.

QUESTION: To get away from the acute political problems that have been under discussion—I wonder if you could give us some outline of the proposed authority to deal with pollution problems. Do you believe that such an international authority should be endowed with powers like those of the Security Council, or perhaps even more effective ones?

THE SECRETARY-GENERAL: I have stated my views on this question from time to time. I think that my most comprehensive statement on this subject was made at Austin, Texas, some two months ago.

As you are aware, the question is before the General Assembly. The General Assembly has decided to convene and international conference on the human environment, in Stockholm in 1972. The matter is under consideration. My personal views have been expressed, particularly in the Texas speech to which I have referred.

There should be an international organization. A very important and crucial question faces the human community. I have no idea about the functioning of that international organization—whether it should be on the lines of the Security Council or on the lines of some of the specialized agencies. It is, of course, for the Member states to debate and decide.

In this connection, I am looking for a secretary-general of the conference. I have been authorized by the General Assembly to appoint such a secretary-general, and I hope to be able to do that very soon, so that he can begin organizing the conference.

QUESTION: I am told that there is a certain malaise among the diplomats accredited to the European Office, including leaders of groups, about the nonexistence of contacts with you, Sir, when you are in Geneva. The diplomats say that they feel discriminated against, in comparison with their colleagues in New York, who usually have opportunities to talk with you. Here there is hardly any possibility of meeting you for informal chats.

THE SECRETARY-GENERAL: Whenever I have come to Geneva, I make it a point to meet the diplomats here. Only the other day I met most of the diplomats in Mr. Vittorio Winspeare Guicciardi's home. I have never before heard of such a complaint as you mention. This is the first time I have heard of it.

QUESTION: I have two questions. First, did Mr. Jarring have a hand in drawing up the new Soviet proposal? Second, do you think that the proposal forms the basis for a lasting peace in the Middle East?

THE SECRETARY-GENERAL: Mr. Jarring had absolutely no hand in drafting the latest Soviet proposal.

With regard to your second question, what I have been saying at this press conference is that, so far as the establishment of a just and lasting peace in the Middle East is concerned, the latest Soviet proposal has concrete and realistic elements.

---

5. Statement to the Press

NEW YORK   NOVEMBER 23, 1970

MY POSITION AGAINST bombing raids on North Vietnam has been often stated and is well known. It remains the same. Naturally, therefore, I find the recent resumption of bombing in the North to be a disturbing development. I trust that the announced official intention in Washington not to continue such operations will prove to be the case in the interest of the pursuit of peace in Indo-China.

SOURCE: *UN Monthly Chronicle,* Vol. VII, December 1970, p. 80.

Speech to the Royal Commonwealth Society
on the Role of the Secretary-General

LONDON   JUNE 15, 1970

U THANT was firmly convinced that quiet diplomacy was often the most productive approach to the settlement of disputes and that the United Nations Secretary-General could—and should—play a major role in such diplomacy. Although he had expressed his views on this subject even before he took office and frequently since then, he felt that both the possibilities and the limitations of the Secretary-General's role were little understood either by the public or by Member states. It was his belief that in part at least this lack of understanding was responsible for a substantial amount of the criticism that had been directed at him and his predecessors. Before accepting a second term, he sought to clarify the role of the Secretary-General by spelling out his understanding that he would have the right to bring to the attention of the Security Council and other United Nations organs basic issues confronting the Organization and disturbing developments in any part of the world. The Council accepted this interpretation of the Secretary-General's role, which in effect was an extension of Article 99 of the Charter. Article 99 simply states that the Secretary-General may bring to the attention of the Security Council "any matter which in his opinion may threaten the maintenance of international peace and security." Thant felt that this Article should be invoked sparingly, but that the Secretary-General should have the unquestioned right to address the Council and the General Assembly without the formality implicit in Article 99, which had been invoked only once in United Nations history—by Hammarskjöld in 1960 on the Congo question.

At a luncheon of the United Nations Correspondents Association on June 11, Thant defended his reluctance to invoke Article 99 in such cases as the Vietnam war. The Secretary-General had the same power as any Member state to request a meeting of the Security Council, he said, but he must consider whether such action would produce positive results. In the face of opposition by some members of the Council, including permanent members, why should the Secretary-General rush in and face disaster, he asked. In an address before the Royal Commonwealth Society in London on June 15, he discussed another phase of the Secretary-General's political potential: the use of his good offices to settle disputes. Although much of this type of quiet diplomacy is conducted in complete secrecy, with only the Secretary-General and the parties aware of it, there are many instances in which the Secretary-General's role has been widely publicized. In some cases, for example, he has been asked publicly by the parties to intervene and in other instances he has been requested by the Security Council to use his good offices. Sometimes he has traveled to the countries involved, accompanied by extensive fanfare. Thant enumerated some of his efforts in his London speech.

IT IS TEMPTING to choose large and sweeping subjects for public speeches. By soaring from peak to peak on a strong up-draft of rhetoric and generalization one may hope to avoid the thickets of detail and the pitfalls of controversy which infest the valleys below, and one may even end up with a sense of exhilaration and euphoria on the final summit of one's peroration, gazing hopefully into the distant future. Today, however, I shall take the valley road and talk about a relatively unknown and specific aspect of the work of the United Nations and of its Secretary-General. This is the sphere of activity known in diplomacy as the exercise of good offices, and it is, I believe, potentially one of the most useful, and least understood, possibilities of the United Nations. It is one way of preventing differences between states from developing into major crises, and of getting results on sensitive problems before they reach the insoluble stage. This is peace-making rather than peace-keeping, and its object is prevention rather than cure. In speaking of the good offices of the Secretary-General, I am, of course, referring only to the action and potential of the office itself, without regard for the individual who may occupy it at any particular time.

It is especially appropriate and timely to speak of this subject here in the United Kingdom because Her Majesty's government, together with the government of Iran, has recently provided an almost classic example of how to use the United Nations and the good offices of the Secretary-General. The two governments had a long-standing difference over the status of the island of Bahrain in the Persian Gulf. This dispute was a serious obstacle to the future tranquillity and stability of the whole Gulf area, and a failure to solve it peacefully could have had a very serious effect on a much wider spectrum of international relationships as well. Iran and the United Kingdom first approached the Secretary-General informally, and ultimately asked him to exercise his good offices in the

SOURCE: *UN Monthly Chronicle,* Vol. VII, July 1970, pp. 122–131.

case and, specifically, to send a personal representative to ascertain the wishes of the people of Bahrain. Both governments took the unusual step of agreeing in advance to accept the findings of the Secretary-General's personal representative after they had been considered and endorsed by the United Nations Security Council. This process was happily concluded on May 11, when the Council endorsed the findings of my personal representative, Mr. Vittorio Winspeare Guicciardi. His conclusion was that "the overwhelming majority of the people of Bahrain wish to gain recognition of their identity in a fully independent and sovereign state free to decide for itself its relations with other states." This is, incidentally, the first time that a good-offices mission has ended in a formal action by the Security Council, which unanimously endorsed Mr. Winspeare's report. The fifteen members of the Security Council, as you know, represent the main regions and national groupings of the world, and its unanimity on any subject is in itself a significant and important achievement. The Council's meeting on Bahrain was also unusual in another way, for the spirit of the occasion inspired the permanent representative of the United Kingdom, Lord Caradon, whose talents and versatility never cease to give us pleasure, to address the Council in verse.

The Bahrain problem was a difficult and delicate one for all the parties concerned, and it is immensely to their credit that they were prepared to settle it in this civilized way in accordance with the precepts of the United Nations Charter. In so doing, they have set an example of enlightened international behavior which is a ray of hope in a world where governments and peoples still seem all too inclined to try to settle their problems by intimidation, threat, and even by force. This latter method tends to be both indecisive and increasingly destructive, and it has produced in various parts of the world a series of situations which poison the present relations of states, jeopardize the future of millions of people, and sometimes result in war.

It is worth noting, in passing, that a successful experiment in civilized international behavior, such as has just been completed over Bahrain, attracts infinitely less attention and interest than the continuing violence and human misery caused by the persistence of other, cruder forms of international conduct. This is, perhaps, as it should be. I hope that my friends in the news media, despite their vested interest in hot news, will not misunderstand me if I say that the perfect good-offices operation is one which is not heard of until it is successfully concluded, or even never heard of at all. One should not, however, underestimate the degree of effort involved in the successful settlement of a difference by peaceful means. The ultimate success of the Bahrain good–offices mission, for example, was the result of nearly a year of intensive and very delicate confidential negotiations and consultations among the parties and the Secretary-General and his staff. Its success, which was by no means a foregone conclusion, can be attributed largely to the good will, restraint and common sense of the parties themselves, and to the discretion, mutual confidence, and respect with which they were prepared, in spite of great political difficulties, to deal with each other. It also required of them political courage and vision, as well as confidence in the integrity of the United Nations. While attracting less attention, the good-offices approach to peace-making is also infinitely cheaper than less civilized approaches to international problems, and, since it has become customary in United Nations good-offices missions for the parties themselves to bear the relatively small costs, the United Nations as such has no financial commitment.

The case of Bahrain is by no means an isolated example of the use of the good offices of the Secretary-General. In fact, the exercise of good offices in one form or another constitutes a very considerable part of the workload of the Secretary-General and his staff. Scarcely a day passes without appeals to the Secretary-General for help in some problem from some corner of the world. These appeals range from approaches from governments for assistance in adjusting difficulties with other governments, through requests from groups of people, usually minorities, for aid in their struggle for just treatment, to calls for help from individuals in a seemingly infinite variety of dilemmas. Some of these latter requests are very strange indeed. There is a surprising number of people in the world who believe themselves to be bewitched or persecuted by supernatural forces and who ask the Secretary-General to break the spell. Others have more sweeping requests. Some years ago, for example, I was interested to receive an urgent request for the abolition of sex as the means of reproducing the species, on the grounds that it was antiquated, inefficient, unhealthy, and discriminatory.

Communications from non-governmental sources often attribute to the Secretary-General a sovereign authority, an influence, or even an omnipotence, which is very far removed from the reality of the powers granted to him in the Charter. In fact, the Secretary-General's resources in these situations are essentially limited to the desire of those concerned to reach a reasonable solution, to persuasion, tact, and discretion, and to the moral authority of his office. His prerogatives include no trace of sovereign power or authority or of the right to interfere in the domestic affairs of states. Thus it is often impossible for him to respond to a request for help, even when, on the face of it, it would seem to merit attention. Nothing is more irresponsible or unhelpful than to raise hopes which cannot possibly be fulfilled.

There are some situations so serious that the Secretary-General himself may decide that his duty requires him to offer his good offices, even if no specific request for them has been made by the parties. The enormous and imminent dangers of the Cuban missiles crisis in 1962 impelled me to offer my good offices, and, in the event, they seem to have served some useful purpose in establishing the contacts through which the United States, the Soviet Union, and Cuba finally reached a solution of the crisis. Although the United Nations as such is not actively involved in the Vietnam situation for obvious reasons, I have also felt obliged to offer my good office in my personal capacity, and to make suggestions concerning the Vietnam situation for a number of years now, unfortunately with little result so far.

Under the heading of good offices, I do not include, of course, the wide variety of tasks which the Secretary-General undertakes at the formal request of the General Assembly, the Security Council, and of the other main organs of the United Nations. Today I am speaking only of situations in which the Secretary-General has no formal mandate from one of the main organs.

Some general rules apply to any exercise of good office. Obviously efforts of this kind must be fully in accordance with the general principles of the United Nations Charter. Then the Secretary-General must reach a considered judgment as to whether his intervention is likely to be helpful, or whether, on the contrary, it will be ineffective, or even positively harmful. On this basis he must himself decide whether or not to accede to a request or take an initiative to exercise his good offices in a particular situation. There have been, for example, occasions in the past when a government has asked the Secretary-General to present warnings, or even threats, to another government or to hold it up for judgment before the bar of world opinion. Such requests must invariably be refused by the Secretary-General as being wholly incompatible with the exercise of his good offices. In 1966 and again in 1967 I felt unable to meet the requests from the government of South Vietnam to provide for

United Nations observation of the elections which were to be held in that country. My reasons for this decision were both practical and constitutional. From a practical point of view and from previous United Nations experience of supervising elections, I saw no possibility, in the circumstances and in the time available, of setting up the necessary and complex machinery required for serious observation of the electoral process. From the constitutional point of view, moreover, since the question of Vietnam is formally on the agenda of the Security Council, I felt that I could not send United Nations observers to observe the elections without the authorization of that body.

Once the Secretary-General has decided to act, some other general rules apply. The kind of problem to be dealt with almost invariably involves the prestige of the governments or other parties concerned, and, in the case of governments, their own political situation at home is not infrequently a primary obstacle to finding a solution. It follows that confidence, mutual respect, and absolute discretion are vital to success, and the less publicity there is the better. Thus it not infrequently happens that while working quietly on a problem, the Secretary-General is publicly accused of ignoring it or of being indifferent to it.

Any hint that an action of the Secretary-General may serve to score political points for one party or another will almost automatically render his efforts useless, and public pressures on him from any quarter are likely to have the same result. The main aim of his effort, after all, must be to keep options open and to afford for the parties concerned a dignified, reasonable, and politically defensible way out of their difficulties. Any effort to seek credit publicly for this or that development is also against the spirit of the good-offices exercise and is liable to be harmful. In any case, a successful outcome is a victory for all concerned and for common sense, so the question of establishing public credit is irrelevant. The purpose of the United Nations and of the Secretary-General in these matters is to harmonize, where possible, the acts and policies of nations in the interest of peace and to provide them with ways of solving their difficulties. This is not a field of activity for those in search of personal triumphs.

There is another good reason for the Secretary-General to exercise extreme discretion and to shun publicity in the exercise of his good offices. The office of the Secretary-General is a relatively new institution, and it is not surprising that governments view it with a certain amount of caution and, on occasion, uneasiness. The key sentence of the

Secretary-General's oath of office, after all, enjoins him not to seek or accept instructions in regard to the performance of his duties from any government or other authority external to the Organization. Some governments have stated on various occasions in the past, including the recent good-offices mission in Bahrain, their contention that any activity by the United Nations in the interest of peace and security should originate in a decision of the Security Council. I fully appreciate the reasons for this point of view even if I cannot agree with it. While the Charter, in Article 98, provides for the Secretary-General to act in pursuance of requests from the main organs of the United Nations, Article 99 gives him a unique right and responsibility, namely, to "bring to the attention of the Security Council any matter which in his opinion may threaten the maintenance of international peace and security." Article 99 has been specifically invoked only once by a Secretary-General—by Dag Hammarskjöld in the Congo crisis of 1960. There are good reasons why Article 99 has been invoked only once, for nothing could be more divisive or useless than for the Secretary-General to invoke Article 99 in a situation where there is no real possibility of the Security Council agreeing on any useful positive action. On various occasions in the past, and no doubt with excellent intentions, one government or another has strongly urged the Secretary-General to use Article 99 in a situation where it has seemed to him that such a course, with all its attendant publicity, would be totally unproductive or even actively harmful. On the other hand, a quiet approach often holds some hope of success. Among the courses of action open to the Secretary-General, the exercise of good offices is at the other end of the spectrum from the use of Article 99, although it is related to the same overall concern for matters affecting peace and security.

Article 33 of the Charter states that the parties to a dispute, the continuance of which is likely to endanger the maintenance of international peace and security, have a duty first of all to seek a solution by negotiation, inquiry, or mediation. This is exactly what the governments of Iran and the United Kingdom did over the Bahrain question. Obviously, if governments request the Secretary-General's help in this process, it is difficult for him to turn them down, and there is no good reason why he should do so. In fact, there is every reason why he should not turn them down, even if practical considerations require that he does not initially inform the members of the Security Council or take the matter publicly to the Council, as some members would wish him to do.

Indeed, one of the main purposes of the quiet approach is to forestall the necessity for public confrontation of the parties in the Security Council or elsewhere, where they will be obliged to adopt hard and intransigent positions. If two governments come to the Secretary-General and ask for his help in settling a dispute, it is often because publicity would inflame feelings at home and in the other countries involved in the issue and cause the governments concerned to take harder positions, which would make a peaceful settlement impossible. If the governments concerned tell the Secretary-General that premature publicity about his good offices will almost certainly destroy their chance of success, what is he to reply? Should he answer that he can be of no help, because one interpretation of the Charter holds that he has no right to act without a mandate from the Security Council, with all the publicity which that entails? Or should he give his help to the governments who have asked for it, with the intention of informing the Security Council as soon as it is prudent to do so? From my point of view as Secretary-General, I cannot have any doubt as to which is the correct alternative.

I do not think that anyone has ever attempted to record publicly and comprehensively all the various instances in which the good offices of the Secretary-General have played a role. In fact, some of these episodes have never been publicly mentioned at all, but they make an interesting and not unimpressive record of conflicts forestalled by common sense and reason. As I mentioned earlier, such efforts, especially when they are successful, are not the stuff of which great news stories are made. They do, however, serve to contradict to some extent the popular suspicion that sovereign governments seldom act with reason and responsibility in their relations with each other. This record also shows the potential value of the United Nations as a meeting place and as an objective and discreet third party in delicate situations.

One of the first important good-offices exercises by a Secretary-General was that conducted in 1955 by my predecessor, Dag Hammarskjöld, to obtain the release of fifteen United States airmen of the United Nations Unified Command in Korea held prisoner by the People's Republic of China. Although he was given this responsibility by the General Assembly, Hammarskjöld made it clear throughout that he was acting in his capacity as Secretary-General, and he himself was left free to choose the method of carrying out his task. His dramatic visit to Peking on this issue was entirely on his own initiative and responsibility, and, if I may so, decidedly at his own risk. Hammarskjöld undertook many other good-offices missions. Some were successful, and others less so. He also delegated good-offices missions to carefully chosen representatives, as for example, the effort, at the request of the United Kingdom and Saudi Arabia, to help solve their dispute over the Bureimi Oasis, and the mission undertaken at the request of Thailand and Cambodia to help resolve their border differences. In 1963, again at the request of the governments of Cambodia and Thailand, I designated a special representative who remained in the area for two years, and a further mission of this kind was undertaken from 1966 to 1968. In 1958, at the request of the British government, Hammarskjöld, using United Nations Military Observers, made arrangements with the Arab governments concerned for the overflight of the British transport aircraft which were carrying the British forces home from Jordan. It was in a final good-offices mission that Hammarskjöld lost his life, flying to meet Tshombé with the purpose of bringing him to Leopoldville for reconciliation talks with Cyrille Adoula, the then prime minister of the Congo.

I myself, during my time as Secretary-General, have undertaken a variety of good-offices efforts, also with varying degrees of success. I mentioned earlier two of these efforts, the provision of good offices in the Cuban missiles crisis, and the later effort, in which I shall persist, to do anything within my power to aid the parties to the struggle in Southeast Asia to cease the fighting and to find a solution to their differences by peaceful means. It may be of interest to recall some others.

In August 1963, I was requested by the governments of Malaya, Indonesia, and the Philippines to ascertain, prior to the establishment of the Federation of Malaysia, the wishes of the people of Sabah (North Borneo) and Sarawak and to ensure that recent elections in those areas had been truly representative of the inhabitants' wishes and had been properly conducted. This very delicate mission was not wholly successful and two of the governments concerned did not formally accept its findings, but it helped, I think, to pave the way for the inclusion of the two territories in the Federation of Malaysia.

In January 1964, when the relations between Rwanda and Burundi had seriously deteriorated, the two governments asked for my help, and I sent a special representative to visit both of them. As a result of his visits and recommendations, the very strained relations between the two governments were improved and a series of practical measures were taken to alleviate the problems which had created tension and discord.

In September 1965, when the war broke out between India and Pakistan and the situation had failed to respond to the Security Council's first call for a cease-fire, the Council called on me, on September 6, to exert every possible effort to give effect to its resolutions calling for a cessation of hostilities and a withdrawal of all forces to the positions held before August 5, 1965. I decided that the only hope of doing anything useful was to talk to the parties on the spot and I left New York for Rawalpindi and New Delhi on September 7. I stayed in the area for a week trying to persuade both sides to agree to a cease-fire, and during my stay both affirmed their desire for peace and for a cessation of hostilities. Before leaving the Indian subcontinent I also proposed a meeting between the two heads of government. The cease-fire demanded by the Security Council finally came into effect on September 22, and the withdrawal of forces took place some months later after the meeting between the heads of the two governments at Tashkent under the auspices of Premier Aleksei Kosygin of the USSR.

The situation in the Middle East has given rise to a number of requests for good offices of one sort or another. Over more than twenty years it has been an almost routine function of the United Nations, often in cooperation with the Red Cross, to do what it can to arrange for the repatriation both of civilians and of military personnel detained by one side or the other. A continuing source of concern, especially since 1967, has been the situation of the small Jewish minorities in some Arab states. After the 1967 war I approached the government of the United Arab Republic concerning the Jewish community in the UAR, of whom some were imprisoned and others were unable to get exit permits. Eventually some 1,400 of them were released and, with the help of the government of Spain, enabled to leave the UAR. My approaches to the government of Iraq on the question of the Jewish minority in that country have been less successful, but my concern continues and I still hope for results. My approach to this situation, like my interventions on behalf of all the accused at the time of the Iraqi trials and public executions last year, can be based only on humanitarian considerations and in the interest of lessening tension in the area, since the Jewish people concerned, being citizens of the countries in which they live, are under the exclusive jurisdiction of the government.

I have been approached by many of the eight governments who have ships stuck in the Suez Canal as a result of the 1967 war, and we have made a number of attempts to get these ships out, so far, unfortunately, without success. Early in 1968, through the efforts of Ambassador Gunnar Jarring, my special representative in the Middle East, and General Odd Bull, the chief of staff of the United Nations Truce Supervision Organization in Palestine, the first stages of a practical effort to extricate the ships were actually undertaken. Unfortunately the effort broke down at the last moment due to the extreme suspicion and hostility which so often prevent constructive developments in that part of the world, and so far we have been unable to revive it.

One of the deplorable and quite recent phenomena of the Middle East crisis has been a variety of attempts to hijack, sabotage, or otherwise interfere with civil aircraft. The United Nations and other agencies and authorities have been working on the general problem of halting this excessively dangerous and irresponsible trend, which is bad enough when it is the work of individuals, but becomes far more ominous when, as in the Middle East, it becomes an instrument of political action or reprisal. I have also exercised my good offices in two specific cases of hijacking, one of an El Al plane to Algiers and one of a TWA plane to Damascus, in which there were difficulties and delays in extricating the crew and passengers and, later on, the aircraft. Securing the release of a hijacked aircraft provides a particularly difficult problem. It is only natural that the governments, families, and companies concerned should wish to get their relatives, crews, and aircraft back as soon as possible and at almost any cost. On the other hand, in securing this end it is, in my view, extremely important that the hijackers should derive no advantage from the criminal act of hijacking by bargaining over, or making deals for, the release of the crew, passengers, and aircraft. If this is allowed to happen, hijacking will be encouraged and will become more widespread. The country which, usually involuntarily and without warning, receives a hijacked aircraft may also find itself trapped in a very delicate position, especially when political feelings run as high as they do in the Middle East. Thus, although it may wish to act in a proper manner, it may find it politically very difficult to do so. Highly publicized international pressures, such as threatened boycotts, can only increase these political difficulties for the recipient government. The primary objective of anyone who really wishes to extricate the passengers, crew, and aircraft must therefore be to make it as easy as possible for the receiving government to release them, even if, as sometimes happens, he is accused of tardiness, appeasement, or ineffectiveness in the process. When these considerations are borne in mind, a number of governments and agencies can be, and are, of assistance in securing a favorable outcome, and once again it is irrelevant who gets the credit.

The Middle East is by no means the only source of recent demands for good offices. Last year, for example, in March, with the agreement of the governments of Equatorial Guinea and Spain, I sent a representative to Equatorial Guinea to help solve the difficulties which had arisen over the presence of Spanish troops and the status of Spanish citizens in that country. With his help, what had been a threatening and even violent situation was resolved within a month to the satisfaction of both governments, thus forestalling the necessity for more drastic moves.

Very often the presence and assistance of a friendly and objective third party can provide the necessary catalyst to resolve a delicate problem. For example, in 1967 when several leading personalities of Guinea had, due to bad weather, unexpectedly landed in the Ivory Coast and had been detained, causing severe tension between the two governments, I sent one of my under-secretaries to the area to facilitate their release and the release of a number of nationals and residents of the Ivory Coast then detained in Guinea. Sometimes no actual physical presence is required on the spot. I was glad, for example, to be able, in response to an approach from the Soviet Government in early 1969, to assist in effecting the release of two Soviet trawlers and their crews which had been detained for four months by the government of Ghana, which explained to me the reasons for their detention.

The latest approach to the Secretary-General for the exercise of his good offices came last Thursday, June 11, at the height of the recent internal crisis in Jordan. Because of the outbreak of violence in Amman and particularly acts against United States nationals there, the United States government, through its mission to the United Nations, approached the Secretary-General for assistance from United Nations personnel and facilities in the area, in arranging for the safety and possible evacuation of United States nationals and other non-Jordanians should the need arise. The Secretary-General responded favorably and promptly with all such assistance as could be given, including approaches to irregular groups as well as to governmental authorities.

There are many other kinds of situations, political or humanitarian, where the Secretary-General's good offices may be of use, but I hope that the examples I have mentioned may give some idea of the nature and possibilities of this particular activity of the United Nations. Nowadays our heads are so full of new subjects—the environment, space, the seabed, the application of technology, and others—that we may tend to forget that in international relations we are still largely dependent, for better or for worse, on old methods of diplomacy and the extension of those methods through a multilateral organization like the United Nations. Until we can take new and major steps toward a more peaceful and stable world order, it is essential to make the best use of what we have got, just as Iran and the United Kingdom have done over Bahrain. If governments are prepared to follow this example they may find that in the United Nations they have a more useful instrument than many of them had realized.

The news is so full of stories of conflict and violence that not enough attention is paid to the steady undercurrent of decency and common sense in the affairs of nations, and people increasingly have the impression that in international affairs nothing ever goes right. This impression makes it even more difficult for governments to choose the road of peaceful settlement, which is the road of the United Nations Charter. Most governments face similar basic problems in solving their differences with other governments. Public emotion, domestic politics, lack of confidence, and the fear of losing face often make it exceedingly difficult for them to take the course of peace, common sense, and mutual understanding. If the United Nations, even in small ways, can help governments, as I am convinced it can, to overcome these difficulties, it is obviously the duty of the Organization and of the Secretary-General to respond whenever it seems that they may usefully do so. If by these methods we can begin to build up mutual confidence among governments and a willingness to follow the principles of the Charter in settling differences, we may not only forestall a number of conflicts, but we may also strengthen the basis of international peace and order which we so desperately and urgently need.

THE TWENTY-FIFTH ANNIVERSARY
OF THE UNITED NATIONS

THE YEAR 1970 was a time for stocktaking. The United Nations had survived for twenty-five years despite the hydrogen bomb, despite the ideological conflict between the superpowers, despite the Korean war, despite the Vietnam war, and despite three Middle East wars. Its image was somewhat tarnished by its failure to live up to the expectations of the generation which had seen the League of Nations collapse and had witnessed the death and destruction of the Second World War. No one could dispute the fact that public disillusionment with the United Nations was a threat to its effectiveness. Perhaps too much had been expected of the Organization, but its shortcomings had become apparent, particularly in the field of peace-keeping, as the big powers ignored or by-passed it. At the age of twenty-five, the United Nations was in the throes of a financial crisis. It was standing on the sidelines of the Vietnam war. It was meeting frustration after frustration in its attempts to bring peace to the Middle East. It had scarcely made a dent in the problem of world disarmament. It had been unable to enforce its mandates to end racial discrimination in southern Africa. Yet there was one predominant factor on the side of the Organization; not a single one of its Members wanted to see it fail and not a single one had written it off to the extent of trying to go it alone without the United Nations. As Secretary-General, U Thant often expressed his disappointment with the performance of the United Nations but he had never faltered in his conviction that its structure was basically sound and that it offered the best hope for a world based on international law and order.

Like many others, Thant seized the occasion of the twenty-fifth anniversary to evaluate the performance of the United Nations, to analyze its strengths and weaknesses, and to offer suggestions for its improvement. In a speech at a dinner in San Francisco on June 26 commemorating the twenty-fifth anniversary of the signing of the United Nations Charter, the Secretary-General acknowledged that the United Nations was facing a crisis of confidence. Much of the trouble, he said, was caused by the refusal of governments to place collective responsibility above national self-interest. "Governments," he said, "especially those of the great nations, have drifted year after year farther and farther away from the basic requirements of the Charter." He concluded with a warning that no nation will ever again be able to live in "splendid isolation" and that governments must cease "to pursue their present outmoded and fratricidal course." He returned to this theme again in a speech before the World Association of World Federalists in Ottawa on August 23. "If there is a crisis today in connection with the United Nations," he said, "it is a crisis of commitment by nation states to the Organization and its purposes. Too many nations still regard the United Nations as peripheral rather than central to their foreign policies. They tend to evaluate it according to its possible use in advancing their own goals rather than the central instrument for forging solutions to world problems in concert with the rest of the world community. The ultimate crisis before the United Nations, therefore, is a crisis of authority."

In a television interview broadcast by the Inter-Nation Television Trust of London on November 5, Thant said the United Nations had not fulfilled the aspirations of the founding fathers in the political field, but he added that if one looked at the Organization in its entirety—including the economic and social fields and the specialized agencies—he must conclude that it had achieved remarkable success. Thant did not agree with critics who sought to blame the shortcomings of the United Nations on the Charter. Although he was fully in accord with the Charter amendments enlarging the Security Council and the Economic and Social Council, he never accepted the idea that the Charter needed wholesale revision. He said on numerous occasions that it was flexible enough to permit a gradual and far-reaching evolution within its existing provisions. It is not the Charter that is inadequate, he said, but "our purposes and policies." Thant had dealt with this problem exhaustively in a speech at the University of Denver on April 3, 1964, saying: "The evolution of an institution as complex and as large as the United Nations . . . will not come about by sudden structural changes or new sweeping innovations. The strength and effectiveness of such an organization must grow gradually in response to the need for it, and in the process there will, more often than not, be much to criticize and much that in retrospect could have been done better. In this process the active support of governments, as well as their scrutiny and criticism, is the essential factor . . ." (see volume VI of this series, p. 562).

---

1. Address at Commemorative Meeting

SAN FRANCISCO   JUNE 26, 1970

IT IS THE CUSTOM in many countries to make a wish on the occasion of an anniversary. In Burma too we have the custom of "Su Taung," or bidding good wishes on the day of anniversaries. Throughout the world such customs reflect the deep unity of men's aspirations.

SOURCE: *UN Monthly Chronicle*, Vol. VII, July 1970, pp. 11–12.

On the occasion of the twenty-fifth anniversary of the United Nations, I would like to express the following wishes for humanity:

• I wish that men cease to hate and kill their fellow men for reasons of race, color, religion, nationalism, or ideology;

• I wish that more love, compassion, and understanding guide the management of human affairs;

• I wish that the rich and privileged share their blessings with the poor;

• I wish that nations enrich each other in the art of governing men in peace, justice, and prosperity;

• I wish that all nations unite to face with courage and determination the unprecedented worldwide problems that lie in store for humanity;

• I wish that the immense progress achieved in science and technology be equaled in the spheres of morality, justice, and politics;

• I wish that the world listen more attentively to the concerned voice of youth;

• I wish that the leaders of the great nations of our time surmount their differences and unite their efforts for the benefit of all mankind;

• I pray for rapid restoration of peace in devastated Indo-China, for a just and lasting peace in the Middle East as prescribed by the United Nations, and for the early involvement of the People's Republic of China in the activities of the world Organization.

I address my best wishes—''Su Taung''—to all of you and to all men and women of good will on this earth.

---

2. Statement at Commemorative Dinner

SAN FRANCISCO   JUNE 26, 1970

ALL OF US who work in the United Nations are deeply grateful for the opportunity which the mayor and citizens of San Francisco have so generously given us to celebrate here the twenty-fifth anniversary of the signing of the Charter of the United Nations.

SOURCE: *Ibid.,* pp. 38–45.

To return to San Francisco is not only to come back to a beautiful, gracious, and civilized city; for us in the United Nations, it is also to return to the birthplace of the Organization and to the congenial and forward-looking atmosphere in which the Charter was created. Here we are reminded of the sense of dedication and urgency, tempered with realism and a vivid awareness of the horrors of war, which inspired the authors of the Charter twenty-five years ago. If we have not yet succeeded in realizing their vision of a world at peace, we can still draw inspiration from the ideals and objectives which they set out with full support from the peoples. Our best tribute to them is to increase our efforts to strengthen the United Nations.

This is the third time that the representatives of the United Nations—national ambassadors and international Secretariat—have come back to San Francisco to celebrate the signing of the Charter.

Fifteen years ago, in 1955, this ceremony took place in an atmosphere of cautious optimism at a time when the world seemed to be awakening from the tribulations of the postwar period and the long winter of the cold war.

Five years ago we gathered here again in a less happy mood to speak of a world in which new problems and new conflicts had dimmed the hopes of a just and peaceful world order—hopes encouraged by the great political emancipation of decolonization and the possibility of emancipation from drudgery made possible by science and technology. At that time, the United Nations itself was in the throes of a crisis which had arisen over the fundamental issue of financing peace-keeping operations.

Now we meet again in a mood of uncertainty and anxiety, with only the knowledge that humanity is moving at an increasing speed in uncertain directions, and that time is running short. I hope we can make use of this opportunity, so generously afforded by the City of San Francisco, to turn the tables on the forces of doubt and gloom, in order to survey calmly, but with a sense of urgency, the course we must take in the next twenty-five years.

Like many institutions, the United Nations is today facing a crisis of confidence. It has been the lot of institutions throughout history to have their usefulness questioned from time to time by the people. This process serves a useful purpose in keeping institutions up to the mark.

In our time, this disillusionment has undoubtedly reached a new pitch. The United Nations, as a relatively young institution, faces a crisis of confidence without ever having emerged, as some older institutions have, from relative impotence to a position of accepted power and authority.

If we are to respond to this challenge, nations, especially the great nations, must improve and change the quality and performance of the United Nations and the way it is used. There can be no question of taking the easy but suicidal way out by consigning the United Nations, along with other institutions, to the dusty attic of history. In an age where physical conservation has become an urgent issue, a degree of institutional conservation may also be in order.

Institutions must constantly adapt and develop in response to new challenges. In our time, the inherent obsolescence of institutions has been emphasized by the extraordinary rate of change in the way we live. I scarcely need to remind you that the membership of the United Nations has grown from 51 in 1945 to 126 today; that the world's population has increased from under two and a half billion in 1945 to well over three and a half billion today; that in the next thirty-eight years this population is likely to be doubled again; that more than half the people of the world were not born when the Charter was signed twenty-five years ago; that in this quarter century we have seen the advent of nuclear energy and weapons, intercontinental missiles, space exploration, computer technology and comparable advances in medicine, biology, biochemistry, and other branches of science, accompanied by revolutionary advances in the techniques of communication.

These, and a hundred other developments, have changed our lives and our prospects on a scale and at a speed never experienced before in history. It is small wonder that those of us who grew up in the twenties and thirties may sometimes be regarded as antediluvian by the youth of today, who are tempted to reject many of the habits and ways of doing things which we have always taken for granted. This reaction should not dismay or surprise us. It should, rather, encourage us to adapt our ideas, our behavior, and our institutions to meet the challenges which we ourselves have created, and to lean on the younger generation to help us meet the urgent demands of change.

The widespread disillusionment of the young with institutions is now more important than ever for another, more encouraging, reason. The younger generation of today is, in general, more widely conscious of what goes on and what is wrong in the world than their predecessors. Much to their credit, they are also far more demanding and concerned about it. It is thus increasingly difficult for institutions which do not fulfill their declared objectives to command respect.

An acute observer of the international scene recently wrote that "All institutions provide a temptation for their members to clothe selfishness in the language of idealism." Our twenty-fifth anniversary is a most appropriate occasion to ponder this uncomfortably shrewd comment.

I do not think that responsible people anywhere doubt the need for a world organization or the validity of the basic ideals and objectives of the United Nations, which were set out here in San Francisco twenty-five years ago. On the contrary, the world has never before so urgently required a universal organization which can build and maintain a peaceful and safe terrestrial society, and the United Nations is undoubtedly the best—in fact, the only—existing organization with the potential capacity for that task. What we should be asking ourselves in this twenty-fifth anniversary year is how we can make the United Nations the organization we know we need, and what changes in attitudes and priorities are imperative for this purpose.

This evening I can only briefly summarize the new approaches which seem indispensable to me.

First and foremost, there must be on the part of governments a radical change from present power politics to a policy of collective responsibility toward mankind. Governments, especially those of the great nations, have drifted year after year farther and farther away from this basic requirement of the Charter.

As matters stand, the management of world affairs lies essentially in the hands of nations. A successful management of the world therefore depends on the behavior of nations. The justice, peace, security, prosperity, health, cleanliness, and the beauty of our world must become the prime preoccupation of governments. The world is too small, its people are too intelligent and the mass problems that lie in store for us are too frightening to allow continued blind acceptance of the sacrosanct concept of national interest.

World affairs are no longer foreign affairs of governments. They have become internal affairs as well.

Where has national interest led us? To an arsenal of ugly weapons, which cost humanity $200 billion a year; to the greatest historical deadlock between big powers that the world has ever seen; to north-south, east-west, ideological, racial and economic cleavages; to a belt of divided countries; to a series of smoldering or active conflicts stretching across the globe.

No big power will be able to solve these problems alone. No big power will ever rule the world alone. No nation will ever be able to live again in splendid isolation.

Since the weight and cleavage of interests is greatest among the big powers, I have recently recommended that their heads of state, heads of government or foreign ministers, including the People's Republic of China, meet from time to time at one of the offices of the United Nations in a neutral country to initiate a change from confrontation and division to the building of a safe and peaceful world. I have made this proposal because I feel that it is high time that the People's Republic of China is involved in international affairs. Are not the events in Southeast Asia, the 750 million people of mainland China and its recent emergence as an atomic and satellite power enough evidence that the People's Republic of China is a key element if we are to move toward a solution of many of the present world problems? This is also why I have recommended a reactivation of the Geneva agreements and, more recently, proposed a new Geneva conference on Southeast Asia in which the People's Republic of China would participate.

Second, and still having the People's Republic of China in mind, I recommend that the United Nations be made universal. The absence of the People's Republic of China and of the divided countries has given to the United Nations a great deal of artificiality.

The simple people in the street, those whose sons are dying in far-away countries, cannot understand why the United Nations is not seized of the most burning issue of 1970, the war in Indo-China. Rhetoric and intelligence are not enough to explain the reasons to them. They demand, as concerned citizens of the world, that their national leaders and international officials find the means, through necessary vision and elevation, to solve urgently this fundamental problem. I therefore urge governments to consider the idea of the universality of the United Nations as the priority item of this year's agenda for world affairs.

Third, we must resolve, with new determination and will, the danger-ously deteriorating situation in the Middle East. The world is increas-ingly alarmed at the trend of events in that theater of hostilities. In this case, the conflict is within the responsibilities of the United Nations. Big-power responsibilities in the context of the Charter of the United

Nations have been acknowledged. But here again we have the vivid illustration of a deadlock nourished by claims, counterclaims, arguments, positions, counterpositions, accusations, denials, attacks and counterattacks. Again the simple man in the street wonders why the people in this region cannot live in peace.

During the three years following the 1967 war, there has been no evidence that the issues of the Middle East conflict can be settled by the parties through their own efforts. Therefore, international assistance should be increased and intensified. Here, the United Nations has a definite role to play, and in the past few days there have been indications that the permanent members of the Security Council have made perceptible progress in their common search for a just and lasting peace.

Fourth, I believe that it is high time that we look more inquisitively into the obstacle of ideologies. From the vantage point of the United Nations, the crisis of extreme inward-looking nationalism is further aggravated by the superimposition of ideologies or political systems which claim that they alone have the key to man's future.

There has been nothing more dangerous and more damaging in human history than the claim of exclusiveness. To it we owe the long religious wars, all waged in the name of exclusive possession of the truth. It is only recently that there has been evidence of tolerance and some mutual understanding in the pursuit of common religious objectives.

Should we again lose precious years in a similar divisive exercise? Is it so difficult to recognize that systems and ideologies are perfect only in theory?

We must realize that adaptation and change are imperative to the survival of social systems and institutions. Indeed the world has become so complex, the pace of change so rapid, and the newly emerging problems so numerous, that no rigid system, however well established on a few sacrosanct principles, is able to cope with all problems. I believe that we are about to embark on the most variegated search for political, institutional, legal, and moral solutions to the social problems of our time.

In a world of many billions of people, who are divided into highly industralized societies as well as regions of extreme poverty, each with their own culture and special problems, there can be no universal recipe or system. Nations must therefore enrich each other with what has proved good in the art of governing men.

Private initiative may be the solution in one case, public initiative may be the answer in another. Many countries have demonstrated that the two can coexist and that one can admirably complement or even correct and stimulate the other. Each system has good and bad aspects.

Those who have the difficult task of governing should recognize that such an art must be highly flexible and nondogmatic in a rapidly changing world. The earlier we recognize this, the sooner we will reach an accord and understanding among nations, and such recognition will conform to one of the basic purposes and principles of the Charter: that the United Nations shall be a center for harmonizing the actions of nations.

It is worth recalling that the primary purpose of the United Nations in the minds of the founding fathers twenty-five years ago was " . . . to save succeeding generations from the scourge of war, which twice in our lifetime has brought untold sorrow to mankind . . ."—this is the language of the Charter. The primary purpose of the founding fathers in 1945 was " . . . to save succeeding generations from the scourge of war, which twice in our lifetime"—once in 1914 and again in 1939—"has brought untold sorrow to mankind . . ."

And in order to achieve that objective the founding fathers also prescribed certain recipes. One of them asks all Member states "to practice tolerance and live together in peace with one another as good neighbors"—this also is the language of the Charter—"and to unite our" common "strength to maintain international peace and security. . . ." That also is the language employed by the founding fathers.

In order to achieve all these objectives the founding fathers enjoined all Member states to see to it that the United Nations serve as a center to harmonize the actions of Member states with a view to the achievement of these common objectives. This harmonizing function of the United Nations, in my view, is one of the most important and basic principles of the Charter. That is why my observations tonight, in my view, are in strict conformity with one of the basic purposes of the Charter.

Fifth, we must look anew at the categories of vast unsolved worldwide problems such as economic and social development, justice and human rights, with which the United Nations, through its system of specialized agencies and the United Nations aid programs, have come to grips during the last twenty-five years. Much more needs to be done. Economic aid must become a matter of international justice and progress and not remain an appendix of divisive power politics and influence. Individual rights must be upheld and protected and not remain the dead letter of lofty declarations. The present anarchy and absence of the rule of law at the international level is a constant invitation to dissension and conflicts. Progress must be made toward the adherence to international law.

Sixth and last, we must diagnose, monitor, and face together the new collective challenges and dangers which arise from a rapidly mushrooming scientific and technological civilization accompanied by unprecedented mass phenomena. If not, while governments are actively bent on spending the best of their intelligence, people, resources and energies trying in vain to advance their respective zones of influence, the world will rapidly deteriorate behind their backs and above their heads.

There is, I am glad to say, a new movement in the United Nations to face these problems through the initiative of various governments, from the largest to the smallest. The Organization has become concerned with such problems as population, outer space, the peaceful uses of the seabed, and, more recently, the most complex question of all, the preservation of our environment.

This is a step in the right direction, but only a step, and it would be naïve, if not dishonest, to pretend that efforts to grapple with these problems of the future are not still seriously impeded by political difficulties and attitudes, which are largely a remnant from the past. For this reason, the advancement from inward-looking nationalism to active international commitment must still have priority among our aims, for our hopes of success depend upon it even in fields which are not primarily political.

When I say "international commitment" I think it is very necessary in these times to bear in mind a basic factor to bring about the successful implementation of this objective. From time to time we used to say that our first allegiance must be to our own states. It is understandable; it is natural; and in many ways it is desirable. Every American must have his first allegiance to the United States of America; every Burmese must have his first allegiance to Burma; every Russian must have his first allegiance to the Soviet Union; every Frenchman must have his allegiance first of all to France. This primary allegiance is understandable, as I have said, natural, and even desirable. But in order to achieve the objectives of the Charter of securing international peace and security, of securing economic and social development, that one single allegiance is not enough.

In my view, if we are to see that the United Nations develops into a really effective instrument for the performance of all the functions outlined in the Charter, the peoples of the United Nations need to develop a second allegiance: that is, the allegiance to the international community as represented by the United Nations. Only when the peoples of the United Nations can develop this double allegiance—allegiance to one's own state and allegiance at the same time to the international community—will the United Nations grow into a really effective instrument for peace, for justice, for progress, and for human rights.

This is my plea, which I have been making from time to time in the last several months; and I am sure these sentiments are shared by all of you who are citizens of the city which gave birth to the United Nations.

Progress in solving the problems of the environment may well show how far this new concern for problems of the future can lead us. A few weeks ago, I suggested that urgent consideration be given to creating a global authority to study and act on environmental problems in the interest of all earth-dwellers, and that, if it were to be of real value, this authority should have powers to police and enforce its decisions. I hope that this suggestion will not be taken simply as a well-meaning idealistic exercise, for I believe that our capacity to preserve and enhance life on our planet may well depend on our ability to set up a new kind of international institution with new authority.

Of course, the possible form and methods of operation of such an institution are very complex and will take time and effort to work out, but that is all the more reason for making an early start, and the hour is already late. I also believe that if this step could successfully be taken, it might help us to find solutions to some of our problems and a way out of some of the emotional, ideological, and political blind alleys in which we, in the United Nations, now spend so much of our time and energy.

Ladies and gentlemen, no one can accuse me of having been impatient during my eight and a half years of service with the United Nations. Some have even accused me of being too patient. I have made every effort in the privacy of my functions to be of help and to bring people and their points of view closer together in conformity with the provisions of the Charter. I will continue this task in the same manner until the end of my mandate.

But, on this solemn occasion, when the eyes of the world are focused on us, I must most emphatically warn nations not to pursue their present outmoded and fratricidal course. Time is running short. People are getting impatient. We need a fresh start: we need a fresh look. Governments must be able, once again, to lift themselves to the same high level of determination and vision as that of the authors of the Charter.

Sages tell us that if there is a will, there is a way. We have the way, but there seems to be diminishing will and increasing discouragement.

The Charter drafted here twenty-five years ago is still our best chance. May nations therefore, especially the powerful ones, give it at last a real chance.

---

3. Statement in the Economic and Social Council

GENEVA   JULY 6, 1970

TWENTY-FIVE YEARS have passed since the birth of the United Nations. For institutions as well as for men, anniversaries are occasions for reflecting upon the past and for setting sights on the future.

It is mostly for its political performance that the United Nations is judged by the man in the street. We often deplore that the public is not sufficiently aware of the extensive work of the United Nations in the economic and social field which, we believe, is inadequately reported by the information media. But let us not deceive ourselves; the people and the mass media have a good instinct for the problems which face our planet. They see conflicts, hatred, dissension, and weapons. And they consider that these are the problems which the United Nations should solve above all others.

Emerging from the holocaust of the Second World War, the drafters of the Charter of the United Nations had the same instinct when they established peace as the paramount objective of the Organization. With

SOURCE: UN Press Release SG/SM/1296 and Corr. 1. The summary record is given in Economic and Social Council Official Records, Forty-ninth Session, 1696th meeting.

the exception of the great emancipation of the colonial peoples and their achievement of independence, which has been one of the most glorious pages in the history of the United Nations, the political record of the Organization has been an uneasy mixture of success and failure. On the credit side, the United Nations can take pride for having been an open channel of access and communication among governments, including those of the two superpowers; for having provided an instrument for preventing local crises from turning into broader, possibly worldwide conflicts; and for having placed the use of force, territorial ambitions, and national misdeeds under the sharp eyes and moral judgment of the world community.

On the debit side, despite such limited successes as the Nuclear Test-Ban Treaty and the Non-Proliferation Treaty, I would list our failure to curb the armaments schizophrenia, which has led to the emergence of such concepts as "overkill capacity" and to a yearly waste of $200 billion—a trend which is now spreading dangerously to the smaller nations; our inability to turn the dissensions and power neuroses of nations into common and constructive endeavors for mankind; our failure to pacify two theaters of conflict—the Middle East and Southeast Asia; and our lack of success in making the Organization universal, leaving outside the realm of worldwide cooperation the People's Republic of China—with its population of 750 million—as well as the several divided countries.

I wanted briefly to recall these few basic political facts before turning to the role of the Economic and Social Council, for I feel that the success of much of what you are trying to do will depend upon a change in the political climate and in the relations between nations.

Looking at the economic and social record of the Organization, there emerges a much brighter picture.

First, hand in hand with the process of decolonization and in conformity with the ideals of the Charter, the concepts of economic and social justice and of human dignity have made enormous progress throughout the world owing to the existence of the United Nations. Two-thirds of the globe were virtually closed to these ideas prior to the Second World War. Today, they have begun to pervade even the most remote villages of the world. The United Nations and its agencies have served, in a way, as a parliament of mankind, where poor nations, like poor people in national assemblies, can raise their voices, proclaim their aspirations, denounce injustice, and demand a remedy. The United Nations has acted as a vent to an explosive force. It has promoted concern for one of the greatest tensions of our time: the existence side by side on the same planet of extreme poverty and affluence. It has compelled the attention of the rich countries and encouraged them to act. It has brought closer together, around a common cause, two deeply divided economic and political systems which emerged from the industrial revolution. It has enhanced the concept of international solidarity and has diverted some of the energies of conquest, power, and influence to a generous world-wide human cause. It has thus been a center for harmonizing the actions of nations, as prescribed by the Charter.

Second, in the pursuit of this objective, the United Nations and the specialized agencies have prepared what can probably be considered as the most complete and most elaborate file of analyses and proposals for action in the history of mankind. Under the guidance of the Economic and Social Council and its functional and regional economic commissions, as well as that of the General Assembly and of the governing bodies of the specialized agencies, an enormous program of data collection, analyses, and recommendations for action has been carried out. In 1945, we knew little if anything about the developing countries. Today we know a great deal about their problems and their needs. A magnificient page of the story of human concern and knowledge has thus been written together by the states Members of the United Nations. This process has not always been easy. It was fraught with frustration, hesitation, and delaying actions. Thus it was only toward the end of these twenty-five years that the United Nations won the battle of recognition of industrialization and trade as two of the main factors of economic progress and greater worldwide justice and equality.

Third, we have witnessed the birth of the first rudiments of true international action. The authors of the Charter can look proudly today at United Nations technical cooperation, at our pre-investment efforts, at the World Food Programme, and at the mobilization of the entire United Nations system of agencies for the development effort. It is a source of great pride and hope for mankind, when one visits the developing countries today, to see that part of their struggle for economic and social betterment is waged under the common flag of the United Nations. Resources, men, ideas, experience, and endeavors from all over the globe are molded together in these magnificent first examples of human solidarity. Embodied in the presence of the United Nations, this solidarity is part of the daily life of the developing countries. Emergence of nationhood and independence has taken place within the broader framework of an interdependent and concerned world. The United Nations has a moral meaning for the children of these countries who are at that age when the mind is receptive to the indelible imprints of love of fellow human beings. Seeds of future understanding and solidarity among men are thus being implanted in the impoverished and more populous two-thirds of the world.

Fourth, a considerable new step forward was made recently with the progressive acceptance of the concept of an international development strategy. In the Economic and Social Council and its Committee for Development Planning, the idea of concerted worldwide action was making progress and had found a first timid expression in the First United Nations Development Decade. But it was the magistral effort of the United Nations Conference on Trade and Development (UNCTAD) that thrust open the door to a development strategy. It revealed for the first time the canvas of a well-structured plan encompassing national and international action, internal and external mobilization of resources, agriculture and industry, trade and finance, and adumbrating for the first time the prospect of an international division of labor conducive to overcoming inequality among men throughout the world. In the Second Development Decade, this vision will be embodied in a timetable of action and commitment. Let us not deceive ourselves and underestimate the difficulties which our colleagues from the developed countries will encounter in their national administrations and parliaments to obtain acceptance of such bold and novel ideas. Their degree of acceptability varies greatly with the progress made toward the concept of solidarity with the poorer regions of the world. This is why the question of the mobilization of public opinion has received such prominence in your deliberations.

Fifth and last, nations during this period have become increasingly aware of the fact that international cooperation is no longer a matter solely of politics. The straitjacket of narrow, inward-looking nationalism is bound to crack under the heavy pressure of a planet which is clamoring for global ways and means. Thus, international cooperation has made its greatest strides during this period not in the field of politics— still nourished by outmoded concepts and dreams—but in those fields in which the world cannot function without such cooperation. We have seen, therefore, the emergence of a remarkable system of international agencies which now cover practically every main sector of human activity. Today fourteen agencies and organizations are active in the additional fields of agriculture, health, education, science and culture, atomic energy, aviation, navigation, meteorology, development, international monetary issues and, last but not least, trade and industry. The creation of these institutions and their contribution to the nonpolitical endeavors of the United Nations represents a cooperative effort without precedent in history. Less obvious, but perhaps just as significant, has been their help in mobilizing the interest and cooperation of national ministries and professionals. The United Nations thus faces the coming decade and the last quarter of the twentieth century with vastly improved and strengthened means of action.

So much for the record of the past.

What is likely to lie in store for humanity in the future? May I be permitted to express on that future a few thoughts that might not be entirely foreign to your preoccupations.

I would first like to comment on the relationship between the political objectives and the economic and social objectives of the Organization. It has been recognized in the Charter that peace is dependent to a large extent on the achievement of social progress and a higher standard of living. The work of the Economic and Social Council has therefore been conceived as a means of reducing tensions and strengthening peace. But, while you have spared no efforts during these many years to study the problems of economic development, to devise remedial action and policies, to set in motion new programs and to try to influence public opinion, the rug has been almost drawn from under your feet, so to speak.

The political relations between nations have not substantially improved. Expenditures on armaments have skyrocketed. Enormously expensive space programs have been launched. The claims for resources have increased everywhere. The demands for ever higher standards of living and consumer goods have not abated. And now sizable expenditures are required due to new mass problems, such as urban concentration and the deterioration of the environment.

The demands for action in favor of the less developed countries are, therefore, likely to encounter increased resistance in the more advanced countries. There might be less money for foreign aid and greater opposition to the entry of goods from the developing countries.

This is why I believe that we must face together with determination during the years to come the problems of priorities on this planet. It will be more and more difficult for the Economic and Social Council to deal with economic and social development in isolation. The Council should review and judge each year a world economy in which armaments are treated as a waste and no longer as a "product." It should not accept passively that the door be slammed on economic and social development by military priorities. It would do little good to prepare additional cases and propose new programs for economic development if they are likely to be rejected outright for overriding military and political reasons. This is why I have advocated recently with a more pressing voice that the leaders of the great nations, including the People's Republic of China, should meet in order to initiate a change from confrontation and division to the building of a safe and peaceful world. It is high time that the main causes of the world's present troubles be faced with intelligence and courage. The people are becoming impatient. New tensions are mounting. How much longer can we continue on the present path of division, suspicion, and waste in a world already united by scientific and technological progress?

The Economic and Social Council has a great role to play in enlightening governments and their leaders. In my view, it should concern itself increasingly with the economic management of the world's resources, human and physical. It should aim at opening the eyes of governments to the obstacles which stand in the way of a more rational utilization of these resources, to a better distribution of income, and to common projects and endeavors of nations aimed at improving life on earth and at preventing its deterioration. For example, data on armaments expenditures should be collected on a yearly basis and reviewed by the Council. A close link should be established between the Development Decade and the Disarmament Decade. There should be fewer theoretical and detailed studies on the development process, since most of what we need to know in order to act is known. Henceforth the primary preoccupation should be with action. The Council should review the list of plans and proposals prepared by the first and second sessions of UNCTAD and, in connection with the Second Development Decade, establish a timetable as well as minimum targets for implementation.

The Council must raise its voice—which is that of reason—and speak out to those who, for outdated political and military considerations, draw the world each year into deeper difficulties. Niko Kasantzakis, in one of his books, has said: "If you were just, O God, you should have given strength to those who fight for right and not to those who are for wrong.'' We in the United Nations must redress the uneven distribution of strength between the forces of negation and the forces of construction. This remains our basic duty to the Charter.

Further progress should also be made during the years to come to strengthen multilateral programs. A much greater part of external aid should be channeled through the United Nations system. The developing countries have said from the beginning to the rich countries: "If you really want to help us, there should be no strings attached to your aid. We would therefore prefer international aid to bilateral aid." It has taken several years to develop the concept of aid through the United Nations system, to prove its merits and advantages, and to transform many disbelievers in the donor countries into convinced adherents to it. The most skeptical among them had even to recognize that, from a purely economic point of view, their countries did not lose anything in this process. But the world has gained enormously in a political way from such aid: whatever human and physical resources have been channeled through it were diverted from the divisive power game of nations. These resources, no matter how modest they may be, are a true enbodiment of worldwide solidarity and a first reassuring image of how nations can work together for a peaceful and rewarding common human cause on our planet. It should be the task of the Economic and Social Council to consolidate this success and to bring it a considerable step forward.

Looking at another aspect of the future, I am sure that during this session my dear friend and colleague, Philippe de Seynes, as well as the heads of the specialized agencies, will want to give you an indication of what lies in store for humanity on what we still call erroneously the "nonpolitical front." Mr. de Seynes has given me recently a short statistical paper highlighting the main changes that have occurred in the world demographic and economic situation during the past twenty years. There can be no doubt about the conclusion deriving from these figures: humanity has already stepped with one foot into a totally new epoch in the history of our planet, the epoch of mass phenomena due to the multiplication of human life.

Here are some of the figures: the number of humans on earth has increased from 2,485 million in 1950, when the first meaningful postwar statistics were available in the United Nations, to 3,632 million today. The world death rate has been reduced from 17 per thousand in 1950 to 14 per thousand in 1970. Thirty-seven percent of the world's people live today in urban areas compared with 28 percent in 1950. World industrial production has tripled since 1950. The volume of world exports has quadrupled. Agricultural production has increased 1.7 times. The phenomenal growth in the production of certain commodities is illustrated by petroleum output, which has increased 5 times since 1950, plastics, which has increased 15 times, aluminum 5 times, cement 4 times, crude steel 2.8 times, motor vehicles 2.7 times, and so forth.

The statistics published by the United Nations and its specialized agencies show a doubling or tripling of most world aggregates during the past twenty years. Projections for the future indicate further accelerated changes in practically every direction. The world population is sure to reach six billion before the end of this century. President [Amintere] Fanfani, in a speech to the recent commemorative session in San Francisco, went so far as to project a world population of 100,000 million in a century and a half if the present growth rate persists.

While the population increase is greatest in the less developed sectors of the world and the consumption explosion greatest in the developed areas, one must foresee a continued spread of the industrial revolution to other parts of the globe. High population figures will then be multiplied by high consumption figures, yielding staggering results. I regard it as quite an interesting exercise in statistics to visualize a world in which individual consumption would be the same everywhere as in the United States. For example, if a world population of six billion were some day to use the same number of passenger vehicles per person as the United States, the number of vehicles in the world would reach two and a half billion!

These are a few illustrations of the age of mass phenomena into which humanity has entered. Many estimates and forecasts do not even exist, since the human mind is not yet fully prepared to project in terms of new time and worldwide dimensions. Little has been done, for example, to calculate the totality of wastes and deleterious materials which are being introduced by nations and international means of transportation into our common atmosphere and oceans.

I believe, therefore, that the moment has come when the Economic and Social Council must daringly look into the problems of the future. Neither these problems nor the mass phenomena problems of the planet can any longer be considered as utopian or visionary. They have become part of a new realism imposed on us by the acceleration of scientific and technical progress and by its consequences on the biology of the human race. At a recent meeting at United Nations Headquarters of a private group of some of the best minds of our time, the proposal was made to create within the United Nations a committee on the future. It would be worthwhile for the Economic and Social Council to look into such a proposal and to broaden considerably the time-horizon of the work of the United Nations system. There are, of course, very great difficulties inherent in such an approach, but we must accustom ourselves as soon as possible to the new and unforeseen challenges of accelerated and interacting worldwide phenomena. We must diagnose sufficiently ahead of time the realities and the dangers of tomorrow. We can save the world considerable resources and difficulties if we detect the emergence and forecast the behavior of new galloping phenomena or tensions and give the necessary warning signals in time. This is the role of the United Nations and of its specialized agencies. No one else in the world is at such a vantage point to perform this task.

The Economic and Social Council could also make further progress in another direction, which might help to reduce present tensions and release resources for the establishment of a safe, peaceful, and prosperous world order: I mean better and reciprocal understanding between different economic and social systems. I have often underlined that ideologies were one of the main reasons for the division of some countries which are otherwise bound by common ties of history, language, and culture. Ideologies, more generally, have split the world into hostile and armed compartments which are contrary to the common nature of man and to the necessity of living in peace together on our small spaceship, Earth.

Much has already been done toward the idea and practice of peaceful coexistence between those groups which are represented in the United Nations. With the impact on the United Nations of the developing countries, which are interested in results rather than in theories, much progress has been made in the United Nations to dissipate the heat out of the earlier ideological debate. There is more understanding for each other today than there was during the cold war. Perhaps the time has come to take a new step forward and to look objectively and without passion into the multiple methods of solving the economic and social problems of our time. In a world of several billion people, who are divided into highly industrialized societies as well as regions of extreme poverty, each with its own culture and special problems, there can be no exclusive universal recipe or system.

We must realize that adaptation and change are imperative to the survival of social systems and institutions. Indeed the world has become so complex, the pace of change so rapid, and the newly emerging problems so numerous, that no rigid system, however well established on a few sacrosanct principles, is able to cope with all problems. I believe that we are about to embark on the most variegated search for political, institutional, legal, and moral solutions to the social problems of our time.

Nations must therefore enrich each other with what has proved good in the art of governing men and managing the environment. Private initiative may be the solution in one case, public initiative may be the answer in another. Many countries have demonstrated that the two can coexist and that one can admirably complement or even correct and stimulate the other. Each system has good and bad aspects.

The Economic and Social Council could look anew at East-West economic relations and establish a new program for better understanding and cooperation. The tremendous changes in science and technology in particular should be capable of bringing the two systems closer together. Science and technology were able to link the earth to the moon and they should be no less capable of uniting people who are living on the same planet, divided essentially by man-made barriers.

Within a new concern for the problems of the world as a whole—developed and underdeveloped, socialist and private enterprise systems—may also lie the key to the future work of the Economic and Social Council. I have often thought that the work of the Council should be less technical and closer to the simple aspirations and understanding of the people. I would hope that the Council should be able to prepare for the General Assembly each year, with the cooperation of the specialized agencies, a broad evaluation of the state of the world and its new emerging trends. Such a report could delineate the main developments and trends in science and technology and in the economic, social, psychological, cultural, and environmental situations of the world.

Now I should like to add a few words as chairman of the Administrative Committee on Co-ordination (ACC).

Mr. President, this is the twenty-fifth anniversary not just of the United Nations Organization itself, but of the United Nations system, the network of international organizations and programs related to the United Nations or forming part of it, which work under the coordinating authority of this Council and the General Assembly. It is not too much to say that most of the United Nations achievements in the economic and social fields have only been possible as a result of the close, active, daily support and cooperation of the members of that system.

It is, I think, well to keep this in mind when reforms are undertaken or explored for the purpose of strengthening our institutional arrangements, at the management level. The main link between the members of the United Nations system is the ACC, through which my colleagues and I supervise a network of arrangements for inter-agency consultation and cooperation in respect of an ever-broadening range of activities. You will note that this body, which had a very useful series of meetings with the Committee for Programme and Co-ordination last week, has decided, in order to increase the assistance which it can render to the Council direct, to establish small panels or groups of its members to deal in depth with particular issues of current importance. The first such group is to study and to anticipate the many implications for the work of our international organizations of that historic breakthrough in plant breeding and the use of high-yielding cereals which is popularly known as the "green revolution." Other groups will be formed on aspects of our international activities for the application of science and technology to development. A preliminary meeting on emergency assistance through the United Nations system, bringing together all interested agencies and senior United Nations officials, has just been held and other such meetings will follow.

The task to which they are addressing themselves is how best to develop and organize the assistance of the United Nations in cases of disaster. The importance and urgency of this question has, alas, been underlined only too poignantly by the terrible natural catastrophes of the past few weeks, and has been confirmed in the resolutions adopted by the Governing Council of the United Nations Development Programme and the Economic Commission for Latin America Committee of the Whole. In the light of the forthcoming discussions in the Council, I trust that our capacity to be of assistance to stricken countries in cases of emergency will be greatly strengthened. Special arrangements may be necessary in connection with a particular disaster; for example, the recent appointment of Dr. Raúl Prebisch as my personal representative in the context of the Peruvian disaster. But in addition, I propose to entrust one of my senior officials with the responsibility of acting for me on a regular basis in developing and coordinating assistance from the United Nations system in this field and ensuring the closest cooperation with the Red Cross and other voluntary agencies.

The discussions in the Governing Council on the capacity of the United Nations development system have provided a great stimulus to our thinking during recent months, and the conclusions reached will naturally figure largely in your coming discussions. Not only are many of the proposals made of direct concern to the Council, but the manner in which the United Nations development work is organized inevitably has profound implications for the functioning of the United Nations as a whole in the context of the Second Development Decade. The United Nations faces the coming decade, and the coming quarter-century, with a machinery of proven value. Some important adjustments and even reforms are clearly required. However, equally important is the question of whether the United Nations machinery is to be fully used by governments, and used by them in the most effective way.

This brings me back, in concluding, to the role and functioning of the Economic and Social Council. It is the hope of the whole system of United Nations organizations that the Council will be strengthened and that it will assume the full role provided for it in the Charter twenty-five years ago.

The Council could thus become again, as it was during the first years after the Second World War, the central organ which judges the main features of the "nonpolitical" situation of the world, which looks daringly into the future, which provides a synthesis of the various directions of change, which detects the constant new tensions that are inherent in human nature and society, which warns the world about collective phenomena that are not discernible to individual nations, which promotes and prompts action by governments, which enhances the creation of new international instruments when necessary and ensures the proper and efficient utilization of those that already exist.

In so doing, the Economic and Social Council will help governments to perform the delicate and increasingly complex task of governing human societies, of foreseeing and monitoring global phenomena, of denouncing and correcting existing and new emerging injustices, and of providing the collective services required to ensure a better, healthier, happier, and more beautiful world.

4. *"The United Nations: Crisis of Authority," from Address to World Association of World Federalists*

OTTAWA   AUGUST 23, 1970

. . .

IF THERE is a crisis today in connection with the United Nations, it is a crisis of commitment by nation states to the Organization and its purposes. Too many nations still regard the United Nations as peripheral rather than central to their foreign policies. They tend to evaluate it according to its possible use in advancing their own goals rather than the central instrument for forging solutions to world problems in concert with the rest of the world community.

The ultimate crisis before the United Nations, therefore, is the crisis of authority. Management of problems which are global in scope requires extension of authority to world agencies, but many nations are extremely reluctant to allow the exercise of that authority. However, if the United Nations is to become effective, we must make the transition from power politics to a policy of collective responsibility toward mankind, as envisaged in the Charter. Of all human activities, the relations between states seem to have been left stranded in old patterns. In most other important fields of activity, men have stepped forward into a more contemporary and more workable world setting. Nothing could increase the effectiveness of the United Nations more than a modification of outmoded and unworkable concepts of unfettered national sovereignty.

In a very important sense, the United Nations is in a transitional stage. Effective and sensible world approaches to world problems are urgently required. The United Nations, for the reasons mentioned, has not yet been charged with that full responsibility or adequate authority to discharge it. But the United Nations has to be the active and vital process within which world policies are made or changed, within which agree-

SOURCE: *UN Monthly Chronicle,* Vol. VII, August–September 1970, pp. 86–92.

ment and consensus must be reached on major issues among Member states, and where agreed decisions must be carried out on behalf of the world community. That process is only embryonic, in comparison with the needs, but we know that it must be fully developed. It is somewhat heartening that a momentum is being created that is moving us in that direction.

I recently said that strengthening the United Nations should be not just a desire but an obsession. That it is a magnificent obsession with your organization has been clearly and constructively demonstrated through the years. This twenty-fifth anniversary year is a particularly appropriate time for stock-taking and for renewed efforts to make the world Organization increasingly effective. I would like to summarize very briefly the immediate steps I see as indispensable.

First and foremost, the decisions of the United Nations, particularly of the Security Council, must be enforceable.

Second, unused provisions of the Charter, which can add greatly to international peace and security, should be activated. Some important measures in this direction have recently been taken, both at the initiative of the government of Finland. The Security Council has agreed to hold periodic meetings at a heads of state or ministerial level, to review the general world situation. Also, the Security Council has submitted a request to the International Court of Justice for an opinion on the responsibilities of governments with regard to the continuing presence of South Africa in Namibia. There are other valuable provisions of the Charter for establishing subsidiary bodies for fact-finding and for purposes of conciliation in political disputes which may be activated far more frequently.

Third, the International Court of Justice must be empowered to interpret the United Nations Charter. Our goal should be the acceptance by all Member states without exception of the compulsory jurisdiction of the International Court of Justice in all international legal disputes.

Fourth, I have mentioned earlier that I consider the idea of the universality of the United Nations the priority item of this year's agenda for world affairs. The lack of universality is an enormous handicap to the effectiveness of the world Organization. Concerned citizens rightly cannot understand why the organization charged with keeping peace in the world cannot deal with the Indo-China war and other matters involving the excluded countries. Can the United Nations and its decisions be credible if the present situation is allowed to persist?

Fifth, I have urgently recommended that global authorities related to the United Nations be established to deal with serious global problems. I have in mind particularly my recommendations for creation of a global authority to deal with the problems of the environment—with the life-support system of our spaceship Earth, now in serious jeopardy. The air and water of the earth circulate universally. They are no respectors of national boundaries or of any other man-conceived barriers. Their protection and purity are the concern of all. Such an authority should become the coordinating and expediting body for international standards and guidelines for control of contamination of the environment and use of its resources. The agency should be able, if necessary, to enforce its decisions for the benefit of the world community. It is my sincere hope that the United Nations Conference on the Human Environment, which is to meet in Stockholm in 1972 on the invitation of the government of Sweden, will take the first steps toward the establishment of such an agency.

Similarly, I hope that steps will swiftly be taken to establish the proposed international régime to administer the resources of the seabed, generally recognized as "the common heritage of mankind."

Sixth, the United Nations urgently needs a stand-by force, a recommendation I made to the General Assembly some years ago. Progress in the Committee of 33 [decolonization committee] may be encouraging, but we have a long way to go before such a force becomes an actuality. In my view, a ready, trained, stand-by force is a prerequisite for effective maintenance of international peace and security.

The most important lesson we have learned from the astronauts and the cosmonauts is that the world is a single unit, a rather tiny place; that the conditions of life are incredibly fragile; and that human life is confined by its own requirements to a very small fraction of the earth's biosphere. The penalty of technological mastery of the earth is that, henceforth, there is no escape from the responsibility of planetary management. Man's future and man's environment must be conceived and managed wisely if he is to survive and to prosper.

I do not criticize national pride. National pride is natural. I say only that the sense of belonging to the human community must now be added to, and become dominant over, other allegiances. Man now has not only the possibility but the necessity for recognizing and for demonstrating his essential unity. This has always been the vision of the great religious teachers, philosophers, sages, and wise men of the past. Today, it is a basic requirement for progress. For mankind cannot proceed, or even survive at all, as a divided and warring species.

Are there any short-cuts to constructing the needed world order and the body of enforceable world law together with the necessary executive, legislative, and judicial functions? I do not think so. It is generally recognized that law derives from norms of behavior accepted by the community, and that in course of time, as usage proves their worth, bodies of law become enforceable. If we accept this concept, then there is no aspect of world affairs and national affairs that does not require the attention of world citizens as they work steadfastly to usher in the new world order. Whatever contributes to the sense of world community, whatever lessens the distance between men, whatever contributes to the well-being and development of the full expression and dignity of the individual, whatever moderates conflict, or brings about concerted action on behalf of the whole community, serves to build the world order we all so earnestly desire. The sense of world community is the matrix for the evolution of enforceable world law and needed world institutions.

We, each of us, will have particular capacities and abilities to work at different aspects of this task. But one need is foremost in my mind above all others, and that is the need to educate the world's peoples to their responsibilities as citizens of the world and the peoples of the United Nations.

You may be sure that in my present capacity and in whatever role life thereafter sets before me, I will be working ceaselessly toward the goal of peace, justice, and progress under effective world order. I have no doubt that your own efforts in our common task will be carried forward even more vigorously than in the past. The will of nations is fundamentally the will of their peoples.

It is up to you to help bring our world into harmony with the requirements of the planetary age.

5. *From Statement at Commemorative Session of the General Assembly*

NEW YORK   OCTOBER 24, 1970

. . . IN WHAT circumstances has the United Nations worked best in the last twenty-five years? On the political side it has worked best only in exceptional situations when the Members have been sufficiently alarmed by a crisis and when they have had confidence enough in the United Nations to give it the authority to do what was needed and to cooperate wholeheartedly in the process. If in the next twenty-five years the United Nations is to live up to its responsibilities for securing peace with justice and advancing human well-being, governments will have to show a far more consistent and sincere confidence in their own ability to cooperate through the United Nations than they have shown in the past. This is not a question of whether the United Nations as such is a success or a failure. If there were any alternatives, the success or failure of the United Nations would be relatively unimportant, and the Organization could be safely consigned to the archives as yet another honorable historical experiment which ultimately failed to live up to its early promise.

But, as far as I can see, there simply is no alternative means in sight for attempting to deal with the swarm of increasingly urgent global problems which now beset us, especially now that survival itself may be the critical question. What other way is there out of the maze of national and special interests, preoccupations and priorities into the larger arena where we can at last face, head on, the monstrous problems of our time? The arms race, with its inexcusable risks and the $200 billion a year which it costs, is at least a familiar and well-documented nightmare compared to some of the other consequences of rapid scientific and technological change which are now running away with our planet at a constantly accelerating pace. Population, poverty, food shortage, urban-

SOURCE: General Assembly Official Records, Twenty-fifth Session, 1883rd plenary meeting.

ization, the squandering of natural resources, the pollution of the whole environment—these are problems we have hardly begun to face, and yet the hour is already very late. As we watch the sun go down, evening after evening, through the smog across the poisoned waters of our native earth, we must ask ourselves seriously whether we really wish some future universal historian on another planet to say about us; "With all their genius and with all their skill, they ran out of foresight and air and food and water and ideas." That is what they are going to say from another planet; or: "They went on playing politics until their world collapsed around them"; or: "When they looked up, it was already too late." If the United Nations does nothing else, it can at least serve a vital purpose in sounding the alarm.

The general directions in which we must move are obvious and, in principle at least, I believe that they are generally acceptable to all governments, even if they have not yet been accepted in practice. We must move from power politics to collective responsibility, from narrow national or commercial interests to a sense of earth partiotism and global solidarity. In the United Nations we must achieve universality, so that all peoples on earth are represented and have a voice here. We must move at all levels of life from international anarchy to a just and respected code of international law and behavior. We must eradicate the last persistent vestiges of colonialism, which is an intolerable anachronism in our time. We must eliminate completely the old forms of racism and ensure that new forms of that insidious disease are not allowed to develop. We must develop—with the minimum delay—adequate new international means to control our new and rapidly changing circumstances. We must build here in the United Nations an organization which can rise above the old quarrels and conflicts of nations and peoples and ideologies, and which can tackle, in the interests of all mankind, the real problems of our planet as a whole, on a scale which will produce real results. . . .

6. Statement at Special Staff Day Meeting

NEW YORK   NOVEMBER 2, 1970

FOLLOWING IS the text of a statement by the Secretary-General, U Thant, at a special staff meeting held today at Headquarters to pay tribute to staff members who have served with the United Nations since its inception:

WE ARE GATHERED here today to honor those of our number who have served with the United Nations since its inception.

The twenty-fifth anniversary of our Organization has given rise to many special events and ceremonies throughout the world. Anniversaries are usually occasions for rejoicing, for congratulations, for blowing candles and forgetting the serious aspects and asperities of life. The anniversary of the United Nations has been a very different event. Seldom has any commemoration been marked by so much soul-searching, evaluation, retrospection, and speculation into the future. We have heard every possible judgment about our Organization. Laud and criticism, hope and impatience, optimism and pessimism have been expressed to every conceivable degree by people from all walks of life, races, creeds, and nations. It is as if the world was commemorating its own anniversary, the anniversary of its coming-of-age, the completion of the first quarter-century of a newborn global society at last in the process of being cemented together by the immense strides of knowledge and communications and by common concerns.

This soul-searching anniversary is far from finished. Let us pray that all those who can change the course of events for the better will draw the appropriate conclusions, live henceforth by the ideals and rules of the Charter, and strengthen our Organization in a way commensurate with the crying needs of our time.

We in the Secretariat, no less than governments, must also make our act of conscience, for we are one of the principal organs established under the Charter. We must ask ourselves if we have exerted our

SOURCE: UN Press Release SG/SM/1366.

maximum efforts, perseverance, imagination, and vision to serve the world community well. We must determine whether we have fulfilled the high hopes of the peoples, of their governments, and of the founding fathers who gave us birth twenty-five years ago in the aftermath of an abominable war. Each of us during these commemorations must ask himself what he has done for peace, justice, and progress and for the Organization.

In a sense we can look rather proudly at the quarter-century passed. We have gone a long way since the first few Secretariat staff members gathered around their first Secretary-General. We have grown in numbers, in national origins, and in quality. We have gained knowledge and experience. We have learned on the job skills which no university or educational establishment in the world can provide. With the increase of membership the scope of our work has come to cover almost the entire globe. New agencies have been established which are active in practically every field of human endeavor. We have seen the creation of regional economic bodies and of important worldwide development programs which give life and blood to the Charter's objectives for greater international cooperation and human solidarity. The Secretariat has actively helped several of the new countries on their road to independence. Many of you were members of peace-keeping operations in troubled areas of the world. And we have given to the world the image of men and women of many nationalities, races, cultures, religions, and social beliefs working harmoniously together, united by their concern for the common good of all peoples on this earth.

Our future looks no less challenging. It is filled with promise and with concern. The world is changing very rapidly around us. Every problem takes on almost from its birth international dimensions. Our globe is criss-crossed by such intense movements of people, goods, means of transportation, capital, news, ideas, fashions, and aspirations that humanity is already much more united than would appear from its political image. Through almost instantaneous communications, not only the good aspects but also the ills and evils of this new global society are spreading overnight; new forms of violence, the alienation of youth, the challenge of institutions, law and order, and even of the very concept of government. Concern is also mounting among the peoples and governments about the global dangers which are menacing humanity: the growing inequality between the rich and the poor, the deterioration of our air, earth, waters, and oceans, the rate of increase of the world's population, the pathological spread of urbanization. Governments are looking at one another and at the international agencies for advice, guidance, and action. National policies begin to be more outward-looking. Nations can no longer stand in splendid isolation in the midst of mounting external and international influences. World affairs become less and less foreign affairs. The eyes and hopes of all increasingly turn to the United Nations. One new problem after the other is being brought to it under the impact of intense worldwide scientific, technological, and social changes. Could any of you who are completing twenty-five years of United Nations service have dreamed in 1945 that this Organization would be dealing today with outer space cooperation, the régime of the ocean floor and seabed, the human environment, criminology, the problems of youth, the non-proliferation of atomic weapons, hijacking of airplanes, and so forth? Can we visualize for a moment what new problems lie in store for humanity and will be brought before this Organization twenty-five years hence?

Each of us is at the same time a force and an anonymous person in this Organization. Since governments and peoples, including those of the highly developed countries, are turning increasingly to the United Nations with newly emerging problems, each of us has become part of the global process of ensuring peace, order, justice, and progress. We are working hand in hand with governments on the same tasks. Our powers are less: we act by persuading, by enlightening, by promoting peace, understanding, generosity, and tolerance. But, basically, we are part of the same old processes of good government which consist in denouncing and redressing injustices, abusive powers, and harmful divisions and in ensuring the good things expected by the people.

For this precise reason, I have often said that we should not lose sight of our national origins. Not only is the world the sum total of a rich variety of beliefs, cultures, and national entities, but we must help the nation-state system adapt itself to the new conditions which prevail on earth and to debouch into enlightened international cooperation to support a stronger United Nations. Our Organization provides a unique opportunity for this historical and ineluctable transition. We must forever cherish our roots in the peoples from whom we come and for whom we work, while maintaining our international integrity to the full. We must be above nations, never subordinated to them or receive their instructions. We should by our example demonstrate that there is no conflict between a sense of national loyalty and an overriding allegiance to the United Nations. But we should not either become an ivory tower cut off from the realities of the world and from those who represent their peoples and try to do the best possible job for them. Our task is to show untiringly that what is good for humanity is also good for each of its component nations.

The need of the world and of Member governments to be serviced by an outstanding international Secretariat requires that our conditions of employment be sufficient to attract and retain the most competent people from all countries. This principle has to be constantly defended. For my part, I have defended it in the past and will do so in the future. The fact that we are located in one of the most expensive and competitive cities of the world must be faced with an open mind, with imagination and generosity. The attraction and retention of competent people for some of the most difficult tasks on earth, often exercised under conditions of expatriation, is becoming year after year more difficult as a result of cumulative erosions and the inevitable delays in reaching fair decisions on the part of our competent organs. I will always be conscious of my special responsibilities in this up-hill struggle against mounting material difficulties. Everything must be done to maintain the highest possible morale in the international civil service. The world needs our unswerving dedication, our enthusiasm, our imagination, our cheerful perseverance, our conviction, and our power of persuasion. For if hope leaves this house where can hope be found in this world? We are constantly judged by the unfailing instinct of the people. We must follow this deep precept of Balzac: "Work for your reputation and your reputation will work for you." But the real judgment will come tomorrow from our children and the children of our children. They may rightly say some day: "You were there when the beginnings of a global human society were in the making; you, more than anyone else, accepted the responsibility and built up the knowledge of peace-keeping and of bringing peoples and nations closer together; you were few, but nothing prevented you from using your skills and minds to signal the trends of events to come on our planet; you were in the center of these events; your role was to speak up, to warn, to propose, to persuade in the name of all nations and mankind and always to press ahead with the cause of justice, peace, and progress, thus preparing a better world for us."

The power lies in each of us as individuals and as composing a totality to help win the praise or contempt of succeeding generations. Each of us is a beginning and an end. Shifting responsibilities or pointing fingers at others above, below, or outside is a sterile attitude which only weakens the image of the concern of which we are part.

The same applies to the phenomenon of bureaucracy. Here again each of us is a beginning and an end. The force lies in ourselves to fight mediocrity, bureaucratic pettiness, sterile pride, and wasteful methods of work. We must be grateful to governments for observing and chiding us whenever deserved. We can be nothing less but a model administration calling for the highest esteem of governments and of the peoples. This is just one more high standard expected from the first group of men and women who are serving peace and the peoples of the world. It is only at this price that we will succeed. And we must succeed, for our success will mean peace and justice and progress for all peoples.

I and many others present in this hall today will no longer be here when our Organization celebrates its second quarter-century. Let us hope that the man who will be in my place and those who will stand in this Assembly hall twenty-five years hence will be serving a world more peaceful, more united, and less dominated by power and self-defeating national interests than is ours today. Our efforts as international civil servants must strive toward this end.

These were the few thoughts which I wanted to leave with you on the threshold of the second quarter-century of our Organization.

One of you, who has served with the Secretariat almost from its inception, has put down some of these thoughts in brief form. I will read them to you, for I consider them fitting words honoring all those who will receive the first scrolls of twenty-five years of service with the United Nations. The text reads:

- We must deeply cherish the privileges of working for an Organization that stands for world peace, justice, and prosperity;
- We must never lose sight of the simple and fundamental hopes and aspirations of the people;
- We must help governments in their arduous tasks of ensuring just, prosperous, and peaceful societies and in harmonizing their actions with each other;
- We must ceaselessly be obsessed with the problems of our planet and of the human community as a whole;
- We must look far into the future and warn nations and men of collective problems that may lie in store for humanity;
- We must speak for mankind and for the community of nations and not for any particular nation or group or interest;
- We must help to preserve humanity's rich legacy of cultures, beliefs, ways of life, and nature and make the world safe for diversity;

• We must always understand, help, and enlighten, never condemn, criticize, or embitter;

• We must be at peace with one another and work relentlessly for the reputation of the noble Organization which we serve; and

• We must never despair, for ours is the most difficult, most challenging, and most rewarding task on earth.

On this day of commemoration and recollection, we must also turn our thoughts and pay our tribute to all those who have given their lives in the service of the United Nations. Let us stand and observe a minute of silence in their memory.

---

7. Transcript of Interview by Inter-Nation Television Trust of London[1]

NOVEMBER 5, 1970

QUESTION: Mr. Secretary-General, might we start out with a point which is particularly relevant to next year, which is quite frankly how have we succeeded or failed to live up to that remarkable Charter which was written twenty-five years ago?

THE SECRETARY-GENERAL: Historians may assess the accomplishments or lack of accomplishments of the United Nations in different ways, of course. If the question is posed, whether the United Nations has fulfilled the aspirations of the founding fathers in 1945, then my answer is: No, the United Nations has not fulfilled the aspiration of the founding fathers in the political field. I want to stress the phrase ''in the political field.'' I think when we assess the accomplishments or lack of accomplishments of the United Nations in the last twenty-five years, it is very necessary to bear in mind that the United Nations was expected to perform certain functions in three spheres; first of all, the political and

SOURCE: UN Press Release SG/SM/1369.

[1]Taped in New York on November 15, 1969, for use during twenty-fifth anniversary of United Nations.

security sphere; second, the economic and social sphere; and third, in the sphere of colonialism. With these purposes in mind, the founding fathers, of course, envisaged the establishment of three principal organs: the Security Council, the Economic and Social Council, and the Trusteeship Council. The Security Council is expected to deal with problems threatening international peace and security; the Economic and Social Council is expected to perform the functions in the economic, social, humanitarian, and human rights fields. The Trusteeship Council is expected to perform the functions of facilitating the emergence of new nations from nonindependent status to independent status.

So if we assess the accomplishments of the United Nations in its entirety, and all its functions, I must say that in the economic and social fields the United Nations and its system of specialized agencies have achieved remarkable success—for instance, in obliterating illiteracy, in eradicating malaria in many parts of the world, and in feeding the hungry. The United Nations, with the cooperation of the specialized agencies, has been able to do very remarkable things.

In the trusteeship field, also, the fact that there were fifty-one Member states in 1945, and 126 Member states today is a testimony to the success of the United Nations in this particular field. Now coming back to the political and security fields, where the Security Council is directly involved, and has been involved, I must say that the achievements of the United Nations have not come up to the expectations of the founding fathers in 1945.

So I think we ought to make a distinction between different functions when we assess the worth of the United Nations. But I must say that even in the political field, because of the emergence of the "cold war," and the discovery of the atomic bomb, I think all the expectations of 1945 were shattered in one year. Then the superpowers or the big powers—the permanent members of the Security Council—who are expected to decide unanimously on issues involving international peace and security, were divided. As a result the most important provision of the Charter regarding the maintenance of international peace and security, that is Chapter VII, was never invoked.

Many don't realize that in the last twenty-five years the provisions of Chapter VII by which the Security Council, with the unanimity of the permanent members, [can take action] to stem aggression, to maintain peace by force, if necessary, by the employment of air force, naval units and army units, have never been invoked. But in spite of that, the

Security Council and the entire membership have devised some procedures by which a form of peace-keeping, not in the sense of the employment of armed force, was established. In this manner, the United Nations has achieved remarkable success in Kashmir, in the Congo, in Cyprus, in the Middle East for a long time, and Lebanon, and in the Dominican Republic, for instance. Although the accomplishments were not spectacular, as expected, I must say that even in this limited sphere of peace-keeping, under Chapter VI of the Charter, the United Nations has achieved some perceptible success.

QUESTION: In view of this fact that the great powers are divided, to what extent is the United Nations in fact held back or foiled by the wishes of the great powers? I mean, how much can they move against the wishes of the great powers?

THE SECRETARY-GENERAL: In matters of maintaining international peace and security, as I have said, under Article VII of the Charter, the small powers cannot do very much against the wish of the big powers. If one permanent member of the Security Council has a definite stand on a particular issue against the position of all the rest of the Security Council membership, then he can block—this particular delegate representing a permanent member can block—any action contemplated by the rest of the membership of the Security Council.

You know, the permanent members of the Security Council have a special status in the Security Council under the Charter, because of their power of vetoing any resolution which they don't like. So with this special status, in my view, the permanent members have a special responsibility to see that the decisions of the Security Council—particularly the unanimous decisions of the Security Council—are implemented. The Security Council in the last few years has been able to come to unanimous decisions on very important issues, and so the first step has been achieved. What is now necessary is to come to the second step, of seeing to it that the unanimous decisions of the Security Council are implemented. With regard to this second step, a lot of dissatisfaction has been expressed by the nonpermanent Members in the United Nations at the lack of achievement by the Security Council regarding the implementation aspect of the resolutions.

I think it is also necessary to remember that there are two types of resolutions of the Security Council. One type may be classified as recommendations. Another can be classified as decisions. As far as the Security Council recommendations are concerned, I don't believe it is mandatory on the part of any parties involved to implement these recommendations. But if the Security Council decides on a particular line of action, especially when this decision is unanimous, then I believe that it is up to the Security Council, particularly the permanent members of the Security Council who have voted for this decision, to see that the parties concerned are obligated to give effect to these resolutions. In this particular step, the Security Council has not been able to accomplish what they should accomplish, what they are expected to accomplish.

QUESTION: In these twenty-five years, the whole balance in the United Nations has changed. There are very, very many more small nations. What effect has this had, for instance, having over forty countries in Africa?

THE SECRETARY-GENERAL: In my view, the principle of one nation, one vote, as far as the General Assembly is concerned, as far as the Economic and Social Council is concerned, as far as the Trusteeship Council is concerned, is completely in line with the principles of democracy, or democratic processes. I am deliberately omitting the Security Council, in this context, because in the Security Council, the permanent members have a special status. The permanent members combined have a greater weight than the rest of the membership collectively. So I am leaving out the Security Council in answering this question. But in the General Assembly, and other deliberative organs, except the Security Council, I believe that this principle of one nation, one vote, is strictly in line with the established democratic processes. In all human societies, you will remember, when it comes to the right vote . . .

(Interruption)

QUESTION: We were talking, sir, about the place of the small nations and the democratic process.

THE SECRETARY-GENERAL: I have made my position very clear on several previous occasions. I believe that this principle of one country, one vote, is in strict conformity with the established democratic procedures. If we take for instance any human organization, like a club or a society or an association, we will find that all members of that particular club or association or society have equal rights under the rules when it comes to the question of voting. Even in national politics, the elevator man, for instance, has one vote, whereas Mr. Rockefeller also has one vote. So I don't think that this criterion of wealth or affluence should have anything to do with the right to vote in any human society, in any human organization. I think this consideration should also apply to the international organizations.

When it comes to the question of voting, I must make this very clear, as I have said a moment ago, that except in the Security Council—of course, in the Security Council the small powers have very little voice compared to the permanent members—in all other deliberative organs of the United Nations, it is just, right, and proper that every Member state must have the same status, if it comes to the question of voting.

I don't think that this practice is in conflict with the established democratic processes, although, perhaps, on some issues, the voice of the small countries, perhaps—countries which are not very experienced or very mature—might have some adverse effect on the functioning of the United Nations. But my experience of the United Nations in the last fourteen years has forced me to come to the conclusion that many Member states have grown with years. They have become more mature, more responsible, and more sensible in their exercise of the vote, particularly on issues not involving the disturbance of international peace and security, which are in many ways the prerogative of the big powers. So I believe the present procedures are very sensible.

QUESTION: Sir, on United Nations Day, you made a speech in the General Assembly, in which you talked about the place of young people in what's going on in the world today, which I think all of us found very exciting. But I was wondering if you could say a bit more about how you feel young people can actually practically do something—because I think very often people talk about young people and they themselves say, "Well, this is all very well but what can we actually do?"

THE SECRETARY-GENERAL: I am glad you have asked this question. I believe very strongly in the future of the younger generation. I think this is one phenomenon about which I am optimistic about the future. As I said on that particular occasion, on United Nations Day, the young people who were born after the Charter was signed, after October 24, 1945, will constitute the majority of the human population when the United Nations celebrates the twenty-fifth anniversary. In other words, on October 24, 1970, more than half the population of the world will be those who were born after the Charter was signed. So I describe this generation as the take-over generation. It should be their responsibility to see to it that they have to fashion the kind of society they want.

The emotions that motivate them—like hatred of war—their dedication to justice and peace, their passion to fashion a more equitable society, their urge for equality of opportunity are in line with the objectives of the Charter. They are raising questions, very legitimate questions, and in my view they are pragmatic idealists, if I may use that

expression. So I am encouraged whenever I think of the younger generation who are posing questions, with a sense of responsibility. Of course,
I must say that when we speak of the younger generation and youth, I
am conscious of two factors about which I have very grave reservations.
I am against obscenity and violence in any shape or form. So long as the
youth movement is not characterized by obscenity and violence—then I
think it should be encouraged.

There is another point. I think it is up to the leaders of thought and
leaders of men to instill in the minds of our young people the spirit of
greater allegiance to humanity than their allegiance to their own state.

I believe that every one of us has two allegiances—our allegiance to
our own state, and our allegiance to humanity as a whole. In order to
fashion a better world, a more peaceful world, it is up to leaders of
thought and leaders of men to instill in the young people of today a
greater allegiance to humanity if it comes to a question of choice. So with
this end in view, I have proposed the consideration of establishing a
United Nations university, an international university, in my Introduction to the annual report which I submitted to the General Assembly in
September 1969. I am developing some ideas in consultation with some
educationists of international repute. I propose to develop this idea
further in my next report to the General Assembly.

You will recall that I am also asked to submit my report on the
International Youth Volunteer Service to the next session of the Economic and Social Council to be held in Geneva in July. And also I think
there is a growing consensus among the membership that a youth
assembly—world youth assembly—should be convened some time next
year, in 1970, in order to devise ways . . .

(Interruption)

QUESTION: We were talking about young people in particular, the
sense you try to instill into them, the feeling that there's a loyalty toward
humanity rather than to your own nation.

THE SECRETARY-GENERAL: Well, I think my conception of the United
Nations is well known. If we analyze the provisions of the Charter of the
United Nations we can summarize these provisions in two words—
human survival and human progress. For the achievement of these twin
objectives of the Charter, it is very necessary for leaders of thought and
leaders of men to instill in the peoples of the United Nations a greater
sense of allegiance to humanity. Of course, everybody has to have
allegiance to his own state, to his own people, but so long as one's
approach to problems is parochial, I don't think we'll achieve the objec-

tives of the Charter, which is for the creation of international understanding and for the creation of conditions for human progress and
human prosperity and international peace and security.

I must say that the national interests of any state cannot be confined
within the frontiers of a particular state. The national interests of all
Member states depend on international peace, international progress,
and the development of international resources. Things are so interrelated that you cannot confine your national interests within the confines
of your own boundaries or territories. Every country's peace and progress depends primarily on international peace, international progress,
and the development of international resources. So with this realization,
we have to instill in the young people particularly that their allegiance to
humanity as a whole—in other words, their allegiance to the United
Nations—their allegiance to the provisions of the Charter, should dominate their allegiance to their own state. This is, of course, very difficult
to achieve, but in my view the objectives of the United Nations Charter
will be achieved only if the peoples of the United Nations realize these
basic facts.

QUESTION: How much do they realize?

THE SECRETARY-GENERAL: It is a very slow process. I think in this
particular sphere I would like to address my appeal to "the peoples of
the United Nations," which is the language of the Charter. I think it is
worth recalling one of the important differences between the Covenant
of the League of Nations and the Charter of the United Nations. The
Covenant of the League of Nations started with the words "We, the
High Contracting Parties" will do this and this and this; the Charter of
the United Nations uses the words "We the peoples of the United
Nations." I think that is the very significant distinction between the two.
So in this particular issue, let me direct my appeal to the peoples of the
United Nations. It should be one of the functions of the United Nations
associations in all Member states, to set it as a priority item, to relate this
item to the educational systems in their own countries and to the mass
education centers that have been established in many parts of the world.
I think this educating process, this process of educating the youth,
should be involved primarily with the conception of humanity as a
whole. Although humanity is divided on the basis of race and color and
creed, in the final analysis, all of us have to realize that our little planet is
an indivisible whole. Only with this realization will the objectives of the
founding fathers in 1945 be achieved.

QUESTION: You've partly answered my next question—How do the economic and social sides of the United Nations relate to the political side? How much is the success of one dependent on the success of the other? How much is one hindered by the failure of the other?

THE SECRETARY-GENERAL: On many previous occasions I used to make one observation—that in my view the division of the world into the north and the south, the haves and the have-nots, the developed and the developing, is much more serious and much more fundamental and in the long run much more explosive than the division of the world based on ideological differences. So in my view, the twin objectives—social and economic development, and the promotion of international peace and security—are interrelated; they cannot be divorced. Many world leaders, including His Holiness Pope Paul VI, said that economic progress and peace are synonymous.

I think this is very basic to our whole conception of peace and progress. I agree completely with His Holiness' statement, assessment—that economic progress and peace are synonymous. Because without the one, the other cannot be accomplished, and, as you are no doubt aware, the breach or the division into the rich and the poor—the gulf between the two—has become wider and wider year after year. Since the end of World War II, the breach, the gap between the rich and the poor, is getting wider every year. This is a very alarming phenomenon, if I may say so. It is primarily up to the rich countries, the affluent societies, the developed countries, to give thought to this particular aspect—that when we launch the Second Development Decade the United Nations must employ what I have called "the global strategy." This global strategy means the recognition of the fact that although the states are divided into the rich and the poor, black and white, in the final analysis, humanity is an indivisible whole.

Only with this realization, I think the developed countries will feel compelled to do more than what they have been doing, because, as I have stated a moment ago, no nation's security is assured without international security. The affluent societies, the rich countries, the developed countries, cannot remain forever rich and affluent and content if two-thirds of humanity are struggling in hunger, in misery, and in poverty. Only when two-thirds of humanity improve their economic and social status, the affluent societies also will feel more secure. This is a two-way street, if I may say so. These repeated resolutions of the United Nations organs appealing to the rich countries to contribute 1 percent of their gross national product in the form of aid to the less fortunate countries should represent the conscience of humanity. This sentiment is being shared by many affluent societies. For instance, the Scandinavian countries particularly realize the importance of this particular aspect of the functioning of the United Nations in the economic field and I am hopeful that the Second Development Decade will be more successful than the first one.

QUESTION: One final question, Sir . . . As you've already said, the United Nations is, in fact, a constantly changing organization. Within this world, how do you see your job developing?

THE SECRETARY-GENERAL: Yes, I agree with the hypothesis that the United Nations is evolving in a way which was not envisaged twenty-five years ago. It is not a static Organization. It is a dynamic, organic Organization. So, in the same way, I think the Secretary-General's functions also have developed in a way which was not contemplated in 1945. First of all, I want to dispel one misunderstanding or misconception about the functions of the Secretary-General. There seems to be a widespread feeling that the Secretary-General of the United Nations is just the chief administrative officer of this Organization and nothing else. I think it is wrong. It is, of course, true that the Secretary-General is the chief administrative officer of this Organization but he is something else, too. For instance, Article 99 of the Charter empowers him to bring to the attention of the Security Council any developments which, in his view, are likely to threaten international peace and security. So from this it is obvious that the Secretary-General has also some political and diplomatic functions to perform, besides functioning as the chief administrative officer. So in my view it is very necessary that the Secretary-General of the United Nations must take diplomatic and political initiatives.

This reminds me of the question of good offices with which I dealt rather comprehensively in my report to the General Assembly in 1969. It is difficult to explain in a brief space of time at our disposal regarding the instances that I have exercised my good offices at the request of the Member states. There are many. At the request of the Member states concerned, I have exercised my good offices privately, informally, and on a personal basis, without publicity in the last eight years and more. I have dealt with governments to ease tensions between two or more Member states or to bring about a normal relationship between two Member states while previously the relationship was not normal. I have exercised my good offices in many areas, for instance between Thailand

and Cambodia, Malaysia and Indonesia, the Netherlands and Indonesia, the Ivory Coast and Guinea, and so on. This is one area where the Secretary-General has to perform his functions privately, informally, and without publicity.

Then, in terms of the Charter the Secretary-General is even empowered to bring to the attention of the Security Countil any developments, as I have said earlier, which, in his view, might threaten international peace and security. Now, coming to Article 99 of the Charter, it is worth recalling that in the course of the United Nations history in the last twenty-five years, there was only one instance when the Secretary-General of the United Nations invoked Article 99, only one instance in twenty-five years. It was when Mr. Dag Hammerskjöld invoked Article 99 to call a Security Council meeting with reference to the developments in the Congo in 1960. At that time, the Secretary-General was on very firm ground. All the African states wanted him to bring this matter to the attention of the Security Council. All the permanent members wanted him to bring this to the attention of the Security Council. So, he had no opposition whatsoever from the membership in bringing this matter to the attention of the Security Council. This reminds me of another case. Some criticism was leveled against my action, for instance, in May 1967, when I did not bring the matter of the withdrawal of the United Nations Emergency Force (UNEF) to the Security Council. It was a completely different basis altogether. The criticism, in my view, was based primarily on the lack of information about the processes of the United Nations. UNEF was established in the Middle East on a completely different basis from the United Nations Force in Cyprus, for instance. To illustrate my point more clearly, if the government of Cyprus were to ask me today to withdraw the United Nations Force from Cyprus, I would have to reply to the government of Cyprus that this is not within my jurisdiction. So I have to refer this request to the Security Council for decision. The bases of the two are completely different. In the case of UNEF, as you well know, it was established by a resolution of the General Assembly, and only with the permission of the host government the Force was stationed on United Arab Republic territory. When the request for withdrawal came, I had no alternative. It is worth remembering that of the 126 Member states of the United Nations, not one single Member state advised me at that time, privately or publicly, that I should refer this matter to the Security Council, not one Member state. Because all the Member states, all the governments know the legal and juridical aspects pertaining to the functioning of the United Nations. Even the government of Israel, through its spokesman in the Security Council, made a public statement that I had no alternative, the Secretary-General had no alternative.

I am making this observation in reference to your question about the functions of the Secretary-General. Because there is still, in my view, some misunderstanding in some quarters regarding my action. As you will recall, I decided on the withdrawal in May 1967. Actual process of withdrawal took six weeks. As soon as I decided, it didn't happen that the withdrawal took place within twenty-four hours. Actual withdrawal took six weeks. In this process of withdrawal, fourteen soldiers of peace serving with UNEF were killed. If I had delayed the withdrawal, for instance, by a week or a month, I don't know how many more soldiers would have been killed. Because the UNEF soldiers were soldiers of peace—they were not armed, they were not equipped for combat duty. Their function was to keep the peace, not to fight. This aspect is also not generally understood by many observers.

So to wind up my answer, I think the Secretary-General's functions have developed in such a way not actually envisaged by those in 1945 who framed the Charter. In some areas where the Security Council is not able to act, or where the Security Council cannot function in the way it was meant to function, then there is a feeling, or even a consensus in my view that the Secretary-General should be permitted to function in the spirit of the Charter in a way which he was not expected to function twenty-five years ago. So in this respect, the Secretary-General has been able to function more independently than it was envisaged in the Charter, particularly in the political field.

For instance, last year, there was a pending crisis, if I may say so, between Spain and Equatorial Guinea, in the first days of the emergence of Equatorial Guinea as a Member state. The problems were critical in my view, and both governments wanted me to use my good offices to ease tensions, and to bring about a normal relationship between the two countries. So I sent a representative there to contact the government of Equatorial Guinea. I was myself in contact with the government of Spain and normal relations were restored. My reports to the Security Council are on record. This is one instance of what the Secretary-General can do in the spirit of the Charter to ease tensions and to prevent a situation from developing into a crisis situation. So in this particular field, in the political field, in the peace-keeping field, in the field where developments might threaten international peace and security, the Secretary-General can perform the functions which were not envisaged in 1945.

WORLD YOUTH ASSEMBLY

DURING ITS early years the United Nations paid little attention to youth as a group. The Charter had been drafted by established experts and statesmen, many of whom had served at the League of Nations. It was not until 1965 that the General Assembly recognized the importance of youth by adopting a Declaration on the Promotion among Youth of the Ideals of Peace, Mutual Respect and Understanding between Peoples. Four years later when plans were being formulated for the 1970 observance of the twenty-fifth anniversary of the United Nations, the Assembly decided that it would be fitting to convene a World Youth Assembly as part of the program. U Thant was heartily in accord with the decision. He soon found himself facing a new problem, however, since he was assigned the task of raising money through voluntary contributions to finance the Youth Assembly. Some of the major powers, who had been expected to give freely, were having second thoughts and contributions were not forthcoming. Countries like the United States saw the possibility that the Youth Assembly might turn into a forum for attacks on the American Vietnam policy. On May 6, just two months before the scheduled date for the opening of the Youth Assembly, Thant warned that if the United Nations was unable to convene the Assembly because of lack of funds "the result will not only be a serious blow to the objectives of the General Assembly resolution, but it is likely to affect the relations between generations for a long time to come." In the end his fears proved groundless. The Assembly was held at United Nations Headquarters from July 9 through July 18 with some 650 young people from 113 countries taking part. Only 68 percent of those attending were twenty-five years of age or younger, as had been suggested, and the young idealistic representatives found the sessions dominated by organized "professional" youth groups who injected ideological issues into the discussions and disrupted the procedings by repeated heckling. Many United Nations diplomats were frankly doubtful as to the value of the Youth Assembly but Thant was among those who believed it had been worthwhile. At the closing session he told the Assembly that "by your behavior and your spirit of cooperation, you have belied the predictions of some people that this gathering would end in utter chaos and disorder."

1. Statement at Opening Meeting

NEW YORK   JULY 9, 1970

MY YOUNG FRIENDS,

I am glad to welcome you to the first World Youth Assembly held under the auspices of the United Nations, which I hereby declare open.

During my lifetime, some of the greatest achievements of mankind have taken place. Man has advanced dramatically into the infinitely large and the infinitely small. Satellites have been placed in outer space. Instruments have been sent farther and farther away into the universe. Humans have set foot on the moon and have returned safely to earth. Instantaneous communications are bringing news, fashions, and new cravings to the most remote villages of the globe. World transportation has expanded dramatically from the limitations of land and sea to the air. Man has reached with his tools the abyss of the seas. My generation has witnessed the birth of electronics, of cybernetics, the breaking of the atom and the harnessing of its energy, as well as hundreds of other advances in medicine, in microbiology, and in other fields of science and technology.

The statistics of the United Nations have reported for the last twenty years a doubling of human lives on earth, a dramatic reduction in the mortality rate, longer lives, better health, a tripling of world industrial production, a quadrupling of international trade and so forth.

But my generation has also seen, side by side with these magnificent success stories, some of the saddest images of evil, injustice, and lack of intelligence. Two world wars in my lifetime have killed several million men. Since the disarmament debate began in the United Nations, world armaments have reached incredible proportions, involving yearly expenditures of $200 billion and using such concepts as "overkill capacity." We have linked the moon to the earth, but we have been unable to conquer the man-made barriers between nations, ideologies, races, and political systems. The world is divided into armed camps which observe

SOURCE: UN Press Release SG/SM/1298.

each other, try to out-distance each other, seek to enlist the support of the smaller nations and claim each to have the sole key to humanity's future. We see living side by side on the same planet, under the same solar system, people amid abundance and overconsumption and masses of people as poor and undernourished as during the times of Buddha or of Christ. Children opening their eyes today in some of the more advanced countries will see the light of life for more than seventy years. Others, born this same moment in some of the poorest countries, will live less than thirty years. And, while we see humanity bent on transforming the physical elements of the world for its benefit, while human groups continue to try to gain power over each other for reasons which year after year become less understandable, the first deteriorations in the mysterious mechanics of our small spaceship Earth have become noticeable: our atmosphere is radioactive and carbon-loaded; our circulatory water system and its biology are being interfered with; and our oxygen-producing oceans are becoming vast receptacles of dumps from all nations of the world. And it did not occur until very recently to any of these nations that its individual action, added to those of other nations, could have a collectively damaging effect.

No wonder that the individual suddenly pauses, as if warned by instinct that something, which tomorrow might be everything, is going silently but inexorably wrong on this planet. The older generation, elated and thrilled with its scientific and technical success, defends itself and points to the tremendous legacy of achievements passed on to the youth of today. The latter points to injustice, waste, lack of love and understanding, blindness to events of the future, antiquated social systems and institutions, and to the absence of a political order commensurate with the profound changes that have taken place on this planet.

I have left to the last any comment on the most important element of all, man himself. The phenomena which we have witnessed since the signing of the Charter have on the whole tended to diminish the status of human beings as individuals and to increase their adherence to or dependence on large groups and categories of people. It is an irony of history that many of the developments which have made life easier for the great majority of people have also tended to reduce both their individuality and the distinguishing qualities of their particular society. It is not nostalgia for the past which concerns me here, but rather, the preservation of the most precious asset of all, the mind, spirit, and extraordinary possibilities of man himself. While the Charter speaks in the name of peoples rather than governments, mankind as such still has no direct voice in the United Nations. In our Organization, ideology calls to ideology; nations declaim their challenges to other nations, and great interests vie for advantage. All too often the forgotten element is man— the people who actually live and die on and around the battlegrounds of ideologies and of conflicting national aims; the people who live and die for the policies of political leaders they are unlikely ever to meet; the masses of men and women for whose hard-won earnings great commercial interests compete; and the silent, suffering millions who still go to bed hungry every night and still have no hope of sharing in the world's riches.

We have an obligation to make new steps forward here too, and I very much hope that, in the years to come, the place of the human individual in the scheme of things will be given the priority that it has so often failed to have in the past. It would indeed be a victory for humanity if our century were to be remembered by succeeding generations not for its wars or its disasters or even for its inventiveness, but as the turning point when, for the first time, it became possible for all mankind to share the advantages of civilization. Today I feel more strongly than ever that our efforts to build better for the future should be centered around the objective of providing a framework for enhancing the life of men and women as individuals in a world where we have, if we use them correctly, the means and the resources to do this for the first time on a large scale. If that can be our central aim, we may begin to hear less talk of alienation and dropping out, which are other words for cynicism and defeatism. And we may also then begin to develop the spirit which we so desperately need to make our international institutions work, a new patriotism which is the patriotism of man.

Let us recognize, however, that every epoch of history has had its brightness and shadows.

To complain of the age we live in, to murmur at the present possessors of power, to lament the past, to conceive extravagant hopes of the future, are the common dispositions of the greatest part of mankind. Such complaints and humors have existed in all times; yet as all times have not been alike, true political sagacity manifests itself in distinguishing that complaint which only characterizes the general infirmity of human nature, from those which are symptoms of the particular distemper of our own air and season.

These words are not mine. They were written in 1770 by Edmund Burke in his "Thoughts on the Cause of the Present Discontents." They still ring true today.

If you are here, if your elders have encouraged you to gather in such an unprecedented worldwide meeting, with principles, objectives, and entirely new methods of your own, it is because the feeling has become very strong that something is not going well in the affairs of the world. Many things have indeed gone increasingly wrong, year after year, before the incredulous eyes of very well-meaning, conscientious, and highly educated men involved in world affairs. It will be your task to come to grips with the fundamental causes of the present discontent.

As you are about to embark upon this formidable task, I would like to tell you what I consider as having gone fundamentally wrong, as being at the root of our present difficulties and as being the possible source of even greater preoccupations in the future, in terms of your own agenda.

I observe that your Assembly has on its provisional agenda four items, namely, world peace, development, education, and environment. These are indeed important subjects and I am glad that you are going to devote special attention to them. Perhaps you will permit me to share a few thoughts on each of these subjects with you.

I need hardly begin by reminding you that the primary objective of the United Nations Charter is peace, and with it the maintenance of international security. The preamble expresses the determination of "the peoples of the United Nations"—as I recalled earlier—and not of Member governments alone, "to save succeeding generations from the scourge of war." Yet—while the United Nations may perhaps claim some credit for the fact that we have not had a third world war in the last twenty-five years—it is in the fulfillment of its primary objective that the Organization has the poorest showing. I must admit this frankly to you so that you may deal with this problem realistically—it is as much your problem as it is mine, because you are the "succeeding generations" to which the Charter relates. In this regard, you may ask what is the main cause of this poor showing. I would say, without in any way trying to make an alibi for the United Nations, that it is not the Charter that has failed the Member states; rather, it is the Member states which have failed to live up to their obligations under the Charter. To a very large extent this flows from the idea of several Member states that they should "use" the United Nations for the purpose of promoting their national interest. I have always held, especially where there is a clash of national interests, that the United Nations should be used as an instrument for "harmonizing the actions of nations." In this way a higher interest, which transcends national interest and which may, in fact, often coincide with the long-term national interest, is served. I am very much afraid that the present unsatisfactory state of affairs will continue as long as nations feel free to act in accordance with the concept of unlimited national sovereignty. Legally, of course, every Member state has freely accepted the restrictions imposed by the Charter on national sovereignty; however, until Member governments, big and small, powerful and weak, live up to their Charter obligations, we shall not have true peace at the international level.

The result of the failure of nations to do so is plain for all to see. We have two major areas of conflict in the world today which are of great concern to all of us. In one area, the Middle East, the Security Council unanimously adopted a resolution over two and a half years ago, but it still remains basically unimplemented. In the other area, namely, Southeast Asia, the tragic conflict has caused a loss of human lives, destruction of property, and suffering of innocent civilians on a scale which is beyond comprehension for most of us. There is, as I have called it before, the mad momentum of the arms race—an exercise of proved wastefulness, in view of the rapid obsolesence of modern strategic arms, and an exercise of proved futility inasmuch as experience has shown that, as the level of armaments piles up, the level of insecurity also increases.

We also have seen that, while such vast resources are diverted to the pursuit of national security through armaments, the United Nations has not been able to agree over the last five years in regard to the financing of its peace-keeping operations, what I may call the "fire-brigade" function of the United Nations, although the funds required for financing these operations are a pittance compared to the vast sums spent on armaments.

In some of the other political activities of the United Nations we have seen some limited success. I refer to the rapid progress of decolonization during the last quarter of a century, which has increased the membership of the United Nations from 51 at the time of its founding to 126 today. But here again we must recognize that there are areas of colonialism which have presented a solid wall of resistance, especially in Africa. Likewise, all forms of discrimination, especially racial discrimination, have been attacked in the United Nations with a measure of success, but there are still areas of the world, again in Africa, where racism is practiced as part of national policy. In the field of disarmament, the nuclear test-ban treaty of 1963 and the Treaty on the Non-Proliferation of Nuclear Weapons, which came into force some months ago, represent some limited success, but there is still a long way to go. I therefore attach particular importance to the success of the strategic arms limitation talks between the two major military powers of the world—the Soviet Union and the United States.

These are some of the aspects of the broad theme of peace to which I wish to draw your attention today. I would like now to turn to the question of development. Several authorities have pointed out that, in the modern world, development is inseparable from security. While security is a precondition to development, development is equally a necessary condition for peace and stability at the political level. I have often referred to the division of the world into the rich and the poor, the "have" and the "have-not" countries, as one of the most potentially explosive forces in the world today. I spoke on the subject at length only three days ago at the opening meeting of the Economic and Social Council. I would not wish, therefore, to take up more of your time on this question except to place one or two thoughts before you. May I refer again to the question of national interest versus international interest. It seems to me that until the rich countries realize that they cannot live in cases of affluence, surrounded by deserts of poverty, and protected against sand drifts from the desert by walls of their own making, be they tariffs, immigration quotas, or whatever else, there will be no movement toward that concept of human solidarity which I regard as essential. In the world of today, which has shrunk in size with the development of technology, all men are truly neighbors, and we have to practice tolerance and learn to live together. This involves inevitably a sharing of our total resources, which is accomplished to some extent in the affluent societies of the West by taxing the rich, providing social security for the poor, and by various other devices. We need to have a similar mechanism at the international level. Further, we have to realize that it is in the long-term interest of all countries, rich and poor, for the rich to help promote the social and economic development of the poor countries. This may involve large-scale transfer of resources, the reduction or elimination of trade barriers and other restrictions, and also enlarged assistance through the international organizations represented by the United Nations development system.

I now come to environment. I am glad to see that this question has attracted the interest of young people the world over. We are all familiar with the facts which have given rise to this problem in such an acute form. In the first place, we must recognize that science and technology, which have done so much to help raise living standards, especially among the affluent countries, have also been largely responsible for the new problems of pollution that we face. The second element is, of course, the rapid growth of population. There is, however, one other element which should not be forgotten. I refer to the wasteful consumption patterns which have developed, in the name of convenience, especially in the advanced countries. This again is an area where we must recognize that every individual, be he a householder, the driver of a motor vehicle, or an entrepreneur, contributes to the problem by his individual actions which produce, unbeknown to him, such a terrible cumulative effect on pollution. If we are to put a stop to pollution and reverse this trend, action has to begin with education at the individual level. In addition to the pollution of the atmosphere, I have also been deeply concerned, as I have observed earlier, by the reports coming in of the dangerous trends toward pollution of the seas. This undoubtedly requires international regulation, and perhaps the United Nations is in the best position to help in establishing such a regimen. However, mere regulation will not succeed until, at the individual level, all of us realize that ultimately we pay an enormous social price for pollution, and this price-tag is probably much higher than the aggregate benefits that we derive as individuals from our current practices. I am convinced that this is an area where individual awareness and cooperation are as essential as national and international regulatory action.

Last, but not least, I would like to refer to the question of education. I have often heard it said, especially by older people, that the young people have a lot to learn. This may be true. I would say, however, that older people also have a lot to learn. Even more, and more important, we of the older generation have a lot to unlearn. We have to unlearn specifically those outmoded concepts to which I have referred, because it is only then that we will succeed in bridging, if not eliminating, the generation gap which has been the cause of so much comment during recent years.

Elsewhere I have paid tribute to the broadmindedness of the younger generation and their freedom from many of the prejudices that have afflicted us of an older generation. I am convinced that true progress toward peace can be made only when the peoples of the United Nations, young and old, are able to unlearn and forget such outmoded ideas as the concept of unlimited national sovereignty and take a broader and more modern view. Basically, we have to recognize that the idea of human solidarity transcends the idea of national sovereignty. Equally, we have to recognize that international responsibility can be realized only by individuals recognizing and accepting responsibility for their own actions toward the common goal. It is with these thoughts in mind that I have proposed that an international university be established where these ideas may be inculcated in young people from all parts of the world, with the hope that over the years such a university may have a great "multiplier" effect.

My young friends! You will no doubt debate these issues and many others and I am sure you will put forward many thoughts and discuss many ideas which I have not included in this statement. I want you to know that I personally await the outcome of your deliberations, and the conclusions that you may reach on these issues, with the greatest interest.

May your youth, your unselfishness, and your idealism bless you with the inspiration of all those earlier generations of youth who throughout history have shown the world its new ways and exits from antiquated beliefs and tensions. May your Assembly be marked by a view of the future of mankind as luminous as those of the revolutionaries who in the past have given us such notable documents as the Declaration of Independence, the declaration of human rights, and the manifesto for economic and social justice.

I wish you a most successful conference.

---

2. Statement at the Closing Meeting

NEW YORK   JULY 17, 1970

As THIS FIRST World Youth Assembly is drawing to a close, I would like to compliment all of you on your hard work. I know it was for you all a race against time, since you were given a very limited period in which to produce your reports and recommendations. Many of us feel that the

SOURCE: UN Press Release SG/SM/1304.

participants in this Assembly, in their nine-day deliberations, have been as productive as the diplomats who meet here each year for the General Assembly.

Generally there has prevailed throughout the Assembly a friendly atmosphere. You have all participated with a sense of purpose in meetings. Many of you have also enjoyed with equal zest the nonconference, extracurricular activities prepared for you. By your behavior and your spirit of cooperation, you have belied the predictions of some people that this gathering would end in utter chaos and disorder.

I would like to commend you in particular for your freedom from insular attitudes toward problems discussed in the plenary, as well as in the commissions. I am told that while there were groups which took a special interest in a certain number of problems, they were not necessarily along strict national or regional lines. Such an approach is a prerequisite for constructive action at the international level.

Many of you expressed your deep individual convictions without regard for the position taken by your respective governments. If a genuine international community is to be established, it is my belief that it can only be on the basis of very deeply held convictions of individuals rather than on the basis of attitudes taken by governments along traditional lines. The opinions you have expressed and the proposals you have made may not always have been in the polished language of diplomats, and many of them may not represent new or fresh ideas. It was, rather, the vigor and frankness with which you expressed these views that made your deliberations so valuable. You have made full use of this international forum, which is an increasingly important factor in the formation of world public opinion.

The debates at the Youth Assembly have made it clear that youth are to be treated not as an isolated element in society but as an integral part of it. As such, the ideological, political, and other preoccupations of the world were bound to reflect themselves in the attitude of youth, sometimes in a way even sharper than the opinions expressed by the older generation. This is natural and should serve to caution those who tend to segregate youth and idealize youth. Youth are very much a part of our world. They are the inheritors of the earth and as such they not only have the right to be heard, but also the duty to contribute in a concrete manner to the creation of a better world.

This Youth Assembly was an entirely unprecedented undertaking on the part of the United Nations. However, we greatly benefited from the advice of certain international youth organizations, and our attitude was from the outset not to impose on you any pattern or preconceived framework. Thus, you were left with a large degree of freedom and initiative in devising the organization, rules of procedure, and other activities. Under the circumstances, some confusion was perhaps inevitable regarding the conduct of meetings, voting, the status of participants, alternates and advisers, the way in which credentials should be handled, etc. With the help of the Steering Committee, however, you overcame many of these difficulties in time to enable the Assembly to tackle its substantive task. In this regard, I would like to pay special tribute to the officers you elected to the Steering Committee and to the four commissions for the way in which they guided this entirely new and difficult conference.

The United Nations will probably never be the same after the World Youth Assembly. Your informal manners, the practice of certain commissions to limit the statements to five minutes or even less, the recognition of speakers by number rather than by country, and most of all the principle of individual participation rather than governmental representation—all of these may affect in some way the practice of United Nations organs in the long run.

Before closing, I would like to ask you most sincerely to persevere in your deep concern over the state of the world today. We need the positive contribution and active cooperation of youth in assuring international peace, in achieving the goals of the Second United Nations Development Decade and in the First Disarmament Decade, in safeguarding human rights, and above all in bringing the present world situation closer to the ideals of the Charter of the United Nations.

I should like to close by thanking all the participants for gathering here for a brief but most intensive period of discussion across national boundaries. I would also like to thank the numerous staff members and volunteers who unstintingly contributed their talents and energy, and who often worked late into the night or even into the small hours of the morning.

I wish you all a safe return to your homes, and every success in your future endeavors.

THE SITUATION
IN THE MIDDLE EAST

It was apparent at U Thant's press conference of February 17, 1970, that the Middle East situation was very much on the minds of the United Nations correspondents and of the Secretary-General himself. Although the end of the Nigerian civil war was still a major public issue, the lack of progress in Middle East peace efforts weighed heavily upon the thoughts of the Secretary-General. His special representative, Gunnar Jarring, had temporarily suspended his peace efforts, but was waiting in Geneva for consultations. Thant had already been conferring in New York with General Odd Bull, chief of the United Nations Truce Supervision Organization in Palestine (UNTSO), who was responsible for the United Nations Observer teams along the Suez Canal. At the time Thant was working closely with the representatives of the four big powers who were trying to agree upon guidelines for reactivated Jarring talks. One of the problems was that the big powers were unable to agree on a common approach. Since his return from Africa in January, the Secretary-General had been in "constant contact" with the representatives of the four powers, seeking to help them come forward with guidelines. One of the immediate concerns of the big four, he said, was to reinstate the 1967 cease-fire, which had broken down completely because of repeated violations. That was the major reason for the presence of General Bull in New York. Thant told the correspondents that "only very strong measures can avert a new catastrophe" in the Middle East. The inescapable conclusion, he said, is that United Nations attempts to maintain a cease-fire in the Suez Canal area had "become increasingly unsuccessful."

The question was raised once again as to whether the United Nations could continue to stand on the resolution of November 22, 1967, as a basis for peace or whether the time had not come for new initiatives. Thant said that he himself did not plan any new approach, but that it was up to the Security Council to take any steps it might consider necessary. He insisted that he had no deadline in mind for new action to implement the 1967 resolution. "I still believe," he said, "that the big four can come up with a formulation of guidelines on certain basic issues, not necessarily a comprehensive agreement on all issues provided for in the Security Council resolution of November 22, 1967. I have been exchanging views with the permanent representatives of the big four, as I have said, since my return from Africa. . . . I am not pessimistic about the outcome of the deliberations of the big four. I do not think it would be realistic to set a timetable or a deadline."

Thant said he had some new ideas to present to Jarring when they met in Geneva, but he made it clear that he had no intention of exercising his rights under Article 99 of the United Nations Charter to call a Security Council meeting on the Middle East situation. Since no member of the Council had indicated to him that a meeting on the Middle East should be held, he said, "I do not think it would be appropriate on my part to invoke Article 99 at this stage."

At a luncheon of the United Nations Correspondents Association on June 11, Thant reported that prospects for peace in the Middle East had continued to worsen. He said the will for an end of the violence was "tragically lacking" and that the positions of the parties appeared to have "hardened." Jarring's efforts were at a standstill at that time and Jarring was back at his post as Sweden's ambassador to the USSR, hopefully awaiting some new guidelines from the representatives of the four big powers who were continuing their private talks at United Nations Headquarters. In mid-June, the Secretary-General received a briefing from United States officials on a new United States proposal, which had been presented to Israel, Egypt, and Jordan, calling on each of them to designate representatives to carry on discussions under Jarring's auspices at places and times to be recommended by Jarring. The United States informed the Secretary-General on August 7 that the three governments had accepted the American proposal and had agreed to a standstill cease-fire for a period of ninety days effective from August 7 until November 5. Jarring was summoned to United Nations Headquarters immediately to reactivate his mission. It seemed that a new phase of the peace efforts was about to begin. Difficulties developed at once, however. Egypt and Jordan designated their representatives for the discussions, but Israel delayed on the ground that the Arab countries were now observing the agreed cease-fire. In the Introduction to his 1970 annual report, issued on September 14, the Secretary-General described the Israeli stand as a "severe setback" to Middle East peace efforts. Thant was convinced, nevertheless, that the United States initiative should be pursued as "the one chance of a breakthrough to peace in the Middle East." On November 4, the General Assembly adopted a resolution urging the parties directly concerned to instruct their representatives to resume contact with Jarring. The resolution also called for a three-month extension of the cease-fire. Jarring sent a letter to Israeli Foreign Minister Abba Eban on November 19 inviting Israel to instruct its representatives to participate in the proposed discussions at United Nations Headquarters. Israel finally agreed on December 30.

1. Statement on Meeting with
Secretary of State William S. Rogers

NEW YORK   AUGUST 4, 1970

IN THE LIGHT of the information, written and oral, available to me thus far, and particularly after the very helpful talk yesterday with Secretary of State Rogers, I am encouraged by recent developments in the quest for peace in the Middle East. There is now, I feel, a real chance to make important advances. Who knows when, or even if, there will be another chance? Over-optimism, however, should be avoided. In such situations, there is often a tendency for some to expect too much, too soon. Ambassador Jarring is here, engaging in intensive consultations as envisaged in the announcement concerning him made last Friday. He is ready to undertake all that may be required of him under his mandate. The United Nations is prepared to provide any other assistance whenever called upon.

There will be, of course, many questions and much speculation about what may lie ahead. Many of the questions are either unanswerable at this stage, or prudence, in the interest of progress, would dictate that they remain unanswered for the time being. Speculation about delicate and sensitive issues knows no bounds and often serves to complicate and confuse matters.

The United Nations is most fortunate to have the services at this time of Ambassador Jarring, a wise and veteran diplomat who is a master of that art of quiet diplomacy most likely to be productive in the Middle East today.

It is my intention, hopefully very soon, to inform the members of the Security Council of current efforts and developments by means of a report to the Council.

SOURCE: UN Press Release SG/SM/1313.

2. Note on the Jarring Mission

NEW YORK   AUGUST 7, 1970

I HAVE BEEN informed by the government of the United States that the peace proposal initiated by that government has been accepted by the governments of Israel, Jordan, and the United Arab Republic. Subsequently, Ambassador Gunnar V. Jarring, my special representative to the Middle East, has been given confirmation of these acceptances by the permanent representatives to the United Nations of those three governments.

In accordance with that proposal and in the light of these acceptances, Ambassador Jarring has addressed to me on August 7 the following letter:

The United Arab Republic, Jordan and Israel advise me that they agree:

(A) that having accepted and indicated their willingness to carry out resolution 242 (1967) in all its parts, they will designate representatives to discussions to be held under my auspices, according to such procedure and at such places and times as I may recommend, taking into account as appropriate each side's preference as to method of procedure and previous experience between the parties.

(B) that the purpose of the aforementioned discussions is to reach agreement on the establishment of a just and lasting peace between them based on (1) mutual acknowledgment by the United Arab Republic, Jordan, and Israel of each other's sovereignty, territorial integrity, and political independence, and (2) Israeli withdrawal from territories occupied in the 1967 conflict, both in accordance with resolution 242 (1967).

(C) that, to facilitate my task of promoting agreement as set forth in resolution 242 (1967), the parties will strictly observe, effective July 1 at least until October 1, the cease-fire resolutions of the Security Council.

Ambassador Jarring and I are of the opinion that there now is a reasonable basis on which to renew immediately his contacts with the parties with a view toward initiating discussions under his auspices on the issues. It may be said, therefore, that the Jarring Mission is now

SOURCE: Security Council Official Records, Twenty-fifth Year, Supplement for July, August and September 1970, document S/9902.

reactivated. In fact, Ambassador Jarring is already intensively at work in this new stage of his peace effort. I may add by way of explanation that the Jarring Mission, since its inception in 1967, has never been suspended or inoperative, although at times, due to unavoidable circumstances, it has been relatively inactive.

This marks, in my view, an important step forward in the search for peace in the Middle East. It is a beginning, a welcome first step. It is already clear, however, that the road ahead is long, arduous, and uncertain. But if only there is a will for peace, all obstacles can be surmounted and peace will be achieved.

I extend to Ambassador Jarring my very best wishes for his success in meeting this new challenge. He may rely on my unfailing support and he certainly merits the support of all governments and peoples in the world who believe in peace.

From Statement on the United States Decision to Dump Nerve Gas into the Atlantic Ocean

NEW YORK   AUGUST 7, 1970

. . . IT IS APPARENT that the safety problems and adverse environmental effects resulting from dumping nerve gases in the Atlantic Ocean are far from clear. There is, so far, no established evidence that the ocean can easily assimilate or dilute these gases beyond their capacity to be harmful.

It is, therefore, understandable that individuals in this country as well as governments, e.g., Barbados and the United Kingdom (on behalf of Bermuda and the Bahamas), have already voiced their concern over the decision of the United States Army to dump nerve gases in the Atlantic Ocean.

This decision, in the Secretary-General's view, clearly contravenes General Assembly resolution 2340 (XXII). This resolution points out, *inter alia,* "the importance of preserving the seabed and the ocean floor and the subsoil thereof . . . from actions and uses which might be detrimental to the common interests of mankind."

This decision also runs counter to the provisions of clause (b) of Article 25 of the 1958 Geneva Convention on the High Seas, which reads as follows:

All states shall cooperate with the competent international organizations in taking measures for the prevention of pollution of the seas or air space above, resulting from any activities with radioactive materials or other harmful agents.

While the Secretary-General is gratified at the prospect of the imminent disposal of quantities of such deadly weapons, he concludes that this is a question which requires further study. He feels that it would

SOURCE: UN Press Release SG/SM/1314.

certainly re-establish public confidence at the international level if the problem could be studied by a group of prominent international scientists—specialists in chemical and bacteriological weapons, oceanography, and ecology—so that safe and acceptable methods of destroying such weapons or rendering them harmless could be evolved for the future.

Transcript of Press Conference Dealing with the Question of a Third Term and Other Subjects

NEW YORK   SEPTEMBER 10, 1970

U THANT's second term as Secretary-General was due to expire on December 31, 1971, but even as early as the spring of 1970 feelers were being put forward privately to ascertain his attitude toward a third term. He had been approached by a number of Member states, including some of the big powers, who let it be known that they would support him if he would consent to serve either another full term or even part of a term. His position was similar to the stand he had taken in 1966, that he believed one term was enough and that he did not intend to offer himself for a third term. Recalling that he had reversed himself in 1966, many did not take his statements as a categorical refusal to accept a new appointment. Speculation continued. At a luncheon of the United Nations Correspondents Association on June 11, he reiterated his belief that no one should aspire to the office for more than one term, but left the way open by saying, "I do not think it is the time or the occasion to make any categorical announcement about my future plans." On July 7, he told a press conference in Geneva that he still was not ready to announce his intentions but he added: "Personally speaking, from a purely selfish point of view, I would be happier if I could leave my post even before the expiry of my present term." Two months later, at a press conference on September 10, he said, "I have no intention of offering myself for a further term," but he added that he would not make a categoric public announcement until later. During a private talk with a newspaper correspondent[1] on October 30, Thant said he had definitely decided to step down at the end of his term and was already making other plans for the future. His reason for delaying a public announcement, he said, was that his advisers felt he would lose some of his effectiveness once he became a lame duck. The Secretary-General authorized the publication of his remarks without direct attribution to him. He continued, however, to withhold the promised public announcement and United Nations diplomats continued to delay their search for a successor.

[1]Max Harrelson, chief United Nations correspondent of the Associated Press.

This, of course, was only one of many subjects covered at the September 10 press conference. Another was the China question.

By 1970 there were signs that the twenty-year deadlock over the representation of China in the United Nations was approaching its end. There was increasing defection of United States allies from the rigid American opposition to the seating of the People's Republic of China. There also was a movement, at least an exploratory approach, toward a possible compromise which would seat the Peking government without expelling the Chinese Nationalists. No such proposal had been put forward formally, but the United States was considering a switch to the so-called "two Chinas" policy, or, as Washington preferred to call it, "dual representation." The United States was aware of the erosion among its supporters and some United States officials were conceding privately that Washington would not be able to hold the line against Peking much longer. Furthermore, relations between the United States and the People's Republic were beginning to thaw perceptibly, adding to the feeling that changes were in the wind.

The question of a possible "two Chinas" solution was raised at Thant's February 17 press conference. He sidestepped a direct reply on the ground that this was a matter for the competent organs of the United Nations to consider and decide, and that it would not be proper for the Secretary-General to venture an opinion. He did say that he was all for greater contacts between the People's Republic and the rest of the world and that "the character of the relationship between China and the outside world will dominate the history of the seventies." Thant was asked whether he had ever considered undertaking any sort of initiative to get the Peking régime in the United Nations. He replied that this was a matter for the Member states. "I am afraid," he said, "that my role in such an enterprise would be minimal." At a press conference in Geneva on July 7, he was asked whether there was any direct contact between his office and the People's Republic with respect to his proposal for a new Indo-China conference. He had no direct line of communications with Peking, he answered, but he used third parties if there were important matters to transmit. He added that some sort of arrangement should be devised by which Peking could be involved in the discussion of international issues while the question of China representation was being debated year after year.

On September 10, as the General Assembly prepared to convene for its twenty-fifth session and for another round of debate on China representation, the Secretary-General was asked whether he foresaw any possible change or whether he intended to take any initiative to speed a settlement. He said he did not expect any change at the 1970 Assembly. His personal guess, he said, was that no change would take place before November or December 1972. This was taken by correspondents to mean that the turning point would be the 1972 presidential election in the United States. He was asked whether this was what he had in mind, but he declined to elaborate. When the issue came before the Assembly for a decision on November 11, the vote was 48 in favor of transferring

China's seat to the People's Republic and 56 against, with 21 abstentions. The question of a "two Chinas" solution was not raised.

THE SECRETARY-GENERAL: I have a short statement to make at the outset of this press conference. It is unusual in that it expresses a wish on my part and makes a request of you which—though exceptional in our meetings—will, in the light of the understanding and candor which have always prevailed in our relations over the years, be readily understood and fully respected by you now.

I shall have a few comments to make on developments in the Middle East. Beyond that I do not wish to say anything further about the Middle East at this meeting, and I very much hope that you will respect my request to you not to press questions on this subject upon me.

The reason for this unaccustomed, indeed unprecedented, restrictiveness is simple enough. As you can imagine, I have had the Middle East very much on my mind in recent days—little else, in fact. The situation is so complicated and delicate, there is so much sensitivity and emotion, everything is so much in a state of touch and go just now, that there is very little that one can say publicly that could be at all helpful. On the other hand, almost any comment at this stage could be harmful in one way or another.

You will understand readily that my overriding concern is to further the cause of peace in the Middle East. I am not willing at this critical juncture to take any risk of saying anything which could be construed as obstructing peace.

The current peace effort in the Middle East, begun only so recently with hope and expectation because there was no other hopeful sign, has now had a severe setback even before it had really got under way. Of this there can be no doubt. But I am not yet prepared to say that it is beyond salvage. This is a time to exert every possible constructive effort—and this we are doing, I assure you.

Ambassador Jarring continues to be here and fully available to all the parties. Indeed, he has been carrying on his effort throughout the crisis of the standstill arrangements, with regard to which he has no relationship and no responsibility. In fact, as you know, Ambassador Jarring

SOURCE: *UN Monthly Chronicle*, Vol. VII, October 1970, pp. 30–38.

was even able to carry on talks with the parties while the cease-fire in the Suez sector was completely broken down—for many months, indeed for a couple of years. Today I am very happy to be able to say that the cease-fire in the Suez sector is being observed scrupulously. There is no fighting.

The matter of the standstill arrangements involves, of course, not Ambassador Jarring or the United Nations, but the United States and the two parties concerned. It bears emphasis that this is an area in which the United Nations has no responsibility because none has been given to it.

My immediate concentration will be on getting the Jarring effort back on the tracks. It is good that, despite the setback, Ambassador Jarring, with his typical resilience and fortitude, is neither hopeless nor despondent. He is persevering in his task in the conviction, which I fully share, that this is the one chance for a breakthrough to peace in the Middle East.

That I deeply deplore hijackings is well known, and my attitude toward them has been often stated, most recently at the beginning of this week, on September 8. Let me repeat what I said then: "However understandable and even justifiable some of the grievances of the perpetrators may be, their acts are savage and inhuman." I am glad that the Security Council, only yesterday, took the first step, which I hope will generate further international action, to put a stop to this return to the law of the jungle.

I am horrified by the sudden increase in the number of incidents involving innocent international air travelers. Let me cite an earlier case. On August 17, 1970, I made an oral appeal to the government of Israel through the mission of Israel to the United Nations for the release of the two Algerian citizens detained in Israel on August 14, 1970, as they were in transit through Lydda airport on a BOAC aircraft. Having had no reply from the government of Israel, I reiterated my appeal on August 26, 1970, by a note handed to the chargé d'affaires of the Israel mission. In the note, I made reference to the wide concern which exists in the international community regarding the need to ensure freedom of air travel. I also recalled that the government of Israel has in the past publicly expressed its strong belief in the unimpaired movement of persons and goods by air. Mention was also made in my note of the representations which the African Group had made to me conveying the grave preoccupation of the African states at the continued detention of the two Algerian citizens in Israel, and requesting me to take all appropriate measures to secure their release.

On the occasion of handing the note to the Israel chargé d'affaires, I expressed to him that it was my intention to send a high-level representative to Israel for the purpose of discussing with the appropriate Israeli authorities the question of the detention of the two Algerian citizens. I regret to have to state that as of this moment, I have received no reply to my appeal, nor any reaction to the sending of a high-level representative to Israel.

In regard to this matter, I have been in touch with the International Civil Aviation Organization (ICAO), with the International Air Transport Association (IATA) and with the International Federation of Air Line Pilots Associations (IFALPA). These organizations have also been active on this question. I shall continue to exercise my good offices for the purpose of obtaining the release of the two detained Algerian citizens.

May I now have your questions other than those relating to the situation in the Middle East, as I have just requested.

QUESTION: Sir, do you expect a meeting of the big four in New York next month and, if so, do you believe that it can produce any political achievements regarding the troubled situation in the world?

THE SECRETARY-GENERAL: As you are aware, the commemorative session of the General Assembly will be attended by many heads of state and heads of government of Member states. It is my belief that it is a historic occasion, and the heads of state and heads of government who happen to be here at this historic occasion should seize the opportunity to exchange views on matters of mutual interest to them and of interest to the United Nations. I have presented some ideas about some of the possibilities, the possible opportunities some heads of state and heads of government might seize. Up to now, of course, I have not issued any official invitation for a meeting, but I am convinced that while they are here, they will take the opportunity of exchanging views, either collectively or bilaterally. And in my view this is one of the most important developments of the twenty-fifth session of the General Assembly.

QUESTION: Mr. Secretary-General, could you share your ideas with us, these ideas on the opportunities the heads of state might utilize?

THE SECRETARY-GENERAL: I have presented some ideas, particularly to the governments of the permanent members of the Security Council.

Since these are privileged, I am sorry that I cannot disclose them at this moment, but at the appropriate moment I am sure I will be able to disclose them.

QUESTION: Mr. Secretary-General, would it violate the restrictions you have requested on this news conference if I were to ask if you have had the opportunity of communicating the Security Council decision last night either directly or indirectly to the Palestinian guerrillas and/or the International Red Cross?

THE SECRETARY-GENERAL: On the basis of the resolution and on the basis of the language employed in the resolution, immediately after the conclusion of the discussions yesterday evening I transmitted the text of the resolution to all Member states and to all those states which are members of the specialized agencies.

As you all know, the consensus was adopted in the form of a resolution.

QUESTION: Do you see anything further that the United Nations can do to prevent future hijackings—that is, is there any action beyond a resolution by the General Assembly or action by ICAO? Is there anything definite that the United Nations can do?

THE SECRETARY-GENERAL: The international community is increasingly anxious to take effective steps to put a stop to these criminal acts. As you know, the convention is before ICAO, and I have been in contact with ICAO and other relevant agencies. An item on hijacking was before the last session of the General Assembly and there may be such an item before the next session, at which time I am sure that concrete and effective measures will be devised by the membership at the forthcoming session of the General Assembly.

QUESTION: Can you tell us whether any member of the United Nations family has been involved in any hijacking anywhere in the world and whether any special precautions are taken in connection with the many people of the United Nations family who travel all over the world now?

THE SECRETARY-GENERAL: To my knowledge no member of the United Nations family—that means the Secretariat of the United Nations and the secretariats of the specialized agencies—has been involved in recent hijacking incidents. Of course, the matter will come up for discussion at the forthcoming meetings of the Administration Committee on Co-ordination here.

QUESTION: Several times this year you have given top priority in some of your statements to the question of the universality of the United Nations, especially with regard to China. Now, with the General Assembly coming, do you see any possible change or do you intend yourself to take an initiative to push this question along?

THE SECRETARY-GENERAL: The question of the representation of China is an item before the forthcoming session of the General Assembly. Personally speaking, I do not see any change in the attitude of the General Assembly this year from that of the membership in previous years. But if I may venture an opinion, I personally do not think that the involvement of the People's Republic of China in United Nations activities will take place earlier than November or December 1972. That is only a personal guess.

QUESTION: In the agenda of the General Assembly session which will open next week, I wonder if you could tell us which of the items on the agenda stand out, in your view, as the most vital that will be debated.

THE SECRETARY-GENERAL: It is very difficult for me to characterize an item or items as being of paramount importance. Of course, to me all items are important. But if I am to categorize the items I would say that the items can be categorized into four or five groups: first of all, the items dealing with disarmament, that is, items involving the consideration of the report of the Conference of the Committee on Disarmament and other items inscribed by Members; then, in the second grouping, I would say items dealing with development, that is, not only items dealing with the report of the Economic and Social Council but other items inscribed by the Member states; and, in the third category, I would say items dealing with colonial problems.

Broadly speaking, those are the three categories of items before the General Assembly. But I must say that the peace-keeping capabilities of the United Nations should, in my view, receive top priority. I have been following the deliberations and discussions in the Committee of 33 (decolonization committee) and I very much hope that that Committee will submit a very positive, constructive, and forward-looking report to the General Assembly.

I attach very great importance to this aspect and also to another aspect, which is basic to the effective functioning of this Organization, that is, the financial solvency of the United Nations. I very much hope the membership will pay very close attention to this particular item.

QUESTION: I was fascinated by your personal forecast of the importance of November or December 1972. Do you have in mind the elections in the United States that fall and perhaps the resulting Vietnam settlement as a precondition to the entry of China, when you are thinking in these terms?

THE SECRETARY-GENERAL: Well, Mr. Halasz,[1] I do not wish to elaborate on the point I have made earlier. At the appropriate time, of course, I hope to be able to elaborate on this idea.

QUESTION: Would you take the time to tell us your latest assessment of the fighting going on in Southeast Asia and the prospects for peace? Things seem to be in a state of complete deadlock there.

THE SECRETARY-GENERAL: Mr. Raghavan,[2] as I have been saying in the last two years, in my view the first priority for peace in Vietnam is the emergence of a broad-based government in Saigon which is likely to have the allegiance of the vast majority of the people of South Vietnam. This view has been expressed by Mr. George Ball[3] and many other eminent Americans who have given a great deal of thought to this problem. Without this first priority for peace I do not believe that there will be any perceptible progress either in the negotiations in Paris or in negotiations in the area. I realize that this priority, this emergence of a broad-based government in Saigon, this idea has been endorsed not only by many thinking Americans, but, to my knowledge, by many leaders in many parts of the world.

QUESTION: You seemed to imply at the last United Nations Correspondents Association luncheon that you will stay on as Secretary-General as long as you feel that you can assist in bringing the Indo-China war to an end. Is this still your attitude or could you give us a more direct answer whether you will be available for another term of office when this one expires?

THE SECRETARY-GENERAL: I think there has been some mistaken assumption in linking the war in Vietnam with my decision regarding the next term. It was not my purpose to link my decision with any particular international development. My views on the job of Secretary-General are well known. I have been saying for several years that nobody should aspire to serve as the Secretary-General of the United Nations for more than one term. I still hold that view. I made this observation not with any

---

[1]Louis Halasz, Radio Free Europe.

[2]Chakravarti Raghavan, Press Trust of India.

[3]Former permanent representative of the United States to the United Nations.

particular development or developments in mind. I am thinking primarily in the context of the nature of the office in which I am functioning. In fact, I have no intention of offering myself for a further term. But I do not believe that this is the time or the occasion for me to make a public announcement categorically. That will be for another occasion.

QUESTION: An American organization calling itself the Jewish Defense League, through its leader on a television program yesterday or the day before yesterday, announced that Arab blood will spill in New York. And this is the same organization that attacked Dr. Saadat Hasan, a member of the Yemen delegation. Still nothing has been done by the American police against this organization. Now you have more than a couple of hundred Arab employees in the United Nations. Have you taken any precautions to protect these Arab employees of the United Nations?

THE SECRETARY-GENERAL: All necessary measures have been taken for the safety and security of the Arab employees of the Secretariat. Beyond that, of course, I do not wish to comment.

QUESTION: Mr. Secretary-General, may I ask you, without violating the vow of silence on substantive Middle East issues, whether the clarification made in your name by the United Nations spokesman as to what you intended, or rather did not intend, to say in your remarks to newsmen on the morning of September 8, whether that clarification stands or whether you are now taking it back or possibly modifying it.

THE SECRETARY-GENERAL: I am not very clear about your question. Clarification on what point?

QUESTION: There was a clarification put out by the United Nations spokesman saying that you did not intend to equate the detention of passengers on regular commercial airlines with the hijacking of planes, the detention of hostages, and the blowing up of planes.

THE SECRETARY-GENERAL: Yes, that was exactly my intention when I made my statement when I came into the office in the morning. I put out a clarification in the afternoon. That is still my attitude.

QUESTION: Sir, it looks likely that both East and West Germany may apply for membership in the United Nations. Do you feel that this is a good move and do you feel that the same thing should take place in the case of other divided countries such as North and South Korea or North and South Vietnam?

THE SECRETARY-GENERAL: I do not think that I can express my views on this, but, personally speaking, the trend in Europe has been most encouraging, thanks to the vision and imagination and wisdom of the leaders, from both the East and the West. If both East and West Germany wish to join the United Nations as Members, of course it is up to the Member states to deliberate, discuss, and decide. But as far as my personal feelings are concerned, the admission of two Germanies would be relatively easier than the admissions of two Koreas or two Vietnams, for reasons you will understand.

QUESTION: I would like to go back to the China issue, if I may, for a moment. I believe you forecast some of your feelings about what would happen on the issue of Chinese representation when you held a press conference in Geneva in July. At that time you cited a need for some kind of arrangement whereby Peking could become involved in discussions on the key issues of war and peace. Do you have any evidence of any interest among the membership and has anything been done by Member states or by your office to forward this notion of an alternative or interim arrangements?

THE SECRETARY-GENERAL: Well, there has been a great deal of interest among the membership on this question. There is a question of the involvement of the People's Republic of China in the important activities of the United Nations, for instance, the discussions on disarmament. I feel very strongly, as you all know, that the Conference of the Committee on Disarmament will succeed, and succeed in the manner in which it was meant to succeed, only with the participation of France and the People's Republic of China. I have been discussing this aspect of the problem with many Member states. There is a very substantial volume of opinion in favor of this. Of course, it is up to the Member states to bring this up publicly and officially in the principal deliberative organs.

QUESTION: As a matter of clarification, would you also tell us whether you distinguish the passengers and crew who were hijacked and detained against their will from those who are being held because of participation in the hijacking. Apparently this three-hour debate behind the scenes seemed to turn largely on wording which the Arabs are reported to believe indicates that all passengers arrested or detained as a result of hijackings shall be freed without exception.

THE SECRETARY-GENERAL: I do not think that it would be helpful if I attempted to interpret the consensus reached yesterday by the Security Council. As far as the type of offenders is concerned, I made my statement on September 8 and my clarification on the afternoon of the same date.

QUESTION: Mr. Secretary-General, in your support of that September 8 clarification by the United Nations spokesman you seem to have taken the position that there is a difference between personnel detained on commercial aircraft and those detained as a result of the action of the hijackers. On the other hand, you yourself devoted a large concluding section of your statement this morning to one aspect of the total situation, to wit, the Algerians detained by Israel; whereas, according to press reports, there are now three hundred civilians being detained by the people whose action you yourself have denounced. Would you kindly help us interpret these two apparently divergent positions by the Secretary-General?

THE SECRETARY-GENERAL: I do not think that one should judge the importance of a matter by the length or shortness of my statements. I have made my position very clear on September 8 in the morning and in the afternoon; I again made my position very clear this morning at the press conference. There is a difference, of course, between the categories of the offenders. When I say that certain actions of certain people are "savage and inhuman," it is just plain common sense to whom I am directing these comments. So please do not judge the importance of the matter on the length of my statement. That is not the right criterion.

QUESTION: Could you tell us, Sir, whether you have had any reaction from China itself to what you might call your initiative in having them participate in decisions?

THE SECRETARY-GENERAL: No.

QUESTION: Mr. Secretary-General, you mentioned important agenda items. I was wondering what new ideas and plans the United Nations has for involving youth in solving some of the world's problems.

THE SECRETARY-GENERAL: These particular problems will be featured in the report of the Committee for the Twenty-fifth Anniversary. The Committee is still actively engaged in drafting papers for the consideration of the membership of the General Assembly and I think that the Members will discuss this particular subject when it is submitted to the General Assembly in the form of the report of the Committee for the Twenty-fifth Anniversary.

QUESTION: Mr. Cy Tung, the Chinese multimillionaire who has made a bid of more than $3 million for the old liner *Queen Elizabeth,* says he would like to turn it into a floating university under the auspices of the United Nations. What do you think of this suggestion?

THE SECRETARY-GENERAL: I am not familiar with this idea, but it is a very interesting one, of course. When the offer is made officially I will refer it to the competent organs of the United Nations. I am sure that the international community will be most grateful for this generosity. As you know, the subject of an international university was before the Economic and Social Council this summer. It was referred for consideration to the United Nations Educational, Scientific and Cultural Organization General Conference and to the United Nations Institute for Training and Research. With the observations of UNESCO and UNITAR, the report will go back to the General Assembly, hopefully, in November. It is up to the Member states to decide on the future line of action.

QUESTION: Mr. Secretary-General, on the eve of the twenty-fifth regular session of the General Assembly, I am sure you know that the charge is constantly being made that the United Nations has failed, that conflicts continue to erupt in various parts of the world. On the eve of the commemorative session I wonder, inasmuch as you have been here some fifteen or sixteen years, with some ten years as Secretary-General, if you would give us your personal opinion about the United Nations and what its future is in the next five to ten years, whether it can really become an instrument for peace in the world.

THE SECRETARY-GENERAL: First of all, I must say that the United Nations has not failed—for the reasons I have stated on many previous occasions. Second, I must say that I am optimistic about the future of the United Nations. In fact, I am optimistic about the trend of events on the international scene, even including the Middle East situation. I say this deliberately because of the events particularly in Europe. The signing of the treaty between the Federal Republic of Germany and the Soviet Union, in my view, is one of the most memorable events in the history of international relations in the postwar period. Speaking of this détente in Europe—Europe, as you know, is the political capital of the world. Two world wars were generated in Europe. So Europe will continue to be responsible for the contribution of peace and stability in other parts of the world also, not only in the political field but also in the economic and colonial fields. And I am hopeful even regarding the Middle East situation.

As I have been saying, I am cautiously optimistic—for two main reasons, among others. First of all, there is an overwhelming body of opinion in the United Nations that the United Nations has a special responsibility to contribute toward a just and lasting peace in the Middle East. The vast majority of the membership subscribes to that view. Second, the permanent members of the Security Council in the course of their periodic meetings in the last two years have developed a kind of consensus, a common approach to the problem. In other words, the area of agreement regarding the final solution of the Middle East situation among the permanent members is much wider than the area of disagreement. This is a very heartening sign, not only from the point of view of the United Nations but also from the point of view of the international community. To my knowledge, in the history of the United Nations over the past twenty-five years there has been not one instance where all permanent members of the Security Council have had such a wide agreement on a major issue as they have now on the Middle East problem. This is a very encouraging sign. I am not suggesting that the four permanent members of the Security Council must institutionalize themselves into an organ or machinery divorced from the Security Council. That is far from my intention. The permanent members of the Security Coundil must operate within the framework of the Security Council and in this particular case within the framework of the relevant resolutions of the Security Council, and I am sure they are moving in that direction. That is why I am optimistic not only about the future of the United Nations but about the future of the human community, because of these trends and evidences.

QUESTION: I should like to return for a moment to your prepared statement. How is one to interpret the fact that the Secretary-General's statement focused on the differences between the Secretary-General and one Member state—that is, Israel—but did not mention the other Member states concerned: Egypt, where a plane was blown up; Jordan, where two or three planes are being held; Lebanon, which, according to all the news reports, including photographs, has aided the hijackers, even to the extent of giving a military escort to a commando who was being loaded on the BOAC plane yesterday?

THE SECRETARY-GENERAL: I am sorry to say that your hypothesis is not correct. I am not attempting to focus attention on a difference between me and a particular Member state. My views on hijacking and on aerial piracy are well known. I have used the strongest possible terms in condemnation of these criminal acts of hijacking, blowing up planes, and detaining innocent passengers. I do not think that I need to reiterate those views at this time. I am now merely reiterating what steps I have taken on the question of the detention of the two Algerians. This is the first time that I have disclosed publicly the action I have taken.

QUESTION: After your expression of optimism it seems that almost any other question will sound a bit like an anticlimax. But, since you have been abroad, I should like to ask you a question with regard to the Pan African Conference and the Conference of Non-Aligned States now in progress. Both of those conferences encompass a very important segment of the United Nations membership. What, in your opinion, is the likely impact on the work of the General Assembly?

THE SECRETARY-GENERAL: I attach very great importance to both those conferences.

As you all know, on September 1 I attended the opening meeting of the Organization of African Unity conference in Addis Ababa. I regard that conference as one of the most successful ever held by the OAU. For instance, the reconciliation between Nigeria and four African states was a testimony to the wisdom and the maturity of African leaders. In my view, the announcement of that reconciliation was a historic one. Many other resolutions have been adopted; I have not seen the text of all of them. I would only say that in my opinion the OAU conferences have a very definite impact on the work of the General Assembly.

In the same way, I attach very great importance to the Third Conference of the Non-Aligned Nations now taking place in Lusaka, Zambia. As you know, about half the membership of the United Nations is represented there. I am sure that the decisions they take and the resolutions they adopt will have a tremendous impact on the consideration of the items before the twenty-fifth session of the General Assembly. I wish the Conference success.

Aerial Hijacking and Terrorism,
from Statement at Dinner Inaugurating
the Twenty-Fifth Anniversary of the
Observance of United Nations Day

NEW YORK   SEPTEMBER 14, 1970

DESPITE ACCELERATED efforts by the United Nations and other international organizations, such as the International Federation of Air Line Pilots Associations, there was a sharp increase in the number of hijackings and attacks on commercial aircraft in 1970. These included an attack on an Israeli plane at the Munich airport on February 12, the explosion of a Swissair plane bound for Israel on February 24, and the hijacking and subsequent destruction of four Israeli aircraft on September 6 and 9. The latter incidents led to a meeting of the United Nations Security Council on September 9 and the adoption of a consensus expressing grave concern at the threat to innocent civilian lives. The Council also (1) appealed to all parties concerned for the immediate release of all passengers and crews, without exception, held as a result of hijackings and (2) called on states to take all possible legal steps to prevent further hijackings or any other interference with international civil air travel. U Thant continued to denounce all interference with international air travel as "savage and inhuman." In the Introduction to his 1970 annual report he said his concern had grown considerably during the year and that hijackings and attacks on civil air transport had reached the point "where confidence in the safety of international civil aviation is being seriously undermined." He said he would support any international action required to prevent and suppress acts of violence against civil aircraft. On September 14, the same day the Introduction was issued, he declared in the following speech that "it is high time that we go to the root of this phenomenon and treat its causes with novel remedies." He urged the creation of an international tribunal with full powers to extradite and punish hijackers, irrespective of their nationality or political affiliation. Thant said some would oppose this as a dangerous breach of national sovereignty, but that his answer would be: "The world has no other choice, because this is only the beginning of an inexorable trend. Nations and people must have the courage to resort to adequate new methods of international law and order. They must face with courage and imagination the new challenges of our times." He expressed the belief that the hijacking menace would end "if hijackers are served notice by all nations that there will be no immunity or amnesty."

. . . I could give numerous examples of the state of legislative, executive, and judicial unreadiness of the world to face the problems of international lawlessness with which we will be increasingly confronted. May I refer to a burning example of what I mean when I speak of the state of lawlessness in which the world finds itself under present-day technological circumstances. The word is on the lips of everyone: hijacking. This is a very revealing new trend of the times in which we live. Many hijackers have not been brought before any court of justice, although the overwhelming majority of peoples and governments have rightly condemned them. Countries which are ready to bring hijackers before a court of justice see their own airplanes hijacked. Any small group of extremists, however justifiable some of their grievances may be, can thus, through hijacking of aircraft or kidnaping of foreign diplomats, receive international attention, remain unpunished, involve innocent people, and sow the seeds of international anarchy.

It is high time that we go to the root of this phenomenon and treat its causes with novel remedies and not with old-time recipes to which it is largely immune. Within a civilized and orderly society, a criminal act is judged for its criminal character and not for its political significance. In your country, a Democrat does not applaud a robber because he has robbed a Republican, and vice versa. But internationally, this is exactly what all too frequently happens. One must start from the premise that international air transportation is an international activity which must be placed under an international rule of law. Airplanes are constructed in one country, owned by another, and may be insured in a third country. They travel from one country to another, use facilities all over the world, carry passengers of all nationalities, and are often piloted by men of many nationalities. I feel that all such passengers should be allowed to go about their business free of any interference, and transit passengers should not be detained under any pretext. Hijacking is of course in a

SOURCE: UN Press Release SG/SM/1333.

totally different category; it is a crime against an international service affecting a diversity of nations, men, women, and interests. This crime must be brought before an international tribunal defending the interests of all peoples and nations and not of any particular people or nation.

It may be of help if all governments pledge themselves to extradite hijackers, irrespective of their nationality or political affiliation, and bring them before an agreed international tribunal. Hijackers should be prosecuted in the name of the peoples of the world, for the benefit of all travelers and all pilots, irrespective of their nationality, and of all nations, irrespective of their political system. Some will tell me: "This will be a dangerous breach of national sovereignty." My answer will be: "The world has no other choice, because this is only the beginning of an inexorable trend. Nations and people must have the courage to resort to adequate new methods of international law and order. They must face with courage and imagination the new challenges of our times." Others will say: "Not all nations will agree to submit their nations to international jurisdiction and not all nations will be able to enforce such a new law." My answer will be: "National or federal justice took the same path and was confronted with the same difficulties at the beginning. These problems will be solved as more and more nations recognize the merit of the system and are ready to implement it. The situation is likely to change if hijackers are served notice by all nations that there will be no immunity or amnesty." . . .

From Introduction to the Twenty-Fifth
Annual Report

NEW YORK   SEPTEMBER 14, 1970

IN THE FOLLOWING Introduction, U Thant reviewed the major problems of the year as usual, but he also took advantage of the occasion to make some additional observations on the changes in the world as the United Nations observed its twenty-fifth anniversary. He noted that during the past quarter-century the "traditional concepts on which human society was based have been swept aside and new values are emerging." One-half of today's world population, he said, was born after the United Nations Charter came into existence. "Although the United Nations has played a significant and constructive role in bringing mankind safely to the threshold of a new age," he said, "it is incumbent upon us now to help the younger generation prepare itself for leadership in a world for which the young will soon assume responsibility." The outlook for the future, in his view, was one of "cautious optimism."

I. General

1. THE YEAR 1970 is a historic one in the life of the United Nations. The need for an effective world organization which can serve as a harmonizing agent for peace has never been so urgently felt by mankind. As we evaluate the past and look toward the future on the twenty-fifth anniversary of the Organization, some very basic questions are uppermost in our minds and are being given thoughtful consideration by governments, groups, and individuals all around the globe. What are the means by which the United Nations can play an increasingly vital role in the world of tomorrow? How can the United Nations make more effective use of its possibilities for reconciling differences between its sovereign Member states? What changes can be evolved in its methods of operation so that

SOURCE: General Assembly Official Records, Twenty-fifth Session, Supplement No. 1A (A/8001/Add.1), sections I, II, IV, VII, IX, X, XI.

its capacity for improving the human condition will be utilized to the full? It is my fervent hope that we shall find the answers to questions such as these and continue to make progress—no matter how slow and painstaking it may at times appear—toward realizing the noble goals set forth in the Charter of the United Nations.

2. In the last two or three years, I have been constrained to report only a general deterioration of the international situation. This year, on the eve of the twenty-fifth anniversary session of the General Assembly, I am happy to be able to express some cautious optimism in this regard, which derives from several factors. Of these, perhaps the most important is the fact that the mission of my special representative, Ambassador Jarring, has been reactivated. I can only hope that the parties concerned will show at last that will to peace which I have observed elsewhere to be indispensable to any hope of progress.

3. Last year I referred at some length to the tragic situation in Nigeria. Toward the very end of 1969 and early in 1970, I was able to undertake at long last my visit to several African countries, a trip which, to my great disappointment, had been deferred more than once. I learned much from this trip, not only of the magnitude of the problems facing Africa, but also of the enormous resources, both human and material, available in that continent. I was deeply impressed by the progress already made under the leadership of the distinguished African statesmen I was privileged to meet. I was equally gratified by the devotion that they all expressed to the purposes and principles of the Charter of the United Nations. It was also a particularly happy coincidence for me that the tragic civil war in Nigeria was brought to a conclusion while I was nearing the end of my trip. I was thus able to visit Lagos and exchange views with General Gowon and other Nigerian leaders before returning to New York.

4. A treaty has recently been concluded between the Union of Soviet Socialist Republics and the Federal Republic of Germany. I believe that this treaty has a positive significance. It is expected to contribute greatly to the improvement of relations between the two parties, to remove many factors of suspicion and promote confidence in their mutual relations and to create a good framework for their future cooperation. In the same context, I may mention other important developments in Europe, especially the bilateral and multilateral negotiations now under way, the objective of which is the solution of major problems of political,

economic, and cultural cooperation. Consideration is being given to the convening of a European security conference, and agreement on the agenda and on possible follow-up action seems to be emerging. It is particularly important to note that economic and cultural cooperation is considered not only as an instrument which could pave the way toward greater confidence among nations, but also as an effort which could greatly benefit from a new security arrangement. The United Nations, and more particularly the Economic Commission of Europe, has acquired considerable experience in this respect. I believe therefore that the United Nations machinery, particularly in the economic field, could perform a very useful function in any comprehensive and expanded program of cooperation which may be established for Europe. I also believe that such use of the existing machinery of the Organization would best link the efforts aimed at regional security in Europe with the global framework of greater security for all.

5. In the field of disarmament I reported only limited progress at this time last year. Since then, the two superpowers have been engaged in strategic arms limitation talks and I am hopeful that these talks will lead to concrete results when they are resumed in November. I am also glad to see the progress that was made in the Conference of the Committee on Disarmament during its recent meetings in Geneva with regard to the formulation of a treaty on the seabed. I hope that the draft treaty which has been submitted by the Conference for approval by the General Assembly will receive wide support from the Members of the United Nations. I have commented elsewhere with gratification on the progress made by the International Atomic Energy Agency in adjusting its safeguards system to the provisions of the Treaty on the Non-Proliferation of Nuclear Weapons.

6. This twenty-fifth anniversary year will also usher in the Second United Nations Development Decade. I hope that the important discussions now under way will enable all concerned to agree upon a global strategy for the Decade which will involve not only the cooperation of the rich and the poor countries, but also a considerable degree of cooperation between the countries of Western Europe, North America, and the socialist countries of Eastern Europe. I very much hope that the required level of cooperation will be forthcoming on the part of all concerned and will help to get the Second United Nations Development Decade off to a good start.

7. In the same context, I am glad to see the increasing interest being taken in some of the basic problems of the human environment not only in various United Nations bodies and other intergovernmental organs, but also by the public at large and especially young people. I have referred at length to this subject in some of my recent public pronouncements, which reflect my deep concern about this problem. I hope that the United Nations will be able to play a very useful role in this regard as a result of the important conference to be held at Stockholm in the summer of 1972 and the follow-up steps that may be taken in the wake of that conference. I am also glad to see the preoccupation of more and more countries and international bodies with the rapid growth of population and the many problems that it presents not only in respect of the living standards of the poor countries, but also in aggravating the problem of pollution, particularly in the advanced countries. In this context, I would like to make an appeal for more support for the United Nations Fund for Population Activities, which is being administered on my behalf by Mr. Paul Hoffman, administrator of the United Nations Development Programme.

8. The elements to which I have referred so far are the hopeful features of the world scene, which have led me to sound the note of cautious optimism with which I began. On the other hand, I must frankly acknowledge that there are many discouraging elements. I referred last year to the signs of improvement that could be seen in regard to devastated Vietnam. These signs have not led to any concrete results and we have actually witnessed not only a continuation of this war with all its tragic concomitants—the loss of life, especially of innocent civilians, and property. We have also seen how easy it is for the conflict to spread to the neighboring countries. I have purposely refrained from public comment so as to avoid prejudicing in any way the Paris talks, but I believe that some bold initiatives need to be taken urgently if the talks are to move forward from the present impasse.

9. Earlier I referred to some progress in the field of disarmament. On the other hand, I must mention the lack of any achievement with respect to a comprehensive test-ban treaty. I should also like to see more progress toward a complete ban on chemical and bacteriological weapons, the importance of which has been rightly stressed during recent months.

10. In the economic and social field I must again take note of the widening gap between the rich and the poor countries and also the risk,

to which I have referred elsewhere, of a virtual global trade war, which statesmanship should be able to avert.

11. Elsewhere I have also noted in detail some of our chronic problems, especially in Africa. The abhorrent practice of *apartheid* has continued in South Africa and it has been extended to Namibia, where the Republic of South Africa continues to defy the will of the international community and has proceeded to extend its authority over that territory. In the case of Southern Rhodesia, I have also mentioned the failure of the policy of economic sanctions to bring down the racist minority régime in that country. The pace of decolonization has been agonizingly slow and there is no progress whatever to report so far with respect to the Portuguese territories in Africa. Even more disconcerting is the fact that Portugal and South Africa have been giving assistance to the minority régime in Southern Rhodesia. In fact it is clear to me that, if it were not for this support, the mandatory economic sanctions imposed by the Security Council would have had a much greater impact on Southern Rhodesia's trade. I am somewhat encouraged by the fact that during recent months the Security Council has taken greater interest in the problems of South Africa. I refer here to the resolutions on Namibia adopted by the Council this year and the resolution redefining the embargo on the sale of arms to South Africa which was recently adopted by the Council.

12. One of the most satisfactory developments in the work of the United Nations during the year under review is undoubtedly the settlement, in May 1970, of a long-standing and potentially dangerous difference between Iran and the United Kingdom over the future status of Bahrain.

13. For some years past, the two governments had been seeking a means for a peaceful settlement of their differences which would also reflect the wishes of the people of Bahrain itself. In March 1970, following informal approaches, they asked me to exercise my good offices in this matter, and specifically to appoint a personal representative to ascertain the wishes of the people of Bahrain concerning its status. In so doing, both governments took the unusual step of agreeing in advance to accept the results of my findings, subject to their endorsement by the Security Council. In pursuance of their request, I appointed a personal representative, Mr. Vittorio Winspeare Guicciardi, director-general of the United Nations Office at Geneva, who, after consulting the people of Bahrain, reached the conclusion that the overwhelming majority of

Bahrainis "wished to gain recognition of their identity in a fully independent and sovereign state free to decide for itself its relations with other states." Following the unanimous endorsement of this report by the Security Council on May 11, 1970, Iran formally renounced its claim to Bahrain.

14. The Bahrain settlement is a striking example of how the good offices of the Secretary-General can be used for the peaceful settlement of international disputes. It also shows that such disputes, difficult and complex as they may be, can be settled peacefully and amicably if the parties concerned are willing to make the necessary concessions to that end. Many differences of this kind between governments might be solved if the parties concerned were prepared to make use of the means available.

15. The Working Group of the Special Committee on Peace-keeping Operations, continuing to hold discussions and consultations with a view to reaching agreement on a model of peace-keeping operations, seems to have gone as far as it can in resolving difficulties by judicious drafting procedures. What now seems necessary is a political consensus at a higher level, among the major powers, on the very difficult outstanding questions relating to the roles of the Military Staff Committee, the Security Council, and the Secretary-General in the management and financing of United Nations military observer groups. It would be unfortunate indeed if the wealth of experience gained by the Secretariat in the management of peace-keeping operations were not taken fully into consideration in the resolution of these remaining problems.

16. While attempts are being made to reach final agreement on a model of peace-keeping operations, I feel that a crucial aspect of the Special Committee's mandate should not be overlooked, namely, the desirability of "overcoming the present financial difficulties of the Organization." The consensus on voluntary contributions reached by the General Assembly in 1965 has not yet been fully implemented. Under the terms of Assembly resolution 2006 (XIX), the president of the General Assembly and I were invited to undertake consultations that finally led to this consensus. Because of my special responsibility, I appeal once again to the members of the Special Committee, as well as to all Member states, to focus their attention on this important aspect of peace-keeping operations. It remains my fervent hope that, in spite of the remaining difficulties, progress will be evident on the vitally important question of peace-keeping during this twenty-fifth anniversary year.

II. Disarmament

17. Twenty-five years ago, as the United Nations was born, mankind witnessed the beginning of the nuclear age. The signing of the Charter took place only days before the explosion of the first atomic bomb, and ever since disarmament has been recognized as an essential condition for the survival and well-being of mankind. Although disarmament is one of the highest priorities of the United Nations, the Organization's achievements in this field hardly measure up to the needs.

18. After fifteen years of seemingly futile discussions, disarmament debates reached a turning point in the 1960s, which witnessed a thaw in the relations between the two superpowers. As a result, four important treaties were agreed upon and have since entered into force: the partial test-ban treaty of August 5, 1963, which prohibited nuclear tests in the atmosphere, in outer space, and under water; the Treaty on Principles Governing the Activities of States in the Exploration and Use of Outer Space, including the Moon and Other Celestial Bodies, of 1967, which banned nuclear and other mass-destruction weapons from outer space and provided for the demilitarization of celestial bodies; the Treaty for the Prohibition of Nuclear Weapons in Latin America, known as the Treaty of Tlatelolco, of February 14, 1967, which established a nuclear-weapon-free zone in Latin America; the Treaty on the Non-Proliferation of Nuclear Weapons of 1968, which prohibited the further spread of nuclear weapons. These treaties constitute real progress toward disarmament.

19. During the past quarter-century, each of the two superpowers has built up its capacity to achieve the total physical destruction of the other at least ten to fifteen times over. In spite of this, new and more sophisticated nuclear weapons are being developed. It would appear, however, that the superpowers have at least recognized that in their own interest, which is also the interest of the entire world, they have compelling reasons to prevent what might become an uncontrollable escalation of the nuclear arms race. There are encouraging reports that the Strategic Arms Limitation Talks between the Union of Soviet Socialist Republics and the United States of America are making progress. All peoples of the world hope for a successful outcome of these negotiations, which have been described as the most important and fateful disarmament discussions since the Second World War. I renew my appeal to the two governments to seize this unique opportunity for

agreement, and meanwhile to respond to the appeal of the General Assembly "to agree, as an urgent preliminary measure, on a moratorium on further testing and deployment of new offensive and defensive strategic nuclear-weapon systems."

20. In the conventional arms race, which absorbs by far the largest portion of all military expenditure, there has been a dangerous trend to produce, accumulate, and disseminate ever more sophisticated and deadly weapons. Limited wars fought with conventional weapons during the past twenty-five years not only have caused terrible death and destruction, but also contain the seeds of the threat of nuclear war. The conventional arms race affects all nations, nuclear and non-nuclear, developed and developing. While at the present time the military expenditures of the industrial countries for both nuclear and conventional armaments represent more than 85 percent of the total world military expenditure, there has been a regrettable tendency in recent years for the military budgets of the developing countries to increase at a greater percentage rate than that of the world total, which now exceeds $200,000 million a year. I believe it is imperative that the tremendous human and economic resources required for human development and progress should be found in very large part from the reduction of allocations to the military sector of national budgets.

21. Turning to recent developments, I am glad to note that a spirit of accommodation has characterized the negotiations of the Conference of the Committee on Disarmament on a draft Treaty on the Prohibition of the Emplacement of Nuclear Weapons and Other Weapons of Mass Destruction on the Sea-Bed and the Ocean Floor and in the Subsoil Thereof. I am confident that a draft treaty will emerge from these discussions, commanding wide support from the Members of the United Nations, and I hope that it can be opened for signature during the course of this year. The treaty would be an important measure to prevent the spread of the nuclear arms race to an area that constitutes two-thirds of our planet and whose significance for mankind is bound to increase greatly. It would also be a step toward further measures in the field of disarmament.

22. In this forty-fifth anniversary year of the Protocol for the Prohibition of the Use in War of Asphyxiating, Poisonous or Other Gases, and of Bacteriological Methods of Warfare, signed at Geneva on June 17, 1925, several countries have ratified or acceded to the Protocol, pursuant to the appeals of the General Assembly, and additional countries have

announced their intention to do so. But the situation is far from satisfactory, since only some seventy states have parties to the Protocol and more than a third of the states belonging to the United Nations family have not yet signed or ratified it. It is my fervent hope that appropriate action will be taken by all states concerned to strengthen the Protocol by adhering to it and by accepting fully its universal obligations.

23. The urgent need to ban the development, production, and stockpiling, and to destroy existing stocks, of these appalling weapons of mass destruction has been universally recognized. The complex problem of verification of a complete ban on these weapons has received detailed attention in the far-reaching discussions at the Conference of the Committee on Disarmament. While no solution has yet been achieved, the dimensions of the problem have been defined and clarified. If persistent efforts are made in search of a solution, I feel confident that one can be found. Pending agreement on a complete ban, I appeal to all parties to the Geneva Protocol which have signed it with reservations to renounce their reservations. Finally, I appeal to all states to cease all further research, production, development, and stockpiling of all chemical and biological weapons for use in warfare.

24. Little progress has been made in recent years toward achieving a comprehensive nuclear test-ban treaty. I hope, however, that my inquiry, conducted at the request of the General Assembly in connection with a worldwide exchange of seismological data, will contribute toward progress in this direction. Seven years have passed since the signing of the partial test-ban treaty—one of the most important disarmament agreements in the history of the United Nations. Yet some states, whose participation is essential if the nuclear arms race is to be curbed and if mankind is to be saved from the hazards of further radioactive contamination, have not put their signatures under the treaty. Time is of the essence. I therefore appeal to those states which have not yet done so to heed the General Assembly's call for adherence to the partial test-ban treaty and I also appeal to all nuclear-weapon states to abide by the Assembly's request for the suspension of nuclear weapon tests in all environments.

25. The United Nations Disarmament Decade has begun auspiciously with the entry into force on March 5, 1970, of the Treaty on the Non-Proliferation of Nuclear Weapons, an event of historic importance. It has been signed by nearly 100 countries and ratified by over fifty. The whole process of signature and ratification should be accelerated, for

only by universal adherence and full implementation can it fully succeed in its objectives. Further substantial progress during the Decade will, to a very large extent, depend upon two developments: first, the full implementation of the Treaty to halt the horizontal proliferation of nuclear weapons; and second, the limitation of offensive and defensive strategic nuclear armaments to halt the vertical proliferation of these weapons.

26. I have been gratified to note certain progress achieved by the International Atomic Energy Agency in promoting the peaceful uses of nuclear energy, including peaceful nuclear explosions, and in adjusting its safeguards system to the provisions of the Treaty on the Non-Proliferation of Nuclear Weapons. The Safeguards Committee of the International Atomic Energy Agency, a committee of the whole, has, in fact, approved a set of safeguard principles to be used in negotiations between the Agency and States Parties to the Treaty on the Non-Proliferation of Nuclear Weapons.

27. It is generally recognized that, in order to achieve agreement on far-reaching measures of disarmament, it is indispensable that all militarily significant powers, and in particular all nuclear powers, including France and the People's Republic of China, should participate in the negotiations. I accordingly feel that the highest priority should be given during the Disarmament Decade to seeking practical means of associating these powers with all disarmament discussions.

28. The Disarmament Decade would acquire real meaning and significance if a comprehensive program for disarmament could be worked out. A request to work out such a program was addressed by the General Assembly to the Conference of the Committee on Disarmament, emphasizing the need for early and continued action so as to hasten progress and increase the momentum of the achievements made in the field of disarmament during the decade of the sixties. This subject has been given full consideration by the Conference of the Committee on Disarmament. Although the Conference has not been able to reach agreement on the contents of such a program, it is my hope that the extensive discussion of this matter and the several constructive ideas and suggestions put forward may facilitate the task of the General Assembly in adopting a comprehensive program. This would be of primary importance in promoting the work of disarmament and would also be extremely opportune in that the program for the Disarmament Decade would coincide in point of time with the proclamation of the Second

United Nations Development Decade, with which it is closely connected in the worldwide struggle for economic and social progress.

29. Finally, in order that the governments and peoples of the world may be more fully informed and may better understand the issues and problems related to the continuing arms race, I would propose that a comprehensive international expert study be undertaken of the economic and social consequences of the arms race and massive military expenditures. Such a study, which would complement a similar study carried out in 1962, could delineate the implications and evaluate the effects on nations and on economies of the growing stockpiles of armaments and the increasing volume of resources being diverted from peaceful to military purposes. It would help toward a better understanding of the needs and the possibilities for reordering both national and international priorities in the decade ahead.

30. On the threshold of the Disarmament Decade and of the second quarter-century of the United Nations, I appeal to the Member states and to the peoples of the world to rededicate themselves to the Charter objectives of establishing and maintaining international peace and security with "the least diversion for armaments of the world's human and economic resources." It is my firm belief that the nations of the world cannot move away from the abyss of self-destruction and fulfill the urgent social tasks facing the rich and poor countries alike, unless they put an early end to the malignancy of the arms race, both nuclear and conventional.

31. If significant progress toward disarmament is to be made, governments must put aside suspicion and mistrust and approach this subject in a new spirit. The Disarmament Decade offers opportunities to speed up the momentum of the agreements achieved during the 1960s and to utilize human creativity and economic resources so that science and technology will become a universal boon and not a bane. If the nations of the world resolve to move ahead in planning specific steps toward the goal of general and complete disarmament, they can succeed in creating a secure and better world for all mankind. . . .

IV. The Middle East and Cyprus

42. A year ago I was obliged to report to the General Assembly that the situation in the Middle East had markedly deteriorated, that there was an unprecedented breakdown of the cease-fire called for by the

Security Council, that the prospect of even a first step toward a peaceful settlement seemed remote, and that the situation, apart from its disastrous effects in the area itself, had also created a crisis of effectiveness for the United Nations and its Members. At that time, I noted the efforts of the Security Council, of my special representative in the Middle East, Ambassador Gunnar V. Jarring, and of four permanent members of the Security Council, and, in commenting on their lack of success, concluded that a will to attain peace by the parties themselves was the decisive factor. That discouraging situation persisted until this summer.

43. It was therefore with satisfaction that I took note, in August 1970, of a more favorable turn of events in the Middle East, which at least gave a chance for progress toward the peaceful settlement which Members of the United Nations had so earnestly desired for so many years. I was aware that this development was only a beginning, a welcome first step, and that the road ahead would be long, arduous, and uncertain. But at least there was a first step. Unfortunately, it was immediately followed by serious and, until now, continuing difficulties which have prevented further progress.

44. Until early August of this year, the Jarring mission, although it was never actually suspended or inoperative, had been relatively inactive for some time. This was because the circumstances seemed utterly unfavorable for a further effort by Ambassador Jarring. The breakdown of the Security Council cease-fire, especially in the Suez Canal sector, had created an impasse related to the differing positions of the parties concerning the cease-fire itself. One side refused to continue to observe the cease-fire, which it regarded as, in effect, perpetuating foreign occupation of its sovereign territory, while the position of the other side was that it would observe the cease-fire as soon as, and as long as, the other party was willing to do so. The efforts of four permanent members of the Security Council, and the separate efforts of the two superpowers, to reach agreement on guidelines which might strengthen Ambassador Jarring's hand seemed doomed to frustration by this impasse. In spite of all the difficulties, however, the governments concerned eventually accepted a proposal initiated by the United States of America, which included a strict ninety-day observance of the Security Council cease-fire and made possible the reactivation of Ambassador Jarring's mission. This agreement provided a favorable opportunity for all concerned with the Middle East problem to make a new effort—an opportunity, I should add, which may not come again. This fact makes the difficulties encountered in early September all the more alarming and deplorable.

45. The agreement of Israel, Jordan, and the United Arab Republic to the peace proposal initiated by the United States, in providing a basis on which Ambassador Jarring was able to renew his contacts with the parties, created at the time an atmosphere of cautious hope which had been conspicuously lacking in recent years. It also served to demonstrate some important truths about the Middle East and about the United Nations itself. In the first place, it was a tentative indication that at long last there might be among the parties a will to peace, which is indispensable for any hope of progress. Now, in mid-September, there can be no doubt that the peace effort in the Middle East has suffered a severe setback. Israel has charged that the cease-fire standstill conditions in the Suez Canal sector have been continuously violated by the United Arab Republic and has insisted that until the original situation is restored Israel will not participate in the talks.

46. Despite all the difficulties, however, I feel very strongly that we should not foresee failure as inevitable, nor should we conclude that there is no longer any scope for constructive peace talks. On the contrary, this is the time to exert every possible effort toward a resumption of the talks. Ambassador Jarring remains at United Nations Headquarters, fully available to all the parties, and he has been carrying on his efforts throughout the crisis of the standstill arrangement, with regard to which he has no relationship and for which he has no responsibility. The matter of the standstill arrangement involves, of course, neither Ambassador Jarring nor the United Nations, but only the United States and the two parties concerned. This is an area in which the United Nations has no responsibility because none has been given to it.

47. On the positive side, at the moment, the actual cease-fire in the Suez Canal sector is being scrupulously observed. There is no fighting.

48. It is to be hoped that the talks can soon be resumed. We must, I feel, persevere in this effort, because I am convinced that this is probably the one chance of a breakthrough to peace in the Middle East. Only when the talks get under way and the parties begin to deal with substance will it become clear whether they are prepared, in the interests of peace, to accept those compromises, and even to take what they believe to be those risks to their vital interests, which are the inescapable price for a peaceful settlement. No one should underestimate the statesmanship and courage which such decisions will require of the governments concerned.

49. The current peace move, even though it has now encountered serious obstacles, has also shown that the Member states, and especially

four of the permanent members of the Security Council, working together both within and outside the United Nations, can reach agreement even on the most difficult and controversial problems and, by reaching that agreement, can provide the firm base upon which United Nations organs and machinery can play a useful and constructive role. In particular, the concurrence of the two superpowers, buttressed by France and the United Kingdom, in a positive course of action is of decisive importance. This is, I firmly believe, the way the United Nations was and is intended to work on difficult and dangerous political problems, and it would be a happy augury for the future if, in its twenty-fifth anniversary year, an impressive demonstration of this process could be given to the world.

50. The great basic problems of the Middle East all still lie before us. To surmount them will require patience, persistence, forebearance, courage, ingenuity, and statesmanship. If the will to peace of the parties and the will to help of the Members of the United Nations can be maintained, I believe that the efforts of the governments concerned, of the Security Council, and of Ambassador Jarring can, in the end, succeed. It goes without saying that the Secretary-General and the Secretariat are always available to assist them in whatever way may seem useful.

51. No significant change has occurred in the situation in Cyprus during the past year. By and large, there has been peace and quiet on the island. Talks between leaders of the two communities continue; however, little progress toward a solution has been made and there are no indications that the parties have bridged to any significant degree their differences on the basic issue of local government. Since there is no other or better procedure available at present in the search for a solution, I welcome the continuation of these talks. I must emphatically state once again, however, that the passage of too much time may hamper rather than facilitate a settlement. As years go by, people learn to live under abnormal conditions and the changed pattern of their lives begins to take root. In addition, there is always the inherent danger that incidents will mar the prevailing calm and create more difficulties in the talks.

52. There was, during this period, an unsuccessful attempt upon the life of President Makarios which, fortunately, had no intercommunal origin. Nevertheless it gave rise to an increase in tension, which subsided rather quickly, thanks to the calm shown by President Makarios, the measures taken by the government, and the restraint demonstrated by the Turkish Cypriot community.

53. The United Nations Peace-keeping Force in Cyprus has steadfastly continued its efforts to maintain quiet on the island and to return the life of its citizens to normality. Although some progress has been made, the fact remains that a complete return to normality will not be possible until the parties find a solution to the basic issues. In the circumstances, I have had no alternative but to recommend periodically to the Security Council the continuation of the stationing of the Force in Cyprus, and the Council has taken decisions to that effect. The financing of the Force by voluntary contributions, however, has proved to be most unsatisfactory and has led to the accumulation of a substantial deficit. This is most regrettable, in view of the fine contribution which the United Nations Peace-keeping Force in Cyprus has made toward peace and stability on the island.

54. As I stated in my report to the Security Council of June 1, 1970, I still believe, in spite of all the difficulties, that the elements necessary for a political settlement in Cyprus do exist. What is now required is that all the parties directly concerned with the question, and particularly the leaders of the two communities, make a determined effort to expedite the talks and to make such mutual concessions as may be necessary to reach a just and lasting solution. . . .

VII. Apartheid

105. On the occasion of the twenty-fifth anniversary of the United Nations, it is with a heavy heart that I must once again report that the efforts made by the Organization to solve the question of the policies of *apartheid* of the government of South Africa have not yet resulted in the elimination of this continuing affront to human dignity. This question has been under discussion in the Organization since its inception. From the outset, the General Assembly has endeavored to uphold in South Africa the basic human and political rights set forth in the Charter of the United Nations and the Universal Declaration of Human Rights.

106. From 1946 to 1952, the General Assembly strove unsuccessfully to prevail upon the government of South Africa to engage in discussions with the governments of India and Pakistan, which had complained about the treatment inflicted upon people of Indian and Indo-Pakistani origin in South Africa in violation of existing agreements. In 1952, in order to deal with the broader question of race conflict in South Africa resulting from the policies of *apartheid,* the General Assembly established the United Nations Commission on the Racial Situation in the

Union of South Africa. At the same time, in resolution 616 B (VII), it enunciated the basic principles for a peaceful settlement, declaring that "in a multiracial society harmony and respect for human rights and freedoms and the peaceful development of a unified community are best assured when patterns of legislation and practice are directed toward ensuring equality before the law of all persons regardless of race, creed or color, and when economic, social, cultural, and political participation of all racial groups is on a basis of equality."

107. The South African government has not only refused to associate itself with all these efforts, withheld its cooperation, and rejected the resolutions of the General Assembly; it has proceeded even further and enacted new measures to consolidate racial discrimination and racial segregation as state policy. It has resorted to arbitrary and repressive measures against opponents of its policies, gradually and steadily transforming South Africa into a police state. No positive results were achieved by direct consultations between the Secretary-General and the government of South Africa in 1961 or by the attempts of some Member states, which maintain friendly relations with that government, to persuade it to reform. By 1962, the General Assembly had come to the conclusion that some coercive measures were necessary. It therefore requested Member states to take a number of diplomatic and economic measures against South Africa and established the Special Committee on the Policies of *Apartheid* of the Government of the Republic of South Africa. In its most recent resolution on the subject, the Assembly once again called upon Member states to enforce a number of measures against South Africa. Whereas some Member states have faithfully implemented those resolutions, a number of states which maintain political and economic relations with South Africa, particularly its major trading partners, have not. I share with the vast majority of Member states the belief that the resolutions in question provide an adequate framework for effective international action.

108. It is gratifying to note that this year the Security Council resumed its consideration of the question of the policies of *apartheid*. It was in the aftermath of the Sharpeville incident in 1960 that the Council first took up the question. From the outset, it condemned *apartheid* and called upon South Africa to renounce these policies and to initiate measures to bring about racial harmony based on equality. It subsequently declared that the situation arising from continued enforcement of the policies of *apartheid* was seriously disturbing international peace and security.

109. A group of experts set up by the Security Council in 1963 to examine methods of resolving the situation in South Africa concluded that only by free and democratic consultation, cooperation, and conciliation could a peaceful and constructive solution be found. It recommended the establishment of a national convention fully representative of all the people of South Africa to set a new future course. It called for the cooperation of the government of South Africa and stated that, in the event of a negative attitude on the part of that government, the Security Council would be left with no effective peaceful means for resolving the situation in South Africa, except the application of economic sanctions. The government of South Africa refused to cooperate and the recommendations could not be implemented. In its search for an alternative solution, the Security Council set up an expert committee to examine the feasibility, effectiveness, and implications of sanctions. The report of that committee, submitted early in 1965, has not yet been considered by the Council.

110. When the Security Council resumed consideration of the question of *apartheid* this year, its deliberations were limited to the question of the implementation of its embargo on the supply of arms and military equipment to South Africa. Since resolution 282 (1970) redefines the embargo on the supply of arms and military equipment to South Africa, I sincerely hope that all Member states will abide by it. The full implementation of this resolution will indeed lessen the danger of violent conflict in southern Africa.

111. It is disheartening to note that all the efforts made by the Organization over the years have not yet resulted in alleviating the situation which still prevails in southern Africa. Disregarding the appeals and demands of the General Assembly and the Security Council, South Africa has evolved a system of government which is entirely inconsistent with the purposes and principles of the Charter of the United Nations and the Universal Declaration of Human Rights. The enforcement of increasingly ruthless and inhuman measures of racial segregation has heightened racial bitterness in the country and created an explosive situation. By suppressing the legitimate opposition to *apartheid* and by resorting to extreme repressive measures, which are clearly in violation of the principles of the rule of law, the government of South Africa has closed all avenues to a peaceful change in the country. The leaders of the oppressed people of South Africa have expressed their determination to resort to violent methods in order to redress the situation and achieve their inalienable rights and freedoms. The situation as it now exists

constitutes a threat to international peace and security. Moreover, by extending its policies of *apartheid* to the international territory of Namibia and by encouraging the other white minority régimes in southern Africa to defy the United Nations resolutions, South Africa has clearly shown its determination to challenge the authority of the Organization in the region.

112. The General Assembly, aware of the seriousness of the situation, has prescribed the enforcement of sanctions against South Africa. The Security Council has recommended that the government of South Africa should either hold consultations among all the people of South Africa with a view to determining a new policy likely to ensure human rights and fundamental freedoms for all or face sanctions by the international community. What is needed above all is the political will on the part of Member states to take effective measures which would induce South Africa to renounce its policies. It is my earnest hope that Member states, particularly those maintaining political and economic relations with South Africa, will realize, before it is too late, that after twenty-five years of debate and deliberation they should come to an agreement and act in concert to alleviate an intolerable situation. . . .

IX. *Financial Situation of the Organization*

127. The Organization's financial situation is worse than ever before and steadily deteriorating. A main cause of the worsening situation is that certain governments continue to withhold contributions apportioned under the regular budget for the cost of servicing United Nations bonds and certain other activities which they consider to be improperly included in the regular budget. In addition, the amounts owed by "slow payers" continue to rise. The actual situation is much graver than is reflected by the cold figures and analysis set forth below. Again at certain times this year the United Nations did not have enough funds in hand from contributions made for that purpose to meet the payment of salaries earned by United Nations staff. Consequently, it was necessary to resort to borrowing from trust funds and special accounts in the custody and control of the Secretary-General. This hand-to-mouth existence scarcely befits the dignity of the world Organization, nor does it permit the conduct of the financial operations of the United Nations on a business-like basis. I again strongly urge that Members concern themselves with this urgent and serious matter on the occasion of the twenty-

fifth anniversary of the Organization and find the means to restore the solvency of the United Nations and to ensure that it has a sound financial basis thereafter. This is indeed an important and necessary step if increased public and governmental support is to be forthcoming for our Organization. Specifically, in respect of the regular budget as at June 30, 1970, current assets (cash, investments, deferred charges, accounts receivable, and amounts due from trust funds) exceeded current liabilities (accounts payable, sundry credits, and amounts due to trust funds, special accounts, and surplus account) by only $3.6 million—less than half of one month's payroll. On the same date, however, $39.8 million had been advanced from the Working Capital Fund, and $15.6 million of voluntary contributions in the United Nations Special Account had been utilized to finance expenditures of the regular budget. There was, therefore, a cumulative shortfall of $51.8 million in contributions received in relation to expenditures incurred as at June 30, 1970, in respect of the regular budget. At the same date, unliquidated obligations, most of which could not be paid, came to a total of $15.8 million.

128. There was some temporary improvement in the situation in July, as a result of the receipt during that month of $26.8 million in assessed contributions to the regular budget. On the other hand, only $5.6 million in assessed contributions was received in August.

129. Unpaid assessed contributions to the regular budget, which amounted to $130 million on June 30, 1969, totaled $135.5 million as at June 30, 1970. Of this amount, $30.3 million, as compared to $26.7 million a year ago, is attributable to the position taken by some Member states of not paying for parts of their regular budget assessments. The balance of $105.2 million represents delayed payments by Member states. On the basis of the pattern of past payments, it is estimated that at least $22.2 million of the balance of $105.2 million is likely to remain unpaid at the end of 1970.

130. With respect to the Special Account for the United Nations Emergency Force and the *Ad Hoc* Account for the United Nations Operation in the Congo, the financial situation remains a matter of serious concern. Unpaid assessed contributions in respect of the United Nations Emergency Force decreased by $1 million between June 30, 1969, and June 30, 1970, to $49.6 million and the amount in respect of the United Nations Operation in the Congo remained unchanged at $82.1 million. At the same date, amounts owed to governments which provided contingents and logistical support to these two operations totaled

$21 million and $10.2 million, respectively, although $4.9 million and $0.2 million of the voluntary contributions in the United Nations Special Account had been utilized to reduce the indebtedness in the respective accounts. Additional net liabilities and unliquidated obligations in the two accounts amounted to $2.4 million and $3 million, respectively. There are no cash balances or investments in these accounts at this time, except for the equivalent of $1.4 million in inconvertible Congolese zaires.

131. Voluntary contributions and interest credited thereon to the United Nations Special Account increased by $0.3 million, thus bringing to $20.7 million the total amount credited to this account as at June 30, 1970.

132. The financial situation in respect of the United Nations Peacekeeping Force in Cyprus, which is to continue in operation until December 15, 1970, under its current mandate, is also of most serious concern. Taking into consideration the amounts paid or pledged as voluntary contributions to the account as at August 31, 1970, and on the assumption that all pledges made will be paid in full, it is estimated that additional contributions of $8.4 million are required in order to meet past commitments and maintain the Force in Cyprus up to December 15, 1970.

133. In my annual report last year, I noted that it would be encouraging if there were a greater degree of optimism and enthusiasm consistent with the signal successes that have attended the efforts of the Organization, particularly as a multinational instrument for promoting economic and social development. I also highlighted the ever increasing reliance of the developing countries on the United Nations for assistance in their development efforts and the growing reluctance on the part of the more affluent Members to provide financial support to the Organization on a scale in keeping with the increased tasks in the economic, social, and human rights fields. I can only report that this dichotomy continues to exist.

134. During the past year, additional steps have been taken toward achieving progress in the matter of program formulation and the establishment of priorities. With respect to program budgeting, it is noted that most of the organizations in the United Nations system have accepted this method in principle and are taking steps to institute medium-term and long-term programming and budgeting.

135. It is my intention to submit to the General Assembly an outline of proposals on a form of budget presentation consistent with the results of

our studies to date. These studies include the discussions which have taken place in a working group of the Consultative Committee on Administrative Questions on the subject of program and budget presentation. Progress is being made on standardized nomenclature for financial and budgetary terms, on standardization of objects of expenditure, and on the revision of the classification of expenditures for the annual report of the Economic and Social Council.

136. In this connection, I wish to call attention to my further view that, if we are to achieve maximum effectiveness from the other programming and budgeting changes which the General Assembly is being asked to consider, any move toward an integrated programming and budgeting system also clearly calls for reconsideration of the budget cycle. By the same token I am persuaded that, as the financial resources available to the Organization are not unlimited, we shall reap the full benefit of the proposed changes in the system only by making a courageous and judicious assessment of priorities.

137. In the Introduction to my report last year, I referred briefly to the survey of manpower utilization and deployment which was being launched at that time with a view to improving the efficiency of the Secretariat. Substantial progress has since been made in this work, and surveys of several major units (the Office of Conference Services, the Office of Public Information, the United Nations Conference on Trade and Development, the United Nations Industrial Development Organization, the Economic Commission for Africa, and the United Nations Economic and Social Office in Beirut) have been completed. Some of the survey teams of the Administrative Management Service are now engaged in the study of the Department of Economic and Social Affairs, while others are about to start work with respect to the remaining regional economic commissions. By the end of 1970, therefore, areas of the Secretariat accounting for roughly 60 percent of the staff will have been brought under scrutiny as part of this operation.

138. I shall be making a report to the General Assembly on the progress of the survey and on the broad conclusions reached so far, including their implications for management beyond the manpower aspects and the strictly budgetary considerations. Meanwhile, the revised budget estimates for 1971 will reflect my decisions in the light of the recommendations made to me by the Administrative Management Service with regard to the manning tables of the units in which surveys will have been completed at that time. In these cases, it will have been possible to decide on a final disposition regarding the provisional posts

which were allocated for 1970 pending the outcome of the surveys. Naturally, with respect to those parts of the Organization for which surveys have not yet been completed, it will be necessary to consider certain staffing requirements for 1971 on a provisional basis. There again a final determination will be made in good time for the 1972 estimates.

139. It goes without saying that the teams of the Administrative Management Service engaged in the survey are working in close liaison with the budget review groups concerned with the area under study. The work of the two is, in fact, complementary. The review groups are spearheaded by budget officers of the Office of the Controller who are directly concerned with the assessment of financial provision to cover additional tasks to be undertaken in the budget year under consideration. In successive years, as the work of the Administrative Management Service proceeds, the appropriate review group will be able to draw on the detailed knowledge acquired in the course of the survey when compiling future estimates for units which have already been surveyed.

140. Earlier I referred to the dichotomy which continues to exist between the wants of the developing nations and the willingness of the more affluent Members to supply a level of resources which would adequately satisfy these wants. This is as true of proposed levels and contributions to the regular budget as it is in other areas. This fact of life has been in the forefront of my mind in preparing and submitting the regular budget estimates this year and it will continue to be so as the amendments to the budget and supplementary estimates are prepared for those program and administrative elements which are yet to be submitted.

141. As can be seen from the above recapitulation, the financial situation of the Organization is far from satisfactory. I very much hope that in this twenty-fifth anniversary year the Member states will make a concerted effort to restore the financial solvency of the Organization. In this connection, I must confess to serious misgivings about the practice of principal organs which has developed whereby resolutions are adopted or decisions taken which require implementation by the Secretary-General, who is then requested to finance the activities involved by soliciting voluntary contributions. I realize that programs financed by voluntary contributions have a proper place in the United Nations system. This would apply particularly to programs like the United Nations Development Programme, the World Food Programme, and the United Nations Children's Fund or, to take a more recent example, the

United Nations Fund for Population Activities, where there can be some matching of programs with the available resources. In other words, it would be possible, so to speak, to cut the coat according to the cloth. There are other programs, however, where there is an irreducible minimum of financial resources required for the carrying out of certain activities. This is true of the United Nations Relief and Works Agency for Palestine Refugees in the Near East, whose expenditures have risen considerably since the middle of 1967 owing to a notable increase in the number of persons needing relief, combined with higher costs; but the General Assembly has decided that the operations of the Agency should continue to be financed by voluntary contributions. The result is that we are facing a situation now when this program may come to a halt, with the enormous hardship and suffering it would involve for nearly one and a half million refugees. The political and psychological consequences of such a setback are incalculable. In the case of the United Nations Peace-keeping Force in Cyprus, the costs have been brought to a minimum by my constant efforts and those of my colleagues to prune down the expenditure. Another recent example was the World Youth Assembly in which, theoretically, the level of participation could have been reduced but, in practice, that would not have been possible unless the United Nations had been willing to face the risk of a complete loss of faith in the Organization by the new generation. In my many reports on the United Nations Relief and Works Agency for Palestine Refugees in the Near East, I have expressed my serious concern in regard to the paucity of financial resources. In my reports on the Cyprus operation, I have again and again pointed to the unsatisfactory financing arrangements. I do so now in regard to the World Youth Assembly. I sincerely hope that the General Assembly and the Security Council will find it possible to review this whole question and agree upon acceptable means for the future financing of these and similar programs.

X. Other Questions

Peaceful settlement of disputes

142. The first aim of the Charter of the United Nations, as stated in the Preamble, is "to save succeeding generations from the scourge of war." If the threat or use of force for settling international disputes is prohibited, it obviously follows that those disputes must be settled by

peaceful means. If they remain unsettled, they grow ever more complex and often develop far beyond the issues of the original dispute, thus increasing serious risks of an outbreak of violence.

143. I recently expressed the view that unused provisions of the Charter, which can add greatly to international peace and security, should be activated. The Charter recognizes the importance of peaceful settlement in the maintenance of world order, and, in Article 33, it obligates all Members which are parties to a dispute, the continuance of which is likely to endanger the maintenance of international peace and security, first of all to "seek a solution by negotiation, inquiry, mediation, conciliation, arbitration, judicial settlement, resort to regional agencies or arrangements, or other peaceful means of their own choice." The Charter leaves the choice of a mode of settlement to the parties, but nevertheless establishes a clear obligation to use some means of settlement rather than to let dangerous disputes persist indefinitely. How well have the Members complied with their obligations under Article 33 during the last quarter-century?

144. Some disputes have been settled by one or another of the means mentioned in the Charter. Negotiation has contributed much to the solution of some disputes. An example of successful negotiation is the dispute between Austria and Italy concerning the status of the German-speaking element in the Province of Bolzano (Bozen). Resort to good offices has also sometimes been successful, as in the case of its recent use by Iran and the United Kingdom in regard to the status of Bahrain. Nevertheless, many disputes, some of which are dangerous, remain unsettled. There is one striking characteristic about international practice over the past twenty-five years: the rarity of recourse to arbitration and judicial settlement. These modes, particularly designed for settling legal disputes—and not all disputes have that character—have been used in only a very few cases where they would have been appropriate.

145. The Charter established the International Court of Justice as "the principal judicial organ" of the United Nations, and its Statute forms an integral part of the Charter. The Court was obviously intended to make a major contribution to the maintenance of peace by settling legal disputes, but states have not often allowed the Court to make this contribution. The president of the International Court of Justice has recently stated that the work of the Court cannot usefully be subjected to quantitative analysis. He has also remarked on the significance of the fact that the number of judgments and advisory opinions that the present

Court has been called upon to give in the past twenty-five years is markedly less than the number given by its predecessor, the Permanent Court of International Justice, in only eighteeen years of effective existence. The fact that some fifty-one cases have been brought before the present Court does not give a true picture of the situation. Thirteen of these cases were requests for advisory opinions. Ten of the contentious cases between states were removed from the Court's list because one party had not accepted the Court's jurisdiction, four were withdrawn by the parties, and nearly half of the remainder were decided on essentially preliminary points rather than on merit. Thus one must conclude that the Court has simply not been asked by states to assist in the settlement of disputes. It is indeed regrettable that, in this anniversary year, not a single contentious case between states is pending before the Court.

146. Another provision of the Charter which I also thought might be activated is the competence of the Court to interpret the Charter of the United Nations. The Security Council has recently made its first request for an advisory opinion—on the important question of Namibia. But this single request by the Security Council is in sharp contrast to the twenty-seven requests made by the Council of the League of Nations between 1922 and 1935. Moreover, this is the only request for an advisory opinion which has been made since 1961. Of the other twelve requests to the present Court, ten were made by the General Assembly, one by the United Nations Educational, Scientific and Cultural Organization, and one by the Inter-Governmental Maritime Consultative Organization. Many of the organs and organizations authorized to request advisory opinions have never done so. There are also many questions on the agendas of the other organs of the United Nations involving legal issues, the clarification of which by advisory opinions of the Court would facilitate solution.

147. It is sometimes said that use is not made of the Court because it is slow and cumbersome or because its composition does not reflect modern realities. The length of proceedings, however, depends largely on the parties, which have frequently asked for long delays. When the duration of a case is more within the control of the Court, as when requests are made for advisory opinions, the Court acts speedily. With one exception, all of its advisory opinions have been rendered within a year of the request. If the full Court is considered too cumbersome, the parties may resort to a Chamber of Summary Procedure, consisting of

five judges, chosen annually by the Court. In twenty-five years, however, no case has ever been brought before this Chamber. There is also a possibility, under Article 26 of the Statute, of forming chambers to deal with particular categories of cases, or with a particular case, but states have made no requests for such chambers. With respect to the composition of the Court, the criterion of the Statute is representation of the main forms of civilization and the principal legal systems of the world, rather than geographical distribution. But, even from the geographic standpoint, it may be noted that the composition of the present Court is exactly the same as that agreed upon in 1963 for the Security Council. Since the composition of the Council is generally considered balanced, there appears little justification for objections to that of the Court.

148. It would seem, however, that the very limited use made of the Court reflects a general aversion to settlement by means of a binding legal decision rather than a specific aversion to the Court, since arbitration has also been little used. According to the information available to the Secretariat, apart from the cases decided by conciliation or property commissions established under certain peace treaties signed after the Second World War, there have been only fourteen decisions or awards by *ad hoc* or other arbitral tribunals since 1945. A few of these dealt with important territorial disputes, such as the one between India and Pakistan over the Rann of Kutch. Most of them, however, concerned minor questions, many of a commercial nature, which were not in the least likely to disturb peace and security.

149. In this twenty-fifth anniversary year, the United Nations will be considering means for increasing its effectiveness and for strengthening international peace. One such means would be for each Member to review its own obligations under the Charter, particularly those of pacific settlement under Article 33, with full attention to the injunction of Article 36 that "legal disputes should as a general rule be referred by the parties to the International Court of Justice." I appeal to the Members to give serious consideration to the advantages of final settlement by an impartial tribunal on the basis of the law binding on both sides. This is the viable alternative to lingering disputes which carry the risk of becoming increasingly inflamed and of involving the parties in explosive violence against their true interests.

150. In addition, states should bear in mind that, in the long run, the cost of compromise resulting in peaceful settlement is considerably less than keeping a dispute open with the consequent diversion of resources which might otherwise be devoted to national development.

151. It would also help if Member states could consider declaring their acceptance of the compulsory jurisdiction of the Court under Article 36, paragraph 2, of its Statute, with as few reservations and limitations as possible. At the present time, only forty-six states—hardly more than a third of the membership of the Organization—have done so. A number of declarations are also accompanied by crippling reservations that make them largely illusory. While acceptance of compulsory jurisdiction is by no means necessary for the submission of cases to the Court, it will tend to promote such submission as a normal procedure in international relations, instead of the very exceptional one it is at present.

152. Member states will have noticed the recent efforts of the Court to make itself better known and its functions better understood in the international community. This end is served by annual reports submitted by the Court to the General Assembly and by closer contacts between the Court and other principal organs of the United Nations. Now the Court is engaged in the important work of revising its rules, the outcome of which will no doubt enable the Court better to meet the needs of modern international life.

153. If these proposals are accepted and implemented, I am confident that during the next twenty-five years we shall see more progress toward eliminating the "scourge of war" and toward achieving another aim set out in the Preamble of the Charter, namely, "to establish conditions under which justice and respect for the obligations arising from treaties and other sources of international law can be maintained."

Unlawful interference with international civil aviation

154. My concern over the increasing incidence of hijacking of civil aircraft has grown considerably during the year, and acts of unlawful seizure of aircraft and of sabotage and armed attacks against civil air transport have now reached unprecedented proportions, to the point where confidence in the safety of international civil aviation is being seriously undermined.

155. A start at least has been made to seek effective measures for combating the problem. Since the adoption, on December 12, 1969, of General Assembly resolution 2551 (XXIV) on the forcible diversion of civil aircraft in flight, the International Civil Aviation Organization has continued its persistent efforts to combat unlawful interference with international civil aviation. The Assembly of the International Civil

Aviation Organization took up the problem as a matter of urgency during an extraordinary session, the second in its history, which was convened last June to deal with the subject of safety in international civil aviation. A wide range of security measures was developed with a view to the protection of air passengers, civil aviation personnel, and civil aircraft. A highly important declaration was adopted by which the Assembly condemned all acts of violence against international civil air transport and urgently called upon states not to have recourse, under any circumstances, to such acts, but rather, to take effective measures to deter and prevent them and to ensure the prosecution of those who commit them. The declaration also requested concerted action on the part of states to suppress acts which jeopardize the development of international civil air transport, and requested application, as soon as possible, of the decisions and recommendations of the Assembly.

156. As in the past, I fully support any international action which is required to prevent and repress acts of violence against international civil aviation. I hope, therefore, that states will give effect at once to the recommendations of the International Civil Aviation Organization for national action. I also hope that those states not yet parties to the Convention on Offences and Certain Other Acts Committed on Board Aircraft, signed at Tokyo on September 14, 1963, will heed the appeal of the General Assembly to ratify or accede to that Convention. The entry into force of a new convention, drafted by the Legal Committee of the International Civil Aviation Organization, which is to be submitted to a diplomatic conference at The Hague in December, is clearly a matter of the utmost urgency and importance. All means which may contribute to accelerating the process by which states will become parties to the new Convention deserve the serious attention of the conference. One suggestion which has been made in this regard is that states which sign the Convention should undertake to submit it within a specified period for whatever constitutional process is necessary in order to enable them to become parties within a specified period, undertake to give notice to the International Civil Aviation Organization, stating their difficulties. Such provisions might perhaps be helpful and would have precedents in international practice.

Conflicting claims to represent a Member state

157. There have been cases in the history of the United Nations when the Secretariat has found itself confronted with the question as to which

of two rival governments is entitled to exercise the rights of a Member state. It has been the normal practice for the Secretary-General to deal with the authorities in *de facto* control of the state in question, without prejudice to the rights of principal deliberative organs to take the final decision on the matter. But this practice does not always lead to a clear answer, particularly in cases where there are fluctuations in regard to control. When the Assembly is not in session, however, some cases can present difficulties, in regard to which the Secretary-General may wish to obtain advice and guidance.

158. The General Assembly attempted to deal with the problem by its resolution 396 (V) of December 14, 1950, which recommended that, when the Assembly was not in session, such questions should be considered by the Interim Committee. This Committee, which has been dormant for twenty years, would not in any case appear to be suited for such a purpose, since its deliberations would presumably lack the participation of some Members which contested its existence on legal grounds and whose views on questions of representation should be considered. To conduct by correspondence a poll of the whole membership of the Organization would require far too much time and would therefore not seem practicable.

159. At this stage, I only wish to bring this problem to the attention of the Members of the United Nations. It would be most useful if some procedures could be generally agreed upon to guide the Secretariat in dealing with such situations.

Assistance in cases of natural disaster

160. A number of serious natural disasters in the past year have required the mobilization of extensive resources from outside the countries afflicted. The United Nations system of organizations has been able to provide assistance in several cases, not the least of which was the recent earthquake in Peru.

161. In this connection, for the first time a Swedish stand-by disaster relief unit, earmarked for service through the United Nations in accordance with General Assembly resolutions 2034 (XX) of December 7, 1965, and 2435 (XXIII) of December 19, 1968, has been made available through the United Nations pursuant to a tripartite agreement concluded between the United Nations, Peru, and Sweden. The catastrophe in Peru underlined only too poignantly the immense destruction and suffering which natural disasters can cause and the need for improved interna-

tional action during the immediate emergency and the subsequent period of rehabilitation. Although systematic scientific research into the whole subject of natural disasters is being given increasing attention, including the application of modern technology in the prevention of these disasters, this requires further development. Disaster preparedness is equally important and, in this connection, I have taken advantage of the General Assembly's authorization to extend modest amounts for assistance in the preparation of pre-disaster plans. National preparedness, however, is often insufficient to meet all the needs at the time of a major disaster, and concerted international action is often required. Effective coordination machinery is essential to enable the United Nations system to provide the speediest and most appropriate assistance in these circumstances. Preliminary consultations have already been undertaken and the Economic and Social Council has commended my intention, which I am now taking steps to implement, to establish a focal point of action within the United Nations Secretariat. This unit will act on my behalf in helping to develop, expand, and coordinate assistance from the whole United Nations system of organizations and in ensuring close and continuing cooperation with governments concerned, as well as with the League of Red Cross Societies, the International Committee of the Red Cross, and other voluntary agencies.

Establishment of an international university

162. In my Introduction to last year's report, I put forward the suggestion that "serious thought may be given to the establishment of a United Nations university, truly international in character and devoted to the Charter objectives of peace and progress." This suggestion was acted upon by the General Assembly and I appointed a consultant to prepare a feasibility study. This study has been the subject of preliminary consideration in the Economic and Social Council, which has asked for the comments of the United Nations Educational, Scientific and Cultural Organization, the United Nations Institute for Training and Research, and other interested agencies and organizations within the United Nations system. I hope that I may soon have the benefit of these comments to enable me to report to the General Assembly. It is, of course, conceivable that further studies might have to be undertaken, but I hope that the value of the function of an international university under United Nations auspices is now generally accepted. I believe

therefore that, whatever further studies may be undertaken, this important function may be kept in mind and eventually come to fruition.

Universality of membership

163. Once again I should like to refer to the importance I attach to the universality of membership in the world Organization, which is increasingly facing problems that can only be resolved on a global basis. This is true not only of questions such as disarmament, but equally of questions like the environment. I quite realize that in respect of some states there are difficult political problems which have to be surmounted before they can participate in the work of the organization as Member states. In this category, however, there are countries which have expressed interest in being represented at the United Nations in the capacity of observers. Once again, I urge that the General Assembly give some attention to this question so that at least those countries which would like to participate in the work of the Organization even without having membership status may be enabled to do so. In the same context, I would like to extend an anticipatory welcome to Fiji, which is due to achieve the status of a sovereign independent state on October 10, 1970.

Periodic meetings of the Security Council

164. In the Introduction to my report on the work of the Organization two years ago, I reiterated the suggestion that I had made in 1967 that "a modest beginning might be made to test the value of holding periodic meetings of the Security Council at which its members might be represented by a member of the government or by some specially designated representative." I am very glad that this idea, which has also been made by my distinguished predecessors, was presented by Finland and that the Security Council finally adopted a decision, on June 12, according to which "the holding of periodic meetings, at which each member of the Council would be represented by a member of the government or by some other specially designated representative, could enhance the authority of the Security Council and make it a more effective instrument for the maintenance of international peace and security." It is gratifying that once again a provision of the Charter—in this case Article 28, paragraph 2—which has for so long remained unused, is being activated. I shall be looking forward with the keenest interest to the

meetings of the Security Council that may take place under this provision in this anniversary year.

Cooperation with regional organizations

165. I have just returned from attending the Assembly of Heads of State and Government of the Organization of African Unity in Addis Ababa. Apart from the opportunity to renew my contacts with African leaders, some of whom I had met earlier in the year in their own countries, it was most grafitying to witness the reconciliation that took place between Nigeria and the four African countries which had broken off diplomatic relations as a result of the recent civil war. I would like to pay tribute to the African leaders for the maturity and wisdom they have shown in this regard. Such a display of amity and willingness to bury the past is essential for Africa to face with confidence the many challenges that lie ahead. I also feel that the value of close cooperation between the United Nations and regional organizations like the Organization of African Unity and the Organization of American States has now been well established, and I look forward to a continued and even closer cooperation in the years ahead.

XI. Concluding Observations

166. Two years ago I suggested that the twenty-fifth anniversary of the founding of the United Nations should be an occasion to rededicate ourselves to the principles of international order and morality set out in the Charter. I am very grateful to the General Assembly and to the Committee for the Twenty-fifth Anniversary of the United Nations for the serious attention they have given to this suggestion. As a result, it is my hope that we may witness during the commemorative period of the twenty-fifth session of the General Assembly the largest gathering of heads of state and heads of government in the history of the United Nations, and perhaps in human history. I believe that, in addition to the ceremony and oratory which are traditional on such occasions, the gathering of so many dignitaries will be a unique opportunity for fruitful contacts and discussions at the highest level. With regard to the political aspect, apart from the general question of relations between East and West, there are also specific crisis areas, such as the Middle East, which world leaders might wish to discuss. In particular, it is my hope that they

will consider ways and means of strengthening the United Nations and promoting its authority and effectiveness as an instrument for achieving international peace, justice, and progress.

167. I would also hope that Member states may give special consideration to re-establishing the financial solvency of the Organization. Compared to the expenditure incurred by Member states for national defense, the financial needs of the Organization would represent only a minute fraction. It seems to me that, without prejudice to the stands taken on principle by the various Member states, they might agree to make a concerted effort to restore the Organization's solvency.

168. The twenty-fifth anniversary of the signing of the Charter has already been celebrated in San Francisco in a manner consistent with the dignity of the organization and the importance of the occasion. I am very glad that the initiative in this regard was taken by the mayor of San Francisco and the Citizens' Committee of that great city, the birthplace of the Charter. Early in July, we also had the opportunity to celebrate the twenty-fifth anniversary of the Organization in Geneva. I am deeply grateful to the president of the Swiss Confederation and his colleagues and to the authorities of the Canton and the City of Geneva for their fine cooperation in making the observance a truly memorable occasion.

169. Another noteworthy event connected with the celebration was the World Youth Assembly, held at Headquarters under the auspices of the United Nations. I was a little concerned at the delay in making final arrangements for this Assembly, owing to disagreement on such important questions as participation, especially from non-governmental youth organizations. This was a particular handicap to me, inasmuch as I had been requested to make arrangements for the holding of the World Youth Assembly on the basis of voluntary contributions, and I could not issue an appeal for funds until early April, only three months before the Assembly was scheduled to meet. However, although it appears that there may be a small shortfall, the greater part of the necessary resources was eventually raised, for which I am most grateful to all the contributors—Member states, non-governmental organizations, foundations, and private philanthropists. In spite of several problems which the World Youth Assembly had to face, I believe that it ended on a positive note and that the experience of holding this Assembly will benefit all of us in establishing contacts with the youth of the world and also perhaps in organizing similar assemblies in the future. Let us not forget that the present generation is the "take-over generation." Let us also remember

that half of today's world population was born after the Charter came into existence twenty-five years ago.

170. During this eventful quarter-century, the world has been transformed. Traditional concepts on which human society was based have been swept aside and new values are emerging. Although the United Nations has played a significant and constructive role in bringing mankind safely to the threshold of a new age, it is incumbent upon us now to help the younger generation prepare itself for leadership in a world for which the young will soon assume responsibility. What better time could there be than this twenty-fifth anniversary year for us to endeavor to overcome our many lingering human afflictions so that we may bequeath to the coming generation a safer and better world?

U THANT
Secretary-General

September 14, 1970

From Report to the Security Council
on Cyprus

NEW YORK   DECEMBER 2, 1970

. . .

115. THE RECORD of the past six months shows neither progress toward further normalization and the elimination of confrontation nor a return to the tense and explosive situation which existed prior to the commencement of the intercommunal talks in June 1968. The situation now prevailing in Cyprus is one of "negative stability," quiet on the surface, but strained, abnormal, and fraught with the serious danger inherent in the continuing close confrontation of well-armed and trained forces. With the passing of time, this situation is threatening to become the way of life of all Cypriots, thus perpetuating the need for UNFI-CYP's [United Nations Force in Cyprus] presence in the island.

116. It is with regret that I have once again to voice my disappointment that, notwithstanding the persistent efforts of my representatives in Cyprus, no significant advance has been made toward a return to normal conditions, especially to freedom of movement along all roads for unarmed citizens. Furthermore, the parties continue to be disinclined to a greater or lesser degree to respond positively to the repeated urgings of my special representative and the Force commander to reduce, if not altogether eliminate, close and dangerous military confrontations in several sensitive areas of the island, as described in detail in the body of the present report. I remain convinced, however, that there are a number of helpful measures which both sides could take without endangering their political and security positions. For instance, a number of suggestions have been made to the Turkish Cypriot leadership which, if agreed to, could, at minimum risk to them, help to generate an atmosphere of increased mutual confidence and contribute significantly to the

SOURCE: Security Council Official Records, Twenty-fifth Year, Supplement for October, November and December, 1970, document S/10005.

improvement in the living conditions of their community. On the government side, I would welcome a determined move to solve the long-outstanding problem of displaced persons and their rehabilitation. This is a humanitarian problem which involves the alleviation of the hardship of several thousand needy people.

117. An encouraging exception to the present immobility is the increased cooperation between the two communities in the economic field. It is significant that a recent severe drought brought the farmers of both communities in the stricken area closer together. This seems to indicate that with good will and when their common interests are involved a rapprochement between the communities is definitely possible. It is my earnest hope that further progress along that road can be made through the establishment of a number of common services and mixed institutions whose main objective would be to serve the people of Cyprus as a whole.

118. Two and a half years have passed since the intercommunal talks began. Unhappily there is, as yet, no real prospect of a long-term settlement. The expectations repeatedly voiced by the Security Council have so far failed to materialize, and the talks themselves have yet to produce any significant agreement on fundamental questions.

119. Despite all the difficulties, it is essential that the intercommunal talks should continue. In the present circumstances they not only remain the sole available method to achieve agreement between the communities, but also provide a useful means for dissipating existing suspicions and tensions. However, what is sorely needed is a new dynamism and direction in the negotiations between the two main parties concerned. There is no road to a settlement other than the arduous one of negotiations steadfastly and honestly pursued with the aim of achieving a reasonable and workable compromise, which would be neither a victory nor a defeat for either side.

120. I believe that both communities in Cyprus now realize that the Cyprus problem cannot be solved by resorting to force and that any attempt to revert to the use of force would only worsen the conflict and prove catastrophic for all on the island and perhaps beyond. The two sides have also indicated that a settlement can be worked out on the basis of an independent, sovereign and unitary state of Cyprus in which the two communities participate. This limited consensus indicates that there is a basis for at least some kind of accommodation. Obviously, in the prevailing circumstances, more than good will and exhortations are

required to reach a reasonable and just agreement. However, as I said in my last report, I believe that the elements necessary for a political settlement in Cyprus do exist and that a compromise solution could be worked out, including the crucial issue of local government.

121. In view of the situation prevailing in Cyprus, I have no doubt that the presence of the Force in the island continues to be necessary and that its withdrawal would involve an acute risk of a return to the pattern of intercommunal violence. In the circumstances, I see no alternative but to recommend to the Security Council the extension of UNFICYP's mandate for another period of six months. The government of Cyprus and the governments of Greece and Turkey have informed me of their agreement to the proposed extension.

122. In recommending a further extension of the UNFICYP mandate, I must once again draw attention to the serious situation concerning the financing of the operation. The deficit in the UNFICYP budget remains high and, as indicated in the body of this report, a slight reduction in the overall deficit is in fact likely to be nullified by certain problems relating to the payment of the pledges of one government. This makes it all the more necessary for governments to give adequate financial support to this important United Nations peace-keeping effort. At the same time, I must again point out that this situation is obviously related to the unsatisfactory method of financing UNFICYP by voluntary contributions.

. . .

Statement to the General Assembly on the
Financial Situation of the United Nations

NEW YORK   DECEMBER 17, 1970

U THANT'S continued concern over the financial plight of the United Nations was reflected in the Introduction to his 1970 annual report. The Organization's financial situation, he said, "is worse than ever before and steadily deteriorating." He urged Member states on the occasion of the twenty-fifth anniversary of the United Nations to find the means "to restore the solvency" of the Organization. "This hand-to-mouth existence scarcely befits the dignity of the world Organization," he said, "nor does it permit the conduct of the financial operations of the United Nations on a business-like basis."

Thant had been plagued by financial problems since he took office in 1961 to find the Organization on the brink of bankruptcy as a result of the massive costs of the Congo operation. As a stopgap measure he had initiated the proposal for a $200 million bond issue, but the problem remained a major one. For almost nine years he had sought to persuade the big powers to restore the Organization to solvency through voluntary contributions, but his efforts had been unavailing. With his second term about to enter its final year, Thant went before the General Assembly to launch a new effort not only to restore the solvency of the United Nations but to work out a formula for keeping it on a sound financial basis. He had enlisted the help of Edvard Hambro, president of the Assembly, who had agreed to work with him and experts in the Secretariat on the problem. He had chosen the final plenary meeting of the twenty-fifth session to announce plans for the joint effort aimed at solving the problem before Thant stepped down from office at the end of 1971. Unfortunately, this initiative was destined to be no more successful than its predecessors.

MEMBERS OF THE Assembly will be aware of the concern I have repeatedly expressed, since assuming office nine years ago, over the Organization's mounting financial difficulties. It is not my intention to

SOURCE: General Assembly Official Records, Twenty-fifth Session, 1933rd plenary meeting.

review these difficulties at this late hour. The facts are already on record—most recently in the Introduction to my report on the work of the Organization and in my statement of October 5 to the First (Political and Security) Committee. I expressed the hope on the latter occasion that arrangements could be agreed upon with a view to resolving these difficulties in this twenty-fifth anniversary year or immediately following it. I said that I had specifically in mind the circumstances that have resulted in the withholding of contributions to the regular budget; the unfunded arrears which remain on the books of the Organization; the problem of the appropriate handling and disposition of certain so-called surplus accounts; and, not least, the obligation owed to governments for which no source of funding is currently available, with the result that the Organization's credit, or even more importantly its integrity, is in danger of being seriously compromised.

As I see the situation, the first essential step is to secure additional voluntary contributions in an amount sufficient to restore the solvency of the United Nations, and that task having been accomplished, to then work out such accommodation as will ensure a sound financial basis for the Organization thereafter. I must admit, in all frankness, that the experience of the past provides little ground for optimism. Yet I see no reason for despair, and still less for resigning ourselves to a policy of drift and deterioration. I am convinced, on the contrary, that there is a common interest in liquidating the past so that a new and generally acceptable course—if one can be found—may be charted for the future. In that connection and in the absence of other initiatives, I therefore intend, with the technical help of my principal aides on budgetary and financial matters, to give special attention as a matter of priority during coming months to the Organization's financial situation and the means by which the difficulties that have plagued us for so long might best be overcome. Since such an endeavor, if it is to yield positive results, will call for much quiet diplomacy through contacts and consultations with Member governments—in particular, prospective contributors—I have also sought the assistance and advice of the president of the twenty-fifth session of the General Assembly, Ambassador Hambro, who has graciously consented to join his good offices with those of the Secretary-General.

I hope that as a result of the joint efforts of the President and the Secretary-General a more hopeful and encouraging report on United Nations finances will be presented to the twenty-sixth session.

❧ 1971 ❧

THE SITUATION IN THE MIDDLE EAST

THE MIDDLE EAST peace talks were resumed at United Nations Headquarters on January 5 under the auspices of the Secretary-General's special representative, Gunnar Jarring. Jarring met separately with the representatives of Egypt, Israel, and Jordan. At the request of Israel, he flew to Jerusalem for discussions with Prime Minister Golda Meir and Foreign Minister Abba Eban. These talks and subsequent talks with the Arab representatives further defined the positions of the two sides but disclosed no substantial movement toward agreement on how to implement the Security Council's resolution of November 22, 1967, which had been accepted by both Israel and the two Arab governments involved in the negotiations. In an effort to break the deadlock, Jarring submitted an *aide-mémoire* on February 8 asking the parties to make prior commitments to him on the key question of Israeli troop withdrawal and acceptance of a peace agreement by Egypt and Jordan. The Egyptian government formally accepted the proposal on February 15, but Israel reacted angrily, asserting that Jarring had exceeded his terms of reference by proposing the withdrawal of Israeli troops to the former international boundary between Egypt and the British Mandate of Palestine. This, the Israelis said, went even further than the November 22 resolution which called for withdrawal to the lines that existed prior to June 5, 1967. Israel told Jarring that it would not agree to withdraw to the former international boundary or to the 1967 boundary, but that it would give an undertaking to withdraw "to recognized and agreed boundaries to be established in the peace agreement."

U Thant had worked with Jarring on the February 8 *aide-mémoire* and had fully approved its contents before its submission to the parties. In a report to the Security Council on March 5, the Secretary-General noted with satisfaction that Egypt had given a positive reply, but he was plainly disappointed with Israel's answer. He appealed to the Israeli government to reconsider its position and to "respond favorably" to Jarring's initiative. Instead, Israel refused to take part in futher peace talks on the basis of Jarring's *aide-mémoire*. Jarring returned to his post as Sweden's ambassador to Moscow. At a press conference in Geneva on April 29, the Secretary-General said he and Jarring had reviewed the situation and that both agreed there "is at present no real basis for Ambassador Jarring's immediate return to New York." It was arranged, however, for Jarring to be in

New York about the middle of May for a further exchange of information with the Secretary-General.

Meanwhile, the United States had undertaken an independent effort to seek an agreement on the reopening of the Suez Canal. The United Nations was not involved, but United States Secretary of State William P. Rogers, who was directing the new talks personally, kept Thant informed on the discussions. At the April 29 press conference, Thant said he had been told by Rogers that the primary United States aim was to help the Jarring mission by trying to remove a major cause of tension. Thant said he did not believe the United States initiative would interfere with Jarring's efforts toward an overall peace agreement.

Both during this press conference and at a later one in Boston, on May 27, the Secretary-General supported Jarring's February 8 initiative. On April 29, he said the representatives of the four big powers felt that Jarring "was strictly within his mandate in taking that initiative" and that "I fully endorsed that position." At the May 27 press conference he again stated that the permanent members of the Security Council had approved of Jarring's *aide-mémoire*. He added: "He has acted fully within his mandate. I have also endorsed his action and initiative . . ."

---

1. Report to the Security Council on Activities of the Special Representative

NEW YORK   JANUARY 5, 1971

I. Activities of the Special Representative during the Period December 9, 1967, to November 26, 1968

. . .

4. WHEN THE special representative first met with the parties in December 1967, he found that the Israeli government was of the firm view that a settlement of the Middle East question could be reached only through direct negotiations between the parties culminating in a peace treaty and that there could be no question of withdrawal of their forces prior to such a settlement. On December 27, the minister for foreign affairs of Israel, Mr. Abba Eban, communicated to the special represent-

SOURCE: Security Council Official Records, Twenty-sixth Year, Supplement for January, February and March 1971, document S/10070.

ative a proposal that Israel and the United Arab Republic representatives should, as a first step, discuss an agenda for peace. The Israeli proposals for such an agenda were:

1. *Political and juridical problems:* The replacement of cease-fire arrangements by peace treaties ending the state of belligerency, ending all hostile acts and threats and embodying a permanent undertaking of mutual nonaggression.

2. *Territorial and security problems:* The determination of agreed territorial boundaries and security arrangements. Agreement on this measure would determine the deployment of armed forces after the cease-fire.

3. *Navigation problems:* Practical methods should be discussed for ensuring free navigation for all states including Israel in the Suez Canal and the Gulf of Aqaba when the cease-fire is replaced by peace. In the light of tragic experience, it is evident that international declarations cannot by themselves solve this problem. Concrete measures and guarantees are required.

4. *Economic problems:* Proposals for terminating boycott practices and instituting normal economic relations.

5. The United Arab Republic and Jordan, for their part, insisted that there could be no question of discussions between the parties until the Israeli forces had been withdrawn to the positions occupied by them prior to June 5, 1967. Reacting specifically to the Israeli proposals for discussing an agenda for peace, the minister for foreign affairs of the United Arab Republic, Mr. Mahmoud Riad, stated that the withdrawal of Israel's forces to the positions held prior to June 1967 was a basic and preliminary step to a peaceful settlement in the Middle East.

6. An Israeli proposal for discussions on an agenda for peace with Jordan was submitted to the special representative on January 7, 1968. It followed the same general lines as the proposal for the United Arab Republic but contained more detailed suggestions for economic cooperation, as well as the following new topics:

Humanitarian problems: In the proposed negotiation, high priority should be given to a solution of the refugee problem with international and regional cooperation.

Religious and historical sites: Access to sites of special religious significance should be discussed. The government of Israel clarified its views on this subject in several verbal and written communications to the United Nations.

It was also stated:

In the meantime, it is urgent that breaches of the cease-fire and activities by El-Fatah and other such organizations should be suppressed and every effort made on both sides to avoid exchanges of fire.

7. The proposals, when communicated to the Jordanian authorities by the special representative, were objected to in the same way as the proposals to the United Arab Republic had been.

8. Faced with these conflicting positions, the special representative sought to obtain from the parties an assurance that they would implement Security Council resolution 242 (1967), in the hope that such a declaration would be regarded as a basis for subsequent discussions between the parties. The special representative received from Mr. Eban a number of formulations of Israel's position on the Security Council resolution, of which the last, dated February 19, 1968, read as follows:

1. The government of Israel, out of respect for the Security Council's resolution of November 22, 1967, and responding affirmatively thereto, assures you of its full cooperation in your efforts with the states concerned to promote agreement and to achieve an accepted settlement for the establishment of a just and lasting peace, in accordance with your mandate under the resolution.

2. Israel's position has throughout been that the best way to achieve the objective of the Security Council resolution is through direct negotiations. However, as a further indication of Israel's cooperation, we are willing that this be done in a meeting convened by the special representative of the Secretary-General.

3. On February 12, 1968, I informed you of Israel's acceptance of the Security Council's call in its resolution of November 22, 1967, for the promotion of agreement on the establishment of peace. The United Arab Republic is also aware of Israel's willingness as explained on February 1 to negotiate on all matters included in the Security Council's resolution. We accept the sponsor's view that the principles recommended for inclusion in the peace settlement are integrally linked and interdependent.

4. We have noted the United Arab Republic's willingness to "implement" the Security Council's resolution and fulfill its obligations thereunder. It is a matter of concern that the United Arab Republic statements, unlike those of Israel, do not specifically use the precise terms of the resolution in such crucial matters as "agreement" and the "establishment of a just and lasting peace," and that the United Arab Republic has not yet agreed to a process of negotiation without which, of course, a declaration of willingness to fulfill the resolution is of no substantive effect. The resolution is a framework for *agreement*. It cannot be fulfilled without a direct exchange of views and proposals leading to bilateral contractual commitments. The United Arab Republic position is, therefore, still deficient in important respects. We are, however, conscious of the importance of the fact that the United Arab Republic and Israel have both responded affirmatively to the call for cooperating with you in the mission laid upon you by the Security Council. At the same time, it would be unrealistic to ignore that there have been sharp differences of interpretation of what the resolution entails. To subscribe to similar declarations does not of itself solve practical issues at stake.

5. It is accordingly urgent to move forward to a more substantive stage and to embark on a meaningful negotiation for achieving the just and lasting peace called for by the Security Council.

In discussions with the special representative, Mr. Eban stated that Israel would not object to an indirect approach to negotiations provided that it was designed to lead to a later stage of direct negotiations and agreement.

9. The United Arab Republic foreign minister gave repeated assurances that the United Arab Republic was ready to implement the Security Council resolution as a whole and to fulfill its obligations under it, but stated that it would not accept direct negotiations. The United Arab Republic accepted indirect negotiations; however, the first step must be an Israeli declaration "in clear language" that it would implement the Security Council resolution.

10. The Jordanian authorities expressed a similar point of view to the special representative.

11. The special representative then proceeded to United Nations Headquarters for consultations with the Secretary-General. Returning to the area at the beginning of March, he informally presented to the parties, to ascertain their reactions, a draft letter from himself to the Secretary-General, which would be worded as follows:

The Governments of Israel and the United Arab Republic [Jordan] have both indicated to me that they accept Security Council resolution 242 (1967) of November 22, 1967, for achieving a peaceful and accepted settlement of the Middle East question and intend to devise arrangements, under my auspices, for the implementation of the provisions of the resolution.

The two governments have expressed their willingness to cooperate with me in my capacity as special representative of the Secretary-General in the discharge of my tasks of promoting agreement and achieving such a settlement.

In view of the urgency of the situation and with a view to expediting efforts to reach settlement, I have invited the two governments to meet with me, for conferences within the framework of the Security Council resolution, in Nicosia. I have pleasure in informing you that the two governments have responded favorably to this invitation.

12. When Ambassador Jarring presented this text to the United Arab Republic foreign minister on March 7, 1968, the latter stated that recent statements by Israeli leaders showed that they were following an expansionist line. It was no longer sufficient to have Israel give an assurance of intent to implement the resolution; the Arabs had to be satisfied that the Israelis were going to "implement it for action." If the Israelis withdrew

completely from the occupied territories, peace could be arrived at by the implementation of the other provisions of the Security Council resolution under the Council's guidance.

13. In a meeting on March 10, the special representative informed the Israeli foreign minister of the United Arab Republic attitude. He then informally showed his draft letter to the foreign minister, who expressed the personal view that it would be fully acceptable to the Israeli authorities if it was also accepted by the other side and led to contacts between them. Subsequently the special representative was informed of Israel's official acceptance, without conditions, of the text.

14. In a meeting on March 14, the Jordanian authorities stated that they were ready to accept the proposed meeting in principle provided that the text was modified to read that the parties had "declared their readiness to implement the resolution."

15. During the following weeks, Ambassador Jarring paid repeated visits to the countries concerned in an endeavor to obtain from the Israelis a more precise formulation of their acceptance of the resolution and from the two Arab states acceptance of the idea of meetings between the parties under his auspices.

16. At a meeting in Amman on April 16, 1968, the Jordanian authorities stated that they were prepared to accept the text of the special representative's draft letter provided that the third paragraph was amended to read as follows:

In view of the urgency of the situation and with a view to expediting efforts to reach settlements, I will meet with representatives of Israel and Jordan for conferences within the framework of the Security Council resolution, in New York. I have pleasure in informing you that the two governments have responded favorably hereto.

The acceptance was based on the assumption that the United Arab Republic would accept an identical text.

17. The Israeli authorities found difficulties in the Jordanian amended text. They had accepted meetings at Nicosia, on the understanding that the special representative's invitation would lead to joint meetings. The new text appeared to give the impression that only meetings between the parties and the special representative were intended. The change of venue, while not objectionable in principle, tended to create the impression that only discussions with the permanent missions in the scope of normal United Nations activities would take place; a change from Nicosia to a European city would be acceptable.

18. The United Arab Republic foreign minister at first continued to insist on a prior declaration by Israel of its intention to implement the Security Council resolution. Finally, however, on May 9, on the eve of the special representative's departure from the area, he replied to the special representative's proposed invitation in the form amended by Jordan in the following written statement:

With reference to your indication to me today of your desire to meet with a representative of the United Arab Republic in New York, I wish to reaffirm the readiness of our permanent representative to the United Nations in New York to meet with you to continue the contacts which you have been conducting with the parties concerned in accordance with Security Council resolution 242 (1967) of November 22, 1967, for the implementation of that resolution.

I have referred in the course of our previous meetings to the importance of the setting of a timetable for the implementation of the resolution of the Security Council, and offered you several alternatives toward that end, one of which was that you present a timetable prepared by yourself for the implementation of the resolution. These suggestions emanate from the United Arab Republic's indication to you of its acceptance and readiness to implement the above-mentioned resolution.

I wish to express anew our willingness to cooperate with you in your capacity as special representative of the Secretary-General in the discharge of your tasks as defined in the Council's resolution of November 22, 1967.

The United Arab Republic foreign minister repeated that the United Arab Republic was ready to implement the resolution as a whole and as a "package deal." It insisted, however, that Israel should do likewise, including complete withdrawal.

19. Ambassador Jarring was faced with a position where there was now agreement, though clearly with considerable differences of interpretation, on the first two paragraphs of his proposed invitation, but where there was disagreement on the third paragraph containing the actual invitation. Further journeying backward and forward between the various countries was unlikely to be productive. In consultations with me, he considered issuing a formal invitation along the lines of his proposal, but with the venue at New York, but it was felt that a forced acceptance obtained by such an invitation would not be helpful. Instead it was decided that the talks in New York should begin without a formal invitation by the special representative or a letter from the special representative to the Secretary-General but on the basis of a short statement to the press in which it would be announced that the special representative was arriving in New York for consultations in continuation of his mission.

20. During his stay in the area, the special representative visited Beirut on three occasions. The Lebanese government expressed its full support for a solution according to Security Council resolution 242 (1967). Lebanon, however, had no territory under occupation and therefore did not have the same detailed involvement in the settlement as the United Arab Republic and Jordan. The special representative did not visit Syria, whose government, as noted above, had not accepted the Security Council resolution.

21. Ambassador Jarring left the area on May 10, 1968, and arrived at Headquarters on May 15, 1968.

22. In the five weeks following his arrival at New York, Ambassador Jarring pursued actively his contacts with the permanent representatives of the parties at both a formal and an informal level. Unfortunately these contacts did not serve in any way to break the deadlock between the parties concerning the interpretation of the Security Council resolution and the manner in which it should be implemented. In that regard, the permanent representative of Israel had stated in the Security Council on May 1, 1968:

In declarations and statements made publicly and to Mr. Jarring, my government has indicated its acceptance of the Security Council resolution for the promotion of agreement on the establishment of a just and durable peace. I am also authorized to reaffirm that we are willing to seek agreement with each Arab state on all the matters included in that resolution.

This statement was not regarded as acceptable by the Arab representatives.

23. Returning to New York on July 22 after a short stay in Europe during which he had met in various capitals the foreign ministers of the United Arab Republic, Israel, and Jordan, Ambassador Jarring decided, with my approval, to return to the Middle East and resume his direct contacts with the parties. This second round of discussions, which began on August 16, 1968, took the form of an exchange of questions and of comments between the parties through the special representative. Some progress in the clarification of the respective positions of the parties had been made when the opening of the twenty-third session of the General Assembly caused the venue of the discussions to be transferred to New York, where they could be carried out with greater convenience. With the arrival of the foreign ministers of the parties for the session toward the end of September, Ambassador Jarring began a series of frequent meetings with them individually, which were at first mainly of an infor-

mal nature but which, following the delivery by the foreign ministers of their speeches in the general debate, assumed a more formal character and concluded with written communications from the foreign ministers of Israel and of the United Arab Republic restating the positions of the respective governments. Those written statements were in amplification of the positions of the parties as publicly stated in the General Assembly and made clear the essential differences between them. On the one hand, Israel regarded the Security Council resolution as a statement of principles in the light of which the parties should negotiate peace and, on the other hand, the United Arab Republic considered that the resolution provided a plan for settlement of the Middle East dispute to be implemented by the parties according to modalities to be established by the special representative. It was also abundantly clear that there was a crucial difference of opinion over the meaning to be attached to the withdrawal provisions of the Security Council resolution, which according to the Arab states applied to all territories occupied since June 5, 1967, and according to Israel applied only to the extent required when agreement had been reached between the parties on secure and recognized borders between them.

24. Discouraging though the prospects seemed, Ambassador Jarring decided to carry out another brief round of discussions in the Middle East. As he explained in a letter to me dated November 26, 1968, he had in mind inviting the parties to a new round of discussions in the middle of January 1969 in order to give them time for reflection and for careful consideration of their respective positions.

II. Activities of the Special Representative from November 27, 1968, to June 1970

25. Ambassador Jarring departed from Headquarters on November 27, 1968, and met with representatives of Israel in Nicosia on December 2 and 3, of the United Arab Republic in Cairo on December 4, and of Jordan in Amman on December 7. Unfortunately these meetings did not reveal a change of position in the attitude of the parties that would have made it expedient for Ambassador Jarring to convene a meeting of the parties in the middle of January 1969, as envisaged in his letter of November 26, 1968.

26. After resuming for a time his duties as ambassador of Sweden to the Union of Soviet Socialist Republics, Ambassador Jarring returned to

Headquarters on January 29, 1969. He there undertook a series of personal contacts with the permanent representatives of the parties and the representatives of other Member states.

27. At that stage, Ambassador Jarring concluded, with my concurrence, that the best contribution which he could make to breaking the existing deadlock was to make a further tour of the Middle East in which he would submit formally to the parties a series of questions designed to elicit their attitude toward Security Council resolution 242 (1967). He accordingly left New York on February 21, 1969, for the Middle East. At meetings with the foreign ministers of the United Arab Republic on March 5, of Jordan on March 8, of Israel on March 9, and of Lebanon on March 14, he submitted the questions which he had previously prepared. The replies[1] of the parties were received by Ambassador Jarring as follows:

Israel: handed to Ambassador Jarring in Jerusalem by the minister for foreign affairs on April 2, 1969.

Jordan: received by Ambassador Jarring in Nicosia on March 24, 1969.

Lebanon: received by Ambassador Jarring in Moscow on April 21, 1969.

United Arab Republic: handed to Ambassador Jarring in Cairo by the minister for foreign affairs of the United Arab Republic on March 27, 1969.

28. It had been the hope of Ambassador Jarring, in submitting his questions, that the replies might show certain encouraging features which might make it possible to invite the parties for a series of meetings between them and him at some mutually convenient place. Unfortunately, the replies were in general a repetition of attitudes already expressed to Ambassador Jarring on numerous occasions from the beginning of his mission. They showed continued serious divergences between the Arab states and Israel both as regards the interpretation to be given to the Security Council resolution and as to the procedures for putting its provisions into effect.

29. Ambassador Jarring was regretfully forced to conclude, with my agreement, that the conditions for convening a useful series of meetings at that time did not exist and that there was no further move which he

---

[1]For the texts of the questions and replies, see Security Council Official Records, Supplement for January, February and March 1971, document S/10070, annex I.

could usefully make at that stage. He therefore returned on April 5, 1969, to Moscow, where he resumed his duties as ambassador of Sweden to the Union of Soviet Socialist Republics.

30. Ambassador Jarring continued to keep in close touch with me and with representatives of the parties and of other interested states.

31. Ambassador Jarring returned to Headquarters from September 12 to October 8, 1969, and from March 10 to 26, 1970, but found no new elements which would permit him to organize active discussions with the parties. On each occasion he returned to his post in Moscow.

32. On April 3, 1969, the permanent representatives of France, the Union of Soviet Socialist Republics, the United Kingdom of Great Britain and Northern Ireland, and the United States of America began a series of meetings on the Middle East question, which have continued at various intervals up to the present time. After each such meeting, the chairman reported to me on the substance of the discussions and I kept Ambassador Jarring informed.

III. The Attempt to Hold Discussions under the Special Representative's Auspices (June 1970–January 4, 1971)

33. In June 1970, the government of the United States of America proposed to the governments of Israel, Jordan, and the United Arab Republic that they should each advise Ambassador Jarring as follows:

(a) that having accepted and indicated their willingness to carry out resolution 242 (1967) in all its parts, they would designate representatives to discussions to be held under his auspices, according to such procedure and at such places and times as he may recommend, taking into account as appropriate each side's preference as to method of procedure and previous experience between the parties;

(b) that the purpose of the aforementioned discussions is to reach agreement on the establishment of a just and lasting peace between them based on (1) mutual acknowledgment by the United Arab Republic, Jordan, and Israel of each other's sovereignty, territorial integrity, and political independence, and (2) Israeli withdrawal from territories occupied in the 1967 conflict, both in accordance with resolution 242 (1967);

(c) that, to facilitate his task of promoting agreement as set forth in resolution 242 (1967), the parties would strictly observe, effective July 1 at least until October 1, the cease-fire resolutions of the Security Council.

34. Having been informed by the United States government that the states concerned had accepted its peace initiative, I invited Ambassador Jarring to return immediately to Headquarters, where he arrived on August 2. I informed the Security Council in a note dated August 7, 1970 (S/9902), that Ambassador Jarring had received confirmation from the representatives of those states of their acceptance and that he had addressed to me a letter as described above. I was informed by the United States representative that his government had received the acceptance of the governments of the United Arab Republic and Israel to a standstill cease-fire for a period of ninety days from 2200 GMT on the same day. Ambassador Jarring and I had previously been informed by the Secretary of State, Mr. Rogers, that his government would take responsibility for organizing the standstill cease-fire.

35. Ambassador Jarring at once entered into contact with the parties and, after considering their views on the time and place of the discussions, on August 21, 1970, addressed to them invitations to take part in discussions opening in New York on August 25, 1970. On the appointed day he met representatives of each of the parties. However, Ambassador Tekoah, who had been designated by Israel as its representative for the initial phase of the talks, then stated that he had been instructed by his government to return to Israel for consultations. On his return on September 8, he communicated to Ambassador Jarring the following decision of his government:

Israel's acceptance of the United States peace initiative according to its decision of August 4, 1970, and the appointment of a representative to the talks under the auspices of Ambassador Jarring are still in effect.

The government of Egypt has gravely violated the cease-fire standstill agreement, and this violation is continuing without let-up.

The strictest observance of the cease-fire standstill agreement is one of the central elements of the American peace initiative and of the talks under the auspices of Ambassador Jarring. Therefore, so long as the cease-fire standstill agreement is not observed in its entirety, and the original situation restored, Israel will not be able to participate in these talks.

Ambassador Tekoah, who is returning to his post as head of the permanent delegation of Israel at the United Nations, has been authorized to bring this decision of the government of Israel to the attention of Ambassador Jarring.

The special representative thus found himself precluded for the time being from holding formal meetings with the Israeli representatives, and his talks with the representatives of the Arab states, though they continued, could not be productive because of the lack of contact with the

Israeli representative. After a brief visit to Moscow from October 6 to 14 to attend to his affairs as ambassador of Sweden there, the special representative returned to New York and had a wide range of contacts with representatives of the parties and of other Member states during the commemorative session of the General Assembly and the debate on the Middle East, which followed that session.

36. Immediately following the adoption of General Assembly resolution 2628 (XXV), Ambassador Jarring entered into contact with the representatives of the parties in order to invite them to re-enter into talks under his auspices for the purpose of reaching agreement on the establishment of a just and lasting peace. The representatives of Jordan and the United Arab Republic informed him that their governments continued to be willing to do so; the representative of Israel stated that the matter was under consideration in the Israeli Cabinet.

37. On November 19 and pending a decision by the Israeli Cabinet, Ambassador Jarring returned to Moscow. On the eve of his departure, he addressed a letter to the Israeli minister for foreign affairs, in which he formally invited the Israeli government to resume its participation in the discussions, as well as letters to the representatives of Jordan and the United Arab Republic, in which he took note of the position of their governments.

38. On December 30, Ambassador Jarring received in Moscow a message from the foreign minister of Israel in which the latter informed him of the readiness of the government of Israel to resume its participation in the talks.

---

2. Transcript of Press Conference

GENEVA   APRIL 29, 1971

THE SECRETARY-GENERAL: Well, ladies and gentlemen, as has been customary on the eve of my departure from Geneva to New York, I just want to see you and extend to you my very best wishes. I look forward

SOURCE: UN Press Release SG/T/347.

to seeing all of you in July when I come here in connection with the Economic and Social Council meetings and, at that time of course, I propose to have a regular press conference and my regular reception for all the members of the press corps. For the moment, I have a brief statement to make.

Yesterday and this morning, I had a useful and comprehensive exchange of information and views with Ambassador Jarring on the situation in the Middle East. We both agree that, although there is at present no real basis for Ambassador Jarring's immediate return to New York, it will be desirable for him to be in New York for a short period about the middle of May for further exchange of information and views, that is, between Ambassador Jarring and myself.

I will be glad to answer a few questions before I leave.

QUESTION: Is this because while [William] Rogers is making an attempt to get some sort of partial agreement that there is no need for Jarring to get into the picture?

THE SECRETARY-GENERAL: No, when we decided on this short announcement, we did not have in mind any particular activity of any particular government for the moment. We took into consideration all factors, and both of us feel that there might be some basis for his return to New York about the middle of next month. Of course, the duration of his stay in New York will depend primarily on the nature of those developments. As you know, the current talks regarding the opening of the Suez Canal have been conducted outside the framework of Ambassador Jarring's activities. I was not involved. Ambassador Jarring was not involved, the United Nations as such was not involved, the four permanent members of the Security Council as such were not involved. But the United States government very kindly briefed me before I left New York last week about the nature of the discussions which are going on between the United Arab Republic and Washington, and Israel and Washington. Ambassador [George] Bush, the permanent representative of the United States to the United Nations, briefed me rather fully on Friday last. The Secretary of State [Rogers] told me personally two weeks ago when I met him in San José in Costa Rica that the efforts of the United States government in bringing about agreement regarding the Suez Canal were directed primarily to help Ambassador Jarring's efforts. As you know, Ambassador Jarring's primary function was and still is to promote agreement. You will also recall that, on the 8th of February, he took some initiative in the form of the dispatch of *aide mémoires* simultaneously to the United Arab Republic and Israel, and, I believe, on the 15th of February, the United Arab Republic responded to his initiative. It was the feeling of the four permanent members of the Security Council, namely, the United States, the United Kingdom, France, and the Soviet Union, that Ambassador Jarring was strictly within his mandate in taking that initiative—I fully endorsed that position—and the four permanent members of the Security Council have also expressed their appreciation to the United Arab Republic for its positive response to Jarring's initiative which asked the two parties to make certain commitments to him simultaneously. These matters were stated in my report submitted to the Security Council on the 5th of March. This is on record.

QUESTION: Do you anticipate a briefing with Secretary of State Rogers on his Middle East visit before you see Ambassador Jarring in New York in mid-May?

THE SECRETARY-GENERAL: Yes, Ambassador Bush briefed me last Friday about the purposes of the Secretary of State's visit to the area.

QUESTION: Sir, do you agree with Mr. Rogers that prospects for peace in the Middle East have never been better—at least not in recent times?

THE SECRETARY-GENERAL: Well, my position was stated only last week, I believe, that now is the moment for the parties to move toward the full implementation of the Security Council resolution of November 1967. Time is not on the side of peace. That is why I have been advocating and urging the parties to come to a speedy settlement.

QUESTION: Who is responsible, Sir, for this impasse in which we seem to be?

THE SECRETARY-GENERAL: Well, I do not want to apportion any blame to any party, but my views on the situation were stated fully in my report to the Security Council, which, as I said a moment ago, was submitted to the Security Council on the 5th of March.

QUESTION: Do you think Mr. Rogers' visit to the Middle East is going to interfere with Gunnar Jarring's efforts?

THE SECRETARY-GENERAL: No, the United States government assured me that the primary purpose of the United States involvement in this particular question of the Suez Canal is to help Ambassador Jarring in his overall effort of seeking peace within the framework of the particular Security Council resolution. I have been assured by the United States government that that was their primary motivation.

QUESTION: What was your own view, Mr. Thant?

THE SECRETARY-GENERAL: I have to make an assessment after Mr. Rogers' return.

QUESTION: Do you have concrete reasons to think that next—the middle of next month—the situation will be better than now?

THE SECRETARY-GENERAL: Both Ambassador Jarring and I have some feelings that there might be some developments in the course of the next one or two weeks which might justify Ambassador Jarring's presence in New York, primarily for consultations with me.

QUESTION: Could you comment on the situation in Pakistan?

THE SECRETARY-GENERAL: I have been in constant touch with the government of Pakistan on the situation, on the tragic situation in East Pakistan. I have assured the government of Pakistan of our willingness, of the willingness of the international humanitarian organizations, to help the government of Pakistan to alleviate the human misery and suffering. Of course, it depends on the consent and permission of the government of Pakistan to get the international humanitarian organizations to be involved. As a matter of fact, I brought up the question at the meeting of the Administrative Committee on Co-ordination on Monday in Berne. This matter is under active consideration by the heads of the agencies primarily concerned with humanitarian activities.

QUESTION: Has the Pakistan government given any reason for not letting in the Red Cross?

THE SECRETARY-GENERAL: As I have said, I have been in touch with the government of Pakistan, and beyond that for this moment I do not think it will be in the public interest to divulge the substance of our contacts.

QUESTION: Do you have a feeling that China will be admitted to the United Nations in 1972?

THE SECRETARY-GENERAL: Yes, I still maintain my position, which I stated some time ago, that the question of the representation of China in the United Nations will be solved at the 1972 session of the General Assembly.

Thank you very much, ladies and gentlemen. My best wishes—I look forward to seeing you again in July.

3. *From Transcript of Press Conference*

BOSTON   MAY 27, 1971

. . .

QUESTION: Is this the final year of your term as Secretary-General, or do you plan to continue in that capacity?

THE SECRETARY-GENERAL: I announced my decision in January of this year in the course of a press conference. In reply to a question at that time, I said that I had no intention whatsoever of serving beyond my present term, which expires on December 31 of this year.

As a matter of fact, many of my colleagues at the United Nations know that, in 1966, when I decided not to serve the second term I had to reverse my decision because of pressures from many governments. Even then, I made it clear that it would not be my intention to serve a further term. Many of my colleagues at the United Nations know that I have not had even two or three days' vacation in the last five years. My last vacation was in January 1966. I planned two or three times in the course of the last five years, but at the last moment I had to cancel it, for international developments, as you know, are unpredictable. That is one of the main reasons why I have decided not to offer myself for a third term. And I very much hope the membership will agree on a successor in time. It is of course too early to assess or even to guess whether or not there will be agreement; but I am sure that, if the membership concentrates its attention on the selection of a successor by September, there will be an agreed candidate.

QUESTION: If they fail to agree, Mr. Secretary-General, and they asked you to stay on, would you do it?

THE SECRETARY-GENERAL: I have made my position very clear on several previous occasions to those government representatives who have very kindly asked me to reconsider my decision. I have explained to them the reasons. Of course there are many reasons. One of them is, as I have explained a moment ago, I have not had even two or three days' rest in the last five years and four months; so I feel that I need

SOURCE: *UN Monthly Chronicle,* Vol. VIII, June 1971, pp. 75–81.

some rest, and I very much hope that the governments will very kindly concentrate their attention on a candidate to succeed me.

QUESTION: As we enter the second decade of international development, do you see this as a real potential for world peace, the hope of this international development?

THE SECRETARY-GENERAL: As Pope Paul, the Holy Father, has said, peace and development are synonymous. One very fine aspect of the international situation today is that there is a growing realization among leaders of thought, leaders of men, leaders of business and leaders of industry, that development is the key to peace. From the vantage point of the United Nations, it is increasingly clear that the membership is beginning to realize a basic fact: that humanity is now at the crossroads of history and there are two choices open before it. One choice is whether the rich countries and the poor countries will march hand-in-hand toward a planned and prosperous future. That is the purpose of the launching of the Second United Nations Development Decade. The other alternative is whether the rich countries and the poor countries will go their own ways without any spirit of togetherness and march haphazardly toward an unplanned and chaotic future. Those are the two alternatives.

I am convinced that if common sense prevails—I believe common sense has begun to prevail—both the rich countries and the poor countries will choose the first alternative, because they have to sink or swim together on this small planet, because all the problems, if I may say so, almost all the problems facing the international organizations—and for that matter the international community—are global problems. They are no longer national problems. For instance, even in financial or fiscal matters, problems in one particular country have repercussions on the whole international community.

A couple of weeks ago, as you will recall, the Swiss government revalued the Swiss franc, and the Austrian government revalued the Austrian schilling. These decisions had repercussions on the United Nations. For this revaluation of their respective currencies, the United Nations, according to a very rough estimate, will have to spend an additional $3 million for this year for the members of the United Nations staff working in Geneva and Vienna because of the post adjustments, the procedure to adjust the salaries of the United Nations personnel in any category they serve. So, the decisions of the Swiss government and the Austrian government have direct repercussions on the United Nations even in the fiscal field. So it is increasingly realized by the United

Nations that almost all problems—political, economic, fiscal, or social, even natural disasters anywhere, in Peru or Iran or Turkey—have repercussions on the international scale. So the basic concept is that almost all the problems we are witnessing today anywhere in the world are no longer national problems. They are international problems.

Only with this realization, particularly on the part of the governments, leaders of party, leaders of men, will the Second United Nations Development Decade be a success.

. . .

QUESTION: Can a development decade succeed if you do not get this money from the United States and the Soviet Union?

THE SECRETARY-GENERAL: I think the success of the Second Development Decade depends on several factors and one of the principal factors is of course this one per cent contribution from the gross national product. But there are indications from the rich countries—particularly from the United States, Canada, and Western Europe. I do not want to pick and choose, but I must say that the Netherlands, for instance, has been very generous, very cooperative with the United Nations in the achievement of the objectives of the Second Development Decade. But many governments have not come out very clearly regarding their policies and their objectives; I am hopeful that, by and large, the objectives of the Second Development Decade will be achieved.

QUESTION: That may be achieved, Sir, without controls of population growth in the poorer nations of the world?

THE SECRETARY-GENERAL: This is also a factor. The problem of population has been receiving the attention of the international community for some time. I believe there is also a growing awareness on the part of many governments of the need for family planning, which is of course a very difficult and delicate problem, particularly in some countries; for instance in Latin America, partly because of religious considerations and partly because of practical considerations. Some governments still feel that their countries do not need to develop family planning policies because of the sparseness of the population. You know that is the feeling of some governments. They feel that the growth of the population in their respective countries has not been sufficiently large. This is the view held by a very small percentage of the membership.

QUESTION: What are your comments, Sir, on this type of a meeting that brings the United Nations and its work to different communities? Do you forsee the possibility of perhaps the Security Council or the General Assembly moving from capital to capital as has been suggested?

THE SECRETARY-GENERAL: Yes, I think this matter has received the attention of many governments and many diplomats and statesmen. For instance, this kind of symposium, which the United Nations is having with the cooperation of the very prominent leaders of the Boston area, will set an example. Personally, I believe similar symposia should be conducted in many other parts of the country, and for that matter in many other Member states. Speaking of the General Assembly and the Security Council, my personal feeling is that it is desirable for the Security Council, from time to time, to meet outside the Headquarters in New York. I think there is also a growing feeling among the delegates of the United Nations that from time to time it will be desirable to conduct Security Council meetings, for instance, in Geneva.

But for the General Assembly, that is a different matter in terms of practical considerations. As you know, for the conduct of the General Assembly, accommodation is a very big question; accommodation not only for the conduct of the meetings involving thousands of delegates and involving seven principal committees of the General Assembly and involving the residential problems of the delegates for their stay and the problems connected with transport. But, as far as the physical resources are concerned, the Geneva office will be completed for the purpose of the General Assembly about the end of next year, about November or December 1972. So I do not see any prospect of a General Assembly meeting outside New York in the foreseeable future. As for the Security Council, of course it is possible and practical and, in a measure, desirable. As many of you are aware, the Economic and Social Council meets from time to time in Geneva, as well as in New York.

QUESTION: Mr. Secretary-General, could we ask another question? This pertains to China. You said at the last press conference that you thought China would be in the United Nations by 1972. Have you had any reason to revise that date? Do you foresee China being in the United Nations this September or October?

THE SECRETARY-GENERAL: I ventured to predict about this question last year, and the matter came up in the course of my press conference in January this year in New York. I still maintained that the question of the representation of China in the United Nations will be solved, in my view, only in 1972.

Of course things are developing at a fast pace. It is difficult to conjecture what will happen in the next four months, before the commencement of the General Assembly; but, as of today, I still maintain that the question of the representation of China in the United Nations will not be solved this year, that is, at the forthcoming session of the General Assembly in 1971.

QUESTION: Sir, on the Vietnam and Middle East issues, are we heading in the right direction, are we easing world tensions in those two major areas?

THE SECRETARY-GENERAL: As regards the conflict in Vietnam and, for that matter, in Southeast Asia, my views are well known. I have made several observations and statements and I have also taken some actions in the last six years or so. My views, my approach to the problem and my activities are on record.

I want to take this opportunity of reiterating my position that the first priority for peace in South Vietnam is the emergence of a broad-based government in Saigon, the kind of government which enjoys the allegiance of the majority of the people of South Vietnam. I have been saying this for the last two and a half years, and I still believe this is the first priority for peace. Without this move, I am afraid there will be no further moves in the direction of peace and justice.

As regards the Middle East, as you are all aware the Security Council resolution 242 (1967) adopted in November 1967 has been accepted by all parties—and for that matter, by the entire membership—as the sole basis on which peace with justice can and must be built. In the beginning stages of the passage of that resolution, there were different interpretations put to it. But in the course of the last two years, a kind of consensus has emerged regarding the interpretation of the principal provisions of that resolution.

As you know, the four permanent members of the Security Council have been meeting in New York almost regularly for the last two years, and whoever presided over the particular meeting invariably reported to me on the proceedings, on the progress or lack of progress of the particular meeting. I transmitted the report to the Secretary-General's special representative, Ambassador Gunnar Jarring, so both Ambassador Jarring and I are fully aware of the attitude of the four permanent members of the Security Council, not only regarding their understanding of the Security Council resolution adopted in November 1967, but also their interpretations of the main provisions of that resolution.

If I may say so, it is of course not a secret matter that the four permanent members of the Security Council are generally in agreement with the interpretation of the principal provisions of the resolution. So, from the vantage point of the United Nations, I want to take this opportunity of making some brief observations.

First of all, I feel very strongly that the United Nations has a special responsibility to contribute toward a peaceful and just solution of the Middle Eastern problem. For that matter, under the Charter, the Security Council has a special responsibility to contribute toward a just and lasting peace in the Middle East. For the Security Council to carry out its legitimate functions, the permanent members of the Council must play a special role. In other words, because of their special status under the Charter the permanent members of the Council have a special responsibility to exert their utmost in order to contribute toward a just and lasting peace in the Middle East. That is my premise.

If this premise is accepted, then one has to accept that the Secretary-General's special representative's initiative taken in February of this year is fully within his mandate; and this view is shared by all the permanent members of the Security Council. He has acted fully within his mandate. I have also endorsed his action and initiative, and I am hopeful that, if the Security Council, and particularly the permanent members of the Council, really exert their utmost to contribute toward a just and lasting peace in the Middle East, there will be a just and lasting peace there. I am convinced of it.

Of course, as I have said on previous occasions, time is not on the side of peace.

From Transcript of Press Conference
Dealing with the Situation in Vietnam
and Other Subjects

NEW YORK   JANUARY 18, 1971

AT HIS FIRST press conference of 1971, held on January 18, U Thant was reminded that he had not commented for some time on the war in Indo-China. He took the occasion to reiterate his view that the "first priority for peace is the emergence of a broad-based government in Saigon, the kind of government which would receive the very wide allegiance of the people of South Vietnam." He added: "Without this prerequisite there will be no move in the negotiations either in Paris or elsewhere." Thant had repeatedly expressed the belief that none of the governments in Saigon, going back to Ngo Dinh Diem, was representative of the people. He had said in 1963, during the Diem administration, that the Republic of Vietnam lacked the two major virtues of democracy: the ability to change governments by peaceful constitutional processes and the ability to conduct public affairs by persuasion, not force. He returned to this subject at a press conference in Boston on May 27, declaring that he still believed a broad-based government in Saigon was the first priority for peace. Thant had little further to say about Vietnam before he left the office of Secretary-General. In the Introduction to his final annual report, issued on September 17, he did say, "If the peoples of China and Vietnam had been represented in this organization, I believe there would have been opportunities for earlier and more fruitful negotiations." As for his own role in Vietnam peace efforts, he was content to let the record speak for itself. In his January 18 press conference, he put it this way: "I stand by every word of what I have said on Vietnam during the past six years and I still stand by every action I have taken regarding that conflict in Vietnam. It is for future historians to assess and evaluate."

. . .

QUESTION: How do you see the most recent developments in the Middle East situation at this time? Can you give us your views on that?

SOURCE: *UN Monthly Chronicle*, Vol. VIII, February 1971, pp. 24–34.

THE SECRETARY-GENERAL: As you all know, the Secretary-General's special representative, Ambassador Jarring, is now at a very delicate stage of the discussions with the parties primarily concerned, and it will not be helpful—I am afraid it would even be damaging to his tireless endeavors to promote agreement—were I to make a substantive statement at this stage. I hope you will understand. As I have been saying for some time, I am cautiously optimistic about the outcome of those discussions. That cautious optimism is shared by Ambassador Jarring.

QUESTION: Mr. Secretary-General, in your opinion, would the introduction into the Middle East of a peace force consisting of big-four troops pose a greater or lesser danger of confrontation among the big powers?

THE SECRETARY-GENERAL: This matter has been receiving the attention of the big four for the last year or so. Of course, the Security Council is the master of its own procedures and the master of its own actions. The Security Council can decide on the composition of the United Nations peace force if it wishes. The Council can even decide that contingents of the four permanent members of the Council should also participate in such a United Nations peace force. Those are all possibilities; they cannot be ruled out.

Regarding your specific question about my attitude to this issue, I must say that the active participation in any United Nations peace force of the two superpowers would create more problems than they set out to solve. That is, of course, only my personal opinion.

As far as British and French participation is concerned, I do not see any difficulty in their functioning. You will remember that in UNFICYP, the Force in Cyprus, the British contingent has been playing a very useful role, and I am sure the French contingent will do an equal job. But I have my personal doubts about the wisdom of active participation by the two superpowers in the United Nations peace-keeping force, particularly in an area like the Middle East. Of course, in the future—perhaps in 1980 or 1990—participation by the United States and Soviet Union contingents, and even participation by a Chinese contingent, may be desirable and even essential in some areas for the purpose of peace-keeping.

QUESTION: Mr. Secretary-General, at one of your press conferences last year you set out as the likely time of the entry of China as 1972. In view of the vote in the General Assembly at its last session, do you stick to that timetable?

THE SECRETARY-GENERAL: I still maintain my position and my anticipation that the question of representation of China in the United Nations
will not be solved earlier than 1972. That remains my position.

QUESTION: Mr. Secretary-General, do you not believe that the peace-
keeping force in the Middle East would be more useful in this respect,
especially if some arrangement were made for the demilitarization of
certain zones? I am thinking of neutral states participating, instead of
any one of the big powers.

THE SECRETARY-GENERAL: These are matters which are the legitimate concern of the Security Council. Of course the Council can decide
on the character and the nature of the composition of the participants in
the United Nations force. So I do not want to project myself into this.
This is the legitimate prerogative of the Council.

QUESTION: How do you view the role of the big four powers now that
the Jarring talks have been resumed?

THE SECRETARY-GENERAL: As I have been saying in the past, the
Security Council has a very important role to play in finding a just and
peaceful solution to the Middle Eastern crisis and the Council will
continue to play a very important role in any future arrangements to
guarantee any kind of agreement that may be arrived at. So, in my view,
for the Council to function effectively in the way it was meant to function
under the Charter, the permanent members of the Council should be
energetic, and because of their special status under the Charter they
have a special responsibility to see to it that the Council is effective.
Therefore, I still feel that the four permanent members of the Council
will have a major role to play sooner or later; but, since Ambassador
Jarring is actively engaged in discussions of a very delicate and difficult
nature, there is some merit in the statements of some governments that
for the moment at least the four permanent members of the Security
Council should not be too active in arriving at a consensus or agreed
principles or guidelines for consideration by the Council. . . .

QUESTION: There has been increased aggression and hooliganism
against certain nations by the Jewish groups in this country, and yesterday a bomb was thrown at the United Arab Republic Mission. Are you
satisfied with the measures taken by the host government in this issue?

THE SECRETARY-GENERAL: All acts of violence, acts of intimidation,
and threats are deplorable and must be condemned; all of those acts are
counterproductive. It is gratifying to note that the whole civilized international community realizes the increasing gravity of the situation aris-

ing out of these acts of hooliganism, particularly in New York. I understand that the government of Israel itself has come out with a strong
condemnation of such acts.

As far as the role played by the city police is concerned, my experience with the New York Police for the past many years has been one of
cooperation, understanding, and willingness to help. That is why I was
so distressed the other day when I learned of the so-called "job action"
taken by the police. Their action, in my view, is against the public
interest and against the norms of the disciplined service which is
expected of the police force in any country, and I hope that common
sense will prevail and that things will be restored to normal very soon.

QUESTION: Mr. Secretary-General, as we move into the next twenty-
five years of the United Nations, I wonder if you would comment for us
on two aspects which we might consider as housekeeping items. One,
how do you feel about the continued talks of moving the Headquarters of
the United Nations to some other country and, second, how do you feel
about the continuous talk to the effect that the United Nations is broke
and that it is kind of up against it economically? What are your views on
this?

THE SECRETARY-GENERAL: Regarding the first question, it is for
Member states to decide where they want the Headquarters of the
United Nations to be. But a development like the one I mentioned a
moment ago will strengthen the arguments of those who want the
Headquarters of the United Nations to be moved, to be shifted some-
where else.

Regarding your second question, the United Nations financial situation is serious, as I have reported from time to time to the General
Assembly. That is why at the closing meeting of the twenty-fifth session
of the General Assembly I made a statement, and I am very glad that
Ambassador Hambro, the president of the session, has promised to
cooperate with me and use his good offices with a view to achieving the
financial solvency of the United Nations. That is one of the aspects of
the United Nations with which I have been very concerned.

You will remember that in 1962 I recommended to the General
Assembly that the United Nations should be militarily disengaged from
the Congo in 1963. My recommendation was not accepted by the
General Assembly and it decided to defer the departure of the United
Nations military forces until the middle of 1964. This postponement
meant that the United Nations had to spend an additional $50 million.

That is one aspect. Of course I am not apportioning the blame to the General Assembly or to any Member state. I am just trying to bring home the fact that there are certain areas of activities of this Organization which could have well been done without necessarily spending what it has spent. For instance, if the United Nations had been militarily disengaged from the Congo in 1963, instead of in 1964, the results would have been much the same. I felt that strongly at the time and I still feel it.

Therefore, whenever we speak of peace-keeping operations or the need for a peace force, I think this financial aspect is more or less ignored. Even now the United Nations owes $21 million to Member states for the supply of contingents to the United Nations Emergency Force (UNEF), which was withdrawn over three years ago. Even now the United Nations owes more than $11 million in cash for the Congo operations, apart from the bond issue which was floated, as you know, in 1962. Now the Cyprus operation, UNFICYP, is in the red. We had a deficit of more than $10 million at the end of last month. Therefore, this financial aspect of peace-keeping operations deserves the very close attention of the Member states. And this explains, of course in part, why the United Nations financial situation has deteriorated over the past years.

QUESTION: Sir, the United States has entered the second decade of its war on the Southeast Asian people. You have not commented on this subject for quite some time. While the United States combat role has been reduced, the aerial and other operations have really increased. Would you care to share your thoughts on this subject with us?

THE SECRETARY-GENERAL: During the war in Vietnam, in the course of the last six years or so, I have made several statements. I have also acted personally for the termination of that tragic conflict. I do not think there is anything new that I can say regarding the Vietnam war. All I can say for the moment is that I stand by every word of what I have said on Vietnam during the past six years and I still stand by every action I have taken regarding that conflict in Vietnam. It is for future historians to assess and evaluate.

For the moment I would say this: since the start of the Paris talks—and my views have been expressed in the past—the first priority for peace is the emergence of a broad-based government in Saigon, the kind of government which would receive the very wide allegiance of the people of South Vietnam. Without this prerequisite there will be no move in negotiations either in Paris or elsewhere. As you know, this feeling is shared by an increasing number of very great Americans and others throughout the world.

QUESTION: Mr. Secretary-General, I have two related questions concerning the future. The first is, under what circumstances would you accept another term in office; and the second is, what do you think is going to happen in 1972 that will make it possible to solve the China problem then?

THE SECRETARY-GENERAL: Regarding my attitude toward a third term, I believe I have stated my feelings on several previous occasions. I still maintain that attitude, namely, that first of all no one should aspire to serve as the Secretary-General of the United Nations for more than one term. When I decided to accept the second term in 1966 I had already decided that it would be my last term. Therefore, I am sure you will not be surprised when I tell you that I have no intention whatsoever of serving beyond the present term.

Regarding the second question, it is difficult to anticipate the nature of arrangements and the nature of problems to be faced by the United Nations after the solution of the question of the representation of China in the United Nations. But, as I said a moment ago, tentative preliminary arrangements have been made in the Secretariat to meet any eventuality.

QUESTION: My question was: What is going to happen in the world in 1972 that will make it possible for the United Nations to solve this problem? Are there any political events that you are expecting in 1972 that will make it possible for the General Assembly thereafter to solve the problem of China?

THE SECRETARY-GENERAL: This is my personal assessment, as I indicated at the last press conference. This is only my personal assessment.

QUESTION: Is the American election the event that will make it possible to solve the problem afterward?

THE SECRETARY-GENERAL: No, I did not have in mind any particular development when I made this assessment.

QUESTION: Could I follow up on the same question? In view of your belief that the Chinese will come in in 1972 or thereabouts, do you not think that the choice of the next Secretary-General should be a matter of consultation with Peking, and would you personally be willing to undertake such a consultation?

THE SECRETARY-GENERAL: Well, regarding the next Secretary-General, I think it is for the Security Council to recommend and for the General Assembly to elect. As far as the nature of the Secretary-General's personality is concerned, I want to make one brief observation. I feel that he should be the kind of man who looks to the future, a futurist, and has a global conception of problems. I do not believe in the importance of regional considerations in the choice of a Secretary-General. I do not believe that only an Asian or an African or a Latin American or a European should be the next Secretary-General. What I believe in are the qualities of the head as well as of the heart, like moral integrity, competence, and his ability to project into the future, to act within the framework of a global unit, and a genuine desire to see this Organization develop into a really effective instrument for peace, justice, and progress.

QUESTION: Mr. Secretary-General, you spoke about the financial crisis recently when you indicated that $21 million is still owed on UNEF and $11 million on the Congo. What strikes me as very strange, since the United Nations has so many Member states; many of them are wealthy. How can these Members stand by and allow such a crisis to exist when they could solve it overnight by joining hands and seeing that these debts were paid, and also could see to it that this was a solvent Organization. This is something which is rather strange to me, Mr. Secretary-General.

THE SECRETARY-GENERAL: Yes, that is one of the things I have in mind when I say that President Hambro has kindly agreed to use his good offices, in cooperation with me, in the course of 1971, to bring back this Organization to financial solvency.

QUESTION: May I go back to the question of your successor? Do you think that if China did not come in this year, and if the big four now choose a successor without Chinese participation, your successor will meet with the same fate as Trygve Lie in his second term? Would it be admissible for you to continue and help with the changeover?

THE SECRETARY-GENERAL: I do not think it would be useful to indulge in these hypothetical issues, since the Member states have ample notice of my intentions. Of course, I have communicated my intentions to almost all the permanent members who asked me this question, and they are aware of my intentions. Unlike in 1966 when I announced officially in September, I am announcing today, and of course some Member states were aware of this decision earlier. Since the membership has ample advance notice of my intentions, I do not think it will be a very big problem for the Members to choose a suitable successor. Of course it is difficult, but it is not impossible, and I do not believe in the concept of indispensability. There is nobody in any job who is indispensable.

QUESTION: You have always spoken of the sanctity of every human life, and the Economic and Social Council has just put on its agenda for the next session the question of capital punishment for a full-scale debate for the first time. Do you feel that it is time for the United Nations to take a stand that would lead to the abolition of capital punishment?

THE SECRETARY-GENERAL: As you know, the question of capital punishment has been before the United Nations for the past eleven or twelve years. Now the question is before the Economic and Social Council. I have done some research about the United Nations involvement in this particular question. I do not think it would be helpful if I were to give a personal opinion on this very delicate and important question. I can—and I should—speak only within the framework of the United Nations activities. This matter has been before the United Nations since the fourteenth session of the General Assembly in 1959. At that time, the General Assembly asked for a study of the question and for information on the effects of capital punishment or its abolition. This led to a series of discussions by the Economic and Social Council at subsequent sessions. If I remember correctly, the General Assembly at its twenty-third session invited Member governments to look again at legal safeguards and other issues. On the basis of that resolution I sent out a questionnaire to Member states regarding their attitude to this matter and, up till now, if I remember correctly, about forty-nine or fifty replies have been received by me. I have to present these replies to the next session of the Economic and Social Council and, in the absence of any observation or recommendation or an expression of views by any principal organ of the United Nations, I do not think I should come out with a personal opinion, although, as you all know, I have a deep-seated conviction about the sacredness of human life.

QUESTION: You have twice mentioned that the Secretariat has been making arrangements for accommodation of the People's Republic of China when it comes in. I wonder if you could tell us what that means beyond something like painting a nameplate.

Second, do you feel, Sir, that the Republic of China should have no room in this Organization in the future?

THE SECRETARY-GENERAL: On the first question I was just referring to the internal Secretariat arrangements, which I do not think I should disclose to the public. Of course those are arrangements, for instance, involving the functions of the Director of Personnel, of the Controller, of the Assistant Secretary-General for Inter-Agency Affairs, and so on. I think pre-planning is essential in all such situations. I am not saying that the People's Republic of China will be coming in this year, or next year, or the year after next. In case the question of the representation of China is solved in this house then I do not want the Secretariat to be taken by surprise, to be unprepared.

Regarding your next question, it is of course for the General Assembly—for the entire membership—to decide. I do not have any official opinion regarding the future status, vis-à-vis the United Nations membership, of the Republic of China. . . .

Statement at Ceremony Proclaiming
Earth Day

NEW YORK   MARCH 21, 1971

IT IS OFTEN said that, in order for mankind to unite and to overcome its wars and divisions, nothing less than in invasion of earth by Martians would be required. This is no longer true. Humanity will be united by the common dangers we all face: the armaments race and its inherent risks of obliterating all life on earth; the outburst of the human species and of its settlements; man's endless passion to change the physical and living texture of our planet primarily for selfish reasons and often needless consumption; the explosive coexistence of wealth and extreme poverty; the predominance of intellectualism and materialism over morality; the widespread prevalence of violence, dissatisfaction, and dissent; the deterioration of our natural environment, and so on.

No wonder that an ''Earth Day'' has become suddenly necessary to remind us of the fact that our small planet is perishable.

All of us, especially the leaders of this world, must have the vision, the courage, and a new broadly based sense of human solidarity to join our thoughts, our hearts, and our forces to change the present course of detrimental man-made events and divisions. Mankind's eternal aspirations for good instead of evil, for peace instead of war, for well-being instead of poverty, for justice instead of injustice, and for friendship instead of hostility have reached worldwide dimensions during this century. From the individual's birthday to the observance of United Nations Day, from personal human rights to universal brotherhood, from the family and the city-state to the international community, at long last the concepts of earth day, of world patriotism, and of the family of man have come into being.

SOURCE: UN Press Release SG/SM/1437.

May this new chapter of united world history be written with determination, tolerance, and deep common concern for all.

May there only be peaceful and cheerful earth days to come for our beautiful spaceship earth as it continues to spin and circle in frigid space with its warm and fragile cargo of animate life.

Happy Earth Day!

Address to the Council for
Foreign Relations Containing a Proposal
for a Big Five Summit Meeting

CHICAGO   MAY 5, 1971

ON NUMEROUS occasions during his ten years in office, U Thant suggested summit meetings of the two superpowers, summit meetings of the big four, and disarmament discussions that would include high-level representatives of the People's Republic of China. It was his belief that high-level contacts, whether at the summit or in periodic meetings of the Security Council or the Economic and Social Council at the ministerial level, could break down barriers that could not be overcome in ordinary diplomatic exchanges. Except for a few bilateral meetings, his desires for summit talks remained unfulfilled because throughout this period the international atmosphere was such that one or more of the big powers felt nothing would be achieved. In the spring of 1971, however, the continued improvement in United States-Soviet relations and signs of a thaw in the relations between Washington and Peking raised hopes for a broadening détente. One hopeful sign was President Richard Nixon's statement on April 29 that he expected one day to visit the People's Republic of China.

In a speech before the Council for Foreign Relations in Chicago on May 5, Thant took the occasion to make a new proposal for a summit meeting of the big five. Noting that he had advanced the idea numerous times without any success, he said the time now appeared to be ripe for him to reactivate the proposal. He suggested that the meeting be held in Geneva and offered his assistance and that of the United Nations. Nuclear disarmament, in his opinion, should head the agenda but the discussions should not be limited. Such a meeting, he said, could even have a great impact on the war in Indo-China among other unresolved problems.

The People's Republic of China was brought into the United Nations a few months later and President Nixon did visit mainland China early in 1972, but the proposed big five summit meeting was still something for the future as Thant left office.

SOURCE: *UN Monthly Chronicle*, Vol. VIII, June 1971, pp. 82–87.

I FEEL A SPECIAL sense of responsibility whenever I am asked to appear before an audience to speak about the United Nations. The courtesy, the kindness, and the understanding with which I am received do not hide from me the severe and often silent questions which are on the minds and in the hearts of the listeners: Why is there still so much horrid killing going on in this world? Why is there war in Indo-China and why does it last so long? Why is there no peaceful and just settlement in the Middle East? Why does the world spend $200 billion a year on armaments? Why are there still colonized people? Why are there divided countries? Why are not all countries participating in the United Nations? Why is there so much poverty, hunger, and illiteracy persisting on the same planet side by side with wealth, abundance, and waste? Why is there racism and *apartheid?* Why are there so many violations of human rights? Why are our common heritages, the oceans, the atmosphere, our rivers, and the beauty of our world suddenly in danger? Why are there still atomic tests? What will the future of mankind be? Where is materialism going to lead us? And so on. . . .

In each hemisphere, on each continent, in each country, these questions are given different weight and urgency. A man dying of hunger or of a bullet in Asia is asking "why" more dramatically than his fellow man who may feel strangled by over-urbanization in Europe or in North America. But each one requests an answer to his interrogations and turns to the institutions and to the leaders of this world who proclaim that they are working for peace, justice, and progress. And each year many millions of people die without having received a satisfactory answer to their question.

The United Nations sees, year after year, more people turn to it and ask this question: Why is not the United Nations doing something about it?

The question is a good one and the United Nations, at any rate, cannot avoid giving an answer. In many instances, of course, the short answer is that the United Nations is indeed doing something about it but, perhaps, not enough. In other cases, the United Nations may have a good reason for not being able to attempt to do something. To begin with, we must understand that the United Nations is but a reflection of the international community, and in effect its success or failure is the success or failure of the international community. The attitudes and tendencies of its components have a profound effect on the functioning of the United Nations; and while it is difficult, if not impossible, to answer the "whys" comprehensively in the brief space of an after-dinner speech, I will try to highlight two fundamental tendencies of our time: the consciousness that the world we live in has become a very small space, where humans and nations have become very dependent on one another; and the increasing feeling that some of the main features of present international relations have become fundamentally wrong and no longer correspond to the aspirations of the people. Both these tendencies have a direct bearing on the functioning of the United Nations. This evening I will attempt to develop my theme with a reiteration of some of my past observations on basic issues.

In October 1964, in the course of a press conference at United Nations Headquarters, in support of a statement made in Columbus, Ohio, by Governor Alfred Landon, who, you will recall, was the Republican candidate for president in 1936, I said, "I feel that it could be very worth while if attempts were made to have a dialogue between the United States, the Soviet Union, the United Kingdom, France, and the People's Republic of China." I received no official reaction from any quarter to the expression of that idea.

In June of last year, in two speeches I made at the World Food Congress in The Hague and in San Francisco on the occasion of the twenty-fifth anniversary of the signing of the United Nations Charter, I asked the following question: "Would it not be possible for the heads of state of the great powers, including the People's Republic of China, or their foreign ministers, to meet from time to time at one of the offices of the United Nations located in a neutral country to initiate a change from confrontation and division to a building of a safe and peaceful world?" I have repeated this question several times and most recently less than a month ago at the first General Assembly of the Organization of American States in San José, Costa Rica.

When I first formulated it, we seemed to be far from any possibility, let us say, of seeing the United States and the People's Republic of China sit at the same table. However, many things have changed since last year. First, you will recall Mr. Leonid Brezhnev's report to the twenty-fourth Congress of the Soviet Communist Party in which he reiterated that the Soviet Union stands "for the nuclear disarmament of all states in possession of nuclear weapons and for the convocation for this purpose of a conference of the five nuclear powers—the USSR, the

United States, the People's Republic of China, France, and Britain." I understand that this conforms to the policy which France has upheld for a number of years. General Charles de Gaulle himself had said in a press conference in 1965 that it was necessary "for Washington, Moscow, London, and Peking to agree to return to the starting point as they had agreed before founding the United Nations. France, for its part, is ready to contribute to such an agreement of the five and considers that Geneva would be the most appropriate place. . . ." Just a few days ago, on April 29, we heard President Nixon say in his press conference that he hoped and, as a matter of fact, expected to visit China some time and in some capacity and wished he could contribute to a policy in which the United States can have some relationship with mainland China.

All this leads me to believe that the time may be ripe for me to reactivate the idea I first expressed in October 1964. I think that the five nuclear powers should take advantage of the present thaw in the international situation to undertake a decisive step forward and agree to meet. Some people will object that many questions should be solved before such a gathering takes place. I would answer that if these questions are solved the meeting would hardly be necessary. Moreover, the problems of our world are of such magnitude that we need some audacity in our search for solutions. Indeed, it is the lack of even a beginning of understanding among all the great powers which is at the source of most of the world's present and seemingly intractable problems.

In my view, as I have previously stated, a five-power conference should be held at a very high level, preferably at the level of heads of state or heads of government, or at least foreign ministers if advance preparation should be necessary. The United Nations and its Secretary-General stand ready for assistance to help such a meeting turn a new page of human history. In that connection, let me say that, in my opinion, Geneva, for many reasons, would technically and politically be the most convenient place for holding such a conference.

Nuclear disarmament could probably be the most urgent theme on which to base a first meeting of the five nuclear powers, since the People's Republic of China itself has expressed interest in the question, and this would constitute the most important element occurring in that field for many years. However, it is in the nature of things that discussions at such meetings would be far-ranging and would go much beyond strict adherence to a limited agenda. I strongly believe that a gathering of the heads of state or heads of government or foreign ministers of the

People's Republic of China, France, the Soviet Union, the United States, and the United Kingdom would have a great impact on such painfully unresolved questions as the conflict in Indo-China.

I must explain that, in making this proposal, it was far from my intention to encourage the big five to form themselves into a club or a consortium to direct the affairs of the world. Such an idea would be in contradiction to the principles of the United Nations Charter, which recognize the sovereign equality of all states. However, in certain areas of activity like nuclear disarmament and peace-keeping, a large measure of agreement or consensus among the big powers is essential. Personally speaking, the final objective of the international community should not be confined to the limitation of the arms race, but directed toward the total prohibition and destruction of all nuclear weapons. Only the nuclear powers can initiate such a discussion, in response to the overriding moral pressure on the part of the non-nuclear nations. . . .

Despite the achievements of the last few years and the hopes for further progress in the near future, the world finds itself in the somewhat paradoxical situation that military expenditures have been escalating at an unconscionable rate. Between 1948 and 1968, world military expenditures have trebled at constant prices. The world is now spending some $200 billion a year for armaments. In addition to the military threats posed to humanity by the spiraling arms race, the diversion of the tremendous economic and human resources from fruitful economic and social purposes to unproductive and wasteful armaments exacts an appalling toll on the living conditions of all people, in the developed as well as in the developing countries. It is highly doubtful whether mankind can successfully deal with the staggering economic and social problems it faces, unless some of the huge sums now being devoted to military expenditures can be redirected to the solution of these problems. I need only mention the problems of poverty in the rich as well as in the poor countries and the widening gap in economic development between them; the increasingly complex problems of the population explosion and of the pollution of the environment; the racial problems on both the national and the international level, which are not unrelated to the questions of poverty and economic development; the problems of health, education, and welfare; the problems of the cities, of inadequate housing, of crime, and of drugs. All of us can readily add to this list.

The massive sums devoted to armaments do not increase international or national or human security or happiness. On the contrary, they serve to feed the escalating arms race, to increase insecurity, and to multiply the risks to human survival. The General Assembly has asked me to prepare a report, with the assistance of consultant experts, on the economic and social consequences of the arms race and of military expenditures. I have appointed a group of experts from fourteen different countries who are presently engaged in studying this question. I am hopeful that the outcome of this study and my report to the next session of the General Assembly will delineate the dimensions and ramifications of the problem and indicate basic guidelines for its solution.

The growing arms race not only puts human survival in jeopardy but, granted that humanity does manage to survive, it is also a cancerous threat to human welfare. The time has certainly arrived when intelligent human beings must at least make a beginning in reordering their national and international priorities so that their wealth and energies can be concentrated on the betterment rather than the possible destruction of life and society on this planet.

Disarmament continues to be one of the top priority subjects on the international agenda and it is under consideration in several forums in addition to the General Assembly. For one and a half years the two nuclear superpowers, the United States and the Soviet Union, have been holding bilateral strategic arms limitation talks, known as SALT, in Helsinki and Vienna. The General Assembly has twice called for a moratorium or a complete cessation of the testing and deployment of offensive and defensive nuclear weapon systems such as the MIRVs and ABMs. It has also repeatedly called for the ending of all nuclear weapon tests, including those underground. All of us most devoutly hope for the success of the negotiations at SALT. But, increasingly, concern is being voiced that SALT might achieve some quantitative limitation of nuclear weaponry but permit a qualitative nuclear arms race to continue without hindrance. No official information has been made public concerning the progress of the discussions at SALT. The time has come, I think, to ask whether these talks might not be better promoted by greater public discussion of at least the issues involved, if not of the details of the day-to-day negotiations.

A number of countries have expressed fears that unless vertical proliferation—i.e., the further development, accumulation, and deployment of nuclear weapons by the nuclear powers—is stopped, an aim which the nuclear powers have themselves pledged in the non-proliferation treaty to pursue, this important treaty might fail and with it the hopes of preventing horizontal proliferation—i.e., the spread of nuclear weapons to non-nuclear countries. I am sure that it is not necessary to explain to this audience the very grave dangers that might threaten the world if that should happen.

Let me now turn to the tragic situation in Indo-China, which is one of the basic issues which have marked my ten years as Secretary-General. You will no doubt recall that the Laotian crisis of 1961–1962 occurred when I was still Acting Secretary-General. Since then, little by little, we have witnessed the extension of the fighting and the gradual involvement of foreign countries in Vietnam, in Laos, and more recently in Cambodia.

In the course of this period, I made use of my position to express the concern of the international community. I also made certain proposals to the parties involved and took certain initiatives—some of which were made public—which I felt might contribute to a solution of the conflict. After the cessation of the bombing of North Vietnam and the beginning of the Paris conversations—two steps which had been the object of concrete suggestions on my part—I emphasized the necessity on the part of both sides for a certain flexibility if they wanted to progress on the difficult road toward peace. I deplore the fact that these talks have been considered as a contest of wills rather than an opportunity rapidly to terminate the sufferings of the peoples of the area. I also regret that, more than two years after a step which was hailed at that time as a harbinger of peace, the conflict has been extended to more areas and that, in spite of measures presented as a de-escalation, there are more refugees and more devastation.

At a time when the United Nations and the peoples and governments of its Member states are increasingly preoccupied with what we now call ecology and the protection of the environment, we are helpless spectators of the systematic destruction in Indo-China not only of innocent men, women, and children but in some cases of all animal and vegetal life and of the remnants of some of the most brilliant civilizations which have ever flourished in Asia.

While the United Nations Organization has set up a veritable shield of texts and mechanisms aimed at protecting human rights, we hear every day of the violation by all sides of the most basic of these rights, the respect of human life and human dignity. As United Nations Secretary-General, I deplore the fact that, despite my various appeals, such elementary rights as access by humanitarian organizations to prisoners of war has not been granted. My heart goes out to wives, parents, and children of those detainees just pining away, thousands of miles from their beloved ones. Nor can I condone the use of some terrifying techniques which have left millions of innocent and defenseless people disabled, displaced, and homeless. In fact, the Indo-China war is the most inhuman war in all history.

The war is waged in the name of certain principles which, as I have repeated many times, the combatants themselves violate every day. The peninsula has become a place of confrontation for the East and the West, in total disregard of the cultural values and traditional ethics of the people of the area.

During my ten years as Secretary-General, I have seen many conflicts, even many armed ones, involving Member states. In many cases, the United Nations has been able to help find a peaceful solution, as for example in the Congo, the dispute between the Netherlands and Indonesia over West Irian, the Cuban missile crisis, the Indo-Pakistani war of 1965, etc. Even when a definite settlement could not be reached, the United Nations has helped in reducing the duration and intensity of the fighting and in organizing or supervising those truces or cease-fires which, however precarious, maintain calm in Kashmir, in Cyprus, and even in the Middle East. These activities of the United Nations save every day a great number of human lives and, hopefully, lay the ground for more durable settlements. The Organization has also been, and is still, often used as a channel for negotiations. This leads me to believe that the fact that most parties to the Vietnam conflict are not represented at the United Nations makes it more difficult to find a solution. I think that if such countries as, for example, the People's Republic of China, had belonged to the world Organization, negotiations on Indo-China— even informal ones—might have taken place much earlier and might have produced more fruitful results. Perhaps some of the confrontation on the battlefield would have occurred across the conference table instead.

I sincerely hope that some new and encouraging developments will take place soon which will help end this tragic conflict in Indo-China. In any case, I believe that when the People's Republic of China participates in the United Nations, as well as perhaps other countries so far excluded from the world Organization, the countries of Indo-China will benefit from the instruments which this Organization has developed to help solve or prevent crisis.

It is also my hope that if the Organization has not been able for various reasons to play a role in the settlement of the conflict, it will at least be able to contribute to the tremendous effort of reconstruction which will be needed after this devastating conflict has ended.

In the course of this address, I have tried to deal with some of the most important political issues that we face today. I am convinced that, if these problems are to be satisfactorily resolved, the United Nations must be enabled to play a part in their solution. This, in its turn, requires the enlightened support of distinguished bodies such as your Council and the other bodies represented here, with whom I have been privileged to share a few thoughts this evening.

EAST PAKISTAN–BANGLADESH

UNTIL MARCH 1971 the growing political differences between East Pakistan and the central Pakistani government were accepted almost universally as an internal problem. The international community was involved in a massive program of assistance in the form of food and medicine for victims of the devastating cyclone of November 1970, but intervention in the political dispute seemed clearly outside the competence of the United Nations. In March, however, peaceful discussions broke down and the situation erupted into mob violence, slaughter, and massacre resulting in the flight of millions of refugees from East Pakistan into the adjacent states of India. Existing political controversies between India and Pakistan were rekindled. Although neither India nor Pakistan was ready to acknowledge that political intervention by the United Nations was required, U Thant expressed his concern to President Mohammed Yahya Khan of Pakistan. He also kept in close touch with both India and Pakistan through their permanent representatives at the United Nations.

The dispute between East Pakistan and the central government had long been smoldering, but three events set the stage for the March violence: (1) the elections of December 7, 1970, which gave a majority in the National Assembly to the Awami League, the powerful Bengali political organization led by Sheikh Mujibur Rahman, (2) the refusal of West Pakistan's most popular leader, Zulfikar Ali Bhutto, to participate in the Assembly, and (3) the postponement of the opening of the Assembly indefinitely by President Yahya Khan. Mujibur Rahman responded by ordering a general strike in East Pakistan. On March 25, Yahya Khan outlawed the Awami League and sent the army to take control of East Pakistan, which later became known as Bangladesh.

Despite the ensuing carnage, no Member state brought the question before the United Nations. As in the case of the Nigerian civil war, Thant limited his initial efforts to the humanitarian field. On April 1, during the height of the fighting, a United Nations spokesman said: "If the government of Pakistan were to request the Secretary-General to assist in humanitarian efforts, he would be happy to do everything in his power in this regard." Pakistan, however, was hesitant to ask for United Nations intervention even to this extent. It was not until some six weeks later that Yahya Khan gave the go-ahead enabling the Secretary-General to appeal for contributions and to designate Sadruddin Khan, United Nation's High Commissioner for Refugees, to coordinate the assistance of the various United Nations agencies. This was only part of the problem. A separate effort was launched to assist the millions of refugees in India and to seek to repatriate them to East Pakistan as soon as the situation permitted. Once again the United

Nations came under severe criticism. At a luncheon of the United Nations Correspondents Association on June 3, one correspondent suggested that the Organization had not come to grips with the real problem. "Does the United Nations deserve public support with such a record?" he asked. Another correspondent asked: "At what point do you think that the United Nations might consider the events as ceasing to be an internal matter of Pakistan's?" Thant did not reply directly to either question. He said it was "for future historians to gather facts and make their own evaluations, but," he added "it has been a very terrible blot on a page of human history." Although he did not say so publicly, Thant by this time had become convinced that the situation was now a threat to international peace and was, therefore, a matter for possible United Nations action. He hesitated to take any initiative on his own under Article 99 of the Charter because, upon consulting members of the Security Council, he found them sharply divided as to whether United Nations intervention would do any good. Although he had decided not to place the matter before the Security Council under Article 99, he took the unusual step of sending all members of the Council a secret *aide-mémoire* on July 20 urging the Council to intervene. "The time is past," he said, "when the international community can continue to stand by, watching the situation deteriorate and hoping that relief programs, humanitarian efforts, and good intentions will be enough to turn the tide of human misery and potential disaster."

The Security Council continued to avoid facing up to the seriousness of the situation. Thant finally made his *aide-mémoire* public on August 2 after distorted versions had appeared in print, but the Council still did not act. At his final press conference on September 14, the Secretary-General expressed regret that the Council had done nothing. He said the basic issue was the repatriation of refugees from India to East Pakistan and that this was not likely to be done unless a climate of confidence was restored. "The restoration of a climate of confidence," he said, "is not within the competence of the Secretary-General." He disclosed that he had proposed to the governments of India and Pakistan on July 19 that a limited number of United Nations representatives be stationed on both sides of the India-Pakistan border to facilitate the voluntary return of refugees to East Pakistan. India rejected the proposal on the grounds that it was not preventing the return of the refugees.

Thant sent messages to the governments of India and Pakistan on October 20, declaring that the situation was so serious it "could all too easily give rise to open hostilities which would not only be disastrous to the two countries principally concerned, but might also constitute a major threat to the wider peace." His immediate concern was the increase of incidents and the massing of troops along the borders. "In this potentially very dangerous situation," he said, "I feel that it is my duty as Secretary-General to do all that I can to assist the governments immediately concerned in avoiding any development which might lead to disaster." He proceded to offer his good offices to the two governments, but they were not accepted. By then they were on the brink of war. Up to the time major fighting began on November 22, the Security Council still had not intervened. By December 3, full-scale warfare was in progress both along India's border with

East Pakistan and along the cease-fire line in Jammu and Kashmir. When the Council did meet, its efforts were stymied by Soviet vetoes. The General Assembly adopted a cease-fire appeal, but it was ignored. On December 7, the Secretary-General went before the Assembly to make a personal appeal to all the parties to the conflict, "no matter what their allegiance, to take every possible measure to spare the lives of the innocent civilian population which is afflicted and threatened by the present hostilities." The fighting came to an end ten days later.

---

1. Appeal for Emergency Assistance to Refugees from East Pakistan in India

NEW YORK   MAY 19, 1971

THE INTERNATIONAL COMMUNITY has been seriously concerned at the plight of the sizable and continuing influx of refugees, including a large proportion of women and children, from East Pakistan into adjacent states of India. I fully share this concern. Mindful that one of the purposes of the United Nations is "to achieve international cooperation in solving international problems of . . . a humanitarian character," I am convinced that the United Nations and its family of organizations have an important role to play in alleviating the serious hardship and suffering which these refugees are undergoing.

In order to ensure a speedy and coordinated response to appeals for assistance addressed by the government of India to me and to various United Nations agencies I decided, following discussions with the executive heads of the various agencies and programs within the United Nations system, that the United Nations High Commissioner for Refugees should act as the focal point for the coordination of assistance from all the organizations of the system. As a first step the High Commissioner for Refugees dispatched a three-man team, led by his deputy, in order to assess the nature and magnitude of the needs of these refugees and to discuss with the Indian government the modalities of assistance

SOURCE: *UN Monthly Chronicle*, Vol. VIII, June 1971, p. 49.

from the United Nations system. The High Commissioner also established standing consultative machinery comprising his office and the United Nations agencies and programs directly concerned in order to assist him in these tasks.

While, in view of the fluid situation, it is not possible at this stage to assess with accuracy the total number of refugees involved there is conclusive evidence of the presence of very large numbers of people from East Pakistan in the neighboring states of India who are in immediate need of assistance. I earnestly hope that these unfortunate people will be voluntarily repatriated at the earliest possible time. It is evident, however, that pending such repatriation, massive external assistance will be required on an emergency basis. The Indian government's preliminary estimates indicate that such assistance might be of the order of $175 million for the next six months for food, clothing, shelter, medical supplies, and other essential relief items.

Several organizations of the United Nations system have already initiated action within their limited resources to provide all possible emergency relief for the afflicted people. At the same time it is clear that these resources will fall far short of the level and scope of the needs to be met.

On behalf of the entire United Nations family I therefore earnestly appeal to governments, intergovernmental and non-governmental organizations, as well as private sources, to help meet the urgent needs for humanitarian assistance in the present tragic situation. I am certain that in responding positively and generously to this humanitarian appeal for contributions in cash and in kind donors, governmental and non-governmental alike, will make use to the greatest possible extent of the established channels and procedures of the United Nations family, in particular the Office of the United Nations High Commissioner for Refugees, the World Food Programme, the United Nations Children's Fund, and the World Health Organization. I also hope that they will keep the Office of the High Commissioner for Refugees informed of all action thus taken or contemplated and will utilize the arrangements made by him to ensure the coordination and to maximize the impact of external assistance.

2. Further Appeal for Assistance, including Aid for the Population of East Pakistan

NEW YORK   JUNE 16, 1971

IT WILL BE recalled that on April 22 I addressed a letter to President Yahya Khan expressing my great concern at the situation in East Pakistan and that, on purely humanitarian grounds, I offered, on behalf of the United Nations family of organizations, all possible assistance to help his government in its task of bringing urgently needed relief for the plight of the population of East Pakistan. President Yahya Khan, in a letter to me dated May 3, 1971, stated that he was touched by my concern for the well-being of Pakistan and added that while the existing situation was that adequate supplies of medicines, foodstuffs, and other daily necessities of life were available, an assessment of future possible international assistance which might eventually be required was under preparation. On May 17, the economic adviser to the president called on me to explain the extent of relief requirements, which were subsequently set out in a communication from the permanent representative of Pakistan dated May 22.

In the meantime, and reflecting the serious concern of the international community at the hardship of the sizable and continuing influx of refugees, including a large proportion of women and children, from East Pakistan into adjacent states of India, I appealed to governments, inter-governmental and non-governmental organizations, as well as private sources, to help to supply the urgent humanitarian assistance which was needed to alleviate that tragic situation. I also decided that the United Nations High Commissioner for Refugees should act as the focal point for the coordination of assistance from the organizations and programs of the United Nations system. I much appreciate the very positive and generous response that my appeal has evoked, and I am satisfied that the arrangements made to channel the assistance given by the international community are proving effective.

SOURCE: *UN Monthly Chronicle,* Vol. VIII, July 1971, pp. 26–27.

As soon as I received the letter of May 22 from the permanent representative of Pakistan I asked the Assistant-Secretary-General for Inter-Agency Affairs to travel to Pakistan to discuss with government authorities the modalities of relief assistance to East Pakistan from and through the United Nations. He was received by President Yahya Khan and held discussions with senior authorities of the government both in Islamabad and in Dacca. There was full agreement on the manner in which the operation should be organized and the president shares my concern that the United Nations must be in a position to assure the international community and the donors in particular that all relief assistance will reach its intended destination—the people of East Pakistan. The president welcomed the arrangements envisaged by the United Nations for the operation, and I have appointed a representative in East Pakistan to act as the focal point for ensuring proper coordination of the work of the agencies and programs of the United Nations. The president of Pakistan has conveyed to me the readiness of his government to extend full cooperation at all levels to the United Nations personnel who will be associated in the planning and implementation of the relief operations.

The assessment of assistance requirements contained in the letter from the permanent representative of Pakistan, and further appraisals of such needs currently being conducted by the government of Pakistan and the United Nations agencies concerned, point to the urgency of mobilizing substantial external resources, notably food and transport, for relief action. Although this is a separate operation from the program of assistance to refugees from East Pakistan in India for which the High Commissioner for Refugees is acting as a focal point, the two operations are, of course, related to the extent that as conditions in East Pakistan are improved, there will be a better possibility of arresting and reversing the flow of refugees.

I am sure that governments, intergovernmental and non-governmental organizations, and private institutions and sources, are conscious of the need to alleviate the suffering which has befallen the population of East Pakistan and I therefore appeal to them to contribute, in cash and in kind, to this challenging humanitarian effort. I hope that donors will avail themselves for this purpose to the largest extent possible of the established procedures of the United Nations family, particularly those of the World Food Programme and the United Nations Children's Fund, whose association in the planning and organization of the task of relief has been expressly welcomed by the government of Pakistan. I trust that the world community will once again rise to the occasion in a manner consistent with the principles of human solidarity and international cooperation embodied in the Charter.

3. Texts of Aide-Mémoire *to India and Pakistan and of Memorandum to the President of the Security Council*

NEW YORK   AUGUST 2, 1971

ATTACHED TO THIS statement are the texts of an *aide-mémoire* which was given by me to the permanent representatives of India and Pakistan on July 19, 1971, and of a memorandum addressed by me to the president of the Security Council on July 20, 1971. I have decided to publish these texts since there has been considerable, and in some cases misleading, speculation and publication of incomplete information about the substance of both of them.

It will be noted that the first text refers to a humanitarian proposal, while the second is related to a concern for international peace and security. The documents are entirely separate, due to the fact that the subject matter of the second one falls within the purview of the Security Council, whereas the first falls within the efforts of the Secretary-General, through the United Nations High Commissioner for Refugees, to assist in the solution of the problem of refugees from East Pakistan now in India. The agreement of the governments concerned is required for such a suggestion to be put into effect.

The *aide-mémoire* of July 19 has a strictly limited and very modest purpose, which is clearly defined in the text. It deals with a humanitarian problem concerning refugees and contains a suggestion related to that problem which, after consultation with the United Nations High Com-

SOURCE: *UN Monthly Chronicle,* Vol. VIII, August–September 1971, pp. 56–59.

missioner for Refugees, I thought fit to make, in my capacity as Secretary-General, to the governments concerned. The *aide-mémoire* is related solely to the problem of the repatriation of the refugees from East Pakistan now in India and has no other implications. There is no question of "humanitarian peace-keeping," nor of the stationing of observers.

The suggestion is simply that a small number of representatives of the high commissioner might take to the field with strictly limited terms of reference and on an experimental basis. The areas in which these representatives might operate would be decided upon by the governments concerned in consultation with the United Nations High Commissioner for Refugees. This suggestion was made with the sole aim of facilitating, if possible, the repatriation of the refugees.

The other document deals with a far-reaching political matter relating to international peace and security and is primarily within the competence of the Security Council. Apart from the Secretary-General's competence under the Charter in such matters, I recall that at its 1329th meeting on December 2, 1966, the members of the Security Council unanimously endorsed a statement that "they fully respect his (the Secretary-General's) position and his action in bringing basic issues confronting the Organization and disturbing developments in many parts of the world to their notice. . . ."

The memorandum is not an official document of the Security Council and was intended to record my own deep concern with the wider potential dangers of the situation in the region and to provide a basis and an opportunity for an exchange of views among the members of the Security Council on this potentially very grave situation.

Text of Aide-Mémoire *to Permanent Representatives of India and Pakistan*

The repatriation of the refugees from East Pakistan now in India is a matter of the utmost concern and urgency. The Secretary-General is anxious to do everything possible, in cooperation with the governments concerned and complementary to their own efforts, to facilitate the voluntary repatriation of the refugees in a secure and orderly manner, which takes due account of their welfare.

One possible method of doing this might be to establish a limited representation of the High Commissioner for Refugees on both sides of the border. The High Commissioner for Refugees is already acting as the focal point for the United Nations effort on behalf of these refugees. The representatives of the high commissioner would be stationed at collecting points on the Indian side, at border crossing points on both sides, and in reception centers on the Pakistan side. It is the feeling of the Secretary-General that before attempting to make such an arrangement on a large scale, it would be desirable to test it in a limited way in order to ascertain whether in practice it would serve a useful purpose in facilitating the process of repatriation.

The Secretary-General therefore wishes to suggest to both governments concerned that representatives of the High Commissioner for Refugees be accepted in two or three selected areas on both sides of the border, the areas to be suggested by the governments in consultation with the high commissioner. Were this arrangement to prove useful, it would then be possible to expand it gradually to include most, or all, of the repatriation points.

The Secretary-General expresses the hope that the government of Pakistan (India) will be prepared to give the necessary cooperation to make this initial endeavor possible. A similar suggestion has been made to the permanent representative of India (Pakistan).

Text of Memorandum to the President of the Security Council

For some months now the members of the Security Council, and many other Members of the United Nations, have been deeply preoccupied with developments in East Pakistan and the adjacent Indian states and their consequences, or possible consequences. I myself expressed my concern over the situation to President Yahya Khan shortly after the events of March 1971 and have been in continuous touch with the governments of Pakistan and India, both through their permanent representatives at the United Nations and through other contacts. In these exchanges I have been acutely aware of the dual responsibility of the United Nations, including the Secretary-General, under the Charter, both to observe the provisions of its Article 2, paragraph 7, and to work, within the framework of international economic and social cooperation, to help promote and ensure human well-being and humanitarian principles.

It was with this latter responsibility in mind that I appealed for assistance both for the refugees from East Pakistan in India and for the population of East Pakistan. In order to channel the assistance given in response to those appeals, I designated the United Nations High Commissioner for Refugees as the focal point for assistance to the refugees in India and appointed, with the agreement of the government of Pakistan, a representative in Dacca, in order to make as effective use as possible of the international assistance made available for the relief of the population of East Pakistan. Both of these humanitarian efforts have been reported upon in detail elsewhere, and the Economic and Social Council held a full discussion on both operations on July 16, 1971, based on statements to the Council by the United Nations High Commissioner for Refugees and the Assistant Secretary-General for Inter-Agency Affairs. I take this opportunity to express my warm gratitude to the governments, the United Nations agencies and programs, and to the voluntary organizations which have responded generously to my appeals. I also wish to express my appreciation to the governments of India and Pakistan for their cooperation with my representatives in the field.

As the weeks have passed since last March, I have become increasingly uneasy and apprehensive at the steady deterioration of the situation in the region in almost all its aspects. In spite of the generous response of the international community to my appeals for assistance for the refugees from East Pakistan now in India, the money and supplies made available are still nowhere near sufficient, and the Indian government still faces the appalling and disruptive problem of caring, for an unforeseeable period of time, for millions of refugees, whose number is still increasing. In East Pakistan international and governmental efforts to cope with the results of two successive disasters, one of them natural, are increasingly hampered by the lack of substantial progress toward a political reconciliation and the consequent effect on law, order, and public administration in East Pakistan. There is a danger that serious food shortages, and even famine, could soon add to the sufferings of the population, unless conditions can be improved to the point where a large-scale relief program can be effective. Equally serious is the undoubted fact that reconciliation, an improved political atmosphere, and the success of relief efforts are indispensable prerequisites for the return of any large proportion of the refugees now in India. The situation is one in which political, economic, and social factors have produced a series of vicious circles which largely frustrate the efforts of the authorities concerned and of the international community to deal with the vast humanitarian problems involved.

These human tragedies have consequences in a far wider sphere. The violent emotions aroused could have repercussions on the relations of religious and ethnic groups in the subcontinent as a whole, and the relationship of the governments of India and Pakistan is also a major component of the problem. The conflict between the principles of the territorial integrity of states and of self-determination has often before in history given rise to fratricidal strife and has provoked in recent years highly emotional reactions in the international community. In the present case there is an additional element of danger, for the crisis is unfolding in the context of the long-standing, and unresolved, differences between India and Pakistan—differences which gave rise to open warfare only six years ago. Although there can be no question of the deep desire of both governments for peace, tension between them shows no sign of subsiding. The situation on the borders of East Pakistan is particularly disturbing. Border clashes, clandestine raids, and acts of sabotage appear to be becoming more frequent, and this is all the more serious since refugees must cross this disturbed border if repatriation is to become a reality. Nor can any of us here in the United Nations afford to forget that a major conflict in the subcontinent could all too easily expand.

In tragic circumstances such as those prevailing in the subcontinent, it is all too easy to make moral judgments. It is far more difficult to face up to the political and human realities of the situation and to help the peoples concerned to find a way out of their enormous difficulties. It is this latter course which, in my view, the United Nations must follow.

I do not think that I have painted too dark a picture of the present situation and of its possible consequences. In the light of the information available to me, I have reluctantly come to the conclusion that the time is past when the international community can continue to stand by, watching the situation deteriorate and hoping that relief programs, humanitarian efforts, and good intentions will be enough to turn the tide of human misery and potential disaster. I am deeply concerned about the possible consequences of the present situation, not only in the humanitarian sense, but also as a potential threat to peace and security and for its bearing on the future of the United Nations as an effective instrument for international cooperation and action. It seems to me that the present tragic situation, in which humanitarian, economic, and political problems are mixed in such a way as almost to defy any distinction between them, presents a challenge to the United Nations as a whole which must be met. Other situations of this kind may well occur in the future. If the Organization faces up to such a situation now, it may be able to develop the new skill and the new strength required to face future situations of this kind.

It is for these reasons that I am taking the unusual step of reporting to the president of the Security Council on a question which has not been inscribed on the Council's agenda. The political aspects of this matter are of such far-reaching importance that the Secretary-General is not in a position to suggest precise courses of action before the members of the Security Council have taken note of the problem. I believe, however, that the United Nations, with its long experience in peace-keeping and with its varied resources for conciliation and persuasion, must, and should, now play a more forthright role in attempting both to mitigate the human tragedy which has already taken place and to avert the further deterioration of the situation.

The Security Council, the world's highest body for the maintenance of international peace and security, is in a position to consider, with the utmost attention and concern, the present situation and to reach some agreed conclusions as to measures which might be taken. Naturally, it is for the members of the Council themselves to decide whether such consideration should take place formally or informally, in public or in private. My primary purpose at this stage is to provide a basis and an opportunity for such discussions to take place and to express my grave concern that all possible ways and means should be explored which might help to resolve this tragic situation.

---

4. Statement by a United Nations Spokesman on the Impending Trial of Sheik Mujibur Rahman

NEW YORK   AUGUST 10, 1971

The Secretary-General feels that it is an extremely sensitive and delicate matter which falls within the competence of the judicial system of a Member state—in this case, Pakistan. It is also a matter of extraordinary interest and concern in

SOURCE: *UN Monthly Chronicle,* Vol. VIII, August–September 1971, p. 69.

many quarters, from a humanitarian as well as from a political point of view. The Secretary-General has received and is still receiving almost every day expressions of serious concern from representatives of governments about the situation in East Pakistan and there is a general feeling that the restoration of peace and normalcy in the region is remote unless some kind of accommodation is reached. The Secretary-General shares the feelings of many representatives that any developments concerning the fate of Sheik Mujibur Rahman will inevitably have repercussions outside the borders of Pakistan.

5. Aide-Mémoire *on Humanitarian Aid to East Pakistan Refugees*

NEW YORK   AUGUST 13, 1971

A. Refugees from East Pakistan in India

1. While assistance to refugees from East Pakistan is separate from the program of international humanitarian assistance to the people of East Pakistan, the two operations are, of course, related to the extent that the possibility of arresting and reversing the flow of refugees depends largely on the improvement of conditions in East Pakistan.

2. On May 19, 1971, the Secretary-General issued an appeal to all governments, intergovernmental and non-governmental organizations, as well as private sources, to help meet the urgent need for humanitarian assistance to refugees from East Pakistan in India. At that time, the Indian government's preliminary estimates indicated that such assistance might be of the order of $175 million for a period of six months. The latest estimate of requirements was provided by the government of India on June 26, 1971, and amounts to $400 million to take care of an average of six million refugees for a period of six months as from the end of March 1971. This average has not yet been attained but account has to be taken of a further inflow of arrivals. The latest figure provided by the government of India on the refugee population is 7.5 million on August 10, 1971.

SOURCE: *UN Monthly Chronicle*, Vol. VIII, August–September 1971, pp. 67–68.

3. To date, pledges in cash and kind to the United Nations system amount to $105 million, composed of $54.5 million in kind and $51 million in cash. In addition to this amount, it is estimated that $75 million have been contributed outside the United Nations system in bilateral contributions from governments and contributions through the Red Cross network and through a great number of non-governmental organizations. It is clear therefore that the total response of the international community falls short of the Indian government's list of requirements by approximately $220 million for the six-month period. However, as a very large proportion of international assistance is made available in kind and is valued at prices which are at variance with the prices used in the list of requirements, the actual shortfall might be less and is possibly closer to $150 million.

4. The most urgent need for the refugees in India is to make immediately available further pledges in cash to the United Nations High Commissioner for Refugees, who is acting as focal point for assistance by the United Nations. These funds are needed to pay for the following essential items: rice, pulses, milk powder, shelter, clothing, blankets, medical care, sanitation, and transport. While some of these items can be contributed in kind, others—such as shelter, clothing, medical care, sanitation, and transport—can only be procured locally.

5. It must be stressed that the list of requirements is for the period from the end of March to the end of September and the main problem is that it has not yet been met. A list of requirements beyond this period has not yet been received from the government of India.

B. Humanitarian Assistance to East Pakistan

6. On June 16, 1971, the Secretary-General issued an appeal to all governments, intergovernmental and non-governmental organizations, and private institutions and donors to alleviate the suffering which had befallen the population of East Pakistan by making contributions in cash and kind. One month later, on July 16, 1971, information was provided by way of a press release based on the report he had received from his officials on the relief needs of East Pakistan and he took that opportunity to reiterate his appeal. That press release set out in detail the immediate requirements, which were estimated at that time at $28.2 million in cash and 450,000 tons of foodgrains in kind.

7. Since that date the United Nations has been actively engaged in

assessing the requirements and establishing the administrative arrangements and modalities for the operation, and the Secretary-General can now report that the operation is proceeding apace. The situation with regard to contributions has improved somewhat since July 16, with the United States, the United Kingdom, France, and Canada making significant pledges. Nevertheless, approximately only $4 million in cash has been contributed to meet the initial requirements of $28.2 million, and the likelihood of a serious food shortage without such assistance forthcoming has not diminished. The Secretary-General is thus taking this opportunity to inform potential donors that he considers that besides the requirement for foodgrains, the most urgent need at this time is for contributions in cash for the purchase of transport, medical supplies, clothing, shelter, and blankets. There is also an urgent requirement for water transport, and particularly for LCT-type craft of between 300 and 500 tons.

8. The Secretary-General hopes that governments will urgently consider early action to respond to this serious challenge to the international community.

6. Text of Identical Messages to the Prime Minister of India and the President of Pakistan

NEW YORK   OCTOBER 20, 1971

ON JULY 19, 1971, as Your Excellency will recall, I addressed a memorandum to the president of the Security Council concerning the situation in East Pakistan and the adjacent Indian states. In that memorandum I expressed my concern at the possible consequences for international peace and security of the situation in that area of the world.

Recent developments have only served to increase my anxiety that

SOURCE: *UN Monthly Chronicle*, Vol. VIII, November 1971, pp. 97–98.

this situation could all too easily give rise to open hostilities which would not only be disastrous to the two countries principally concerned, but might also constitute a major threat to the wider peace. I have in mind both recent indications of a worsening situation on the borders of East Pakistan and reports of growing tension on the border between West Pakistan and India and on the cease-fire line in Jammu and Kashmir.

I wish to emphasize that I have full confidence in the sincere desire of both governments to avoid a senseless and destructive war. I have noted the efforts which leaders on both sides have made, in spite of the severe pressures upon them, to discourage developments which might lead to open conflict. In the prevailing circumstances, however, where feelings run high and where both governments are under exceptional stress and strain, a small and unintentional incident could all too easily lead to more widespread conflict.

The Chief Military Observer of the United Nations Military Observer Group in Pakistan, UNMOGIP, with my full backing, is doing all that he can on the cease-fire line in Jammu and Kashmir to ease tensions, to avert misunderstandings, to prevent military escalation, and to avoid confrontations that might lead to open hostilities. On the borders of East Pakistan and on the international frontier between India and West Pakistan there is, of course, no comparable United Nations mechanism.

In this potentially very dangerous situation, I feel that it is my duty as Secretary-General to do all that I can to assist the governments immediately concerned in avoiding any development which might lead to disaster. I wish Your Excellency to know, therefore, that my good offices are entirely at your disposal if you believe that they could be helpful at any time. Naturally the Chief Military Observer of UNMOGIP will continue to do his utmost to assist in maintaining the peace in the area of his responsibility.

I have addressed a similar communication to the president of Pakistan (prime minister of India).

THE SECOND UNITED NATIONS
DEVELOPMENT DECADE

ON UNITED NATIONS DAY, October 24, 1970, the General Assembly voted to launch the Second United Nations Development Decade, beginning January 1, 1971. It also adopted an ambitious plan, known as the International Development Strategy for the Decade, which had been drafted over a two-year period by a special preparatory committee set up by the Assembly in 1968. This document spelled out in detail development goals and again urged the more developed countries to provide a minimum of 1 percent of their gross national product annually to the developing countries to provide capital for economic development. The prospects for achieving the goals for the Decade were dimmed somewhat by the numerous reservations made by such potential contributors as the United States which said it could not give any assurances that it would meet the 1 percent target. The United Kingdom and Japan said they could not accept any targets and France said the target was too high. It may be noted here that the results obtained by United Nations efforts during the First Development Decade were extremely disappointing. For one thing, the growth rate in the developing countries was substantially below that of the developed market economies, leaving the gap even wider than before. Further, the net flow of financial resources to developing countries, as a percentage of gross national product, had declined rather than increased as had been hoped. One of U Thant's major concerns was the widening gap between rich and poor countries. He frequently commented that this gap had widened during the 1960s despite the efforts of the international community. He made a number of statements during 1971 on this problem and other aspects of the Second Development Decade.

On May 27, he addressed an International Symposium of the Second Development Decade in Boston. At a press conference prior to his speech, he said humanity was faced with two choices: "One choice is whether the rich countries and the poor countries will march hand-in-hand toward a planned and prosperous future. That is the purpose of the launching of the Second Development Decade. The other alternative is whether the rich countries and the poor countries will go their own ways without any spirit of togetherness and march haphazardly toward an unplanned and chaotic future." In his speech Thant stressed that the main effort would have to come from the developing countries themselves. "It is sometimes thought," he said, "that the poor countries are not doing their share in this undertaking. The record shows most emphatically that this is not the case." In the Introduction to his 1971 annual report, issued on

September 17, he said: "The world, for all its wealth, is still divided into rich and poor, and the gulf between them is growing. Just as the poorer nations are aspiring to technological and industrial progress, the richer ones are beginning to wonder whether they are not tired of affluence and frightened by some of its effects. The developing countries must be helped to develop and to avoid some of the worst consequences of development. A balance must be found which will at the same time meet their needs and avoid putting an impossible strain on the natural resources and on the life-sustaining systems of our planet."

---

1. From Statement to the International Symposium on the Decade

BOSTON   MAY 27, 1971

. . . BEFORE LOOKING at the future, may I be permitted to recall briefly a few significant events which have taken place during the past years:

First, on the positive side, a great page of human history has been turned by placing the fate of the vast majority of developing countries in their own hands. More than one billion people have achieved independence since the end of the Second World War;

Second, the industrial revolution which was outside the reach of most developing countries a mere quarter of a century ago, has continued its inexorable worldwide spread and has brought progress, better and longer lives to innumerable people. The industrial revolution no longer knows any races, frontiers, political systems, or ideologies;

Third, it looks as if the fundamental nutritional and agricultural basis for further industrial progress in the developing countries will at long last be secured through the "green revolution" and through the protein breakthrough;

Fourth, since under prevailing human aspirations and endeavors, economic and technological progress induces further progress, the developing countries are beginning to be interesting investment, produc-

SOURCE: UN Press Release SG/SM/1486.

tion, and marketing grounds for the firms of the developed countries, especially the multinational corporations for which the world is becoming a borderless single economic unit;

Fifth, the international community can be reasonably proud of the collective institutional instruments making up the United Nations development system, which have been created to tackle the problem of underdevelopment.

And yet—in spite of all this progress, in spite of the vast steps forward taken through our inventive genius—as we stand at the beginning of the 1970s mass poverty is still the most characteristic feature of human existence. Hundreds of millions of our fellow human beings suffer from almost every kind of deprivation. The problem is represented by the remarkable and vivid contrast between the comfort and affluence many countries enjoy, surrounded by a veritable sea of the impoverished, the hungry, the illiterate, and the miserable. In many parts of the world, the condition is still deteriorating. . . .

What I think is needed now, today, is to help history in a further jump ahead by believing strongly in new dreams, some of which are embodied in the Second Development Decade. To prepare the minds of people and governments for indispensable changes in thinking, in behavior and in worldwide human cooperation is the duty of all those who are deeply concerned with the future of our planet.

May I be allowed to develop before you briefly some of the hopes which I would like to see materialize within the next decade.

Above all, I hope most fervently that, after twenty-five years of unstable world peace, but of peace nevertheless, however numerous, persistent, and tragic local conflicts may have been, the major powers of the world will now embark upon the road of peaceful cooperation and understanding instead of armed coexistence. Poverty and the future of our small planet must receive without any further delay absolute precedence over the present ruinous military and ideological priorities. Nations spent last year $204 billion on armaments, that is to say, the equivalent of a total year's income of all the developing countries. This is an unprecedented and even an intolerable waste of resources, to maintain a mere stalemate of power, when so many crying needs are prevailing in the world: poverty at home and abroad, hunger, unemployment, educational needs, aspirations for better health and housing, and the sword of Damocles hanging over the natural environment and beauty of our world.

I know, of course, that much of the savings from disarmament will go to meet the pressing demands at home in the affluent societies. But is it really too much to hope that, in the redeployment of the vast resources which would result, sufficient care would be taken to provide what is necessary for the developing countries?

I think, too, it bears repeating that the effort required from the rich to enable the poor to improve their lot is not a monumental one. The monumental effort of development—not only for greater production but also for fundamental social and economic transformation—must emanate from the developing countries themselves. The successful examples we have seen, in the last twenty years, of impoverished countries achieving a significant, at times spectacular, measure of progress and welfare, show clearly that we are not thinking in terms of Utopia. There have been, of course, the lapses, the mistakes, the failings, the turbulence, but this should not prevent us from taking seriously the commitment of the poor countries to the international development strategy, their will, their dedication and discipline. It is sometimes thought that the poor countries are not doing their share in this undertaking. The record shows most emphatically that this is not the case. Their own effort in creating a capacity for further growth and development is most impressive and will yield tangible results in the years to come. . . .

2. From Statement to the St. Louis Symposium on the Decade

ST. LOUIS, MISSOURI   DECEMBER 16, 1971

. . . TO THE IMPATIENT voices from all quarters calling for an end to the United Nations and its replacement with a more dynamic and more effective instrument for peace, this Secretary-General can only reply: take care; in today's troubled world there might not even be a chance to establish a new international organization—much less one better than the United Nations. Cherish it, improve it, but do not forsake it!

SOURCE: UN Press Release SG/SM/1613.

The Secretary-General can find some hope in the fact that there has been no world war in the last twenty-six years, that there has been no major nuclear accident, that a major part of humanity has been freed from colonialism, that racism and discrimination are retreating, that the world is gradually being unified by science and technology, that a growing number of nations are beginning to grasp the merits of harmony in diversity, that the world organization is very close to being universal, and that the leaders of the great nations are beginning to talk directly to each other.

While my ten years in office have been marked by the cold war, by local conflicts—some of which are still unresolved—by an unabating armaments race, by persisting pockets of racism and intolerance, by innumerable violations of individual human rights, and by so many other continuing obstacles to peace and justice on our beautiful planet, the achievements of the Organization in the economic field have been to me precious pillars of support and a source of hope.

Although deeply involved in political issues, I was greatly encouraged by these achievements and, whenever possible, I gave them my fullest support and encouragement. I commend the generous approach of several great nations to the needs of the poorer countries, and the work of dynamic and forward-looking delegates in the economic and social bodies of the United Nations. They are the life work and pride of some of my dearest colleagues in the Secretariat and in the specialized agencies. The world can never be grateful enough for what they have done. The name of Paul Hoffman evokes the model of a great world citizen and pioneer for peace which the United Nations is proud to count among its ranks.

Let me recall to you briefly some economic landmarks which I consider most significant.

First, at the outset of my tenure, and even during my term as permanent representative of my country, I witnessed the fruition of protracted earlier efforts to provide new forms and greater means of international assistance to the developing countries, above and beyond classical loans and technical assistance. I refer to the creation of the International Development Association, the World Food Programme, and the United Nations Special Fund (for pre-investment) which was later merged with technical assistance into the United Nations Development Programme. What magnificent stories of success, progress, solidarity, and collective human creativity have been engraved in the world's history by these endeavors, which represent, at most, contributions of a few cents per year by the peoples of the more privileged countries! Together with the United Nations Children's Fund and other humanitarian aid programs, they are a living testimony to the fact that the affluent in the better half of the world can care for the poor elsewhere in an unselfish and disinterested manner.

Second, I have seen the strengthening of the international institutional system in two fields of paramount importance for the developing countries, the fields of trade and industrial development. Let us not forget that 85 percent of the income of the poorer nations derives from the sale of their products, mostly unprocessed and at cheap, fluctuating world prices; and let us not forget that nowadays industrial skill is at the root of any significant progress of any country. There has been significant progress toward more enlightened trade policies and toward a more rapid worldwide diffusion of scientific and technological knowledge.

I leave the Organization with the deep satisfaction of seeing the world equipped with a minimum of worldwide institutions and cooperative arrangements in almost every field of human endeavor—ranging from the atom to outer space, from industry and labor to art and culture, from aviation to postal services, from health and agriculture to telecommunications. If the potential for action and especially enforcement by these agencies is still in its early stages, at least the world has at its disposal the necessary gauges and warning systems on collective phenomena which encompass and might endanger the entire planet.

Third, we have seen in the economic field, for the first time in history, the birth of a worldwide strategy for development. We still lack such strategies in the political, environmental, and cultural fields, but in the face of oppressive poverty and economic disparity, the community of nations has reacted well and has now launched a second development decade based on a concerted strategy of developed and developing countries alike.

The precise measures by which the developed countries may extend a helping hand to the developing countries are enumerated in some detail in the strategy. They range from purely domestic policies, which have an effect on the rest of the world, to trade and aid policies, which have direct bearing on the life line of the less affluent. With the growing sentiment for political independence and the jealous protection of national sovereignty everywhere, many developed nations are finding it practical and advantageous to channel an increasing amount of aid through multilateral institutions, such as the United Nations system. The multilateral approach assures freedom from foreign-power domination and allows for an even-handed, businesslike and long-term program not subject to political vicissitudes.

This strategy is being brought to the attention of people and leaders in this series of symposia devoted to the presentation of the Second Development Decade. The strategy now exists, its goals have been defined, the means have been measured. But enlightened support by the people is important in a world of manifold priorities and in the face of an all too easy tendency to fall back on narrowly defined interests and isolation.

At the beginning of the 1970s we are in great need of vision and foresight to cope with the challenge of development. Your beautiful Gateway Arch recalls to us that St. Louis was the point of embarkation for many pioneering ventures in the development of this country. I hope that this symposium will mark the beginning of renewed efforts on the part of every individual in this large and distinguished audience to mobilize public support in favor of a great venture in world development. You might look upon this moment as the launching of a new "Spirit of St. Louis."

Last but not least, during recent years I have observed the emergence of new needs for worldwide solidarity with respect to which the affluent societies are for the first time seeking help as, for example, in the two fields of population and environment. For a series of historical reasons, the population base of the developing and of the developed world show a vast discrepancy which is likely to mar profoundly the future course of international human relations unless a harmonious growth of population in relation to resources endowment and future progress is assured. Here the affluent and demographically more disciplined countries are seeking the cooperation of the developing ones. In the field of the environment the same phenomena occur: the developed world knows that, if the heavily populated poorer countries will follow the same course of development as the affluent countries, the entire resources endowment of our planet might be endangered. United Nations data tell us, for example, that the annual population increase in the world requires an additional consumption of water equal to that carried by a midium-sized river; or that each day twenty pounds of river-borne pollution reaches the ocean for every man, woman, and child in the United States and Canada. In a week this represents the approximate equivalent of the average person's weight.

What would be the end-result for a world of seven billion people within a few decades, similarly developed with insufficient regard for the environment? Here again the affluent societies need international cooperation while the developing countries are still striving toward assuring minimum levels of decent living for their people.

These are all signs of new preoccupations which encompass the world as a whole and which have grown beyond the interest of any single nation. But in these global concerns, we also find potent ingredients for greater cooperation among all nations. If religion, morality, education, and ethics have not been able to bring about permanent peace and order, perhaps these new common dangers which come closer and closer to the daily life of each person on this earth will finally teach us to live together in greater understanding and with less greed and intolerance. . . .

From Transcript of His Final Press Conference

NEW YORK   SEPTEMBER 14, 1971

U THANT held his final press conference as Secretary-General on September 14, 1971, almost ten years after he had met the United Nations press corps in the same conference room for the first time on December 1, 1961. The opening remarks of Louis Foy, president of the United Nations Correspondents Association, reflected the warm and friendly relations that had continued between the Secretary-General and the press during this period. Speaking for the United Nations Correspondents Association executive committee and for all members of the association, Foy expressed their "feelings of deep affection and respect." He added, "If indeed you are no longer Secretary-General after January 1, I want you to carry those feelings throughout the future." As a former journalist, Thant not only felt a close personal tie to the press, but he knew the value of the mass media as a vehicle for transmitting his views both to the public and to Member states. Except for one or two critical periods, he met the press regularly both at Headquarters and on his travels. In 1971, for example, he held three press conferences at Headquarters, one in Boston, and one in Geneva. A comparison of the questions asked at his first and last press conferences shows that world attention was focused on some of the same issues in 1971 that had been brought up in 1961. The big question in 1961 had been the Congo. This dominated the Secretary-General's initial press conference. It was a dead issue, of course, in 1971. In both press conferences, however, Thant expressed his views on Chinese representation, Southeast Asia, and the United Nations financial problems. There was only a passing reference to the Middle East in the 1961 meeting. In his final press conference, he was asked whether he felt the time had come to reactivate the peace mission of his special representative, Gunnar Jarring. He replied that this depended primarily on whether Israel gave a "more positive response" to Jarring's *aide-mémoire* of February 8. He added, however, that he felt Jarring's presence in New York during the twenty-sixth session of the General Assembly might be useful in view of the expected presence of the foreign ministers of Israel and the Arab countries. In response to another question, Thant said the biggest problems he would pass on to his successor would be "the restoration of the financial solvency" of the United Nations and the problem of financing future peace-keeping operations. These were problems that he himself had inherited and had lived with for ten years.

THE SECRETARY-GENERAL: In accordance with a long-established tradition—a very useful tradition—we are meeting today on the eve of the General Assembly session. Unless the developments in the next three months warrant another press conference immediately after the session—that is, before Christmas—this will be my last press conference in my present capacity. . . .

MR. LOUIS FOY (President, United Nations Correspondents Association): Mr. Secretary-General, after your statement you will understand that I open this press conference with deep emotions, and I want to express to you, in the name of our executive committee and of all our members, our feelings of deep affection and deep respect. And if indeed you are no longer Secretary-General after January 1, I want you to carry those feelings throughout the future.

Nevertheless, Sir, there is still a lingering hope that you might agree to remain for a short period—several months, or maybe a year or two— especially if the five big powers were deadlocked on the choice of a successor.

As friends and as journalists we should very much like to have your answer on that so that we may know whether such a hope may be entertained.

THE SECRETARY-GENERAL: Mr. Foy, I thank you for your very gracious remarks about me. Regarding your question, I believe I stated my decision very clearly in January of this year in the course of a press conference. Since then I have reiterated my decision on several occasions. I just want to reiterate my position and my decision.

As you will recall, on September 1, 1966, I decided to retire at the end of my first term. At that time, for reasons known to all of you, I had to reverse my decision, but even at that time I made it very clear that the second term would be my last term. I also said that nobody should aspire to serve as the Secretary-General of the United Nations for more than one term, because of the nature of the work involved and because of the tremendous responsibilities—without authority, if I may say so.

So this is not a new decision. I just want to make it very clear that I will not serve beyond my present term even for a limited period of one year or two years or two months, under any circumstances.

At the same time, I want to take this opportunity of expressing my thanks and gratitude to those governments which have asked me to

SOURCE: *UN Monthly Chronicle,* Vol. VIII, October 1971, pp. 167–177.

reconsider my decision and particularly to the Organization of African Unity, which collectively transmitted to me through its chairman, His Excellency the President of Mauritania, its desire that I stay on even for a limited period. Of course, I have replied to all governments and to all organizations that my decision is final and categorical. I am convinced that if the membership realizes that my decision is irrevocable it will concentrate on the selection of a suitable successor. I do not think the question of a draft will arise.

QUESTION: Have you had any contact at all, either direct or indirect, with the Peking government on the possibilities of the coming Assembly? To be more specific, are you aware of Peking's thinking now about United Nations membership this autumn?

THE SECRETARY-GENERAL: Let me say that I am aware of Peking's thinking, although I have no contact with Peking either directly or indirectly.

QUESTION: Mr. Secretary-General, in line with that same question, President Nixon has indicated that he will make a trip to Peking next spring. In your opinion, what effect will this have—and even the added membership of the People's Republic of China—to the ongoing work of the United Nations in the years ahead?

THE SECRETARY-GENERAL: It is very difficult to anticipate the outcome of the projected visit of President Nixon to Peking early next year. But my personal feeling is that such a visit could be very useful not only in establishing a relationship between two great countries, but also in contributing toward the solution of many outstanding problems. What effect this visit will have on the United Nations is difficult to predict because this is tied up with many issues.

Regarding this question of the representation of China in the United Nations, I said last year and early this year that I did not foresee the solution of this question earlier than 1972. But in the course of the last few weeks, I had to revise my position and I said, through a spokesman, that the prospects of the solution of the question of the representation of China at the United Nations were much brighter than before.

As you know, things are moving very fast, and it is unpredictable what will happen between now and the time the question is brought up before the General Assembly, which I believe will be in the latter part of October. It depends primarily on the attitude of the Member states. According to my information, some Member states have not made up their minds regarding the draft resolutions to be tabled before the General

Assembly. Some Member states have informed me that they might make up their minds only on the eve of the discussion at the General Assembly. So it is very difficult to predict what the outcome will be at the coming session of the General Assembly. Of course, as you know, I have been advocating the principle of universality of the United Nations for many years. I will be the happiest person if this question is solved this year.

QUESTION: Mr. Secretary-General, in the light of your definitive statement today, do you see on the horizon the possibility of an acceptable and suitable successor? Second, I would like to ask whether you feel that the time has come for the reactivation of the Jarring mission?

THE SECRETARY-GENERAL: On the first question, I think your guess is as good as mine. It is difficult to anticipate the results of the deliberations which will take place in late September when the foreign ministers are here. Of course, I will be in contact with them and exchange views with them on the question of my successor. But I believe that there will be a solution in the course of the coming session of the General Assembly.

Regarding your second question, the reactivation of the Jarring mission depends primarily on certain factors, including a more positive response by Israel to his *aide-mémoire* of February 8. This has been made known to everybody and all the governments are aware of it. But I feel that his presence here at the commencement of the twenty-sixth session of the General Assembly might be useful, particularly in view of the fact that most of the foreign ministers directly concerned with the conflict in the Middle East will be here. I feel that he should take advantage of the presence of the foreign ministers here. I have been in contact with him from time to time and he agrees with me that his presence at the United Nations next week could be very useful.

QUESTION: Mr. Secretary-General, you say that you are aware of Peking's thinking about coming into the United Nations. I wonder if you could tell us what it is?

THE SECRETARY-GENERAL: I do not think it would be in the public interest if I were to make a public statement on what Peking thinks, but Peking's feelings have been brought to the attention of the international community through the mass media, and the publications in several newspapers accurately reflect the views of Peking. Beyond that I do not think it will be helpful for me to elaborate.

QUESTION: Mr. Secretary-General, as you know, on August 20 the foreign ministry in Peking issued a statement which again restated its position concerning Chinese representation here, and it said, as we all know, that any resolution of the problem which left Taiwan in while inviting Peking was unacceptable to the Chinese. I would like to ask you two short questions. First, do you regard this as a firm working position on the part of the Chinese; and second, what justification would there be, historically or otherwise, for assuming, as some states have, that this is not a firm position on the part of the Chinese?

THE SECRETARY-GENERAL: I believe that that particular statement reflects the official views of Peking and I believe that it is a firm statement of policy. . . .

QUESTION: Mr. Secretary-General, you have been advocating universality throughout the years. Last year, if I remember correctly, you stated that the problem of the admission of the divided states may be even easier to solve this year. First, how do you assess the prospects for achieving universality in the light of the recent developments, especially in Europe? Second, I wonder if you would like to comment on the recent Soviet proposal for convening a world disarmament conference? How do you assess the prospects for such a conference?

THE SECRETARY-GENERAL: On your first question, I had thought that the principle of universality would be achieved before the end of my term. Unfortunately, that will, of course, not be the case. Perhaps in the case of China, a solution may be arrived at during the forthcoming session of the General Assembly. In the case of the divided countries, my assumption is that they will all be admitted to the United Nations in 1972, although my hope—which was expressed two or three years ago— was that the divided countries would be full Members of the United Nations before the end of my term. However, a trend is unmistakable.

Regarding your second question on the Soviet item on a world disarmament conference, reflected in Mr. Andrei Gromyko's letter addressed to me last week, there are some new features in the Soviet proposal, particularly the stress on the universality of participants. It is a very interesting one, and I hope this item will receive the close attention of the membership it deserves. Personally speaking, I welcome this Soviet initiative.

QUESTION: Would you consider the expulsion of the Taiwan government an abrogation of the principle of universality?

THE SECRETARY-GENERAL: Since this is before the General Assembly, I do not think I should venture an opinion on it.

QUESTION: What is, in your opinion, the biggest problem that your successor will inherit from you?

THE SECRETARY-GENERAL: It is very difficult to categorize the problems as biggest or smallest. I think most of the problems are big. I would say that the financial problem, the restoration of the financial solvency of this Organization, must receive priority attention and, second, the potency of the United Nations vis-à-vis the peace-keeping operations. That is, agreement by the membership, particularly by the big powers, on the administrative, financial, and supervisory aspects of the peace-keeping operations is essential. I think agreement should be reached as quickly as possible. Then of course, as I have said on many previous occasions, he should be one who looks to the future. I shall develop some of these ideas regarding the role of the Secretary-General, as I said a moment ago, on Thursday at your lunch.

QUESTION: Mr. Secretary-General, to go on with the idea of the divided nations, do you think it is possible that duality of representation will solve that problem, and can it also solve the problem with China— duality of representation, one nation with more than one set of representatives?

THE SECRETARY-GENERAL: The two things are different, I think. When you say "the divided countries," the countries are divided. When you speak of duality of representation, that means something else. So I do not think that it would be proper on my part to assess or evaluate the concept of duality of representation.

QUESTION: Mr. Secretary-General, for some time you have not expressed yourself on the subject of Vietnam, and just now you have indicated that you feel that all the divided countries will come in—I suppose that means Vietnam as well. Do you see any special opening now, either politically or in negotiations locally or otherwise?

THE SECRETARY-GENERAL: There have been some encouraging signs regarding the Vietnam war in the last few weeks. To cite an instance, Mrs. Thi Binh's proposals submitted on July 1 can, in my view, serve as a basis for negotiations. Of course, clarifications are necessary. In my view, Mrs. Thi Binh's proposals constitute a very good opportunity— perhaps the best opportunity so far—for breaking the deadlock. I very much hope that the parties concerned will look into these proposals very seriously, of course after eliciting clarifications on some points. This is one encouraging sign of the Vietnam war.

QUESTION: Mr. Secretary-General, in your remarks you referred to your responsibility without authority. Would you say what in your ivew is the realistic possibility of any change in the status of the Secretary-General to implement his authority?

THE SECRETARY-GENERAL: First of all, the Secretary-General is not only a chief administrative officer, as many people think he is. The Secretary-General also has to perform political functions. That is more than implied in the provisions of the Charter. I am developing all these ideas in the speech that I propose to deliver on Thursday.

QUESTION: On July 20, in an unusual step, you sent a memorandum to the president of the Security Council warning that the situation in Pakistan constituted a potential threat to the peace. How do you view that situation today, and are you satisfied with the steps that have been taken by members of the Council?

THE SECRETARY-GENERAL: I still maintain that position. The situation in East Pakistan vis-à-vis the adjoining Indian states constitutes a threat to international peace and security. That was the main reason why I submitted a confidential memorandum to the president of the Security Council on July 20. I still maintain that view, but to my regret the Security Council has not taken any action so far.

Of course, up till now the United Nations has been involved in only the humanitarian aspects of the problem, but the basic issues are political, as everybody knows. Unless a climate of confidence is restored in East Pakistan there will be no prospect of the return of the refugees—at least, most of the refugees—to Pakistan; and that is the basic issue. The restoration of a climate of confidence is not within the competence of the Secretary-General. But everybody with whom I talk agrees that this is the first prerequisite to the restoration of peace, and that it would be the only inducement for the return of the refugees from India to Pakistan. Of course, as I have said, this is not within the competence of the Secretary-General. . . .

QUESTION: Mr. Secretary-General, as you come to the end of this term you must have thoughts about the kind and quality and number of Member states which will constitute this United Nations in the years to come. Of the two latest candidates, one has a population of 200,000; the other, of 130,000; and, as you know, in the background there is China, with over 700 million. Do you foresee that this trend of fragmentation on one side will be good for the United Nations?

THE SECRETARY-GENERAL: I am a strong believer in parliamentary democracy. When we think of the exercise of the right to vote—in the United States or any other country—that right is not predicated on property, or even on education or literacy, in many countries: every adult, man or woman, has the right to vote. For instance, as I said some years ago, in elections in New York, when it comes to voting, Mr. Rockefeller has one vote; the elevator girl has one vote. That principle should be applicable to the international scene. That means that the membership of the United Nations—implying the membership of the General Assembly, not necessarily of the Security Council—should be democratic and broad-based, irrespective of affluence or the size of population, or the nature of the wealth or gross national product, and so on.

When it comes to voting in the General Assembly, the expression of the views of the international community, I think all countries, large and small, should have one vote. This—the sovereign equality of all states—is more than implied in the Charter. But when it comes to decision-making and peace-keeping operations involving mandatory resolutions, that is another matter. I am, of course, speaking in terms of the democratic principles being applied to the membership of the United Nations.

It is true that one aspirant to membership has a population of 200,000 and another has a population of 130,000; at present there is a Member with a population of less than 100,000. When it comes to membership, I believe in the elimination of all qualifications such as wealth, population, gross national product, and balance of payments. With reference to the Security Council, however, that is a different matter.

THE ROLE OF THE SECRETARY-GENERAL

As U THANT'S FINAL term approached its end during the fall of 1971, he summed up his views on the office of the Secretary-General in two important speeches and in the Introduction to his final annual report. On September 16, he addressed a luncheon of the Dag Hammarskjöld Memorial Scholarship Fund on the role of the Secretary-General. The next day, the tenth anniversary of Hammarskjöld's death, he praised his predecessor for his courage in pursuing his efforts to project a strong United Nations regardless of opposition. He said he had "little doubt that the verdict of history will in the end be resoundingly favorable to Hammarskjöld's concept of the United Nations as a dynamic and active force in international life." In the Introduction to his 1971 annual report, issued on September 17, Thant devoted an entire section to the office of the Secretary-General.

Since the texts of these statements are published here in full, it is not necessary to go into detail in this commentary. The editors, therefore, will simply summarize a few of Thant's conclusions, most of which were part of Hammarskjöld's concept. Both men held, for example, that the Secretary-General must have the power, including the right of inquiry, to reach a seasoned and independent opinion on whether or not a particular matter might threaten international peace and security. Both also believed that the Secretary-General should endeavor, through the exercise of his good offices, to carry on "preventive diplomacy" designed to prevent a matter from becoming a threat to peace. Thant too was a strong advocate of "quiet diplomacy." "When the Secretary-General decides that he may usefully act," he said, "it is in nearly every case essential that he should, in the initial stages, act privately and without public fanfare. Governments are not likely to entrust a matter to him or to entertain any of his proposals, in the full glare of publicity." No one more than Thant was aware that the Secretary-General's political role had its limitations, both legal and practical, and that the public often expected more of him than he was able to do. "The Secretary-General has no means of enforcement," he pointed out, "no economic power at his disposal: he can rely only upon the prestige of his office and his own powers of persuasiveness. These are fragile instruments with which to tackle an international conflict, and it is important that they should be preserved. If a move by the Secretary-General were to give rise to the impression that he was intervening in a matter essentially within the domestic jurisdiction of a Member state, or taking a particular side in a conflict, or that he was abandoning his impartiality, his usefulness would be at an end. . . ."

1. From Speech at Luncheon for the Dag Hammarskjöld Memorial Scholarship Fund

NEW YORK   SEPTEMBER 16, 1971

. . . TEN YEARS AGO tomorrow, Dag Hammarskjöld died in Africa. In his eight years at the United Nations, he gave the Office of the Secretary-General a new meaning and a new place in international life. He died at the height of a controversy over the nature and function of the United Nations as a political organization and over the role of the Secretary-General—a controversy which is still by no means resolved. Today, I shall speak of the role of the Secretary-General as it appears to me, ten years after Hammarskjöld's death and in the light of my own experiences as his successor.

Hammarskjöld brought to the Office of the Secretary-General the gifts of a scholar, a visionary, and of a man of great practical experience in public affairs. He deployed these gifts with energy and realism in his work as Secretary-General, using the challenges and opportunities of international life to develop the potential of the United Nations as an instrument of multilateral diplomacy. He was a diplomat of extraordinary skill and perception, as well as an indefatigable and resourceful negotiator. All his work was based on a thorough and penetrating study of the problems he faced and on a deep insight into the difficulties of those he was dealing with. His mastery of political matters, law and economics, which he had first gained in academic life, was constantly tested and enhanced by practical application. He had an unequaled intellectual grasp of the complexities of international affairs and of the United Nations as an embryonic system of world order.

These great gifts were complemented by human qualities which gave Dag Hammarskjöld an extraordinary stature in the world. He felt a sense of total vocation in the secretary-generalship and devoted all of his strength and skill to its problems. Although he was anything but a

SOURCE: *UN Monthly Chronicle,* Vol. VIII, October 16, 1971, pp. 178–187.

moralist and disliked moral judgments on public matters, he had an unshakable integrity and a clear and determined view of what was right. He new that in public life there is no substitute for individual courage and conviction, and he demanded of himself far more than he expected of others. Though sensitive to public opinion and criticism, he steadfastly refused to compromise his principles for the sake of popularity.

Some of the human qualities which gave Hammarskjöld his exceptional position in the world shine through a passage in *Markings,* published after his death, in which he sets out some rules for those engaged in the pursuit of peace. These rules remain valid for all of us who work in the United Nations and in the struggle for a better world:

It is more important to be aware of the grounds for your own behavior than to understand the motives of another.

The other's "face" is more important than your own.

If, while pleading another's cause, you are at the same time seeking something for yourself, you cannot hope to succeed.

You can only hope to find a lasting solution to a conflict if you have learned to see the other objectively, but, at the same time, to experience his difficulties subjectively.

The man who "likes people" disposes once and for all of the man who despises them.

All first-hand experience is valuable, and he who has given up looking for it will one day find—that he lacks what he needs: a closed mind is a weakness, and he who approaches persons or painting or poetry without the youthful ambition to learn a new language and so gain access to someone else's perspective on life, let him beware.

A successful lie is doubly a lie, an error which has to be corrected is a heavier burden than truth: only an uncompromising "honesty" can reach the bedrock of decency which you should always expect to find, even under deep layers of evil.

Diplomatic "finesse" must never be another word for fear of being unpopular: that is to seek the appearance of influence at the cost of its reality.[1]

Every Secretary-General brings to the office his own personality, ideas, and methods. The efforts and experiences, achievements and failures, of successive secretaries-general are the raw materials out of which the office has developed over the years on the basis of the very general description which is given in the Charter. While the fundamental objectives of the Charter remain, circumstances change, new opportunities for development present themselves—and sometimes new obsta-

---

[1] Dag Hammarskjöld, *Markings,* translated from the Swedish by Lief Sjöberg and W. H. Auden (New York, 1964), p. 114.

cles appear. Things that were possible for one Secretary-General are no longer possible for his successor, and vice versa. There are times when action, dynamism, and innovation are in demand, and other times when governments shun them like the plague. The office is, of necessity, developed through trial and error and in response to the demands and challenges of the passing years. Each Secretary-General must build as best he can on the office as he inherited it. If he cannot hope to repeat all the successes of his predecessors, neither should he fear to try again where they failed.

No Secretary-General can afford to lose a sense of obligation to the human community in its broadest sense—an obligation to give his utmost to make the principles and aims of the Charter a reality and to do whatever he can to improve the general condition of the community of nations. Hammarskjöld never lost for a moment this sense of obligation, and I myself have regarded it, during my ten years in office, as the primary rule which nothing can be allowed to obscure. While it is debatable whether the Secretary-General is—or should try to be—the conscience of mankind, he must certainly never lose a strong personal sense of justice, of humanity, and of the importance of human dignity.

The other quality which a Secretary-General can never afford to lose is an urgent sense of political realism. The Secretary-General operates under the Charter in a world of independent sovereign states, where national interests remain dominant despite ideological, technological, and scientific changes, and despite the obvious dangers of unbridled nationalism. He works within the paradox that as these sovereign states in fact become increasingly interdependent, the forces of nationalism often lead them to assert more and more stridently their rivalries with each other.

These are the two poles of the Secretary-General's world—at one extreme the idealism and the global objectives of the Charter; at the other the pragmatic, and on occasion downright selfish, nature of national sovereignty. Working between these two poles, the Secretary-General cannot afford to lose touch with either. This is, I suspect, the reason why the first Secretary-General, Trygve Lie, in a moment of understandable exasperation, once called the secretary-generalship "the most impossible job in the world." Although I do not agree with his assessment, I can easily understand what he meant.

In every critical situation, the Secretary-General's activity will seem to some governments to be too much and to others too little. He must thread his way through the jungle of conflicting national policies with the Charter as his compass, and, if he is lucky, with a directive from one of the main deliberative organs as his guide. Even if such a directive exists, it is unlikely to insure him against governmental objections to his actions, for the most explicit and straightforward resolution on a controversial matter will inevitably contain compromises, silences, and ambiguities which the organ concerned is unlikely to wish to elucidate. In such situations, there is often a large difference between what some governments wish the Secretary-General to do, or not to do, and what other governments and public opinion expect of him. While he has a general obligation to act in accordance with the principles of the Charter, to act effectively he must also work with and through sovereign governments. The luxury of judgments and moral declarations, so freely engaged in by national politicians and by the press in troubled times, must be foresworn by the Secretary-General if he is to maintain that degree of cooperation from governments through which alone he may be able eventually to get some results. And when he refuses to make public moral judgments, he will be widely accused of callousness, insensibility, and worse. National sovereignty and national interest, humanitarian considerations, governmental susceptibilities and the principles of the Charter form the elements of an insoluble equation, which nonetheless the Secretary-General must continually, and in all sorts of situations, attempt to solve. I think this is what Trygve Lie had in mind.

There is a persistent illusion that the Secretary-General's position is in some way comparable to that of the head of a government, and that clear-cut and decisive action can, and should, be taken by him on problems which have defied the collective wisdom of the 127 Member governments. The truth, of course, is that the United Nations, and the Secretary-General, have none of the attributes of sovereignty, and no independent power, although the Secretary-General has, and must maintain, his independence of judgment, and must never become the agent of any particular government or group of governments. No parliament enacts for the Secretary-General the detailed and enforceable legislation which provides a prime minister with precise and continuous directives. No clear-cut policy illuminates his course of action. He is supported by none of the great permanent establishments of a state, and lacks the firsthand sources of information upon which governments can base their plans. More often than not he faces the conflicts of the present or the problems of the future with vague or nonexistent directives, with an exiguous budget, and, in the case of some peace-keeping operations or of vast relief problems, with resources based solely on voluntary contributions. These are some of the limitations of the secretary-generalship.

The constitutional basis for the role of the Secretary-General is contained in five short articles of the Charter—Articles 97 to 101. Article 97 establishes the Secretary-General as chief administrative officer of the Organization. This in itself is more than a full-time job. It is sometimes overlooked that the United Nations, which is intended to deal with the problems of sovereign governments, many of which are centuries old, itself started from scratch only twenty-six years ago. To build a truly international civil service and to maintain the requisite balance between efficiency, competence, and integrity, on the one hand, and equitable geographical distribution, on the other, is in itself a tremendous challenge. To attend to the myriad administrative and political details involved and to make a complex and embryonic international civil service system actually work in the context of the day-to-day, worldwide political and other developments is heavy and time-consuming work. Like my predecessors, I have constantly had cause to regret that other pressures leave the Secretary-General far too little time for a task which in the long run will have a decisive effect on the successful development and performance of the Organization.

While there has been real progress in establishing the nucleus of a truly international civil service in the Secretariat, an immense amount remains to be done. Such a service, to be fully effective, must also be fully accepted by governments, and here progress is disappointing and slow. In some respects, in fact, there have been setbacks in the past few years, and the spirit of internationalism has tended to be in retreat before the forces of nationalism. Questions of nationality, and governmental suspicions about the objectivity of Secretariat members in particular situations, however unjustified, all too often make it impossible to use the existing staff to its full potential. I hope the day will soon come when all members of the Secretariat, whatever their country of origin, are equally accepted in all situations as the impartial and objective officials which the Charter and their oath of office require them to be. Even fifty years ago, at the inception of the League of Nations, it was soon recognized that a Secretariat composed entirely of seconded national officials would not satisfactorily meet the challenges of international problems. Whatever the difficulties, I am more than ever convinced of the basic and urgent necessity for the creation and acceptance of a truly international civil service if our Organization is to be able to meet the demands of the future, whether in the political, economic, social, or technological sphere. I believe that very serious thought should be given to new methods of helping the Secretary-General to fulfill his responsibilities in this fundamental task.

Article 98 is the first of two articles setting out the political responsibilities of the Secretary-General. This is a radical departure from the nonpolitical concept of the secretary-generalship to be found in the Covenant of the League of Nations. Article 98, by providing that the Security Council, the General Assembly, and the other main organs may entrust the Secretary-General with unspecified "other functions," has brought him—and the Secretariat—into the arena of political conflict. As I said just now, even the most apparently straightforward resolution often contains ambiguities and compromises, and most resolutions on controversial subjects could not have been passed without such twilight areas. Thus, the Secretary-General often finds himself faced with the necessity of taking actions under Article 98 which will be disliked or contested by one government or another. His only guide here is his judgment as to the intentions of the majority which voted the resolution, his application of the principles of the Charter to the situation at hand, and the confidence that his integrity will be respected even if his conclusions are disputed. I count myself fortunate that, in my ten years as Secretary-General, the many governments who have at one time or another disagreed with my interpretations of, or actions on, the decisions of the main organs have also recognized my obligation to discharge my duty as I see it.

I feel strongly that the Secretary-General, irrespective of his personal views on any issue, is obliged to stand by every resolution or decision of the main deliberative organs of the United Nations. As I have said many times, the United Nations will not become the effective instrument its founders intended it to be until its Members abide by its rules and give real attention to its decisions and resolutions. This is especially true in the most complex and difficult situations, such as the Middle East problem, where the failure to reach a solution is not so much the failure of the United Nations to take decisions as the failure of its Members to abide by those decisions. The Secretary-General has no option whatsoever in this regard, whatever may be the temporary effect on his relations with individual Member states. Nor can he seek an escape from a resolution of an organ of the United Nations because it may appear to be unpractical or even unfair. The Organization can only mature and develop a sense of responsibility through experience and cooperation in collective decision-making. Mistakes and false starts are an inevitable part of this process. The correction of such mistakes is another essential part of the process, which hitherto has not figured large in the activities of the United Nations.

It is Article 99 of the Charter which gives the Secretary-General explicit political responsibility in his own right. The Preparatory Commission of the United Nations elaborated on Article 99 in its report as follows:

The Secretary-General may have an important role to play as a mediator and as an informal adviser of many governments, and will undoubtedly be called upon from time to time, in the exercise of his administrative duties, to take decisions which may justly be called political. Under Article 99 of the Charter, moreover, he has been given a quite special right which goes beyond any power previously accorded to the head of an international organization, viz: to bring to the attention of the Security Council any matter (not merely any dispute or situation) which, in his opinion, may threaten the maintenance of international peace and security. It is impossible to foresee how this Article will be applied; but the responsibility it confers upon the Secretary-General will require the exercise of the highest qualities of political judgment, tact, and integrity.

This is virtually the only official guidance available to the Secretary-General on the implications of Article 99, which, surprisingly enough, was adopted with very little debate at San Francisco. The right to bring matters to the attention of the Security Council implies a watching brief and a broad discretion to conduct inquiries and to engage in informal diplomatic activity in regard to matters relating to the maintenance of international peace and security. Article 33, which enjoins parties to any dispute to seek a solution by peaceful means of their own choice, is also relevant to the Secretary-General's duty under Article 99.

Article 99 is both far-reaching and vague. It has been specifically invoked only once, when Hammarskjöld used it to call the Security Council into session over the Congo, but its implications are central to the day-to-day political functioning of the Secretary-General. In December 1966, when the Security Council requested me to continue as Secretary-General, the president informed me that the members of the Council "fully respected the Secretary-General's position and his action in bringing basic issues confronting the Organization and disturbing developments to their notice." I have continued to act in accordance with my interpretation of Article 99 as reinforced by this statement, most recently in my memorandum to the president of the Council concerning the situation in East Pakistan and the adjacent Indian states. Although there is a difference of opinion as to the Secretary-General's rights to take independent initiatives, Article 99 leaves no doubt that any potential threat to peace and security must be of concern to him, and that he has a duty to do what he can to mitigate it.

There are, of course, many ways of fulfilling the wide but imprecise responsibilities of the Secretary-General under Article 99. These responsibilities must be seen in the broader context of the nature of the secretary-generalship as it has developed over the years. In the early stages of drafting the Charter, President Franklin D. Roosevelt suggested that the chief officer of the United Nations should be called the "Moderator," and I know of no better single word to describe my own idea of the office. I have always felt that the most important political duty of the Secretary-General was to concentrate on the harmonizing functions of the United Nations as set out in Article 1, paragraph 4, of the Charter. I have tried to use my office, with all the discretion that the importance of the task requires, to allay unnecessary fears and suspicions, to establish communication between conflicting parties, and to do whatever I could to bridge the gulf between East and West. With this end in view, I have been at pains to understand, and to remain on cooperative terms with all the governments concerned, even when, as often happens, an easier and more popular course might be to take sides and make public judgments. I would hope that when the full record can be written, this continuous and discreet activity may prove to have made some contribution to international peace and understanding in our time.

I have never had any doubt that the Secretary-General, with Article 33 in mind, must exercise his good offices in the settlement of disputes or difficulties, even without specific authorization from the Security Council or another organ of the United Nations, when the states concerned request it. As I was obliged to point out to the president of the Security Council over the case of Equatorial Guinea in March 1969, my informing him of my intention to send a representative to that country at the request of the governments concerned was in no sense a consultation, and I was merely following the previously established practice of taking action and keeping the Security Council informed of what I was doing.

The exercise of good offices has proved on occasion to be a useful method of preventing differences between states from developing into major crises and of getting results on sensitive problems before they reach the insoluble stage. Preventive diplomacy of this kind is far more effective—and incidentally much cheaper—than attempting to cure a conflict which has been allowed to reach an acute stage. It requires total discretion and the cooperation, restraint, and good will of the parties concerned. It also requires from them courage and vision, as well as confidence in the discretion and integrity of the Secretary-General. When these conditions are present, much can be done quietly. The settlement of the question of Bahrain, whose application for membership was recently unanimously approved by the Security Council, is a case in point.

Much of the Secretary-General's time is spent in attempts to exercise good offices in one form or another, and the less publicity there is during or after these efforts, the more successful they are likely to be. Scarcely a day passes without appeals to the Secretary-General for help from some corner of the world. These appeals range from approaches from governments for assistance in adjusting difficulties with other governments through requests for help from minority groups, to calls from individuals in an infinite variety of dilemmas. Sometimes the Secretary-General can help, and sometimes he must frankly state that he cannot, because in his judgment his intervention will be ineffective, or even positively harmful, or perhaps outside the scope of his functions under the Charter.

In the last ten years I have also offered my good offices in situations which seemed to me to be so serious as to require me to do so even without a specific request from the parties. I did this in the Cuban missile crisis, for example, and on a number of occasions, such as over Vietnam, as well as in the Nigerian civil war.

This quiet method of forestalling conflict seems to me to be a part of the Secretary-General's role which should be continuously developed as an alternative to the specific—and much more dramatic—invocation of Article 99. There are good reasons why Article 99 has been specifically invoked only once. Nothing could be more divisive and useless than for the Secretary-General to bring a situation publicly to the Security Council when there is no practical possibility of the Council agreeing on effective or useful action. On the other hand, a quiet approach which avoids a public confrontation may often hold some hope of success. In this context, I hope that it may be possible to develop further the procedure of quiet consultations among members of the Security Council on threatening situations, a process which I recently attempted to initiate over the situation in East Pakistan and the adjacent Indian states.

A development which was not foreseen when the Charter was written has become an important, and positive, element in discharging the political responsibilities of the Secretary-General. The establishment of permanent missions to the United Nations, which has vastly increased the day-to-day usefulness of the United Nations as an instrument of multilateral diplomacy, also gives the Secretary-General immediate and permanent access to highly skilled and experienced representatives of the Member governments. In my view, this largely unpublicized development is one of the most important institutional advances of our first twenty-five years. It has greatly facilitated the political work of the Secretary-General, for it makes possible the discussion of the most sensitive problems in private and on impartial ground, where the Secretary-General and his senior colleagues are available, if required, as objective go-betweens and middlemen. The close relationships built up among the permanent representatives and the Secretary-General are an invaluable asset, especially in difficult times. I take this opportunity to pay tribute to the hundreds of devoted permanent representatives with whom I have been lucky enough to deal. They have made and will, I am sure, continue to make an incomparable contribution to the building of a reliable system of world order here in the United Nations.

I sometimes think that the drafters of the Charter were overly obsessed with political and military conflict. No doubt that obsession was justified in the situation prevailing at the time. In the world of today, it might be useful to add an Article 99(a), which would authorize the Secretary-General to bring to the attention of the membership global threats to human well-being other than those to peace and security. I have tried to do this, without specific authorization, in matters such as population growth or the environment. Some of these threats are now so grave and all-encompassing that they deserve a place of their own in our Charter. Much more could be done through the United Nations if its Members paid as much attention to relatively noncontroversial, but nonetheless appalling, threats to humanity as they do to political conflicts which may become threats to the peace. The spirit and practice of international cooperation and solidarity might also be strengthened through such efforts.

Then there are the great humanitarian emergencies which the United Nations is still not equipped to meet. I am glad that steps are now being taken to fit the Organization to deal with natural disasters. The next step is to expand its capability to cover unnatural disasters. The current situation in East Pakistan and the adjacent states of India has brought this necessity vividly to light. In an effort to do something about these immense disasters, I have, on my own initiative and without any supporting resolution from any United Nations organ, launched two relief operations which are concerned with millions of people and expenditures of hundreds of millions of dollars. I have felt that an initiative on my part was essential to fill the gap until more regular arrangements can be made, and that the Secretary-General's obligations under the Charter must include any humanitarian action that he can take to save the lives of large numbers of human beings. The political aspects of such situations, on the other hand, must obviously fall, as far as the United Nations is concerned, primarily within the competence of the Security Council.

There is one aspect of the role of the Secretary-General which is no less important for being fortuitous or for lacking any description in the Charter. I mention it at the end of ten years of service not in any spirit of rancor, but because I know it to be an important part of the Secretary-General's role. In a world of frustrated and short-sighted nationalism, where the superpowers are armed against each other to a degree so suicidal as to seem insane to any reasonable person, a pretext is often necessary to avoid proceeding to the logical conclusion of national policies—or, to put it more crudely, there comes a time in the affairs of nations when it is eminently desirable to pass the buck. The United Nations as an organization is often an ideal recipient of the buck, and it follows that the Secretary-General can easily become a scapegoat in dangerous situations where no solution can be found.

These are by no means contemptible functions. I feel, however, and I have often said it before, that the peoples of the world should be very clear as to what is involved in this process. The process is a part of the character of the United Nations itself, of the way governments use it and of the nature of the situations with which the Organization has to deal. The United Nations, lacking any attributes of sovereignty, must work by persuasion, argument, negotiation, and a persistent search for consensus. For all the high ideals in the Charter, it is a very down-to-earth and pragmatic organization, which for the most part deals with hard political realities rather than with sweet reason or ideal aspirations. The opportunities for inspirational leadership or crusading are exceedingly rare.

The Secretary-General must usually operate within these highly realistic limits if he is to achieve any useful results at all.

For the governments of Member states, the United Nations is a place where responsibility can be shared or shifted—where concern can be publicly expressed and a valid formal reason for not taking unilateral action can be created. It is a place to which the moral demands of public opinion can be redirected when those demands become too oppressive for an individual government to bear. It is a place where, behind the smokescreen of exhaustive debate, positions can be gradually changed and faces saved. Working in private, the Secretary-General may play some useful part in this process, but his usefulness will usually vanish as soon as he proclaims it publicly.

Great problems usually come to the United Nations because governments have been unable to think of anything else to do about them. This applies equally to the Middle East and to the environment. The United Nations is a last-ditch, hard-core affair, and it is not surprising that the Organization should often be blamed for failing to solve problems which have already been found to be insoluble by governments. That is a part—admittedly a somewhat negative part—of the *raison d'être* of the United Nations. There is, I may add, no excuse for the Organization or the Secretary-General to give up the attempt to find solutions to apparently insoluble problems.

The secretary-generalship is at the same time an absorbing, a thrilling, and a deeply frustrating task. No one who is lucky enough to be given the opportunities it offers has the right to complain of the difficulties. At the same time, the Secretary-General can never for a moment underestimate what is at stake. In matters relating to international peace and security, the Secretary-General's responsibility requires a continuous examination of the possibilities of effective action. In this examination, two simple considerations are inescapable. First, the Secretary-General must always be prepared to take an initiative, no matter what the consequences to his office or to him personally may be, if he sincerely believes that it might mean the difference between peace and war. In such a situation, the personal prestige of a Secretary-General—and even the position of his office—must be considered to be expendable. The second cardinal consideration must be the maintenance of the Secretary-General's independent position, as set out in Article 100 of the Charter, which alone can give him the freedom to act, without fear or favor, in the interests of world peace. Such an independence does not imply any disrespect for the wishes or opinions of Member governments. On the contrary, his independence is an insurance that the Secretary-General will be able to serve, in full accordance with his oath of office, the long-term interest in peace of all the Members of the Organization.

There is no easy way to discharge the duties of the secretary-generalship, but that does not detract from the immense privilege of being allowed to attempt the job. In my view, it is the most varied, most interesting, and most challenging political job on earth. In one way, the Secretary-General is fortunate, for he is allowed to consider the problems of peace and war, the problems of the present and the future of mankind, from a position which is, and must be by its very nature, independent of national considerations. Impartiality, principle, and objective truth are his strongest weapons. He is, and must be, at the same time a realist and a man of idealism and hope, with his mind more concentrated on a better future than preoccupied with a baneful past.

I feel strongly that my successor should be a man who will look to the future and to a global concept of the problems we all face. In our interdependent world, his continent or country of origin seems to me to be far less important than his integrity, his competence, and his ability to look toward the future and to help make this Organization into a really effective instrument for peace, justice, and progress. He should be impartial and objective without necessarily being neutral. He should be responsive to the movements and preoccupations of world public opinion and especially of young people, but he must also retain the confidence of the Member governments, where, I need hardly say, the average age tends to be a good deal higher. He must have that political judgment, tact, and integrity which the Preparatory Commission mentioned. He must also have an unassailable conviction of the importance of individual human dignity and value as a balance to the impersonal forces of national or group interests. He must have a sense of proportion and of humor to protect him against the bitterness of frustration and the discomfort of perennial, and sometimes unjustified, criticism. The secretary-generalship is not the most impossible job in the world, although it is certainly one of the most difficult. It is without any question one of the most rewarding.

2. From Statement on the Tenth Anniversary
of the Death of Dag Hammarskjöld

NEW YORK   SEPTEMBER 17, 1971

. . . I WELL REMEMBER the August day in 1957 when I presented my credentials to Dag Hammarskjöld. I was immediately impressed by his interest in the moral and spiritual aspects of life. His knowledge of Buddhist philosophy was far from superficial and he was interested in the affinities between the Buddhist thought and the writings of Martin Buber. I remember that I tried to straighten him out on the theory of Karma. It was a most pleasant and rewarding thirty minutes.

Dag Hammarskjöld's death left an aching void in the life of the world community, and few of those who knew him, whether they agreed with him or not, remained untouched by his death. By his dedication, his integrity, his courage, and his intellect, he had made an unprecedented place in the world for himself and for his office. He was in a very real sense the world's first public servant, and a long string of achievements in the most difficult task of all, the search for peace, attested to his extraordinary qualities. He left the Organization immeasurably enriched by his efforts.

It is the irony of success that it often carries within itself the seeds of a temporary setback. So it was with Hammarskjöld, for he died at a time when his achievement was being questioned, his concept of his office attacked, and the validity of the secretary-generalship itself being challenged. Progress in human institutions is seldom achieved without struggle and anguish, and this was true of the stewardship of Hammarskjöld at the United Nations.

When I was appointed to succeed him as Acting Secretary-General, I was vividly aware both of the legacy of achievement and example which he had left behind and of the extreme difficulty of the task which I had inherited. Hammarskjöld had set an extraordinary standard of dedica-

SOURCE: UN Press Release SG/SM/1533.

tion, diplomatic skill, intellect, energy, and courage. He had worked for eight years to develop, often in novel ways, the potential of the United Nations for keeping the peace. He had developed techniques of multilateral diplomacy which had not been tried before. He was a tireless champion of the principles of the Charter and an indefatigable seeker after its objectives. He had set the stamp of his powerful and unusual personality on much of the activity of the Organization and had gained for it, by his actions as well as by his words, the respect and involvement of millions of people all over the world.

Hammarskjöld was also a staunch defender of the unity and independence of the Secretariat. He helped us to have a better understanding of the duties, obligations, and responsibilities of international civil service, a concept which he himself embodied to the outside world. By his actions and leadership he infused a new meaning into the provision of the Charter which makes the Secretariat one of the main organs of the United Nations.

Hammarskjöld did not hesitate to take risks if he thought it was necessary to take them. Nor did he fear the disapproval of various sections of the membership if he believed that the course he was taking was right. He was strongly criticized almost as frequently as he was highly praised, and was thought by some to be pushing the development of the Organization too fast and too far. His untimely death left his work incomplete at a time of division and controversy in the United Nations.

It is still too early to assess properly Hammarskjöld's contribution to the development of the world Organization. A longer perspective will be necessary before it is possible to judge where he made real advances toward a system of world order and where his ideas and experiments failed. As with the real achievements of all people who look to the future and are ahead of their time, there must be a long pause before a valid and lasting judgment can be made. Those who knew and worked with Dag Hammarskjöld, however, myself included, can be in no doubt as to the quality and the magnificent vision of the man—his steadfast courage, his imaginativeness, his enormous skill, and his total devotion to the United Nations. These qualities are in themselves a legacy of inestimable value to our Organization, whatever may be the ultimate verdict on some of his ideas and policies. I may add that, personally, I have little doubt that the verdict of history will in the end be resoundingly favorable to Hammarskjöld's concept of the United Nations as a dynamic and active force in international life.

In my ten years as Secretary-General I have, of course, been considerably influenced by my predecessor's ideas and actions. Most of all I have been impressed by the personal qualities which upheld him in a formidably difficult task. We remember him today with the greatest respect and honor as an outstanding pioneer of our Organization, which he liked to describe as the greatest adventure on earth.

RETROSPECT

LONG BEFORE THE WORLD had accepted his decision to leave the office of Secretary-General at the end of his second term, U Thant was at work on a comprehensive review of his ten years in office. He had decided to make this a major part of the Introduction to his final annual report so that his views would be perpetuated in the official records of the General Assembly. His comments ranged over all the principal problems of the decade—the Congo, the Middle East, Cyprus, Vietnam, disarmament, United Nations finances, decolonization, human rights, and economic development—and on the performance of the United Nations itself. Despite the Organization's disappointing performance in the political field, Thant expressed his conviction "that the institution itself is sound, and that it can, must, and will be made to work." He attributed most of the Organization's difficulties to the fact that the big powers "have all too seldom shown themselves able to rise above the suspicions, fears, and mistrust that spring from their different ideologies, different objectives, and different conceptions of the best interests of the world. By and large, the rivalry of nations continued to be the dominant factor in international life." Nevertheless, Thant concluded: "I have never been so convinced as now of the usefulness, the potential, and the absolute necessity of the United Nations."

From Introduction to the Twenty-Sixth Annual Report

NEW YORK   SEPTEMBER 17, 1971

Part One. Retrospect

I. General

1. WHEN THIS Introduction is published, I will have been in office for ten consecutive years as Secretary-General of the United Nations. I assumed these responsibilities in a period of great difficulty for the Organization, following the death of my predecessor. During my tenure of office, I have greatly benefited from the legacy of Dag Hammarskjöld, his historic vision of our Organization and his conception of the world of tomorrow. Looking back at the ten years during which I have known the rewards and frustrations of the office of Secretary-General, I feel compelled to pay·a special tribute to the immense task accomplished by the two men who preceded me in this office. Both, with their different personalities, made outstanding contributions to our world, consolidated the United Nations, determined its orientation, and gave it much of its present shape.

2. A reflection upon this past decade arouses in me memories of many hopes and satisfactions, and some disappointments; the results of these years of personal experience also evoke some thoughts and considerations that I would like to share with Member states on the eve of the expiration of my mandate.

3. The twenty-fifth session of the General Assembly was an occasion for drawing up a balance-sheet of the activities, achievements, and shortcomings of the Organization. It is not my intention to undertake a similar task here. Nor do I want to duplicate my annual report, which covers the activities of the Organization since June 1970. I shall here

SOURCE: General Assembly Official Records, Twenty-sixth Session, Supplement No. 1A (A/8401/Add. 1), part one; and part two, sections I, II, III, and IV).

limit myself to some remarks on events and institutions which I have had the opportunity of observing closely for the past ten years and with which I have been closely associated.

4. I shall first take up the political aspects of the period under consideration, then the economic and social problems. I would also like to express some thoughts concerning the structure and functioning of our Organizations, and I will conclude with some observations on its future.

5. In my previous nine introductions, I have been compelled to report more failures of the Organization than successes in the political field, more disappointment than satisfaction at the result of our combined efforts.

6. Looking back on the past ten years, I cannot help reaching the conclusion that during that period the most powerful nations have all too seldom shown themselves able to rise above the suspicions, fears, and mistrust that spring from their different ideologies, different objectives, and different conceptions of the best interests of the world. By and large, the rivalry of nations continued to be the dominant factor in international life. Precisely for that reason, many promising developments have not reached fulfillment, and results still remain far below the hopes and aspirations of the world community. Responsibility for this state of affairs has often been laid publicly at the door of the United Nations.

7. I profoundly disagree with those who try to belittle the achievements of the world Organization. The United Nations is only capable of being what its Members want it to be and, despite the many handicaps and obstacles, its influence on the great trends of our era has been considerable. For example, during the past ten years there have been many conflicts, some of them armed conflicts, involving Member states. In several cases the United Nations has been able to help find a peaceful solution, as for example in the Congo, in the dispute between the Netherlands and Indonesia over West Irian, in the Cuban missile crisis, and in the India-Pakistan war of 1965.

8. Even when a lasting settlement could not be reached, the United Nations helped in reducing the duration and intensity of the fighting. It organized and supervised those truces or cease-fires which, however precarious, maintain calm in Kashmir, Cyprus, and the Middle East. The United Nations may pride itself on the fact that every day, owing to these activities, a great number of human lives are saved, discussion is substituted for armed conflict, and the ground is prepared for more

durable settlements. The Organization has also often been used as a channel for negotiations and it contributes, in a way perhaps not specifically provided for in the letter of the Charter of the United Nations but very much in its spirit, to the pacific settlement of many disputes.

9. As I have pointed out on other occasions, it is in the conflicts that take place outside the framework of the United Nations that there usually seems little prospect of an immediate end to the bloodshed. This is true of the war which ravages Indo-China, a war involving several parties that do not belong to the Organization. If the peoples of China and Vietnam had been represented in this Organization, I believe there would have been opportunities for earlier and more fruitful negotiations.

10. It is well to remember that the decade under review has seen a number of encouraging trends in the political life of the international community. These developments justify reasonable hopes that the climate in which the United Nations operates is improving and will continue to improve. It is worth mentioning a few of these trends. After the traumatic experience of the Cuban missile crisis, the superpowers, greatly to their credit, made a determined effort to improve their relations with each other and to reduce to manageable proportions some of the more dangerous issues that existed between them. Thus they were able to achieve the limited nuclear test-ban agreement, the agreement not to place weapons of mass destruction in outer space, as well as some other partial agreements relating to arms control. Despite the embittering effects of the war in Vietnam, they were able to improve their relationships on various political, economic, cultural, and scientific matters and to embark on the Strategic Arms Limitations Talks, which make it possible to envisage the limiting and the eventual ending of the possibility of a nuclear war between them. Perhaps it is not too much to hope that these steps may be the beginning of a realization that in the modern world massive armaments are no longer the decisive factor of power.

11. We have also seen in this decade a movement toward a détente in Europe, culminating in progress on the German question and, most recently, the four-power agreement on Berlin. If this progress continues, it is to be hoped that the long-planned conference on European security may at last become a reality. We are also beginning to see developments in relation to the People's Republic of China which could be the beginning of a decisive step toward peace in Asia and the Pacific. In the Middle East, although unfortunately no long-term settlement is yet in

sight, we have seen the superpowers show a common desire to avoid a confrontation in the area and a recognition that peace can best be achieved with their strong and positive support for the actions of the United Nations.

12. Considerations such as the preceding ones give me confidence in the future of the United Nations and in its eventual ability, with the support and assistance of its Member states, to help solve the vast majority of the political problems of our generation and prevent conflicts that would threaten the future of mankind.

II. The Congo

13. The most urgent problem confronting the United Nations at the time I became Acting Secretary-General, and one that severely tested the peace-keeping capability of the Organization, was that of the Congo.

14. When the people of the Congo gained their independence from Belgium on June 30, 1960, it was an occasion for joyful celebration after the long period of colonial rule. Only a few days later, the country was plunged into a nightmare of mutiny and lawlessness, of secession and senseless bloodletting, followed by the collapse of public order and services. The Belgian administrators departed and the Belgian troops arrived, uninvited.

15. The new government appealed to the United Nations for help on July 12, 1960, and the Security Council authorized the requested United Nations military assistance. Within forty-eight hours, the first elements of the United Nations Force arrived on the scene. During the four years of the United Nations Operation in the Congo, thirty-four countries supplied military contingents or personnel. The Force reached a total of more than 20,000 at its peak strength. All but a very few of the 93,000 who served as "blue helmets" performed admirably as soldiers of peace. In establishing and later widening the mandate of the Operation, the Security Council conferred upon it responsibilities to prevent external interference in the Congo, assist in restoring and maintaining law and order, defend the country's independence and territorial integrity, and provide advice and assistance to the young nation through the most extensive civilian operations program every undertaken by the United Nations.

16. When the complex task of guiding the Operation was passed to

me, the situation had already undergone rapid changes. The tragic events between July 1960 and November 1961 had been marked by internal chaos—a total breakdown of governmental authority and the maneuvering of rival groups, each claiming to be a lawful government; misunderstandings and falsifications as to United Nations objectives and actions; attacks from various quarters upon the Organization, the Secretary-General, and the staff; division among the major powers and even among the Member states supplying personnel; mounting evidence of the involvement of mercenaries and foreign interest; and, for Patrice Lumumba as for many Congolese and non-Congolese, civilian and military, sudden and violent death.

17. Whatever progress had been made at that time had come about with painful difficulty. The withdrawal of Belgian troop units had been carried out, as called for by the Security Council, although the process took two months. In some parts of the country the mere presence of the United Nations Operation exerted a calming influence. The Force was able to protect many endangered people—individuals, threatened minority groups and refugees, and both national and provincial officials. Although attempts to train the national army and provide it with a corps of officers and the needed discipline had met with little success, United Nations civilian operations were furnishing not only advice but operational personnel in many essential fields, maintaining the country's basic services and dealing with the added burdens of economic paralysis, a growing stream of refugees, floods, and famines. The arrival of United Nations units in Katanga had achieved a symbolic restoration of the Congo's integrity, but the secessionist movement went on—inspired, instigated, financed, and armed by non-Congolese elements in connivance with certain members of the Katanga provincial administration. After eleven months without an accepted legal government—a period during which the United Nations Operation in the Congo sought to encourage conciliation and to prevent the various camps from using force against one another—a national unity government had at last been formed in August 1961, but without the participation of Katanga.

18. Three weeks after my appointment as Acting Secretary-General, the Security Council, on November 24, 1961, reaffirmed the purposes of the United Nations in the Congo—to maintain its territorial integrity and political independence, to assist the central government in the restoration and maintenance of law and order, to prevent the occurrence of civil war, to secure the immediate withdrawal and evacuation of all foreign

military, para-military, and advisory personnel not under United Nations command, by the use of the requisite measure of force if necessary, and to render technical assistance. It may be recalled that hundreds of foreign personnel remained in the Katanga forces, and efforts to deal with the mercenary problem by way of negotiations, or by entrusting the matter to consulates within the Congo, had been inadequate. Another objective, generally accepted as such although not formally expressed, was to prevent a confrontation of the great powers in this vast, mineral-rich country. No one can state with certainty whether, or to what extent, the Congo might have become an area of direct struggle between East and West if the United Nations had not responded to the request for aid. At the time, however, there were sufficient indications that such a possibility did in fact exist.

19. In pursuing its mandate the United Nations was governed by certain basic principles: that it would not intervene in the Congo's internal affairs, that force was to be used only as a last resort—in self-defense or for the specific purposes stated by the Security Council—and that the United Nations Force was to be neither an arm of the government nor an occupation army.

20. It is well to recall the Council's underlying position in this regard, one with which I fully agreed. As stated in its resolution of February 21, 1961, the Council was convinced "that the solution of the problem of the Congo lies in the hands of the Congolese people themselves without any interference from outside, and that there can be no solution without conciliation," and "that the imposition of any solution, including the formation of any government not based on genuine conciliation, would, far from settling any issues, greatly enhance the dangers of conflict within the Congo and the threat to international peace and security."

21. The difficulty in balancing all the United Nations aims and principles was demonstrated by the challenge of Katanga, which had become the most crucial aspect of the Congo problem, once the central government under Prime Minister Adoula had been formed. As I declared in 1962: "The core of the Congo problem is that of the secession of Katanga; the problem of the Katanga secession is primarily a problem of finance; the problem of finance, in turn, is the problem of the major mining companies."

22. In the Kitona declaration of December 21, 1961, Katanga's President Tshombé agreed to end the secession. But as the weeks and months went by, it became increasingly apparent that Mr. Tshombé was

employing dilatory and evasive tactics, refusing to implement the declaration and evading the questions of the expulsion of mercenaries and freedom of movement. It was clear that neither the United Nations nor the central government could tolerate such tactics indefinitely. Nevertheless, the United Nations continued to seek conciliation and mutual understanding. In consulting the Advisory Committee on the Congo, composed of members supplying forces for the Operation, I warned in July 1962 that the Organization might have to decide whether to withdraw the Force or go to the other extreme and specifically authorize the United Nations Operation to end the secession. I suggested the possibility of strengthening the mandate, but the Advisory Committee's consensus was that the existing mandate was adequate. As for the support of the Member states concerned, under Articles 25 and 49 of the Charter of the United Nations, I declared that the time had come for these obligations to be honored in action. In August 1962, I proposed the Plan of National Reconciliation, which was promptly accepted by Prime Minister Adoula and Mr. Tshombé; but once again the Katangese authorities failed to take any steps to implement this plan for a federal system of government. Finally, in December 1962, the lack of cooperation led me to propose various measures for applying economic pressure by preventing the export of Katanga's copper and cobalt and ensuring that payments of revenues to Katanga would be withheld.

23. Before these proposals could be acted upon, however, the final stage of the Katanga chapter began, in the form of a military show-down provoked by Katanga's *gendarmerie* and mercenaries. United Nations troops were fired at but did not retaliate. After four days of this, I reluctantly authorized the military action that began on December 28 and culminated in the peaceful entry of the Force into Kolwezi on January 21, 1963. Fortunately, there was little resistance and the action was carried out successfully and with a minimum of fighting. Mr. Tshombé and his ministers then stated their readiness to end the secession, and the arrival of the Minister Resident on January 23 symbolized the restoration of the central government's authority. Katanga's secession had come to an end, and the major elements of the mandate of the Operation had been fulfilled. It was a moment of deep satisfaction to me and, I am sure, to most Members of the United Nations.

24. With its units scattered across a country the size of western Europe, the Operation was also called upon to maintain order and to undertake humanitarian missions in other parts of the Congo. These

episodes were too numerous to review in this brief summary. It was recognized, however, that stability in the Congo ultimately would have to depend upon the effectiveness of the Congolese National Army. Unfortunately, despite repeated United Nations efforts to persuade the Congo to accept its assistance in retraining and reorganizing the Army, it was not possible to reach agreement on arrangements for this purpose. The problem of maintaining law and order remained; yet the United Nations Force could not stay on for long solely as an auxiliary police force. In a report of June 19, 1964, I stated: "The United Nations cannot permanently protect the Congo, or any other country, from the internal tensions and disturbances created by its own organic growth toward unity and nationhood." With the dangers of external interference largely removed, this undertaking would have to be carried out by the government and people of the Congo. Purely for financial reasons I recommended that the United Nations should be militarily disengaged from the Congo by the end of 1963. However, at the request of the central government, the General Assembly approved expenditures for a further period of six months ending on June 30, 1964, thus extending the Operation and entailing an additional expenditure of over $40 million. The United Nations was under great financial strain as a result of the Congo operations, but it was clear that the Congolese National Army was not yet ready to deal with the intertribal conflicts, pillaging, assaults and murders, and increasing activities against the government. The United Nations Force, during the transitional period, continued to assist the central government on various occasions, even in its final days, although the Force had been reduced to a strength of less than 6,000 by the end of 1963.

25. As many had feared, the Congo's internal security situation deteriorated following the withdrawal of the Force. For a time it even appeared that the turmoil of 1960 might return, with a rebellion movement growing after Mr. Tshombé became prime minister. Again a dissident government was set up in Stanleyville; again Mr. Tshombé recruited foreign mercenaries, this time to assist the Congolese National Army; and again, in November 1964, Belgian para-commandos arrived (with the government's declared approval), for the stated purpose of rescuing hostages held by the rebels. Many United Nations Members decried the operations as an intervention in African affairs; the Congo government in turn charged that certain states were aiding the rebel movement. After considering the matter, the Security Council called for

an end to foreign intervention and appealed for a cease-fire and the withdrawal of mercenaries. The government of the Congo, meanwhile, sought the assistance of the Organization of African Unity and the Council gave its support to that organization's efforts. Late in 1964, I expressed the hope that the Congo would muster the will and the ability to attain both security and political stability. Eventually, after the period of unrest which followed the departure of the United Nations Operation, the Democratic Republic of the Congo made considerable progress toward achieving those goals.

26. Although the Force had completed its tasks, the extensive United Nations program of technical assistance continued to provide thousands of experts and training activities. The momentum gained through the civilian operations program, carried out by the Organization in collaboration with the specialized agencies, was kept up when the regular channels of United Nations technical cooperation took over the work financed earlier under the United Nations Fund for the Congo. These activities provided the backbone of the Congo's public administration and services. Doctors, teachers, agricultural advisers, meteorologists, telecommunications experts, magistrates, airfield controllers, public works experts, and many others carried out their assignments under trying and often dangerous conditions. Gradually the in-service training programs, special institutes, and other educational efforts assisted by the United Nations enabled more and more Congolese to replace the United Nations personnel.

27. The costs of the Congo involvement were great. United Nations casualties included 126 killed in action and 75 in accidents. In the course of its implementation, the Congo operation claimed the lives of my distinguished predecessor, Dag Hammarskjöld, and other senior officials. Expenditures (including those for the civilian operations) totaled more than $400 million. And the controversy over financing created an unprecedented crisis for the United Nations.

28. The Security Council had made no special provision for financing the operations it authorized in the Congo, and it was the General Assembly which apportioned expenses among Members, taking the position that these were "expenses of the Organization" within the meaning of Article 17 of the Charter. This signified that Member states were obligated to pay their assessed shares. The International Court of Justice, in an advisory opinion requested by the Assembly, confirmed

that the costs were expenses of the Organization. But certain Members refused—and still refuse—to pay their designated shares, for various reasons of policy. As an extraordinary measure to provide needed resources, the Assembly in 1961 authorized the sale of up to $200 million worth of United Nations bonds, while stating that such measures should not be deemed a precedent for future financing of United Nations expenses. As of 1970, unpaid assessed contributions in respect of the United Nations Operation in the Congo amounted to $82.1 million. The total cash expenses of the Operation came to $337 million. Only $159 million was collected from Member states in assessed contributions for the Force, while the bond issue provided $143 million and voluntary contributions an additional $36 million.

29. But for the presence of the United Nations in the Congo, I commented in 1963, that country would have collapsed. The United Nations presence was the decisive factor in preserving the Congo's territorial integrity and in preventing full-scale civil war engineered from outside; it also helped the people of the Congo establish a bridge from the desperation of 1960 to a more solid beginning for their young nation.

III. Indo-China

30. For almost the entire duration of my mandate, I have been deeply preoccupied with the situation in Indo-China. Not only has the conflict in the peninsula cost the lives of hundreds of thousands of people— combatants and civilians alike—but it has also displaced and left homeless millions of others and brought intolerable suffering and hardships to an entire generation in the countries involved.

31. This conflict constitutes a direct challenge to the principles and authority of our Organization. Moreover, it diverts the energies and the technical and financial capacity of some of the most powerful nations in the world toward the barren task of advancing or consolidating so-called zones of influence. Even now, despite some positive elements, it is still difficult to forecast when and how this tragic war will end; indeed, its consequences for the peoples of Indo-China and for the countries involved are unforeseeable.

32. The absence of the People's Republic of China and both parts of Vietnam from our Organization has largely deprived the parties themselves of United Nations channels of communication and the world community of the means of exerting a mediatory role. Nevertheless, I

have made it clear time and again to the parties involved that the Organization and the Secretary-General are ready to use their best efforts in the service of peace in the area. On several occasions I have lent my good offices. It is with deep regret that I have seen so many efforts to promote peace achieve such limited success.

33. For a long time I advocated the cessation of the bombing of North Vietnam and the beginning of negotiations between the parties. The United States decision to halt the bombing and the opening of the Paris talks were encouraging elements, as was, later, the withdrawal of important contingents of foreign troops from Vietnam. Despite these steps, the war is still raging on the peninsula. It is more necessary than ever, therefore, for both sides in the conflict to show flexibility, adaptability, and tolerance as expressions of their will to progress on the difficult road toward peace. It is regrettable that the Paris talks have been considered a contest of wills rather than an opportunity to put a speedy end to the sufferings of the peoples of the area.

34. A distressing development during recent years has been the increasing use of systematic techniques of destruction which affect not only the combatants, but also innocent men, women, and children and sometimes animal and vegetable life, and threaten the remnants of some of the most brilliant civilizations of Asia. The violations by all sides of the most basic human rights and of respect for human life and dignity must also be the cause of concern and distress to the human community. Despite some hopeful indications, there has also been little progress so far on the question of the prisoners of war detained by both sides. It is doubtful that any appreciable headway will be achieved on this question as long as prisoners are used as pawns or instruments of propaganda.

35. Can we seriously expect an end to the tragic situation in Vietnam as long as the peoples of the area are not allowed to attempt to reconcile their differences and to express freely their wishes without any interference from outside powers? Let us hope that it will soon be possible for all trends of opinion in Vietnam to participate in the elaboration of decisions at the national level and for political discussions to be substituted for armed confrontations between factions. A lasting settlement, whatever its form, will undoubtedly have to take into account a political reality which is also one of the reasons for the present conflict, namely the community of language, civilization, and interest, and the close kinship between North and South Vietnam. This is why, after so many years of violence and suffering, I still consider that no durable solution

will be found without the application of the principles decided upon in Geneva when the peoples of Vietnam became independent.

36. Another distressing factor in the situation in Indo-China in the last two years is the extension of the conflict to two neighboring countries, which have become battlefields where soldiers of foreign countries confront each other.

37. In Laos, one of the few positive elements has been the agreement between the Pathet Lao, headed by Prince Souphanouvong, and the Royal Government of Prince Souvanna Phouma to renew their dialogue. I have urgently requested both parties to put aside the bitterness and suspicion generated by years of war and to hold discussions in a spirit of give-and-take, with the primary purpose of terminating the sufferings of the people for whom they are responsible.

38. With some parts of Laos being subjected to intensive bombing and with foreign intervention resulting in more foreign intervention, the kingdom is now the theater of a conflict of interest alien to the Laotians themselves. No solution to the Laotian conflict will be found as long as the bombing lasts and as long as the kingdom is denied the actual exercise of sovereignty over parts of its territory. It is high time for the international community, and particularly for those powers which signed the Geneva agreements on Laos, to fulfill the responsibilities they accepted at that time.

39. No strategic or other outside interests can justify the afflictions of the people of Cambodia which we are now witnessing. Cambodia, as well as the other countries of Indo-China, should be free from foreign intervention and should be allowed to live in peace.

40. In the midst of the tragic situation now prevailing in Indo-China, a positive note is struck by the United Nations through the accomplishments of the Economic Commission for Asia and the Far East and the Mekong Committee. Despite the fighting and with considerable personal risk, United Nations personnel and the contracting organizations are patiently establishing a network of irrigation and hydro-electric facilities for the purpose of ensuring a more prosperous future for the area. It is encouraging to note that these operations and achievements have so far been respected by all the parties to the conflict. This is an example of what the Organization can do for the real well-being of the peoples of Indo-China, and it is my hope that if, for various reasons, our Organiza-

tion has not been able to play a role in the settlement of the conflict, it will at least be able to contribute to the tremendous effort of relief and reconstruction that will be needed after this devastating conflict has ended.

IV. Disarmament

41. During this period, the Members of the United Nations have devoted a considerable portion of time and attention to the most important question of disarmament. The agreement during this decade on five major treaties in the field of disarmament is a noteworthy achievement that should inspire greater efforts during the Disarmament Decade of the 1970s.

42. There are, however, other factors which are a cause for concern. Not only have the nations of the world failed to halt or slow down the arms race—particularly the nuclear arms race—but they have escalated this disastrous course at a greater rate and to a higher level than ever before in history. During this period, world military expenditures have increased from $120,000 million to over $200,000 million per year. Each of the two nuclear superpowers has at its disposal sufficient nuclear "overkill" to destroy each other and the world many times over. They are still engaged in testing and producing nuclear weapons and in testing and deploying more sophisticated delivery systems.

43. There is an urgent need to make even more determined efforts to adopt effective measures that are conducive to nuclear disarmament. All nuclear-weapon powers have the duty to work out and implement a practical program for the total prohibition and destruction of all nuclear weapons. In the meantime, the world manages to survive in a precarious balance of nuclear force while material and human resources, which could immeasurably improve the standards of living and the quality of life for all people, have been diverted from productive peaceful purposes to an unproductive and dangerous arms race.

44. In the final analysis, disarmament must remain unattainable and all blueprints remain scraps of paper unless all negotiators cast aside unwarranted fears and suspicion and proceed with determination toward achieving essential security at ever lower armament levels. During my years in office there have been signs that such a spirit is developing. This offers some hope that both the real and imagined obstacles to concrete progress in disarmament may be overcome.

45. In order that the governments and peoples of the world might better understand the complex problems related to the arms race, I have been requested by the General Assembly at various times during the past ten years to prepare expert studies on various aspects of disarmament that are of overriding and worldwide concern. The most important of these were a study on the economic and social consequences of disarmament, in 1962; one on the effects of the possible use of nuclear weapons and the security and economic implications for states of the acquisition and further development of these weapons, in 1967; and a third, on chemical and bacteriological (biological) weapons and the effects of their possible use, in 1969. Two very important aspects of these reports are that the experts were unanimous in the writing of them and that the Assembly accepted them unanimously. I hope that this pattern will be continued in the future, as these studies provide practical guidelines for the solution of the great global issues confronting the world in the field of disarmament.

46. As the years go by, a most unfortunate tendency appears to have developed for nations and peoples to be lulled into accepting the steadily mounting weapon stockpiles and the drastically escalating military budgets as tolerable features of modern life, or ones which they are incapable of changing. Despite the manifold and repeated warnings about the perils and evils involved and the undercurrent of deep anxiety that afflicts almost everyone, and in particular the younger generation, those who wish to turn down the spiral of the arms race have not thus far been able to compete successfully with those who lay the principal stress on armaments as the means of ensuring national and international security. For this reason I believe that my forthcoming report on the economic and social consequences of the arms race and of military expenditures, prepared with the assistance of a distinguished group of international experts, can help to focus the attention of the international community on this important question, and also provide useful guidelines for its solution.

47. There have been disquieting reports that some of the current proposals considered at the Strategic Arms Limitation Talks provide for a ceiling on anti-ballistic missiles higher than their present level and for no limitation on the development of multiple independently targetable re-entry vehicles. Any agreement between the two powers to put a limit on the production and deployment of offensive and defensive nuclear systems would have great significance, particularly if it served to break the vicious action-reaction chain and if it in fact marked the start of a real

disarmament process. But an agreement that would fix higher ceilings than current levels would seem to provide, at least to some extent, for continued nuclear armament rather than for a limitation on armaments. What is needed is a halt in both the quantitative accumulation and qualitative sophistication of nuclear weapons and missiles, a reduction in their present numbers, and the beginning of the process of their drastic reduction and eventual elimination.

48. At present, the Members of the United Nations have to rely on unofficial and unconfirmed press reports about the negotiations at the Strategic Arms Limitation Talks. But questions concerning a possible nuclear war and human survival, as well as the economic and social burdens of the arms race, directly and intimately affect every human being on earth. Let us recall that the United Nations under the Charter has been given specific responsibility in the field of disarmament. Accordingly, in my opinion the time has come to inquire whether the United Nations should not be officially informed about the progress of the arms limitation discussions, to enable the Members to understand and consider the issues involved, even if they do not discuss the details of the day-to-day negotiations.

49. The world would also welcome an announcement by the Soviet Union and the United States that they would concentrate in 1972 on working out a treaty banning all underground nuclear weapon tests.

50. If the world is to survive and to prosper, progress must be made during the 1970s in both disarmament and development. Both the Disarmament Decade and the Second United Nations Development Decade have related objectives; progress in each of them will have a beneficial effect on the other and will facilitate the establishment of conditions of peace, justice, and progress in the world. Because of the central importance of questions of armaments, disarmament, and development to international peace and security, I would recommend that a study on the economic and social consequences of the arms race and of military expenditures be undertaken, with the assistance of consultant experts, every three years. Such periodic studies could provide current information and a study of the trends, and help to bring about a fuller understanding of the harmful effects of the arms race and the need, and perhaps also of the modalities, of converting the arms race into a peace race.

51. One additional way of helping to deal with the nuclear arms race may be found in a rather simple institutional device. As Members of the Organization are aware, the Secretary-General has since 1954 had avail-

able a United Nations Scientific Advisory Committee to advise and assist him on all matters relating to the peaceful uses of atomic energy with which the United Nations might be concerned. My predecessor and I found the advice and assistance of this small group of scientists invaluable in our understanding of the possibilities for peaceful uses of atomic energy. I have, however, often felt the need for more scientific advice and assistance in coping with the problems of the nuclear arms race and of nuclear disarmament. I would accordingly suggest that it would be useful to expand the numbers and functions of the existing Scientific Advisory Committee, so that the Secretary-General could have the benefit of the best scientific advice at his disposal in the field of nuclear weapons and nuclear disarmament, as well as in the related field of peaceful uses of nuclear energy.

52. There is one aspect of the operation of the Conference of the Committee on Disarmament on which I would like to comment. The institution of the co-chairmanship is unique in United Nations practice and indeed very rare on the entire international scene. The Soviet and United States co-chairmen have performed extremely valuable service since 1962 in providing substantive leadership and procedural guidance to the Eighteen-Nation Committee and to the Conference of the Committee on Disarmament. There appears to be considerable sentiment among the members of the Conference, however, that its work and achievements might be better promoted if the number of co-chairmen were to be expanded. The three groups of countries represented in the Conference—the Soviet Union and its allies, the United States and its allies, and the twelve non-aligned members—hold three separate caucuses. It would accordingly seem that the addition of a non-aligned co-chairman might provide more balanced leadership and ensure that all points of view were more truly reflected in the guidance given to the Conference. Since the Conference in any case does not take decisions by vote but operates only on the basis of unanimous agreement or consensus, a change in the co-chairmanship, such as I am suggesting, might also tend to facilitate the reaching of agreement among the twenty-five members who participate in the Conference. I would accordingly hope that this idea will be given full consideration.

V. Decolonization

53. It is commonly agreed that one of the great achievements of the United Nations has been its part in the process of decolonization. Since I

took office, twenty-four new Members have joined our Organization. At times, misgivings have been expressed about the emergence in the United Nations of a new majority of nations which had only recently attained independence. Certainly, these new countries have had an important impact on the Organization not only in the pattern of voting but also in the conception of the role and goals of the United Nations. For the last decade, the Organization has gone through a period of adjustment and we may already discern some definite trends. Conscious of the inequalities of wealth and power throughout the world, these new nations have questioned the established international system. It is my strong belief, however, that, far from having a disruptive effect, they have made an important contribution to a more representative and balanced view of the world in the United Nations.

54. Not only have the new countries loyally and steadfastly supported the United Nations, but they have often produced useful and constructive initiatives in the search for solutions to the pressing political, economic, and social problems of our time. Some of my ablest colleagues and staff members, as well as some of the international personalities most dedicated to our Organization and to the world community, come precisely from these newly independent countries.

55. These positive aspects make it all the more ironic that the last few years have been marked by a slowing-down in the pace of decolonization. It is a source of deep concern to this Organization and to me personally that millions of people have not yet been able to exercise their right to self-determination. These remaining territories under colonial rule should not be considered as an inevitable residuum of a past era but, on the contrary, as a direct challenge to the Charter and an anachronism unacceptable to the membership of this Organization.

56. I must report with particular regret that the question of Namibia, a territory for which the United Nations has a special responsibility, is still the object of complete deadlock despite repeated resolutions of the General Assembly and the Security Council and a recent advisory opinion delivered by the International Court of Justice at the request of the Security Council. Once more, I appeal to the Member states, especially to those vested with special responsibilities by the Charter, to undertake the steps well within their scope which will put an end to this intolerable situation.

57. If the governments of South Africa and Portugal have ignored the decisions of the United Nations, they have not shown themselves any more responsive to the positive initiatives undertaken by the Organiza-

tion of African Unity in the past years or by some groups of countries. The situation in the southern part of Africa involves principles which neither the United Nations nor the neighboring African countries can renounce. Those governments which condone the attitude of South Africa and Portugal in order to protect short-term national interests should be aware that if the problem of austral Africa is not solved in conformity with the legitimate rights of the black population, it will generate intolerable racial tensions that will inevitably affect the future relationships between black Africa and the rest of the world.

58. On the other hand, if the governments of South Africa and Portugal undertook the first steps toward the implementation of the decisions of the Security Council and the General Assembly, they would certainly receive the assistance and cooperation of the Organization and of the international community, and ways could then be found to protect the legitimate rights of all the communities, whatever their color, in this part of Africa.

59. During the last years of my tenure, I have been particularly distressed by the situation in Southern Rhodesia, where an illegal régime was instituted in 1965 in defiance both of the administering power and of world public opinion as expressed through the United Nations. This régime has so far succeeded, notably with the help of South Africa and Portugal, in surviving the economic sanctions imposed by the Security Council, and has even managed to maintain, and more recently increase, the value of the territory's external trade.

60. Although recent negotiations between the government of the United Kingdom and the *de facto* authorities in Salisbury raised some hope that a negotiated solution could be reached, it remains incumbent upon the administering power to restore constitutional government in Southern Rhodesia and ensure that the black majority can enjoy all political and economic rights. I would like also to recall that it is the duty of all Member states to see to it that the sanctions imposed by the Security Council are enforced more rigorously, in particular by exercising greater vigilance in the prevention of clandestine trade.

61. As I have recalled elsewhere in the Introduction, the General Assembly adopted on October 12, 1970, a program of action for the full implementation of the Declaration on the Granting of Independence to Colonial Countries and Peoples, and it called upon Member states to intensify their efforts to give effect to General Assembly and Security Council resolutions on colonial questions.

62. I cannot conclude these considerations on colonial problems without paying here a special tribute to the Organization of African Unity. Its contribution to the task of decolonization has been exceptional, and its efforts over many years in this field and the field of *apartheid* have resulted in the formulation of the historic Manifesto on Southern Africa, which was endorsed overwhelmingly by the General Assembly at its twenty-fourth session. My personal relations with its successive presidents and officials have been particularly fruitful and, in my opinion, beneficial to both the United Nations and the African states. The confidence in the United Nations and its Secretary-General expressed every year by the African heads of state in their annual conferences has been for me a source of gratification and encouragement, as well as one of the most constant and straightforward expressions of support for the work of our Organization.

VI. *International economic and social cooperation*

63. The spirit of internationalism, embodied in the Charter, has in recent years found its most far-reaching expression in the efforts of the United Nations in the economic and social fields. Ten years ago, the concept of "development decades" came into being in order to mobilize all available resources to combat poverty, illiteracy, and disease, which continue to plague two-thirds of the world's population. This formidable task caused the Organization to appraise its capacity for action, to define its priorities, to adopt new methods of operation in order that an International Development Strategy could be successfully implemented in this decade and the next.

64. The impact of modern science and technology upon the world is being taken into account in the United Nations, where the major concern is, of course, to ensure that scientific discoveries and technological inventions are used peacefully and for the benefit of all mankind, whether on earth, under the sea, in and beyond the earth's atmosphere far into the reaches of outer space. The extension of the principles of international law to these new areas, which are being recognized as the heritage of all mankind, augurs particularly well for the future.

65. Frustrated by the slowness of progress in some important domains, the Organization has used its growing resources to improve the lot of people in areas where its services are at present more welcome: education, child care, relief, social justice, demography, environment,

agriculture, health, safety, employment—the list is endless. These concerns, which transcend national boundaries, are increasingly attracting the interest and involvement of the younger generation, which now includes the majority of the world's people.

66. The population explosion which has continued during this past decade remains a major obstacle in the pursuit of political stability and orderly development. During the decade, the world's population increased by 650 million people. More than 80 percent of this increase took place in the less developed areas. This accelerating growth in population makes it ever more imperative and more difficult to rectify the dangerous imbalance between world affluence and poverty. In the 1960s, the resources of the United Nations system were mobilized and the machinery has been set in motion for the Herculean task of raising the standard of living of the vast majority of human beings to at least an acceptable level.

67. As a source of technical assistance and an investment instrument to serve the needs of developing countries, as an international mechanism for achieving national development objectives, the United Nations Development Programme constitutes a unique partnership between the countries of the world and the organizations of the United Nations system. Its operations are of unprecedented range and scope, as is the volume of its resources for noncapital development aid. The Programme and its partner organizations have demonstrated their readiness and ability to assist activities in nearly all sectors of economic and social development identified in the International Development Strategy for the Second United Nations Development Decade. The administrator is also responsible for the administration of the United Nations Fund for Population Activities.

68. It has become apparent in the past decade that the size and complexity of the tasks which the United Nations has undertaken in economic and social development require the intensive and well-coordinated efforts of the entire United Nations system. Notwithstanding the pattern of functional decentralization on which the United Nations system is based, the arrangements for coordination that have been carefully evolved in recent years on the basis of Articles 58 and 63 of the Charter have led to greater interagency cooperation in an increasing number of program areas and to considerable improvement in performance and administrative efficiency within the system.

69. I should like to cite a few examples to illustrate how overall planning and cooperative action by United Nations agencies, coordinated with national development efforts, have yielded some very dramatic results during the past ten years.

70. The world community may be proud of the progress made in freeing mankind from a scourge which, wherever it existed, proved a veritable obstacle to human development. I refer, of course, to malaria, which was considered the world's greatest single cause of disablement. With the discovery of DDT and other residual insecticides, it was possible to extend anti-malaria measures to large areas. As a result, over 1,000 million people are now living in areas in which this disease has been completely eradicated. This achievement, unparalleled in the annals of public health and possibly in the annals of human society, would not have been possible without the efforts of national governments assisted by the World Health Organization working in conjunction with the United Nations Children's Fund and the United Nations Development Programme. It is a milestone in international cooperation.

71. By preventing incapacity and death due to malaria, the anti-malaria campaign has broken the vicious circle of poverty and disease in many areas of the world. Specifically, it has contributed to a greater rice production in some countries by increasing the work output of the labor force. In many previously virgin areas, it has led to the opening of vast tracts of land for agricultural production and has augmented land value in areas where only subsistence-level agriculture could previously be sustained.

72. I trust that no effort will be spared by national governments in liberating the total population of the world from the scourge of malaria in due time and that the dramatic progress which has been made during the past five years in the World Health Organization's global campaign to eradicate smallpox will culminate in the elimination of this disease from the face of the earth during the present decade.

73. Ten years ago, almost one-half of the world's people were either hungry or suffered from the effects of poor diet, or both. Today, the threat of actual famine has been largely exorcised, although the percentage of people affected by under-nutrition and malnutrition has not diminished, owing to the increase in world population during the period. An important feature of United Nations assistance to economic and social development during the past ten years has been the creation of the

World Food Programme, a joint undertaking of the United Nations and the Food and Agriculture Organization of the United Nations, for multilateral food aid to developing countries. Since January 1963, the World Food Programme has committed more than $1,000 million in food aid to a total of almost 500 development projects in some 83 countries. I hope that the momentum gained by the World Food Programme as an instrument of international assistance to development will not be lost in the next few years.

74. The success of the efforts by private foundations, by the United Nations Development Programme and the Food and Agriculture Organization of the United Nations, in developing and cultivating high-yield cereals has dramatically improved the food supply in a number of areas where the food situation in recent years stood at the very edge of disaster. This "green revolution" has proved conclusively that the scientific and technological bases for increased agricultural productivity and, therefore, an abundant world food supply are indeed available. Although this multilateral effort has grown sevenfold during the past ten years, an even greater effort is required by the agencies, national governments, and individual farmers in order that world agricultural development may fulfill its promise of doubling world food production during the next decade. By improving substantially the nutritional value, yield-potential, and disease-resistance of various cereals and legumes and promoting their use in the less developed areas of the world, the United Nations can help 300 million children grow up healthy in body and in mind.

75. The decade also witnessed a thorough re-examination and re-orientation of the program and structure of the International Labour Organisation designed to enhance its capacities to meet the increasing needs of Member states for practical assistance in the fields of concern to it. Comprehensive long-term programs were initiated in the areas of human resources development, employment promotion, conditions of work and life, development of social institutions, and research. Important developments in the field of human rights included the adoption of the Declaration concerning the Policy of *Apartheid* of the Republic of South Africa, the formulation of a program for the elimination of *apartheid* in labor matters in that country, and the launching of an intensive program of action with a view to promoting equality of opportunity and treatment in employment. In addition, a large number of conventions and recommendations were adopted, with a view to the further realiza-

tion of socioeconomic rights. With regard to technical cooperation, there were two major breakthroughs in institution-building at the international level which are of particular interest to the developing countries. These were the establishment of the International Institute for Labour Studies in Geneva and the International Centre for Advanced Technical and Vocational Training in Turin. Of particular importance also as one of the highlights of the fiftieth anniversary of the International Labour Organisation was the launching of the World Employment Programme. It is my confident hope that this ambitious and yet realistic venture will prove to be a notable contribution to the solution of the problems of galloping unemployment and under-employment evident in so many of the developing countries.

76. The period from 1961 to 1971 witnessed scientific and technological developments which significantly advanced meteorology in theory and in practice. Artificial earth satellites now serve as meteorological observing platforms and high-speed electronic computers permit numerical weather prediction. The World Weather Watch, operated by the World Meteorological Organization since 1967, is an outstanding example of a highly useful and successful international endeavor on a truly global scale.

77. During these past ten years, enthusiasm for the potential benefits of modern scientific and technological advances has been tempered by a growing realization that these wondrous tools are also increasing man's capacity to destroy the human and natural resources of the earth. It has become quite clear that a unified global endeavor to control and preserve man and his environment is urgently required. One specialized agency of the United Nations, the Inter-Governmental Maritime Consultative Organization, is already helping to prevent pollution of the sea by oil and, hopefully, its activities will be extended to cover other ship-borne pollutants. Marine pollution will be only one of many topics to be included in the agenda of the forthcoming United Nations Conference on the Human Environment. Let me reiterate my hope that as a result of this Conference, some form of global system will be established, which will be associated with the United Nations and entrusted with negotiations among governments and private interests on matters affecting the environment, and that new international environmental standards, guidelines, and legislation will gradually emerge from its activities.

78. The establishment of the United Nations Industrial Development Organization on January 1, 1967, with its headquarters in Vienna, must

be counted as one of the successes achieved by the United Nations system during the decade. The organization undertakes three basic types of activities: first, operational activities in the field involving direct assistance; second, related activities in support of field operations or in seminars, symposiums, etc.; and third, promotion activities. After four years of operation, it is clear that there has been increasing recognition of the organization's efforts and its contribution to the industrial development of the developing countries and a wide acceptance by governments, both developed and developing, of its role in the area of industrial development. This has been reflected in the growing demand for its services and the widening of the scope of its activities.

79. During the past decade there has been an unprecedented expansion of world trade, and total exports have tripled since 1961. The activities of the United Nations during this period have been characterized by special efforts, fostered by both the General Agreement on Tariffs and Trade and the United Nations Conference on Trade and Development, to adapt the rules of trade to the needs of the developing countries. The latter are no longer expected to offer trade concessions inconsistent with their development needs in return for those made by developed countries. The partial suspension of the most-favored-nation clause of the General Agreement offers the prospect of a mutually advantageous expansion of their exports. The past ten years have witnessed great progress in trade liberalization with protective tariffs being slashed all over the world. However, the rising protectionist tendencies discernible in certain quarters during the past two years threaten to halt, or even reverse, the growth of international trade, which has brought such benefits to so many nations.

80. During the same period, the developing countries have also been able to rely increasingly on the financial institutions of the United Nations system for development assistance. These institutions themselves have forged much closer ties with other organizations in the United Nations family and have carried their financing operations into many new fields. I cite this example of international cooperative action because, in the field of international finance, a most significant development during the decade was the institution, in 1969, by the International Monetary Fund of Special Drawing Rights. By means of this new facility, the international community has for the first time by deliberate decision created a form of internationally acceptable reserves. The new facility, created to provide additional funds for governments to use in

settling international debts, is of particular importance to the developing countries, because it promises to strengthen their reserve positions so that they can proceed with their development plans with fewer worries about the fluctuations to which their trade and payments are subject. At the same time, the developed countries are less likely to adopt trade restrictions or to reduce the quality and quantity of their financial contributions to development assistance because of their own balance-of-payments difficulties.

81. Recent developments which have overtaken the international monetary system have been described by the Managing Director of the International Monetary Fund as giving great cause for concern while at the same time creating the opportunity for strengthening the system which has been the basis for effective collaboration for a quarter of a century.

82. During recent years, the International Bank for Reconstruction and Development and its affiliates, the International Development Association and the International Finance Corporation, have also greatly expanded and accelerated their activities. It is particularly important that the Bank should be able to finance not only normal "bankable" projects, but also projects in the public health, educational, and other fields which have great social as well as economic impact, but which would not normally be self-financing. For this reason I commend the efforts of the president of the Bank to secure periodically the replenishment of the resources of the International Development Association.

83. During the decade, I have also seen the emergence of new regional development banks. They have already shown their capacity for assisting the economic development of their respective regions. I hope that they will continue to work closely with the United Nations development system and that their activities may help maintain the momentum of the economic and social development of the poorer countries.

84. Frequently, in reviewing the accomplishments of the United Nations system, the steady and significant but seemingly unspectacular contributions of the technical agencies are not given sufficient prominence. Their contributions are nevertheless remarkable. They include the work of the International Atomic Energy Agency in promoting the peaceful uses of nuclear energy and in fostering the use of nuclear techniques in, for example, hydrology, agriculture, medicine, and industry; the establishment of regulations in the field of space telecommunications and in working toward the creation of a global automatic telephone

network by the International Telecommunication Union; the activities of the International Civil Aviation Organization in the planning of major air navigation surveys, the study of the economy of air transport and the development of international air law; the dissemination of information on technological progress and the conveyance of mail and in encouraging the use of air conveyance by the Universal Postal Union; and finally, of equal importance, the provision of technical assistance to the developing countries by all these organizations.

85. The preservation of mankind's cultural heritage is another of the many areas in which international action has proved feasible and successful during recent years. The international campaigns sponsored by the United Nations Educational, Scientific and Cultural Organization to protect endangered art monuments—the salvage of Abu Simbel, Florence, Borobudur, and now Philae and Venice—indicate that peoples and nations are capable of pooling their resources and ingenuity in an effort to save the glories of human civilization for future generations.

86. Elsewhere I have stated my belief in the need for a United Nations university. I believe that such a university would have a beneficial influence among the younger generation and contribute to the development of international understanding. The proposal is under consideration both in the United Nations Educational, Scientific and Cultural Organization and in the United Nations. I hope that, ultimately, it may be possible to establish this university with several campuses and institutions of higher learning in a number of countries, both developed and developing.

87. Before bringing this section to a close, I would like to pay a tribute once again to the spirit of cooperation shown me at all times by my colleagues, the executive heads of agencies constituting the United Nations system. They have realized, as I have, that the system is greater than the sum of its individual parts. This friendship and cooperation so generously extended to me by my colleagues in the Administrative Committee on Co-ordination will remain one of my cherished memories.

VII. Structure and functioning of the United Nations

88. Although ten years is a short time in the life of an institution, it is enough to perceive trends in the evolution of the United Nations.

89. Since 1961, the structure of the Organization has been affected by the emergence of new subsidiary bodies, such as the United Nations Development Programme, the United Nations Conference on Trade and

Development, the United Nations Industrial Development Organization, and the United Nations Institute for Training and Research. These outgrowths represent indispensable—and often courageous—steps forward, and demonstrate the vitality of our Organization and its capacity to cope with new issues.

90. The structure of the Secretariat itself has been modified in the past ten years, notably because of the increasing importance of problems related to development. With a limited expansion of personnel, and by changing the balance between staff involved in administrative, political, and economic tasks, and between those working at Headquarters or in the field, the Secretariat has been able to set up new services dealing with matters little known a few years ago and, in so doing, to keep abreast of the changes taking place in the world.

91. The United Nations must face the increasing complexity of our societies and their problems and it may be necessary, in the near future, to envisage new subsidiary organs or substantive departments to deal with global issues. This need may be felt more specifically in regard to questions concerning the environment or in the fields of science and technology, space or maritime problems. The creation of such new bodies, which may often be only the regrouping in a coherent organ of services dispersed among various departments or agencies, should be viewed by the membership as an appropriate response to the ever new challenges of our world. The setting up of new entities, however, should not be detrimental to the coordination and coherence of the activities of the United Nations family, and provision should be made to ensure the overall authority in their respective domains of the Secretary-General, the Economic and Social Council, and the General Assembly.

92. It is so commonly said that the United Nations is increasingly ineffective that it hardly bears repeating. It is argued that the Security Council meets less and less frequently and, when it does, it fails to take effective action. It is said that the great powers seek more and more to resolve disputes outside the Organization. Furthermore, the argument runs, the General Assembly concentrates increasingly on economic matters. With respect to difficult political problems, the Assembly adopts a spate of resolutions which have little to do with reality and which attract little interest and achieve little compliance. The degree to which these points are true is a matter for personal assessment, but the very fact that they are made requires that they be taken seriously.

93. The various alleged failings of the Organization are sometimes

attributed to the great increase in membership, to the admission of many small states and, basically, to the principle of "one state, one vote." To find the latter principle embodied in the United Nations is hardly surprising. On the national plane, it is to be found in many bicameral systems, where one legislative body is based on population, that is, power, and the other on equal provincial or state representation. On the international plane, in the United Nations, the realities of power are recognized by the permanent membership and the great powers' right to veto in the Security Council, the organ with the authority to make binding decisions. The equitable idea of an equal voice for each nation is expressed in the representation and equal voting rights of all Member states in the General Assembly, which has for the most part only the power of recommendation.

94. To have the right to vote as such cannot be harmful, although the irresponsible exercise of that right—as of any other right—is bound, in the long run, to have undesirable consequences.

95. In my many years with the United Nations as both delegate and Secretary-General I have become increasingly convinced of the great potential for influence which lies in the General Assembly. It is futile to adopt recommendations which everyone knows from the start will have no effect. To adopt recommendations which are realistic, which are fair to all the interests involved, is bound to influence world opinion and to affect the course of events. The Assembly thus offers the smaller and the medium powers not only a voice, but also a way of influencing the course of events far in excess of what was previously available to them. To really exercise this influence, however, the majority must make it plain that they will listen to both sides of a case and not only to the larger faction. The majority must prove that they will seek a realistic way out of difficulties rather than resort to condemnations or threats.

96. It would be a grave pity if the smaller and medium powers throw away their opportunity and fail to establish some collective credibility through a more realistic approach to what they can or cannot do. Such failure would strengthen the criticisms of the United Nations, which are increasingly heard and which could, in the long run, destroy the Organization. On the contrary, if the opportunity is grasped by those concerned, the Organization can look forward to a future bright with hope and success. The General Assembly, in particular, could become increasingly effective over the whole field of United Nations operations, including the maintenance of peace and security, primary responsibility

for which is vested in the Security Council. The Assembly also has responsibilities in this field, however, and any balanced and sober recommendations which it can adopt will surely not go unheeded even in the most powerful nations of the world.

97. If the United Nations is to become a center for harmonizing the action of nations, it must keep abreast of political developments occurring in the world. For that purpose, governments should continue more systematically the practice of reporting on the efforts and progress they make toward the maintenance of peace and security and on their foreign policy programs. This would enable the Organization to have a more balanced view of the world political situation showing not only the unsolved problems, but also the progress achieved.

98. The General Assembly and the Security Council would also benefit from a better knowledge of the accomplishments of the regional organizations such as the Organization of American States, the Organization of African Unity, the League of Arab States, and the Council of Europe, among others. Ways could also be found to enable institutions with no links with the Organization to inform the General Assembly when they undertake politically important initiatives such as the mutual reduction of forces at present envisaged in Europe between the Warsaw Treaty Organization and the North Atlantic Treaty Organization.

99. An important step forward in international cooperation was the holding last year of the first periodic meeting of the Security Council. The practice thus instituted on October 21, 1970, should be continued, but such meetings should be more than mere formal occasions and should provide the members of the Council with an opportunity to carry out effectively their responsibilities for the maintenance of international peace and security. In my opinion, these periodic meetings should enable this body to take stock of the international situation and review the achievements made in the implementation of previous decisions. The Council could also take advantage of such meetings, held privately, if need be, to assess potential threats to the peace in areas of instability, make recommendations to the governments concerned and thus fulfill its role in the prevention of international crises. In cases when, by means of a general consensus or as a result of the position of certain governments, an important question is withheld from public discussion at the United Nations, I believe that the situation could usefully benefit from consideration by the Council in the course of its periodic meetings.

100. The United Nations has been suffering from what I would call a "documentation explosion." There has been a vast increase in the number of meetings of United Nations bodies and conferences and, although many efforts have been made, an effective means of controlling the conference program has yet to be found. These meetings generate large quantities of documents, and there has been little reduction in the documentation of the permanent organs. The result is the continuous output, rising to a peak during the General Assembly, of an enormous mass of paper. The costs of writing, editing, translating, reproducing, and distributing this mass are correspondingly enormous; the facilities of the Secretariat are at certain periods badly overstrained; and many delegations complain—privately and publicly—that they cannot digest the contents of the quantity of paper they receive. The only alleviation of this situation lies in self-discipline by both the delegations and the Secretariat, which should avoid producing or calling for the production of documents that are not worth their cost in labor, money, and reading time. This discipline, if its necessity is understood, can possibly be reinforced by rules adopted by the General Assembly which, while allowing the various organs the necessary power to decide on the best means of performing their tasks, will still help to bring the quantity of documentation within manageable limits. This whole problem has been examined by the Special Committee on the Rationalization of the Procedures and Organization of the General Assembly and by the Joint Inspection Unit. These reports, and the recommendations made therein, raise issues which merit the close attention of the General Assembly.

101. Communications covering a vast range of subjects are sent to the Secretary-General by governments of Member states with the request that they be circulated either as documents of the General Assembly and its subsidiary organs or under cover of a *note verbale*. The rule has been applied that a communication can be circulated as a document of an organ only if it relates to an agenda item or if it requests the inclusion of a new item in the agenda. This rule has been more or less generally accepted. As regards circulation under cover of a *note verbale,* the Secretary-General has in principle been willing to issue in this form any communication which a Member state has asked him to circulate. This liberal policy has given rise on a number of occasions to the question of whether certain criteria should be established to determine what material is appropriate for circulation under cover of a *note verbale*. As the

General Assembly is about to undertake new efforts with a view to the limitation of documentation, this problem could appropriately be dealt with in that context.

102. I have become increasingly concerned about the slowness and unreliability of the Organization's operational communications system, which utilizes a number of short-wave relay stations and is extremely limited in extent. There have been several occasions during the past year when direct contact was lost altogether between Headquarters and politically sensitive missions or operations in other parts of the world. Against this background, I have explored the possibility of transferring the Organization's operational communications, or at least part of them, to communications satellites, which provide instant communication of high reliability and are increasingly used by Member states. In view of the cost involved, I have approached the International Telecommunications Satellite Consortium with the request that a limited number of satellite circuits be placed at the disposal of the United Nations free of charge.

VIII. Membership of the United Nations

103. At a time when the participation of the People's Republic of China in the United Nations seems to be within reach, I very much hope that no more time will be lost in sterile debate on this question and by the use of legalistic arguments to conceal political realities. Although the nature of the solution depends on Member states, it has always been my firm conviction that our Organization would have undoubtedly been more efficient had it not kept the door closed to one of the largest nations in the world and to those states which—precisely because they were divided and belonged to opposing ideological systems—needed to participate in the United Nations, where they could have found a common ground for working together to overcome their differences.

104. The participation of the People's Republic of China will no doubt increase the United Nations capability of working for the objectives of the Charter. It will also bring closer to realization the goal of universality of membership of the United Nations, which has been one of my cherished personal aspirations during the past ten years. In this regard, I feel strongly that the admission of the divided countries to the United Nations should not be linked to the solution of the problems resulting

from their division. Their accession to membership should, on the contrary, be considered as likely to facilitate the search for solutions to these problems.

105. I should also like to reiterate the views I have expressed on several occasions, notably in the Introduction to my annual report on the work of the Organization for 1966–1967, regarding the problem of micro-states, since this question is likely to become more acute in the years to come. While universality of membership is most desirable, like all general concepts it has its limitations, and the problem should be considered in the light of the Charter and of the future effectiveness of the United Nations as well as the interests of the states concerned. It is, of course, desirable and legitimate that even the smallest territories, through the exercise of their right to self-determination, should attain independence. Nor should any political entity be deprived of the right to have its voice heard in our Organization. On the other hand, there are many ways in which the views of very small states can be channeled to the Organization without their carrying the burden of the status of full membership, and it is incumbent upon the Member states to find an appropriate solution. This problem certainly deserves the closest attention of the membership on its own merits and without reference to political alignments.

106. I should also like to reiterate a suggestion that I have made on several occasions that the question of observer status and the criteria for such status should be examined by the membership so that the present institutional arrangements may be put on a more regular and practical basis.

IX. *The Secretariat*

107. Although the world's attention is directed mainly to the deliberative bodies and the Secretary-General, I believe it is proper to make some observations on the Secretariat staff who prepare and implement, at Headquarters and in the field, the decisions of the main organs.

108. After my ten years as head of the Secretariat, I am convinced that a true "international civil service" exists. It is staffed, by and large, with persons who have the interests of the United Nations only in view and who are not influenced in their work by the policies of the states of which they happen to be nationals. The last quarter of a century has shown that such a Secretariat is essential if the Organization is to be a

viable and dynamic institution. Either from within or from without, such a civil service must not be eroded.

109. Erosion from within could result from a departure from the standards and restraints that are incumbent upon an international civil servant. Until now, service at every level of the Secretariat has been generally regarded as more than just "another job." It has been considered a calling or vocation, with its concomitant satisfactions and rewards. Such an attitude, in turn, imposes certain restraints and standards which may not be required in many other occupations. It would be disastrous for the Secretariat, and thus for the United Nations as a whole, if this approach were changed under the influence of labor developments outside the Organization.

110. Erosion from without could arise from the failure of Member states to respect fully the Secretary-General's freedom of choice in the appointment of staff or from the competent deliberative organs' disregard of the principle that the "conditions of service" should be determined by "the necessity of securing the highest standards of efficiency, competence, and integrity." Such is the importance of this principle that all Member states should consider it essential to their own interests, as well as those of the international community, to have their ablest people serve the Organization. For this purpose, the conditions of employment should be sufficient to draw and retain the most competent men and women from all countries. I have always been conscious of my responsibility as head of the Secretariat to help assure the well-being and financial independence of staff members, and I still believe that everything necessary must be done to maintain the highest possible morale in the international civil service.

111. Much of the originality and spirit which characterizes the United Nations comes from the fact that its staff is representative of a wide variety of beliefs, cultures, and national entities. The Organization cannot yield on the principles of independence and integrity of the staff contained in Chapter XV of the Charter and in the Staff Rules, and on rare occasions it has been the Secretary-General's duty to remind governments and staff members of these principles. On the other hand, the exclusively international character of the responsibilities of the staff need not conflict with their legitimate pride in their national origins. A sense of national loyalty is not incompatible with overriding allegiance to the United Nations.

112. I should like to take this opportunity to pay an unreserved tribute

to the devotion, quality, and initiative of all those who have served the United Nations—at all levels and in all capacities—during my two mandates. Despite difficulties inherent in the work of an international organization and despite inevitable frustrations, I have found among my colleagues unswerving faith and enthusiasm in the goals of the United Nations, dedication to their tasks, and skill and competence in the performance of their work. It has been my experience that staff members can cope with the most difficult problems or situations. Many have accepted service in the United Nations at great personal risk—in the Congo, the Middle East, Southeast Asia, and elsewhere. Some of them have given their lives for peace and for a better world, and they deserve our deepest gratitude and that of future generations.

X. Non-governmental support

113. One of the most remarkable occasions during my years as Secretary-General, and one which I shall always remember as a truly historic occasion, was the visit of His Holiness Pope Paul VI to the United Nations on October 4, 1965. It was in the cause of peace that I invited him and it was in the cause of peace that he came. He brought a message from the gospel of peace and made a stirring appeal—"Never again war." The appeal of the Pope represented for me not only a call for peace by the head of the Catholic Church, but an appeal to the conscience of all men to support the international Organization. As the Pope said, "We wish Our message first of all to be a moral and solemn ratification of this high institution."

114. I have been equally gratified by the support given to the world Organization by the World Council of Churches. It is a source of great satisfaction to me that many other religious groups have also identified their goals with those of the United Nations, having as one of their basic objectives support for the Organization. I wish also to avail myself of this opportunity to pay a tribute to the various non-governmental organizations which have been so active in bringing to the people of the world a deeper and wider understanding of the United Nations by familiarizing them with its limitations as well as its possibilities, its achievements as well as its areas of doubtful accomplishment. Several of these non-governmental organizations have, of course, their special fields of interest and activity. I commend them for their good work in the past and hope that they will continue their activities with even greater intensity

and enthusiasm in the years ahead. My particular appreciation goes to the World Federation of United Nations Associations and the United Nations associations in the various Member countries. Their support has indeed been invaluable.

115. In spite of the activities of the non-governmental organizations and also of the public information offices in the United Nations and the various agencies, there still remains considerable ignorance among the public about the peace-building activities, especially through economic and social development, and the global services rendered by the world Organization. There is a tendency, on the other hand, to place too much emphasis on crises and sensationalism. Since global problems, such as peace, disarmament, development, the environment, and many others, affect the daily lives of peoples everywhere, it is essential that world affairs and international instruments be made the daily concern of news media and of educators.

116. In this regard, I should like to pay my warmest tribute to the corps of correspondents accredited to the United Nations for their untiring work of information, education, and enlightenment about the United Nations. They have also been for me personally a great source of strength and belief in the future of our Organization.

XI. United Nations finances

117. During my entire period of office, I have been deeply concerned with the financial position of the Organization. Ten years ago the first signs of major difficulties appeared on the financial horizon of the United Nations. Efforts were made to resolve these difficulties by appeals to governments, by the sale of United Nations bonds to Member states, and by requesting an advisory opinion of the International Court of Justice on the legality of certain assessments. Some of these efforts were moderately successful; but no solution emerged to meet the political and juridical differences which lay at the heart of the Organization's financial plight.

118. In 1965, after some years of steady deterioration, the General Assembly responded by establishing the *Ad Hoc* Committee of Experts to Examine the Finances of the United Nations and the Specialized Agencies. In its first and second reports this Committee analyzed the financial situation and related matters and provided the Assembly with a factual basis for dealing with the growing financial crisis. It was only on

the assumption that action would be taken and that assurances of cooperation from all sides would be honored that I agreed reluctantly to serve a second term as Secretary-General. I made it clear at that critical stage that implicit in my acceptance was the understanding and expectation that the Organization would be restored to solvency and that its finances would be placed again on a sound and viable basis.

119. It is with deep regret that I report a continuing deterioration to the point at which hard and unpalatable decisions can no longer be responsibly postponed. There exists no real basis for optimism or for the expectation that an overall and comprehensive solution is imminent or likely to be found in the foreseeable future. This, despite the efforts that have been made during recent months by the president of the twenty-fifth session of the General Assembly, who had graciously consented, as I informed the Assembly at its last plenary meeting, to join the Secretary-General in also using his good offices in a search for "the means by which the difficulties that have plagued us for so long might best be overcome." The approach has been predicated on the assumption that, while positions of principle which Member governments have taken must be fully respected, there is nevertheless a lively common interest in ensuring that the prestige and capabilities of the United Nations should not be irreparably weakened. It was therefore inescapable that we should seek to establish a recognition of the need to liquidate once and for all the unfortunate legacy of the past and thereby provide a more secure political and financial basis for the Organization's continued existence.

120. Instead, it is a melancholy fact that the cumulative shortfall in regular budgetary receipts continues to grow. The Organization's Working Capital Fund has been fully utilized. Debts incurred for past and present peace-keeping operations remain unpaid. The authority provided annually to borrow from "special funds and accounts" in the Secretary-General's custody has been nearly exhausted. I have been forced to utilize balances in such "funds and accounts" beyond the clear intent of the authorizing resolutions, namely, to make possible the temporary borrowing of funds which are not needed at the time to finance the programs for which they were specifically provided. With the depletion of working capital and the erosion of net liquid assets, this need to borrow has in fact tended to become permanently recurrent. Nor, in the absence of effective remedial measures, is there any firm assurance that the substantial sums currently owed to these special funds and accounts can be repaid.

121. Even so, great difficulty has been experienced in meeting a number of payrolls during the past year. They were met only as a result of the cooperation of a number of Members in paying their assessed contributions in advance of the dates on which they were due. I am bound to report that, on the basis of past payment patterns of Member states, serious and disturbing difficulties must be expected in meeting the regular payroll and certain other obligations in the last months of 1971. This, of course, also assumes that collections of current and arrear contributions are not unexpectedly and significantly increased or accelerated and that I am not counseled or instructed to borrow funds whose repayment, irrespective of their source, cannot be guaranteed. The situation, in short, is that the United Nations, after ten or more years of deficit financing of peace-keeping operations, must very soon face the fact that it is a bankrupt Organization.

122. It would cause me deep personal sorrow and regret if my service as Secretary-General were to end on this note. Unfortunately, the tragedy far transcends any personal aspect: what is at stake is the Organization, for which we have all held, and continue to hold, such high hopes despite the fact that its credit standing and reputation have already been seriously impaired by its financial plight.

123. Against this background of urgency and crisis I must once more appeal to Member governments to give priority to considering ways and means of dealing definitively with the Organization's financial problems. I hope that at least some of the necessary steps may be taken early in the General Assembly's twenty-sixth session. I stand ready, as does my staff, to support this process in any way possible, but real progress can only be achieved if there is a willingness to accept certain political compromises and accommodations.

XII. The office of the Secretary-General

124. Ten years ago, shortly before his tragic death at Ndola, my predecessor, in the Introduction to his annual report on the work of the Organization dated August 17, 1961, gave a brilliant analysis of the different concepts then prevalent regarding the character, authority, and structure of the United Nations and the role of the Secretary-General. My own experience has confirmed in every way Dag Hammarskjöld's philosophy concerning the powers of the Organization and, in particular, the role of the Secretary-General. There may still be some, as there were ten years ago, who consider that the role of the Secretary-General

should be purely a technical one, as the servant of the principal deliberative organs. This attitude does not, in my view, tally with the law or with
the facts. Therefore, as I come to the end of my second term of office, I
feel it incumbent upon me to review briefly the political role of the
Secretary-General, as I have found it to be in law and in practice.

125. To turn first to the law, under Article 7 of the Charter the
Secretariat is itself established as a principal organ. Article 97 defines the
Secretariat as comprising "a Secretary-General and such staff as the
Organization may require." That same Article and the ones which
immediately follow enumerate, in the broadest terms, the wide variety of
functions which, taken together, make up the role of the Secretary-
General. Article 97 covers the technical, or "housekeeping," function
by specifying that the Secretary-General "shall be the chief administrative officer of the Organization." Article 98 goes further, in not only
providing that the Secretary-General "shall act in that capacity in all
meetings" of the principal deliberative organs but also that he "shall
perform such other functions as are entrusted to him by these organs."
These "other functions" are not expressly limited to ones of a technical
nature and, indeed, practice confirms that these also encompass political
functions inherent in the responsibilities of both the Security Council
and the General Assembly. Article 99 goes furthest of all, in clearly and
expressly conferring a political role on the Secretary-General, independent of the decisions of the deliberative organs, by authorizing him to
"bring to the attention of the Security Council any matter which in his
opinion may threaten the maintenance of international peace and
security."

126. As a matter of common-sense interpretation, in order to exercise
his right under Article 99, the Secretary-General must necessarily have
all the powers, including those of inquiry, to reach a reasoned and
independent opinion on whether or not a particular matter may threaten
international peace and security. He may also endeavor, through the
exercise of good offices, to play a part in "preventive diplomacy"
designed to ensure that a matter does not become a threat to international peace and security.

127. Particularly important, in the present context, are the obligations
under Article 33 of the Charter for the parties to any dispute, the
continuance of which is likely to endanger international peace and
security, to seek "a solution by negotiation, inquiry, mediation, conciliation, arbitration, judicial settlement, resort to regional agencies or

arrangements, or other peaceful means of their own choice." There is no prohibition in the Charter preventing parties to a dispute from seeking the Secretary-General's help in resolving their difficulties. It would be anomalous, at the very least, if the head of a principal organ of an Organization designed "to save succeeding generations from the scourge of war" were excluded from any political role in the realization of this aim. Therefore, I have come to the clear conclusion that I am competent, under the Charter, to use my good offices.

128. The political role of the Secretary-General, in addition to his administrative functions, was expressly recognized by the Preparatory Commission of the United Nations. In chapter VIII, section 2, of its report the Commission stated:

The Secretary-General may have an important role to play as a mediator and as an informal adviser of many governments, and will undoubtedly be called upon from time to time, in the exercise of his administrative duties, to take decisions which may justly be called political. Under Article 99 of the Charter, moreover, he has been given a quite special right which goes beyond any power previously accorded to the head of an international organization, viz: to bring to the attention of the Security Council any matter (not merely any dispute or situation) which, in his opinion, may threaten the maintenance of international peace and security. It is impossible to foresee how this Article will be applied; but the responsibility it confers upon the Secretary-General will require the exercise of the highest qualities of political judgment, tact, and integrity.

On February 13, 1946, by its resolution 13 (I), adopted unanimously, the General Assembly transmitted the foregoing section to the Secretary-General for his guidance. The Security Council, for its part, has also expressly recognized the political role played by the Secretary-General. At the 1329th meeting, on December 2, 1966, in a statement made by the president on behalf of the Council, it was recorded that the members of the Council "fully respect [the Secretary-General's] position and his action in bringing basic issues confronting the Organization and disturbing developments in many parts of the world to their notice. . . ."

129. What follows from the law is also borne out by the facts. During my tenure of office alone, at the request of deliberative organs, I have been entrusted with tasks, carried out frequently under my direction by my personal representatives, involving political elements varying from the entire administration of a territory, as in West Irian, or the establishment, running, and supervision of a peace-keeping force, as in Cyprus, to the observation of and reporting on elections, as in Aden. At the

request of governments, I have assisted in the determination of the wishes of the inhabitants of certain territories regarding their future status, as in Sabah (North Borneo) and Sarawak and, most recently, in Bahrain. I have sought, through personal representatives, to resolve certain specific differences between particular states, such as Cambodia and Thailand in the period from 1961 to 1968, Rwanda and Burundi in 1963 and 1964, India and Pakistan in 1965 and 1966, Guinea and the Ivory Coast in 1967, Equatorial Guinea and Spain in 1969, Ghana and the Soviet Union, also in 1969. Differences with which I have been concerned have been as diverse as charges of aggression, territorial disputes, the placement of atomic weapons, the impounding of fishing vessels, the hijacking of airliners, and the imprisonment of individuals. This is not a comprehensive list, there being other cases such as the Congo and the Middle East where the record is now already largely public. There have also been the humanitarian missions in situations such as the Nigerian civil war and East Pakistan where political elements are naturally involved.

130. It may be that any such enumeration sounds rather thin in relation to the great issues or hard-core problems of our times—such as those of the Middle East, Kashmir, Cyprus, *apartheid*, or Namibia—but it does serve to underline that what the law permits the facts bear out regarding a political role for the Secretary-General. On the negative side, it also shows that the Secretary-General cannot resolve those hard-core problems which even the strongest nations do not wish to face head-on.

131. I do not assert that the Secretary-General's political role is unlimited or is possible in every circumstance. Indeed it is subject to legal and, in many cases, severe practical limitations. It is here that the level of expectation, particularly of the general public, is often so much greater than reality will permit. The general public expects the Secretary-General to act in crisis situations, and when he makes no pronouncements there is a consequent reaction of disappointment and an assumption that the Secretary-General is doing nothing. The requirements of discretion and the essential need for "quiet diplomacy," if useful results are to be achieved, are not always adequately recognized.

132. When a specific mandate is given to the Secretary-General by the Security Council or the General Assembly, he must necessarily act in accordance with the terms of that mandate. Some element of discretion may remain in interpreting such a mandate, which is often laid down in the broadest terms, or in dealing with unexpected situations which may

subsequently arise, but this discretion has to be exercised in the light of an honest and impartial appreciation by the Secretary-General of what he considers to be the wishes of the organ concerned. In some instances it may be possible, in case of doubt, to seek further instructions or interpretations from the relevant deliberative organ. In others, it may be clear that, because of differences between Member states, such recourse would be fruitless. It is only in these extreme instances that it falls upon the Secretary-General, in carrying out a particular mandate, to exercise a wider discretion in determining what he believes to be the true international interest and in acting accordingly.

133. When the Secretary-General considers exercising a political role on his own initiative, or at the request of the parties, he must necessarily arrive at his decision taking into account specific legal limitations, such as Article 2, paragraph 7, of the Charter, and practical limitations such as a determination whether action on his part would be likely to produce useful results. The Secretary-General has no means of enforcement, no economic power at his disposal: he can rely only upon the prestige of his office and his own powers of persuasiveness. These are fragile instruments with which to tackle an international conflict, and it is important that they should be preserved. If a move by the Secretary-General were to give rise to the impression that he was intervening in a matter essentially within the domestic jurisdiction of a Member state, or taking a particular side in a conflict, or that he was abandoning his impartiality, his usefulness would be at an end, as any measure of success is in turn a measure of the confidence which he enjoys with the governments concerned.

134. When the Secretary-General decides that he may usefully act, it is in nearly every case essential that he should, in the initial stages, act privately and without public fanfare. Governments are not likely to entrust a matter to him or to entertain any of his proposals, in the full glare of publicity. This is not to say that, at an appropriate stage, the Secretary-General should not inform—as has always been my policy— the competent deliberative organs either privately or in a public report; but the element of confidentiality is an essential one at the start, or when a matter is at a stage when public opinion on both sides is strongly committed.

135. Although the Secretary-General's powers of initiative in political matters are circumscribed and rather modest, practice has shown that many governments appreciate the availability of an institution such as

the office of the Secretary-General as a possible means of seeking a solution to particular international differences. In a world so crowded with differences any new possibility for finding solutions—even a circumscribed and modest one—should be welcomed.

136. For the sake of the next Secretary-General, I feel that I should plead with delegations for understanding of the fact that the increasing burdens of the Secretary-General's office leave him less and less time for contacts with individual permanent representatives. In the early days when there were no more than sixty Members of the Organization and its activities were much less complex, the Secretary-General had some time for the simple purpose of exchanging views on matters of common interest with the representatives. Nowadays, however, when there are 127 Members and still more are expected, and when not a year passes without adding new problems, new organs, and new programs to the sphere of United Nations concern, the responsibility of the Secretary-General to keep himself informed and the performance of his duties have become so increasingly heavy that little chance remains for conversations without an immediate and practical object, however useful they might be if there were less pressure of time. If the delegations sympathetically realize this, they will seek individual interviews with my successor only when there are specific substantive points to be discussed, and only when it is he in person, and not any of his senior colleagues, who can deal with the matter involved.

137. An international organization charged with the great responsibilities of peace has existed, first through the League of Nations and now the United Nations, for little more than half a century. This is but a brief moment in history, and there remains an awesome gap between the Organization's responsibilities under the Charter and the role which states permit the Organization to play. However, among the traditions and expectations which have begun to develop are those regarding the role of the Secretary-General. Given the brevity of their existence, such traditions and expectations could be swept away if there was to be a return to a concept of the Organization as nothing more than a static conference machinery. I have wished to make these remarks so as to place on record my fervent conviction that the incumbent of the office of Secretary-General must play a political role, necessarily circumspect and judicious, if he is to be of real assistance to Member states in a dynamic and imaginative search for peace and for the realization of the purposes and principles of the United Nations.

XIII. Concluding remarks

138. This year, after ten years of service as Secretary-General, I shall briefly make a few general concluding remarks in this Introduction. Simple and obvious as most of them are, they express some of my own feelings at the end of my term.

139. The United Nations and the concept of internationalism as embodied in the Charter are sometimes viewed with less than enthusiasm, and even on occasion, with resentment by governments. I am convinced more than ever, however, that it is a dangerous illusion to believe, in the present state of the world, that life can be safe without that concept and without a world organization which embodies it. Much of the usefulness of the United Nations is unknown and indeed intangible. But, however faulty, it represents an aspiration and a method of trying to realize a great ideal. Nations and peoples will turn their backs on this great endeavor at their gravest peril.

140. At this stage the United Nations system provides the best available and workable method by which nationalism and national sovereignty can evolve in order to keep pace with the vast changes that have made the nations of the world interdependent. If this evolution can succeed we may achieve a world concert of nations which preserves the best elements of nationalism. In a concert of nations where each plays its rightful part, the relations between states should at last be based on reality and fact, rather than on conflicting ideology, prejudice, and xenophobia. This simple hope may be said to be naïve and unrealistic, but how immensely productive and practical its realization would be in terms of the better use of our resources, our talents, and our brief span of life on this planet!

141. If a genuine concert of nations could be achieved, the world Organization could at last become the instrument for harmonizing the policies and actions of states and the center for joint enterprises on all those matters—and there is no shortage of them—which are of the deepest concern to human beings all over the world.

142. No one can deny that the performance of the political organs of the United Nations is disappointing, although great changes have taken place in the methods of operation both of the Security Council and of the General Assembly. The return to consensus in the Security Council has disadvantages as well as advantages, for it has often meant that when the Council cannot agree on an important question it may not even take up

that question. Neither the Secretary-General nor any other organ can satisfactorily fill the gap created by the failure of the Security Council to comprehend the responsibilities given to it in the Charter. The primary function of our Organization—the maintenance of international peace and security—cannot be fulfilled by a retreat from collective weakness and collective impotence.

143. It is unquestionably a step in the right direction that the General Assembly has broken out of its former preoccupation with cold-war topics and now devotes most of its time to a vastly wider range of subjects, on which the voting is refreshingly unpredictable. It is however a weakness when resolutions are adopted which have no prospect of implementation, and the authority and prestige of the world's greatest deliberative body is thereby eroded.

144. Perhaps the most decisive change in the last twenty-five years is the change in the scale of world problems and the accelerating pace of that change. Developments in population, technology, and damage to the environment have shown us what the authors of the Charter perhaps did not sufficiently appreciate, namely that scientific and technological advance is the most important single factor in bringing about changes not only in the lives of peoples, but also in the balance of power in the world. The United Nations as a global organization has a vital role to play in the control of the new breed of worldwide mass phenomena which we are now, almost helplessly, witnessing. A system of management of questions such as our planet's vital resources, including air and water, is an urgent and long overdue necessity. Such questions can only be tackled effectively on a global scale. To curb the current waste of resources, including human time and energy, may also require a new and comprehensive look at the life style of the human race.

145. The world, for all its wealth, is still divided into rich and poor, and the gulf between them is growing. Just as the poorer nations are aspiring to technological and industrial progress, the richer ones are beginning to wonder whether they are not tired of affluence and frightened by some of its effects. The developing countries must be helped to develop and to avoid some of the worst consequences of development. A balance must be found which will at the same time meet their needs and avoid putting an impossible strain on the natural resources and on the life-sustaining systems of our planet.

146. I feel more strongly than ever that the worth of the individual human being is the most unique and precious of all our assets and must be the beginning and the end of all our efforts. Governments, systems,

ideologies, and institutions come and go, but humanity remains. The nature and value of this most precious asset is increasingly appreciated as we see how empty organized life becomes when we remove or suppress the infinite variety and vitality of the individual.

147. In this connection I feel obliged to mention a problem which has been almost daily in my mind during my time as Secretary-General. I refer to the violation of human rights within the frontiers of a state. Theoretically the United Nations has little standing in such situations— and they are all too common. Legally, the membership of the United Nations has done an admirable job on human rights. The necessary texts exist. But practically, where does an individual or a group of individuals find recourse against oppression within their own country? World public opinion has become an increasingly important factor in such problems. I myself have privately done the best I could in many such situations, knowing full well the weakness of my own position, and I know that many national leaders have done the same. But this can never be enough, and the time has surely come when governments in the United Nations must make a determined effort to give justice a worldwide dimension.

148. A related problem which often confronts us, and to which as yet no acceptable answer has been found in the provisions of the Charter, is the conflict between the principles of the integrity of sovereign states and the assertion of the right to self-determination, and even secession, by a large group within a sovereign state. Here again, as in the case of human rights, a dangerous deadlock can paralyze the ability of the United Nations to help those involved.

149. I am increasingly persuaded that, whatever the size and strength of governments or the awe-inspiring achievements of technology, we are more and more reliant for a decent future on the seriousness and responsibility of the individual citizens of the world. It is in the end their sense of decency and justice, their tolerance and human kindness, their talent and their will to live in peace, that is our best hope for a just, orderly, and creative society. Education in its broadest sense is the key to such a society, which will be supported and sustained not by the dominance of its rulers but by the character and wisdom of its citizens. Perhaps we have more to learn in this field than in any other.

150. These are a few random thoughts arising out of an absorbing ten years of service to the community of nations. I have never been so convinced as now of the usefulness, the potential, and the absolute necessity of the United Nations. The Organization is evolving, as all

vital institutions must evolve, through a process of trial and error toward a goal and an ideal which all can accept. It is customary now for radicals to join with reactionaries in condemning the United Nations as an ineffective, outmoded, and hypocritical instrument for peace and justice. What they would be able to put in its place is not clear. I too, like most of the Member governments, am critical of much that goes on, or does not go on, in this house. But I am convinced that the institution itself is sound, and that it can, must, and will be made to work.

151. In fact, after ten years in office, my conviction stands undiminished that the United Nations remains the best instrument with which nations may cooperate for the development and the peace of their peoples. I have directed all my faith and efforts toward maintaining and developing this Organization as an indispensable center for harmonizing the actions of nations in the attainment of our common ends and as an increasingly effective instrument for peace and development.

152. For the duration of my tenure I have worked ceaselessly toward the goal of peace, justice, and progress and, in whatever role life thereafter sets before me, I will continue to do so.

153. I cannot close without expressing my profound appreciation to the Member governments which have given me such unfailing support and cooperation during these ten years. I have received this cooperation at every level from the head of state or government through the foreign minister and the permanent representative and his colleagues. This support was displayed most notably in 1966, when I had announced my intention not to accept a second term. At the present time, when there seems to be a feeling among many of the Member governments that I should somehow be persuaded to accept a third term, I only wish that, apart from thanking them most sincerely for their continued confidence, I were in a position to accede to their wish. I much regret that this is not possible.

Part Two. Current Issues

I. General

Twenty-fifth Anniversary

154. The twenty-fifth anniversary of the founding of the United Nations provided a solemn occasion for reflection and evaluation, for consolidation of the progress already made, and for a rededication to the

principles of international order and morality set forth in the Charter. I am pleased that the twenty-fifth anniversary of the United Nations was so widely observed in 1970—at the United Nations and by the specialized agencies and other organizations in the United Nations family, and in Member states by non-governmental organizations and concerned individuals throughout the world.

155. The first World Youth Assembly to be convened under United Nations auspices was held at Headquarters in July 1970. The Assembly served to draw the attention of youth to the principal problems before the United Nations and gave young people an opportunity to express their views concerning peace and progress. Most of the more than 640 participants from all over the world came from Member states, some came from major non-self-governing territories, and some represented international youth organizations. In an atmosphere free from external constraints, they addressed themselves to subjects of major international concern such as peace, development, education, and the environment. I trust that before any similar Assembly is convened in the future, adequate financial support will be assured well in advance of the event and that most of the procedural difficulties encountered last year in the conduct of the debate will be avoided. I hope that this initial step to establish a dialogue with representatives of the world's youth, who now constitute more than half of the world's population, will be followed by others.

156. The climax of the anniversary was the commemorative session of the General Assembly, which took place from October 14 to 24. An impressive number of heads of state and government, as well as their deputies and foreign ministers of Member states, came to Headquarters and addressed themselves to the past record, present problems, and future tasks of the Organization. The very presence at the United Nations of such eminent statesmen from all over the world gave proof of their faith in the Organization. All the speakers emphasized the urgent need to strengthen the United Nations and render it more effective in meeting the great challenges that will face the Organization in the years ahead.

157. The commemorative session culminated in the adoption on October 14, 1970, of three major documents. In the Declaration on the Occasion of the Twenty-fifth Anniversary of the United Nations, the representatives of Member states reaffirmed their dedication to the Charter and their will to carry out its obligations. They reviewed the overall record and declared that, despite its limitations, the United

Nations, as a center for harmonizing the actions of nations, had made an important contribution to the maintenance of international peace and security, to developing friendly relations based on respect for the principle of equal rights and self-determination of peoples, and to achieving international cooperation in the economic, social, cultural, and humanitarian fields. In closing, they expressed full confidence that the actions of the United Nations would be conducive to the advancement of mankind along the road to peace, justice, and progress.

158. In the International Development Strategy for the Second United Nations Development Decade, governments of Member states reaffirmed their unswerving resolve to seek a better and more effective system of international cooperation so that the prevailing disparities in the world might be banished and prosperity secured for all. The Declaration on Principles of International Law concerning Friendly Relations and Co-operation among States in accordance with the Charter of the United Nations was the fruit of several years' intense efforts for the codification and progressive development of the principles of international law.

159. Since the twenty-fifth anniversary of the United Nations coincided with the tenth anniversary of the adoption of the Declaration on the Granting of Independence to Colonial Countries and Peoples, the General Assembly, at a special meeting, adopted a program of action for the full implementation of this historic Declaration.

160. The anniversary was also a welcome occasion to give special recognition to the members of the United Nations Secretariat who have participated in the work of the Organization since its inception. Scrolls were given to them as tokens of appreciation for their loyal and valued service. The message of peace, justice, and progress was carried throughout the world by the commemorative stamps and medals issued by the United Nations, as well as by stamps issued in ninety-five countries to mark the occasion. The specialized agencies and other organizations of the United Nations system also observed the occasion, some with special publications and others by convening commemorative meetings. Among the extensive anniversary activities in a number of Member states, special national committees were established to prepare and coordinate various programs and events to broaden and deepen understanding of the United Nations.

161. The anniversary celebrations occasioned extensive official and unofficial debate on the role of the United Nations during the remaining years of this century. There appeared to be general agreement that, in

order to have survived the many vicissitudes of the postwar years, the Organization must have been endowed with a good measure of resilience and flexibility. Viewed in the light of the present state of the world, the need to strengthen it has never been more urgent. In the interdependent world of the 1970s, the security and welfare of all peoples can only be assured through the concerted efforts and cooperative action that the United Nations alone can provide at present. I believe that the anniversary has served to place past achievements in a clearer perspective and to point to the directions which must be taken if the principles set forth in the Charter are to be put into practice. . . .

East Pakistan

177. The civil strife which erupted in East Pakistan in March 1971, and its aftermath, are matters of deep concern to me as Secretary-General of the United Nations. While the civil strife in itself is an internal affair of Pakistan, some of the problems generated by it are necessarily of concern to the international community. The recent events in East Pakistan, following on the cyclone disaster of last November, have resulted in extensive loss of life, destruction, and disruption. The plight of much of the population is serious, and millions of people have fled to the adjacent states of India, bringing to the Indian authorities overwhelming health and relief problems and imposing an intolerable burden upon their already strained resources. International assistance on an unprecedented scale was urgently needed both for the relief of the distressed people in East Pakistan and for aid to the East Pakistan refugees in India.

178. I expressed my concern over this situation to President Agha Mohammed Yahya Khan shortly after the events of March 1971 and have been in continuous touch with the governments of Pakistan and India, both through their permanent representatives at the United Nations and through other contacts. In these exchanges I have been acutely aware of the dual responsibility of the United Nations, including the Secretary-General, under the Charter both to observe the provision of Article 2, paragraph 7, and to work, within the framework of international economic and social cooperation, to help promote and ensure human well-being and humanitarian principles.

179. It was with this latter responsibility in mind that I appealed for assistance both for the East Pakistan refugees in India and for the

population of East Pakistan. In order to channel the assistance given in response to those appeals, I designated the United Nations High Commissioner for Refugees as the focal point for assistance to the refugees in India and assigned, with the agreement of the government of Pakistan, a representative in Dacca in order to make as effective use as possible of the international assistance made available for the relief of the population of East Pakistan. In addition to those two emergency relief operations, the High Commissioner has initiated, with my full concurrence, an effort to facilitate the voluntary repatriation of the refugees now in India.

180. At its meeting on July 16, 1971, the Economic and Social Council held a full discussion of these operations, based on the statements made in the Council by the High Commissioner and the Assistant Secretary-General for Inter-Agency Affairs. At the conclusion of this discussion, the president of the Council expressed full support for the action taken by the Secretary-General.

181. Substantial contributions have been promptly offered in response to my appeal for the refugees in India. However, the money and supplies made available are not nearly sufficient, and the Indian government still faces the appalling and disruptive problem of caring for millions of refugees in its territory for an unforeseeable period of time.

182. The response to my appeal for the relief operation in East Pakistan, particularly in its initial phase, has been far from sufficient or adequate to the magnitude of the task. In this connection, I should mention that in my dealings with the government of Pakistan, as well as in the organization of the relief effort in East Pakistan, I have been at pains to emphasize the necessity of being able to give to the donor countries appropriate assurances that their contributions will reach their intended destination—the people of East Pakistan.

183. Efforts to bring about the repatriation of refugees have so far been unavailing. Since President Yahya Khan announced his agreement to allow the East Pakistan refugees to return on May 25, only an insignificant number of refugees have done so, and, according to Indian and other sources, the total number of the refugees in India has steadily increased.

184. The crux of the matter is that international and government efforts in East Pakistan are increasingly hampered by the lack of substantial progress toward a political reconciliation and the consequent effect on law, order, and public administration in the region. There is a danger that serious food shortages, and even famine, could soon add to

the sufferings of the population unless conditions can be improved to the point where a large-scale relief program can be effective. Equally serious is the undoubted fact that reconciliation, an improved political atmosphere, and the success of relief efforts are indispensable prerequisites for the return of any of the refugees now in India. The situation is one in which political, economic, and social factors have produced a series of vicious circles which largely frustrate the efforts of the authorities concerned and of the international community to deal with the vast humanitarian problems involved.

185. These human tragedies have consequences in a far wider sphere. The violent emotions aroused could have repercussions on the relations of religious and ethnic groups on the subcontinent as a whole. The relations between the governments of India and Pakistan are also a major component of the problem. The conflict between the principles of the territorial integrity of states and self-determination has often before in history given rise to fratricidal strife and, in recent years, has provoked highly emotional reactions in the international community. In the present case, there is an additional element of danger, for the crisis is unfolding in the context of the long-standing and unresolved difficulties between India and Pakistan—difficulties which gave rise to open warfare only six years ago. Although there can be no question of the deep desire of both governments for peace, tension between them shows no sign of subsiding. The situation on the borders of East Pakistan is particularly disturbing. Border clashes, clandestine raids, and acts of sabotage appear to be becoming more frequent, and this is all the more serious since refugees must cross this disturbed border if repatriation is to become a reality. Nor can any of us in the United Nations afford to forget that a major conflict on the subcontinent could all too easily expand.

186. In tragic circumstances such as these, it is all too easy to make moral judgments. It is far more difficult to face up to the political and human realities of the situation and to help the people find a way out of their difficulties. It is the latter course which, in my view, the United Nations must follow.

187. In the light of the information available to me, I reluctantly came to the conclusion, by mid-July, that the time was past when the international community could continue to stand by, watching the situation deteriorate and hoping that relief programs, humanitarian efforts, and good intentions would be enough to turn the tide of human misery and

potential disaster. I was deeply concerned about the possible consequences of this situation, not only its humanitarian aspect, but also the potential threat to international peace and security and the bearing it might have on the future of the United Nations as an effective instrument for international cooperation and action. It seemed to me that the tragic situation arising from these events, in which humanitarian, economic, and political problems were mixed in such a way as almost to defy distinction, presented a challenge to the United Nations as a whole which must be met.

188. For these reasons I felt it was my duty, as Secretary-General, to bring this problem to the attention of the Security Council. I did so on July 20 by means of a memorandum to the president of the Council. In the memorandum, after outlining the considerations set forth above, I stated that the political aspects of this matter were of such far-reaching importance that the Secretary-General was not in a position to suggest precise courses of action before the members of the Security Council had taken note of the problem. I believed, however, that the United Nations—with its long experience in peace-keeping and with its varied resources for conciliation and persuasion—must and should play a more forthright role in attempting both to mitigate the human tragedy and to avert a further deterioration of the situation. I expressed the view that the Security Council, the world's highest body for the maintenance of international peace and security, was in a position to consider, with the utmost attention and concern, the situation on the subcontinent and to reach some agreed conclusions as to measures which might be taken. My primary purpose was to provide the basis and opportunity for such discussions to take place and to expresss my grave concern that all possible means should be explored to resolve this tragic situation.

189. At about the same time as I submitted this memorandum, which is related to a concern for international peace and security, I made a humanitarian proposal, also in the exercise of my responsibilities and within my competence as Secretary-General, aimed at facilitating the process of voluntary repatriation of refugees by establishing on both sides of the border a limited representation of the United Nations High Commissioner for Refugees. As an initial step, I suggested that such representatives should be stationed in two or three areas to be selected by the two governments, in consultation with him. The government of Pakistan accepted my suggestion, but the government of India did not on the grounds that it was not preventing the refugees from returning to East Pakistan.

190. Recently I also took an initiative for the strengthening of the United Nations relief operation in East Pakistan. On the recommendation of my representative in Dacca, I approved a plan to increase considerably the United Nations personnel for this operation, thus greatly improving its effectiveness. This would also put the Organization in a better position to assure the international community, and donors in particular, that all supplies reach their destination—the people of East Pakistan. It is my hope that with this strengthening of the United Nations operation, more contributions will be obtained for the relief and rehabilitation that are so urgently needed in East Pakistan.

191. In a disaster of such vast proportions, the international community has a clear obligation to help the governments and peoples concerned in every possible way. But, as I have indicated, the basic problem can be solved only if a political solution based on reconciliation and the respect of humanitarian principles is achieved.

II. Disarmament

192. The designation of the 1970s as the Disarmament Decade serves to underline the fact that general and complete disarmament remains the goal of all discussions and negotiations, despite the recent tendency to concentrate on certain collateral measures for the prevention or limitation of armaments. The General Assembly last year requested the Conference of the Committee on Disarmament to give specific consideration to a comprehensive program of disarmament. In the time available to it, however, the Committee's efforts were devoted mainly to the problems of chemical and biological weapons and to the comprehensive test ban. I hope that the Assembly will devote full attention to the important measures contained in the comprehensive program with a view to speeding up the consideration of a number of items. There is much work to be done in both the nuclear and conventional fields. If momentum is to be maintained during the Disarmament Decade, and indeed it must be not only maintained but increased, then simultaneous consideration must be given to more than one or two disarmament measures at a time. Progress should be made in respect of collateral measures leading toward the goal of general and complete disarmament.

193. There is also a great need for more information and publicity regarding both armaments and disarmament so that peoples and governments can better understand the problems with which they are obliged to cope. Here, I believe that my report on the economic and social conse-

quences of the arms race and of military expenditures, prepared with the assistance of a distinguished group of international experts, can help to focus the attention of the international community on this important question, as well as provide useful guidelines for its solution. This report emphasizes the great dangers of the arms race, both nuclear and conventional, and illustrates the dimensions and ramifications of the crushing burden of military expenditures. I hope that it will convince people and their leaders that they must begin to rearrange their national and international priorities and concentrate their resources and energies on the solution of the staggering economic and social problems facing humanity, rather than on the feverish accumulation of the means for destroying life and society on our planet.

194. During the past year, because of the insistent demands for an end to underground weapon tests, a number of ideas have been put forward for facilitating the achievement of a comprehensive test ban, which I consider the most important measure that can be taken to halt the nuclear arms race. It was felt that if, against all hope, there was any further delay in achieving an immediate comprehensive test ban, a number of temporary transitional measures could be undertaken immediately to limit and reduce the magnitude and number of underground nuclear tests, and to phase them out, pending the achievement of a comprehensive agreement. Such transitional measures can certainly help to reduce the dangers and risks inherent in continued testing, while negotiations proceed urgently for the complete cessation of all tests except those that are permitted for peaceful purposes.

195. Some modest progress in the field of nuclear disarmament was achieved during the past year. At its twenty-fifth session, the General Assembly, by an overwhelming vote, commended the Treaty on the Prohibition of the Emplacement of Nuclear Weapons and Other Weapons of Mass Destruction on the Sea-Bed and the Ocean Floor and in the Subsoil Thereof. It is a matter of satisfaction that more than eighty states have signed the Treaty and almost a score have already ratified it. Its early entry into force would ensure that an area covering almost two thirds of the surface of the earth would remain free of nuclear weapons. The Treaty also contains a pledge to pursue further measures of disarmament in this area, whose importance will increase in future years.

196. There was also some continued progress with regard to the Treaty for the Prohibition of Nuclear Weapons in Latin America, which established the first nuclear-free zone for an inhabited area of the earth.

Additional countries became parties to the Treaty or ratified its two protocols. In accordance with the several resolutions of the General Assembly to that effect, I appeal to all nuclear powers to guarantee the nuclear inviolability of the zone by signing and ratifying Additional Protocol II of the Treaty of Tlatelolco.

197. In the field of chemical and biological weapons, more progress has been made during the past few years than at any time since the adoption of the Protocol for the Prohibition of the Use in War of Asphyxiating, Poisonous or Other Gases, and of Bacteriological Methods of Warfare, signed at Geneva in 1925. The General Assembly has called for universal adherence to the Protocol and has affirmed that it prohibits the use in international armed conflict of all chemical and biological weapons. I am gratified to note the growing number of countries that have ratified or acceded to the Protocol. Last year alone more countries became parties to it than in any year since its signature. I am also pleased to note the progress made by the Conference of the Committee on Disarmament in working out a draft convention on the prohibition of the development, production, and stockpiling of bacteriological (biological) and toxin weapons and on their destruction, as a first step toward achieving a similar ban on chemical weapons. Such a convention would represent the first time that any treaty had been agreed to that provided for the actual destruction and elimination of existing weapons. While welcoming and looking forward to the complete prohibition and elimination of biological weapons and toxins, I would like to stress the overriding importance of also achieving as soon as possible the complete prohibition and elimination of all chemical weapons, which are far more important and dangerous.

198. On May 20, the United States and the Soviet Union announced that they had agreed to concentrate this year at the bilateral Strategic Arms Limitation Talks on working out an agreement for the limitation of the deployment of antiballistic missiles, together with an agreement on certain measures with respect to the limitation of offensive strategic systems. This announcement was welcomed as an encouraging development and gave rise to the hopes that reason would prevail and that both superpowers were becoming convinced of the futility of the nuclear arms race. All of us fervently hope that this is indeed the case.

199. In our preoccupation with weapons of mass destruction, we should not lose sight of the urgent need for curbing the conventional arms race throughout the world. I have previously expressed my con-

cern that the rate of increase of these weapons has been markedly greater in recent years than that of nuclear weapons and more rapid in developing areas, where the burden of arms is particularly difficult to bear. Special efforts should be made to reverse this unfortunate trend everywhere, especially in areas of conflict, where the upward spiral has been particularly steep. In addition, each individual country should re-examine its position to determine whether or not its arms expenditures are truly essential for its security.

200. With respect to Europe, there are encouraging signs that both opposing military groups seem to be reaching the conclusion that the mutual reduction of troops and arms would not only eliminate a totally unnecessary arms burden, but would also release funds for other press-ing peaceful purposes. I hope that the endeavors to bring this positive venture in Europe to fruition will continue and that they will meet with success.

201. For many years I have had the feeling that there was great need for regional disarmament measures—in the nuclear field as well as in the conventional field—and that additional nuclear-free zones should be created. I would welcome the convening of regional conferences, not only in Europe but also in other regions of the world, on the initiative of the states of those regions, for the consideration of the reduction and regulation of armaments and forces, and for the establishment of nuclear-free zones in areas other than Latin America.

202. During the Disarmament Decade, it is not only important that intensive and uninterrupted work proceed in the field of disarmament; it is also important that all the existing treaties should be strengthened. I should like to appeal for universal adherence to and the full implementa-tion of all the existing treaties. The strengthening of these treaties and their becoming accepted standards of international law will not only ensure that they will be observed and have continuing validity, but will also serve to make additional agreements more readily attainable and acceptable. The full implementation of each agreement will have a synergetic effect on the overall field of disarmament.

203. A special word is in order about the Treaty on the Non-Prolifera-tion of Nuclear Weapons, which was acclaimed as the most important international agreement in the field of disarmament since the nuclear age began. The Treaty can only achieve its full purpose if it is universally observed, and I accordingly renew my appeal to all countries to become parties to it. The International Atomic Energy Agency has made good

progress in working out the contents of the safeguards agreements and for financing arrangements, which will facilitate the negotiation of the safeguards agreements envisaged by the Treaty. For the Treaty to remain full viable and valid, all of its provisions must be fully implemented and the proliferation of nuclear weapons must be prevented. If nuclear weapons should continue to proliferate, then not only the Treaty but our very survival would indeed by jeopardized. The risk of nuclear war by accident, miscalculation, or mad intent would be multiplied to an extent that might make it unmanageable.

204. For many years I have stressed the importance of bringing France and the People's Republic of China into the disarmament negotiations. It is obvious that there can be no far-reaching measures of disarmament, either nuclear or conventional, unless all the nuclear powers participate in the negotiations. The anticipation of the early participation of the People's Republic of China in the work of the United Nations brings the hope of a new situation. I look forward to procedural and institutional developments that will facilitate the participation of both the People's Republic of China and France in the work of disarmament. It is a requisite for achieving measures of actual disarmament, and not merely measures of arms control and limitation, for all five nuclear powers to play an active role in the discussion and negotiation of further treaties on disarmament. I am sure that all Members of the United Nations and all people interested in rapid progress in the field of disarmament will look forward to the advances that can be made if all important powers make their full contribution to the work.

III. Outer space and the seabed

205. The year under review has also brought renewed progress in international collaboration in the peaceful uses of outer space. Of major importance is the fact that the General Assembly at its present session will have before it a draft Convention on International Liability for Damage Caused by Space Objects.

206. After years of detailed study and extensive negotiations on the many complicated problems involved, the draft Convention was finalized in June 1971 by the Legal Sub-Committee of the Committee on the Peaceful Uses of Outer Space. It is heartening to note that through this Convention a reasonable expectation of prompt and fair compensation will be offered to those who might be injured by space activities. At a

time when such activities have become an everyday occurrence, it is of paramount importance that they be conducted in the interest and for the welfare of mankind. To this end, the establishment of a legal order for the exploration and use of outer space is indispensable. It is with satisfaction, therefore, that I anticipate that this liability convention will take its place alongside the Treat on Principles Governing the Activities of States in the Exploration and Use of Outer Space, including the Moon and Other Celestial Bodies and the Agreement on the Rescue of Astronauts, the Return of Astronauts and the Return of Objects Launched into Outer Space as another major step in the progressive development of the law of outer space.

207. In the past, the Committee on the Peaceful Uses of Outer Space and its Scientific and Technical Sub-Committee have, with Secretariat assistance, encouraged Member states to establish programs in the application of space technology. In such specific areas of space technology as communications, meteorology, and earth resources surveys, the United Nations has taken necessary measures to encourage the effective utilization of these new space applications which can benefit man on earth.

208. Under the impetus created by the United Nations Conference on the Exploration and Peaceful Uses of Outer Space in 1968, a United Nations Panel Meeting on Remote Sensing Systems for Earth Resources Surveys was held in the United States in May 1971, with a related topic to be studied by another United Nations panel later this year in Brazil. Future panels organized by the United Nations on the use of satellite broadcasting for educational purposes, the use of meteorological data obtained from satellites, and the applicability of space and other remote sensing techniques to the management of food resources are already planned for 1972. Such programs assist nations, particularly those not yet involved in space activities and technology, in achieving a fuller understanding of the practical benefits to be derived from space applications. I trust that these efforts will commend themselves to the Member states and that they will continue to participate in and support them.

209. The United Nations must also assess the extent of its own role in meeting the challenges posed by new technological promises and outer space exploration. I am, therefore, gratified to note that, under General Assembly resolution 2733 C (XXV), a Working Group on Remote Sensing of the Earth by Satellites has been established this year, *inter alia* to consider whether there are operational systems which might be of

special value in meeting international, regional, and global requirements, and to make recommendations for possible development, provision, and operation of data collection and utilization systems within the framework of the United Nations or other international organizations.

210. I am equally pleased to note the contribution of the specialized agencies in the field of space application. The World Meteorological Organization has established a comprehensive program for the utilization of meteorological data through its World Weather Watch and has responded to the request, made by the General Assembly at its twenty-fifth session, to discover ways and means of mitigating the harmful effects of typhoons and storms in various parts of the world, particularly in Asia. The United Nations Educational, Scientific and Cultural Organization, in cooperation with the International Telecommunication Union, has carried out several comprehensive surveys on the feasibility of using communications satellites for educational purposes on a regional basis. The Union, through its recently concluded World Administrative Conference for Space Communications, has helped to provide a firm basis for equitable international collaboration in the exploration of outer space and the applications of space technology by the regulation of a limited natural resource—the Radio Spectrum. In other agencies, such as the Food and Agriculture Organization of the United Nations and the World Health Organization, increasing attention is being given to the practical applications of space technology.

211. When fully developed, the applications of space technology will no doubt prove a most effective tool in controlling and utilizing man's environment and his resources. Because of their potential usefulness in alleviating such major problems as food shortage, ignorance, communication, misunderstanding among people, and the quality of the human environment, I am pleased that these applications have been receiving the full attention of the Committee on the Peaceful Uses of Outer Space, the Economic and Social Council, and the specialized agencies. I trust that the General Assembly will continue to encourage these activities and set guidelines for new and even more meaningful programs.

212. Broad and significant developments have taken place during the past year with regard to the seas and the seabed. The two most noteworthy are the adoption by the General Assembly, at its twenty-fifth session, of the Declaration of Principles Governing the Sea-Bed and the Ocean Floor, and the Subsoil Thereof, beyond the Limits of National Jurisdic-

tion, and the adoption of another resolution concerning the convening of a new conference on the law of the sea in 1973. The preparatory work for this conference was entrusted to the Committee on the Peaceful Uses of the Sea-Bed and the Ocean Floor beyond the Limits of National Jurisdiction, and its membership was substantially enlarged for this purpose. Another major development was the opening for signature and ratification of the Treaty on the Prohibition of the Emplacement of Nuclear Weapons and Other Weapons of Mass Destruction on the Sea-Bed and the Ocean Floor and in the Subsoil Thereof, which has been referred to above.

213. The adoption of the Declaration of Principles Governing the Sea-Bed and the Ocean Floor, and the Subsoil Thereof, beyond the Limits of National Jurisdiction, which covers the status and use of the major part of the surface of the globe, is an important achievement of the United Nations. It constitutes a convincing demonstration both of the ability of Member states to reach broad agreements through arduous and complex multilateral negotiations and of the capacity of the Organization to confront, within a remarkably short time, the challenge posed by new and, until recently, unexpected consequences of rapid technological advance. The historic nature of the principles which contain, in particular, the declaration that the area of the seabed beyond national jurisdiction, as well as its resources, is the common heritage of mankind, is underlined by the provision, in the resolution convening a new conference, that the draft treaty articles embodying the international régime for the area are to be prepared on the basis of the Declaration.

214. In this second resolution, the General Assembly decided to go still further and to include in the scope of the new conference on the law of the sea not only an equitable international régime—including an international machinery—for the area and resources of the seabed beyond national jurisdiction and a precise definition of that area, but also a broad range of related issues including those concerning the régimes of the high seas, the continental shelf, the territorial sea (including the question of its breadth and the question of international straits) and contiguous zone, fishing and conservation of the living resources of the high seas (including the question of the preferential rights of coastal states), the preservation of the marine environment (including, among other things, the prevention of pollution), and scientific research. At its twenty-sixth and twenty-seventh sessions, the General Assembly is to review the preparatory work of the Committee in order to determine the

precise agenda of the conference, its definitive date, locations, and duration, and related arrangements. It has been specified that if, at its twenty-seventh session, the General Assembly determines the progress of the Preparatory Committee to be insufficient, it may decide to postpone the conference.

215. The Committee on the Peaceful Uses of the Sea-Bed and the Ocean Floor beyond the Limits of National Jurisdiction has started this preparatory work. At its March session, it established three subcommittees to deal with various aspects of the preparation of draft treaty articles in accordance with the decision of the General Assembly. The Committee and its subcommittees have available to them various background papers prepared by the Secretariat. Because of the diversity of the issues involved, staff in a number of departments and offices of the Secretariat have been assigned to assist in the preparatory work for a new conference, and close cooperation between the departments and offices concerned has been established. At a suitable stage, the expertise of staff in other components of the United Nations system will also be called upon.

216. The magnitude of the task undertaken by the international community is patent. The importance and extent of the issues involved here clearly appeared in the debates of the Committee on the Peaceful Uses of the Sea-Bed and the Ocean Floor beyond the Limits of National Jurisdiction in 1971, as well as in the proposals and suggestions submitted to that body. A major effort to produce new and far-reaching international institutional arrangements is now under way and the outcome of this effort is of direct concern, not only to all Members of the Organization, but also to the entire international community.

IV. The Middle East and Cyprus

217. More than four years have now elapsed since the outbreak of the June 1967 hostilities in the Middle East, and yet a peaceful and agreed settlement is still not in sight.

218. A year ago the situation took a turn for the better. Following the acceptance by Israel, Jordan, and the United Arab Republic of a United States peace initiative, quiet was re-established along the Suez Canal on August 7, 1970, after sixteen months of fierce fighting, thus opening the way for the resumption of the peace talks under the auspices of my special representative to the Middle East, Ambassador Gunnar V. Jarring. Unfortunately the high hopes raised by this turn of events were

short-lived. The talks began on August 21, 1970, but shortly thereafter Israel refused to continue to participate in them because it alleged that the United Arab Republic had violated the cease-fire standstill agreement in the Suez Canal area. The talks were resumed in January 1971 and continued until the beginning of March, when they were forced once again into abeyance.

219. While the resumed talks did not achieve the breakthrough that had been hoped for, some progress was made. In February, Ambassador Jarring took the important initiative of breaking the existing deadlock by seeking from Israel and the United Arab Republic parallel and simultaneous commitments that seemed to him necessary as preconditions to progress in the talks. In brief, he sought a commitment from Israel to withdraw its forces from occupied United Arab Republic territory to the former international boundary between Egypt and the British Mandate of Palestine, and a commitment from the United Arab Republic to enter into a peace agreement with Israel with various undertakings and acknowledgments arising from the relevant principles mentioned in Security Council resolution 242 (1967). The United Arab Republic accepted the specific commitments requested of it, but so far Israel has not responded to the special representative's request. Ambassador Jarring feels, and I agree with him, that, until there has been a change in Israel's position on the question of withdrawal, it would serve little useful purpose to attempt to reactivate the talks. It is still my hope that Israel will find it possible before too long to make a response that will enable the search for a peaceful settlement under Ambassador Jarring's auspices to continue.

220. It is a matter of gratification that, despite this impasse, the quiet which was re-established in the Suez Canal sector on August 7, 1970, has continued to this day. It began with an agreement for a ninety-day cease-fire as part of the United States peace initiative, and although this cease-fire agreement was allowed to lapse, after two extensions, in March 1971, quiet has nevertheless been maintained. In the Israel–Syria sector there have been almost daily exchanges of fire, but these have generally been minor isolated incidents, and by and large quiet also prevailed in that sector. The United Nations has no observation machinery in the cease-fire sectors between Jordan and Lebanon, but all the available information indicates that these sectors, too, have generally been quiet during the period under review, although there were reports of incidents

along the Israel–Lebanon borders involving activities of Arab guerrilla groups based in Lebanon against Israel and incursions by Israeli forces into Lebanese territory.

221. It is not possible to predict how long this quiet will last, but there can be little doubt that, if the present impasse in the search for a peaceful settlement persists, new fighting will break out sooner or later. Since the parties have taken advantage of the present lull to strengthen considerably their military capabilities, it is only too likely that the new round of fighting will be more violent and dangerous than the previous ones, and there is always the danger that it may not be possible to limit it to the present antagonists and to the confines of the Middle East.

222. I see no other way to forestall such a disastrous eventuality than by intensifying the search for a peaceful and agreed settlement. I believe there is still a chance of achieving such a settlement. I do not overlook the formidable difficulty of the problems to be tackled, but there exist several important assets on the side of peace efforts as well. The Security Council's cease-fire resolutions of June 1967 and its resolution 242 (1967) of November 22, 1967, if implemented simultaneously and fully, should provide the framework for achieving a peaceful and agreed settlement of the present conflict. To promote agreement for such a settlement, we are fortunate to have the services of Ambassador Jarring, who is uniquely qualified for this almost impossible task.

223. Ambassador Jarring has clearly defined the minimum conditions that are required to move the peace talks ahead and, until those conditions are met, it is hard to see what else he can do to further his efforts. Steps to ensure that those conditions are met must be taken by the parties concerned and, failing this, by the Security Council itself or by states Members of the United Nations and, particularly, the permanent members of the Security Council, both because of their special responsibility within the United Nations and of their influence on the parties concerned.

224. The United States government, whose peace initiative last year led to the re-establishment of the cease-fire in the Suez Canal sector in August 1970, recently took a second initiative with the objective of securing an interim agreement from Israel and the United Arab Republic for the reopening of the Suez Canal. In this connection, the United States has assured me that its initiative aims at promoting and facilitating the resumption of Ambassador Jarring's mission and is within the frame-

work of Security Council resolution 242 (1967). The information so far available does not indicate that an agreement can be reached in the near future.

225. But time is of the essence. I feel that if moves for even a partial solution do not bear fruit before too long, the United Nations, and particularly the Security Council, will have to review the situation once again and find ways and means to enable the Jarring mission to move forward.

226. Despite many difficulties, the United Nations Relief and Works Agency for Palestine Refugees in the Near East has continued to provide assistance to refugees. Of the many difficulties encountered during the past year, two were particularly serious. The Agency's operation in East Jordan was disrupted during the armed clashes that erupted between the Jordanian army and the *fedayeen* in the autumn of 1970 and again, though on a much lesser scale, in July 1971. The Agency, however, was able to resume its services to the refugees after brief periods of suspension. More recently the Agency was confronted with another serious problem, this time in the Gaza Strip, when the Israeli authorities decided, for what they considered as compelling security reasons, to demolish large numbers of shelters in three refugee camps and to remove the occupants, some of them to places outside the Gaza Strip. The Commissioner-General of the Agency has protested against these measures, not only because of the personal hardship inflicted upon the refugees and the resulting disruption of the Agency's services, but also because they are contrary to certain provisions of the Geneva Convention of August 12, 1949, relative to the Protection of Civilian Persons in Time of War and to General Assembly resolution 2675 (XXV), which affirmed a number of basic principles for the protection of civilian populations in armed conflicts. On August 18, I approached the Israeli government through its permanent representative to the United Nations and requested that it undertake promptly all measures necessary to ensure the immediate cessation of the destruction of refugee homes in the Gaza Strip and to halt the removal of the refugee occupants to places outside the Gaza Strip. According to the information received from the Commissioner-General, the Israeli operation was suspended as of August 26.

227. The persisting financial difficulties of the Agency are also a matter of great concern to me. Last year the General Assembly set up a working group to look into this problem. Thanks to the efforts of the

chairman and the other members of this group, to the assistance provided by the specialized agencies concerned, and to the generous response of a number of governments, the deficit for 1971 has been considerably reduced and the Commissioner-General has been able to defer new reductions in the Agency's services. However, the long-term problem remains unsolved. If new resources are not found, the deficit for 1972 will probably exceed $6 million and the Agency will have no alternative but to reduce some of its essential services to the refugees. Once again I must commend this problem to the serious attention of the General Assembly.

228. I cannot conclude my comments on the situation in the Middle East without making a reference to the question of Jerusalem. This question is of direct concern to me not only because it is one of the most complex and difficult problems in the Middle East conflict, but also because both the General Assembly and the Security Council have requested me to report to them any developments which tend to change the city's legal status.

229. During the year under review, there were many reports from the press and other sources concerning a master plan prepared by Israeli authorities for the construction of housing projects in the Jerusalem area, including the sector controlled by Jordan before June 1967 and the area between the armistice demarcation lines. As soon as I heard of those reports, I sought from the Israeli authorities detailed information of the reported master plan, but those authorities have not yet responded to my request. Thus I have not been able to fulfill the reporting responsibilities laid upon me by the General Assembly and the Security Council. In this connection, I have also been in correspondence with the Israeli authorities concerning the United Nations premises at Government House.

230. I am also deeply concerned over the situation in Cyprus. When the two communities on the island agreed, three years ago, to enter into talks in an attempt to bridge their differences, the expectations were high that these talks would eventually lead to a peaceful and agreed settlement of the Cyprus problem. After some initial progress, the talks slowed down considerably and, on August 10, 1971, President Makarios stated publicly that they had reached a deadlock.

231. While the intercommunal talks drifted toward an impasse, ominous signs of growing frustration and tension appeared on the island.

The attitudes of the leaders on both sides hardened perceptibly, and each side made statements that the other found provocative or at least incompatible with the search for an agreed solution. The possibility of a collapse of the local talks seemed all the more dangerous as it might encourage irresponsible elements in both communities to make trouble with a view to aggravating the conflict, which could bring about intervention from outside.

232. So far, however, quiet has been maintained, thanks in substantial measure to the efforts of the United Nations Peace-keeping Force. My special representative in Cyprus, the commander of the Force and their staff have been watching developments on the island with the utmost vigilance, attempting to reconcile difficulties between the two communities whenever they arise, keeping any minor clashes from escalating, and ceaselessly urging restraint upon the government and the Turkish Cypriot leadership. As a result of these endeavors, the trend from negotiation to confrontation has for the time being been slowed down. If, however, the situation were to become more unstable, intercommunal relations in general, as well as the chances of a negotiated settlement, would be adversely affected.

233. It is both imperative and possible to reverse this trend before it leads to irreparable consequences. The differences which divide the communities in Cyprus are substantial and complex, involving as they do not only conflicting vital interests, but also deeply rooted emotional issues. I am convinced that they could be resolved if the parties concerned were to accept certain necessary compromises and accommodations which need not jeopardize what they consider their vital interests. This would be a small price to pay for attaining an agreed, peaceful, and lasting settlement based on an independent, sovereign, and unitary state in which the two communities participate.

234. It is no longer possible, however, to ignore the evidence that the parties' willingness or ability to make the necessary mutual concessions has not so far been sufficient to lead them to agreement, and that such an agreement may indeed require more time and greater efforts than had been anticipated heretofore. I am confident that in the meantime the government of Cyprus and the Turkish Cypriot leadership, as well as the other governments concerned, will exert every effort to maintain the peace in Cyprus.

235. At the very time when it seems more necessary than ever to continue the presence of the United Nations Force in Cyprus, the Force

is undergoing a crisis of its own. When the Security Council established the Force in March 1964, it stipulated that the operation was to be financed by voluntary contributions. As I have stated repeatedly to the Council, I have deep misgivings about this method of financing. My objection in this regard is, first of all, based on a question of principle, as I strongly feel that the maintenance of international peace and security is a collective responsibility of the United Nations, which must be shared by all its Members. There is also a practical reason which has taken on even greater weight with the passing of time. Initially the Security Council established the Force for a period of three months. The cost involved was therefore relatively modest and could easily be covered by voluntary contributions. For reasons beyond its control, the Force has had to be repeatedly extended, and more than seven years of continued operation have resulted in a very substantial expenditure. While the costs of the Force grew, the number of donors and the amount of new contributions steadily decreased. The result has been an increasing deficit, which has now reached a critical level. The problem of financing should be an important factor in the Security Council's review of the general problem of the United Nations commitment in Cyprus in the light of the present situation on the island. . . .

U THANT
Secretary-General

September 17, 1971

Statement to the Press on the Question
of a Third Term

NEW YORK   OCTOBER 18, 1971

U THANT had promised several times during 1970 that he would make an announcement at the appropriate time about his intentions regarding a third term as Secretary-General. As early as October he had told friends privately that he definitely would step down at the end of 1971. At a press conference on January 18, 1971, he said that when he decided to accept a second term in 1966 he had already decided that this would be his last. "Therefore," he said, "I am sure you will not be surprised when I tell you that I have no intention whatsoever of serving beyond the present term." Even though this declaration appeared to be unequivocal, neither the Member states nor the press took it as the final word. They recalled that he had reversed himself in 1966 after making a similar statement and they believed he might be prevailed upon again if he became convinced that no agreement could be reached on a successor. Actually little attention had been given to the search for a successor and those interested in the job were reluctant to come forward until they were sure Thant really meant to leave.

At the January 18 press conference Thant said he had communicated his intentions to representatives who asked him, including most of the big powers. "Since the membership has ample advance notice of my intentions," he added, "I do not think it will be a very big problem for the Members to choose a suitable successor. Of course, it is difficult, but it is not impossible, and I do not believe in the concept of indispensability." In response to another question, as to whether the People's Republic of China should be consulted and whether he would personally undertake such a consultation, he replied that it was a matter for the Security Council to recommend his successor and for the General Assembly to elect him. He took the occasion to make some observations on the qualities his successor should have. Among these, Thant said, were moral integrity, an ability to project into the future, a genuine desire to see the United Nations develop into an effective instrument for peace, justice, and progress, and the ability to act within the framework of a global unit. "I do not believe in the importance of regional considerations in the choice of a Secretary-General," he said.

The question of his future was raised again at a press conference in Boston on

May 27 and he repeated his statement of January 18. Noting that he had not had a vacation since January 1966, he said "this is one of the main reasons why I have decided not to offer myself for a third term." He said it was too early to guess whether the Member states would agree on a successor, but he expressed confidence that agreement could be reached if the membership concentrated its attention on the problem. Asked whether he would stay on if the Member states failed to agree on a successor, he replied: "I have made my position very clear on several previous occasions to those government representatives who have very kindly asked me to reconsider my decision." Did this mean that he would not stay on under any circumstances? Some wondered why he had not replied with a flat "no."

As was his custom before each session of the General Assembly, Thant met the press on September 14. Realizing that his own future plans were still a very live question, he began by saying that unless unusual developments in the next three months warrented another press conference at the end of the session "this will be my last press conference in my present capacity." The president of the United Nations Correspondents Association, Louis Foy, wished him well on behalf of the press "if indeed you are no longer Secretary-General after January 1." He added, however, that "there is still a lingering hope that you might agree to remain for a short period—several months, or maybe a year or two— especially if the five big powers were deadlocked on the choice of a successor. As friends and as journalists we should very much like to have your answer on that so that we may know whether such a hope may be entertained." This time the Secretary-General replied in language that seemed to leave no doubt that he was determined to step down. "I will not serve beyond my present term," he said, "even for a limited period of one year or two years or two months, under any circumstances." He noted that many governments had asked him to reconsider his decision and that the Organization of African Unity had transmitted to him a formal request that he stay on for a limited period, if not for a new term. "I have replied to all governments," he said, "that my decision is final and categorical." He expressed the belief that the question of a draft would not arise.

Despite his apparent firmness, efforts persisted to prevail upon him to change his mind. In a statement to the press on October 18, he mentioned that during the general debate in the Assembly some delegations were still urging him to reconsider his decision and to remain for a limited period. "I very much regret," he said, "to have to restate that my decision is final and unequivocal, and that under no circumstances could I agree to serve beyond my present term even for a limited period. I do not share the feelings of many Member governments that my departure at this juncture will engender a crisis in the United Nations." He concluded by appealing to the Member governments to begin "serious consultations on the question of my successor as soon as practicable." Even more convincing than this statement was a serious ulcer attack suffered by Thant two weeks later. He had been hospitalized by such an ailment in 1964, but since his recovery, his health had been excellent. However, when he was stricken on November 2 with a recurrence of the ulcer, the chances of his staying on became dim indeed. In fact, he remained in the hospital for some time and after that he convalesced at his residence until December 6. When he did return to his duties, he still did not have the strength to work full time. It was only after he left office that he regained his normal vigor and health.

The Member states finally accepted his decision and on December 21 the Security Council agreed to recommend that Kurt Waldheim of Austria be named the fourth Secretary-General of the United Nations. The Assembly formalized the appointment the following day and Waldheim was sworn in for a five-year term beginning January 1, 1972.

IN THE COURSE of the general debate which was concluded last week, almost all chairmen of delegations made very kind references to me in connection with my announced decision to retire at the end of my present term. Some delegations even expressed the hope I might still agree to serve beyond my term. In the course of my meetings with many chairmen of delegations they expressed the view that it would be very difficult for the membership to agree on my successor, and they requested me to reconsider my decision and agree to serve for a limited period before a widely acceptable candidate is forthcoming. Once again I wish to reiterate my declared decision not to serve beyond December 31, 1971. It may be recalled that I announced my decision not to serve beyond my present term in January of this year, and have restated it in categorical terms on several occasions since then.

Words fail me when I attempt to express my deeply felt appreciation and gratitude to the Member governments for their continued trust and confidence in me and for their gracious recognition of my services to the international community, but I very much regret to have to restate that my decision is final and unequivocal, and that under no circumstances could I agree to serve beyond my present term even for a limited period. I do not share the feelings of many Member governments that my departure at this juncture will engender a crisis in the United Nations. I am confident that with the interest of United Nations only in mind, a solution can be found in time. Let me once again appeal to all Member

SOURCE: *UN Monthly Chronicle,* Vol. VIII, November 1971, p. 95.

governments to start serious consultations on the question of my successor as soon as practicable.

I pledge once again my unswerving allegiance to the United Nations and to the principles of its Charter, and offer my continued and dedicated service for the cause of the United Nations in the future.

Address at United Nations Day Concert

NEW YORK   OCTOBER 24, 1971

ONE OF THE MOST unusual initiatives taken by U Thant as Secretary-General was to persuade Pablo Casals and W. H. Auden to collaborate in writing the music and lyrics for a "Hymn to the United Nations." The premier performance of the new work took place in the General Assembly Hall on United Nations Day, 1971, with Casals conducting. In a brief address to the audience of distinguished diplomats and guests, Thant noted that the United Nations had fallen short of expectations, but he reaffirmed his confidence in the Organization and appealed to the Member states to "breathe new life into the principles to which they have all subscribed." And he added, "For the United Nations remains indispensable to survival on this planet; it remains our only hope for building the kind of life we all desire for ourselves and for future generations."

EACH YEAR on October 24, we mark the anniversary of the United Nations with the performance of great music by master musicians. For an hour or two on that day, we borrow this General Assembly Hall from the delegates and invite musicians to speak to us in the universal language of music, thus filling our hearts with joy and lifting our spirits in harmony. Today we have the rare and memorable privilege of celebrating this birthday with Maestro Pablo Casals and some of his closest musical associates and friends. These distinguished artists require no praise from me. Their eminent names are symbols of the highest musical achievement throughout the world. I speak for us all in thanking them for coming here and sharing with us their consummate artistry.

No less warmly do I express our gratitude to our United Nations Singers and to the Chorus of the Manhattan School of Music, who have joined with them in the first performance of our new "Hymn to the United Nations."

SOURCE: UN Press Release SG/SM/1561.

This composition has brought together the vision and talents of Pablo Casals and of the distinguished poet W. H. Auden. Both responded graciously to my suggestion that they should collaborate on this work; and now they have carried their generosity even further, by agreeing to donate royalties from the new "Hymn" for the benefit of the United Nations International School. This is a cause very close to my heart and, I hope, to yours. Don Pablo is here to conduct the "Hymn" and thus he receives personally our heartfelt thanks; Mr. Auden is in Europe, perhaps listening to his radio: so let me say "thank you" to both of these great humanists for the work which they have created for us.

Twenty-six years have gone by since the historic founding ceremony in San Francisco. Those who were alive when the Charter was written are now a minority of the world's people. A full generation has passed; the world has changed and so has the Organization which was created to heal its divisions and balance its forces. The United Nations today is not what the architects of San Francisco had planned it to be. It has fallen short of expectations. This much we can claim: another world holocaust has thus far been avoided and much has been accomplished in improving the lot of billions of men, women, and children on earth.

Those of us who believe profoundly in the principles of the Charter as the civilized and humane way of settling differences among nations are witnessing with infinite sorrow the gradual erosion of the authority and prestige of this great Organization. Violence and lawlessness continue to prevail in the relations among nations despite our efforts to keep peace. The gulf between rich and poor remains menacingly wide despite our efforts to close it. The arms race continues to accelerate at a disastrous rate despite our efforts to halt and reverse it. Millions of human beings still suffer the humiliation of discrimination and injustice despite our efforts to uproot these evils from the hearts of men.

This is no time for cynicism, for disillusionment, for apathy. This is the time when Member states of the United Nations should honor their pledges and breathe new life into the principles to which they have all subscribed. Let us make the necessary adjustment—in our attitudes and in our practices—to the conditions of the world in 1971. Let us muster the moral strength and the wisdom to move forward toward the noble goals on which we all are agreed.

As we gather here today, joining with millions all around the earth, we reaffirm our deep conviction of the need for harmony and balance in our existence.

After bearing the burden of the office of Secretary-General for a decade, I remain firm in my conviction that the United Nations can help mankind achieve the peace which it has always sought. For the United Nations remains indispensable to survival on this planet; it remains our only hope for building the kind of life we all desire for ourselves and for future generations.

Before returning this occasion to our superb musicians, I wish to take this opportunity to pay special tribute to Maestro Casals and to Mr. Auden:

Don Pablo, you have devoted your life to truth, to beauty, and to peace. Both as a man and as an artist, you embody the ideals symbolized by this United Nations Peace Medal. I present it to you with my deep respect and admiration.

Although Mr. Auden is not with us in person, his spirit graces this occasion. In appreciation of his profound commitment to humanistic values in an era which he has characterized as "the age of anxiety," I take great pleasure in presenting to W. H. Auden the United Nations Peace Medal.

Statement to the Press on the Seating of the Representatives of the People's Republic of China

NEW YORK   OCTOBER 26, 1971

MORE THAN TWO DECADES of diplomatic conflict over the representation of China in the United Nations ended on October 25, 1971, when the General Assembly voted to expel the representatives of the Taiwan government and to seat the representatives of the People's Republic of China. The United States had sought to save a place for the Nationalists by backing a dual representation plan which would have given China's important Security Council seat to the Peking régime but would have permitted both governments to remain in the United Nations. Many Member states, however, felt that this was a rearguard action which, at best, could only delay the seating of the People's Republic as the sole representative of China. The anti-Peking bloc had already begun to disintegrate as a result of the defection of staunch NATO allies of the United States such as Italy, Belgium, and Canada. The decision of President Nixon to visit Peking early in 1972 made it clear that the fight was all but over. U Thant, long an advocate of seating the People's Republic, had been predicting for months that this would happen by late 1972. Even at his press conferences on January 18, April 29, and May 27 Thant stuck to his prediction that the Peking government would not be seated in the United Nations before November or December, 1972, although in the May 27 conference he acknowledged that "things are developing at a fast pace." When he met the press on September 14, just before the General Assembly opened its twenty-sixth session, he said he had had to revise his prediction and that prospects for a solution of the China question were "much brighter than before." He declined to make a definite guess, but said, "I will be the happiest person if this question is solved this year." It was well known among his associates that he wanted to see Peking in the United Nations before he stepped down as Secretary-General on December 31. In response to a question, he expressed the belief that the People's Republic meant what it said when it stated that it would not take a seat in the United Nations as long as Nationalist China remained in the Organization. Despite his belief in the universality of membership in the United Nations, he did not consider a "two-Chinas" solution to be realistic. He did not regard China as being in the same category as

SOURCE: *UN Monthly Chronicle,* Vol. VIII, November 1971, p. 96–97.

the so-called divided countries: Germany, Korea, and Vietnam. When the decision was finally taken Thant welcomed it as "an essential step toward a more effective and realistic international system." In a statement to the press on October 26, he said he felt sad at the departure of Nationalist China's representatives, but that he strongly believed the presence of the Peking government's delegation "will eventually lead to the strengthening and betterment of the Organization." One of Thant's most satisfying moments came when he, as Secretary-General, personally welcomed the first delegation of the People's Republic.

THE UNITED NATIONS has been confronted for over twenty years with the problem of the participation of the People's Republic of China. Over the years the representatives of nearly every country in the world have on many occasions expressed the positions, the hopes, and also the misgivings of their governments concerning the solution to this fundamental problem. The debate which we have witnessed during the last ten days has shown very clearly that the issue is one which still involves deep emotions and strong convictions. As Secretary-General of the United Nations, I have always advocated the participation of the People's Republic of China in the work of this Organization, but I have also always respected, as I still do, the opinion of every Member state, even when I personally do not agree with it.

Now that the Assembly has taken a decision, that the question has been settled, let us not lose time and energy by falling into the temptation of judging attitudes which now belong to the past, of awakening suspicions which have already been overcome. Let us unanimously and resolutely engage on the new road which opens today before us. I solemnly appeal to all Member states to leave no room for bitterness, but on the contrary to abide by the decision of the General Assembly and endorse the tremendous step forward which was taken last night.

I strongly believe that the presence among us of the People's Republic of China, which is now to become a reality, attests to the considerable improvement in the international situation, and will eventually lead to the strengthening and betterment of the Organization. I have always said that room should be made in the United Nations for Member governments with widely differing economic and social systems. Now, at the close of this debate, it seems that the Organization will fulfill more fully one of the basic purposes of the Charter, "to be a centre for harmonizing the actions of nations." Whatever their sentiment as to the desirable outcome of the debate, I think almost all Member states agreed that the absence of the People's Republic of China from the Organization gave it a certain artificiality and adversely affected its authority. The decision reached last night may enable us to solve more effectively the international problems with which we are confronted. However, this will imply that no Member turns its back on the new tasks and new prospects which are now facing the international community.

It is indeed necessary for our Organization to reflect the changes which occur in the international arena. We have been gratified to see new trends towards détente and cooperation. The bold decision made by the President of the United States to visit the People's Republic of China, thereby overlooking two decades of hostility, is one of the positive and hopeful developments which we have watched recently. Also, the readiness of the government of the People's Republic of China to overcome long-standing fears and suspicions and to accept this dialogue, gives us a clear image of its maturity and constructiveness.

It is my hope that last night's decision by the General Assembly will be considered in the light of all these developments, and that the true statesmanship already displayed by the leaders of both sides will once again be reflected in their continued acceptance of the goals of the United Nations.

I feel sad at the departure of the members of the Permanent Mission of "the Republic of China" from the halls of the United Nations. My personal relations with its permanent representative and his colleagues for the past ten years have been very warm, and I have always held Ambassador Liu Chieh in high esteem for his great human qualities. However, the international community through its forum has pronounced its decision, and it has to be respected.

The recognition of the new role that the People's Republic of China is now playing in international life has been expressed by the ever-growing number of Member states who have normalized their relations with that country.

Last night's vote should not be considered in terms of either victory or defeat, but as an essential step toward a more effective and realistic international system. The twenty-sixth session of the General Assembly will thus have been a session of decision.

From Final Report to the Security Council
on the Situation in Cyprus

NEW YORK   NOVEMBER 30, 1971

As U THANT prepared to leave office, one of his concerns was the failure of peace efforts in Cyprus. Not only had a United Nations peace force been stationed on the island since 1964; Thant himself had been involved personally through a number of mediators and special representatives named by him to seek peace between the Greek and Turkish communities. He also had struggled with the task of raising money to finance the operation year after year, a task he had never relished. In the Introduction to his 1971 annual report, issued on September 17, he reported that the peace negotiations had once more reached an impasse and that the attitudes of the leaders on both sides had hardened perceptibly. "It is both imperative and possible," he said, "to reverse this trend before it leads to irreparable consequences." Once more he states his deep misgivings about the Security Council's insistence that the United Nations operation in Cyprus be financed by voluntary contributions. He objected both as a matter of principle and for practical reasons. In Thant's opinion costs of such operations should be shared by all Member states, not by a few. On the practical side, he noted increasing difficulties in getting donors. "While the costs of the Force grew," he said, "the number of donors and the amount of new contributions steadily decreased. The result has been an increasing deficit, which has now reached a critical level." He urged the Security Council to take a new look at the problem of financing the operation.

In his final report on the Cyprus operation he expressed disappointment in the rigid attitude of the Greek and Turkish communities, which he blamed for the continued deadlock. "After nearly eight years," he said, "the solution of the Cyprus problem is still not in sight, conditions in the island remain precarious, and I have come once more before the Security Council—in fact for the twentieth time—to recommend a further extension of the mandate of UNFICYP [United Nations Force in Cyprus]. It is obvious that this situation cannot continue indefinitely, to the detriment of the people of Cyprus and as a lingering threat to international peace and security."

SOURCE: Security Council Official Records, Twenty-sixth Year, Supplement for October, November and December 1971, document S/10401.

. . .

108. THIS IS the last report which it is incumbent upon me, as Secretary-General, to submit to the Security Council on the question of Cyprus. It will be one of my lasting regrets that I cannot report, in accordance with Security Council resolution 186 (1964) of March 4, 1964, that there has been found "a peaceful solution and an agreed settlement of the problem confronting Cyprus, in accordance with the Charter of the United Nations, having in mind the well-being of the people of Cyprus as a whole and the preservation of international peace and security."

109. I remember well the hopes and expectations engendered by the unanimous adoption of the Council resolution of March 4, 1964. It provided both for a United Nations Peace-keeping Force and for mediation. The Force, intended to be of only the most temporary nature—indeed, three months—was "to use its best efforts to prevent a recurrence of fighting and, as necessary, to contribute to the maintenance and restoration of law and order and a return to normal conditions." The mediator, in the meantime, was to "use his best endeavors with the representatives of the communities" and with the governments concerned to achieve the peaceful solution and agreed settlement to which I have already referred. Not only did the mediation called for by the Security Council meet with no success, but it also proved impossible to resume the search for an agreed solution in full measure.

110. Thus the hopes and expectations of 1964 are yet to be fulfilled. After nearly eight years, the solution of the Cyprus problem is still not in sight, conditions in the island remain precarious, and I have to come once more before the Security Council—in fact, for the twentieth time—to recommend a further extension of the mandate of UNFICYP. It is obvious that this situation cannot continue indefinitely, to the detriment of the people of Cyprus and as a lingering threat to international peace and security.

111. Despite the difficulties involved, I am deeply convinced that, given the necessary good will, the Cyprus problem is capable of solution. It is my earnest hope that, in accordance with the principles of the Charter, the parties to this problem will soon find it possible, in the interest of the well-being of the people of Cyprus and the cause of international peace and security, to make those necessary compromises and accommodations without which no settlement can be achieved. . . .

Statement on the Proposed
United Nations University

NEW YORK   DECEMBER 10, 1971

THE IDEA of creating a United Nations university was put forward by U Thant in the Introduction to his 1969 annual report (see pp. 309–10). He said he felt that the time had come "when serious thought may be given to the establishment of a United Nations university, truly international in character and devoted to the Charter objectives of peace and progress." At that time he was thinking in terms of a single campus institution where students from many countries and cultures would live together in an international atmosphere. "The location of the university," he said, "should be in a country noted for its spirit of tolerance and freedom of thought." The primary object, in his view, would be to "promote international understanding both at the political and cultural levels." The Secretary-General suggested that the United Nations Educational, Scientific and Cultural Organization (UNESCO) might study the matter and, if feasible, develop it. Within a few weeks the proposal was raised in the General Assembly, which adopted a resolution on December 13 welcoming the Secretary-General's initiative and asking him to prepare, in cooperation with UNESCO and in consultation with the United Nations Institute for Training and Research, a study on the feasibility of an international university. This report was ready for discussion at the summer session of the Economic and Social Council. As disclosed in the report, the concept had changed somewhat since Thant had made his original proposal. The institution, for example, would have a number of campuses located in the various regions of the world instead of a single campus. The university would be supported by contributions from Member states, foundations, international business concerns, and other organizations with international interests. The report suggested a fund of $100 million as the initial target. The Secretary-General expressed the hope that the Assembly would authorize him to proceed further with his studies, possibly with the assistance of a panel of experts. On December 11, 1970, the Assembly approved the idea that the establishment of an international university "could contribute to the achievement of the objectives" of the United Nations. It requested Thant to continue his studies and authorized him to set up a panel of experts on the establishment of an

SOURCE: UN Press Release SG/SM/1607.

international university. This panel was to consist of ten experts nominated by Member states to be designated by the President of the Assembly and five experts to be named by the Secretary-General. The Assembly further asked Member states to submit to the Secretary-General by the end of May 1971 their preliminary views on the creation of an international university, including what contribution, if any, they might make to help finance it.

The panel of experts was headed by Andrew W. Cordier, president emeritus of Columbia University and former executive assistant to Trygve Lie and Dag Hammarskjöld during their terms as Secretary-General. The following statement, read in the Second (Economic and Financial) Committee by Martin Hill, consultant to the Secretary-General, was the last made by Thant on the proposed international university before he left office at the end of 1971.

THE PROPOSAL for the establishment of a United Nations university, truly international in character and devoted to the Charter objectives of peace and progress, is one in which I have taken a great personal interest. When I suggested to the General Assembly two years ago that serious thought be given to such a proposal, it was in the context of the darkening situation for the maintenance of international peace and security. The primary objective of the proposed university was to promote international understanding, and I felt strongly that such an institution would radiate a beneficial influence throughout the world, especially among the rising generation, and that it would help to break down moral and intellectual barriers between nations.

This remains my firm belief, and I was gratified that it was echoed in the preamble to the General Assembly's resolution on the subject 2691 (XXV), last year. Since that time, the concept of a United Nations university has evolved considerably as a result of the intensive and fruitful process of study and consultation with governments, universities and academic personalities, and organizations, which was launched by the General Assembly in resolution 2691 (XXV). One now sees more clearly than ever the immense potentialities of such an institution, the contribution it should be able to make to the work of the United Nations itself, to the strengthening and widening of scholarly effort in the developing world, and to stimulating the creative thinking of institutions of higher learning in different parts of the world on problems of global concern.

There has emerged, moreover, an unconventional and imaginative model for the university around which a wide consensus has gathered and which would require only modest funds to enable it to start functioning.

This plan envisages the development, under a light programming unit, of a flexible and dynamic system of cooperation among scholars and institutions engaged in higher learning and research throughout the world. It would be concerned with stimulating study, and encouraging training for research and consultations at a high postgraduate level, of certain vital subjects of international concern. The research program under the auspices of the proposed university would be organized, not in terms of traditional disciplines, each pursued on a particular campus, but in relation to specific and urgent problems confronting the world community, e.g. problems of international organization and peace, human rights, development, transfer of science and technology, and the environment. Existing research institutions within and outside the United Nations system should benefit, through exchanges, joint study, and in other ways, from voluntary participation in, or affiliation with, the proposed network of cooperation.

The General Assembly requested me last year to submit a report to the twenty-sixth session on the studies undertaken at its behest, together with any recommendations, "so that the Assembly may take decisions on the question of the establishment of an international university at the earliest possible date." You have my report before you, which includes the report and comments of the Director-General of the United Nations Educational, Scientific and Cultural Organization (UNESCO) on the results of the UNESCO feasibility study, the decision of the UNESCO Executive Board, the note by the United Nations Institute for Training and Research (UNITAR) on organizational and financial aspects, and the report of the Panel of Experts which I had been authorized by resolution 2691 (XXV) of the General Assembly to establish for the purpose of assisting me in my consultations and studies. You also have my recommendations, which are in fact those put forward by the Panel of Experts. On the basis of the findings of the Panel, the Director-General of UNESCO, the UNESCO Executive Board, and UNITAR, it was my hope that the General Assembly would now be able to endorse the view that the establishment of a United Nations university is both desirable and feasible. I also asked that the General Assembly agree to set up a Committee of Experts—along the lines of the Panel, which has done such an effective job in the past year—to carry forward the preparatory consultations and to find solutions for issues which still remain to be examined before a final decision on the establishment of the university can be taken.

The scope of this needed preparatory work is indicated by the Panel, which suggests that the Committee of Experts be requested "to propose a detailed structure and scheme of relationships for the United Nations university," including relationships with the intergovernmental organs of the United Nations and UNESCO and with existing institutes; to consult and advise on the university's initial program; to advise on the principles of administration and finance and determine the availability of financial contributions and facilities from governments, non-governmental organizations, and other sources; to advise on the locations of units of the university; and to formulate such recommendations regarding other practical modalities as may be required. This will make it possible to deal with the problems to which the UNESCO Executive Board has called attention as being in need of further examination, such as guarantees of academic freedom and the methods of coordination and cooperation with affiliated institutions. Both the Executive Board and the Panel have asked for further consultations with the academic community and with youth and student organizations in particular.

It has seemed very desirable that such essential studies and consultations, instead of being carried out independently by UNESCO and the United Nations as heretofore, should henceforth be undertaken jointly by the two organizations. For this reason, in particular, I favor a somewhat broader membership than that of the Panel to allow for additional representation of educationists and the academic world, as well as, perhaps, experts in other professional areas.

I regret that the unavoidably late issuance of my report, due entirely to the schedule of studies and consultations which had been called for, prevented detailed consideration of the subject by the Economic and Social Council at its recent resumed session. I can understand and sympathize with the Council's recommendation that the General Assembly defer consideration of the item to its twenty-seventh session, in order that the Council may have an opportunity to submit to the General Assembly its concrete recommendations. I feel, however, that such a recommendation should not hold up the further consultations and studies to which I have alluded, and which would surely be essential for the Council's own consideration of the matter. I also hope that a preparatory committee or some form of enlarged panel will be authorized to assist me in carrying them out, in close cooperation both with the Director-General of UNESCO and the Executive Director of UNITAR, as well as the executive heads of other interested United Nations organs and agencies.

One last point: for the realization of this plan, wide support by governments will be of decisive importance. It would be very helpful indeed if governments in a position to do so could indicate their interest in the plan in the course of the coming debate, a debate which—I need scarcely say—I shall follow with the closest attention.

FAREWELL TO THE UNITED NATIONS

In his farewell statements to the staff and to the representatives of the Member states, U Thant went beyond the routine leave-taking to make a number of substantive observations. In his remarks to the staff, he stressed the need for preserving the international character of the Secretariat by strict adherence to Article 100 of the Charter. He noted that this Article contained the two-way provision that the staff would not seek or receive instructions from any government or outside authority and that the Member states would not seek to influence the staff in the performance of its duties. "The integrity, impartiality, and effectiveness of the Secretariat," he said, "are essential if the United Nations is to survive as a lasting force for peace, justice, and progress." In his statement to the General Assembly, he proposed the creation of a new post, that of Deputy Secretary-General, to take over the responsibilities of the office during absences of the Secretary-General. He said he was not making a formal proposal, but added that "in the interests of good management and his own health the next Secretary-General might be well advised to consider such a proposal." The post could be established, he said, without an amendment to the Charter and with little added expense. His successor, Kurt Waldheim, did not follow up his suggestion.

1. From Statement to the Staff

NEW YORK   DECEMBER 17, 1971

. . . During my past 3,697 days as Secretary-General of the United Nations, my greatest source of strength and, if I may say so, solace in difficult times has been the unswerving loyalty, commitment, and devotion to duty shown by all the staff members of the United Nations.

In saying this today, my thoughts are filled with the courage and fortitude shown by so many of our colleagues in distant lands. Even as

Source: UN Press Release SG/SM/1612.

we are gathered in this hall, we are all aware of the example of steadfastness and devotion to duty being shown by so many of our staff members in South Asia. Concern for their welfare has been uppermost in mind during these last few difficult days.

In my expression of gratitude, I also wish to include the thousands of international civil servants who have served with us in various projects in the economic and social development fields, and who have also borne hardship—but of a different kind—in distant corners of the world. They outnumber those of us who serve in established duty stations, not only in New York, Geneva, and the regional economic commissions but in the various field offices in the United Nations and its Development Programme.

I would also like to recall that the Secretariat, of which I am the chief administrative officer, is a principal organ under the Charter. While the Secretariat, of course, derives its mandate and work program from the decision of the principal intergovernmental organs, let us remember that the Secretariat is an independent entity with a status of its own. The integrity, impartiality, and effectiveness of the Secretariat are essential if the United Nations is to survive as a lasting force for peace, justice, and progress.

You have referred, Dr. Rathore,[1] to the Charter requirement that "the paramount consideration in the employment of the staff and in the determination of the conditions of service shall be the necessity of securing the highest standards of efficiency, competence, and integrity. . . ." This, of course, is very important.

Equally important is Article 100 of the Charter, which deals with the integrity of our service. Paragraph 1 of this Article states: "In the performance of their duties the Secretary-General and the staff shall not seek or receive instructions from any government or from any other authority external to the Organization. . . ."

I would also draw the attention of Member states to paragraph 2 of Article 100, which states: "Each Member of the United Nations undertakes to respect the exclusively international character of the responsibilities of the Secretary-General and the staff and not to seek to influence them in the discharge of their responsibilities." I draw special attention to this provision because I feel that it is an essential counterpart to paragraph 1 of Article 100 of the Charter.

You have also referred to my abiding concern for the welfare of the

[1]Naeem G. Rathore, chairman of the Staff Committee.

staff. I have always felt that the United Nations should be more than just a good employer, and particularly that the conditions of service at the lower levels of the Secretariat need serious consideration. I hope that the Salary Review Committee will give due thought to this aspect of staff concerns.

I realize that whatever might be done to improve the conditions of service, there will always be a few elements in regard to which the staff as a whole, or sections of the staff, might feel that more could be done for them. This to me is quite understandable, but I would urge that the staff keep in mind at all times their special status as international civil servants. This status confers on them certain rights and privileges, and, equally, certain responsibilities. I regard it as one of these important responsibilities that the staff should at all times make use of the established machinery to obtain due redress of all their just grievances and demands.

Once again, I wish to thank all of you, in New York and all over the world, for your fine spirit of cooperation and solidarity. I know that my successor will be able to count equally on your cooperation and whole-hearted support. It is with a full heart that I wish you all a happy holiday season after the conclusion of this demanding session of the General Assembly. In the years ahead, may you and your families enjoy the fulfillment and satisfaction of lives devoted to the pursuit of peace and human welfare.

2. *From Statement at the Closing of the General Assembly*

NEW YORK   DECEMBER 22, 1971

I AM MOST GRATEFUL to you all for your very kind words and cordial sentiments on this occasion when I take leave of the Member states represented in the General Assembly. . . . My emotions on this occasion

SOURCE: General Assembly Official Records, Twenty-sixth Session, 2031st plenary meeting.

are deep and, understandably, mixed. On the one hand, it is sad for me to take leave of so many friends, many of whom I might still continue to meet, but with whom I do not expect to have that close and friendly association which has brightened my 3,702 days as Secretary-General. On the other hand, I would be less than candid if I did not tell you that I feel a sense of great relief bordering on liberation, upon my impending retirement and upon laying down the burdens of this office.

During recent months, I have reiterated my gratitude to all my many friends and colleagues who have expressed the wish that I should reconsider my decision to step down. I am sure they will agree with me, on further reflection, that I was right to insist that I should leave my office at this time. In doing so I am greatly heartened and encouraged by the thought that I should be leaving this office in such capable hands.

I have known Ambassador Waldheim ever since he first came to New York as permanent representative of Austria to the United Nations in 1964. Subsequently, he has been foreign minister of his own country, and I was personally very pleased when he was reappointed as permanent representative of Austria to the United Nations last year. I know that he is held in very high esteem by all of those who have come to know him during his many years in New York. Apart from his well-known diplomatic ability he has also shown a special talent for conciliation in his work as chairman of the outer space committee and in other United Nations bodies. I wish him every success in his new and high responsibilities.

I leave at a time when the Organization has many unresolved problems and much unfinished business on its hands. First, there is the long-standing problem of the Middle East. In this case, I feel it is imperative that resolution 242 (1967), which was unanimously adopted by the Security Council on November 22, 1967, should be fully implemented. More recently, and especially during the current month, all of us have been preoccupied with the situation in South Asia. Let us hope that a fair and just settlement may be negotiated among the parties principally involved and that a new era of peace and stability may lie ahead for that vast sub-continent. . . .

I must also express my sense of personal disappointment that more progress has not been made by the Special Committee on Peace-keeping Operations, which has been doing its best to formulate some guidelines over the last six years and more. As I have observed recently, this is a vital issue, and it is important that a firm agreement be reached on this question before long.

The Organization continues to face a serious financial situation, despite my best attempts over many years to resolve this problem, and more recently the dedicated efforts of Mr. Hambro, president of the twenty-fifth session of the General Assembly. I hope that the financial difficulties may be resolved, at least in part, under my successor, because I feel it will not be possible for anyone to preside with any sense of satisfaction over the activities of a bankrupt Organization.

In my statement of November 3, 1961, when I first assumed office as Acting Secretary-General of the United Nations, and in my statement of December 2, 1966, when I accepted a fresh five-year mandate, I paid tribute to the Secretariat of which I have been the head for the last ten years and more. I have also recently had the opportunity to take leave of the staff and I have been able to express my profound gratitude to all the members of the staff both in New York and in the far-distant corners of the world, for their dedication and devotion. They represent a priceless asset which I am sure my successor can count upon.

During all these years, I have pursued a policy of consulting with my colleagues, the Under-Secretaries-General and Assistant Secretaries-General, individually, in groups, or at meetings as appropriate to the occasion. They have shared their thoughts and problems with me as freely as I have, for my part, shared my difficulties and problems with them. I feel that in this way we have had an understanding of each other's positions and I think I can also say that during all these years the decisions I have taken were based on careful consideration and prior consultation, and my colleagues have found them generally acceptable.

There is, however, one aspect of my work as chief administrative officer of this Organization on which I would like to make a few observations. I feel that, before laying down my office as Secretary-General of the United Nations, I should in all candor inform the Member states that it is a very unsatisfactory position for the Secretary-General not to have a deputy who can act on his behalf with full authority and full responsibility during his absence, whether for a rest or for a holiday, or on official travel. I say this although I have been well served by my own senior colleagues who have cooperated with me in every possible way whenever it has been necessary for me to absent myself on official travel. However, I have no doubt in my own mind that the absence of a deputy has been one of the main reasons why I myself felt inhibited from taking an occasional holiday, and Members are aware of the resultant consequence to my own health.

I understand that in every major specialized agency there is at least one deputy who is able to relieve the executive head of some bureaucratic responsibilities on a day-to-day basis and who is also authorized and fully able to act for him during his absence. With the phenomenal growth in the Secretariat during recent years and the expected growth of activity in such fields as environment, the seabed and outer space in the future, I feel it is even more important that in the next ten years the Secretary-General should be able to rely upon the services of one deputy.

While the Preparatory Commission in 1945 realized the necessity for a deputy, the actual recommendation which involved a kind of rotation of acting responsibilities of the Secretary-General would be impractical under present circumstances. The relationship between the Secretary-General and his deputy has to be one of complete confidence, and it follows that the deputy should be one individual appointed by and responsible to the Secretary-General. At the same time, in view of the fact that a variety of responsibilities might devolve upon the Secretary-General's deputy in the absence of the Secretary-General, I believe he should be acceptable to the Security Council and also, of course, to the membership in general.

I do not feel that the Deputy Secretary-General need be paid a higher salary then an Under-Secretary-General, since I regard his function basically as a clearly recognized *primus inter pares* position. However, in order to take care of his additional representational responsibilities, I would suggest that he be paid a higher representation allowance than the other Under-Secretaries-General.

This is, of course, not a formal proposal. I want to make it quite clear that I am not making an official proposal. But I feel that in the interests of good management and his own health, the next Secretary-General might be well advised to consider such a proposal and, of course, it should receive the closest attention of the membership in general and particularly the members of the Security Council. This would not require an amendment of the Charter and the financial implications would be minimal.

I wish to conclude by saying *au revoir* rather than farewell to my friends and colleagues assembled here. I hope to be around for some time, and I also intend to use my leisure for the active propagation and advancement of the purposes and principles of the United Nations Charter, to which I have such a deep sense of personal commitment.

Index

Adoula, Cyrille, 610, 611
Aerial hijacking, *see* Hijacking
Africa: major problems of, 71–75, 243–48, 469, 474; *see also* Organization of African Unity; United Nations Operation in the Congo; *names of countries*
Africa Day (1968): Thant statement on, 71–75
Alberta, University of: Thant speech at, 41–45
Algeria: detention of Algerian citizens in Israel, 459–60, 466, 469; El Al plane incident, 249
Algerian war (1950s), 84
Algiers Charter, 52
Allegiance to international community, 402–3, 416–19, 433
American Broadcasting Company, 205n
Angkor Wat, Cambodia, 356
Angola, 73, 146, 301, 477
Annual Reports: Introductions: *22d* (1967), 23, 160; *23d* (1968), 7, 107, 116, 118, 130–59, 160; *24th* (1969), 226, 263, 274–313, 684; *25th* (1970), 450, 470, 473–506; *26th* (1971), 1, 10–11, 535, 571–72, 587, 604–71, 682
Antarctic Treaty, 95
Apartheid, 65, 73, 145, 245–46, 275, 276, 296–99, 477, 487–90
Apartheid, Special Committee on Policies of South Africa on, 297
Associated Press, 329n
Auden, W. H., 676, 677, 678
Authority: crisis of, for United Nations, 416–19

Bahrain: status of, 381–83, 386, 477–78, 596
Ball, George: Vietnam situation, 4, 117, 463
Bandung Conference of Asian-African States (1955), 63, 204
Bangladesh: established, 9: *see also* East Pakistan

Beer, Henrik, 322, 327, 328
Bhutto, Zulfikar Ali, 555
Biafra, Republic of, 6; background summary of secession movement, 201–2, 241, 321–22; Nigerian civil war and Biafran secession, 35, 89–92, 100–5, 120, 128, 186–87, 207–9, 241–43, 246–47, 266–67, 274, 312, 449; reconciliation following civil war, 321–28, 336–38
Big power discussions of common problems proposed, 160–63, 546, 548–50
Biological weapons, 138–39, 286, 476, 480–81
Blue Helmets, 93
Bogotá, Colombia: International Eucharistic Congress in, 109–10
Boren, Per, 175, 176
Brezhnev, Leonid, 36, 548
Briand, Aristide, 222
Brown, Lord George, 6, 36
Bruce, David, 374
Buber, Martin, 601
Budapest Declaration, 207
Bulgaria: Czechoslovakia, invasion of, 7–8, 106; *see also* Czechoslovakia
Bull, Odd, 85, 332, 333, 449
Bunche, Ralph, 262, 270, 332
Burke, Edmund, 442
Burundi: Rwanda-Burundi situation, 388
Bush, George, 526, 527

Camara, Archbishop Helder, 187
Cambodia, 5, 32; extension of Vietnam war into, 353, 354–56, 358–59, 367–69, 374–75; neutrality of, 28–29
Canada, 5, 106; fur seal trade in, 361
Capital punishment, 542
Caracas Conference of American States (1954), 63
Caradon, Lord, 215
Casals, Pablo, 676, 677, 678
Castro, Fidel, 269

Catholic Inter-American Co-operation Programme: Conference of, 188
Cecil, Viscount, 222
Chalfont, Lord, 36
Charter of United Nations, 9, 68, 112, 124, 146, 148, 164, 165, 176, 185, 204, 207, 217, 218, 237, 240, 246, 255, 267, 302, 346, 438, 440, 441, 442, 473, 474, 483, 590, 597, 598, 619, 635, 636, 646, 648, 651, 675, 677, 690, 694; *apartheid* and, 296, 297; decolonization and, 299; economic and social questions and, 623; fundamentals of, 314–20; human rights and, 299; International Court of Justice competence to interpret, 496–99; vs. League of Nations Covenant, 433; peace-keeping operations, 495–96; regional organizations and military alliances and, 7; role of Secretary-General, 384, 359–60, 437, 585, 589, 592, 593–94, 596; and Secretariat reorganization, 127; Security Council and, 429, 596–97; twenty-fifth anniversary observances, 393–437; violations of, 7
——Chapter I: Article *1*, 12, 595: Article *2*, 563, 645, 653
——Chapter II: Article *7*, 90, 100
——Chapter IV: Article *13*, 305; Article *15*, 637; Article *17*, 613
——Chapter V: Article *25*, 611; Article *26*, 498; Article *28*, 160
——Chapter VI, 429; Article *33*, 11, 307, 386, 498, 595, 642, Article *36*, 498
——Chapter VII, 315, 316, 428, 429, 643; Article *49*, 611
——Chapter IX: Article *58*, 624
——Chapter X: Article *63*, 624
——Chapter XI, 239
——Chapter XV: Article *97*, 11, 592, 642; Article *98*, 11, 386, 592; Article *99*, 11–12, 15, 80, 306, 334, 359–60, 380, 386, 435, 450, 556, 594–95, 596–97, 642, 643; Article *100*, 13, 599, 689, 690; Article *101*, 592
Chemical and biological weapons, 138–39, 286, 476, 480–81
Chiang Kai-shek, 269
China, People's Republic of, 5; admitted to United Nations, 679–81; India-Pakistan conflict, 9; in international community, 376–77, 395, 399, 405, 661; Sino-Soviet relations, 212–13, 270–71

China, Republic of (Taiwan), 542–43, 583; expelled from United Nations, 679, 681
China representation in United Nations, 119, 126–27, 183–84, 262–63, 271–72, 335–36, 376, 457–58, 462, 465, 528, 532–33, 536–37, 540, 542–43, 581–82, 582–83; People's Republic of China admitted to United Nations, 679–81
Chou En-lai, 263, 271
Christian Science Monitor, 26n, 80n
Clerides, Glafcos, 77, 86, 294
Commonwealth Secretariat, 86
Conference Services, Office of, 254, 256, 258
Congo, 100, 207; *see also* United Nations Operation in the Congo
Coordination, Administrative Committee on, 60, 413, 414, 461
Coordination in United Nations system, 413–15
Cordier, Andrew W., 685
Council for Foreign Relations: addressed by Thant, on current political issues, 546–54
Couve de Murville, Maurice, 37
Cuba: in international community, 187–88, 212–13
Cuban missile crisis, 15, 384, 596
Cyprus situation, 2–3, 76–78, 85, 86–87, 142–44, 172–73, 275, 24–95, 486–87, 669–71, 682–83; Thant reports on, 76–78, 172–73, 226–31, 507–9, 682–83; *see also* United Nations Force in Cyprus
Czechoslovakia: invasion of (1968), 7–8, 106–8, 120, 121–22, 125–26, 127, 154–56, 182, 202–3, 209, 311, 339, 340

Dag Hammarskjöld Scholarship Fund, 1, 11, 107; Thant statements at luncheons for, 264–67 587–600
Damascus, Syria, 249
Declaration on the Granting of Independence to Colonial Countries and Peoples, 62, 68, 144, 148–49, 243–44, 299, 302, 303
Decolonization, 71–72, 74–75, 144–49, 243–48, 275, 299–303, 405, 462; African problems and, 243–48; ten-year survey, 620–33; *see also* Declaration on the Granting of Independence to Colonial Countries and Peoples
Denktash, Raul, 77, 86, 294

Denmark, 106

Development Decade, *see* United Nations Development Decade

Development questions, 122–23, 280–81, 406–8, 414; economic, 67, 404–15, 576–77, 623–30; Economic and Social Council and, 54–60; industrial development, 576; strategy for, 576–77; ten-year survey, 623–30; *see also* United Nations Conference on Trade and Development; United Nations Development Decade (2d); United Nations Development Programme; United Nations Industrial Development Organization; United Nations Institute for Training and Research

Diem, Ngo Dinh, 535

Disarmament, 20–24, 119, 134–39, 196–200, 275, 282–89, 341–44, 462, 475, 476, 479–83, 657–61; arms race, 480, 550–52, 659–60; Conference on Politics of Disarmament, 343–44; *Report on Economic and Social Consequences of Disarmament* (1962), 197; SALT talks, 196–200, 340, 475, 479, 551, 659; ten-year survey, 617–20; world disarmament conference proposed, 583; *see also* Nuclear weapons; United Nations Disarmament Decade

Disarmament Commission, 372

Disarmament Committee (18-Nation), 20–24, 119, 196, 199, 286–87, 288–89; Conference of, 20–24, 136, 139, 284, 289, 475, 480, 481, 482, 659; Thant messages to, 21–22, 197–98

Disaster relief: cooperation in, 414–15, 501–2, 598

Divided countries, 187, 325–26, 336–40, 500–1, 584, 679–80

Dominican Republic, 7, 107, 123, 127

Dubček, Alexander, 7, 106, 202–3

Earth Day; Thant statement on, 544–45

Eastern Region, Nigeria, *see* Biafra

East Germany (German Democratic Republic), 7–8, 106

East Pakistan (Bangladesh): dispute with central government and problem of refugees in India, 555–70, 585, 595, 597, 653–57 (summary); establishment of Bangladesh, 9

East-West relations, 210–11, 214–15, 413

Eban, Abba, 450, 513, 515, 516, 517; letters from Thant on El Al plane attack by Palestine Liberation Front, 179, 189–93

Economic and Social Affairs Department (United Nations), 256

Economic and Social Council, 299, 369, 428, 430, 432, 444, 462, 467, 684, 687; capital punishment, 542; future objectives and role, 410–15; Thant statement to, on development questions, 54–60; Thant statement to, on United Nations twenty-fifth anniversary, 404–15

Economic and social objectives; relation of political objectives to, 408–10, 433–35

Economic Commission for Europe, 475

Economic Commission for Latin America, 414

Economic development, *see* Development questions; Economic and Social Council; United Nations Development Programme

Eden, Anthony, 44

Education: youth and, 445–46

Effiong, Philip, 321

Egypt, 6, 17–18; *see also* United Arab Republic

El Al plane incidents: hijacked to Algiers, 249; Zurich airport, 179–80, 189–93, 249

El Salvador: Honduras hostilities, 308–9

Environment, *see* Human environment

Equatorial Guinea: Spaniards in, 194–95, 299, 303, 311, 391, 437, 595

Eshkol, Levi, 31

Estabrook, Robert, 32

Europe: Economic Commission for Europe, 475; general problems of, 474–75; security problems of, 206–7

European Atomic Energy Community (EURATOM), 372

Evatt, Herbert, 62

Fifth (Administrative and Budgetary) Committee, 257–60, 279–80, 510–11

Finances (UN), 132, 231, 259, 277–80, 478, 490–95, 510–11, 539, 541, 583–84; ten-year survey, 639–41

First (Political and Security) Committee, 22–24

Foell, Earl, 26, 80

Forsberg, O., 251

Foy, Louis, 579, 580, 673
France, 106, 661; letter from Thant proposing high-level meetings for discussion of common problems, 160–63; *see also* Middle East: big four talks
Fur seal trade in Canada, 361

Gandhi, Indira, 25, 36
de Gaulle, Charles, 37, 92, 548
General Assembly: *apartheid,* 296, 489–90; capital punishment, 542; China, People's Republic of, admitted to United Nations, 679; China representation in United Nations, 457–58; commemoration of United Nations twenty-fifth anniversary, 420–21; Czechoslovak invasion, 7; decolonization, 72; Development Decade (2d), 571; disarmament, 196–98, 199, 482; Fifth (Administrative and Budgetary) Committee: Thant statement to, 257–60; finances (United Nations), 279–80, 510–11; First (Political and Security) Committee, 22–24; General Assembly vs. Security Council action, 377; hijacking of planes, 250, 252; human environment, 345; human rights, 61, 62; international security, 360; Middle East situation, 450; non-proliferation of nuclear weapons, 20, 22–24, 284, 285; Palestinian refugees, 169; role of, 10; Second (Economic and Financial) Committee, 685
——sessions: *23d* (1968), 7; *25th* (1970), 457, 462, 605, 693; *26th* (1971), 679, 681
——Thant statements to: farewell to United Nations, 691–94; on United Nations finances, 510–11
——United Nations University, 684–87; voting system in, 430–31, 585–86; Youth Declaration, 438
Geneva Conference: *1954,* 5, 25, 29–30, 31, 44, 353, 365, 375; *1962,* 5, 353, 375
Genocide, 91–92
German Democratic Republic (East Germany): Czechoslovakia, invasion of, 7–8, 106; *see also* Czechoslovakia
German representation in United Nations, 335, 464–65
Germany, Federal Republic of (West Germany): treaty with USSR, 474
Global strategy for United Nations, 393–94, 403, 407–13, 418–19, 420–21, 434, 600

Goldberg, Arthur, J., 25, 37
"Good offices" concept of United Nations Secretary-General, 305–7, 380–92, 435, 478, 595–97
Gowon, Gen. Yakubu: Nigeria-Biafra situation, 6, 86, 89, 100, 101, 158, 321, 326, 327, 328, 474
Grant, Donald, 30
Greece, *see* Cyprus situation; United Nations Force in Cyprus
Gromyko, Andrei A., 36, 583
Guinea (Portuguese), 73, 146, 301, 477
Gussing, Nils-Goran, 100, 158, 159

Haile Selassie, 89, 100, 209; Spaniards in Equatorial Guinea, 194–95; *see also* Equatorial Guinea
Halasz, Louis, 127, 463
Hambro, Edvard, 510, 511, 693
Hammarskjöld, Dag, 2, 11, 12, 160, 175, 292, 322, 334, 338, 380, 386, 436, 587, 594, 605, 613, 641; as diplomat and Secretary-General, 588–89; good offices missions, 387–88; quotation from *Markings,* 589; Thant statement on tenth anniversary of death of, 601–03
Hammarskjöld, Knut, 252
Hanoi, 3–4
Harriman, Averell: Vietnam negotiations, 79, 88
Hasan, Saadat, 464
Heath, Edward, 36
High-level meetings for discussion of common problems, 160–63, 546, 548–50
Hijacking, aerial, 249–53, 267–68, 307–8, 459–60, 461, 464, 465, 468–69, 470–72, 499–500
Hill, Martin, 685
Ho Chi Minh, 45, 272
Hoffman, Paul, 476, 575
Honduras: El Salvador hostilities, 308–9
Human environment, 444–45, 476, 577; Earth Day, 544–45; pollution problems, 378; United Nations role in protection of, 345–52
Human Environment, United Nations Conference on, 418, 476; Prepartory Committee addressed by Thant, 346–49
Human rights, 237, 299–300; European Convention for Protection of, 63; International Covenants on (1966), 64; Inter-

national Year for, 61, 65, 70, 148; Universal Declaration for, 61–70
Human Rights, International Conference on: Thant address to, 61–70
Human Rights Day (1967), 69
Human well-being: global threats to, 597
Hungary: invasion of Czechoslovakia, 7–8, 106; *see also* Czechoslovakia
Husain, Zakir, 36
Huu Chi, Nguyen, 25, 37
"Hymn to the Nations" (Auden, Casals), 676, 677

Ideologies: divisiveness of, 412
Ifni, 299
India, 5; East Pakistani refugees in India, 555–70, 585, 595, 597, 653–57 (summary); war with Pakistan, 8–9, 389
Indo-China, 5; extension of Vietnam war in, 353, 354–56, 357, 358–59, 363–66, 367–69, 374–75, 395, 399, 405, 443, 463, 535, 552–53, 692; neutrality of, 45; ten-year survey of situation, 614–17; *see also* Cambodia
Indonesia: West Irian situation, 92, 131–32, 311
Institute on Man and Science: Thant statement to Conference on Politics of Disarmament, 343–44
International Air Transport Association, 179, 190, 249, 252, 308, 460
International Atomic Energy Agency, 286, 475, 482
International Bar Association: addressed by Thant, 94–99
International Bill of Rights, 64
International Civil Aviation Organization, 179, 190, 249, 250, 251, 252, 268, 308, 460, 461, 499–500
International civil service, 219, 592–93, 636–38; *see also* Staff (UN)
International Committee of the Red Cross, 415; Biafran aid, 89, 100, 101, 102, 103, 104, 120, 158, 202, 209, 241, 242
International Control Commission, 5, 32, 353–54, 364, 375
International Court of Justice, 149, 417; competence to interpret United Nations Charter, 496–99
International Development Association, 575

International Eucharistic Congress: message from Thant, 109–10
International Federation of Air Line Pilots Associations: and hijacking problem, 249–52, 267–68, 460, 470
International Labour Organisation, 63, 151; Fiftieth Anniversary Conference addressed by Thant, 232–38
International University, *see* United Nations University
International Year for Human Rights (1968), 61, 65, 70, 148
International Youth Volunteer Service, 432
Inter-Nation Television Trust of London: Thant interview by, 427–37
Ireland: Ulster question, 312, 376
Israel, 17–18; detention of Algerians in, 459–60, 466, 469; El-Al plane incidents, 179–80, 189–93, 249; *see also* Middle East situation; Suez Canal

Jackson, C., 251
Jarring, Gunnar: Middle East mission, 2, 17–19, 32–33, 34, 84–85, 86, 93, 125, 140, 141, 142, 160, 166, 179, 181, 183, 190, 201, 205, 206, 211, 262, 270, 271, 291, 330, 333–34, 357, 362, 370, 373, 379, 449; reactivation of Middle East mission, 450–53, 458–59, 474, 484–86, 526–28, 535–36, 537, 582, 665, 667; Thant report on Jarring's activities in Middle East, 514–25
Jewish Defense League, 464
John XXIII (Pope), 109
Johnson, Lyndon B.: Vietnam situation, 4–5, 25–26, 27, 34, 37, 117, 118
Joint Inspection Unit, 112
Jordan, 17; internal crisis, 361, 391; *see also* Middle East situation

Kasantzakis, Niko, 409
Kennan, George, 350
Kennedy, John F., 15
Kennedy Round (tariff talks), 48, 49, 58
Khrushchev, Nikita, 15
Korea, North: shooting down of American plane, 204–5
Kosygin, Aleksei, 36, 196, 199, 263, 270
Ky, Nguyen Cao, 32, 45

Labouisse, Henry R., 158, 322, 327, 328, 337
Laird, Melvin, 367

Landon, Alfred, 548

Laos, 5; extension of Vietnam war into, 353, 354–56, 367, 374–75; *see also* Indo-China

Latin America: non-proliferation of nuclear weapons in, 96–97, 137, 287, 479, 658–59; *see also* Economic Commission for Latin America

Law, international: codification of, 303–5; peace-keeping and, 94–99

Law of Treaties Conference, 97, 303–4

Law of Treaties Convention, 304

League of Nations, 220, 393, 497, 592; Covenant of, 222, 306, 593; Covenant vs. United Nations Charter, 433; Thant address on fiftieth anniversary of, 221–23

League of Red Cross Societies, 322, 327n, 328

Lebanon, *see* Middle East situation

Lewis, Anthony, 322, 339

Lie, Trygve, 13, 160, 541; Thant tributes on death of, 175–78

Littlejohns, Michael, 180, 267

Liu Chieh, 681

McVane, John, 205

Mai Van Bo, 3, 25, 36

Makarios, President, 486, 669

Malaysia, Federation of, 388

Malik, Yakov, 370

Manhattan School of Music, 676

Mao Tse-tung, 269

Markings (Hammarskjöld), 589

Martola, A. E., 231

Mass phenomena, age of, 410–11

Meir, Golda, 513

Membership in United Nations: university of, 150–51, 335–36, 417, 503, 583, 584

Michelmore, Laurence, 361

Micro-states, 307

Middle East situation (general), 2, 31–33, 92–93, 125, 139–42, 160–61, 166–71, 181–82, 183, 184, 185, 188–89, 205–6, 211–12, 265–66, 271, 274, 289–94, 357–58, 362–63, 369–74, 377–78, 389–91, 395, 399–400, 405, 443, 665–69, 692; background summaries, 17–18, 179–80, 201, 262, 449–50, 513–14; big four talks, 201, 262, 268–69, 330–32, 332–35, 340, 369–70, 373–74, 379, 449, 450, 533; Palestine

Liberation Front attack on El Al plane at Zurich (1969), 179; standstill cease-fire and new peace talks (1970), 450–53, 458–60, 474, 483–86; Thant report on activities of special representative, 514–25; United Nations' special responsibility toward, 534; work of United Nations special representative to, 2, 18–19, 32–33, 34, 84–85, 86, 93, 125, 140, 141, 142, 160, 166, 179, 181, 183, 190, 201, 205, 206, 211, 262, 270, 271, 291, 330, 333–34, 357, 362, 370, 373, 379, 449, 450–53, 458–59, 526–28, 535–36, 537, 582, 665, 667; *see also* United Nations Emergency Force

Military observer operations (United Nations), 281–82, 478

Morse, David, 235

Motta, Giuseppe, 223

Mozambique, 73, 146, 301, 477

Mujibur Rahman, Sheikh, 555; trial of, 566–67

Namibia (South West Africa), 497; *apartheid* in, 296–97; South Africa and, 73, 85–86, 145–46, 244–45, 300, 417, 477

National Liberation Front (Vietcong), 5, 32, 79, 82, 83, 211, 224, 273, 365, 374, 375

National pride: international commitment and, 418–19

Natural disasters: coordination of aid in, 414–15, 501–2, 598

Navy League: Thant address to, 314–20

Nerve gas: dumping into Atlantic Ocean, 454–55

Netherlands, *see* West Irian

New Delhi, India: United Nations Conference on Trade and Development (2d session) held at, 25, 36, 46–54, 56, 57

New York Times, 205, 322

Nguyen Hoa, 3, 25, 36

Nicolaeff, V., 251

Nigeria: background summary of internal strife, 201–2, 241, 321–22; civil war and Biafran secession, 5–6, 35, 89–92, 100–5, 120, 128, 157–59, 186–87, 207–9, 241–43, 246–47, 266–67, 274, 312, 449, 474, 596; national reconciliation following civil war, 321–28, 336–38

Nixon, Richard, 179, 182, 186, 196, 199, 224, 263, 269, 272, 374, 546, 548, 581, 679

Non-Aligned States Conference, 469

Non-Governmental Organizations, 638–39; Thant statements at Conference of, 53–54, 198–200

Non-Nuclear-Weapon States Conference (1968), 119, 197, 199, 285

North Atlantic Treaty Organization, 4, 156, 679

North-South relations (rich-poor nations), 215–16

North Vietnam, 3–4; *see also* Vietnam situation

Norway: Thant message to, on death of Trygve Lie, 176–77

Novotny, Antonin, 106

Nuclear weapons, 134–38, 282–86, 288, 372; Non-Proliferation Treaty, 20–24, 96–97, 131, 134–35, 196, 263, 282, 285, 405, 475, 479, 481–82, 660; Non-Proliferation Treaty, entry into force, 341–42; partial test-ban treaty, 405, 479, 481

Oatis, William N., 329

Ogrady, J., 251

Ojukwu, Odumegwu, 101, 321, 324, 337, 338

Organization of African Unity, 74, 89, 580–81; addressed by Thant, on African problems, 243–48; Nigerian civil war and, 6, 35, 100, 101, 120, 128, 186, 202, 208–9, 241, 242, 266, 321, 322, 323–24; territorial integrity of member states, 336–37; United Nations cooperation with, 504

Organization of American States, 7, 123, 127; El Salvador-Honduras hostilities, 308–9

Orlando, Vittorio, 222

Ortiz-Sanz, Fernando, 131

Outer space: peaceful uses of, 95–96, 287, 479, 661–63

Pakistan, 528; Bangladesh established, 9; dispute with central government and problem of refugees in India, 555–70, 585, 595, 597, 653–57 (summary); war with India, 8–9, 389

Palestine, *see* Middle East situation; Palestine liberation movements; Refugees; United Nations Relief and Works Agency for Palestine Refugees in the Near East; United Nations Truce Supervision Organization

Palestine liberation movements, 189, 211, 461

Palthey, George, 251

Pan African Conference, 469

Paraguay, 106

Paris talks, *see* Vietnam situation

Paul VI (Pope), 434, 530, 638; *Encyclical Letter on the Development of Peoples,* 234; message from Thant, 109–10

Peace and peace-keeping operations (general), 110, 133, 139–44, 149–51, 218, 281, 462, 478, 495–96, 530–31, 539; international law and, 94–99; machinery for, 94; relation between world peace and economic progress, 434–35; Security Council role, 203–4; United Nations and, 164–65, 422–25; *see also* United Nations Emergency Force; United Nations Force in Cyprus; United Nations Operation in the Congo; United Nations Truce Supervision Organization

Peace-keeping Operations, Special Committee on, 692; Working Group, 281, 478

Peking, *see* China, People's Republic of

Podgorny, Nikolai V., 36

Poland, 5; invasion of Czechoslovakia, 7–8, 106; *see also* Czechoslovakia

Pollution, *see* Human environment

Pompidou, Georges, 322

Population questions, 476, 495, 531, 577; Declaration on Population, 69

Portugal, 73; Southern Rhodesia and, 239; territories administered by, 73, 146, 301–3, 477

Portuguese Guinea, 73, 146, 301, 477

Portuguese territories, 73, 146, 301, 477

Prebisch, Raúl, 46, 53, 56, 414

Programme and Co-ordination, Committee for, 60, 112, 414

Public Information, Office of (UN), 254, 256, 258, 276

Racial discrimination, 216, 246; Declaration on (1963), 64, 68; International Convention on (1965), 64; see also *Apartheid*

Raghavan, Chakravarti, 463

Rathore, Naeem, 690

Refugees: Pakistani, 555–70, 585, 595, 597, 653–57 (summary); Palestinian, 140–1, 166–71, 293

Regional organizations: United Nations and, 7, 504

Representation of Member states by rival governments, 500–1; *see also* Divided countries

Reuters, 180n

Rhodesia, *see* Southern Rhodesia

Riad, Mahmoud, 515

Richardson, Elliot, 359

Rogers, William, 196, 200, 205, 451, 514, 526, 527, 528

Roosevelt, Franklin D., 595

Royal Commonwealth Society: addressed by Thant, on Secretary-General's role, 380–92

Rusk, Dean, 25, 37

Rwanda-Burundi situation, 388

Sadruddin Khan, 555

Said-Uddin Khan, 100, 322, 327, 328

St. Bernard's School, New York City: addressed by Thant, 177–78

St. Louis Post-Dispatch, 30

St. Louis Symposium on Second Development Decade: addressed by Thant, 574–78

SALT talks, 196–200, 340, 475, 479, 551, 659

San Francisco, Calif.: United Nations twenty-fifth anniversary observances in, 393–404

Science and technology, 69, 414

Sea-bed and ocean floor: peaceful uses of, 96, 138, 286, 475, 480, 658, 663–65

Secession of states and problem of divided countries: United Nations and, 187, 325–26, 336–40, 500–1, 584, 679–80

Second (Economic and Financial) Committee, 685

Secretariat (UN), *see* Staff

Secretary-General of United Nations: Deputy Secretary-General post proposed, 689, 693–94; essential qualities of, 590–91; "good offices" concept, 305–7, 380–92; implementing authority of, 584–85; initiative and independence of, 599–600; as "moderator," 595; political responsi-bilities of, 593–97; role of, 1, 6, 11–13, 175, 359–60, 380–92, 435–37, 585, 587–600, 641–46; selection of, 540–41, 541–42; *see also* Hammarskjöld, Dag; Lie, Trygve; Thant, U; Waldheim, Kurt

Security, international, 360; *see also* Peace and peace-keeping operations; Security Council

Security Council: *apartheid* and South Africa problems, 477, 488–89; and Article 99 of United Nations Charter, 596–97; Bahrain, 477–78, 496; Cyprus situation, 682, 683; Czechoslovakia, invasion of (1968), 7, 106–7, 182; hijacking of planes, 249, 250, 252, 470; internal affairs of Member states, 91–92; maintaining world peace, 203–4; micro-states, 307; Middle East situation, 17–19, 181, 190, 205–6, 289–91, 333–35, 449, 461, 468, 484, 534, 536, 537; nuclear weapons, 20–21; periodic meetings, 149, 160, 161, 503–4; resolutions by, 210, 273–74, 429–30; role of, 10, 317–18, 428–30; Security Council vs. General Assembly action, 377; Southern Rhodesia situation, 239, 301; terrorism, 253; Thant memorandum to, on threat to international peace by East Pakistan (Bangladesh) situation, 562, 563–66

——Thant reports to: on activities of special representative in Middle East, 18–19; 514–25; on Cyprus situation, 76–78, 172–73, 226–31, 507–9, 682–83

——voting system in, 430–31

Self-determination of peoples, 72

de Seynes, Philippe, 410

Sihanouk, Prince, 375

Smith, Arnold, 100, 101

Smith, Gerard C., 199

Smith, Ian, 239

Souphanouvong, Prince, 375

South Africa, 10; arms shipments to, 297–98, 372, 477; Sharpeville massacre, 246, 296; Southern Rhodesia and, 239, 245; United Nations Conference on Trade and Development and, 188; see also *Apartheid;* Namibia

Southeast Asia, *see* Indo-China

South East Asia Treaty Organization, 127

Southern Rhodesia question, 73–74, 146, 245, 296, 300–1, 477; background summary, 239; sanctions against Southern Rhodesia, 301; Thant statement on 1969 Constitution for, 240

South Vietnam, *see* Vietnam, Republic of

South West Africa, *see* Namibia

Soviet Union, *see* Union of Soviet Socialist Republics

Spain: Spaniards in Equatorial Guinea, 194–95, 299, 303, 311, 391, 437, 595

Special Political Committee: Thant statement to, on Middle East situation, 167–71

Staff (United Nations), 275–76, 636–38; Administrative Management Service, 254, 258; clearance for public statements by, 211–12; composition of Secretariat, 113–14; manpower utilization, 254, 256, 257–60, 493–94; observance of United Nations twenty-fifth anniversary, 422–27; reorganization of Secretariat, 113, 133–34; salary system, 115, 691

——Thant addresses to: farewell to, 689–91; Staff Day, *1968,* 111–16; Staff Day, *1969,* 254–57; tribute to staff who served from inception of United Nations, 422–27

Strong-weak countries, 216–17

Suez Canal: breaches of cease-fire and new peace talks, 331–32, 362, 373, 449, 459, 485, 514, 526–27, 666, 667; reopening of, 514

Syria; *see* Middle East situation

Tafall, Osorio: Cyprus situation, 86–87

Tamayo, Marcial: Spaniards in Equatorial Guinea, 194–95, 311

Tariff talks: Kennedy Round, 48, 49, 58

Technical cooperation: need for, 406

Technology, 69, 414

Teheran, Iran: Human Rights Conference (1968) held in, 61–70

Tekoah, Yosef, 179, 191, 192, 524

Tensions, world: sources of, 214; United Nations and, 214–20

Territorial asylum: Declaration on, 64

Terrorism, international, 250, 253, 464, 470–72; bombing of United Arab Republic Mission, New York, 537–38; *see also* Hijacking, aerial

Texas, University of: Thant address at, on international role in protecting environment, 345, 350–52

Thant, U:

——*aides-mémoires,* letters, memorandum, note relating to official concerns: *aide-mémoire* on humanitarian aid to East Pakistan refugees, 567–69; *aide-mémoire* to India and Pakistan, on refugee problem, and India-Pakistan threat to international peace, 8, 561–63, 569–70; letter to France, United Kingdom, United States, Soviet Union, proposing high-level meetings for discussion of common problems, 160–63; letter to Haile Selassie, on Spaniards in Equatorial Guinea, 194–95; letters to Israel, on El Al plane attack by Palestine Liberation Front, 179, 189–93; memorandum to Security Council, on threat to international peace by East Pakistan (Bangladesh) situation, 562, 563–66; note on reactivation of Jarring Middle East mission, 452–53

——biographical data: assessment of Thant, 14–15; "Two-Thant" doctrine, 184

——major issues and concerns as Secretary-General: Africa problems (general), 71–75, 469, 474; Angola, 73, 146, 301, 477; *apartheid,* 65, 73, 145, 245–46, 275, 276, 296–99, 477, 487–90; arms to South Africa, 297–98, 372, 477; Bahrain problem, 381–83, 386, 477–78, 596; Biafran secession, 6, 89–92, 100–5, 120, 128, 157–59, 186–87, 201–2, 207–9, 241–43, 246–47, 266–67, 274, 312, 321–28, 336–38, 449, 596; "birthday wishes" for humanity, on United Nations twenty-fifth anniversary, 394–95; Cambodian neutrality and extension of Vietnam war, 28–29, 353, 354–56, 358–59, 367–69, 374–75; Charter of United Nations and responsibilities of nations under it, 7 (*See also* *main entry* Charter of United Nations); chemical and biological weapons, 138–39, 286, 476, 480–81; China in international community, 376–77, 395, 399, 405, 661; China representation in United Nations, 119, 126–27, 183–84, 262–63, 271–72, 335–36, 376, 457–58, 462, 465,

Thant, U.: Major issues and concerns as Secretary-General (*Continued*)

528, 532–33, 536–37, 540, 542–43, 581–82, 582–83; China representation question: admission of People's Republic to United Nations, 679–81; coordination in United Nations system, 413–15; Cuba in international community, 187–88, 212–13; Cuban missile crisis, 15, 384, 596; Cyprus situation, 2–3, 76–78, 85, 86–87, 142–44, 172–73, 226–31, 275, 294–95, 486–87, 669–71, 682–83; Czechoslovakia, invasion of (1968), 7–8, 106–08, 120, 121–22, 125–26, 127, 154–56, 182, 202–3, 299, 311, 339, 340; decolonization, 71–72, 74–75, 144–49, 243–48, 275, 299–303, 405, 462, 620–23; Development Decade (2d), 53–54, 59, 119, 236, 278–79, 288, 407, 409, 434, 435, 448, 475, 483, 530–31; Development Decade (2d) launched, 572–78; development questions, 54–60, 122–23, 280–81, 404–15, 623–30, 690; disarmament, 20–24, 119, 134–39, 196–200, 275, 282–89, 340, 341–44, 372, 462, 475, 476, 479–83, 617–20, 657–61; disarmament: arms race, 480, 550–52, 659–60; disarmament: world disarmament conference proposal, 583; Disarmament Decade, 263, 288, 341, 343, 409, 448, 481–83, 657–58, 660; disaster-relief coordination, 414–15, 501–2, 598; East-West relations, 210–11, 214–15, 413; El Al plane incident (Zurich, 1969), 179–80, 189–93; El Salvador-Honduras hostilities, 308–9; Equatorial Guinea, 194–95, 299, 303, 311, 391, 437, 595; farewell messages to United Nations, 689–94; finances of United Nations, 132, 259, 277–80, 478, 490–95, 539, 541, 583–84, 639–41; German representation in United Nations, 335, 464–65; global strategy for United Nations, 393–94, 403, 407–13, 418–19, 420–21, 434, 600; "good offices" of Secretary-General, 305–7, 380–92, 435, 478, 595–97; Guinea, 73, 146, 301, 477; high-level meetings for discussion of common problems, 160–63, 546, 548–50; hijacking of planes, 249–53, 267–68, 307–8, 459–60, 461, 464, 465, 468–69, 470–72, 499–500; human environment, 345–52,

418, 444–45, 476, 544–45, 577; human rights, 61–70, 237, 299–300; implementing authority of Secretary-General, 584–85; India-Pakistan conflict, 8–9, 389 (*see also* Pakistan, problem of refugees in India); Indo-China and Vietnam war, 353, 354–56, 357, 358–59, 363–66, 367–69, 374–75, 395, 399, 405, 443, 463, 535, 552–53, 614–17, 692; international civil service concept, 219, 592–93, 636–38; Jordan crisis, 361, 391; Laos and Vietnam war, 353, 354–56, 367, 374–75; Latin America denuclearization, 137, 287, 479, 658–59; law, international, 303–5; Law of Treaties, 303–4; Malaysia, 388; microstates, 307; Middle East big-four talks, 201, 205–6, 262, 268–69, 330–32, 332–35, 340, 369–70, 373–74, 379, 449, 450, 533; Middle East: reactivation of peace discussions, 450–53, 458–60, 474, 483–86, 526–28, 535–36, 537, 582, 665–69; Middle East situation (general), 2, 17–19, 31–33, 84–85, 86, 92–93, 125, 139–42, 166–71, 179–80, 181–82, 183, 184, 185, 188–89, 211–12, 265–66, 268–70, 271, 274, 289–94, 335–36, 357–58, 362–63, 369–74, 377–78, 389–91, 395, 399–400, 405, 513–25, 692; military observer groups, 478; Mozambique, 73, 146, 301, 477; Namibia (South West Africa) question, 85–86, 145–46, 244–45, 296–97, 300, 417, 477, 497; Nigerian civil war, 5–6, 35, 89–92, 100–5, 120, 128, 157–59, 186–87, 201–2, 207–9, 241–43, 246–47, 266–67, 274, 312, 321–28, 336–38, 449, 474, 596; Non-Proliferation Treaty, 20–24, 96–97, 131, 134–35, 196, 263, 282, 285, 341–42, 405, 475, 479, 481–82, 660; North-South relations, 215–16; nuclear weapons, 20–24, 96–97, 131, 134–38, 196, 263, 282–86, 288, 372, 405; nuclear weapons partial test-ban treaty, 479, 481; outer space: peaceful uses of, 95–96, 287, 479, 661–63; Pakistan situation and East Pakistani refugees in India, 555–70, 585, 595, 597, 653–57; Palestinian refugees, 140–41, 166–71, 293; peace and peace-keeping operations, 94–99, 110, 133, 139–44, 149–51, 218, 281, 442–44, 462, 478, 495–96, 530–31, 539, 606–7, 692; peace objectives in relation to world economic progress, 434–35; population questions, 476, 495, 531, 577; racial discrimination, 216, 246 *(see also Apartheid);* regional organizations, 7, 504; role of Secretary-General, 1, 6, 11–13, 175, 359–60, 380–92, 435–37, 587–600, 641–46; Rwanda-Burundi relations, 388; SALT talks, 196–200, 340, 475, 479, 659; science and technology, 69, 414; seabed and ocean floor: peaceful uses of, 138, 286, 475, 480, 658, 663–65; secessionist movements and problem of divided countries, 187, 325–26, 336–40, 584, 679–80; Southern Rhodesia situation, 146, 239–40, 245, 296, 300–1, 477; staff (UN) questions, 111–16, 133–34, 211–12, 254–60, 275–76, 493–94, 636–38; staff (UN): farewell statement to, 689–91, staff tribute by Thant on United Nations twenty-fifth anniversary, 422–27; Suez hostilities and cease-fire, 331–32, 362, 373, 449, 459, 485, 666, 667; survey of ten-year term as Secretary-General (Introduction, *26th Annual Report*), 604–71; terrorism, 250, 253, 464, 470–72, 537–38 *(see also* Hijacking); "third moral force" concept, 204; third term as Secretary-General, 456–57, 463–64, 529–30, 540, 580–81, 672–75; United Nations: assessment of, 9–11, 203, 314–320, 393–437, 547–48, 647–50, 677–78; United Nations: authority and development of, 393–437; United Nations: crisis of international commitment to, 402–3, 416–19, 433; United Nations: future direction of, 410–15, 420–21, 467–68, 473–74, 608; United Nations: twenty-fifth anniversary of, 312–13, 393–437, 470, 504–6, 650–53; United Nations: universality of membership, 150–51, 335–36, 417, 503, 583, 584, 635–36; United Nations: world tensions and, 214–20; United Nations Conference on Trade and Development (2d session, New Delhi), 25, 33–34, 36, 46–54, 55, 56–59, 407, 409; United Nations Force in Cyprus, 76–78, 132–33, 143, 144, 172–73, 226–31, 278, 295, 339, 377, 436, 487, 492, 670–71, 682–83; United Nations University, 309–10, 466–67, 502–3, 684–88; Vietnam situa-

tion, 3–5, 25–45, 79–84, 86, 88, 117–18, 119–21, 124–25, 127, 128–29, 130, 152–54, 184, 210, 224–25, 261, 271, 272–73, 274, 310–11, 332, 353–54, 358–59, 363–69, 374–75, 385, 463, 476, 533, 535, 539–40, 584, 596, 614–17; voting system in United Nations bodies, 430–31, 585–86; West Irian situation, 92, 131–32, 311

——official visits: Africa, 321–28, 338, 474; New Delhi (United Nations Conference on Trade and Development), 25, 36, 46

——press conferences, 26–35, 79–93, 119–28, 180–89, 201–13, 321–26, 329–40, 356–69, 369–79, 456–69, 525–43, 579–86; African problems (general), 469; American plane shot down by North Koreans, 204–5; arms to South Africa, 372; Biafran secession, 35, 89–92, 120, 128, 186–87, 201–2, 207–9, 321–28, 336–38; Cambodia and Vietnam war, 28–29, 353, 354–56, 358–59, 367–69, 374–75; capital punishment, 542; China as part of international community, 376–77; China representation in United Nations, 119, 126–27, 183–84, 271–72, 335–36, 376, 457–58, 462, 465, 528, 532–33, 536–37, 540, 542–43, 581–82, 582–83; Cuba as part of international community, 187–88, 212–13; Cyprus situation, 85, 86–87; Czechoslovakia, invasion of, 120, 121–22, 125–26, 127, 182, 202–3, 299, 339, 340; decolonization, 462; Development Decade (2d), 119, 530–31; development questions, 122–23; disarmament, 119, 340, 462, 583; Disarmament Commission, 372; divided nations (Germany, Korea, Vietnam), 584; East-West relations, 210–11; European security problems, 206–7; financial situation of United Nations, 539, 541, 583–84; German representation in United Nations, 335, 464–65; hijacking of planes, 267–68, 459–60, 461, 464, 465, 468–69; implementing authority of Secretary-General, 584–85; Indo-China situation, 353, 354–56, 357, 358–59, 363–66, 367–69, 374–75, 463, 535; international security, 360; Jordan internal crisis, 361; Laos and Vietnam war, 353, 354–56, 367, 374–75; Middle East big-four talks, 201, 205–6, 268–69, 330–32, 332–35, 340,

Thant, U.: press conferences (*Continued*) 369–70, 373–74, 379, 533; Middle East reactivated peace talks, 458–60, 526–28, 535–36, 537, 582; Middle East situation (general), 31–33, 84–85, 86, 92–93, 125, 179–80, 181–82, 183, 184, 185, 188–89, 211–12, 269–70, 271, 357–58, 362–63, 369–74, 377–78; Nigerian civil war, 35, 89–92, 120, 128, 186–87, 201–2, 207–9, 321–28, 336–38; Nixon trip to Peking, 581; nuclear proliferation, 372; Pakistan internal strife, 585, 595, 597; peace and peace-keeping operations, 462, 530–31, 539; population questions, 531; relationship with United Nations Correspondents Association, 479–80; role of Secretary-General, 359–60; secession of states and problem of divided countries, 325–26; Security Council resolutions, 273–74; Sino-Soviet relations, 212–13, 270–71; South West Africa question, 85–86; staff questions, 211–12; Suez hostilities and cease-fire, 362, 373, 459; terrorism, 464, 537–38; third term as Secretary-General, 456–57, 463–64, 529–30, 540, 580–81; Ulster situation, 376; United Nations: future prospects of, 467–68; United Nations Conference on Trade and Development, 33–34; United Nations Emergency Force, 339, 371, 377; United Nations Force in Cyprus, 339, 377; United Nations University, 466–67; universality of United Nations membership, 335–36, 583, 584; Vietnam situation (general), 26–32, 34–35, 79–84, 86, 88, 119–21, 124–25, 127, 184, 210, 271, 272–73, 332, 358–59, 363–69, 374, 463, 533, 535, 539–40, 584; Vietnam situation and new peace conference proposal, 353–54, 364–66, 374–75; voting system in General Assembly, 585–86; youth, in world affairs, 466

——radio and television appearances: interview by Inter-Nation Television Trust of London, on United Nations twenty-fifth anniversary, 427–37; statement on Vietnam, 39

——reports: *Annual Reports:* Introductions: *22d* (1967), 23, 160; *23d* (1968), 7, 106, 116, 118, 130–59, 160; *24th* (1969), 226, 263, 274–313, 684; *25th* (1970), 450, 470, 473–506; *26th* (1971), 1, 10–11, 535, 571–72, 587, 604–71, 682; to Security Council, on activities of special representative to Middle East, 18–19, 514–25; to Security Council, on Cyprus situation, 76–78, 172–73, 226–31, 507–9, 682–83

——speeches, messages, statements, *notes-verbales:* Africa Day (1968), 71–75; appeals for emergency assistance for East Pakistani population and for East Pakistani refugees in India, 557–58, 559–61; to Conference on Politics of Disarmament, 343–44; to Council for Foreign Relations, on current political issues, 546–54; on Czechoslovak invasion, 108; at dinner inaugurating United Nations twenty-fifth anniversary observance, on hijacking and terrorism, 470–72; to Disarmament Committee (18-Nation), 21–22, 197–98; on dumping of nerve gas into Atlantic Ocean by United States, 454–55; on Earth Day, 544–45; to Economic and Social Council, on development questions, 54–60; to Economic and Social Council, on United Nations twenty-fifth anniversary, 404–15; on entry into force of Non-Proliferation Treaty, 341–42; to Fifth (Administrative and Budgetary) Committee, on staff questions, 257–60; in First Committee, on nuclear weapons, 22–24; in General Assembly: farewell to United Nations, 691–94; at General Assembly commemoration of United Nations twenty-fifth anniversary, 420–21; to General Gowon, on Nigerian civil war, 102–3; at Hammarskjöld Memorial Scholarship Fund Luncheon, on role of Secretary-General, 587–600; at Hammarskjöld Memorial Scholarship Fund Luncheon, on United Nations and world problem areas, 264–67; on hijacking problem, 251–52; on humanitarian relief to civilian victims of Nigerian conflict, 242–43; on impending trial of Sheikh Mujibur Rahman, 566–67; to International Bar Association, on role of international law in peace-keeping, 94–99; to International Conference on Human Rights, 61–70; to International Labour Organisation, on fiftieth anniversary, 232–38; to International Symposium on Second Development Decade, 572–74; on League of Nations fiftieth anniversary, 221–23; on Middle East situation, following meeting with William Rogers, 451; to Navy League, on assessment of United Nations, 314–20; to Non-Governmental Organizations Conference, on disarmament, 198–200; to Non-Governmental Organizations Conference, on trade and development, 53–54; to Organization of African Unity, on African problems, 243–48; to Organization on African Unity, on Nigerian civil war, 103–5; to Pope Paul VI, on International Eucharistic Congress, 109–10; on preliminary studies for establishing United Nations University, 684–88; to Preparatory Committee for United Nations Conference on Human Environment, 345, 346–49; to Press, on admission of People's Republic of China to United Nations, 679–81; to Press, on bombing of North Vietnam, 379; to Press, on decision not to stand for third term of office, 674–75; to Press, on Nigerian national reconciliation, 326–28; to Press, on Nixon-National Liberation Front initiatives regarding Vietnam war, 224–25; to Press, on Vietnam situation, 36–38, 39–41, 128–29; to Press, on Vietnam war extension in Indo-China, 354–55; to Prime Minister of Norway, on death of Trygve Lie, 176–77; to Royal Commonwealth Society, on Secretary-General's role, 380–92; at St. Bernard's School, on Trygve Lie, 177–78; to Security Council, on terrorism, 253; on Southern Rhodesia's 1969 Constitution, 240; in Special Political Committee, on Middle East situation, 167–71; on tenth anniversary of death of Hammarskjöld, 601–3; to United Nations Association of Great Britain, on world tensions, 214–20; at United Nations Conference on Trade and Development (2d session, New Delhi), 47–54; at United Nations Correspondents luncheons, 80–87, 201–13, 356–69; on United Nations Day (1968), 164–65; at United Nations Day Concert (1971), 676–78; to United Nations Staff: farewell statement, 689–91; on United Nations Staff Day: *1968,* 111–16; *1969,* 254–57; *1970,* 422–27; at United Nations twenty-fifth anniversary events in San Francisco, 394–404; to University of Alberta, on

Vietnam situation, 41–45; at University of Texas, on international role in protecting environment, 345, 350–52; to World Association of World Federalists, on United Nations twenty-fifth anniversary, 416–19; to World Youth Assembly, 439–48

Thermonuclear weapons, *see* Nuclear weapons

Thi Binh, Mrs., 584

Thieu, Nguyen Van, 32

"Third moral force" concept, 204

Third term for Thant as Secretary-General, 456–57, 463–64, 529–30, 540, 580–81; background summary, 672–74; decision by Thant, 674–75

Thomas, Albert, 234

Thomson, George, 36

Trade, international, 98, 576; *see also* United Nations Conference on Trade and Development

Trans World Airlines plane hijack, 249

Trusteeship Council, 428, 430

Tshombé, Moïse, 208, 322, 338, 610, 611, 612

Tung, Cy, 466

Turkey, *see* Cyprus situation; United Nations Force in Cyprus

Twenty-fifth anniversary observances of United Nations, 312–13, 393–437, 470, 504–6, 650–53; Thant address to World Association of World Federalists, 416–19; Thant interview of Inter-Nation Television Trust of London, 427–37; Thant statement in Economic and Social Council, 404–15; Thant statement at General Assembly commemorative session, 420–21; Thant statement at special staff meeting, 422–27; Thant statements at San Francisco commemorative events, 394–404

"Two-Thant" doctrine, 184

Ulster question, 312, 376

Union of Soviet Socialist Republics (USSR): India-Pakistan conflict, 9; letter from Thant proposing high-level meetings for discussion of common problems, 160–63; military intervention in Czechoslovakia, 7–8, 106–8, 120, 121–22, 125–27, 154–56, 182, 202, 209, 311, 339, 340; nuclear weapons, 20, 23; on regional organizations, 7; SALT talks, 196–200,

Union of Soviet Socialist Republics (USSR): (*Continued*)
340, 475, 479, 551, 659; Sino-Soviet relations, 212–13, 270–71; treaty with Federal Republic of Germany (West Germany), 474; world disarmament conference proposed by, 583; *see also* Middle East: big four talks

United Arab Republic: bombing of Mission in New York, 537–38; *see also* Egypt; Middle East situation

United Kingdom: letter from Thant proposing high-level meetings for discussion of common problems, 160–63; nuclear weapons, 20; *see also* Middle East: big four talks; Southern Rhodesia question

United Nations: assessment of, by Thant, 9–11, 203, 314–20, 393–437, 547–48, 647–50, 677–78; authority and development of, 393–437; crisis of international commitment to, 402–3, 416–19, 433; decolonization role, 148; environmental protection role, 351–52; future direction of, 410–15, 420–21, 467–68, 473–74, 608; global strategy for, 393–94, 403, 407–13, 418–19, 420–21, 434; insoluble world problems and, 598–99; peace role, 203, 547–48, 678, 606–7; permanent missions to, 597; regional organizations and, 504; relation between political and economic and social objectives, 408–10, 433–35; secession of states and problem of divided countries, 187, 325–26, 336–40; structure and functions of United Nations (ten-year survey), 630–35; ten-year survey of United Nations and world conditions (Thant's Introduction to *26th Annual Report*), 604–71; universality of membership, 150–51, 335–36, 417, 503, 583, 584, 635–36; world tensions and, 214–20; youth and, 431–33, 466; *see also* Staff; Twenty-fifth anniversary observances of United Nations

United Nations Association of Great Britain: Thant address to, 214–20

United Nations Children's Fund, 278, 494, 576; Biafran aid, 89, 90, 101, 120, 128, 158, 202, 209, 242, 247, 337

United Nations Commission on International Trade Law, 98

United Nations Conference on Trade and Development (2d session, New Delhi), 25, 33–34, 46–54, 55, 56–59, 254, 256, 258, 278, 407, 409; background summary, 46; South Africa and, 188; Thant statement to, 47–54

United Nations Correspondents Association, 180, 241, 264, 329, 380, 450, 556, 673; luncheons for Thant, 80–87, 201–13, 215, 353, 356–69

United Nations Council for Namibia, 145,300

United Nations Day (1968): Thant message on, 164–65

United Nations Day Concert (1971): address by Thant at, 676–78

United Nations Development Decade (2d), 53–54, 59, 119, 236, 278–79, 288, 407, 409, 434, 435, 448, 475, 483, 530–31; International Symposium on, addressed by Thant, 572–74; launching of, 571; St. Louis Symposium on, addressed by Thant, 574–78

United Nations Development Programme, 122–23, 215–16, 278, 281, 414, 494, 575, 690

United Nations Disarmament Decade, 448, 481–83, 657–58, 660; proposed, 263, 288, 341, 343, 344, 409

United Nations Economic Commission for Africa, 243, 248

United Nations Educational and Training Programme for Southern Africa, 298

United Nations Educational, Scientific and Cultural Organization, 63, 310, 467, 684, 686, 687, 688

United Nations Emergency Force, 6, 339, 377, 541; finances, 277; withdrawal of, 371, 436–37

United Nations Force in Cyprus, 132–33, 143, 144, 172–73, 295, 339, 377, 436, 487, 536, 670–71, 682–83; background summary, 76; finances, 231, 278, 492, 539; Thant reports on, 76–78, 172–73, 226–31, 507–9

United Nations Fund for Population Activities, 476, 495

United Nations Industrial Development Organization, 256, 278

United Nations Institute for Training and Research, 278, 467, 684, 686, 688

United Nations International School, 677

United Nations Military Observer Group in Pakistan, 570

United Nations Operation in the Congo, 322, 323, 334, 338, 380, 386, 541; finances, 277–78; summarized, 608–14

United Nations Relief and Works Agency for Palestine Refugees in the Near East, 140, 166–71, 293, 361, 495

United Nations Special Account, 278, 492

United Nations Truce Supervision Organization, 139, 332, 449

United Nations Trust Fund for South Africa, 298

United Nations University, 466–67, 502–3; preliminary studies for establishment of, 684–88; proposed, 309–10

United States of America, 106; American plane shot down by North Koreans, 204–5; dual representation plan for China, 679; dumping of nerve gas into Atlantic Ocean by, 454–55; letter from Thant proposing high-level meetings for discussion of common problems, 160–63; nuclear weapons, 20, 23; SALT talks, 196–200, 340, 475, 479, 551, 659; *see also* Middle East: big four talks; Suez Canal; Vietnam situation

Universal Declaration of Human Rights: twentieth anniversary (1968), 61–70

Vance, Cyrus: Vietnam negotiations, 79, 88

Vietcong, *see* National Liberation Front

Vietnam, Democratic Republic of (North Vietnam), 3–4; *see also* Indo-China; Vietnam situation

Vietnam, Republic of (South Vietnam), 4, 5; Provisional Revolutionary Government, 365; *see also* Indo-China; Vietnam situation

Vietnam situation (U.S.-Vietnam involvement), 3–5, 25–45, 117–18, 119–21, 124–25, 127, 128–29, 152–54, 184, 211–12, 271, 272–73, 358–59, 363–69, 374, 385, 463, 476, 533, 535, 539–40, 584, 596; background summaries, 25–26, 79, 117–18, 261, 353–54, 614–17; bombing of North Vietnam, 118–19, 128–29, 353; new peace conference proposed by Thant, 353–54, 364–66, 374–75; Paris peace talks, 4–5, 25, 39, 41, 45, 79–84, 86, 88, 117–18, 130, 153–54, 210, 224–25, 261, 274, 332, 374, 539; San Antonio formula, 25–26, 37; *see also* Indo-China

Violence: Vietnam war and, 43

Voting system in United Nations bodies, 430–31, 585–86

Waldheim, Kurt: elected Secretary-General, as successor to Thant, 674, 689, 692

Warsaw Pact, 7, 106, 122, 125, 156

Washington, D.C., *see* United States of America

Washington Declaration, 207

Washington Post, 32n

Weak countries, 216–17

Weapons, *see* Chemical and biological weapons; Disarmament; Nuclear weapons

West Irian situation, 92, 131–32, 311

Wheeler, Earle G., 367

Wilson, Harold, 36

Wilson, Woodrow, 222

Winspeare Guicciardi, Vittorio, 378, 382, 477

Women: Declaration on discrimination against, 64

Woods, George, 55

World affairs: youth and, 431–33

World Association of World Federalists: addressed by Thant, on United Nations twenty-fifth anniversary, 416–19

World Economic Survey, 55, 59

World Food Programme, 406, 494, 575; Biafran aid, 202, 209, 247

World Youth Assembly (1970), 438, 495, 505, 651; addressed by Thant, 439–48

Xuan Thuy: Vietnam negotiations, 79, 88

Yahya Khan, Mohammed, 555, 559, 560, 563, 653, 654

Youth: Declaration on, 438; role in world affairs, 431–33; *see also* World Youth Assembly

Zeckendorf, Arthur, 177n

Zeckendorf, Guri Lie, 177n

Zeckendorf, William, 177n

Zurich: attack on El Al plane at, 179–80, 189–93

Index by Lisa McGaw